XML Application Development with MSXML 4.0

Danny Ayers
Michael Corning
Steven Livingstone
Stephen Mohr
Darshan Singh

Wrox Press Ltd. ®

XML Application Development with MSXML 4.0

January   2002

Published by Wrox Press Ltd,
Arden House, 1102 Warwick Road, Acocks Green,
Birmingham. B27 6BH. UK
Printed in the United States
ISBN 1-861005-89-X

Trademark Acknowledgements

Wrox has endeavored to provide trademark information about all the companies and products mentioned in this book by the appropriate use of capitals. However, Wrox cannot guarantee the accuracy of this information.

Credits

Authors
Danny Ayers
Michael Corning
Steven Livingstone
Stephen Mohr
Darshan Singh

Additional Material
Sean Schade

Category Managers
Simon Cox
Louay Fatoohi
Dave Galloway

Technical Architect
Dianne Arrow

Technical Editors
Dianne Arrow
Phillip Jackson
James Robinson

Author Agents
Marsha Collins
Beckie Stones

Project Managers
Christianne Bailey
Vicky Idiens
Beckie Stones

Technical Reviewers
Kapil Apshankar
Dave Beauchemin
Martin Beaulieu
Richard Birkby
Jon Duckett
Teun Duynstee
Sachin Kanna
Sing Li
Gareth Reakes
Alex Schiell
David Schultz
Stan Scott
Ian Stokes-Rees
Kevin Westhead

Production Coordinator
Emma Eato

Additional Layout
Natalie O'Donnell

Figures
Emma Eato

Indexing
Martin Brooks

Proof Reader
Chris Smith
Lisa Stephenson

Cover
Chris Morris

About the Authors

Danny Ayers

Danny Ayers is an independent consultant and author on Internet technologies, specializing in server-side information engineering. He lives in northern Italy with his wife Caroline and a bilingual cat. His personal web site is at http://www.isacat.net.

Dedicated to autonomous astronauts and pan-galactic peace.

Danny Ayers contributed Chapters 8 and 16.

Michael Corning

Michael Corning is a Memetic Engineer at Microsoft busy building a software test infrastructure for the Server Manager Team based on XML Web Services. At night he writes for Wrox Press (he coauthored "*Professional XSL*") and writes a monthly column in *XML Developer Magazine* called, "*Confessions of an XSLT Bigot*". His first book was "*Working with Active Server Pages*", Que, 1997. Corning speaks at conferences around the world preaching the good news of schema-based programming.

When he's not working he's going out on dates with his wife, Katy, (whom he adores), sailing his brand new West Wight Potter named *Finally*, or reading. He is the proud father of three handsome sons, Christian, Seth, and Casey; and he's the property of three cats, Minnie, Dixie, and Chica.

Michael Corning contributed Chapter 13.

Steven Livingstone

Steven Livingstone is an author and consultant in XML and .NET technologies, and is currently working on a meta data portal at http://www.deltabis.com.

He is also an avid Celtic supporter and supported them from afar while writing this book in Chile.

He would like to thank everyone at Wrox for their help on this book. He would especially like to thank the patience of his new fiancée, Loreto, for putting up with the long days and late nights. Te Amo.

Steven Livingstone contributed Chapters 3, 4, 5, 7, 10, and 14.

Stephen Mohr

Stephen Mohr is a senior software architect with Omicron Consulting and XMLabs in Philadelphia, USA. He has over twelve years' experience developing software for various platforms. Currently focusing on XML and related technologies as they apply to applications and computing systems, he has research interests in distributed computing and artificial intelligence.

Stephen holds BS and MS degrees in computer science from Rensselaer Polytechnic Institute.

Thanks to my wife Denise for her support and tolerance, and the challenges and questions of my sons James and Matthew.

Stephen Mohr contributed Chapters 1, 2, and 11.

Darshan Singh

Darshan Singh is a Senior Developer at InstallShield Software Corp. He also manages the XML community web site www.PerfectXML.com and can be reached at darshan@PerfectXML.com.

I would like to dedicate my work on this book to my beloved parents, Surjan Singh and Sumitra Kaur. Their love and blessings are the best gift to me from my God.

Sincere thanks to the Wrox team: Dianne Arrow, James Robinson, Beckie Stones, Vicky Idiens, Marsha Collins, and Christianne Bailey.

Darshan Singh contributed Chapters 6, 9, 12 and 15. (Sean Schade contributed the "Working in a Distributed Environment" section in Chapter 9.)

XML Application Development with MSXML 4.0
SOAP
XHTML
XML Schemas DTDs XPath CSS
XML Namespaces
XML 1.0
MSXML

Table of Contents

Table of Contents

Table of Contents

Table of Contents

Table of Contents

XML Application Development with MSXML 4.0
SOAP
XHTML
XML Schemas DTDs XPath CSS
XML Namespaces
XML 1.0
MSXML

Introduction

In its relatively short history XML has managed to infiltrate a surprising number and range of applications. Developers have found many ways to use it, mainly because most programming activity involves managing data in some way and XML is a flexible but simple data markup format. The success of XML has been helped by the fact that it is just plain text – so all applications can easily work with it regardless of the platform or language upon which they are based. Such interoperability, aided by well-developed specifications for defining, interrogating, and transforming data structures and content, has ensured a widespread adoption of XML. These days many developers use it as if it had been around forever.

But it was only a few years ago that XML first burst through the "hype bubble" and became widely accepted as *the* data format to use, for both raw data and wrapping existing formats for messaging and investigation. In those early days specifications and tools were fairly scarce. One of the first was the Microsoft XML parser built in to Internet Explorer (early uses of XML concentrated on manipulating the data in a browser client). Rightly or wrongly (depending on your personal point of view), the first incarnations of MSXML supported draft versions of some XML-related specifications, and Microsoft filled any gaps with its own proprietary solutions. MSXML has since been incorporated in other Microsoft products.

Today there are many XML processors available, but none as comprehensive as MSXML in their support for a full range of XML-related features. Installed as a COM component on a server, MSXML can be used from script and full-blown programming languages. This latest version is highly compliant with W3C and other major specifications. It still has some proprietary features to further enhance applications, but the choice of whether to use them and risk future compatibility with other products is entirely up to the developer. Installed on the client embedded in the IE browser it offers potential for shifting some of the application's workload away from the server and improving the user's experience.

Overall MSXML 4.0 (or the Microsoft XML Core Services 4.0 as it is now called) is a high-performance, feature-rich, component for use as the engine behind many powerful XML-based applications.

What Does This Book Cover?

This book covers XML standards from the point of view of what is supported in MSXML 4.0, and shows what you can achieve with such technologies. It covers typical tasks that need to be achieved in your applications and shows how best to implement this functionality using MSXML.

The first section of the book is devoted to describing the DOM, XML Schemas, XPath, XSLT, and SAX – showing the most useful aspects supported by MSXML. Although no prior experience of working with these technologies is required, for those who already understand the basics this section will serve as a handy reference to what is and is not supported.

The middle section of the book is more task-focused, showing how MSXML and its support for XML technologies can be put into practice to achieve typical application functionality such as styling for presentation, generating and transmitting data, linking web pages, validating data, and manipulating data structures.

The final section provides case studies bringing together a range of such tasks and demonstrating complete applications based around MSXML 4.0.

Who Is This Book For?

This is a book for programmers who are interested in learning about developing applications based on XML technologies, for the Windows platform. It assumes that you are already familiar with basic XML concepts, including the XML 1.0 Recommendation and Namespaces in XML.

> *If you are new to XML and surrounding standards like XSLT and XML Schemas, you might consider reading an introductory or advanced XML title first, such as the "Beginning XML" or "Professional XML" titles (ISBN 1-861005-59-8 and 1-861005-05-9 respectively).*

We also assume that you are familiar with general web technology, concepts, and jargon. Examples are given in a variety of languages – Visual Basic, Visual C++, JavaScript, and VBScript, and we also use ASP and ADO. The code is explained but we do not aim to teach any of these languages in this book.

What You Need To Use This Book

The main requirement is to have MSXML 4.0 (the Microsoft XML Core Services 4.0 component). This can be downloaded from:

http://msdn.microsoft.com/downloads/default.asp?URL=/code/sample.asp?url=/msdn-files/027/001/766/msdncompositedoc.xml

It is crucial that you read the Notices on the product download page if you have been working with a previous version of MSXML. There is a public mailing list to support this product, available at:

http://msdn.microsoft.com/newsgroups/default.asp?url=/newsgroups/loadframes.asp?icp=msdn&slcid=us&newsgroup=microsoft.public.xml.msxml-webrelease

This is a particularly useful source of information if you have any problems downloading and installing MSXML. For example, at the time of writing the download files needed to be renamed from msxml4 *to* msxml *in order for the installer to successfully run.*

To try out all of the examples you will also need Internet Explorer and occasionally Netscape Navigator, Visual Basic and Visual C++, SQL Server, and some other free downloads as mentioned in the appropriate chapters.

The code included in this book can be downloaded from http://www.wrox.com/. More details are given in the *Customer Support* section.

How Is This Book Structured?

This book is organized into three sections:

❑   Section 1 – a reference to XML standards and support in MSXML.

❑   Section 2 – practical uses of XML technologies to achieve typical application functionality.

❑   Section 3 – case studies.

Section 1: Reference Section

Chapter 1: Introduction to MSXML
Stephen Mohr
Chapter 1 introduces the MSXML parser, its history and purpose. It briefly discusses the core XML technologies and MSXML's support for them. We discuss common application architectures in which MSXML can be employed. Finally, the future of MSXML is considered, with regard to the XML support in the .NET Framework

Chapter 2: Document Object Model in MSXML
Stephen Mohr
Chapter 2 is a comprehensive guide to the DOM, the W3C's recommended API to XML. We describe the W3C's view of the DOM and its interfaces, then look in detail at Microsoft's extensions. Common DOM tasks are demonstrated – such as loading, navigating, and modifying documents.

Chapter 3: Schemas in MSXML
Steven Livingstone
Schemas are used to define data and document structures, and to validate the content of XML files. MSXML 4.0 implements the XML Schema Language from the W3C, and Chapter 3 focuses on providing a reference to the supported features. An earlier specification, XML-Data Reduced, was also used in previous versions of MSXML so we take a brief look at that too. The practical use of schemas is demonstrated, and the Schema Object Model (MSXML 4.0's API for schemas) is introduced.

Chapter 4: XPath in MSXML
Steven Livingstone
In Chapter 4 we look at the XML Path Language, XPath, which allows us to access data in XML documents, and select and filter it according to our requirements. XPath is used in XSLT and the DOM, as well as with other XML technologies. This chapter covers the W3C specification and Microsoft extensions. It provides comprehensive examples of XPath expressions, and an example of XPath in use with Schemas and the DOM.

Chapter 5: XSLT in MSXML
Steven Livingstone

The Extensible Stylesheet Language Transformations (XSLT) is the subject of Chapter 5. This is used for transforming data and data structures, and is often used for changing raw data into a suitable format for presentation. MSXML 4.0 supports the W3C XSLT specification as well as an early version based on a Working Draft. We first cover the latter, with examples of its syntax, before providing a comprehensive reference to the support for the W3C XSLT elements and functions.

Chapter 6: Simple API for XML (SAX) in MSXML
Darshan Singh

Chapter 6 is a practical reference to the Simple API for XML (SAX). MSXML 4.0 supports SAX2, and this chapter has extensive examples to show how to use each of the interfaces from a range of languages. The examples include using SAX for parsing and creating XML documents, locating data and handling errors, and working with XSLT and XML Schemas. A full reference is provided to the SAX2 interfaces as implemented in MSXML 4.0.

Section 2: Practical Applications

Chapter 7: Styling XML Content
Steven Livingstone

Chapter 7 takes a look at various technologies for presenting XML data to users. Cascading Stylesheets (CSS) is introduced, and we both compare and integrate it with XSLT. We look at IE behaviors for encapsulating reusable code for use within web pages. Finally we learn how to create dynamic graphics with the Vector Markup Language (VML), and take a brief look at the as yet unsupported Scalable Vector Graphics format (SVG).

Chapter 8: Linking and Pointing
Danny Ayers

In Chapter 8 we briefly look at some of the technologies that will one day allow us to define links between XML documents and to identify arbitrary parts of XML documents: XLink, XPointer, and Resource Description Framework (RDF). These standards are not supported in MSXML 4.0 but, to illustrate how some of the ideas of linking and pointing might be emulated in MSXML, we develop an exploratory prototype that approximates some of the functionality of a web annotation system developed by the W3C.

Chapter 9: Sending and Retrieving XML Data
Darshan Singh (plus contribution from Sean Schade)

Chapter 9 focuses on generating XML data on the server or on the middle tier, sending it to the client, and also retrieving XML data posted by the client. We introduce ServerXMLHTTP, an important class for requesting or posting HTTP data using MSXML, used extensively in later chapters. We also consider data transmission in a distributed environment, and see how ServerXMLHTTP can help us when communicating with remote servers.

Chapter 10: Transformations on the Server
Steven Livingstone

In this chapter we recap on what was covered in Chapter 9, but in the context of XSLT. Some advanced MSXML concepts and techniques are demonstrated for working with XML data and XSLT on the server. These include selecting appropriate stylesheets based on browser detection, improving stylesheet performance, selecting threading models, use of the XSLTemplate and XSLProcessor objects, and passing parameters and objects. We also consider interacting with other servers to perform complex manipulation and transformation of source XML files. The chapter concludes with a look at Microsoft's ISAPI filter and MSXSL.exe tool, performing bulk transformations, and handling errors.

Chapter 11: Schemas on the Server
Stephen Mohr
In Chapter 11 we discuss using MSXML and document validation on the server. This includes a more detailed look at MSXML threading models. Schema caching with the `IXMLDOMSchemaCollection` and `IXMLDOMSchemaCollection2` interfaces is the main focus of the chapter, and we include a simple application for illustration.

Chapter 12: Working with Data on the Client
Darshan Singh
In Chapter 12 we assume our client is an IE 5.0+ browser (MSXML version 2.5+) and look at what tasks can be handled client-side. After a brief overview of XML encoding issues with MSXML, and some simple examples of processing and transforming XML documents client-side, we move on to look at dealing with MSXML version incompatibility issues. Sending HTTP requests and receiving the response using the `XMLHTTP` class are demonstrated. We then look at the data binding functionality of Internet Explorer and show how to use XML Data Islands.

Chapter 13: Performance, Scalability, and Security
Michael Corning
Chapter 13 considers three inter-related issues faced when moving from development to deployment. In this chapter we look at the factors that affect performance, scalability, and security. Several practical techniques are presented for addressing each issue when using MSXML 4.0.

Section 3: Case Studies

Chapter 14: An Information Portal
Steven Livingstone
In this case study we build an information portal system that registers, indexes, and generates content for multiple browsers. This includes content syndication and batch retrieval for obtaining HTML or XML content from a remote site and validation against local schemas. Content is converted to the required XML format and an index of available documents is created. Device detection is used to retrieve the appropriate XML and XSLT to create the front page, which links to pre-generated HTML pages. The application also demonstrates how to link in other utility processes. Most of the features covered throughout the book are put to use in this application.

Chapter 15: Attendance Tracking System
Darshan Singh
In this case study we develop an intranet-based application for tracking time-off for personnel at a fictional company. Employees are able to log on and view holiday information, then submit requests for time-off. The system allows managers to approve or reject requests, automatically e-mailing the employee, and HR can produce reports from the data. The application demonstrates using XML as a data transfer mechanism, and separating content from presentation. MSXML is used on the server-side and on the middle tier, so the application does not rely on any client-side manipulation of XML.

Chapter 16: Helpdesk XML Messaging System
Danny Ayers
In the final case study we build a custom XML messaging application for a helpdesk system. The web interface allows clients to report problems and helpdesk personnel to provide solutions. Different views are available to check the status of helpdesk jobs. A message broker takes care of responding to submissions, storing messages, and sending e-mail notifications. Again, a broad range of MSXML functionality is put to use.

Conventions

To help you get the most from the text and keep track of what's happening, we've used a number of conventions throughout the book.

For instance:

> **These boxes hold important, not-to-be forgotten information, which is directly relevant to the surrounding text.**

> *By contrast, this indented italicized style is used for asides to the current discussion.*

As for styles in the text:

- ❑ When we introduce them, we **highlight** important words
- ❑ We show keyboard strokes like this: *Ctrl-A*
- ❑ We show filenames, and code within the text, like this: `sample.xml`
- ❑ Text on user interfaces is shown like this: File | Save
- ❑ URLs are shown in a similar fontm for example: http://www.wrox.com/
- ❑ Namespace URIs, however, are shown like this: `http://www.w3.org/2001/XMLSchema`
- ❑ When referring to a chapter section or title, like the *Introduction*, we italicize it

We present code in two different ways. Code that is new or important is shown as so:

```
In our code examples, the code foreground style shows
new, important, and pertinent code
```

Code that is an aside, or has been seen before is shown as so:

```
Code background shows code that's less important in the present context,
or that has been seen before.
```

In addition, when something is to be typed at a command line interface (for example, a DOS/Command prompt), then we use the following style to show what is typed:

```
> set WSTK_HOME=c:\wstk-2.3
```

Customer Support

We always value hearing from our readers, and we want to know what you think about this book: what you liked, what you didn't like, and what you think we can do better next time. You can send us your comments, either by returning the reply card in the back of the book, or by e-mail to feedback@wrox.com. Please be sure to mention the book title in your message.

How to Download the Sample Code for the Book

When you log on to the Wrox site http://www.wrox.com/, simply locate the title through our Search facility or by using one of the title lists. Click on Download in the Code column, or on Download Code on the book's detail page.

The files that are available for download from our site have been archived using WinZip. When you have saved the attachments to a folder on your hard-drive, you need to extract the files using a de-compression program such as WinZip or PKUnzip. When you extract the files, the code is usually extracted into chapter folders. When you start the extraction process, ensure your software (WinZip, PKUnzip, etc.) is set to extract to Use Folder Names.

Errata

We've made every effort to make sure that there are no errors in the text or in the code. However, no one is perfect and mistakes do occur. If you find an error in one of our books, like a spelling mistake or a faulty piece of code, we would be very grateful for feedback. By sending in errata you may save another reader hours of frustration, and of course, you will be helping us provide even higher quality information. Simply e-mail the information to support@wrox.com, your information will be checked and if correct, posted to the errata page for that title, or used in subsequent editions of the book.

To find errata on the web site, log on to http://www.wrox.com/, and simply locate the title through our Advanced Search or title list. Click on the Book Errata link, which is below the cover graphic on the book's detail page.

E-mail Support

If you wish to directly query a problem in the book page with an expert who knows the book in detail then e-mail support@wrox.com, with the title of the book and the last four numbers of the ISBN in the subject field of the e-mail. A typical e-mail should include the following things:

❑ The **name**, **last four digits of the ISBN**, and **page number** of the problem in the Subject field.

❑ Your **name**, **contact information**, and the **problem** in the body of the message.

We **won't** send you junk mail. We need the details to save your time and ours. When you send an e-mail message, it will go through the following chain of support:

❑ Customer Support – Your message is delivered to one of our customer support staff, who are the first people to read it. They have files on most frequently asked questions and will answer anything general about the book or the web site immediately.

❑ Editorial – Deeper queries are forwarded to the technical editor responsible for that book. They have experience with the programming language or particular product, and are able to answer detailed technical questions on the subject. Once an issue has been resolved, the editor can post the errata to the web site.

❑ The Authors – Finally, in the unlikely event that the editor cannot answer your problem, he or she will forward the request to the author. We do try to protect the author from any distractions to their writing, however, we are quite happy to forward specific requests to them. All Wrox authors help with the support on their books. They will mail the customer and the editor with their response, and again all readers should benefit.

The Wrox Support process can only offer support to issues that are directly pertinent to the content of our published title. Support for questions that fall outside the scope of normal book support is provided via the community lists of our http://p2p.wrox.com/ forum.

p2p.wrox.com

For author and peer discussion join the P2P mailing lists. Our unique system provides **programmer to programmer**™ contact on mailing lists, forums, and newsgroups, all in addition to our one-to-one e-mail support system. Be confident that your query is being examined by the many Wrox authors and other industry experts who are present on our mailing lists. At p2p.wrox.com you will find a number of different lists that will help you, not only while you read this book, but also as you develop your own applications.

To subscribe to a mailing list just follow these steps:

1. Go to http://p2p.wrox.com/.

2. Choose the appropriate category from the left menu bar.

3. Click on the mailing list you wish to join.

4. Follow the instructions to subscribe and fill in your e-mail address and password.

5. Reply to the confirmation e-mail you receive.

6. Use the subscription manager to join more lists and set your mail preferences.

XML Application Development with MSXML 4.0
SOAP SOAP SOAP SOAP SOAP SOAP
XHTML XHTML XHTML XHTML
XML Schemas DTDs XPath CSS
XML Namespaces XML Namespaces
XML 1.0 XML 1.0 XML 1.0
MSXML MSXML
MSXML

1

Introduction to MSXML

Understanding MSXML necessarily means understanding XML, the Extensible Markup Language. However, this is not a book about XML; the popularity of XML in the programming community means bookstore shelves are filled with books that will teach you the finer points of XML and its supporting technologies. MSXML is an XML processor, a component that parses XML documents and exposes the document to applications through standard Application Programming Interfaces (APIs). It is Microsoft's original XML processor, built as a COM component and bundled with a variety of applications. The .NET classes also implement the key XML standards, but MSXML remains the XML workhorse of the Windows platform. Without MSXML, products as diverse as Internet Explorer and BizTalk Server could not function. Developers throughout the world have written sophisticated XML-based applications using MSXML that range from personal applications to mission-essential products.

MSXML is no ordinary XML processor. It takes a comprehensive approach to XML. As you first learn about XML you quickly realize that XML itself is just the first standard on which additional, complementary technologies are layered to create a powerful, flexible foundation for applications. MSXML, now in its fourth generation, supports not only XML but also the most common XML-related technologies you need to develop great applications, including:

- ❑ XML 1.0
- ❑ XML Namespaces
- ❑ XML Document Object Model (DOM)
- ❑ Simple API for XML (SAX)
- ❑ XML Path Language (XPath)
- ❑ Extensible Stylesheet Language Transformations (XSLT)
- ❑ XML Schemas

In addition, Microsoft included a series of interfaces and utilities that, while proprietary, greatly assist developers in programming web applications using XML. There are client- and server-side HTTP implementations for retrieving documents, server-side optimizations for XSLT and schemas, multi-threading support, and ADO-aware data binding. Some vendors take a lean approach, requiring a multitude of components or classes to accomplish tasks that span more than one technology. MSXML is the "Swiss Army knife" of XML components. As your XML skills grow, you will use new interfaces but not necessarily another component, though there are arguments to be made for both the lean and multi-purpose approaches. While MSXML does not currently offer certain functionalities, it does offer the virtue of providing a complete XML run-time toolkit in a single component. MSXML is also a high-performance XML processor. Since version 3, Microsoft has put considerable emphasis on optimizing the component, particularly in server-side usage scenarios. This makes it one of the most useful and widely used XML processors available today in the Windows environment.

This book is intended for the intermediate to expert XML programmer who needs a powerful processor for Windows applications and web applications hosted under Windows servers. It focuses on the traditional COM-based development model, although we'll point out similarities to and contrasts with the .NET XML classes as we go along. You will gain a deep understanding of all the interfaces supported by MSXML and consequently a broad exposure to XML technologies and techniques. You will also learn best practices and architectures for XML development using MSXML. Although the specific syntax used applies to COM and traditional Windows development, the techniques and XML technologies are the same in the .NET classes. As a result, you can use this book as a guide to current practice, then transfer the underlying knowledge to the .NET classes when they move into mainstream usage.

Overview

In the light of what is often wild hype surrounding XML, it is easy to forget that all XML applications build on the XML 1.0 Recommendation of the World Wide Web Consortium (W3C), and that document mainly describes a text format with no reference to any sort of programmatic access. It talks about software only to the extent that some points are clarified by describing how a processor will respond under certain circumstances. At its core, then, XML is just text that obeys a certain set of markup rules. This situation does not begin to explain the popularity and utility of XML in the programming world. Programmers need two additional things: a real processor implementation and supporting technologies.

As we have seen in the introduction to this chapter, MSXML is the processor implementation for the classic Windows platform (in which development is based on COM+ rather than .NET). By this point, any deficiencies it may have in conforming to the XML 1.0 Recommendation are a matter of conflicting interpretations of ambiguous parts of the Recommendation.

> *A detailed discussion of MSXML's conformance and Microsoft's interpretation of the finer points of XML 1.0 is found at http://www.xml.com/pub/a/2000/08/30/msxml/index.html.*

Just as we sometimes speak of "thin" and "fat" clients, we can also have "thin" and "fat" XML processors. MSXML definitely takes the fat approach, supporting 27 COM+ interfaces, five major XML-related technologies, and a host of utility features. Before we can appreciate MSXML's "fat architecture" approach and delve into its use in XML applications, we must understand how XML technology is layered and what the key supporting standards are. There are well over a dozen main supporting technologies. Apart from their relation to the XML 1.0 Recommendation, there is little formal architectural guidance from the W3C in terms of an XML technology model. We might, though, consider the model presented in the following diagram:

SOAP	XHTML	Other	**Applications**
XSLT	DOM	SAX	**Manipulation**
XML Schemas		XPath	**Structure**
XML Namespaces			
XML 1.0			**Core**

The foundation is XML 1.0. Closely related is the XML Namespaces Recommendation, a way to bring modularity to XML documents and schemas (and something of an afterthought to XML 1.0). That is, namespaces are clearly *core* technology and they are not part of the main XML Recommendation only because they were, by necessity, developed in parallel with XML 1.0.

> *We believe that the two will be merged in some later release of the XML Recommendation, but that is strictly a matter of personal opinion and not a reflection of the W3C XML Activity.*

Classification of technologies beyond this core increasingly becomes a matter of opinion, including our own, the community's, and that of various members of the W3C. Indeed, much depends on what you are trying to accomplish. Rather than take our model as a rigid representation, think of it more as a flexible attempt to orient you to XML-related technologies.

Leaving the core, we next encounter information about *structure*. XML Schemas are XML syntax for describing the structure and data types of XML vocabularies. They are a highly evolved replacement for the Document Type Definitions (DTDs) that are the way this information is specified in XML 1.0.

> *Though XML Schemas are now the W3C recognized standard for describing XML in data and documents, DTDs are still favored by some people due to familiarity and their relative simplicity. Furthermore, XML Schemas do not allow you to perform certain tasks such as defining your own entities, though Schemas generally have some feature permitting you to meet the same underlying requirement. Future versions of XML may allow DTDs to be dropped entirely, but for the time being DTDs will still be used.*

XPath is a language for describing a path through an XML document to a node or set of nodes. Classifying XPath at this level – structure – is somewhat controversial. XPath does nothing to describe structure (that is completely accomplished by XML Schemas), but it is dependent on structure and defines a query or retrieval in terms of structure. Equally important, a number of technologies at higher levels rely on XPath.

Beyond structure we find technologies designed to traverse and *manipulate* XML documents. This is where XML becomes useful to application developers. Without a means of accessing a document through a processor and altering the document, XML would hold no interest for programmers. The most conventional APIs are the Document Object Model (DOM) and the Simple API for XML (SAX). The former is a fairly conventional API that treats a document as a tree structure in memory. SAX – which has the distinction of not being a W3C-controlled technology – is an event driven interface that processes an XML document as a stream. A more radical approach is the Extensible Stylesheet Language Transformations (XSLT). This is a declarative language, in that we don't need to tell our computer *how* to perform required tasks, but simply tell the processor what tasks to perform. With XSLT, the author is permitted to specify rules for the transformation of a class of XML documents into another form. XSLT grew out of the effort to provide visual styling for XML documents, but is widely used for non-visual data conversion tasks.

Beyond the manipulation layer of our model we reach the realm of *applications*. We cannot stop here as the W3C has interesting work in a number of areas. One absolutely critical application of XML is SOAP, formerly known as the Simple Object Access Protocol (and now just an acronym with no meaning, which is being brought under W3C guidance under the name of XML Protocol). SOAP is a means of accessing programmatic services over the Web using request-response pairs of XML documents to conceal the platform-specific details of clients and servers. It is the basis for web services and the subject of much attention from all the major software vendors. SOAP, in turn, will be used by other applications as a communications protocol.

XHTML is an application of XML to HTML, bringing more structure and discipline to the latter.

There are many more applications, and you will undoubtedly write some of your own. That is the purpose of this book. By introducing you to MSXML's implementation of the various technologies, we will be preparing you to write your own applications of XML. MSXML is an excellent tool for the task as it takes in the whole of the core, structure, and manipulation layers of our model.

Let's take a few moments and consider these technologies in a little more depth. The next few sections will describe the technologies, tell you how they can be used in applications, and point you to the chapters of this book that show you how to work with them in detail using MSXML. Following those discussions, we'll consider the nature of XML processors and briefly mention some competing implementations. We'll move on to show how processors and technologies are tied together by discussing common architectures for XML applications. Finally, we'll have a few words on the future of MSXML and XML processing in .NET.

> *The following sections and the detailed chapters in the rest of the book will give you a working knowledge of XML, but cannot possibly cover all of its related technologies in depth. In part this is due to a desire to keep this book small enough for an ordinary human being to lift without mechanical assistance, and in part to the fact that different processor implementations shed light on different facets of XML and related technology. This book will be enough to make you productive using MSXML, but if you want to really grasp XML in its entirety, you should follow this book with "Professional XML, 2nd Edition" (Wrox Press, 2001, ISBN 1-861005-05-9).*

Core Technologies

Without the XML 1.0 Recommendation, there is no XML technology. That document defines elements, attributes, processing instructions, and all the other primitive constructs of XML. It defines the rules for well-formed documents (crudely, the minimum set of rules that make up a "legal" XML document that is fit for processing) and valid XML documents (that is, well-formed documents that obey the constraints of some specified DTD or schema). XML 1.0 puts the pointy brackets into text to get the whole game going.

XML namespaces are deceptively simple. They are a way of saying that a group of names belong together. Purists will rightly advocate that this is all that namespaces say. In practice, there is usually some DTD or schema associated with a namespace to provide structural information. Without namespaces, it is very hard to specify large, complex XML vocabularies, and nearly impossible to write XML applications. The Namespaces in XML Recommendation provides a mechanism of prefixes and namespace scope to avoid collision between identical names with different meanings. At their most basic, namespaces are a way to distinguish one XML vocabulary from another within the same document, even if the two use the same name for different concepts. It is this mechanism that allows MSXML to distinguish between your definition of some element named `Product` and my element named `Product` when both are used in the same `Catalog` document. Namespaces allow us to modularize structural declarations by some criteria such as functionality or use. With namespaces, we can take common declarations from a variety of sources to construct XML documents. We can also build schemas that declare structures for widely used concepts, such as people and places, then reuse them throughout our applications. MSXML is fully compliant with XML 1.0 and XML namespaces.

The W3C XML Recommendation is found at http://www.w3.org/TR/REC-xml, while Namespaces in XML is found at http://www.w3.org/TR/REC-xml-names/.

Structure

As noted earlier, XML 1.0 has a mechanism for formally defining and restricting the permissible content of arbitrary XML vocabularies. This mechanism was carried out through a formal document, similar in intent to a schema, known as the Document Type Definition (DTD) – part of the core XML technology. That should have been that, but DTDs have their limits. From a programming perspective, DTDs lack a wide range of data types. Since everything is text, the authors of XML 1.0 seemed satisfied with a limited range of text-oriented types. These types were perfectly adequate for publishing documents, and no one wanted to let XML get bogged down in a debate over metadata on the off chance that XML might prove wildly popular for applications. However, programmers need numeric, date, and time types, among others. Ideally, we'd like to have the ability to create our own types as well. Furthermore, the constraints you may place on the particular values an element or attribute may take are limited. The process of validating a document against a DTD should eliminate the sorts of field-level validation we practice in conventional applications. Given the limits on constraining content with DTDs, this is not the case.

From an XML standpoint, there is an additional drawback to DTDs. The syntax used to write DTDs is not XML. XML processors – those that support validation, anyway – must be able to parse two syntaxes: XML and DTD notation. Not only does this place a burden of extra work on processor developers, but it also closes off DTDs to application developers in the normal course of things. Regardless of what sort of development you are doing, DTDs mean more work. These factors and others drove the development of XML Schemas. As XML Schemas are specified in XML notation, they provide an XML vocabulary and type system for the specification of XML vocabularies.

XML Schemas have been a very long time in coming. Programmers have been pressing for their standardization, a fact that led many vendors and independent developers to offer their own proposals for the expression of structure in XML documents. Microsoft was one of them, and two early draft proposals from Microsoft were among the sources used as input to the W3C XML Schemas effort. While that effort continued, a streamlined form of the proposals, termed XML Data-Reduced (XDR), was implemented in MSXML 2.0. Support for the structures and types of XDR remains in the version 4.0 processor. While the syntax of W3C XML Schemas is different from XDR, everything in an XDR schema may be expressed using XML Schema syntax. Although there are numerous Microsoft products using XDR notation – BizTalk Server and ADO are among them – there is no longer any reason to continue writing XDR schemas for your own use as MSXML 4.0 supports a substantial subset of the XML Schemas Recommendation.

XML Schemas is a complicated area, leading to a primer document as well as separate documents for structures and data types. These documents are found at http://www.w3.org/TR/xmlschema-0/, http://www.w3.org/TR/xmlschema-1/, and http://www.w3.org/TR/xmlschema-2/, respectively. The basics of XML Schemas are covered in Chapter 3, "Schemas in MSXML". Special optimizations and techniques for using XML Schemas on the server are discussed in Chapter 11, "Schemas on the Server".

Once you know the structure of an XML document, you can navigate it and retrieve information using XPath. XPath is an expression language that allows developers to specify relative or absolute paths through a document to get to a node of interest. Consider the following XML fragment:

```
<DriverRegistration>
   <Alabama>
   </Alabama>
. . .
   <Pennsylvania>
      <Berks suspended="1500" adult="800000"
             learnersPermits="10000"/>
   </Pennsylvania>
. . .
</DriverRegistration>
```

This sample document records information about licensed drivers by US state and county. If we wish to know how many drivers have suspended licenses in Berks county, Pennsylvania, we could write the following XPath expression:

```
/DriverRegistration/Pennsylvania/Berks/@suspended
```

This expression is independent of the implementation language. In JavaScript, using MSXML and skipping some preliminaries, we might have:

```
node = root.selectSingleNode("/DriverRegistration/Pennsylvania/Berks/@suspended");
if (node != null)
   alert(node.nodeValue);
```

The XPath implementation does all the work for us after we pass the expression to the processor using the selectSingleNode method. It will always return the information we desire – 1500 in the example above – or null if that attribute does not appear. Now consider the following JavaScript sample needed to retrieve the same thing using the Document Object Model:

```
node = root.childNodes(2).childNodes(0);
for (i = 0; i < node.attributes.length; i++)
{
   if (node.attributes(i).nodeName == "suspended")
      alert(node.attributes(i).nodeValue);
}
```

There is more code, and we have to test each attribute node to find the one we are looking for. Worse, we have hard-coded the indices in the childNodes collections – which contain the state and county elements. To get the desired county, we would need to introduce additional checks. Perhaps worst of all, the performance of the DOM version will suffer greatly when called from a scripting language as each method call or property access must pass through all the steps of late binding in COM+. The XPath implementation makes this journey just once. The XPath representation expresses the desired node in terms of the document's structure, while the DOM version expresses it in terms of an arbitrary tree structure. Which you use will depend on your application requirements, but by offering both technologies in a single component, MSXML allows you to freely mix the two as needed.

XPath also lets us return multiple nodes and constrain our search by some criteria. Using the sample document, we could get a collection of all counties included in the XML document whose population of suspended drivers exceeds 1000, with the following XPath expression:

```
/DriverRegistration/*/*/@suspended[. > '1000']
```

XPath is covered in Chapter 4, "XPath in MSXML". The W3C XPath Recommendation is found at http://www.w3.org/TR/xpath. The simple examples above are included in the code download as DemoXPath.html.

MSXML has offered an XPath implementation since version 2.0. It offers extensions to the DOM, which we've used in the code above, such that XPath expressions may be evaluated in the midst of DOM code. This is a flexible alternative to using DOM traversal and is a valuable shortcut for XML developers. The W3C's current specification of the DOM has no links to XPath.

As of August 2001, the DOM Working Group has published a Working Draft entitled "Document Object Model (DOM) Level 3 XPath Specification" that seeks to offer XPath expression evaluation through future DOM interfaces. These interfaces differ substantially from the XPath extensions in MSXML. The current draft may be found at http://www.w3.org/TR/DOM-Level-3-XPath.

Manipulation

Now that we have provisions for XML documents and ways to declare their structure, we need APIs to access and manipulate their contents. These APIs are the point at which your applications interface to the document processor. There are two APIs that use classic procedural interfaces: DOM and SAX.

The DOM loads an entire document into memory as a tree structure. This has the advantage of combining document parsing with a common data structure, but also requires more system resources than SAX. All DOM implementations must use more memory to represent the document than is required on disk, so as to record information about structure that it obtained through parsing and to reflect the overhead of its data structures. MSXML, for example, requires 1–4 times the document size to store the DOM tree. (A more exact formula is given in "*Inside MSXML Performance*" found at http://msdn.microsoft.com/library/en-us/dnexxml/html/xml02212000.asp.) There are interfaces for the document as a whole, each node of the tree, an error handling object, and some collections of nodes. The DOM allows a programmer to traverse a document, modify the contents of a document, and create and delete portions of the document. You may, in fact, create entire documents using the DOM, bypassing disk files entirely. MSXML has offered a DOM implementation since version 2.0. Its implementation includes a number of proprietary extensions that facilitate common tasks and interface to some of the non-DOM technologies implemented by MSXML, such as XSLT.

Chapter 2, "Document Object Model in MSXML", discusses the DOM in detail. MSXML's implementation is primarily that of the W3C's Level 1 Recommendation at http://www.w3.org/TR/REC-DOM_Level_1/. That is to say, it implements the interfaces of DOM Level 1, but many of its proprietary methods are duplicated in DOM Level 2 under different names and parameter lists. DOM Level 2 was published as a W3C Recommendation on 13 November 2000, so MSXML's adherence to Level 1 is beginning to look a bit dated. One problem is that many programmers have become accustomed to using the proprietary extensions for namespace support and would have to recode to achieve the same functionality under DOM Level 2. DOM Level 3 is currently in progress, but has not yet moved beyond the Working Draft stage.

While waiting for the W3C to produce the DOM, the XML community, centered on the XML-DEV mailing list and under the leadership of David Megginson, developed an event-driven set of Java interfaces called the Simple API for XML (SAX). Using SAX, an XML document is exposed as a stream of events that are fired as the document is being parsed. Developers write implementations for events they wish to process. For example, the `ContentHandler` interface has methods signaling the start and end of elements. If you were interested in processing a particular element, you would implement this interface and test for the name of the desired element in your implementation of the `startElement` method. SAX has the advantage of consuming minimal system resources. As such, it is suitable for processing very large documents. The drawback is that if you need context, or access to large subsections of the document, then you must implement your own data structures. Once an event occurs, SAX has no further knowledge of that particular item in the document. MSXML has supported the latest version of SAX, SAX2, since version 3.0.

> *The XML-DEV list home page may be found at http://www.xml.org/xml/xmldev.shtml. The SAX home page is at http://www.megginson.com/SAX/, with a list of related resources at http://www.xml.org/xml/resources_focus_sax.shtml.*

The W3C effort to provide visual styling for XML documents uncovered an interesting need early in its work: the need to transform one XML vocabulary into another. This is because it was following a rule-based approach similar in spirit to cascading stylesheets (CSS). That is, the styling effort wanted to allow an author to specify a context or condition – all `<Person>` elements, for example – and a series of one or more actions to take when that context was reached in a document. The input document is an instance of one XML vocabulary, while the document resulting from the application of all the rules is an instance of another XML vocabulary. You may generate well-formed XML, for example, which is a very common application of this technology. The activity focused on this transformation task, producing the XSLT Recommendation in November 1999. Using XSLT, you may start with the following document:

```
<Person role="student">
    <Age>18</Age>
    <Name>
        <First>John</First>
        <Last>Doe</Last>
    </Name>
</Person>
```

After applying an XSLT stylesheet, you can have the following document:

```
<Student age="18">
    <Name first="John" last="Doe"/>
</Student>
```

The data is equivalent, but the form of the two vocabularies is different. Such transformations are particularly common in e-commerce. Everyone has the notion of a purchase order, for example, but every e-commerce partner seems to have their own notion of the exact form of such a document. With XSLT, e-commerce software can dynamically transform the internal purchase order representation into the form favored by the partner receiving the document. MSXML offered a preliminary implementation of the XSLT Working Draft, starting with version 2.0. The syntax of XSLT has changed substantially since then. Version 3.0 of MSXML supported both the Microsoft early implementation and the W3C XSLT Recommendation. Version 4.0 drops the Working Draft implementation and supports only the final Recommendation.

The XSLT Recommendation is found at http://www.w3.org/TR/xslt. The fundamentals of XSLT are covered in Chapter 5, "XSLT in MSXML", with additional coverage of the common task of server-side transformations in Chapter 10, "Transformations on the Server". Two excellent XSLT resources are "XSLT Programmer's Reference 2nd Edition" (Wrox Press, ISBN 1-861005-06-7) and "Professional XSL" (Wrox Press, ISBN 1-861003-57-9).

Applications

With XML documents and their structure in place, and an interface to them through DOM, SAX, and XSLT, we are ready to begin programming applications. We are not the first, of course, so there are already a number of generally useful applications of XML. In fact, some of them are under the guidance of the W3C. XHTML, for instance, recasts HTML as an XML application. Different facets of the HTML experience are segregated into modules, thereby facilitating the delivery of web browsers on different user devices. A handheld device that cannot support the entire feature-set can implement only those modules that make sense for its hardware. Additionally, the mathematics community developed a vocabulary for expressing mathematical expressions, called MathML, so that academic papers could be freely exchanged on the Web without resorting to various dodges like turning formulae into images.

XHTML 1.1 is a W3C Recommendation published at http://www.w3.org/TR/xhtml11/, while the modularisation of that vocabulary is explicitly discussed at http://www.w3.org/TR/xhtml-modularization. MathML version 2.0 is a Recommendation, presented at http://www.w3.org/TR/MathML2/.

While applications of XML for visual presentation are interesting, programmers will be much more excited about SOAP. Originally a vendor-based initiative, SOAP is an example of an appropriate technology coming along at the right time. XML was enjoying the full flush of marketing hype, and there was high interest in distributing computing services via the Web. SOAP offers an RPC-like mechanism for making function calls over HTTP (and other protocols in the future), using XML documents to pass parameters and function names, and receive responses. Faced with the curious circumstances of such bitter rivals as Sun and Microsoft backing the same technology, the W3C bowed to the general clamor for standardization and brought SOAP under its development process. The W3C is not immune to human vanity, of course, so future versions will be renamed XML Protocol and will have a greatly expanded feature-set developed through the W3C. SOAP is the communications protocol for Microsoft's web services architecture and Sun's competing Sun ONE architecture. Both expose useful software functions, smaller than complete applications, over the Web. Some examples of these services would be single sign on and Web-based address books. With SOAP and XML, these services are available to any authorized user without regard for hardware platform and operating system. Although MSXML does not directly support SOAP, the Microsoft SOAP toolkit relies on MSXML for its XML processing. The toolkit, then, is an XML application that creates and consumes XML documents using the DOM as the interface to the document. This is the same sort of programming you will do in your applications.

A major area remaining for the W3C is interoperability between SOAP implementations. The current version, 1.2, has significant areas requiring clarification and does not directly address the issue of describing the services offered by a SOAP-based web service. SOAP 1.2 is a W3C Working Draft published at http://www.w3.org/TR/soap12/. The Web Services Description Language (WSDL) is an XML vocabulary designed to address the service description issue. It may be found at http://www.w3.org/TR/wsdl. XML Protocol, also a Working Draft, will likely include WSDL. Its conceptual model is described at http://www.w3.org/TR/xmlp-am/.

XML Processors

Since this book is about a particular XML processor, we should really specify what we mean by the term "XML processor". This term pops up again and again in the XML 1.0 Recommendation. In the Introduction to that document we find the following definitions:

> *[Definition: A software module called an **XML processor** is used to read XML documents and provide access to their content and structure.] [Definition: It is assumed that an XML processor is doing its work on behalf of another module, called the **application**.] This specification describes the required behavior of an XML processor in terms of how it must read XML data and the information it must provide to the application.*

According to this, then, the processor combines the core layers and some or all of the manipulation layers of our model. The XML 1.0 Recommendation makes no assumptions as to the particular interface used to expose the document, which is a good thing as each of the interfaces we discussed are specified elsewhere. Still, the definition is certainly adequate at a high level. Some component consumes XML documents and gives our applications access to them. The processor is not the final user of the document. This accords well with the implementation of MSXML as a COM+ component. It cannot stand alone, but rather is created by, and on behalf of, some application like Internet Explorer, the SOAP toolkit, or an application of our own devising.

The Recommendation goes on to distinguish between processors that are validating, reporting conflicts between a document instance and a DTD's declarations, and non-validating. Both classes of processors must enforce the basic rules of well-formedness. A non-validating processor is a very lightweight component, indeed. It has no ability to parse DTDs, let alone implement the advanced features of XML Schemas. Since MSXML implements so many other layers and interfaces, it is not only *useful* to be a validating processor, but *essential.*

MSXML is broadly characterized in terms of the layered model with which we started the chapter, as follows:

- ❑ **Core**: Validating processor fully implementing XML 1.0 and namespaces.

- ❑ **Structure**: Validating processor, extending validation to include XML Schemas, with support for XPath.

- ❑ **Manipulation**: Implements XSLT, DOM Level 1, and SAX 2.

- ❑ **Application**: As with any processor, MSXML does not implement the application layer, but provides utility interfaces and exposes its lower-layer features through COM to facilitate application programming.

Let's consider how MSXML's "fat" architecture integrates the various layers.

Core Features and Structures

Processing of the core layers is strictly according to the W3C standards. XML 1.0 provides a standard syntax for associating a DTD with an instance document. If you use it, MSXML will load the DTD and perform validation. A document that fails validation will trigger an error. Similarly, XML Schemas provide a standard mechanism for associating all or part of a document with a schema, and using that mechanism triggers schema-based validation.

Things are a bit tricky with XPath support. There is no standard mechanism for invoking an XPath expression. Microsoft has brought it into MSXML through non-standard extensions to DOM interfaces, a pattern that will be commonplace as we consider the higher-layer implementations in MSXML.

Manipulation

SAX2 and DOM interface implementations are straightforward. You can readily transfer SAX programming experience in Java to MSXML provided you have some minimal knowledge of COM. Everything in the standard is there. The DOM implementation is also faithful, though those interfaces are somewhat more complex. DOM also lacks a number of features in Level 1 that MSXML needs. In fact, DOM Level 1 makes no provisions for loading documents! The standard explicitly says that it assumes the document has been parsed and is resident in memory. *Every* XML processor supporting a DOM implementation therefore requires at least one proprietary extension.

Some of the extensions to the DOM offered by MSXML are intended to make DOM programming easier for experienced Windows programmers. For example, events are a common part of the Windows platform, especially in COM and Visual Basic. Also, COM makes common use of enumeration interfaces. If you have spent any time at all programming in Visual Basic, you have used these interfaces, though you may not know them under that name. They are the COM+ feature that supports the For Each … In … language construct. In consequence, MSXML supports a number of events and collections that are extensions to the DOM, but which facilitate Windows development. Nevertheless, there are standard alternatives, and every common XML programming task may be accomplished while sticking to the standard features of the DOM and SAX implementations in MSXML.

Microsoft did make one very interesting design choice when it comes to SAX and DOM. They took advantage of the fact that MSXML, a single component, implements both APIs to address the problem of data structures for SAX-based applications. It is possible to selectively write SAX events to a DOM-based document. That is, you can use the low-resource SAX processor to parse a very large XML document and capture as a tree structure only that subset of the document in which you are interested. With the DOM tree, you may use the DOM interfaces to traverse and manipulate the XML fragment. It is also possible to go in the other direction, passing a DOM document tree to the SAX processor in order to generate SAX events for processing.

It was convenient for us to treat XSLT as a manipulation API and not an application. Many applications use XSLT this way, and it is a simple and effective way to manipulate XML documents in certain common usage scenarios. XSLT, however, is like XPath in that there is no formal mechanism for invoking it. The Recommendation loosely assumes that there is an XSLT processor analogous to the XML processor. Indeed, some vendors provide standalone XSLT processors as part of a "thin" architecture approach to XML technology. The problem here is that an XSLT stylesheet is an XML document. It is useful, indeed powerful, to have DOM access to an XSLT stylesheet. A number of interesting applications have been written in which stylesheets are dynamically modified through DOM before being applied to an input document. Since MSXML supports both, it is worthwhile to be able to access XSLT from DOM. MSXML adds extended methods to its DOM interfaces so that programmers may directly invoke an XSLT transformation.

Schema-based programming makes extreme use of this feature of MSXML to implement entire applications as a series of event-driven XSLT transformations invoked from the DOM. This technique is described in Chapter 13 of "Professional XML, 2nd Edition" (Wrox Press, ISBN 1-861005-05-9), Chapter 15 of "Professional XSL" (Wrox Press, ISBN 1-861003-57-9), and Chapter 16 of "Professional XML Schemas" (Wrox Press, ISBN 1-861005-47-4). All the applications presented take advantage of the fusion of XSLT and DOM in MSXML.

Processors for Supporting Technologies

Now things really get murky. Once we enter the applications layer, there is no definite way to tie MSXML to core technologies except through the application's use of one of the standard APIs. That is, there is no provision for calling out to applications from the core functions, nor should there be any such feature. Applications drive components, not the other way around. Even highly standardized applications like SOAP and MathML are just that – applications that use standard technology – and not part of the technology itself. Still, there are many common usage scenarios for XML applications. The designers of MSXML have considered these and added utility interfaces and extensions to make the programmer's life easier.

The appallingly uneven level of XML support among web browsers recently has driven many programmers to perform XML processing on the server, passing the resulting HTML to the client. This reduces the need to offer competing implementations of the same XML-related feature and means that the developer need not rely on the presence of an XML processor on the client. This approach means that performance is at a premium. Transformations and schema processing must be optimized for server-side usage at all but the smallest web sites. For example, it is common to store content, such as an online newspaper, in XML and render platform-appropriate versions. Simply modifying an XSLT stylesheet may change the style of the site, and multiple versions may be available to suit different device display capabilities. MSXML meets this need through optimizing the component for server-side usage and offering proprietary interfaces for caching stylesheets. In the case of a newspaper with different styles (for example, headlines only, full text, full text without illustrations) to suit different devices, you load and parse the different XSLT stylesheets once and cache the compiled templates on the server. By "compiled", incidentally, we mean the stylesheet as represented in MSXML's internal, binary structures rather than as text in the XSLT syntax. As each request comes in, the appropriate cached stylesheet is used to perform the desired transformation. This eliminates the disk access and parsing tasks that you incur without caching.

Similar server-side optimizations exist for schemas. In applications that use the exchange of XML documents as a means of distributed computing, such as SOAP and BizTalk Server, server-side schemas act as a sort of semantic firewall. Validating incoming documents against a well-known schema ensures that requests from ill-behaved clients do not cause problems for the server. Invalid documents are discarded with a warning to the client. Here again, servers that lack optimizations for server-side use would have to load and parse the same small set of documents, that is, XML schemas, over and over to the detriment of server throughput. MSXML supports an interface that allows you to load and parse a schema once, then reuse it multiple times. This is particularly useful when a document takes advantage of namespaces to build a vocabulary from several existing schemas. The time to retrieve, load, and parse multiple schemas files is avoided every time an instance document conforming to the new, combined vocabulary arrives on the server.

XSLT and XML Schemas are standard technologies that exist below the application layer in our model. The proprietary extensions to support them in MSXML are fairly obvious optimizations. What does MSXML do to support less obvious applications of XML technology? Many types of XML applications rely on HTTP, either to get XML documents or send XML documents to another application. MSXML offers not one but two HTTP implementations, one intended for client-side use and one that is suitable for use in the server environment. XML documents may be loaded asynchronously, allowing an XML client to begin work while a large document continues to load. Larger applications may require multi-threading support server-side, allowing multiple clients to update different portions of an XML document concurrently. MSXML has a free-threaded DOM interface for just this purpose. Finally, the proprietary data binding architecture found throughout Windows and the Active Data Objects (ADO) interfaces is extended to MSXML, allowing data binding to XML documents. This directly facilitates one of the architectures we'll consider in the next section.

The common thread tying application-layer support together in MSXML is the fact of the "fat" architecture. As MSXML supports so many related and useful XML technologies, it is able to add proprietary features that allow one technology to complement another. If you merely want to parse and read an XML document, this will do you little good. If, however, you are committed to using XML throughout your application, MSXML is a powerful addition to your toolset. With one component, you have access to optimized implementations of the common XML technologies. Since these technologies are integrated in MSXML and the Windows operating system, it is easy to apply the appropriate technology to the tasks you face in your applications. Let's see how this works in practice by considering some common architectures for XML-based applications.

Some Alternatives

It is worth considering some alternative processors as a contrast to the fat architecture of MSXML. The list below is far from exhaustive, but mentions a few of the more popular XML processors available. Consider especially the feature set of each and contrast them with the features offered in MSXML. We believe you will begin to see why MSXML is a fat processor. Whether that is good or bad is a matter for individual programmers. Note that some are optimized for performance and sacrifice features. Two support both SAX and DOM interfaces, but only one supports XML Schemas. None support other XML technologies such as XSLT or XPath, deferring that support to other components.

A list of free tools is found at http://www.garshol.priv.no/download/xmltools/, while a broader (though dated) list can be found at http://wdvl.com/Software/XML/parsers.html.

XP, Expat

Originally created by James Clark, these processors have gone on to further development by others. Expat is a C-language processor optimized for performance. Supporting XML 1.0 and namespaces, it offers its own stream-oriented interface to XML document processing. Expat is the processor underlying the Mozilla browser effort. XP is a Java-language, non-validating processor that supports XML 1.0. Both processors support the UTF-8, UTF-16, ISO-8859-1, and US-ASCII character encodings. Expat is available from http://expat.sourceforge.net.

Xerces

This is a validating XML processor offered in several forms for C++ and Java. The C++ version offers wrappers that make it accessible from Perl and COM+. The latest version, in late beta, supports DOM Level 2, as well as a custom interface designed to facilitate the creation of specialized processors and processor configurations using Xerces. The beta version for Java is available from http://xml.apache.org/xerces2-j/index.html.

IBM XML Processors

IBM's alphaWorks effort offers XML4J and XML4C, processors for the Java and C++ languages, respectively. Both offer support for XML Schemas, SAX 2, and DOM Level 2 (with partial Level 3 support), though the C++ version lags slightly behind. XML4J is available from http://www.alphaworks.ibm.com/tech/xml4j.

Architecture

The technologies you use and the sort of XML processor you require is driven, of course, by your application architecture. In this section we'll present some common architectures that you can implement using MSXML as your processor. The choice of architecture depends on how XML is being used in your application and what clients you expect to access the application.

Addressing the former issue, how XML is used, we have the following typical usages:

❑ Platform-neutral data exchange and application integration.

❑ Separation of data from representation.

❑ Data extraction and caching.

The first use is typified by business-to-business (B2B) e-commerce. You have issues of differing platforms (for example, Sun Solaris versus Windows) and data formats (like the purchase orders we mentioned earlier) that cannot be resolved by standardizing on a common platform and format. Business partners will wish to retain their current technology infrastructure. Worse, when the B2B exchange is many-to-many, you will need to support many differing formats. In addition, you will almost certainly be using HTTP and the Web for communications, so you need a format that is amenable to delivery over this medium, in other words, text.

The online newspaper scenario mentioned earlier is an example of the separation of data from presentation. Sales and product support literature is another application. In each case you have a common core of data (the news content or support literature) and many different delivery channels. In the case of the newspaper, we assumed delivery over a variety of hardware devices with differing bandwidth and display capabilities. In the support literature case, we have different target users. When promoting or marketing our products, we wish to present a succinct subset in a rich, visually appealing user interface. An established customer looking for support wants a less elaborate presentation and more detailed content. If the data (common core content) is separated from the visual delivery by XSLT, we can maintain one set of data and dynamically render the appropriate interface. It is easier to maintain data integrity without losing the appeal of multiple delivery channels tailored to the users' needs.

Data extraction and caching focuses more on implementation than user requirements. We may need to extract a subset of data from a relational source for delivery to the client in XML format as a local data cache. In the past we would have used a native binary format, but that would tie our application to a particular platform. XML allows us to leverage all the supporting technologies, such as XPath, in using the data extract. In a widely distributed system, we might find it useful to pass such an extract to a client application or some other server to flatten the service load across the various tiers of the system. If we know the target client has its own XML processor supporting the required technologies, we can offload some processing from the server to the client.

The second issue – client support for XML – was the strongest driver of architecture in early XML-based applications. Many web developers wanted to use XML but couldn't rely on client support due to a lack of an XML processor or the use of differing, proprietary implementations of features not yet addressed by the W3C. For example, there is no W3C-approved way to associate an XSLT stylesheet with an XML instance document. Internet Explorer uses an XML processing instruction (PI) to convey this information. Processing instructions in XML 1.0 are explicitly application-dependent and exist to pass processing hints along to a particular application. When Internet Explorer downloads an XML document with the appropriate processing instruction, it retrieves the referenced stylesheet, performs the transformation, and displays the results in the browser window in lieu of the raw XML. A processing instruction like the following would therefore take the place of some client-side code in the delivery of an online newspaper:

```
<?xml-stylesheet type="text\xsl" href="fullnews.xslt" ?>
```

Internet Explorer gained rich support for XML, beginning with version 5.0, but Netscape Communicator has only slowly come around to supporting XML, chiefly through the Mozilla open source effort. Where Communicator/Mozilla have embraced XML, they have often chosen differing features or implementation syntax. Rather than sense the type of requesting browser and serve different content, it is frequently easier to perform all the XML processing on the server and return only HTML (or other formats when the requesting application is not a browser).

We often combine some of the solutions we just presented in order to devise architectures for real-world systems and applications. There are at least four common architectural patterns in XML systems, which we will now consider. Here are the architectures we will examine in more detail:

❑   Clients that process XML directly, including caching of data.

❑   Server-side XML manipulation on behalf of thin clients.

❑   Hybrids of client and server-side processing.

❑   XML in the backend enterprise infrastructure.

Client-Side Uses of XML

Client-side XML processing is an ideal solution when we can guarantee a minimum level of software and computing capability for XML processing support on the client device. Server software is clean and free of presentation software, sending and receiving XML documents. Errors are minimized as the client can perform validation prior to sending data to the server. While it remains beneficial to perform validation on the server in order to trap errors from bad clients, the share of server resources consumed by error handling is diminished, and the network is spared a high volume of traffic devoted to resolving errors. Most importantly, the burden of converting data from user inputs to XML is shared with the client, allowing the server to handle more clients with the same processing resources. In short, the server is a pure XML application, and the issue of how the XML emitted by the server will be consumed is left to the device closest to the user.

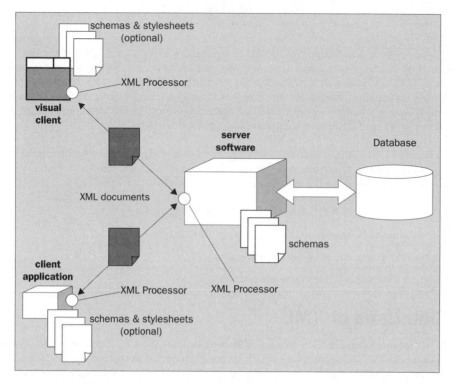

In this case, both client and server must have XML support, although the technologies supported may differ. Here are the server's responsibilities:

❑ Generate valid XML from server resources such as databases, according to recognized schemas.

❑ Validate incoming documents according to recognized schemas.

❑ Parse XML documents from clients and convert the data into server-side activities, for example, perform data retrieval.

❑ Potentially perform transformations between schemas to accommodate external partners.

Note that the server does not become involved in presentation issues at any time. While XSLT support may be required, it is strictly for data transformation. This is independent of the nature and capabilities of the requesting client, so client sensing and conditional processing logic is not required.

Server involvement in data integrity can generally be limited to document-level validation (as opposed to field-by-field checks) as they are typically generating documents from trusted sources on the server-side. If a database is the source of data for outgoing XML documents, it will usually have performed integrity checks at the column level. As long as constraints in the XML Schemas do not contradict database constraints, inputs from the database may be presumed to be at least as good as the schema requires, and document-level validation serves as a final check to catch obscure problems.

Now consider the responsibilities of client devices:

❏   Perform field-level validation on user or application inputs.

❏   Generate XML from user or application inputs.

❏   Parse (and optionally validate) XML documents received from the server.

❏   Perform processing to convert XML into human-readable form.

When the client application originates an XML document, it must perform checks on individual inputs from the user interface to ensure that the data conforms to constraints in the schema for the final document. The application must provide these checks prior to processor-based validation of the complete document to avoid rejecting a document resulting from lengthy user operations. Users will soon lose interest in an application that waits to reject an input until all data is collected and the user wishes to submit it to the server.

With the field-level validations performed, the client must use an XML processor to create an XML document for submission to the server. It may elect to validate the document prior to submission, although this will only be a redundant check on the accuracy of the field-level validations and the integrity of the code used to generate the XML document. If validation is performed, the issue of keeping client-side schemas synchronized with those on the server arises. If the client is required to download schemas prior to every session, additional network traffic arises and the system must also have a mechanism for advising the client if a schema changes during a session.

When receiving data in XML format from the server, the client must parse (and optionally validate) the documents. The validation issues are the same as previously discussed. If the client is another application, code must be available to convert the XML document into native formats and perform appropriate actions. If the data is intended for visual display to a human user, the client must support some technology (XSLT for example), for rendering the data visually. Although this imposes a processing burden on the client, it allows the client to provide the form of rendering most appropriate to the resources of the client hardware, the requirements of the client application, and the current state of the user session. In short, the client is the software best positioned to select the optimal form of rendering for the data.

Server-Side Uses of XML

In a server-side architecture, all XML processing occurs on the server. The client is isolated from this, either because it has no capability to process XML or because it is a legacy application that predates our use of XML. XML is still valuable, however. The system gets the benefit of a single data format while supporting the ability to render that data in many different formats. We also get the benefits of XML's supporting technologies, such as XPath and XSLT, thereby simplifying our development efforts.

The scheme of processing is depicted in the diagram overleaf. A request arrives from the client as an HTTP GET or POST operation. The request parameters are encoded under the rules of that protocol and are accessible only to a compliant web server. The server software performs native-format retrieval, typically from a relational database, and then converts the results of processing into XML. XML Schemas may be used to validate the final reply document. So far, the sequence of events on the server is the same as for the previous architecture. At this point, however, rather than return the XML document, the server continues to process it. Based on its knowledge of the requesting client, the server selects a representation format and converts the XML into that form. The server usually maintains a collection of stylesheets, one for each format it supports. This will usually be an HTML document, although some servers support PDF or another visual format.

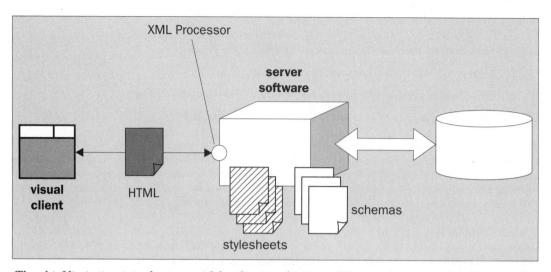

The chief limitation is in the nature of the client applications. Whereas the client-side architecture supports diverse client applications, clients in a server-side architecture are limited to visual clients like web browsers. The end user must be a human consumer of visual data. XML is not returned to the client, so no further processing of the data *as data* is possible. The server has made all the decisions, and all flexibility is lost once the server is finished with the data.

Here is a list of the server's responsibilities:

- ❑ Parse client HTTP requests.
- ❑ Detect or identify client capabilities.
- ❑ Perform server-side processing, for example data retrieval.
- ❑ Create XML response documents.
- ❑ Validate XML documents.
- ❑ Render data in a form suitable to the target client.

In contrast, the list of client responsibilities is quite short. A forms-based web page will satisfy these requirements:

- ❑ Compose HTTP requests.
- ❑ Render HTML.

The benefit of this architecture is that it simplifies client-side development and effectively eliminates concerns regarding client capabilities and platforms. This benefit, though, is purchased at a significant cost. The request-response mechanism in a client-side architecture is transparent: both sides of the exchange are XML documents. If the architect has done their job, the markup will be descriptive and therefore accessible to any developer with the proper toolset. In server-side architectures, the request is concealed within the communications protocol, HTTP, used to communicate with the server. To understand the exchange, a developer has to distinguish between the part of the request that deals with the application and the parts needed just to communicate with the server. For example, an HTTP POST includes header information followed by field and value pairs. This structure is specific to HTTP, but contains information – the field values – the application needs. The developer has to have tools for HTTP and XML.

So why would we select this architecture? The issue is chiefly one of control. A distributed application tends to put parts of the system outside the control of the programmer. A server-side solution brings more parts of the application onto the server where the programmer has control over them. The system developer knows the entire XML portion of the application, and can be sure of the level of support for XML and XSLT available to the system. The only significant part of the solution that is not under the control of the programmer is the step in which the user's intentions are converted into an HTTP request. The page that performs this task is served, though, and HTML form processing in browsers is standardized, so this step presents few risks.

Hybrid Architectures

Purity is lost somewhere between the whiteboard session and the programmer's development environment. Most systems, consequently, will be hybrid forms of the preceding architectures. It is also not the case, as you might suppose, that a hybrid system starts out as server-side and migrates toward a client-side architecture. There are many reasons why hybrid architecture might come to be implemented, including:

❑ Accommodating critical legacy applications in a generally client-side environment.

❑ Supporting novel use cases, for example a business-to-consumer store front in an otherwise automated, business-to-business system.

❑ Adding applications to a server-side system that previously supported only web browsers as clients.

❑ Adding external partners and clients to a previously client-side, internal system.

❑ Enabling disconnected client processing in an otherwise server-side system.

❑ Distributing processing load in a system of web browser clients when up-level browsers are known to be available.

The key to developing hybrid architectures is determining how much control the system designers choose to exercise over the system. If you are developing an intranet application, you will naturally gravitate toward the advantages of a client-side system as you control the selection of client software. Since robust XML capabilities are available, you will want to distribute the processing load and simplify the server software. If, however, you have a significant body of users who are not under your administrative control then you will need to add a server-side solution. This leads to an overall hybrid architecture. Sometimes this takes the form of supporting down-level clients or legacy applications, while in other cases, it may mean that the server is itself the client – and a very sophisticated one from the standpoint of XML – of other servers. The latter case is at the heart of so-called web services. A server may obtain data from another server not under its control (with a common native data format and security permissions) by exchanging XML documents.

XML in the Infrastructure

The models just described look at XML in terms of where document processing occurs in the architecture of a particular application or system. A useful alternative is to consider XML as part of the computing infrastructure – the products installed to support computing regardless of specific applications. Regardless of how you distribute tasks to process documents, it is instructive to consider where XML might be useful and how it fits in as an enabler of a system's applications. In this case, rather than consider what each tier does in a given application, we are considering how various resources may be used and ensuring the key resources are enabled for XML data exchange. If a resource is something that should be publicly accessible or may be broadly used across a number of applications, it needs to be amenable to XML processing. For data resources, this means exporting an XML format. Communications resources need to work well with XML. Consider the following system assets and how they might be XML-enabled:

❏ Relational data – XML formats for exchanging recordsets; optionally, an XML syntax for performing data operations on the database.

❏ Messaging – ability to pass XML documents cleanly; optionally, the ability to work seamlessly with XML processors.

❏ Content – perform XSLT on XML – format content for visual presentation.

❏ E-Commerce systems – exchange data as XML messages with outside systems and perform XSLT transformation dynamically.

❏ Standalone applications – support an XML vocabulary as a secondary file format as an alternative to the application's native file format, for purposes such as facilitating data exchange, migration, and interoperability.

❏ Search engines – ability to use an XML Schema to permit element-specific searches of XML documents.

Since MSXML is a COM+ component, it is widely leveraged throughout the Microsoft product line to provide XML-oriented features. SQL Server, for example, uses MSXML to provide very rich XML services. Not only can recordsets be exposed as XML documents rather than in the traditional binary format (a feature also available through ADO COM+ objects), but there is also a query format allowing normal operations to be submitted to the database engine as XML documents. This helps web developers, for example, to provide a thin front-end to a SQL Server database through a web page without resorting to ActiveX objects on the client. In addition, by exposing the data as XML, data can be passed back in a form amenable to processing locally, even if the client is not running Windows. The alternative, an ASP performing the data retrieval, would require significant coding that is eliminated with the XML option.

Microsoft Message Queuing (MSMQ), of course, handles XML very well as it can handle text messages up to several megabytes in size. The COM+ object model for MSMQ goes a step further. Since both MSMQ and MSXML support certain streaming interfaces, programmers can simply assign an instance of MSXML containing a document to the body of an MSMQ message. The object models cooperate behind the scenes to stream the document into the message, and also stream it back out on the other end into MSXML. This feature, also available in ASP, eliminates a few lines of code each time an application needs to move XML documents via MSMQ.

The entire Office suite uses XML as an alternative file format. It utilizes namespaces as a means of saving an Office document as HTML while retaining the specialized formatting options that Office supports and HTML does not. This allows for publishing to a web site, then bringing the document back into Office for editing. Once again, MSXML is the XML processor underlying this feature.

The lesson for programmers and architects is to consider when XML is valuable to a system or application. If data needs to be shared or used in various ways across a variety of applications, it is worthwhile to incur the performance penalty and add an XML layer to the service or application hosting the data. A wise precautionary move is to include XML support in your evaluation criteria when selecting major software. When developing custom software, you must make a choice between enabling future XML capabilities and avoiding the cost of building such features.

The benefit of using MSXML in such a situation is not only in offering pre-built XML tools, but also in making standardized support available via COM+ to all your applications. The latter point may not be entirely obvious at first glance. After all, a major consideration in choosing XML in the first place is standardization. Commercial XML processors, though, differ in two areas: proprietary extensions and their interpretation of ambiguous points in W3C Recommendations. Since MSXML is available across languages through COM+, using it as your XML workhorse will reduce disparities between applications and increase productivity slightly.

The first area is obvious. Even if you make it a practice to stick closely to the standard methods and avoid proprietary extensions in the interest of portability, you will find occasions when you will resort to extensions. They may provide useful shortcuts to some key feature of your application. In other cases, such as the matter of loading a document into a DOM implementation, you will need to resort to extension methods because there is no standard. Regardless of the reason, standardizing on a common XML processor allows you to leverage your investment in learning the proprietary extensions over all your projects. If you are using a processor that is tied to a particular language, you may easily find yourself involved in a project that does not permit you to use your chosen processor.

The last point – interpretations of ambiguous points – is much more obscure. XML itself is only in its first version. Supporting technologies are necessarily newer. There are inevitably subtle areas in which the guiding W3C document leaves room for interpretation. Different processor vendors make different choices, and there is considerable contention among the faithful on the XML-DEV mailing list as to who is right in various disputes. In fact, in MSXML 4.0, the interpretation of non-essential whitespace (for example "pretty printing" formatting) is different between the DOM and SAX2 interfaces of MSXML. The SAX2 implementation embraces the emerging consensus regarding this issue – preserving the whitespace. Since SAX2 support is relatively new (it became fully supported with version 3.0), Microsoft is able to make the change with less chance of breaking existing applications.

> *While you will want to focus on a particular processor for reasons of commonality and productivity, you should spend some time with other processors. This will help you avoid the common error of assuming that a non-standard implementation in your favorite processor is, in fact, the standard. In particular, if your application or system involves external partners, you must make it a practice to use different processors in testing to ensure that you have not unknowingly locked your application into a proprietary extension to XML.*

History and Future of MSXML

MSXML has an unusual past, beginning as a tool designed only to support one of Microsoft's products and progressing to become one of the lynchpins of Microsoft software. As one tee shirt making the rounds in Redmond has it: "*MSXML – the component that is turning this company around 360°*". Even after turning completely around and returning to its starting point – going forward, hopefully – Microsoft and MSXML are forever changed. The commitment to XML began with the earliest version of MSXML, continued through the current, highly robust release and is going forward into the .NET world.

Origins

Internet Explorer 4.0 was released with the "channels" feature – Microsoft's take on pushed web content. A format for encoding the structure and update frequency of channels was needed. As this was around the time XML 1.0 became a W3C Recommendation, one of the developers proposed XML as the syntax for encoding this information. Although this was a bold move at the time, the proposal was adopted. MSXML was written as a component that Internet Explorer could call on to parse the stored information and properly maintain channels. The first version was comparatively primitive, and there was no intention of publicly releasing the interface.

Nevertheless, COM components (COM+ had yet to be invented) expose information to system tools, and developers became aware of MSXML. There was a clamor, both inside and outside Microsoft, to make MSXML a formal, public tool with developer support. At the same time, the DOM was progressing in the W3C standardization process and it would be necessary to add DOM support to Microsoft's original, wholly internal, API to XML documents in MSXML.

MSXML's Public Debut

MSXML was quickly upgraded and released with public acknowledgement of its interfaces with Internet Explorer 4.01. Though initially tied to Internet Explorer releases, tension between that product's release schedule, the developer community, and the needs of other products that took to using MSXML has served to give the component an identity that is partially distinct from Internet Explorer. There have been separate web releases, and newer products have bundled MSXML upgrades for their own use. The following list gives the highlights of MSXML releases and the products with which they were released:

- ❑ Windows 95 OSR – MSXML version 1.0
- ❑ Windows 95 OSR with Internet Explorer 4.01 – version 2.0a
- ❑ Office 2000 with Internet Explorer 5.0a – version 2.0a
- ❑ Internet Explorer 5.01 or Windows 2000 – version 2.5
- ❑ Windows 2000 SP1 (Internet Explorer 5.5) – version 2.5
- ❑ BizTalk Server – version 2.6

MSXML 3.0 was released on the Web as a separate distribution in March 2001. MSXML 4.0 went into beta release in July 2001, with a second beta in August. MSXML 4.0 (now referred to as Microsoft XML Core Services Component version 4.0) was released in October 2001.

> *The comprehensive list from which the above is adapted includes file version numbers and an expanded list of products. The list is found on the Microsoft Knowledge Base in article Q269238 (http://support.microsoft.com/support/kb/articles/Q269/2/38.asp).*

MSXML, .NET, and the Future

At this point, you may have some questions regarding the continued viability of MSXML as a development tool. The new .NET architecture is destined to be the basis for future Windows-platform development. So where does this leave traditional COM+ components?

First, Microsoft remains committed to XML as it moves forward into the .NET architecture. Indeed, as the communications mechanism for web services, XML is fundamental to .NET. It should not be surprising, then, to learn that the capabilities exposed in MSXML are available as system-level classes in the .NET framework.

Currently, the run-time classes provided with a .NET system support the following:

- ❑ XML 1.0
- ❑ XML Namespaces
- ❑ XML Schemas
- ❑ XPath
- ❑ XSLT
- ❑ DOM Level 2
- ❑ SOAP 1.1

DOM Level 2 lies at the heart of XML support in .NET and is supported by the classes belonging to the `System.Xml` namespace. All the functionality and features you find in MSXML with respect to DOM processing are found there. This includes XML namespace processing. `System.Xml.Schema` supports XML Schemas in their entirety, both structures and data types. The `System.Xml.XPath` namespace implements XPath. Several classes are performance-optimized and work with XSLT-supporting classes. These latter classes belong to the `System.Xml.Xsl` namespace. Finally, a non-standard namespace, `System.Xml.Serialization`, is provided to read and write the persistent information about objects as XML documents.

Early in this chapter we said that one of the benefits of using a robust implementation of an XML processor such as MSXML was having a single-source toolkit for most of the technologies you will need in order to work with XML. The outline above would suggest that Microsoft is turning away from this approach. Does this contradict the architecture of MSXML? If it does, how will developers migrate from MSXML to the standard .NET classes for XML? The answer to this lies in the nature of .NET development and its key component, the **Common Language Runtime** (**CLR**). Like COM+, .NET strives to be language-neutral. The means by which it accomplishes this goal is the CLR. .NET classes are compiled into a byte-code that is the same for all languages. At run time, the byte-code is executed using the CLR. The CLR is similar to the Java Virtual Machine (JVM) at the heart of the Java world. Having a common interpretive entity allows different classes to be included and invoked as easily as COM+ makes a new interface available to Windows programmers. Unlike a JVM, though, the CLR's language neutrality brings the language independence of COM+ to the flexibility of Java. Since the XML support in .NET is built into the system classes, XML interfaces are always available to .NET developers. Basically, the path from MSXML to .NET is quite short and has the following characteristics:

❑ Common interfaces for standard APIs, such as the DOM – apart from the differences peculiar to the two environments, your standardized code should look quite similar.

❑ Language flexibility – the same wide range of languages that can use MSXML is also available in .NET.

❑ Ease of use – you can get a new interface in .NET as easily as in COM+ (and if you are a C++ programmer concerned with reference counting, then .NET is a good deal easier).

So for brand new, custom development, MSXML is a training ground for .NET XML programmers. The world, though, is not restricted to new code. Since MSXML is so widely used, by Microsoft and others, we will be dealing with code designed for MSXML for some time to come. MSXML will continue to be deployed by Microsoft software, and the .NET system classes will likely be informed by the experience and design choices of MSXML, even if inadvertently. You cannot disrupt such a massive code base lightly. Further, the .NET development tools are not yet released. Once they are, programmers will need to become experienced with them, vendors will need to modify their products for compatibility, and new applications will have to be phased in to replace old ones. This will not happen soon. MSXML experience will continue to be a good thing to have for quite a while.

Summary

MSXML is the workhorse of XML development for Windows programmers. Originating in the earliest days of XML, it has evolved to become a high-performance, feature-rich component offering support for all the key technologies related to XML. It is hard to imagine doing native Windows development with XML support without strongly considering using MSXML. Best of all, it is available free of charge.

MSXML is suited to all the common XML application architectures. It is accessible from all major programming languages available on Windows, making client-side development easier. It contains performance-oriented interfaces suited to server-side development. It is also well suited to web development, supporting not one but two HTTP interfaces, one intended for client-side work and one for the server environment.

Hopefully we have convinced you that MSXML is the component you need in order to do serious XML development within a Windows environment. In this introduction we have listed the technologies it supports, and described the more common application architectures enabled by those technologies. There are no high-level surprises left, only interfaces to learn and technologies to practice. That is the task of this book. You will be given a thorough grounding in the technologies MSXML supports and experience in working with them as interpreted and implemented by MSXML. We will start by reviewing each of the major supporting technologies for XML: DOM, XML Schemas, XPath, XSLT, and SAX. Next, we'll build on that foundation by demonstrating some of the application architectures with a focus on how to perform different tasks with MSXML on each tier of the system. Finally, several case studies that combine the technologies, architectures, and MSXML will be presented to show this component in action from start to finish. XML-based development is an exciting type of programming, and MSXML is an excellent tool with which to do this development.

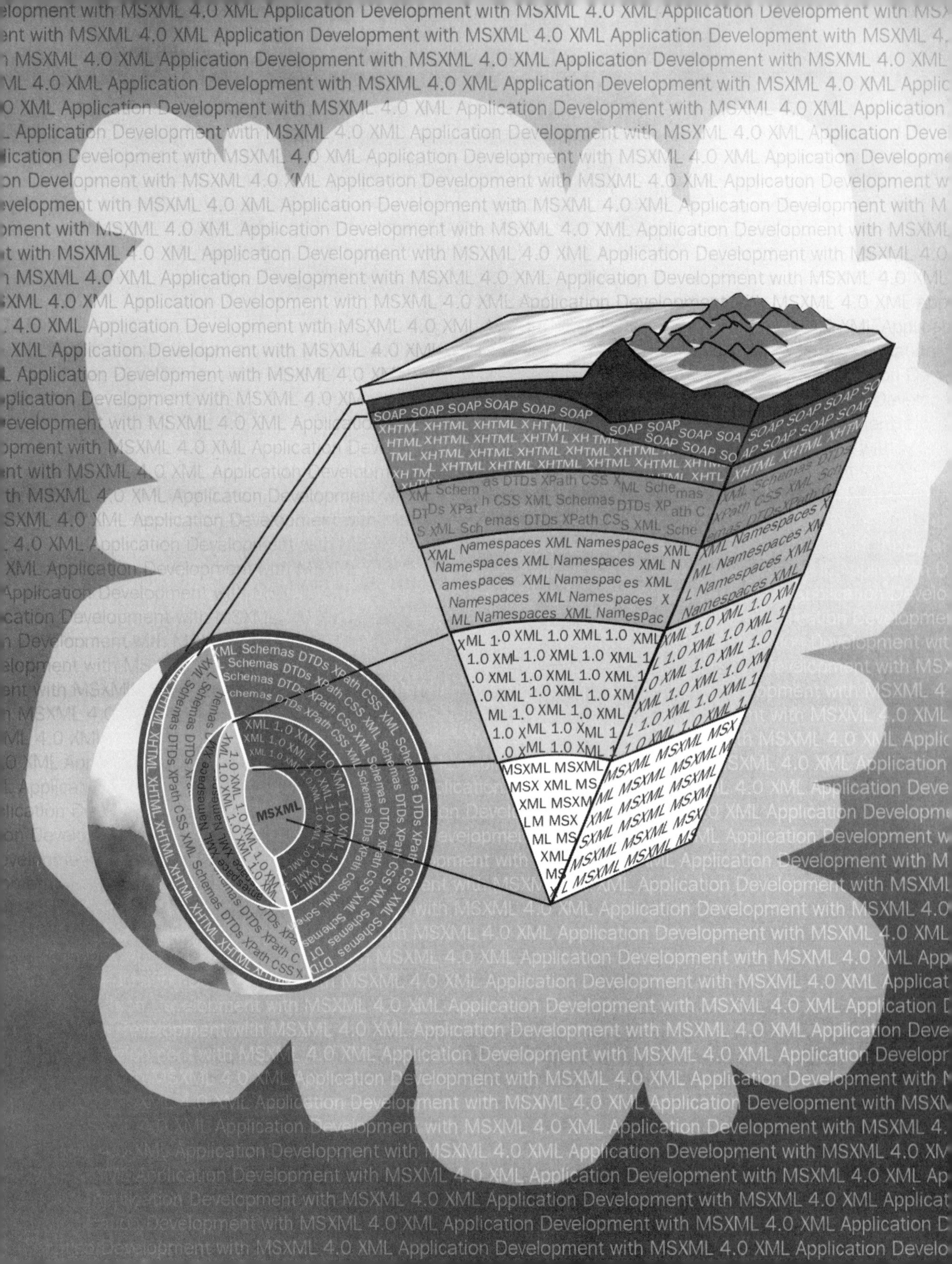
XML Application Development with MSXML 4.0
SOAP
XHTML
XML Schemas DTDs XPath CSS
XML Namespaces
XML 1.0
MSXML

2

Document Object Model in MSXML

Any non-trivial component or technology has an application programming interface (API) that programmers must use to program the technology. The API serves as a clean interface between the programmer's application and the technology they wish to use. MSXML is no different. In fact, MSXML has many APIs in the form of related COM+ interfaces.

In this chapter we will focus on the **Document Object Model** (**DOM**) API. This group of interfaces is unique in that it is Microsoft's implementation of the W3C's API to XML itself. While MSXML supports another API for working with XML documents (SAX – the subject of Chapter 6), the DOM is the only API controlled and published by the W3C.

This chapter will introduce you to the DOM, its interfaces, and the basic tasks you must perform to work with the DOM effectively. In particular, you will learn the following:

- ❑   The W3C's involvement in the DOM.

- ❑   The overall structure of the DOM object model.

- ❑   Properties and methods of the principal objects of the object model.

- ❑   How to perform the more common DOM programming tasks.

As we cover the DOM object model we will be careful to distinguish between the properties and methods the W3C *mandates* in its DOM Recommendation and the *extensions* MSXML offers. This will help you write code that is as portable as possible although, as we shall see, no DOM code can be completely portable due to certain omissions in the DOM as it exists today. Before we dive into the DOM as seen by Microsoft, let's go back to the source – the W3C – and see what it has to say about it.

W3C and DOM

The DOM looks at an XML document as a tree composed of nodes representing the individual items of markup that constitute an XML document. These include elements, attributes, processing instructions, and all the other parts of XML 1.0. The top of the tree is the document root. Its immediate children are nodes representing the prolog elements (for example, XML declaration, comments, processing instructions, or DOCTYPE declarations), if any, and the document element. The XML document element has child nodes, which may in turn have their own child nodes, and so on down the structure until the innermost elements and text nodes are modeled. A simplified view of this is depicted here:

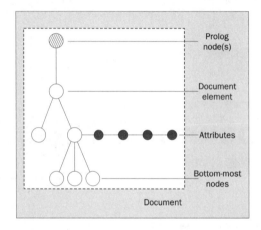

> Note that attributes, unlike all other types of markup, have their own special collection. You cannot navigate from attributes to other content, nor will you reach attributes if you are following the main body of the tree. This makes sense; after all, attributes in XML are unordered properties wholly belonging to the element on which they appear.

The **W3C DOM Activity** is the body responsible for ongoing development of the Document Object Model. It has taken to describing different versions of the DOM as **levels**. The DOM is divided into **modules** within each level. Modules *compartmentalize* features, while levels *extend* features.

The DOM provides a series of **interfaces** that collectively describe an object model for the tree-structured document concept we discussed above. The DOM interfaces are divided into two groups: **principal** and **extended**. All DOM implementations must support the principal interfaces, but extended interfaces are optional. For reasons that will become clear in a moment, MSXML implements both sets of interfaces fully.

Level 1 became a Recommendation in October 1998. Broadly speaking, it supported XML 1.0 and HTML. Level 2 reached Recommendation status in November 2000. Its major changes were namespace and cascading style sheet support, an event model for user interface interaction and tree manipulation, and some other useful features for tree manipulation. Level 3 is under development in Working Draft status. Among its projected enhancements are: alignment with the newer theoretical models underlying XML, more events, support for XML Schemas and XPath, and the standardized ability to load and save a document.

MSXML adheres to DOM Level 1, although some of its extensions closely parallel DOM Level 2 additions. For example, MSXML's named node map interface supports a method, `getQualifiedItem()`, which permits you to retrieve a namespace-qualified node. DOM Level 2 added the method `getNamedItemNS()` to the same interface, with equivalent functionality.

In order to focus on how MSXML implements the W3C DOM as a way of reading and manipulating XML documents, we'll describe the interfaces from DOM Level 1. We will not delve into the properties and methods of these interfaces, but will defer that until we discuss the DOM implementation provided by MSXML. This will allow us to cover the information once, including the proprietary extensions offered by that component. For now, it is enough to get an idea of what interfaces are available, how they map to the tree-structured view of an XML document, and for what, in general, they can be used in applications.

Principal Interfaces

The principal interfaces deal with the basic constructs of a markup document – whether HTML or XML – in a tree structure. There are several categories of objects:

❑ Document – the entire document as a whole.

❑ Nodes in the tree – component constructs within the document.

❑ Collections of nodes – useful groupings of nodes.

The following table lists the W3C principal interfaces and their implementation equivalents in MSXML 4.0:

W3C Interface	MSXML 4.0 Implementation	DOM Concept
DOMImplementation	IXMLDOMImplementation	XML processor.
DocumentFragment	IXMLDOMDocumentFragment	Fragment of a document, which need not have a single root element.
Document	IXMLDOMDocument, IXMLDOMDocument2	Document.
Node	IXMLDOMNode	Any node in the tree.
NodeList	IXMLDOMNodeList	Integer-ordered list of nodes.
NamedNodeMap	IXMLDOMNamedNodeMap	Collection of nodes ordered by name.
CharacterData	IXMLDOMCharacterData	PCDATA.
Attr	IXMLDOMAttribute	Attributes.
Element	IXMLDOMElement	Elements.
Text	IXMLDOMText	Textual content of elements and attributes.
Comment	IXMLDOMComment	Comments.

There is also an interface in the W3C DOM called DOMException. This interface, however, is nothing more than an unsigned short integer value with a list of predefined values. MSXML accommodates these in the IXMLDOMParseError interface. DOMException is intended for languages that offer an exception mechanism. The Recommendation explicitly allows passing the error values defined in DOMException through alternative, native error reporting mechanisms. Since DOM does not provide any sort of error object, MSXML offers IXMLDOMParseError as a proprietary interface, which includes line and column numbers where the error occurred, making it easy to handle error information in COM+-compliant languages.

The DOM authors made an interesting design decision that is directly relevant to MSXML and, indeed, any web development using COM+ or Java. There is substantial overhead in obtaining new interfaces from a component. Java requires a cast, while COM+ requires a call to the QueryInterface() method of the IUnknown COM+ interface. Most of the methods and properties of the various tree-node-related interfaces are the same, differing only where the underlying markup constructs differ. (For example, an element can have child content whereas an attribute cannot. Consequently, Element needs some sort of collection object as one of its properties while Attr does not.)

The DOM authors provide an alternative to the overhead of obtaining interfaces by permitting considerable overlap between the features of Node and those of the other interfaces. In this way, the DOM is "flattened" – rather than using many different interfaces, it uses two principal ones (Document and Node) and two interfaces for collections. Nodes become extremely versatile, standing in for all sorts of markup items smaller than a document. Where an instance of Node represents some markup item for which a particular property is inappropriate, the property will be empty. If you look at the collection for child content on a Node representing an attribute, you will find an empty collection object, and if you try to append children to an attribute an error will occur.

Extended Interfaces

The W3C DOM applies to both XML and HTML. Thus, the W3C DOM Activity members concluded there would be DOM implementations intended strictly for processing HTML (for example, browser object models). Consequently, they distinguished between those interfaces required by all DOM implementations (termed the **DOM Core**), in other words the principal interfaces just discussed, and extended interfaces required for XML processing. The extended interfaces are not required in HTML-only implementations of the DOM. Since we are dealing with XML, however, there is little distinction for our purposes. As you can see from the following table, MSXML 4.0 covers the extended interfaces as well as the principal ones:

W3C Interface	MSXML 4.0 Implementation Interface
CDATASection	IXMLDOMCDATASection
DocumentType	IXMLDOMDocumentType
Notation	IXMLDOMNotation
Entity	IXMLDOMEntity
EntityReference	IXMLDOMEntityReference
ProcessingInstruction	IXMLDOMProcessingInstruction

MSXML Object Model

MSXML implements DOM Level 1 with extensions. Many of these extensions, particularly those related to namespace support, are implemented in the W3C DOM Level 2 Recommendation, albeit under different names. We'll survey the major objects in DOM Level 1 and list their properties, methods, and events. Additionally, we'll discuss the extensions added in MSXML's implementation of the DOM. There's a lot here, but bear with us. Once we have the reference material out of the way, we'll tie it together and demonstrate how to use the object model to accomplish the most common tasks involved in XML-related programming.

Common Objects

In the flattened, node-centric view, the DOM consists of the following basic objects:

- ❑ Document (IXMLDOMDocument, IXMLDOMDocument2) – a representation of the document as a whole, and the object that creates new nodes.

- ❑ Node (IXMLDOMNode) – all-purpose object representing any markup construct smaller than the document, that is elements, attributes, text, etc.

- ❑ NamedNodeMap (IXMLDOMNamedNodeMap) – a collection object used for iteration by name, which offers namespace support.

- ❑ NodeList (IXMLDOMNodeList) – a sequential collection object offering iteration by ordinal index.

Additionally, MSXML offers the IXMLDOMParseError object to provide error information for failures arising from the parsing and validation process. The relationships between these objects are illustrated in the following diagram:

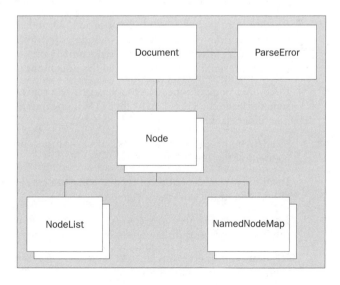

Document

This object represents the document as a whole. In MSXML it does double duty as the processor. That is, you receive an object of this type when creating a new object with the ProgID `MSXML2.DOMDocument.4.0`. You may use this object to load an existing document, or create new nodes to assemble a document dynamically.

In MSXML this object has the W3C DOM Level 1 standard properties and methods, as well as some extended, proprietary properties and methods that foreshadow DOM Level 2 and 3. The COM+ interface for this object is `IXMLDOMDocument`. Version 4.0 of the component also supports the `IXMLDOMDocument2` interface, which has some extensions to support XPath and performance enhancements in the area of schemas and namespaces.

Standard

The standard properties and methods are compliant with the W3C Recommendations for the DOM, differing only where a parameter is a COM+ interface. In such a case, the parameter's type in the interface deviates from the W3C parameter's type. The `IXMLDOMDocument` interface derives from (or is said to *inherit* from, in COM+ terminology) `IXMLDOMNode`. This means that all the properties and methods of the parent interface are present on the derived interface. For document objects, this means that a number of properties and methods are picked up that have little or no use on the document object.

Document objects have the following standard properties, as specified in the W3C DOM Level 1:

Properties	Description
attributes	Read-only collection (`IXMLDOMNamedNodeMap`) of attribute nodes. This property is inherited from the `Node` interface; as document objects cannot have attributes, this property is always `null` for this interface.
childNodes	Read-only collection (`IXMLDOMNodeList`) of nodes representing child content (in other words, does not include attributes). For document objects, this collection contains the document element as well as any nodes representing markup items in the document prolog.
doctype	Read-only node of type `IXMLDocumentType` representing the document type declaration. This is `null` for HTML documents and XML documents lacking a DTD.
documentElement	Read/write property of type `IXMLDOMElement` representing the top-most element of the document tree.
firstChild	Read-only; returns a node of type `IXMLDOMNode` representing the first child node of the document element.
implementation	Read-only; returns an `IXMLDOMImplementation` interface representing the XML processor, independent of the loaded document.
lastChild	Read-only; property of type `IXMLDOMNode` representing the last child node of the document element.
nextSibling	Inherited from `IXMLDOMNode`, this property is `null` for documents.

Properties	Description
nodeName	Read-only; returns #document for document objects; present through inheritance from IXMLDOMNode.
nodeType	Read-only property returning the enumerated value NODE_DOCUMENT (9) when invoked for document objects.
nodeValue	Inherited from IXMLDOMNode, this property returns null for document objects.
ownerDocument	Also inherited from IXMLDOMNode, this read-only property returns the document object itself when invoked on document objects. For all other nodes, it returns the object representing the containing document.
parentNode	Read-only property of type IXMLDOMNode; inherited from IXMLDOMNode, this property returns the document node when invoked on document objects.
previousSibling	Read-only (IXMLDOMNode); returns null for document objects.

The following W3C standard methods are supported by MSXML for document objects:

Methods

Methods	Description
appendChild()	Appends a single node to the list of child nodes for the document element. Takes a single parameter of type IXMLDOMNode (or any interface derived from it) and returns the same node. Namespace information is not changed by moving a node, but the identity of the owning document is updated if the new parent belongs to a document other than the node's old parent, as when a node is removed from one document instance and appended within the node tree of another document instance. Similarly, any entity references belonging to the appended node are updated as needed.
cloneNode()	Copies a node and, optionally, its child sub-tree. Takes a single Boolean parameter. When this parameter is true, the sub-tree is copied. If false, only the node and its attributes are copied. Returns the cloned node. If the node is an element, any attributes belonging to the element will also be cloned regardless of the value of the parameter.
createAttribute()	Takes a string whose value is the name of the attribute to be created and returns a node of type IXMLDOMAttribute. Note that the attribute is created without setting a value.
createCDATA Section()	Takes a string representing the data content of the new CDATA section and returns a node of type IXMLDOMCDATASection. The string parameter's value is subsequently returned when the value of the CDATA section object's nodeValue property is queried.
createComment()	Accepts a string representing a comment and returns a node of type IXMLDOMComment.

Table continued on following page

Methods	Description
createDocument Fragment()	Creates and returns an empty IXMLDOMDocumentFragment object, an interface for independently building and manipulating sections of documents; no parameters.
createElement()	Accepts a string parameter representing the case-sensitive name of the element and returns a newly created element (IXMLDOMElement object) of that name.
createEntityRe ference()	Creates and returns a new IXMLDOMEntityReference object when passed a string representing the name of the entity referenced. This string value is subsequently available as the nodeName property of the created entity reference node.
createProcessing Instruction()	Creates and returns a node of type IXMLDOMProcessingInstruction. Takes two parameters: target – target part of the PI, subsequently available as the new node's nodeName property. data – data portion of the PI, subsequently available as the nodeValue property.
createTextNode()	Accepts a string value and creates a new IXMLDOMText object containing the value.
getElementsBy TagName()	Takes a single string parameter and returns an IXMLDOMNodeList containing all elements with that name (the literal * returns all element nodes in the document).
hasChildNodes()	Returns true for non-empty document objects.
insertBefore()	Inserts a node immediately before, that is to the left of, a reference node. Takes two parameters of type IXMLDOMNode: new – new node to be inserted. ref – reference node. Rules regarding child content and siblings (for example, elements and attributes cannot be siblings) are observed and an error will be generated when an illegal operation is attempted.
removeChild()	Takes a single parameter of type IXMLDOMNode and removes it from the child content of the document element if found.
replaceChild()	Takes two parameters of type IXMLDOMNode: new – node with which to replace old. old – node to be replaced. Rules regarding permissible child content and sibling types are observed and will generate an error if an illegal operation is attempted.

The methods listed above are the ones you will use most frequently and are sufficient to handle most of the tasks you will need to perform in loading, creating, traversing, and manipulating XML documents. The DOM does not provide a mechanism for loading documents (in Levels 1 and 2), and there is no support for namespaces. This is where MSXML's extended properties and methods come in to play.

Extended

The properties and methods listed in this section are wholly proprietary and therefore non-portable. Some, like namespace support, foreshadow and closely resemble the additions of DOM Level 2. Others exist solely to enhance performance or improve programmer productivity.

Now that the W3C has Recommendations in place for namespaces and schemas, as well as support for this in the DOM, we may expect the following to undergo some change in future versions. For the near future, however, you will see these properties used extensively in code written for MSXML.

The new .NET Framework classes dealing with XML adhere to DOM Level 2. We take this as an indication of Microsoft's stance toward the evolving DOM API.

The extended properties for the document object are:

Properties	Description
async	Boolean that, when `false`, forces the processor to block while loading documents (in other words, not return from `load` or `loadXML`). When `true` (the default), loading proceeds in the background and events are fired while this continues.
baseName	Inherited from `IXMLDOMNode`, this property returns an empty string for document objects. Read-only.
dataType	Denotes the proprietary data type of a node. For document objects, this property is `null`.
definition	Returns a node representing the declaration (in a DTD or schema) of the current node; for documents, this property is `null`.
namespaceURI	Inherited from `IXMLDOMNode`, this read-only property is always an empty string for document objects as only element and attribute nodes can belong to namespaces.
nodeTypedValue	Inherited from `IXMLDOMNode`, this property is `null` for document objects.
nodeTypeString	String representation of the type of the node. For document nodes, this is `document`. Read-only.
ondataavailable	Write-only property taking the name of the event handler function to call when the `ondataavailable` event is fired, in other words, a new chunk of the document has been parsed; used only when `async` is `true`.
onreadystatechange	Write-only property providing a reference to the event handler function to call when the `onreadystatechange` event is fired, that is, document processing has transitioned from one state to another; used only when `async` is `true`.
ontransformnode	Write-only property taking the name of the event handler function to call when the `ontransformnode` event is fired, that is, just prior to applying an XSLT transformation to the document.

Table continued on following page

Properties	Description
parsed	Read-only Boolean; true when the entire document has been parsed.
parseError	Read-only property returning an IXMLDOMError object for inspecting error information.
prefix	Document objects always return an empty string for this property as it relates to namespaces. See the discussion under Node, below, from which this property is inherited. Read-only.
preserveWhite Space	Boolean value controlling whitespace handling. By default, this value is false, and any xml:space attributes in the document's DTD (if any) are obeyed. If none appear, non-essential whitespace, for example, "pretty printing" formatting, is stripped. If true, xml:space is overridden and whitespace is preserved. This property is read-write, but once whitespace has been stripped by setting this property, it cannot be restored.
readyState	Long integer value denoting the current loading state of the processor: LOADING (1) – XML data is loading, but parsing has not begun. LOADED (2) – XML is being parsed, but the tree's DOM object model is not yet available. INTERACTIVE (3) – Partially parsed document; the object model is available for those items which have been parsed. COMPLETED (4) – Fully parsed document with object model; note this does not imply the document was successfully parsed – errors may have occurred. Generally speaking, you will want to wait for the COMPLETED state to begin processing the document as it lets you avoid code that checks for incompletely loaded documents. Other application processing, such as initializing the interface or data structures, may go on while the processor is in earlier states.
resolve Externals	Boolean, read write. When true, external definitions (including resolvable namespaces, external DTD subsets, and external entity references) are resolved at parse time. Default value is true.
specified	Boolean indicating whether the node was explicitly specified or inferred from DTD or schema defaults. For documents, this property is always true.
text	For document objects, concatenation of all textual (PCDATA) content in the document.
url	URL of the last loaded document; if the document is being built dynamically and entirely in memory, this property will be null. Note that if the document is loaded from a string via the loadXML() method, this property will be an empty string.
validateOn Parse	Boolean indicating whether validation should be performed when the document is loaded (true) or merely checked for "well-formedness". Read write.
xml	Entire XML content of the document as a string; read-only.

Asynchronous loading is useful for very large documents retrieved over slow connections. It is relatively easy to accommodate in languages like C++ and Visual Basic, but trickier in scripting languages on web pages or earlier versions of Visual Basic due to the lack of multi-threading. That is not to say that it cannot be done. You might, for example, start an asynchronous load in response to the document onload event, then defer DOM processing until the user interacts with the page. The following code (found in the download as async_test.html) also works. It assigns a JavaScript function to the onreadystatechange property as an event handler:

```
var proc;
function test()
{
    proc = new ActiveXObject("msxml2.DOMDocument.4.0");
    proc.async = true;
    proc.onreadystatechange = flashWarning;
    proc.loadXML("<rootOfAllEvil><cause>money</cause></rootOfAllEvil>");
    proc = null;
}
function flashWarning()
{
    switch (proc.readyState)
    {
        case 1:
            sState = "LOADING";
            break;
        case 2:
            sState = "LOADED";
            break;
        case 3:
            sState = "INTERACTIVE";
            break;
        case 4:
            sState = "COMPLETED";
            break;
    }
    alert("Boink! goes the readyState: " + sState);
}
```

Even though the document is trivially short (not to mention silly), the document object will still fire multiple events. These events cause MSXML to call the function flashWarning(), which pops up a really annoying message. In production, you might check the progress of parsing a document of known size to provide a status bar in the user interface, or begin DOM-related tasks following transition to the INTERACTIVE state, taking care not to make assumptions about the presence or absence of nodes while the document is in this state.

If you are using the IXMLDOMDocument2 interface (which you will get in scripting languages if you use the MSXML2.DOMDocument.4.0 ProgID, or in Visual Basic if you don't type the object as IXMLDOMDocument), you have two additional properties related to performance enhancements and validation. These enhancements cache schemas and namespace references loaded in conjunction with a document. Programmers may copy these cache collections to avoid future loading or parsing, or control when schemas are loaded in order to better tune an application's performance. The additional properties are:

Properties	Description
namespaces	Read-only; returns an IXMLDOMSchemaCollection interface reference containing all namespaces used in the document. If none are declared, the collection will be empty.

Table continued on following page

Properties	Description
schemas	A variant value containing an IXMLDOMSchemaCollection interface to a collection of all schemas parsed during the loading of a document or programmatically pre-loaded; typically used to cache frequently used schemas.

The use of these properties is discussed at length in Chapter 11, "Schemas on the Server".

Returning to the IXMLDOMDocument interface, you also get the following extended methods:

Methods

Methods	Description
abort()	An asynchronous document load (async = true) is terminated by this method and any parsed nodes are discarded. IXMLDOMParseError reflects the aborted load. No parameters.
createNode()	In contrast to the type-specific create*XXX*() methods provided in the standard DOM interface, this method creates nodes of any supported XML type. It takes three parameters, as listed below, and returns a reference to the IXMLDOMNode interface of the newly created node.
	type – variant containing an enumerated value (see below) denoting the type of node to create.
	name – string containing the value for the new node's nodeName property (for example, tag name for elements); for types where this information is not relevant, such as comments, this parameter is ignored.
	ns_uri – string containing the namespace URI in whose context the node is to be created. If name has no prefix, this will be considered the node's default namespace.
load()	This critical method, completely omitted from DOM Levels 1 and 2, accepts a single variant parameter whose value is a URL and loads the document located by that URL. Alternatively, the variant may contain an IStream reference, allowing MSXML to load documents directly from components supporting streaming interfaces, for example, the ASP Request object.
loadXML()	Takes a single string parameter and loads the XML document contained therein.
nodeFromID()	This method is used in documents associated with a schema or DTD. The method takes a single string parameter presumed to contain the value of an attribute typed in the DTD or schema as ID. If an element exists with such an attribute, the node element is returned.
save()	Saves the current document to the location denoted in the value of the single variant parameter. This parameter may be a string (filename), or IStream interface (such as an ASP Response object), or DOMDocument interface.

Methods	Description
selectNodes()	Accepts a string whose value is an XPath expression and returns an IXMLDOMNodeList containing all the nodes matching the expression.
selectSingleNode()	Takes a string containing an XPath expression and returns the first node matching the expression.
transformNode()	Takes a single parameter, consisting of an IXMLDOMNode representing an XSLT stylesheet or document sub-tree containing such a stylesheet, and performs the transformation on the current document, returning the resultant document as a string.
transformNodeToObject()	As for transformNode, except the second parameter is a variant containing an IXMLDOMDocument or IStream instance to be used as the output document:
	Stylesheet – IXMLDOMNode (document root of stylesheet or root of document sub-tree containing XSLT templates).
	Output – variant containing IXMLDOMDocument or IStream; if a document, the results of the transformation are a DOM tree; if a stream interface, the results are written as XML to the stream.

This is where MSXML makes the crucial addition to the DOM of loading documents. Early versions of MSXML supported only load(), but loadXML() was added in version 2.6 in response to developer feedback and has proven useful. Note also the addition of createNode(). This directly supported the flattened view of the DOM document tree envisioned by the W3C and helps us parameterize code. That is, we can write common code that looks at the value of nodeType and branches only when different markup constructs require different actions. Otherwise, everything is treated the same – as a Node object – when the differences do not matter.

The enumerated values used in conjunction with createNode() to direct MSXML in the creation of XML items are the same as those reported by the nodeType parameter and are as follows:

Name	Constant value	Node type created
NODE_ELEMENT	1	Element.
NODE_ATTRIBUTE	2	Attribute.
NODE_TEXT	3	PCDATA, that is, textual content.
NODE_CDATA_SECTION	4	CDATA section.
NODE_ENTITY_REFERENCE	5	Reference to an entity.
NODE_ENTITY	6	Expanded entity other than numeric and XML built-in entities.
NODE_PROCESSING_INSTRUCTION	7	Processing instruction.
NODE_COMMENT	8	Comment.
NODE_DOCUMENT	9	XML document; note this is not the same as the document element, which is a child of this node.

Table continued on following page

Name	Constant value	Node type created
NODE_DOCUMENT_TYPE	10	Document type declaration, that is, `<!DOCTYPE>` tag.
NODE_DOCUMENT_FRAGMENT	11	XML document fragment; the fragment must conform to all "well-formedness" rules except the one requiring a single root element node.
NODE_NOTATION	12	XML notation within the document type declaration.

The IXMLDOMDocument2 interface adds the following methods:

Methods	Description
getProperty()	Takes a single string parameter and returns the internal property value named by the string. Values of properties supported by MSXML 4.0 are listed in the next table.
setProperty()	Takes a property name string and sets that property to the value passed in the second, variant parameter. Property names are listed in the next table. name – string naming the predefined internal property. value – variant containing the value to be set.
validate()	Performs on-demand document validation using the DTD, schema(s), or schema collection currently associated with the document. No parameters. Returns an IXMLDOMParseError interface.

The following properties may be set and retrieved with setProperty and getProperty:

Properties	Description
SelectionLanguage	The string XPath. MSXML versions prior to 4.0 permitted the use of the proprietary XSL Pattern language; this property was used to control which language was to be used in conjunction with selectNodes() and selectSingleNode().
ServerHTTPRequest	Boolean value that, when true, directs MSXML to use the server-safe ServerXMLHTTP component in conjunction with load(). When this property is true, async must be false.
Selection Namespaces	String containing a whitespace-delimited set of namespace declarations. This enables selectNodes() and selectSingleNode() to operate with qualified names. This is a means of associating namespace URIs with prefixes prior to making an XPath-based selection.
NewParser	Boolean denoting whether the new or old parser was used. Now set to true in all cases, this property was used during beta to control whether the older, feature-complete parser was used or the newer, less stable and less complete parser implementation was used.

The meaning and usage of the `SelectionNamespaces` property as set or retrieved by the `setProperty()` and `getProperty()` methods may not be immediately obvious. Since prefixes may be arbitrarily assigned to namespace URIs in a document, it is important to tell MSXML what namespaces go with the prefixes in our expression so that the proper items will be selected in the document. Consider the following markup expressing the document element of some XML document:

```
<p:parent xmlns:p="urn:schemas-xmlabs-com:1">
   <child type="1"/>
</p:parent>
```

This document element will be selected by the following lines of code even though the expression uses a different prefix for the namespace from the one that appears in the document (q instead of p).

```
doc.setProperty("SelectionNamespaces",
   "xmlns:q='urn:schemas-xmlabs-com:1' xmlns:r='urn:schemas-xmlabs-com:2'");
var node = doc.selectSingleNode("/q:parent");
```

This is because both prefixes point to the same namespace. Under the rules of XML Namespaces, this makes the two equivalent. We have used the `SelectionNamespaces` property to tell MSXML what prefix we are using for the selection. It will then compare this with the prefixes it parsed from the document and make the appropriate mapping. Note the use of single quotes around the URI in the call to `setProperty()`; this avoids conflict with the double quotes enclosing the property value string.

`IXMLDOMDocument` and `IXMLDOMDocument2` support the following events:

Event	Description
ondataavailable	Fired as new chunks of XML data become available during an asynchronous load.
onreadystatechange	Fired whenever the value of `readyState` changes, in other words a load state transition in the document.
ontransformnode	Fired before an XSLT transformation is applied to the document.

Node

The `Node` object is a real workhorse; you will spend considerable time with this interface as you work with MSXML. This object implements the flattened view of the document tree in the DOM, and it is certainly more flexible than the specialized interfaces particular to the type of node in question. Everything in the document will be represented as a node. If you check the `nodeType` property, you can perform the actions appropriate to the type of markup you are processing. You still have a reference to an `IXMLDOMNode` interface, but you can account for the fact that the value of an element, say, is handled differently from the value of an attribute. In contrast, if you wish to use the specialized interfaces, you must still check this property, but then you must obtain a reference to the proper interface, an expensive task in processing terms. The value of having the specialized interface is minimal. Usually, all you gain is the omission of irrelevant parameters from certain method calls.

Standard

The standard DOM properties and methods of the `Node` object are the heart of XML processing in the DOM and MSXML. Let's look at the properties first:

Properties	Description
attributes	Read-only property that returns an IXMLDOMNamedNodeMap containing the attributes of element, entity, or notation nodes. On nodes that do not support attributes this property is null. For nodes that may support attributes but have none, an empty NamedNodeMap is returned.
childNodes	Read-only property returning an IXMLDOMNodeList containing the child nodes of the current node. Node types that cannot have children, such as comments, return empty lists.
firstChild	Returns an IXMLDOMNode object representing the first child node (left-most in the tree) of the specified node. If no such child exists, this property is null. Read-only.
lastChild	Returns the IXMLDOMNode object representing the last child node (right-most in the tree) of the specified node. If no such child exists, this property is null. Read-only.
nextSibling	Node maintains an internal pointer for iterating over the child nodes of the object. Each time nextSibling is accessed, the pointer advances. If the node has no children, or nextSibling has previously reached lastChild, nextSibling is null. Read-only.
nodeName	Returns the name of the node. If namespace-qualified, the string returned by this property is the fully qualified name. For nodes of type other than attribute, document type, element, entity, or notation, a fixed string denoting the type of the node is returned. Read-only.
nodeType	Read-only property returning the long enumerated value indicating the node type (that is, the XML 1.0 type, not the Microsoft-proprietary data type). Values are as listed under the Document object above (in the discussion of createNode).
nodeValue	Returns a string whose value is the text associated with the node. The nature of this string depends on the type of node. For attributes, it is the attribute value. For elements, documents, document fragments, entities, entity references, and notations, this property is null. For PCDATA, CDATA sections, comments, and processing instructions, it is the textual content of the node. Read write. Attempting to set a value for one of the node types just listed results in an error.
ownerDocument	Read-only property returning the owning IXMLDOMDocument object.
parentNode	Read-only property returning the IXMLDOMNode that is the parent of the specified node. For the document element, this property is null. If a node is newly created and not yet added to the tree, or if it has been removed from the tree, this property will also be null.
previousSibling	Works with firstChild, lastChild, and nextSibling to return the node immediately preceding (to the left in the tree) the current child node. Read-only.

The list of standard methods of the Node object is somewhat shorter, and devoted to managing a node's child nodes:

Methods	Description
appendChild()	Takes a single IXMLDOMNode parameter and inserts it at the end of the list of child nodes. Returns the newly inserted node.
cloneNode()	Creates and returns a copy of the node. The sole parameter controls whether the node's sub-tree is copied.
	deep – Boolean; when true, a deep copy is made (node and all child nodes, recursively, until the entire sub-tree rooted by the node is traversed); if false, only the specified node and its attributes are copied.
hasChildNodes()	Returns true if the node has child nodes, false otherwise.
insertBefore()	Inserts the new node before the reference node and returns the new child node. If XML rules regarding what types may be children of other types are violated, an error is generated.
	new – IXMLDOMNode to insert.
	ref – address of node the new node should precede; if null, this is the same as a call to appendChild().
removeChild()	Removes and returns the node passed as a parameter.
	discard – node to remove.
replaceChild()	Replaces old with new and returns new.
	new – IXMLDOMNode to add.
	old – IXMLDOMNode to replace; if null, this is the same as a call to removeChild().

Extended

MSXML's extensions to this interface are chiefly concerned with namespace support, but also add some useful capabilities. The xml property, for example, is a useful way of getting at the markup text during debugging. The extension methods make XPath and XSLT available to DOM programmers. While not part of the "pure" DOM, both are powerful techniques and widely used in day-to-day XML programming tasks.

The current draft of DOM Level 3 attempts to provide XPath access as a layer over the DOM core. The current draft of DOM Level 3 XPath is found at http://www.w3.org/TR/DOM-Level-3-XPath/.

Properties	Description
baseName	Returns the base name of a namespace-qualified node; read-only.
dataType	Read write variant property controlling the strong typing of the node. Note: these types are those provided in the proprietary XML Data Reduced (XDR) schema data types, not the W3C XML Schemas data types (see Chapter 3 for more explanation of these data types).
definition	Read-only; returns the IXMLDOMNode from the DTD or schema that declares this node.

Table continued on following page

Properties	Description
namespaceURI	Returns a string value containing the URI value of the namespace from which the node is drawn. Read-only.
nodeTypedValue	Returns a variant containing the value of the node cast into the data type specified by dataType. Note: this pertains to XDR data types (see Chapter 3 for more information). Read write.
nodeTypeString	Returns the type of the node expressed as a string. The types referred to are the node type enumerations, for example, "element", "attribute", etc. Read-only.
parsed	Read-only Boolean; when true, the node and all its children have been parsed. Used when async is true for the document object.
prefix	Read-only; returns the namespace prefix for the node.
specified	Read-only Boolean; when true, the node (typically an attribute) appears explicitly in the document. When false, the node's value is implicitly drawn from a default in the DTD.
text	String containing the concatenated PCDATA content of an element and all its children; read write.
xml	String containing the XML markup for the node and all its children; read-only.

The four extended methods of Node serve to bring the supporting XML technologies of XPath and XSLT to bear on common programming tasks. While the W3C is bringing XPath to DOM Level 3, no such moves are planned for XSLT as at the time of writing. Both technologies offer high-performance alternatives to native DOM calls in certain situations, such as document format translation (XSLT) and node location (XPath).

Methods	Description
selectNodes()	Applies the XPath expression passed in and returns an IXMLDOMNodeList containing any matching nodes. The context is based on the calling node. expr – string containing a valid XPath expression.
selectSingleNode()	Returns the first IXMLDOMNode matching expr. expr – string containing a valid XPath expression.
transformNode()	Applies the supplied XSLT transformation to the node and its children and returns a string containing the resultant document. style – IXMLDOMNode representing an XSLT stylesheet.
transformNodeToObject()	As for transformNode(), except the result is placed into an IXMLDOMDocument object. style – IXMLDOMNode representing an XSLT stylesheet. outdoc – IXMLDOMDocument to receive the resultant document.

There are no events for this interface.

NamedNodeMap

This object is used to collect nodes whose nodeName property is the key to accessing them in the collection. The most important use for this object is as the type of the attributes property of the Node object (though it is also used to collect entities and notations in the IXMLDOMDocumentType interface). The attributes of an element have meaningful names, which are guaranteed to be unique (within the scope of the element) by the rules of XML 1.0. There is no implicit order to the attributes. When dealing with them, we need to be able to supply a name and retrieve the corresponding node.

While named, random-access retrieval is the most common way to access nodes in the NamedNodeMap collection, we also need a way to iterate through nodes without knowing their names. You might, for example, need to traverse the attributes of an element whose structure is unknown to you. On the other hand, you may simply be writing a general-purpose routine to process a variety of elements. You know which attributes they are supposed to have, but you don't want to put that knowledge into a lot of special purpose code. NamedNodeMap makes provisions for both sorts of access. Consider the following XML element:

```
<Person ssn="059-11-1234">. . .</Person>
```

If I located the <Person> element in the document and placed it in a variable, node, then I could retrieve the ssn attribute node using the attributes property of the node (a NamedNodeMap object):

```
var ssnAttr = node.attributes("ssn");
```

Standard

This interface has exactly one property, and it is read-only. This is the length property, which is the count of items in the named node map. The standard methods of this interface are dedicated to retrieval and modification of the nodes in the collection:

Methods	Description
getNamedItem()	Accepts a string parameter and returns the node, if any, whose nodeName parameter is equal to the parameter value.
item()	Takes a single integer parameter as an index into the collection and returns the node at that position in the collection. The index is zero-based.
removeNamedItem()	Takes a single string parameter and removes the corresponding attribute from the map. The removed node is returned, or null if no attribute with that name exists in the collection.
setNamedItem()	Takes an IXMLDOMNode object and adds it to the collection, returning the node. If a pre-existing object has the same name, it is replaced.

Extended

There are no extended properties for this interface, and no events. There are, however, four extension methods, offered chiefly for namespace support:

Methods	Description
getQualifiedItem()	Takes a base name and namespace URI and returns the corresponding node. Returns null if no such attribute exists.
	base – base, that is, un-prefixed, name of the attribute.
	uri – URI value for the namespace from which the desired attribute is drawn.
nextNode()	Returns the next node in the map, beginning with the first. Returns null once every node in the map has been accessed.
removeQualifiedItem()	Takes the same parameters in the same order as getQualifiedItem(), removes the corresponding node (if found), and returns the newly removed node.
reset()	Works with nextNode() to reset the internal pointer to the first node in the collection.

Note the presence and nature of nextNode() and reset(). We said at the outset that there is no implicit order to a NamedNodeMap object. This is true from a theoretical standpoint, but of course any implementation has to keep track of its constituent nodes. It therefore imposes an order that is completely arbitrary from the viewpoint of XML and the DOM, but useful for practical iteration.

NodeList

This object gives ordered access to a collection of nodes through an integer index. As such, it is particularly well suited to handling child nodes. This is because they have an explicit left-to-right order in the node tree, an order that is more important than the name of the node. Some nodes, like comments, do not have a useful name, whereas named nodes, particularly elements, may occur in various places in the node tree depending on the document schema or DTD. What is important, in terms of accessing them in a meaningful way, is the position of the node in the document's node tree.

Another use for this object is the return type for the selectNodes() method of the Document and Node objects. Here again, names may or may not be important; what is important is the ability to easily iterate through the collection.

Standard

Like the named node map, the NodeList interface has a single standard property, length. This property, which is read-only, gives the count of items in the list. It also has a single standard method, item(). Like the item() method in the named node map interface, this method allows random access to the nodes in the list by passing a zero-based index in and receiving a Node object in return.

The childNodes collection is the most common use for the NodeList object. Here is a code fragment showing array-based access to all the immediate child nodes of a given node, named testNode:

```
var i, child;
For (i = 0; i < testNode.childNodes.length; i++)
{
   child = testNode.childNodes.item(i);
   // do something with child here
}
```

Extended

There are no extension properties and no events for this interface. The following extension methods are offered:

Methods	Description
nextNode()	Used to iterate through the collection. After the last node in the collection is returned, subsequent calls will return null. No parameters.
reset()	Used to reset the collection to the first node for use with nextNode().

ParseError

COM+ (not to mention scripting languages) does not handle exceptions. Instead, error information is returned in the HRESULT value passed with every COM+ call. Microsoft, therefore, took the W3C's leave in the DOM Level 1 Core Recommendation and created an error handling object. Programs may check the properties of this object to detect errors in loading and validating documents. Note that since XML processors may terminate parsing upon detecting certain errors, this object will not detect all errors in the document, only the most recent. Your MSXML code should always check this object's properties after loading a document.

Since this interface is unspecified by the DOM, all its properties (there are no methods) are proprietary. In addition, since the object exists solely for reporting errors detected by the processor, the properties are read-only.

Properties	Description
errorCode	Decimal code associated with the error.
filepos	Integer index into the document's character stream locating the source of the error.
line	Line index into the document locating the source of the error. The index is one-based.
linepos	Position (one-based) in the line where the error was detected.
reason	String containing a human-readable error message.
srcText	String containing the fragment of the document in which the error was detected.
url	URL of the document in which the error was detected.

A few observations about XML error detection are in order. First, the error indices filepos, line, and linepos are only approximate and depend on the internal working of the parser. They serve to localize the error, not point you to the absolute, single character causing the problem. The same holds true for srcText. You will typically see the markup construct, such as the element opening tag, in which the error was detected.

The errorCode property can be distinctly unhelpful. Neither the SDK documentation nor the type library for MSXML contain a reference for the permissible values of errorCode. Experience may teach you these values, in which case the property can be useful shorthand for certain errors. If you are exposing the error condition to your program's user, however, you are far better off presenting reason.

Finally, you might wonder why url is included. After all, we can obtain the URL of the last loaded document from the document object. The URL value contained in this property is subtler than that. If your document references multiple schema documents, through namespace declarations, and one of these schemas has an XML error, its URL will be reported in the url property. The reason, line, and linepos properties will refer to the schema document.

Note also that only a single error is reported. Under XML 1.0 rules, XML processors must not pass along document information to an application after a fatal error is detected, though they may, optionally, continue parsing to detect additional errors. MSXML terminates parsing and reports only the fatal error.

Here's a sample use of the ParseError object to see if a document has been loaded correctly:

```
doc.load("catalog.xml");
if (doc.parseError.errorCode != 0)
{
    msg = "Load error at line " + doc.parseError.line + " position " +
            doc.parseError.linepos;
    msg += "\r\nReason: " + doc.parseError.reason;
    alert(msg);
    return false;
}
else
    // work with the document here
```

If the document is loaded without error, the errorCode property will be 0. Any other value signifies an error, so we have used the line, linepos, and reason properties to give the user an indication of what the problem is and where it occurred in the file.

Stronger Typing for Nodes

As we noted previously, Node is the workhorse object of the DOM and represents the flattened view of the object model hierarchy. The DOM, however, also supports specialized interfaces that directly correspond with the basic markup constructs of XML 1.0. For the most part, the properties and methods of these interfaces are the same as those for Node. However, relevant additions are made that simplify programming when you explicitly know what sort of node you are dealing with.

Note that this convenience comes at the price of a QueryInterface call on MSXML.

The following table lists the specialized interfaces and summarizes what type-specific additions are available in each beyond the core features of the Node interface:

Interface	Nature of additions
IXMLDOMAttribute	Adds the value property to access the attribute's value.
IXMLDOMCDATASection	Adds data and length properties to get the CDATA sections content and character count, respectively.
IXMLDOMCharacterData	Provides methods for sub-string manipulation.

Interface	Nature of additions
IXMLDOMComment	Provides methods for sub-string manipulation.
IXMLDOMElement	Adds methods to retrieve the tag name and deal explicitly with attribute nodes without iterating through the attributes collection.
IXMLDOMEntity	Adds properties for dealing with the notation name of unparsed entities, as well as retrieving the public and system IDs of entities.
IXMLDOMEntityReference	Inherits from IXMLDOMNode without adding any properties or methods of its own.
IXMLDOMNotation	Adds properties for retrieving the public and system IDs of XML notations.

Note that some of these interfaces offer real convenience. The sub-string manipulation methods of the interfaces for handling character data and comments, in particular, make life easier for the practicing programmer. The methods for retrieving public and system IDs retrieve valuable information without having to resort to string manipulation in your code. Interfaces like IXMLDOMAttribute and IXMLDOMElement, however, offer very little and exist mainly for conformance with the DOM.

Other Objects

There are a number of other interfaces prescribed by the DOM (and one, Selection, that is proprietary to MSXML) that are seldom encountered in normal practice. Depending on your needs, however, you may find them useful. These objects and their COM+ interfaces in MSXML are:

❑   DocumentFragment (IXMLDOMDocumentFragment) – fragment of XML markup.

❑   DocumentType (IXMLDOMDocumentType) – reports information regarding a document's DTD.

❑   Implementation (IXMLDOMImplementation) – reports information regarding the XML processor independent of any document instance.

❑   Selection (IXMLDOMSelection) – represents the results of an XPath expression evaluation.

DocumentFragment

The cloneNode() method of the IXMLDOMNode interface allows you to make copies of a portion (or all) of a document. If Document permits us to create nodes of all sorts, why do we need an object intended to represent a part of a document? If copying an entire document, or creating parts, Document would seem sufficient. If copying whole sub-trees, Node would suffice. DocumentFragment does not offer any properties or methods that are not found on Node.

The answer lies in one important characteristic of nodes and documents: the tree structure must be rooted by a single node. DocumentFragment removes this restriction. Suppose you have a common set of nodes that are used throughout a document instance as child content for each of several different elements. You could use DocumentFragment to create the child content. For example:

```
        var elt;

        g_frag = doc.createDocumentFragment();
        elt = doc.createElement("Instructor");
        elt.appendChild(doc.createTextNode(" "));
        g_frag.appendChild(elt);

        elt = doc.createElement("CourseTitle");
        elt.appendChild(doc.createTextNode(" "));
        g_frag.appendChild(elt);

        elt = doc.createElement("Scheduled");
        elt.appendChild(doc.createTextNode(" "));
        g_frag.appendChild(elt);
```

We created a document fragment consisting of three elements – <Instructor>, <CourseTitle>, and <Scheduled> – and their text node children. Note there is no node serving as a parent to these nodes. They are peers, which may be inserted as children of a node in an existing document.

You would traverse to the element needing the content, then insert a clone of the fragment (after setting the appropriate values) directly into the child content of the element. To do the same thing with Node, you would need to create a Node object to serve as an artificial tree root, then access each child, inserting it individually into the child content of the destination node. Using DocumentFragment under the right circumstances will avoid several lines of code.

IXMLDOMDocumentFragment inherits from IXMLDOMNode. Its methods and properties are, therefore, identical to those described under the Node object.

DocumentType

As noted in the introductory chapter, the only mechanism in XML 1.0 that allows developers to formally specify the syntax of an XML vocabulary is the DTD. Despite the drawbacks of DTDs, they remain an important source of information. Since they are not XML syntax, we cannot work with them as easily as we might with a schema, but some information resides in DTDs and nowhere else. This includes information about the entities and notations that may be declared in the DTD.

The IXMLDOMDocumentType interface adds three properties, all read-only, to those it inherits from IXMLDOMNode. These properties are standard DOM Level 1 properties:

Properties	Description
entities	A read-only NamedNodeMap of entity declaration nodes. The nodeName property of each node is the name of the entity.
name	Read-only string containing the name of the document type, that is, the name of the document element specified in the DTD.
notations	Read-only NamedNodeMap of IXMLDOMNotation nodes.

It is easy to get carried away and think that DocumentType objects will allow us to traverse DTDs the same way we navigate actual XML documents. This is not so. If you check the xml property of the doctype node, you will indeed see the entire text of the DTD. If you check that node's childNodes collection, however, you will find that it is empty. Robust manipulation of XML metadata requires XML Schemas.

Implementation

All the interfaces described so far pertain to specific document instances. XML processor compliance and feature support is an important question, and you should be able to query a processor for this information without loading a document into the processor. This is the motivation for the Implementation object.

Standard

This interface has just a single member, the standard method hasFeature(). This method takes two parameters, feature and version. Both are strings. The feature parameter names some feature of the DOM. The version parameter lists the version of the DOM Level you are testing. The purpose of the method is to return the Boolean value true if the processor supports that DOM Level version of the feature. In other words, you are checking the DOM compliance of the processor.

At present, the only valid specific version you can test in MSXML is DOM Level 1.0. For DOM Level 1, the version must always be 1.0. If you supply null as the value of version, all versions of the DOM Level in question are checked. Since MSXML is based on Level 1, and Level 1 has only a single version, 1.0 and null are the only values you can use with MSXML.

There are three values for feature: XML (for support of XML itself), DOM (for support of the W3C DOM), and MS-DOM (for support of MSXML extensions to the DOM). This parameter's value is used in a case-insensitive fashion.

Selection

This object is added to the standard DOM interfaces because MSXML offers XPath support to programmers working with the DOM. You can certainly work with the node-list returned by selectNodes() or the node returned by selectSingleNode() directly using those interfaces, but Selection offers a few properties and options to make your life (in programming, anyway) a little easier.

> *The IXMLDOMSelection interface inherits from IXMLDOMNodeList, so the properties and methods of that interface – item, length, nextNode(), and reset() – are available to the Selection interface in addition to those listed below.*

The two properties of this interface are:

Properties	Description
context	Returns or sets the IXMLDOMNode from which the XPath selection was or is to be made. Read write. Calling this property has the side effect of resetting the NodeList pointer, in other words it is equivalent to calling reset().
expr	String representation of the XPath expression. Read write.

One of the problems of dealing with the results of an XPath selection is looking ahead to the next node without moving the node-list pointer. This is dealt with in the Selection interface. Another common task addressed by this interface is removing selected nodes from the document. With this capability available, XPath can be used to quickly locate nodes and prune them from the tree. The same can be done with NodeList and Document, but it requires additional lines of code and additional trips through the COM+ layer. By encapsulating this in a single method, removeAll() or removeNext(), the task can be performed entirely within the highly optimized C++ code of MSXML. The methods for the Selection object are:

Methods	Description
clone()	Clones the Selection object, maintaining NodeList position and context. No parameters.
getProperty()	Returns the value of a property set using setProperty() on the Document interface.
	propname – string containing the name of the property to check. The only valid value for this interface is SelectionLanguage, which will always return XPath in MSXML 4.0. Earlier versions supported a proprietary alternative expression language.
item()	Allows random access to the collection based on ordinal position. The node list pointer is not affected by calls to this method.
	index – zero-based index into the collection.
matches()	Checks to see if the given node appears in the Selection. If it does, the context node that would return the given node in response to the expression is returned. If not, the return is null. The current context of the XPath evaluation is not used when checking for a match.
	testnode – IXMLDOMNode to check for in the Selection.
nextNode()	Returns the next node in the collection and advances the node list pointer one position. No parameters.
peekNode()	Returns the results of a call to nextNode() without the side effect of advancing the node list pointer. No parameters.
removeAll()	Removes all nodes in the Selection from the document object. No parameters.
removeNext()	Removes the node that would be returned by nextNode() from the document and returns it, or null if nextNode() would return null, such as when the node-list pointer is past the end of the collection. Side effects are as follows: the node-list pointer is not advanced, that is it has the effect of peekNode() rather than nextNode(), and length is decreased by one.
reset()	Resets the node-list pointer to the beginning of the collection.

Common DOM Tasks

We've just covered the object model. It's a great volume of reference material, and we haven't even begun to show you how it works in action. The best way to learn the DOM is to work with it. We'll focus on the following key tasks:

❑ Loading a document into MSXML.

❑ Navigating the document tree.

❑ Manipulating the document tree.

To do this we'll start with an XML document and show you how to load it. Once it is there, we'll show you how to reach every node in the tree starting with the document element. Finally, we'll dynamically extend the document by creating some new nodes. When we're finished, we'll display the original document and the revised document in a client-side web page so that you can see that the document has indeed changed.

Let's consider the problem of a course catalog. We want to create an XML document consisting of a series of <Class> elements. Assume that the original designer of this document decided to record all their critical information as attributes, with a textual description of the course residing in a child element, <Description>. Here's a fragment of such a document. It is found in the code download for this chapter in the file catalog.xml:

```
<?xml version="1.0"?>
<Catalog>
    <Class classCode="481C" instructor="Prof. Freamish"
           title="Reformation and Revolution" meets="Tue Thu">
        <Description>A survey of Europe in the aftermath of the Protestant
                     Revolution</Description>
    </Class>
    . . .
</Catalog>
```

The choice of using attributes rather than elements to convey the bulk of our data is not ideal, giving us an excuse later to change it. The instructor's name would be better modeled as an element or series of elements. This would allow us to include whitespace in the name without having to declare the attribute as type IDREFS, which is the only type in XML 1.0 that would accommodate this (though the string type in W3C XML Schemas will handle this). We might even have an <instructor> element elsewhere in the document, linked to the class by an IDREF attribute. The course title definitely should be a <PCDATA> element given the amount of whitespace present.

For now, we need to load this document into MSXML. Once there, provided there are no validation errors, we want to iterate through each <Class> element and touch each attribute in turn. When we have done that, we'll revisit the design issue and take matters into our own hands.

We'll develop two HTML pages. The first, TraversalOnly.html, loads a document and recursively traverses it. It looks as shown overleaf.

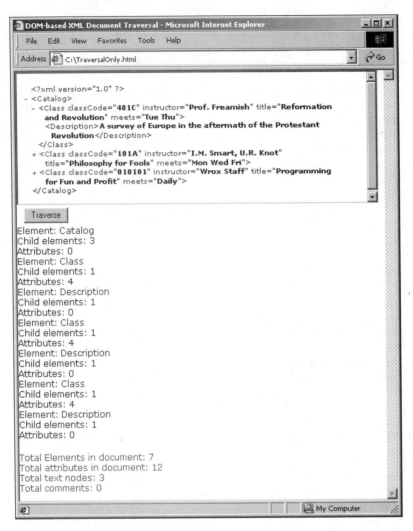

We take advantage of the built-in support for XML found in Internet Explorer 5.0 and later to display the original document in an IFRAME at the top of the page. When the Traverse button is clicked, we navigate the document tree. As we go, we list the attribute and child element counts. This gives us a minimum of user interface code, allowing us to focus on the DOM tasks we really want to show.

Loading and Validating Documents

We mentioned earlier that the W3C does not provide a method in either DOM Level 1 or Level 2 for opening an XML document file and directing the XML processor to parse its contents. In fact, this was a deliberate design omission. The assumption of the first two DOM Levels is that a document tree exists for manipulation. Eventually, Level 3 will correct this problem. Until then, there is no such thing as a "pure" DOM processor. Every processor has at least one proprietary extension used to load documents. MSXML, in fact, has two. The load() method loads a document from disk, and the loadXML() method loads from an in-memory string.

Loading from a File

We begin our implementation of `TraversalOnly.html` with a few words about the interface. The `IFRAME` that displays the original document is in part a proprietary feature of Internet Explorer, not MSXML. The `IFRAME`'s `src` attribute, a standard part of HTML 4.0, links the XML file to the page. Internet Explorer, recognizing an XML format document, applies a stock XSL stylesheet (in Microsoft's proprietary technology preview syntax that pre-dated the XSLT Recommendation) to display the document in a collapsible hierarchy. This is just the easiest way to display the XML with some structure and is not used in the code for DOM manipulation.

Our study of DOM methods begins with the event handler for the button, a JavaScript function named `OnClickTraverse()`. We begin by instantiating an instance of MSXML 4.0:

```
function OnClickTraverse()
{
  output.innerHTML = "";
  var parser = new ActiveXObject("MSXML2.DOMDocument.4.0");
```

The first line clears any previously existing text in the `DIV` named `output`; this is useful when running the sample more than once. The next line declares a variable and sets its value to a new instance of MSXML 4.0.

Note that we must use the version-specific ProgID for the component. With version 4.0, Microsoft abandoned a lot of proprietary capabilities that have since been superseded by W3C standards, so we want to be sure we are dealing with the proper version of the component.

Whenever you are dealing with a COM+ component, we want to check that an instance of the component was successfully created by the COM+ runtimes in the operating system. When we have that, we want to load the document and perform our manipulations if, and only if, the processor successfully loaded and parsed the document:

```
    if (parser != null && LoadDoc(parser))
    {
        // work with DOM here
        parser = null;
    }
    else
        alert("No document available");
}
```

The first half of the conditional clause checks for a component instance. The second is a call to another function where we've hidden the code for loading the document. We've written it so that it returns a Boolean value indicating success or failure. If it returns `true`, we are free to go about our processing. We've commented that out here, but we do show the assignment of a `null` value to the processor variable, `parser`, which allows the JavaScript runtime to perform COM+ cleanup tasks for us. Let's have a look now at `LoadDoc()`:

```
function LoadDoc(doc)
{
    var msg = "";

    doc.async = false;
    doc.load("catalog.xml");
```

This function takes as its sole parameter an instance of an `IXMLDOMDocument` interface. We presume it has been checked (as we did above) and proceed to load a known document. To keep things simple, we've stuck to synchronous loading by assigning the `async` property of the processor the value `false`. The same object's `load()` method takes the name of the file to load (assumed to be in the same folder as the HTML page for simplicity). When `load` returns, the processor is finished, but we cannot assume success. For that, we need to inspect the document's `ParseError` object:

```
if (doc.parseError.errorCode != 0)
{
   msg = "Load error at line " + doc.parseError.line +
         " position " + doc.parseError.linepos;
   msg += "\nReason: " + doc.parseError.reason;
   alert(msg);
   return false;
}
else
   return true;
```

If the document was successfully parsed, `errorCode` will have a value of zero. Any non-zero value is related to an error code. In the next two lines (inside the `if` statement), we take advantage of the `ParseError` object's properties to set up an error message for display to the user. We report the line, position within the line, and the human readable text of the error detected. The character `\n` is JavaScript's way of calling for a newline. Finally, we return `true` or `false` depending on the value of `errorCode`. The event handler, as we saw a moment ago, uses this to decide whether to continue processing.

> *The `load()` method may also accept a COM+ component that implements the `IStream` interface. This is useful when you are doing classic ASP development because the `Request` object supports the `IStream` interface. If your client POSTs an XML document, you may load it into the processor with this call: `parser.load(Request)`. This presumes that the parser holds an instance of MSXML. ASP and COM+ will work behind the scenes to obtain the `IStream` interface and retrieve the data that MSXML needs.*

Loading from a String

An early omission in MSXML was the ability to load a document from a string. This omission seems reasonable at first glance. Due to the component's close ties to Internet Explorer, we simply assume we are dealing with web development. In the web world, you just supply a document's URL and load it. A document is a remote resource, not a string in local memory.

Developers were quick to call Microsoft's attention to the problem. MSXML quickly saw use in non-web applications. Frequently, such applications will build documents using string manipulation, or receive them from non-COM+ sources via strings. The `loadXML()` method handles this situation for us. In the line below we have provided the `Catalog` document to the processor as a string literal:

```
Parser.loadXML("<?xml version='1.0'?><Catalog><Class…</Class></Catalog>");
```

Note that we've abridged the string to fit it on one line. More importantly, you need to remember to keep the quotes that delimit the string distinct from the quotes that delimit attribute values. We've used a single quote for the latter. Any attributes in the string would be in single quotes.

Simple Validation

So far, we haven't said anything about XML validation. This is easy to remedy. MSXML, like any validating XML processor, can be directed to perform validation when the document is loaded. If the Document object's validateOnParse property is set to true prior to calling load() or loadXML(), the processor will perform validation using any associated meta data. It will look for the following and use it if found:

❑   Internal or external DTD linked via the DOCTYPE instruction.

❑   XDR schema linked via a namespace declaration whose value begins x-schema:, for example, xmlns:p="x-schema:myschema.xdr".

❑   XML Schema linked via the schemaLocation attribute.

If none of these links are found, the effect is as if validateOnParse had the value false. If an external schema or DTD is referenced, MSXML will attempt to load that document and apply the information contained to the document instance.

Navigating Document Trees

Now that we have a document loaded into a DOM tree structure we need to move around the tree to inspect individual nodes. Let's replace the comment in our event handler with calls that do this:

```
if (parser != null && LoadDoc(parser))
{
    Traverse(parser.documentElement);
    Summary();
    parser = null;
}
```

Traverse() is a function that performs a depth-first, recursive traversal of the tree. If you haven't taken Computer Science 201 in the last few years or you simply want that in English, we're going to call a function recursively to dive down through the child elements of the root and their children until we reach the bottom-most layer of the tree. When that happens, we want to pop back up again and dive down through the next child of the document element until we reach the bottom of that sub-tree. The fact that we go all the way to the bottom before moving to the next sibling node makes it depth-first. It is recursive since our function will call itself repeatedly to perform the traversal. Here is the body of Traverse():

```
function Traverse(node)
{
    var child;

    ProcessNode(node);
    child = node.firstChild;
    while (child != null)
    {
        Traverse(child);
        child = child.nextSibling;
    }
}
```

The function receives a `Node` object as its sole argument. Remember that we called `Traverse()` from the event handler, passing it the document element to start things off at the very top. The function `ProcessNode()` does something with the node. Put that aside for a moment so we can focus on the navigation aspects of the DOM. We start things off by setting the variable `child` to the first child of node. Next, we go into a `while` loop until every child node is exhausted, at which time `child` will have the value `null`. Within the body of the loop, the function calls itself – that's the recursion – but this time the parameter is `child`. This takes us down to the next layer of the tree. Eventually, we will reach the bottom, the node will have no children, and `Traverse()` will terminate. The call stack will unwind one call, and the previous call to `Traverse()` will move to the next line. When that happens, `child` takes on the value of the next sibling node. If we have reached the end, `child` becomes `null` and the loop and the function terminate. Otherwise, if there are siblings to be processed, we move on to the next sibling and call on `Traverse()` to work its way through the sibling's children.

This use of recursion is a simple and elegant way to ensure every element in the document node tree is reached. This is useful in practice when a document must be exhaustively processed. As such, it suits our current purposes quite well. In practice, you are much more likely to need to traverse some small subset of the document tree. The same calls are used (firstChild, nextSibling), but you may not need to use recursion. The main point to take away from the Traverse function is the use of the DOM to iterate through child nodes.

We've used `firstChild` and `nextSibling` because MSXML's code is more efficient that way. Array-based access (via the `childNodes` collection) is less efficient than simply following a pointer in a linked list. What `childNodes` gives up in performance, though, it gives back in terms of random access. We could also use the `childNodes` collection and array iteration to make the code look like this:

```
function Traverse(node)
{
    ProcessNode(node);
    for (var i=0; i < node.childNodes.length; i++)
        Traverse(node.childNodes(i));
}
```

MSDN's Extreme XML column has two excellent articles on MSXML performance dating from version 3.0 of the parser. They are found at http://msdn.microsoft.com/library/en-us/dnexxml/html/xml02212000.asp and http://msdn.microsoft.com/library/en-us/dnexxml/html/xml03202000.asp.

What we do with the node in `ProcessNode()` is task-specific, but our implementation will uncover a few useful points of DOM usage. The `Node` object's `nodeType` property is key to how we work with the document. We therefore employ a `switch` statement to distinguish between the various types of nodes based on the value of that property:

```
function ProcessNode(node)
{
    switch (node.nodeType)
    {
        case NODE_ELEMENT:
            //alert("Current node subtree: " + node.xml);
            g_attrs += node.attributes.length;
            //TraverseAttrs(node.attributes);
            g_elements += 1;
```

```
            OutLn("Element: " + node.nodeName, "blue");
            OutLn("Child elements: " + node.childNodes.length, "black");
            OutLn("Attributes: " + node.attributes.length, "black");
            break;
        case NODE_TEXT:
            g_text += 1;
            break;
        case NODE_COMMENT:
            g_comments += 1;
            break;
    }
}
```

Note that there is no line that reads case NODE_ATTRIBUTE. That is because we reach
ProcessNode() through the child nodes of other nodes. The childNodes collection does not contain
attributes, the latter having been segregated into the aptly named attributes collection. If we want to
traverse attribute nodes – and we do – we have to iterate through the attributes collection when we
have a node of type NODE_ELEMENT. First we increment the global count of attributes, g_attrs, by the
length of the attributes collection. Then we increment the global count of elements in the document,
g_elements, by one to account for the current node. Finally, we call the utility function OutLn() to
make DHTML calls to report the information we have found so far into the user interface.

You may wonder at the two lines we've commented out of the listing. These are useful debugging lines.
The first uses the xml property of the Node interface to preview the node and all its child content as
markup. You can use it to follow the progress of the recursive descent and check the code's count of
various items against your own inspection. The next debugging line makes a call to code that makes a
point about attributes versus child content. We previously said there is no case NODE_ATTRIBUTE
because attributes are stored in their own collection. We updated the count of attributes using the length
property, but what if we want to inspect individual attributes? Traversing the attributes of an element is a
simple matter of using the array index-based item() method of the NamedNodeMap interface:

```
function TraverseAttrs(nodeMap)
{
    var i;
    var attrLen = nodeMap.length;
    for (i=0; i < attrLen; i ++)
    {
        alert(nodeMap.item(i).nodeValue);
    }
}
```

The item() method gives us access to the contents of the map without knowing the names of the attributes.
The return value is a Node object, so we take advantage of that object's nodeValue property to push the
value of the attribute into the user interface as an alert box. This is really annoying, though effective, so you
will surely want to comment out the call to TraverseAttrs() after you have seen it execute once.

Along the way, you may have noticed calls to two utility functions, OutLn() and Summary(). OutLn()
generates a color-coded line of output given a string message and a color. It does so by generating the
appropriate HTML:

```
function OutLn(str, sColor)
{
    top += 4;
```

```
output.insertAdjacentHTML("beforeEnd",
    "<FONT style='font-family:verdana;font-size:10pt;color:" +
    sColor + ";'>" + str + "</FONT>
    <BR style='position:relative;top:" + top + ";'/>");
}
```

The parameter sColor is used directly, so it must be one of the predefined colors in HTML. We use relative positioning to position the message in the lower DIV, named output. This relies on a global variable, top, which is initialized at zero when the script loads and is updated by four whenever OutLn() is called.

Summary() makes a few hard-coded calls to OutLn() to display the results of the cumulative counts of elements, attributes, text, and comments in the document:

```
function Summary()
{
    OutLn("<P/>Total Elements in document: " + g_elements, "red");
    OutLn("Total attributes in document: " + g_attrs, "red");
    OutLn("Total text nodes: " + g_text, "red");
    OutLn("Total comments: " + g_comments, "red");
}
```

Creating, Modifying, and Deleting Nodes

Now you know how to load a document and get around in it. It's time to cut the XML document apart in code and put it back together in a form more to our liking. We want to convert those ugly attributes into child elements of each <Class> element. Instead of listing summary information as we did in TraversalOnly.html, we want to display the final document so you can compare the two forms visually. We start by converting the former sample into a new file, Traverse_and_Build.html:

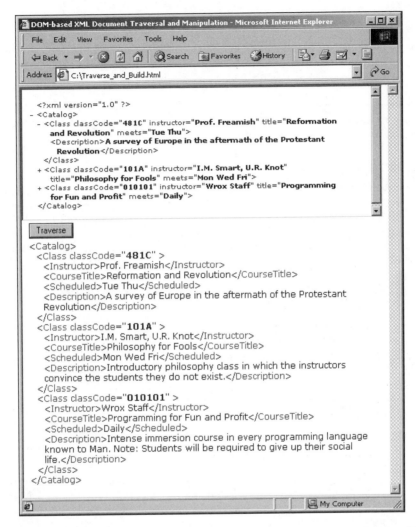

As with our previous example, we load the XML document into the IFRAME at the top of the page using Internet Explorer's native support for rendering XML. When the user clicks the Traverse button this time, however, we will not only traverse the DOM tree, but also modify the document structure. We were not fond of the attribute-centric approach to modeling the <Class> element, so we will convert three of the four attributes found in the <Class> element to elements. As you can see from the screenshot, the classCode attribute remains, but instructor, title, and meets must be removed and replaced with <Instructor>, <CourseTitle>, and <Scheduled> elements with the same content.

> *The design decision to leave classCode as an attribute does not effect the code in this chapter, but such a unique ID is useful in linking the declaration of a class to its uses through the XML ID and IDREF attribute types.*

This is an ideal use for the `DocumentFragment` object. We'll modify the event handler so that it calls a function to set up a fragment to serve as a template for the new elements. During traversal, we'll set the values found in the attributes, clone the fragment, and insert the clone into the child content of the `Class` node. When we're finished, we'll use an XSLT stylesheet to create an HTML document similar to what Internet Explorer creates for native XML documents.

As we are dynamically inserting the HTML into an existing page, there is no way to make use of the native support feature in Internet Explorer. We will have similar indenting and color-coding, but the resultant structure will not be collapsible.

Modifying the Event Handler

We need just minor changes in the body of the event handler. After creating the processor instance and loading the document successfully, we make a call to `MakeFrag()`, passing the function the component instance. After traversal, we load an XSLT stylesheet, `Output.xslt`, then call `transformNode()` to perform the transformation that creates the output document. This means we have to modify our traversal code to perform the XML modifications, but that is the right place for that task. Here's what the relevant section of the event handler looks like:

```
var stylesheet = new ActiveXObject("MSXML2.DOMDocument.4.0");
if (parser != null && LoadDoc(parser))
{
    MakeFrag(parser);
    Traverse(parser.documentElement);
    stylesheet.load("Output.xslt");
    if (stylesheet.parseError.errorCode == 0)
        output.innerHTML = parser.transformNode(stylesheet);
    else
        alert(stylesheet.parseError.reason);
    parser = null;
}
```

Creating and Preparing the Document Fragment

Since we're going to create three new elements for each `<Class>` element, it makes sense to create a document fragment and populate it with three elements of the appropriate name. Recall from our discussion of the `DocumentFragment` interface that we do not need a document root element. This is how the `MakeFrag()` function starts:

```
function MakeFrag(doc)
{
    var elt;

    g_frag = doc.createDocumentFragment();
```

The variable `g_frag` is global in scope and declared in the script outside the functions without giving it any value. The method `createDocumentFragment()` is called on the `Document` object instance we passed in to create an empty fragment. We have declared a local variable, `elt`, because we will be creating three new elements.

The sequence of events for each element is to create the element, append an empty text node to it, and then append the element to the document fragment:

```
function MakeFrag(doc)
{
    var elt;

    g_frag = doc.createDocumentFragment();
    elt = doc.createElement("Instructor");
    elt.appendChild(doc.createTextNode(" "));
    g_frag.appendChild(elt);

    elt = doc.createElement("CourseTitle");
    elt.appendChild(doc.createTextNode(" "));
    g_frag.appendChild(elt);

    elt = doc.createElement("Scheduled");
    elt.appendChild(doc.createTextNode(" "));
    g_frag.appendChild(elt);
}
```

The text node might as well be whitespace because we will need to set its value based on the value of the corresponding attribute as we traverse the tree. createElement() and createTextNode() create the nodes we need while appendChild() connects the text node to the element and the element to the fragment. When MakeFrag() concludes, we have the following markup in memory as a document fragment (newlines have been added for clarity on the page):

```
<Instructor> </Instructor>
<CourseTitle> </CourseTitle>
<Scheduled> </Scheduled>
```

Changing the Document

Most of the code changes are found in ProcessNode(). Everything is stripped out except the case for elements. Within that case, we need to test for the name Class, and if found, assign the value of the PCDATA content of the elements based on their corresponding attributes. When that is done, we clone the fragment, insert the clone into the child content of the <Class> element, and remove the attributes from the <Class> element:

```
case NODE_ELEMENT:
    if (node.nodeName == "Class")
    {
        g_frag.childNodes(0).childNodes(0).nodeValue =
            node.attributes.getNamedItem("instructor").nodeValue;
        g_frag.childNodes(1).childNodes(0).nodeValue =
            node.attributes.getNamedItem("title").nodeValue;
        g_frag.childNodes(2).childNodes(0).nodeValue =
            node.attributes.getNamedItem("meets").nodeValue;

        node.insertBefore(g_frag.cloneNode(true), node.childNodes(0));

        node.attributes.removeNamedItem("instructor");
        node.attributes.removeNamedItem("title");
        node.attributes.removeNamedItem("meets");
    }
    break;
```

This is less imposing than it appears at first glance. The `Node` object's `nodeName` property lets us distinguish between the `<Catalog>`, `<Class>`, and `<Description>` elements, performing the DOM manipulation only for `<Class>` element nodes. The call to `childNodes` on the object in `g_frag` locates the `<Instructor>`, `<CourseTitle>`, and `<Scheduled>` elements in the template, respectively. We can get away with hard coding the indices as we know the structure of the fragment as created in `MakeFrag()`. The call to `childNodes(0)` locates the first – and, as we know, the only child of these elements. That is the text node that will receive our content. Assigning a string value to the `nodeValue` property of the text node changes the `PCDATA` content that will appear.

The value we want to assign is the value of the attribute of which we are disposing. The `attributes` property of the node is, as we have seen, a `NamedNodeMap` object. This time, since we cannot guarantee the order of the content, we must use named access rather than index-based random access. Fortunately, we know the names of the attributes we need. This approach also protects our code if the attributes appear in some order other than what we have defined. The `getNamedItem()` method gets us the value we need. Once the values have been set, we make a deep clone of the document fragment with the `cloneNode()` method, then insert the clone into the element's child content. We want this to appear before the existing `<Description>` element, so we need to use `insertBefore()`. That method takes the new node to insert – in this case, the cloned fragment – and a reference node. Until the insertion is performed, the only child of the `<Class>` element is the `<Description>` element. Since it is the only child, `childNodes(0)` will find that node for us.

With the new element created, it is time to remove the old attributes from the node. That is accomplished by calling `removeNamedItem()` on the `attributes` `NamedNodeMap` with the name of the attribute to remove as a parameter.

Summary

We've presented a great deal of reference material in this chapter and a little bit of code. We've accomplished more than you might think, however. You now know the following:

❑   The W3C work regarding the DOM.

❑   The principal interfaces of the only standard XML API, as well as numerous secondary interfaces.

❑   How to load, traverse, and manipulate XML documents using the DOM.

In short, you have seen 70 – 80% of the tasks you will ever perform with the DOM, and certainly all of the routine tasks. We've covered the W3C-prescribed interfaces, and also separately listed the extensions MSXML brings to bear on the problem of manipulating document trees. The extensions include a number of methods that exist solely for the convenience of programmers, but they also bring in two powerful XML-related technologies – XPath and XSLT – that will be of enormous value to you in practical programming but which are not yet formally integrated with the DOM as published by the W3C.

We hope you appreciate the power and scope of the DOM, but you should also be thinking about some of the limitations of what we have seen. We've alluded to the resources issue in the introduction of the chapter. MSXML has to bring the entire document into memory before you can use the DOM. Very large documents, or moderately sized documents from which you only want a few items, are very expensive in terms of system resources when the DOM is used. Chapter 6 looks at the Simple API for XML (SAX), which addresses these issues. Neither API is inherently "better" for all uses; you must contrast the strengths and weaknesses and select the one that is right for your problem.

When we modified the sample catalog document in the last part of the example, you may have got the idea that a lot of lines of code were needed to do simple things. That is entirely correct. In fact, a single line of code, calling `transformNode()`, caused much larger changes through XSLT. Here too, we have an alternative to DOM manipulations. The DOM is the workhorse of XML programming with MSXML, but it is far from your only tool. With that in mind, we'll move on to the next chapter and see what else MSXML has in store.

XML Application Development with MSXML 4.0
SOAP
XHTML
XML Schemas DTDs XPath CSS
XML Namespaces
XML 1.0
MSXML

3

Schemas in MSXML

As you will already be aware, XML is a highly flexible data format. It allows you to create elements and attributes that contain many different types of ASCII and binary content, in various structures nested to arbitrary depths, as long as you conform to the simple rules of the XML Recommendation. This flexibility, however, poses some obvious problems (and some not so obvious) when it comes to making sure that the markup is used as originally intended and when sharing data between different parties.

For example, users and applications can create multiple XML documents that contain the same information, yet are structured entirely differently; the elements and attributes may differ between documents, or they may have the same names but in a different structure. Consider a document describing a customer – it may be structured like this:

```
<Customer CustomerID = "C3223">
   <CustomerName>
      <FirstName>Bob</FirstName>
      <LastName>Stone</LastName>
   </CustomerName>
   <CustomerAddress>
   ...
   </CustomerAddress>
</Customer>
```

While another document may use the following structure:

```
<Customer CustomerID = "C3223" FirstName = "Bob" LastName = "Stone">
   <Address>
   ...
   </Address>
</Customer>
```

Interpreting the markup can be difficult, even when done manually. It is therefore extremely helpful if we can create *rules* that can be shared that describe how the markup we create can and should be used. By creating these rules of how we intend our documents to be marked up, we can not only aid sharing between *human* consumers and authors of documents, but also programs that need to use our markup.

The problems of ensuring correctness of data and data structure can be addressed, and even overcome, with **validation**. By this we mean checking that XML conforms to the rules concerning what elements it can contain and in what order they may be used, as well as the attributes they may have and what types of content may appear within them. This is the basics of what we can do – as this chapter will show you, there is a lot more.

Validation is not a new concept – when the XML 1.0 Recommendation was published it included a mechanism for defining certain rules about the intended use for our XML vocabularies. This mechanism was the **Document Type Definition**, or **DTD**. Soon after XML was published, however, the XML community decided that it was important to have a different way of describing the rules and constraints of XML documents. The W3C took a long time creating an alternative, known as the **XML Schema** language (often referred to as **XSD**). During this period many alternatives were proposed, notably **XML-Data Reduced**, which Microsoft used in many products (such as MSXML, BizTalk, and SQL Server) to facilitate features that customers required, and to fill the gap until the W3C released its recommendation.

XML schemas greatly improve on what was offered by DTDs, and are the way forward for validating XML. In this chapter we will be looking at the validation of XML using both the W3C's XML Schema Recommendation and also the Microsoft XML-Data Reduced implementation that can still be found in MSXML. We will briefly discuss the emergence from the old DTDs through the newer XDR and how this leads to the prime language for developing schemas, the official XML Schema language (XSD).

We move on to discuss XSD in detail, looking at how to create an XML Schema and use the elements, attributes, and built-in types available to us, as well as how to create our own custom types. You will learn how to create simple type and complex type definitions, and how to use these to define a complex schema that can be used to validate XML instances.

Finally, the chapter will cover how schemas are used in practice, in particular with namespaces, validation, and how to import and include other schemas. The chapter will conclude with a brief look at the **Schema Object Model** (**SOM**) – an API for schemas – and a simple example of how it is used in practice.

History of Schema Support in MSXML

Before we begin discussing the details of any of the validation languages, it would be useful to be aware of the support for schema validation in the various MSXML parsers. This is shown in the following table:

Version	Support	Other Information
MSXML	No support for schemas.	
MSXML 2.0	Support for Microsoft's XML-Data Reduced (XDR).	Used in IE 5.0 and IE 5.5.
MSXML 2.6	Support for XDR.	Used in BizTalk, SQL Server 2000, Office 2000, and ADO.

Version	Support	Other Information
MSXML 3.0	Support for XDR.	Directly integrated with IE 6.0.
MSXML 4.0	Support for W3C XML Schema Language (XSD) and XDR.	

Throughout the chapter, when we refer to the W3C XML Schema Recommendation (XSD), we will use 'Schemas' with an upper case 'S'. When we refer to schemas in general, including XDR, we will use a lower case 's'.

Overview of XML Schemas

To recap our introduction, schemas simply describe what can occur in an instance of a document. Before we begin to see how they do this, let's first look at where XML schemas started, with Document Type Definitions (DTDs).

DTDs

XML DTDs use a subset of the same constraint mechanisms employed in SGML, known as **Extended Backus-Naur Form** (**EBNF**). It was recognized that, for the wide deployment of XML, a different solution was required and hence the work on XML schemas began. Let's take a look at the problems inherent in DTDs that caused the evolution of today's XML Schema Recommendation.

Non-XML Syntax Used

Since the syntax of DTDs is different from the syntax of markup found in instance documents, DTDs need to be parsed by a different processor from that which parses the XML document. This is because the separate syntax of DTDs does not follow the 'standard' XML syntax of elements, attributes, comments, text, and so on. However, if your schema of choice uses an XML syntax, then other XML technologies such as XSLT can be used to transform your schemas if required.

DTDs Can't Be Easily Extended

Although you can use entities and files to include declarations from many sources, extending the DTD can introduce a whole array of problems. The DTD can get very complex, with many interdependencies, becoming difficult to change and follow. This can lead to an increase in processing time and more disorder.

Only One DTD Per Document

An XML file may have only one DTD per document and so it is almost impossible to validate against multiple descriptions. External parameter entities can be used to get round this and modularize the DTDs. However, to do this, all modules must be designed to share a single namespace, making extension and reuseextremely difficult.

Limitations of Using Namespaces

Namespaces provide us with the ability to prevent element types with the same names from conflicting, and also to resolve element names intended to have the same meaning. The advantages of using XML namespaces are:

❑ Reusability – you can reuse the namespace definitions across multiple schemas where the namespace definition is well understood.

❑ Modularity – you can mix and use namespace definitions from other schemas to provide more modular documents.

❑ Extensibility – you can even extend your schemas by incorporating schema information from other sources.

However, in DTDs, if you intend to use namespaces, every element type from each namespace must be included within that DTD, which counters all of the above points. Furthermore, element names cannot be reused within a single document, so you could not have <Total> and <Total> having two different meanings depending on where they are located.

Basic Data Typing

Documents that are to be validated against DTDs really have only one data type, and that is text. This seriously limits the validation of certain values within the document. We can apply some constraints on attribute types, such as indicating an ID, NOTATION, or other attribute, but we cannot validate some common types such as integers, Booleans, or dates, as well as more complex types such as lists and complex custom types. Later we will look at how schemas introduce data type validation to solve many of these problems.

Internal DTD Subsets Can Override External DTDs

When a document has an internal DTD (such as that illustrated in our first example, which we'll see shortly) it actually takes precedence over any external DTD you may specify. This can be a huge problem for distributed scenarios, which are commonplace today; you would be unable to override this document-centric validation if the document rules changed.

This would be an even bigger problem when trying to manage a *set* of documents. You would have to ensure each document had synchronized and/or updated internal DTDs if and when the rules changed.

When working with schemas you can override internal definitions and inline schemas with an external schema file – note, however, that MSXML 4.0 does not yet support inline XSD Schema definitions (more information is given later in the chapter in the "*Known Bugs*" section). An internal definition is where you specify the location of the XSD Schema that is to be used for validation at the root of the XML document being validated; an inline Schema is when the actual XSD constraints are present in the XML document being validated.

No DOM Support

It seems a sensible option to allow you to access the rules defining the constraints of an XML document you are modifying, particularly for adding and updating the validation rules that apply to the document. Although you can use the DOM to manipulate XML data that you are working with, you are unable to access the rules of the DTD.

Limited Tooling

Over the last few years there has been rapid adoption of tools for creating and editing XML. Editing DTDs has very little support (if any) in popular XML editors. Although SGML tools offer varying levels of support for this, they are often complex and targeted at specialized markets.

However, if the validation document we are using also uses XML (as is the case with schemas), many of the tools used for XML could also be used for these schemas. Indeed, support in Visual Studio .NET for editing XML works on this basis, and most other editors have the ability to specify the XML parser you want to work with – this is useful when a particular feature is available within a parser that is not available in another. A good example is that the support of inline schemas may be important for some application and so you could specify another parser to provide validation for this (as it is not yet supported by MSXML). Similarly, there will be other features available in MSXML, not available in other parsers (or the editor's default parser).

You can view a comprehensive list of schema editing software (including some for DTDs) at http://www.xmlsoftware.com/dtd/.

Are DTDs Still Useful?

In some respects they are. In addition to the huge amount of legacy XML built using DTDs, they allow compact representation of your document rules and can be included directly in instances of XML documents. This can be useful if any other users need to override certain data types. Additionally, they are the only definition mechanism that is included in the XML Recommendation. Consider the following XML, indtd.xml, which, if using schemas, would require that the definition be in an external schema file (because MSXML does not yet support inline XSD Schema definitions):

```
<?xml version="1.0"?>
<!DOCTYPE author [
  <!ELEMENT author    (firstname,surname)>
  <!ATTLIST author     age     CDATA      #REQUIRED  >
  <!ELEMENT firstname (#PCDATA)>
  <!ELEMENT surname   (#PCDATA)>
]>
<author age="26">
    <firstname>Steven</firstname>
    <surname>Livingstone</surname>
</author>
```

Whether including the schema within the instance document is a practice you would want to adopt is another question, as it breaks all the rules of reusability and modularity. Since the constraints on the markup are within the XML file, they cannot be used by another XML document (they are not in an external DTD that multiple documents can refer to). However, as we mentioned above, it is useful in the sense that it provides a compact representation of document rules.

XML-Data Reduced (XDR)

XDR (XML-Data Reduced) was an early schema language proposed as an alternative to DTDs and submitted to the W3C by several companies including Microsoft. Rather than wait for the final XML Schema Recommendation (which was announced on 2 May 2001), Microsoft implemented support for XDR, as can be seen in the versions table at the start of the chapter. Microsoft has received much criticism over not waiting for the full version, and there is no doubt it has created some confusion. However, there is also no doubt that it pushed through the idea of schema adoption within enterprises working with MSXML and IE 5, as well concepts such as XML data types (in ADO etc.) and processing schemas using the DOM on the server.

XDR offers many advantages over DTDs, such as:

❑ It is written entirely in XML, so can be read by an XML parser and displayed like an XML document in IE (5+).

❑ It supports namespaces. MSXML (2+) has support for namespaces and allows you to directly validate an XML document containing namespaces against its schema.

❑ It supports data types. XDR provides a host of data types that can be used to validate element content and attribute values of an XML document. These include those found in DTDs, as well as many of the data types we discussed above when looking at the shortcomings of DTDs, such as integers, Booleans, and dates.

Now that XML Schemas has become a full Recommendation, Microsoft has fulfilled its commitment to schemas by implementing a substantial proportion of the Recommendation in MSXML 4. However, as XDR is supported in IE5 and other products, it has a considerable client base and will have exposure for a while to come yet. For new projects that are not tied to legacy applications, XML Schemas should be the preferred choice over XDR. The following sites offer conversion utilities/programs:

❑ IBM – http://alphaworks.ibm.com/tech/xdrtoxsd

❑ XMLSpy – http://www.xmlspy.com

❑ Microsoft – http://msdn.microsoft.com/downloads/sample.asp?url=/msdn-files/027/001/539/msdncompositedoc.xml&frame=true

Simple Example of XDR Schema (Compared to DTD)

As an example of an XDR schema, let's convert the XML document we saw earlier, which used an internal DTD. The following example will work with IE 5 and above.

When you use IE to view an XML document that has an associated XDR schema, validation is not performed against that schema – you must do it through some client script and the DOM. However, you can test that the documents you create are valid by using the **'Internet Explorer Tools for Validating XML and Viewing XSLT Output'** available for download from the Web Development/XML section at http://msdn.microsoft.com/downloads.

Back to our example, the XML content and the schema definition are now in separate documents. We are going to add a reference to our new XDR schema (don't worry too much about the syntax). This is simpleXDRXML.xml:

```xml
<?xml version="1.0" ?>
<n:author n:age="26" xmlns:n="x-schema:simpleXDR.xml">
<n:firstname>Steven</n:firstname>
<n:surname>Livingstone</n:surname>
</n:author>
```

All you should really take from this at the moment is that a reference has now been put in pointing to the external schema document, simpleXDR.xml, which is defined as follows:

```xml
<?xml version="1.0" ?>
<Schema xmlns="urn:schemas-microsoft-com:xml-data"
        xmlns:dt="urn:schemas-microsoft-com:datatypes" >
```

```
    <ElementType name="firstname" dt:type="string"/>
    <ElementType name="surname" dt:type="string"/>

    <AttributeType name="age" dt:type="int"/>
    <ElementType name="author">
        <attribute type="age"/>
        <element type="firstname"/>
        <element type="surname"/>
    </ElementType>
</Schema>
```

Once again, don't concern yourself with the details as we are not interested in the syntax here, but look at how we can now specify exactly what data types we are working with. As you can see, this schema is in fact an XML file itself. The constraints applied by the schema are contained in the <Schema> element. Elements are declared with an element called <ElementType>, while attributes are declared using an element called <AttributeType>:

```
<ElementType name="surname" dt:type="string"/>
<AttributeType name="age" dt:type="int"/>
```

This requires that, for example, the value of the age attribute in an instance document be an integer if it is to be validated successfully against the XDR schema. In our DTD we simply had the following entry, which accepts any CDATA type:

```
age     CDATA        #REQUIRED
```

When we view simpleXDRXML.xml in IE, provided you have installed the validation tools, you can right-click on the document in the browser, then click Validate XML, and you will get a "Validation Successful" message:

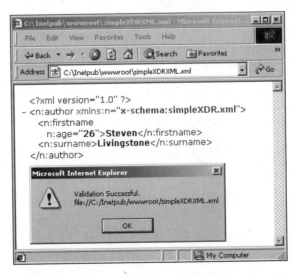

Let's change the value of the age of the author, from 26 to X (where "X" is something other than an integer age value). You will receive an error message telling you it is not a valid integer type:

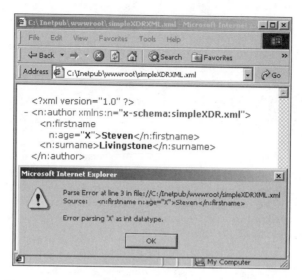

Of course, we wouldn't expect a user to download a validation tool and validate the XML file beforehand in the real world; we would use the DOM to perform the validation programmatically in an HTML page. We will look at this shortly in the detailed XSD section below.

All we have to understand for now is that the XML processor that comes with Internet Explorer (MSXML) has loaded the source XML document. That source document includes a reference (internal or, as in this case, external) to some XDR schema, which is itself loaded by the processor. The source XML file is validated against the constraints dictated in this XDR schema. In our case, it checked if the age attribute was an integer and outputted the problem that X was not an integer data type.

At this point you should have a basic understanding of how XDR schema validation is accomplished. We won't be looking at XDR any further in this chapter, as we will focus our attention on the official W3C XML Schema Language Recommendation (XSD) that is to be used in future.

XML Schema

The **W3C XML Schema** Recommendation, often given the term **XSD** – XML Schema Definition, or **XSDL** – XML Schema Definition Language, is a very comprehensive standard, set to become the dominant constraint and validation mechanism for instances of XML documents.

The XML Schema Recommendation consists of two parts: **Structures** and **Datatypes**. The normative descriptions for these are found in two documents. A supplementary **Primer** is also provided by the W3C in order to help people get up to speed quickly with XSDL, given its complexity (and the complexity of the normative Structures and Datatypes definition documents). Below are some links to the Primer and the two parts of the XML Schema Recommendation:

❑ An introduction to XML Schema concepts, at http://www.w3.org/TR/xmlschema-0.

❑ A document defining all of the structures used in XML Schemas, at http://www.w3.org/TR/xmlschema-1.

❑ A document describing XML Schema Datatypes, at http://www.w3.org/TR/xmlschema-2.

Why XML Schemas Came About

The W3C XML Schema Recommendation is the official alternative to DTDs, and the future language for defining and constraining XML documents. It is built into MSXML 4.0 and is Microsoft's recommended way forward for working with XML Schemas.

It also forms part of many of Microsoft's products, including Exchange Server 2000 (which uses the earlier 2000/10 XML Schema Proposed Recommendation) and the .NET Framework. It is likely to play a huge role in XML applications, in areas ranging from electronic commerce and business information exchange to content creation and management.

The XSD Schema language has undergone transitions during its move towards a full Recommendation, and different versions were implemented in various Microsoft products before MSXML 4.0. They are identified by separate namespaces, as below:

❑ http://www.w3.org/2000/XMLSchema – the Official Recommendation and used in .NET Framework and Visual Studio .NET technologies.

❑ http://www.w3.org/2000/10/XMLSchema – used in Microsoft Access 2000 Export Wizard.

❑ http://www.w3.org/1999/XMLSchema – used in Microsoft Office 2000.

MSXML 4.0 supports the latest version of these, namely http://www.w3.org/2001/XMLSchema. The W3C offers an online tool to help convert from older versions of the W3C Schema specification (prior to the recommendation). This is at http://www.w3.org/2001/03/webdata/xsu. It attempts to convert valid schema documents with the namespace URI http://www.w3.org/2000/10/XMLSchema to valid schema documents with the namespace URI http://www.w3.org/2001/XMLSchema.

The W3C also maintains an application for validating your Schemas online. You can test against any of the versions of XSD that were released prior to the Recommendation, as well as the recommendation itself. You can find this at http://www.w3.org/2001/03/webdata/xsv.

Schema-Related Limitations and Known Bugs in MSXML 4.0

❑ One of the most notable omissions in MSXML 4.0 is that you cannot use inline Schema validation in the same way you can use DTDs and XDR schemas for including the constraints within the XML file itself. Although it is recommended that you don't include schemas within XML files, there are situations where self-contained documents may be useful (such as self-contained recordsets going directy to SQL Server). This is to be fixed with MSXML 4.0 SP1.

❑ The SDK documentation mentions the XSD Boolean built-in data type where it should be boolean (small "b").

How Does XSD Improve on XDR and DTDs?

Let's consider why XML Schema is so important and why it will become the dominant schema validation language. We will discuss XSD in detail below, but in brief, it offers many advantages over DTDs and improves on MSXML's schema predecessor, XDR. Notably, the advantages are:

❏ It is written in XML. Like XDR, XSD is written entirely as XML and can be read by an XML parser and displayed like an XML document in IE (5+). In turn, this means it can be read and manipulated using standard XML technologies such as the DOM, SAX, and XSLT. Additionally, you can also use it with standard XML editors, parsers, and other readily available XML tools.

❏ It supports namespaces. XSD has support for namespaces; this allows you to directly validate an XML document that contains markup from multiple namespaces against its schema.

❏ It supports data types. XSD has huge improvements on the data types offered by both DTDs and XDR, providing a host of primitive data types (such as `string`, `boolean`, `date`, etc.), derived data types (`nonNegativeInteger`, `language`, etc.) and the ability to create your own complex types made up of simple types and other complex types. It also supports regular expressions, which are used for recognizing patterns within textual data such as ZIP codes, telephone numbers, product codes, etc.

❏ It is self-documenting. XSD has built-in documentation elements that can be used to describe the purpose of elements or attributes. This means that a stylesheet or DOM can be used to generate documentation for a given Schema.

❏ It is extensible. XSD provides the ability to reuse parts of other schemas, define complex structures to reuse in other schemas, derive new types from existing types, and reference multiple schemas.

XML Schemas (XSD) in Detail

XSD is a very powerful and flexible language, improving dramatically on both the conformance and capability offered by DTDs and XDR. The examples in this section use only the MSXML 4.0 parser as this was the first version to support XSD.

Creating a Simple Schema

Let's start by looking at how to create a simple Schema using XSD. Following this, we will create an instance based on this Schema and use some very simple script to check whether the document instance is valid according to the constraints of the XSD. This section is intended to give you a basic understanding of how to build an XSD Schema – more in-depth details are given in a later section, "*Building XSD Schemas*".

The example files required for this are `simpleSchema.xsd`, `simpleSchemaInstance.xml`, and `validateXSD.htm`, available in the code download. It is based on the capabilities of MSXML 4.0. However, you can still view (that is, without validating) both the XSD file (`simpleSchema.xsd`) and the XML instance (`simpleSchemaInstance.xml`) in IE 5+. You can run the sample directly from `validateXSD.htm` by choosing `simpleSchemaInstance.xml` from the drop-down list – note that there are two samples; this first instance validates against the Schema and the second instance (`simpleSchemaInstanceB.xml`) is in fact invalid.

The code for `simpleSchema.xsd` is shown below:

```
<?xml version="1.0" encoding="utf-8" ?>
<xsd:schema xmlns:xsd="http://www.w3.org/2001/XMLSchema">
    <xsd:annotation>
```

```
                <xsd:documentation xml:lang="en">
                    Wrox author information.
                </xsd:documentation>
        </xsd:annotation>
        <xsd:element name="author">
            <xsd:complexType>
                <xsd:sequence>
                    <xsd:element name="firstname" type="xsd:string" />
                    <xsd:element name="surname" type="xsd:string" />
                </xsd:sequence>
                <xsd:attribute name="age" type="xsd:int" />
            </xsd:complexType>
        </xsd:element>
    </xsd:schema>
```

The Schema is itself an XML file with the constraints defined within a <schema> root element. The xsd prefix is associated with the XML Schema namespace http://www.w3.org/2001/XMLSchema and qualifies any elements, attributes, or types associated with XSD. At a high level, you should notice how structured documentation is possible with the <annotation> element. Elements are defined by <element> tags and attributes using <attribute> tags, but more complex constraints can be created using <complexType> elements to group elements and attributes together.

Within the Schema, elements are declared using two methods: directly and using the <complexType> element. We will look at <complexType> elements later on, so let's first consider the most basic way to create an XSD element. When we created the <firstname> element in our DTD we declared it as follows:

```
<!ELEMENT firstname (#PCDATA)>
```

and using XDR, this element could be declared as follows:

```
<ElementType name="firstname" dt:type="string"/>
```

To define a similar element in XSD, the following definition is used:

```
<xsd:element name="firstname" type="xsd:string" />
```

Attributes in XSD are defined in a similar way to how they are in XDR. In the DTD we had:

```
age    CDATA       #REQUIRED
```

and in XDR it would be:

```
<AttributeType name="age" dt:type="int"/>
```

In XSD a similar element is used to define the age attribute with type int:

```
<xsd:attribute name="age" type="xsd:int"/>
```

A valid XML document (`simpleSchemaInstance.xml`) based on this Schema is shown below:

```
<?xml version="1.0" ?>
<author age="26" xmlns:xsi="http://www.w3.org/2001/XMLSchema-instance"
    xsi:noNamespaceSchemaLocation="simpleSchema.xsd">
  <firstname>Steven</firstname>
  <surname>Livingstone</surname>
</author>
```

This XML instance is a little more complex than a typical XML document when you reference the XML Schema within the document – this is what we are doing with the `xsi:noNamespaceSchemaLocation` attribute. Ignore this for the moment as it will be discussed in the "*Namespaces in XML Schema and Validating XML Instances*" section below; for the moment just understand that we are saying this document does not use any namespaces (other than the `XMLSchema-Instance` namespace) and specifiying the location of the Schema at `simpleSchema.xsd`.

Beyond this, a simple XML instance is created using the element and attribute constraints defined in the Schema. How can we test this? The script in `validateXSD.htm` will cause the validation to occur because MSXML validates the XML file by default (`validateOnParse=true` is the default) – it is quite basic and although I suggest you have a quick look at the file, it does nothing more than load the desired XML. A message box is displayed indicating whether the XML document successfully validated and, if not, what the problem was.

However, have we really seen any validation? How do we know it even validated and didn't just display a message box saying everything was fine without actually ensuring that was so? The following example (`simpleSchemaInstanceB.xml`) is almost identical to the XML document instance above, but we have changed the value of the `age` attribute in the following line from:

```
<author age="26"
    xmlns:xsi="http://www.w3.org/2001/XMLSchema-instance"
    xsi:noNamespaceSchemaLocation="simpleSchema.xsd">
```

to:

```
<author age="twentysix"
    xmlns:xsi="http://www.w3.org/2001/XMLSchema-instance"
    xsi:noNamespaceSchemaLocation="simpleSchema.xsd">
```

If you run this (select it from the drop-down list in `validateXSD.htm`), you will get the following:

When you run the **`validateXSD.htm`** page, you will see a **TEXTAREA** element containing the XML that was contained in the source file. This is intended to allow you to easily change the XML file to test the validation (for example put in wrong values and see that it doesn't successfully validate). However, one important note is that the **`xsi:noNamespaceSchemaLocation`** attribute contains just the local file name to ensure that the samples run immediately. If (and only if) you change the XML in the TEXTAREA element and click the **"Validate my Changes"** button, you must ensure that the **`xsi:noNamespaceSchemaLocation`** has the full URL to the XSD file. In other words change **`xsi:noNamespaceSchemaLocation="simpleSchema.xsd"`** to **`xsi:noNamespaceSchemaLocation="http://yourserver/folder/simpleSchema.xsd"`**. This is true for all examples that use **`validateXSD.htm`**.

The <schema> Root Element

The chapter does not cover every element and attribute available in XSD due to space limitations – in fact, an entire book has been devoted to the subject. Rather, we will concentrate on those most used when working with XSD day-to-day. For further information consult the MSXML SDK or "Professional XML Schemas" (Wrox Press, ISBN 1-8-6005-47-4).

The <schema> element is the root of any Schema and contains the constraints of the Schema, as well as the XSD Schema namespace definition, other namespace definitions, version information, language information, and some other attributes.

In the sample case above we defined the <schema> element as follows:

```
<xsd:schema xmlns:xsd="http://www.w3.org/2001/XMLSchema">
```

The `xmlns:xsd="http://www.w3.org/2001/XMLSchema"` namespace definition is essential in creating the constraints of the Schema and allows us to associate the elements, attributes, and types that have been defined within the Schema as part of the XSD vocabulary – we use `xsd` as the prefix, but this can be anything you want.

There is a `version` attribute that is useful in the version management of your Schema files, and an `id` attribute to uniquely identify the element within the document.

One more very important attribute is the `targetNamespace` attribute, which we will look at in more detail later, in the section on "*Namespaces in XML Schema and Validating XML Instances*". Briefly, the `targetNamespace` attribute allows you to specify the namespace to which this Schema will be associated.

Elements

Elements in XSD are declared using the `<element>` tag, but in comparison with DTDs and XDR, the actual definition of elements is very flexible. The exact details on the attributes that can be applied to the `<element>` tag can be found in the MSXML SDK, but let's look at some examples of how elements can be defined.

We have already seen the simplest way to define an element when we looked the example above:

```
<xsd:element name="firstname" type="xsd:string" />
```

However, there are a number of attributes that can be used to control the usage of an `<element>` definition. The `type` attribute we see here is quite flexible and can refer to the many built-in XSD data types, or it can have the name of a simple or complex type defined within this Schema (or another namespace-qualified simple or complex type). So the following definition would limit the value of the `<InsuranceNumber>` element to the constraints imposed by the `InsNo` type defined in the Schema associated with the namespace definition `"xmlns:nums='uri:insnos'"`:

```
<xsd:element name="InsuranceNumber" type="nums:InsNo" />
```

Two more of the most commonly used `<element>` attributes are the `minOccurs` and `maxOccurs` attributes which define the minimum number of times and maximum number of times that the element can occur within its parent. (These can not be applied to the `<schema>` element because the root element must appear once and only once.) The `minOccurs` attribute must be an integer value greater or equal to zero (zero states that the element itself is optional). So, if you have set a `minOccurs` of zero and a `maxOccurs` value, this would say that the element might not appear, but if it does there is a limit on its number of appearances. The `maxOccurs` attribute must also be an integer greater or equal to zero – additionally, this can have the value `unbounded`, which indicates that there is no limit on the maximum number of appearances. The following table outlines the effect of `minOccurs` and `maxOccurs` on elements:

CardinalityOperator	minOccursValue	maxOccursValue	Number of Child Element(s)
[none]	1	1	One and only one.
?	0	1	Zero or one.
*	0	unbounded	Zero or more.
+	1	unbounded	One or more.

So, we could modify part of the XSD sample above to state that the `<firstname>` element is optional (minOccurs is zero), but can appear as many times as required (maxOccurs is unbounded); and the `<surname>` element must appear once and only once, with the following lines:

```
...
    <xsd:element name="author">
        <xsd:complexType>
            <xsd:sequence>
                <xsd:element name="firstname" type="xsd:string"
                    minOccurs="0" maxOccurs="unbounded"/>
                <xsd:element name="surname" type="xsd:string"
                    minOccurs="1" maxOccurs="1"/>
            </xsd:sequence>
            <xsd:attribute name="age" type="xsd:int" />
        </xsd:complexType>
    </xsd:element>
...
```

Another important attribute is the `ref` attribute, allowing you to reference a previously defined element in the Schema (or another Schema using namespace qualification). We can now update our XSD from earlier to incorporate a new `<Address>` element using the `type` attribute, and this `<Address>` element definition itself uses the `ref` attribute, as shown below. This example can be run from `validate.htm` (the Schema is called `simpleSchemaRef.xsd` and the instance `simpleSchemaInstanceRef.xml`). The code of the XSD file is:

```
...
    <xsd:element name="author">
        <xsd:complexType>
            <xsd:sequence>
                <xsd:element name="firstname" type="xsd:string"
                    minOccurs="0" maxOccurs="unbounded" />
                <xsd:element name="surname" type="xsd:string"
                    minOccurs="1" maxOccurs="1" />
                <xsd:element name="Address" type="Address"
                    minOccurs="1" maxOccurs="1" />
            </xsd:sequence>
            <xsd:attribute name="age" type="xsd:int" />
        </xsd:complexType>
    </xsd:element>
    <xsd:element name="house" type="xsd:int" />
    <xsd:element name="flat" substitutionGroup="house" type="xsd:int" />
    <xsd:complexType name="Address">
        <xsd:sequence>
            <xsd:element ref="house" />
            <xsd:element name="street" type="xsd:string" />
            <xsd:element name="city" type="xsd:string"
                default="Rio De Janerio" />
            <xsd:element name="country" type="xsd:string"
                nillable="true" />
            <xsd:element name="continent" type="xsd:string"
                fixed="South America" />
        </xsd:sequence>
    </xsd:complexType>
...
```

You may notice that the `nillable="true"` attribute is set in the XSD Schema, but the actual instance document used the `xsi:nil="true"` attribute (`<country xsi:nil="true"></country>`). The `nillable` attribute in XSD defines whether or not a given element can be defined to have an explicit "nil" value – to actual set an element value as "nil" in an instance document, you use the `xsi:nil="true"` attribute.

The new `<Address>` element sets its `type` attribute to the complex type `Address` – don't worry too much about this yet, we cover complex types in detail below. More importantly for now, the example shows how you can use the `ref` attribute within the `<Address>` element to reference the `<house>` element defined above in the Schema (we look at this element again below). The element that is referenced is defined in the same way as we define any other `<element>` element, and within the instance it is used as though the element were defined directly as a child of the `<Address>` element. The updated instance reads as below:

```
<?xml version="1.0" ?>
<author age="26" xmlns:xsi="http://www.w3.org/2001/XMLSchema-instance"
        xsi:noNamespaceSchemaLocation="simpleSchemaRef.xsd">
    <firstname>Steven</firstname>
    <surname>Livingstone</surname>
    <Address>
            <house>123</house>
            <street>Santiago Bay</street>
            <city>Santiago</city>
            <country xsi:nil="true"></country>
            <continent>South America</continent>
    </Address>
</author>
```

Beyond the simple introduction of the `ref` attribute, some of the other XSD `<element>` attributes have been introduced to give you a better idea of what is possible. For example, the `substitutionGroup` attribute can be used on an `<element>` to define an element that this element can substitute. Imagine that some creators of an instance may prefer to use "flat" (another term for an apartment) rather than "house", although in respect of our Schema they are really the same thing. Therefore, at a global level, we can define the `<house>` element and then the `<flat>` element with a `substitutionGroup` value of `house`:

```
<xsd:element name="house" type="xsd:int" />
<xsd:element name="flat" substitutionGroup="house" type="xsd:int" />
```

Also, in the definition of the `<city>` element, we stated a `default` attribute with value "Rio De Janerio", which simply means that if no value is given then "Rio De Janerio" is the assumed value. In contrast, in the `<continent>` element definition, we said it had a `fixed` attribute of value "South America", which means that this is the default value and cannot be changed – so it will always be "South America". Finally, the `<country>` element definition was defined with the `nil` attribute set to `true`, indicating that some instances can explicitly declare the value of this to nill as follows:

```
<country xsi:nil="true"></country>
```

Here we will stop looking explicitly at element definitions, but as they form the basis for creating XML Schemas, it won't be our last look at them. We will see them next in our discussions of `simpleType` and `complexType` definitions.

Before we move on to look at XSD data types, let's look briefly at how attributes can be defined.

Attributes

Defining attributes in XSD is very much like defining elements, but there is a much greater restriction. They may contain only text, annotations, or simple type definitions, and have similar but fewer attributes that can be applied. In fact, the attributes that can be used on an <attribute> definition are as listed:

- ❑ default – initial value that can be overridden.
- ❑ fixed – default value that cannot be overridden.
- ❑ form – determines the local value of attributeFormDefault.
- ❑ id – unique ID in the document.
- ❑ name – the name of the attribute.
- ❑ ref – reference to a prior attribute definition.
- ❑ type – XSD built-in type or simple type definition.
- ❑ use – how the attribute is used.

We'll be looking at the form attribute later, so let's just outline the other attribute we haven't met yet – use. This attribute takes one of the values optional, prohibited, or required; optional indicates that the attribute isn't mandatory, prohibited is used when you are reusing some pre-defined set of attribute definitions and don't want a given attribute to be reused from within that group (for example if we want to use the age and taxNumber attributes, but not the identityNumber attribute from the personalInformation set of attributes; more on this later), and required means the attribute is mandatory. So we may define the age attribute within our sample as follows:

```
<xsd:attribute name="age" type="xsd:int" use="required"/>
```

The other definitions work in a very similar manner to that of elements and you will meet many of them within the chapter. You can also find out specific details on them in the MSXML SDK.

XSD Data Types

Data types within XML Schemas offer all capabilities provided by DTDs, but also offer more choice of data types and the powerful ability to use **data type facets** to specify valid values much more effectively.

XSD defines two types of data type: **simple** types and **complex** types, from which Schemas are made. A simple type is used if you are talking about element content that only contains character data and no child elements or attributes, and for all attribute values. Otherwise, when you want to create a content model for an element that contains child elements or if you want an element to carry attributes, you have to define a complex type.

The building blocks of any XSD Schema are simple types, as they are used in elements that only contain character data, and for all attribute values.

Simple Types

The <simpleType> element is used to define XSD simple types, which can be derived from existing built-in simple types and other derived simple types (in this case the new type would likely be a subset of the derived type). You use simple types to build more simple types and complex types (discussed below).

There are two ways a simple type can be used – the first is directly on an `<element>` element, if it has no attributes or child elements. (This is like an XDR `<ElementType>` element.) The second is as a defined `<simpleType>` element. The latter is a great improvement on what was available in XDR.

So we could define an element called age that takes any valid positive integer, as follows (infants less than one are rounded up to one):

```
<xsd:element name='age' type='xsd:positiveInteger'/>
```

Similarly, you may define an element for a person's first name as follows:

```
<xsd:element name='firstname' type='xsd:string'/>
```

However, this is the same as what you can do in XDR – with XSD you can do a lot more, such as restrict the valid integer values, or the length of a person's name. For this you can use a `<simpleType>` element, defined as follows:

```
<simpleType
   id = "ID"
   name="NCName"
   final="(#all | (list | union | restriction))" />
```

The id should uniquely identify the `<simpleType>` element within the document and the name must be a non-colon-name, which means any XML name that does not contain a colon character (:). A simpleType cannot contain elements and cannot have attributes – it is basically a value, or set of values, according to the rules defined within the `<simpleType>` definition, and is derived from existing XSD data types or existing simple types. We discuss these below, but first let's look at the most common child element when defining `<simpleType>` elements – the `<restriction>` element.

The `<restriction>` element within a `<simpleType>` definition is used as follows:

```
<restriction
   id = "ID"
   base="QName" />
```

The id attribute is a unique identifier for the `<restriction>` element within the document. The base attribute takes a built-in data type or simple type definition (and can use namespaces) and this is the type that is restricted in order to produce a resultant type for the `<restriction>` element. Within the `<restriction>` element are constraining facets (discussed in detail in the "*Data Type Constraining Facets*" section below) such as length, minInclusive, and maxInclusive, and many others. These define the constraints (restrictions) on the type that is being restricted.

> The following examples can be seen by running the `simpleSchemaInstanceST.xml` entry in `validate.htm`. The XSD file `simpleSchemaST.xsd` contains the updated Schema information.

For example, the above age example could be redefined to limit the values to integers between 1 and 125, like so:

```
<xsd:simpleType name="PersonsAge">
   <xsd:restriction base="xsd:integer">
      <xsd:minInclusive value="1"/>
```

```
        <xsd:maxInclusive value="125"/>
    </xsd:restriction>
</xsd:simpleType>
<xsd:attribute name='age' type='PersonsAge'/>
```

In this case, a `<simpleType>` element has been created with the name `PersonsAge`. The `<restriction>` element has been used with a `base` type of the built-in XSD `integer` data type, which now restricts possible values to integer types. However, we further restrict the integer types using the `minInclusive` and `maxInclusive` facets (discussed below). The `<minInclusive>` element says that the minimum value of `PersonsAge` is the number one, including one. The `<maxInclusive>` element says that the maximum value of `PersonsAge` is the number 125, including 125. We can then use this simple type as the value of a `type` attribute on an `<attribute>` (or `<element>`) definition.

Similarly, the `firstname` string may be defined as follows to restrict its length to 7 characters:

```
<xsd:simpleType name="PersonsFirstname">
    <xsd:restriction base="xsd:string">
        <xsd:maxLength value="7"/>
    </xsd:restriction>
</xsd:simpleType>
<xsd:element name='firstname' type='PersonsFirstname'/>
```

This uses the XSD `string` built-in data type as the `base` for `<restriction>` and the `maxLength` data type facet with a value of 7 to restrict the maximum number of characters of the `PersonsFirstname` simple type to seven characters.

We have discussed some simple examples of working with `<simpleType>` elements thus far and we mentioned there were a lot of data types that can be used as the `base` for restrictions to create new simple type definitions. Let's have a look at these now.

Primitive Data Types

The primitive data types available in the XML Schema language are discussed below:

Data type	Description
anyURI	Represents a URI as defined by RFC 2396. It can be absolute or relative, and may have an optional fragment identifier.
base64Binary	base64-encoded binary data BLOB.
boolean	Can be true, false, 1, or 0.
date	An ISO 8601 abbreviated date without the time part – from the Gregorian calendar, in the form CCYY-MM-DD (for example, "2001-09-25").
dateTime	An ISO 8601 abbreviated date with optional time part and time zone as CCYY-MM-DDThh:mm:ss. For example, "2001-09-25T07:27:59-11:00" which means that the time given (after T) is 11 hours behind Universal Coordinated time (UTC). You can also write this as "2001-09-24T18:27:59Z" where the Z indicates the time is with respect to UTC, and so the 11 hours difference defined above is taken away from the local time (just after the T).

Table continued on following page

Data type	Description
decimal	Represents arbitrary precision decimal numbers.
double	Represents double-precision 64-bit floating-point numbers (for example, "-2E3, 4.5E-3, 19").
duration	Represents a duration of time in the format PnYnMnDTnHnMnS, where P must always be the first character, nY is the number of years, nM the months, nD the days, T the date time separator, nH the hours, nM the minutes, and nS the seconds (for example, "P2Y7M0DT13H12M23S" means 2 years, 7 months (and zero days), 13 hours, 12 minutes, and 23 seconds).
float	Standard concept of real numbers corresponding to a single precision 32-bit floating-point type.
gDay	Represents a day in the Gregorian calendar in the form –DD (for example, -24 is the 24th day of a month).
gMonth	Represents a month in the Gregorian calendar in the form –MM (for example, -8 is the 8th month of the year).
gMonthDay	Represents a day in a month in the Gregorian calendar in the form –MM-DD (for example, -11-27 is the 27th day of the 11th month).
gYear	Represents a year in the Gregorian calendar in the form –CCYY (for example, -2001 for the year 2001).
gYearMonth	Represents a month in a year in the Gregorian calendar in the form –CCYY-MM (for example, -2001-11 is the 11th month of the year 2001).
hexBinary	Hexadecimal digits (0-9, a-f, A-F) representing binary data (for example, "8F").
NOTATION	A declaration of non-XML data corresponding to a `<!NOTATION..>` declaration in some DTD.
QName	Represents an XML Namespace QName (for example, `xsd:element` or `urn:ns`).
string	Character data (for example, "Glasgow Celtic"). In DTD it was CDATA. For example, `<!ATTLIST author age CDATA #IMPLIED>`.
time	An ISO 8601 abbreviated time with optional time zone, in the format HH:MM:SS (for example, "07:27:98").

Derived Data Types

The derived data types in XSD are shown below alphabetically and are based on either the primitive types above or another pre-defined derived data type:

Data type	Description
byte	A one byte signed integer (-128 to +127). Derived from short data type.
entities	List of whitespace-separated "entity" types.
entity	Reference to a pre-defined unparsed entity.
id	Unique identifier for an element in a document; can't be all numeric and must be valid XML.
idref	A reference to an element with an "id" type attribute. Allows links within a document.
idrefs	List of whitespace-separated "idref" types.
int	Represents an integer with a minimum value of -2,147,483,648 and maximum of 2,147,483,647. Derived from long derived type.
integer	A signed integer (for example, -8). Based on decimal primitive type.
language	Language identifiers as defined in RFC 1766 (for example, en or fr). Based on token derived type. Note that this doesn't actually validate against the RFC 1766 language values.
long	Represents an integer with a minimum value of -9,223,372,036,854,775,808 and maximum of 9,223,372,036,854,775,807.
Name	Represents XML names (for example, Country). Based on token derived type.
NCName	Represents XML names, but cannot begin with a colon (:) character. Based on Name derived type.
negativeInteger	Represents an integer that is less than zero. A negativeInteger consists of a negative sign (-) and sequence of decimal digits (for example, -72). Derived from nonPositiveInteger derived type.
nmtoken	Values conforming to the name token (like a single enumeration), but as valid XML without the first character restrictions.
nmtokens	A list of whitespace-separated nmtoken values – like enumeration, but without the first character restrictions.
nonNegativeInteger	Represents an integer that is greater than or equal to zero (for example, 72). Derived from integer derived type.
nonPositiveInteger	Represents an integer that is less than or equal to zero. A nonPositiveInteger consists of a negative sign (-) and a sequence of decimal digits (for example, -72). Derived from integer derived type.
normalizedString	Represents whitespace-normalized strings; the strings do not contain carriage return, line feed, or tab characters. Based on string primitive type.

Table continued on following page

Data type	Description
positiveInteger	Represents an integer that is greater than zero (for example, 1). Derived from nonNegativeInteger derived type.
short	Represents an integer with a minimum value of -32,768 and maximum of 32,767. Derived from int data type.
token	Represents a tokenized string, which does not contain line feed or tab characters, leading or trailing spaces, or internal sequences of more than two spaces. Based on the derived data type normalizedString.
unsignedByte	A one byte unsigned integer (0 to +255). Derived from unsignedShort derived data type.
unsignedInt	A four byte unsigned integer (0 to +4,294,967,295). Derived from unsignedLong derived data type.
unsignedLong	An eight byte unsigned integer (0 to +18,446,744,073,709,551,615). Derived from nonNegativeInteger data type.
unsignedShort	A two byte unsigned integer (0 to +65,535). Derived from unsignedInt derived data type.

Other Data Types

There are three data types also available in XSD, but which we have not yet covered. These are atomic, list, and union data types.

An **atomic** data type is one that is not divisible within the context of the XML Schema language – in other words a given data type cannot be broken down into some sub-data type defined as part of the XML Schema Data Types specification. Since XML Schema does not define a character as a data type, rather a string, the following is an atomic data type of type string: "<s>I represent some string</s>". Also, the NMTOKEN value "UK" is considered indivisible and hence atomic because "U" and "K" make no sense as individual characters. The following is an atomic derived data type that is a date (it cannot be derived further than this) and could have been derived from the primitive type string: "<s>2001-09-25</s>".

XSD also has the concept of **list** data types. XSD has some built0in list types that we have already discussed, namely NMTOKENS, IDREFS, and ENTITIES. XSD also allows you to create new lists derived from existing finite lists of atomic types, for example "<vals>1 2 3 4 5</vals>".

Finally, **union** data types allow the valid values of an element or attribute for one or more instances of multiple atomic and list types. In other words, we can define a data type as a combination of atomic and list types.

Data Type Constraining Facets

Further enhancing the power and flexibility of XSD is the ability to apply **data type facets**. These allow us to further constrain the values of the data type on a <simpleType> element, as we saw above with the <restriction> element. The following facets can be used to constrain the permissible values:

Facet	Description
enumeration	A specified set of values separated by whitespace (for example, 1 2 3 4 5). This constrains a data type to the specified values.
fractionDigits	Value with specific maximum number of decimal digits in the fractional part (for example, fractionDigits=1 would mean that 36.4 and 45.9 are valid).
length	Number of units of length. Units of length depend on the data type, so the length of a string is measured in characters, whereas the length for base64Binary is measured in octets (8 bytes). This value must be a nonNegativeInteger.
maxExclusive	Upper bound value, so all values are less than this value (for example, a maxExclusive value of 10 would mean all values should be under 10). This value must be the same data type as the inherited data type.
maxInclusive	Maximum value (for example, a maxInclusive value of 10 would mean all values should be under, or equal to, 10). This value must be the same data type as the inherited data type.
maxLength	Maximum number of units of length (for example, a maxLength of 5 would mean there could be a maximum of 5 units of length). Units of length depend on the data type. This value must be a nonNegativeInteger.
minExclusive	Lower bound value, so all values are greater than this value (for example, a minExclusive value of 10 would mean all values should be greater than 10). This value must be the same data type as the inherited data type.
minInclusive	Minimum value (for example, a minInclusive value of 10 would mean all values should be greater than, or equal to, 10). This value must be the same data type as the inherited data type.
minLength	Minimum number of units of length (for example, a minLength of 5 would mean there could be a minimum of 5 units of length). Units of length depend on the data type. This value must be a nonNegativeInteger.
pattern	Specific pattern that the data type's values must match. The pattern value must be a regular expression. A regular expression uses pattern matching techniques to determine whether some string matches a given pattern.
totalDigits	Value with specific maximum number of decimal digits.
whiteSpace	This constrains the values derived from the string data type. Its value can be preserve which means that no normalization is done and so the value is not changed. It may be replace, which means all tabs, line feeds, and carriage returns in the value are replaced by a single space. Finally, its value may be collapse, in which the same things done by replace are carried out, but then contiguous whitespace characters are collapsed to a single space and leading and trailing spaces are removed.

Complex Types

In contrast to simple type elements, complex types may contain elements and use attributes, and are what we use to create the structure of an XSD Schema – basiclly if you want an element to have child elements or attributes, then you must work with <complexType> definitions. We tie together the simple types that have already been defined with other complex types to create a **content model**.

<complexType> elements declared at a global level (direct children of the <schema> element) should have a name attribute so they can be referred to and an id attribute which uniquely identifies them within the document. A mixed attribute also says whether character data is allowed as a child of the element (it defaults to false). If a complex type is declared as a child of an <element> tag and contains no name attribute, then it is known as an **anonymous** type – anonymous type definitions generally contain few constraints and aren't reused in the Schema. They save on the overhead of naming and referencing types, but have none of the reuse that is a major part of XSD.

We have in fact been using the <complexType> element within our sample files for quite a while now and we haven't really discussed it. The sample defines the Address complex type as follows:

```
<xsd:complexType name="Address">
        <xsd:sequence>
                <xsd:element ref="house" />
                <xsd:element name="street" type="xsd:string" />
                <xsd:element name="city" type="xsd:string"
                        default="Rio De Janerio" />
                <xsd:element name="country" type="xsd:string"
                        nillable="true" />
                <xsd:element name="continent" type="xsd:string"
                        fixed="South America" />
        </xsd:sequence>
</xsd:complexType>
```

The definition we have here for the Address complex type contains elements, and so we must use a <complexType> definition rather than a <simpleType> definition. Within the complex type, however, there can be a set of grouping elements (in our case we defined a sequence of elements) and attributes, plus restrictions and extensions decribing the content that is allowable. Let's look at these details, starting with grouping and attribute definitions in <complexType> elements.

Grouping and Attributes

> The examples in the following section can be run using **validateXSD.htm** by choosing the **simpleSchemaInstanceGroup.xml** file from the drop-down list – the XSD file is **simpleSchemaGroup.xsd**.

Grouping can be used to group elements and attributes to extend complex type definitions and promote reuse and inheritance of element definitions. A <group> element definition can use a name attribute so that it can be referenced by the ref attribute in some other group. The minOccurs and maxOccurs attributes define how many times the group may be repeated in the containing element. Both of these default to 1, minOccurs must be an integer value equal to or greater than 0 (0 implies the group is optional), and maxOccurs also takes a value greater to or equal to 0, with unbounded meaning there is no limit. These should be used when the group is used (or a reference to the group) within a containing element.

To group elements, we use the <group> element combined with a <sequence>, <choice>, or <all> child element, which are known as **compositors**. The <sequence> element, which is a sub-element of the <group> element, states that elements defined within it must appear in the order they are shown. In the sample file for this section, a new global <group> element has been created, called Addresses, which groups together the elements required to create an arbitrary address:

```
<xsd:group name="Addresses">
    <xsd:sequence>
        <xsd:element ref="house" />
        <xsd:element name="street" type="xsd:string" />
        <xsd:element name="city" type="xsd:string"
            default="Rio De Janerio" />
        <xsd:element name="country" type="xsd:string" nillable="true" />
        <xsd:element name="continent" type="xsd:string"
            fixed="South America" />
    </xsd:sequence>
</xsd:group>
```

This uses the <sequence> element to say that the <house> (or <flat>) element must come first, followed by <street> then <city> and so on. To reference the <group> within a <complexType> definition, we simply do the following:

```
<xsd:complexType name="Address">
    <xsd:group ref="Addresses" />
</xsd:complexType>
```

As you can see, you simply define a <group> element and use the ref attribute to reference the <group> definition.

Alternatively, to create a <group> element where the selected value should be *one* of those listed we use the <choice> child element. Within the example, the following code defines a <group> where either <postcode> *or* <zipcode> can appear in the instance:

```
<xsd:group name="postcode">
    <xsd:choice>
        <xsd:element name="postcode" type="xsd:string" />
        <xsd:element name="zipcode" type="xsd:string" />
    </xsd:choice>
</xsd:group>
```

This is then included in the <group> definition of Addresses, as shown below:

```
<xsd:group name="Addresses">
    <xsd:sequence>
        <xsd:element ref="house" />
        <xsd:element name="street" type="xsd:string" />
        <xsd:element name="city" type="xsd:string"
            default="Rio De Janerio" />
        <xsd:group ref="postcode" minOccurs="1" maxOccurs="1" />
        <xsd:element name="country" type="xsd:string" nillable="true" />
        <xsd:element name="continent" type="xsd:string"
            fixed="South America" />
    </xsd:sequence>
</xsd:group>
```

The `minOccurs` and `maxOccurs` attributes are used to explicitly define that this group may only appear once, although this is the default and so not necessary – however, it is easier to read. An example instance (`simpleSchemaInstanceGroup.xml`) corresponding to the newly updated Schema is shown below:

```
<?xml version="1.0" ?>
<author age="26" xmlns:xsi="http://www.w3.org/2001/XMLSchema-instance"
     xsi:noNamespaceSchemaLocation="simpleSchemaGroup.xsd">
     <firstname>Steven</firstname>
     <surname>Livingstone</surname>
     <Address>
          <house>123</house>
          <street>Santiago Bay</street>
          <city>Santiago</city>
          <postcode>G13 4JA</postcode>
          <country xsi:nil="true"></country>
          <continent>South America</continent>
     </Address>
</author>
```

Finally, the `<xsd:all>` element implies that all elements may appear once and only once (or not at all), in any order, and must be unique throughout the content model. Its content can only be elements and it is limited to the top level of a content model.

The following is an example of a valid use of the `<xsd:all>` element, which allows the various names a person may have to be in any order:

```
<xsd:complexType name="FullName">
   <xsd:all>
      <xsd:element name="firstname" type="xsd:string" />
      <xsd:element name="surname" type="xsd:string" />
      <xsd:element name="madidenname" type="xsd:string" />
      <xsd:element name="middlename1" type="xsd:string" />
      <xsd:element name="middlename2" type="xsd:string" />
      <xsd:element name="middlename3" type="xsd:string" />
   </xsd:all>
</xsd:complexType>
```

Note, however, that the following declaration is invalid because it does not appear at the top of the content model (it comes after the `<sequence>` element):

```
<xsd:complexType name="FullName">
   <xsd:sequence>
      <xsd:all>
         <xsd:element name="firstname" type="xsd:string" />
         <xsd:element name="surname" type="xsd:string" />
         <xsd:element name="madidenname" type="xsd:string" />
         <xsd:element name="middlename1" type="xsd:string" />
         <xsd:element name="middlename2" type="xsd:string" />
         <xsd:element name="middlename3" type="xsd:string" />
      </xsd:all>
      <xsd:element name="age" type="xsd:integer" />
   <xsd:sequence>
</xsd:complexType>
```

Of course, if we find ourselves wanting to group elements, we are also going to want to group attributes for inheritance and reuse, and we do this using the `<xsd:attributeGroup>` element.

> **The examples in the following section can be run using `validateXSD.htm` by choosing the `simpleSchemaInstanceAtt.xml` file from the drop down list – the XSD file is `simpleSchemaAtt.xsd`.**

So, if we had a group of attributes that were used often it would be easy to reuse them – it also makes the Schema much easier to read. Say in the sample we wanted to group the personal details of a person as a set of attributes to be applied to the `<author>` element definition. An attribute group could be created as follows:

```
<xsd:attributeGroup name="PersonalDetails">
     <xsd:attribute name="age" type="xsd:integer" />
     <xsd:attribute name="dob" type="xsd:date" />
     <xsd:attribute name="birthplace" type="xsd:string" />
</xsd:attributeGroup>
```

We would then reference this attribute group within an `<author>` element like so:

```
<xsd:element name="author">
     <xsd:complexType>
          <xsd:sequence>
               <xsd:element name="firstname" type="xsd:string"
                    minOccurs="0" maxOccurs="unbounded" />
               <xsd:element name="surname" type="xsd:string"
                    minOccurs="1" maxOccurs="1" />
               <xsd:element ref="Address" minOccurs="1" maxOccurs="1" />
          </xsd:sequence>
          <xsd:attributeGroup ref="PersonalDetails" />
     </xsd:complexType>
</xsd:element>
```

Then within the instance we could have the following:

```
<?xml version="1.0"?>
<author age="26" dob="1974-09-25" birthplace="glasgow"
     xmlns:xsi="http://www.w3.org/2001/XMLSchema-instance"
     xsi:noNamespaceSchemaLocation="simpleSchemaAtt.xsd">
...
</author>
```

Other attribute groups can be nested within an attribute group and the attribute group must appear at the end of a complex type definition, just before the closing `<complexType>` tag.

`<simpleContent>` Extension and Restrictions

> **The examples in the following section can be seen using `validateXSD.htm` by choosing the `simpleSchemaInstanceSC.xml` file from the drop-down list – the XSD file is `simpleSchemaSC.xsd`.**

The `<simpleContent>` element is used to restrict or extend an existing built-in data type or simple type within the new complex type. It must contain a `<restriction>` or `<extension>` element as its child. Say we wanted to add some information about members of the family within a `<FamilyMember>` element in the `<author>` element definition, as shown below:

```
<xsd:element name="author">
    <xsd:complexType>
        <xsd:sequence>
            <xsd:element name="firstname" type="PersonsFirstname"
                    minOccurs="0" maxOccurs="unbounded" />
            <xsd:element name="surname" type="xsd:string"
                    minOccurs="1" maxOccurs="1" />
            <xsd:element name="Address" type="Address"
                    minOccurs="1" maxOccurs="1" />
            <xsd:element name="FamilyMember" type="FamilyInfo"
                    minOccurs="0" maxOccurs="unbounded" />
        </xsd:sequence>
        <xsd:attributeGroup ref="PersonalDetails" />
    </xsd:complexType>
</xsd:element>
```

We have defined it as type `FamilyInfo`, which is a named complex type defined later in the Schema. This makes use of some of the `<simpleType>` elements previously defined in the Schema and the built-in data types. This `<complexType>` element is shown below:

```
<xsd:complexType name="FamilyInfo">
    <xsd:simpleContent>
        <xsd:extension base="PersonsFirstname">
            <xsd:attribute name="relation">
                <xsd:simpleType>
                    <xsd:restriction base="xsd:string">
                        <xsd:enumeration value="mother" />
                        <xsd:enumeration value="brother" />
                        <xsd:enumeration value="sister" />
                        <xsd:enumeration value="cat" />
                    </xsd:restriction>
                </xsd:simpleType>
            </xsd:attribute>
            <xsd:attribute name="AdultFamilyAges">
                <xsd:simpleType>
                    <xsd:restriction base="PersonsAge">
                        <xsd:minInclusive value="15" />
                        <xsd:maxInclusive value="60" />
                    </xsd:restriction>
                </xsd:simpleType>
            </xsd:attribute>
        </xsd:extension>
    </xsd:simpleContent>
</xsd:complexType>
```

We are going to *extend* the `PersonsFirstName` simple type that we defined earlier, so a `<simpleContent>` element is required as a child of the `<complexType>` element. An `<extension>` element is then required, with a `base` value of `PersonsFirstName` (the type we mean to extend) – this means the element defined by this complex type will have the same base type as the `PersonsFirstName` simple type, which is a `string` of `maxLength` 7 (as we defined earlier).

The first extension we make is to add a new attribute called `relation` to the type, with a simple type value restricted to `string` types (using the `<restriction>` element), which must be one of the contained `<enumeration>` values (see the "*Data TypeConstraining Facets*" section above for further information).

Furthermore, to illustrate that we can use existing simple types, we have defined an attribute called `AdultFamilyAges`, which uses a `<simpleType>` and `<restriction>` child element of base type `PersonsAge`. If we left the `<restriction>` element empty, this would mean that values of `AdultFamilyAges` were restricted to those defined in the simple type `PersonsAge` definition; for example integer values between 1 and 125. However, we impose further restrictions on allowable values by using the `minInclusive` and `maxInclusive` facets to limit the range from 15 to 60.

An instance can now be created as shown below:

```
<?xml version="1.0"?>
<author age="26" dob="1974-09-25" birthplace="glasgow"
      xmlns:xsi="http://www.w3.org/2001/XMLSchema-instance"
      xsi:noNamespaceSchemaLocation="simpleSchemaSC.xsd">
...
      <FamilyMember relation="mother">
            Eileen
      </FamilyMember>
      <FamilyMember relation="brother" AdultFamilyAges="24">
            Graham
      </FamilyMember>
      <FamilyMember relation="sister" AdultFamilyAges="25">
            Cathy
      </FamilyMember>
      <FamilyMember relation="cat" AdultFamilyAges="16">
            Rambo
      </FamilyMember>
</author>
```

Sometimes we may want to extend or restrict types that are not built-in data types or simple types – for example, extend the `Address` complex type to create an `EmploymentInfo` complex type that includes some information about the floor number and office number. To do this, we need to use a `<complexContent>` element.

<complexContent> Extension and Restrictions

> The examples in the following section can be demonstrated using `validateXSD.htm` by choosing the `simpleSchemaInstanceCC.xml` file from the drop-down list – the XSD file is `simpleSchemaCC.xsd`.

The `<complexContent>` element is used to restrict or extend an existing complex type definition containing mixed content or just elements. It can only be the child of a `<complexType>` element. When using the `<restriction>` child element, you may remove optional elements or attributes from a previously defined complex type, set a `default` or `fixed` value where one didn't exist before, assign a type where one was not previously defined, or impose restrictions using `minOccurs` or `maxOccurs`.

The following example shows how you could assign a `default` value to an element, restrict an element's type to an assigned `type`, and restrict the `maxOccurs` and `minOccurs` – note that all element definitions must be repeated in the restricted `<complexContent>` element just as they appear in the `<complexType>` element defining them:

```
<xsd:complexType name="someType">
    <xsd:element name="firstelement" type="xsd:string"/>
    <xsd:element name="secondelement"/>
    <xsd:element name="thirdelement" type="xsd:int"/>
</xsd:complexType>

<xsd:complexType name="someSubType">
    <xsd:complexContent>
        <xsd:restriction base="someType">
        <xsd:element name="firstelement" type="xsd:string"
            default="XYZ"/>
        <xsd:element name="secondelement" type="xsd:boolean"/>
        <xsd:element name="thirdelement" type="xsd:int"
            minOccurs="1" maxOccurs="1"/>
        </xsd:restriction>
    </xsd:complexContent>
</xsd:complexType>
```

Continuing, we are going to extend the `Address` complex type as we mentioned in the last section, to create an `EmploymentInfo` complex type that includes some information about the floor number and office number. The XSD fragment for this (also in the sample XSD file for this section) is shown here:

```
<xsd:complexType name="EmploymentInfo">
    <xsd:complexContent>
        <xsd:extension base="Address">
            <xsd:sequence>
                <xsd:element name="CompanyName" type="xsd:string"
                    default="SK Inc" />
                <xsd:element name="office" type="xsd:unsignedByte" />
            </xsd:sequence>
            <xsd:attribute name="EmployeeID"
                type="xsd:positiveInteger" />
            <xsd:attribute name="IsManager" type="xsd:boolean" />
        </xsd:extension>
    </xsd:complexContent>
</xsd:complexType>
```

The new complex type is declared as a global type (direct child of the `<schema>` element) and because we are to extend the `Address` complex type we need to use a `<complexContent>` element below our new complex type definition. Within this, the `<extension>` element is used with a `base` type of `Address` – the element we are extending. We then define the elements and attribute to add to the existing `Address` definition to create the new type. First a `<sequence>` element is defined with the definition of a `<CompanyName>` element (a string) and an `<office>` element (an `unsignedByte` type – 0 to 255). Additionally, as a child of the `<extension>` element, two new attributes are created, namely `EmployeeID` (`positiveInteger` data type) and `IsManager` (`boolean` type). This new definition is referenced as a child of the `<Author>` element definition as:

```
<xsd:element name="author">
    <xsd:complexType>
...
        <xsd:element name="EmploymentInformation" type="EmploymentInfo" />
    </xsd:complexType>
</xsd:element>
```

An element is defined called <EmploymentInformation> with its type defined as the complex type EmploymentInfo. Within the instance we can then create the <EmploymentInformation> element as though it was explicity defined with all child elements within it (rather than an extended complex type definition).

```
<?xml version="1.0" ?>
<author age="26" dob="1974-09-25" birthplace="glasgow"
    xmlns:xsi="http://www.w3.org/2001/XMLSchema-instance"
    xsi:noNamespaceSchemaLocation="simpleSchemaCC.xsd">
...
        <EmploymentInformation EmployeeID="232484" IsManager="false">
            <house>9332</house>
            <street>Calle Miranda</street>
            <city>Rio De Janerio</city>
            <postcode>U897 A</postcode>
            <country>Brazil</country>
            <continent>South America</continent>
            <CompanyName>ST News Corp.</CompanyName>
            <office>72</office>
        </EmploymentInformation>
</author>
```

We will now move on from looking explicitly at simple type and complex type definitions to look at how they are used in the overall XSD language to build Schemas.

Building XSD Schemas

When building Schemas, there are two different types of mark up:

❑   Definitions that create new simple and complex types.

❑   Declarations that describe the content models of the elements and attributes defined, and the declaration of elements or attributes associating a type with a name.

We looked at the first of these above, so we will now look at the second. First of all we have a reference to the elements available to us.

Elements Reference Section

This section will discuss the main elements and features available to you when building your XSD Schemas.

For more detailed information, see "Professional XML Schemas" (Wrox Press, ISBN 1-861005-47-4) or the MSXML 4.0 SDK.

❑   all – allows the elements in the group to appear (or not appear) in any order in the containing element.

❑   any – enables any element from the specified namespace(s) to appear in the containing <complexType>, <group>, <sequence>, <all>, or <choice> element.

❑   anyAttribute – enables any attribute from the specified namespace(s) to appear in the containing <complexType> element.

❑   annotation – defines an <annotation> element, which can contain a <documentation> element or an <appInfo> element to pass information up to the application.

❑ appInfo – used within an <annotation> element, this can be used by applications for processing instructions.

❑ attribute – declares an attribute to be used on an element in the Schema. It has the name specified in the name attribute and its type attribute defines the built-in type or simple type to constrain the attribute value.

❑ attributeGroup – allows you to group attributes so that they can be incorporated as a group into complex type definitions.

❑ choice – is a child of a <complexType> element and dictates that one and only one of the elements within the <choice> element can be present in the instance.

❑ complexContent – contains extensions or restrictions on a complex type that contains mixed content or elements only.

❑ complexType – defines a complex type. You need to define a complex type for any element that has element content or mixed content, or that can carry attributes. Once you have defined a complex type you can use the type attribute of the <complexType> element to refer to the name of the complex type when building complex content models.

❑ documentation – provides some information about the application that can be read by users. This is what allows XML Schema to be self-documenting through the addition of a stylesheet.

❑ element – declares an element with the name specified in the name attribute, which can be associated (in the type attribute) with a complex type or simple type definition, as well as the XSD provided types.

❑ extension – contains extensions on complex content or simple content definitions, which can also extend a complex type.

❑ field – specifies an XML Path Language (XPath) expression that specifies the value (or one of the values) used to define an identity constraint when using <unique>, <key>, and <keyref> elements. (XPath is covered in Chapter 4.)

❑ group – groups a set of element declarations so that they can be incorporated as a group into complex type definitions.

❑ import – identifies a namespace whose Schema components are referenced by the containing Schema, and promotes the reuse of Schema type and element definitions.

❑ include – includes the specified Schema document in the target namespace of the containing Schema and promotes Schema reuse. The Schema to be "included" has to have the same value for the targetNamespace attribute or else must be a no-namespace schema.

❑ key – specifies that an attribute or element value (or set of values) must be a key within the specified scope. The scope of a key is the containing element in an instance document. A key must be unique, non nullable, and always present. It is like an XML ID, but with the extra power that it can be used only within a specified range of the document, and that it can begin with a number. Similar to a primary key in a relational database.

❑ keyref – specifies that an attribute or element value (or set of values) corresponds to those of the specified key or unique element. Similar to a foreign key in a database.

❑ list – defines a <simpleType> element as a list of values of a specified data type.

❑ notation – contains the definition of a notation.

❏ redefine – allows simple and complex types, groups, and attribute groups that are obtained from external Schema files to be redefined in the current Schema.

❏ restriction – defines constraints on a simple type, simple content, or complex content definition.

❏ schema – contains the definition of a Schema and must be at the root of a Schema document.

❏ selector – specifies an XML Path Language (XPath) expression that selects a set of elements for an identity constraint using the <unique>, <key>, and <keyref> elements.

❏ sequence – requires the elements in the group to appear in the specified sequence within the containing element. Can also be used directly within a <complexType> element.

❏ simpleContent – contains either the extensions or restrictions on a <complexType> element with character data, or contains a <simpleType> element as content.

❏ simpleType – defines a simple type, which determines the constraints on and information about the values of attributes or elements with text-only content.

❏ union – defines a <simpleType> element as a collection of values from specified simple data types.

❏ unique – specifies that an attribute or element value (or a combination of attribute or element values) must be unique within the specified scope.

Content Models

The content models in XSD define allowable content within XSD elements that may appear in the structure of your Schema. In XDR, the default content model is "open" which means that you can use (or not use) any text, elements, or attributes within your Schema. There are also methods in XDR to restrict empty elements, only text within the elements, only elements within elements, or a mixture of elements and text. In fact, the content model of XSD doesn't vary much from this. There are the following options:

Any

This is the default content model when an element is declared in XML Schema, and it can contain text, elements, and whitespace. (This is similar to the "open" content model in XDR.) In XSD, it is called an "anyType" type rather than "open", and is optional as it is the default. An element can be defined as follows:

```
<xsd:element name="SomeElement" type="xsd:anyType" />
```

This is the same as writing:

```
<xsd:element name="SomeElement" />
```

This is the reason for using the built-in types and defining our own custom simple type and complex type definitions – otherwise anything could be used. One of the major difficulties when writing a Schema is being too restrictive and not allowing the author of an instance (or user of the Schema within some other Schema) enough flexibility. This is useful when unconstrained element content is required, such as prose with embedded markup or when you want to restrict the user of any kind of type (often used with attribute-only elements).

Empty

Empty elements prevent any text or elements from appearing as children on the element that is declared as being empty. (This is like the XDR "empty" attribute value.)

However, it is slightly more complex to define an empty type in XSD as you don't explicitly declare that the element should be "empty", rather you restrict it using the xsd:anyType type discussed above – doing this means that the element may only carry attributes. The following is an example of a complex type that is empty and allows only the "age" attribute:

```xsd
<xsd:element name="person">
   <xsd:complexType>
      <xsd:complexContent>
         <xsd:restriction base="xsd:anyType">
            <xsd:attribute name="age" type="xsd:integer" />
         </xsd:restriction>
      </xsd:complexContent>
   </xsd:complexType>
</xsd:element>
```

This should look fairly familiar to you, but note two points. The <complexContent> element is required to indicate that the content for the complex type is to be extended or restricted – in our case, it is to be restricted and so the <xsd:restriction> element is used. The <restriction> element takes the base type you wish to restrict, and because we want to restrict everything, we use the xsd:anyType type. This allows an instance like the following:

```
<person age="78"><!--Nothing allowed in here --></person>
```

Element

This is what we have been previously discussing when we looked at creating complex types. Note that complex types can be either named or anonymous. They are named when they are given a name attribute (as crazy as that may sound) so they can be reused throughout the Schema.

```xsd
<xsd:complexType name="sometype">
...
</xsd:complexType>

<xsd:element name="myname" type="sometype" />
```

They are anonymous when they are defined without a name within an <element> tag and defined only for that element:

```xsd
<xsd:element name="myname">
   <xsd:complexType>
      ...
   </xsd:complexType>
</xsd:element>
```

Mixed

The final content model is mixed, which can contain a mixture of text, content, and attributes. (This is similar to the "mixed" content type in XDR schema). We declare a content type of mixed by setting the mixed attribute on an <xsd:complexType> element to true. The default is false.

For example, the following is a mixed complex type for describing a person:

```
<xsd:element name="Person">
   <xsd:complexType mixed="true">
      <xsd:sequence>
          <xsd:element name="firstname" type="xsd:string" />
      </xsd:sequence>
   </xsd:complexType>
</xsd:element>
```

An instance of this element could be:

```
<Person>His Christian name is <firstname>Steven</firstname></Person>
```

Notice that the `<Person>` element contains text as well as the `<firstname>` element.

Documentation of Schemas

Typically, XML Schemas are documented using the traditional XML comment syntax (which was also used in HTML) of the form `<!-- some comment -->`. However, this is typically for comments aimed at an editor or author of the Schema and such comments are generally passed over by any application working with the Schema. XML Schemas introduce two forms of documentation that can be used by an interpreting application. However, they are both children of the `<xsd:annotation>` element which can appear anywhere within the Schema. The children of this element are:

❑   `documentation` – this is very similar to the traditional comment, but is part of the Schema markup. It can be interpreted by applications for users or just serve for automated documentation purposes, for which the simplest method would be to add an XSLT stylesheet.

   An example of a `<documentation>` element is shown below, which references an external XML document containing the documentation. An alternative way is to simply put text within the `<documentation>` element and omit the `source` attribute. The `xml:lang` attribute is part of XML 1.0 and simply specifies the language in which the documentation is written.

```
<xsd:annotation>
   <xsd:documentation source="http://tempURI.org/somedoc.xml"
      xml:lang="en" />
</xsd:annotation>
```

❑   `appInfo` – this element can be used to provide information to external applications. It is somewhat similar to a processing instruction in that it can pass information to tools, stylesheets, and other applications (for example, it is used in XLANG – an XML language for describing processes, and is used in the BizTalk Server to define how to pass property definitions).

We have now covered how we can manually create Schemas and the various rules governing their structure. Let's now look at XSD Schemas in practice.

XSD Schemas in Practice

The use of XSD Schemas in practice is still in its early stages, but is going to be one of the most important areas of XML applications, in everything from content creation and validation to e-business message exchange.

Namespaces in XML Schema and Validating XML Instances

When working with MSXML 4.0, there are two ways to validate an XML instance against some XSD Schema – one we have already seen is to declare the Schema location details on the root element, and the other is to validate programmatically (for example, VBScript, JScript, Visual Basic, C++, VB .NET, C#, etc.).

Let's consider the first method, which is to enter the Schema location details directly into the XML instance. You will generally use one of the following templates when entering your XML Schema validation information directly into your XML instance. The first, which we have been using in all of the examples so far, is as follows:

```
<?xml version="1.0" ?>
<rootElement xmlns:xsi="http://www.w3.org/2001/XMLSchema-instance"
    xsi:noNamespaceSchemaLocation="uri">
    ...
</rootElement>
```

The `xmlns:xsi="http://www.w3.org/2001/XMLSchema-instance"` is the XML Schema namespace for instances and must be present if you intend to validate your XML instances directly (in other words without using programmatic techniques to assign a Schema for the instance to be validated against – discussed below). The `noNamespaceSchemaLocation` contains the URI of some XSD document that the instance can be validated against – this is used when no namespace is defined in the Schema. This allows the file to be validated as it is loaded into a `DOMDocument` without having to specify any other information. An important point to note – it is *not* compulsory that the Schema defined in the `noNamespaceSchemaLocation` actually be used to validate the document; it acts only as a hint. The processor itself, or some external programmatic means, can override any of the XML Schema files referred to within the XML instance. You can see an example of this working (the same as the last example we worked on above) by viewing the version of `validateXSD.htm` from the `adv` directory of the chapter's code download and choosing the `SchemaInstance.xml` file from the drop-down list.

The second method is slightly more complicated, but will be the most common technique used when entering Schema information within your XML instances. This is because it deals with namespaces, which are becoming increasingly important. A template for this technique is shown below:

```
<?xml version="1.0" ?>
<rootElement xmlns:x="namespace1" xmlns:y="namespace2" xmlns:Z="namespaceN"
    xmlns:xsi="http://www.w3.org/2001/XMLSchema-instance"
    xsi:SchemaLocation="namespace1 uri1 namepsace2 uri2 namespaceN uriN">
    ...
</rootElement>
```

The `schemaLocation` attribute in your XML instance document is used as a hint for the Schema processor when locating the correct Schema for a specific namespace. This means that the value of the `schemaLocation` attribute has to contain both the namespace URI and the file location (as a URI). The two values are separated by a space and if you use more than one namespace in your instance document the value is a space-separated list of namespace URI's and schema file location URIs. So in the template above, the location of the Schema associated with `namespace1` is `uri1`, `namespace2` is at `uri2`, and `namespaceN` is at `uriN`. Also, each namespace in the `SchemaLocation` should map to a namespace declaration in the XML instance. In the case of the template above, `namespace1` in the `SchemaLocation` attribute maps to the `xmlns:x` namespace declaration as they are both the same namespace. This means that any elements or attributes in the instance prefixed with "x" (or more correctly in the `namespace1` namespace), will be validated against the `uri1` Schema (or as we hinted at above – it doesn't *have* to validate against this).

The Schema is generally viewed as a collection of vocabulary types and definitions that belong to a particular namespace called the **target namespace**. The target namespace "associates" the definitions and declarations in the schema with a single namespace URI, independent of the other namespace declarations within the document. This is the namespace to which you want the vocabulary you are creating in the Schema to belong. In the simplest case, a template for the root of a Schema that uses namespaces is shown below:

```
<xsd:schema xmlns="namespace1" xmlns:xsd="http://www.w3.org/2001/XMLSchema"
    targetNamespace="namespace1">
    ...
</xsd:schema>
```

The `targetNamespace` has specified `namespace1` as the target namespace for the Schema – the `targetNamespace` attribute should have the value of one of the namespace declarions in the Schema and in this case we use `namespace1`.

Let's look at how our example changes when we start to use namespaces – the example files are called `SchemaInstanceNS.xml` and `SchemaNS.xsd` in the `adv` folder and can be run from the version of `validateXSD.htm` found in the `adv` folder. The following fragment shows how the XSD in the sample is modified to set the default namespace to `uri:personal-info`, which is defined as the Schema's `targetNamespace`:

```
<xsd:schema xmlns:xsd="http://www.w3.org/2001/XMLSchema"
    targetNamespace="uri:personal-info" xmlns="uri:personal-info">
    ...
</xsd:schema>
```

The instance is also updated, as shown below:

```
<per:author xmlns:per="uri:personal-info" age="26" dob="1974-09-25"
  birthplace="glasgow" xmlns:xsi="http://www.w3.org/2001/XMLSchema-instance"
  xsi:schemaLocation="uri:personal-info SchemaNS.xsd">
    ...
</per:author>
```

Ignore the `per` prefix on the `<author>` element for the moment. A namespace association is defined to associate the prefix `per` with the namespace `uri:personal-info` – notice this is the same as the default namespace in the Schema. A mapping between this namespace and the one in the Schema is done using the `schemaLocation` attribute, which maps the `uri:personal-info` (also the `targetNamespace` of the Schema) to the Schema `SchemaNS.xsd`.

You may be wondering why we use the `per` prefix and those of you who have looked at the source will see that some elements are prefixed while others are not. Well, on the `<schema>` root of the XSD there are two attributes that we never looked at – `elementFormDefault` and `attributeFormDefault`.

The `elementFormDefault` attribute acts as a switch as to whether the element must be qualified in a document instance – the `<schema>` element also has the `attributeFormDefault` attribute, which does the same for attributes. These attributes must have the value `qualified` or `unqualified`. These attributes are used as a mechanism for hiding namespace definitions from someone creating an instance of a Schema where you want the creator of instances to explicitly use the namespaces defined in the document. It is most useful when you have a main Schema composed of multiple Schemas with different namespaces and you want someone creating an instance of the main XML Schema to use just one namespace rather than all the namespaces defined in the other Schemas. This method can also be used to preserve rights on a Schema (particularly if a Schema is composed of multiple Schemas from different companies) as you are explicitly declaring each namespace URI within the instance document.

The `elementFormDefault` attribute is used to declare that all elements must be qualified in the instance document that conforms to this Schema in order to be validated. It is set at the parent level of the Schema, otherwise only the global declarations would have to be qualified. Globally declared elements and attributes are immediate child elements of the root `<schema>` element and in the example XSD file, this would be elements such as `<author>` and `<house>`, while we have no global attributes.

Locally declared elements and attributes are nested within other elements, `<complexType>` or `<simpleType>` definitions, such as the `<street>` or `<postcode>` elements and the `relation` and `AdultFamilyAges` attributes. If the attribute `elementFormDefault` is set to `qualified`, then in an instance of that document all elements must be qualified by a namespace if they are to be validated. Also, note that if the value of `elementFormDefault` is `unqualified`, then all global elements *must* be qualified in a namespace in the instance document, whereas locally declared elements do not have to be qualified. All globally declared elements must always be qualified in a instance, although you can use the `form` attribute on locally declared elements to state that they should be qualified.

So, as both of these attributes default to `unqualified` and the `<schema>` element in the sample doesn't declare them, we have to qualify only the global elements in the instance – this is where the `per` prefix comes in. We have two globally declared elements in the instance that have to be explicitly qualified in the namespace `uri:personal-info` that is associated with `per` – these are `<author>` and `<house>` (notice that if we had used `flat` then this is also globally declared). So the instance must be updated as follows (fragment only, see `SchemaInstanceNS.xml` for the full XML):

```xml
<?xml version="1.0" ?>
<per:author xmlns:per="uri:personal-info" age="26" dob="1974-09-25"
   birthplace="glasgow" xmlns:xsi="http://www.w3.org/2001/XMLSchema-instance"
   xsi:schemaLocation="uri:personal-info SchemaNS.xsd">
        <firstname>Steven</firstname>
        <surname>Livingstone</surname>
        <Address>
                <per:house>123</per:house>
                <street>Santiago Bay</street>
                ...
        </Address>
        ...
        <EmploymentInformation EmployeeID="232484" IsManager="false">
                <per:house>9332</per:house>
                <street>Calle Miranda</street>
                ...
        </EmploymentInformation>
</per:author>
```

You can see how the elements that were globally declared within the Schema have been prefixed with `per` and hence qualified, whereas the locally declared elements (and attributes) don't need to be qualified.

In contrast, say we wanted to ensure that all elements *are* qualified, then we would set the value of the `elementFormDefault` attribute to `qualified` as shown below (the example files are called `SchemaInstanceNSQual.xml` and `SchemaNSQual.xsd` in the `adv` folder and can be run from `validateXSD.htm`):

```
<xsd:schema xmlns:xsd="http://www.w3.org/2001/XMLSchema"
     elementFormDefault="qualified" targetNamespace="uri:personal-info"
     xmlns="uri:personal-info">
...
</xsd:schema>
```

This dramatically affects our sample instance as now all global and locally declared elements must be qualified – although it does provide us with the benefits namespaces were intended for! A fragment of the XML sample file is shown below:

```
<?xml version="1.0" ?>
<per:author xmlns:per="uri:personal-info" age="26" dob="1974-09-25"
   birthplace="glasgow" xmlns:xsi="http://www.w3.org/2001/XMLSchema-instance"
   xsi:schemaLocation="uri:personal-info SchemaNSQual.xsd">
     <per:firstname>Steven</per:firstname>
     <per:surname>Livingstone</per:surname>
     <per:Address>
          <per:house>123</per:house>
          <per:street>Santiago Bay</per:street>
          <per:city>Santiago</per:city>
          ...
     </per:Address>
...
</per:author>
```

In this case we would be better defining the `uri:personal-info` namespace as the default for the instance to save the repeated `per` prefixes; but in many cases we would be mixing elements from different namespaces and so we would be better qualifying them explicitly.

If we can use namespaces in the instances we create, then they play an equally important part when creating the Schemas themselves – in fact, most Schemas will also be composed of multiple namespaces from many documents – we are going to look at this shortly. But before we do, let's just demonstrate how you could use a namespace in your XSD to explicitly qualify types rather than using the default namespace as we have done so far. (The example files are called `SchemaInstanceNSExp.xml` and `SchemaNSExp.xsd` in the `adv` folder and can be run from `validateXSD.htm`.)

The namespace `<schema>` element is now changed from the default namespace of `uri:personal-info` to being associated with the namespace `pinfo`. When this is done, all types that refer to globally declared elements or types must also be qualified, such as `type="prefix:type"`. A fragment of the updated sample is shown next:

```
<?xml version="1.0" encoding="utf-8" ?>
<xsd:schema xmlns:xsd="http://www.w3.org/2001/XMLSchema"
     elementFormDefault="qualified" targetNamespace="uri:personal-info"
     xmlns:pinfo="uri:personal-info">
```

```
        . . .
      <xsd:element name="author">
          <xsd:complexType>
              <xsd:sequence>
                  <xsd:element name="firstname"
                        type="pinfo:PersonsFirstname" minOccurs="0"
                        maxOccurs="unbounded" />
                  <xsd:element name="surname" type="xsd:string"
                        minOccurs="1" maxOccurs="1" />
                  <xsd:element name="Address" type="pinfo:Address"
                        minOccurs="1" maxOccurs="1" />
                  <xsd:element name="FamilyMember"
                        type="pinfo:FamilyInfo" minOccurs="0"
                        maxOccurs="unbounded" />
                  <xsd:element name="EmploymentInformation"
                        type="pinfo:EmploymentInfo" />
              </xsd:sequence>
              <xsd:attributeGroup ref="pinfo:PersonalDetails" />
          </xsd:complexType>
      </xsd:element>
      <xsd:element name="house" type="xsd:int" />
      <xsd:element name="flat" substitutionGroup="pinfo:house"
            type="xsd:int" />
      . . .
  </xsd:schema>
```

Notice how all element or attribute definitions (including group definitions, etc.) that refer to some globally defined type (or element/attribute, group, etc.) must qualify the reference.

At this point it would be quite reasonable for you to ask the question as to *why* you would do such a thing and not just stick with the default namespace technique we used earlier. Well, the first and perhaps most obvious reason is that you may have something else as the default namespace – a common example is the preference to declare the W3C Schema namespace as the default (and hence omit the xsd prefixes). A much stronger argument is the ability within XML to mix namespaces, and Schemas may be composed of elements in multiple namespaces, likely coming from a set of different XSD documents. All of the definitions in one of those documents may belong to the same target namespace or different target namespace. Let's look at how this is accomplished.

Modularization of XSD Schemas

Schemas can be modularized using the <include> or <import> elements, which allows reuse of elements in Schemas rather than redefining them each time. include is the simplest way of doing this and simply adds the elements in the included Schema to the Schema doing the including. It is important to note that for this to work, the targetNamespace property in the included Schema must either be the same targetNamespace as the importing Schema or have no targetNamespace defined – all elements are effectively brought into the targetNamespace of the including Schema. This last point means that your XML instance document does not need to know about these modularized Schemas and hence does not need to be any different from that which we have been working with so far.

So, in our example, we may remove all simple type definitions from our Schema and put them into another more generalized Schema. This means that you can then use your user-defined simple types in other Schemas that you are creating, and that they would then become part of the targetNamespace of the including Schema. If the Schema we include borrows from other Schemas, we only have to reference the topmost Schema for it to pull in other Schemas it references.

In the case of the example (the example files are called `SchemaInstanceInc.xml`, `SchemaInc.xsd` and `SchemaTypesInc.xsd` in the adv folder and can be run from `validateXSD.htm`), we have chosen to put all simple types in the XSD file `SchemaTypesInc.xsd` and we can then include these as follows in the main `SchemaInc.xsd` file:

```
<?xml version="1.0" encoding="utf-8" ?>
<xsd:schema xmlns:xsd="http://www.w3.org/2001/XMLSchema"
    elementFormDefault="qualified" targetNamespace="uri:personal-info"
    xmlns:pinfo="uri:personal-info">
    <xsd:include schemaLocation="SchemaTypesInc.xsd" />
    ...
</xsd:schema>
```

Then, `SchemaTypesInc.xsd` is defined as follows:

```
<?xml version="1.0" encoding="utf-8" ?>
<xsd:schema xmlns:xsd="http://www.w3.org/2001/XMLSchema">
    <xsd:simpleType name="PersonsAge">
        <xsd:restriction base="xsd:integer">
            <xsd:minInclusive value="1" />
            <xsd:maxInclusive value="125" />
        </xsd:restriction>
    </xsd:simpleType>
    <xsd:simpleType name="PersonsFirstname">
        <xsd:restriction base="xsd:string">
            <xsd:maxLength value="7" />
        </xsd:restriction>
    </xsd:simpleType>
</xsd:schema>
```

You can see that no `targetNamespace` has been specified and so the namespace of these types when included will be the same as the importing Schema (in other words `uri:personal-info`). Additionally, if any types were included in this file via another include within itself, they would only be valid if they have the same target namespace as the main including Schema.

The other method of reuse is the `<import>` element. This is useful when you want to reference types without necessarily bringing them into your target namespace. In this case, you can identify the namespace to be imported as well as the location of the Schema. In the example files (the example files are called `SchemaInstanceImp.xml`, `SchemaImp.xsd`, and `SchemaTypesImp.xml` in the adv folder and can be run from `validateXSD.htm`), the file containing the simple types is imported as shown below:

```
<?xml version="1.0" encoding="utf-8" ?>
<xsd:schema xmlns:xsd="http://www.w3.org/2001/XMLSchema"
    elementFormDefault="qualified" targetNamespace="uri:personal-info"
    xmlns:pinfo="uri:personal-info"
    xmlns:ptypes="uri:personal-info-types">

    <xsd:import namespace="uri:personal-info-types"
        schemaLocation="SchemaTypesImp.xsd" />
    ...
</xsd:schema>
```

To use type definitions from the imported namespace, that namespace must be associated with a prefix in the normal manner:

```
<?xml version="1.0" encoding="utf-8" ?>
<xsd:schema xmlns:xsd="http://www.w3.org/2001/XMLSchema"
     elementFormDefault="qualified" targetNamespace="uri:personal-info"
     xmlns:pinfo="uri:personal-info"
     xmlns:ptypes="uri:personal-info-types">

        <xsd:import namespace="uri:personal-info-types"
              schemaLocation="SchemaTypesImp.xsd" />
        ...
</xsd:schema>
```

Notice that, now the imported namespace is defined with the prefix "ptypes" in the importing Schema, types defined in this document are referenced via the "ptypes" prefix being appended to the type. This applies to the types that reference externally defined data types. For example:

```
...
<xsd:element name="firstname" type="ptypes:PersonsFirstname"
     minOccurs="0" maxOccurs="unbounded" />
...
```

All of this has no effect on the creation of an instance and these are seamless to the importing of simple types. However, imagine we wanted to import an element that had been defined in the SchemaTypesImp.xsd file – remember that it has its elementFormDefault attribute set to qualified, so all elements must be qualified explicitly in the instance.

To demonstrate this with a very simple example (this is in fact included in the code for the previous example), an element called `<sometype>` (very imaginative I know) has been defined with a type of int:

```
<?xml version="1.0" encoding="utf-8" ?>
<xsd:schema xmlns:xsd="http://www.w3.org/2001/XMLSchema"
    elementFormDefault="qualified" targetNamespace="uri:personal-info-types"
    xmlns="uri:personal-info-types">
...
        <xsd:element name="sometype" type="xsd:int" />
</xsd:schema>
```

The element is then included within the definition of the `<author>` element by defining an element with a ref attribute with a qualified reference to the element `<sometype>`:

```
...
<xsd:element name="author">
     <xsd:complexType>
            <xsd:sequence>
                  ...
                     <xsd:element ref="ptypes:sometype" />
            </xsd:sequence>
            <xsd:attributeGroup ref="pinfo:PersonalDetails" />
     </xsd:complexType>
</xsd:element>
...
```

Finally, the actual author of the instance must include a definition of the namespace uri:personal-info-types, which is associated with the prefix vals, and thus we can correctly qualify the `<sometype>` element, as shown below:

```
<?xml version="1.0" ?>
<per:author xmlns:per="uri:personal-info"
      xmlns:vals="uri:personal-info-types"
      age="26" dob="1974-09-25" birthplace="glasgow"
      xmlns:xsi="http://www.w3.org/2001/XMLSchema-instance"
      xsi:schemaLocation="uri:personal-info SchemaImp.xsd">
      ...
      <vals:sometype>123</vals:sometype>
</per:author>
...
```

Programmatic Validation with XSD Schemas

We have mentioned throughout the chapter that as well as putting the Schema location information within the XML file itself, you can use programmatic techniques to validate against the Schema. There is more on this in Chapter 11 "*Schemas on the Server*", but it is worth familiarizing yourself with it client-side also as it is an essential part of Schema development with MSXML. We will illustrate with a practical example of ensuring that the XML file SchemaInstanceImp.xml actually validates against the Schema definition in SchemaImp.xsd via programmatic means.

These are the same files we worked with earlier but the code in ClientValidate.htm overrides any definitions within the XML file – so it is effectively a completely different Schema. If you want to you can even remove all Schema references from the XML file and validate purely using the programmatic methods discussed below.

We are only going to look at the JavaScript section of the HTML page – the rest is simple HTML, which you can have a look at if you are interested. All the work is done by the function ValidateXML(). Firstly, because we are working with Schemas defined using XSD, we have to create an instance of the MSXML 4.0 DOMDocument and the XSD Schema is loaded as a DOMDocument instance:

```
function ValidateXML()
{
      var xmlXSD = new ActiveXObject("Msxml2.DOMDocument.4.0");
      xmlXSD.async = false;
      xmlXSD.load("SchemaImp.xsd");
```

Following this, an instance of the Schema cache object is created, which allows you to cache one or more Schemas. This object has the add() method, which allows you to associate a namespace (the first parameter) with some Schema (the second parameter). The namespace should be the target namespace of the Schema (uri:personal-info in our case) and the second parameter can either be a DOMDocument object or the URI to the Schema. We have already loaded our Schema into a DOMDocument so this is the method we will use:

```
      var cache = new ActiveXObject("MSXML2.XMLSchemaCache.4.0");
      cache.add("uri:personal-info", xmlXSD);
```

If the URI you specify here (as the first parameter) is different from the target namespace of the Schema then you will get an error indicating exactly that. We next have to create a DOMDocument object, which the XML file we intend to validate will be loaded into. Because we want to validate it immediately, we set the validateOnParse property to true. We could equally have set this to false and enforced validation after the XML instance had loaded, using the validate() method.

119

```
        var xmlDoc = new ActiveXObject("Msxml2.DOMDocument.4.0");
        xmlDoc.async = false;
        xmlDoc.validateOnParse = true;
```

Next we want to ensure that the XML instance uses the Schemas we loaded into the Schema cache and hence override the Schemas mentioned in the XML instance. To do this we set the `schemas` property of the `DOMDocument` instance to the `cache` object:

```
        xmlDoc.schemas=cache;
```

Finally, the XML instance can be loaded and tested for validity – as the instance we have been working with is perfectly valid against this Schema, you will get a "File is valid" message:

```
        var strXML = document.all("XMLfile").value;
        bol = xmlDoc.load(strXML);

        if (xmlDoc.parseError.errorCode != 0)
        {
                alert(xmlDoc.parseError.reason + "\n" +
                        xmlDoc.parseError.srcText);
        }
        else {
                        document.all("XML").value=xmlDoc.xml;
                        alert("File is valid.");
        }
}
```

Any error messages when the validation is performed are also displayed – these are the same as the errors you would get when the document uses its own Schema details (as we have seen throughout the chapter). In contrast you will have noticed that, when your instance uses a reference to a Schema using the `xsi:schemaLocation` attribute, the errors are not reported since they are just hints for the validation engine.

One additional and very powerful piece of functionality offered in MSXML 4.0 is the ability to create Schemas dynamically in memory and validate XML instances against them. This is called the Schema Object Model, or SOM for short.

Schema Object Model (SOM)

This is intended only as an introduction to the ability of the MSXML 4.0-specific **Schema Object Model** (**SOM**), and you should look through the latest MSXML SDK for more detailed and reference information. The SOM can access all areas of the XML Schema and can be very useful not only in creating dynamic Schemas, but also in navigating existing ones, and even modifying them.

Overview of SOM

The following interfaces are available to the developer when working with the SOM:

❑   `ISchema` interface – this interface provides information about each schema in the cache, such as the version, and simple and complex types defined in the Schema and `schemaLocations`.

❑ `ISchemaAny` interface – provides further information on an `anyAttribute` declaration, such as the namespaces and `processContent` instructions for the attribute (what kind – if any – of validation should be performed).

❑ `ISchemaAttribute` interface – provides information about attribute items, such as their type, scope, and default value.

❑ `ISchemaAttributeGroup` interface – gives us access to information on `attributeGroups`, such as the `anyAttribute` object if one has been declared and any collection of attributes declared within the group.

❑ `ISchemaComplexType` interface – allows us to access information about complex type definitions within the Schema. It gives access to the attributes declared, content types, content models, and some of the objects that can be retrieved.

❑ `ISchemaElement` interface – provides information on element items such as the element type, its default value, and identity constraints.

❑ `ISchemaIdentityConstraint` interface – gives access to identity constraint properties such as the `selector` and `field` properties.

❑ `ISchemaItem` interface – we can access all of the individual items in a Schema through this interface. Through this we can access information such as the item name, its `id` attribute, and the type of the Schema item.

❑ `ISchemaItemCollection` interface – stores collections of objects that are returned from various SOM interfaces, such as the collection of attributes or elements returned from the `ISchema` interface.

❑ `ISchemaModelGroup` interface – returns a combination of `ISchemaElement`, `ISchemaModelGroup`, and `ISchemaAny` based on the `modelGroups` property of the `ISchema` interface, `contentModel`, or `ISchemaComplexType`.

❑ `ISchemaNotation` interface – gets the notation objects of the Schema, which can then be accessed to provide the `systemIdentifier` and `publicIdentifier` URIs for programs declared.

❑ `ISchemaParticle` interface – this returns the cardinality of a given item (`maxOccurs` and `minOccurs`) that tells us how many times an item may appear in a given document.

❑ `ISchemaStringCollection` interface – allows you to store indexed collections of strings such as fields, schema namespace URIs, enumerations, and namespaces.

❑ `ISchemaType` interface – provides basic information about base types and constraints set on attributes and elements, such as the `maxInclusive` value, pattern, or length of the restriction.

Example of Working with the SOM

In this example we will show how the SOM can be useful to interrogate a simple Schema and output some simple validation rules for the elements to be input. The example files needed to run this are `validate.htm` and our previous sample Schema `simpleSchemaCC.xsd`.

In this case, the user interface is extremely simple and just asks the user to enter the `PersonsAge` of the author – the XSD Schema rules state that a person can be a minimum age of 1 and a maximum age of 125. Typically, some HTML validation rules would be created, using some JavaScript perhaps. It would be so much more powerful if we could dynamically create what needs to be entered as well as our validation rules from a single source – the Schema. The Schema fragment that defines the `PersonsAge` simple type, which is deliberately simple, is shown below. It is part of the Schema we looked at earlier, so we won't walk through it again:

```
<xsd:simpleType name="PersonsAge">
    <xsd:restriction base="xsd:integer">
            <xsd:minInclusive value="1" />
            <xsd:maxInclusive value="125" />
    </xsd:restriction>
</xsd:simpleType>
```

The following figure shows the user interface after the user clicks the "CreateHTML" button to dynamically generate the entry form:

The following code shows the state of the page the user will see when they first view it:

```
<HTML>
   <HEAD>
      <TITLE>Create HTML</TITLE>
      <SCRIPT LANGUAGE="JAVASCRIPT">
         <!--
```

The `CreateHTML()` method first creates an instance of the XML `SchemaCache` object – this will be used to cache the XSD Schema we are going to work with.

```
function CreateHTML()
{
    var oSchemaCache = new ActiveXObject("Msxml2.XMLSchemaCache.4.0");
```

Next, the Schema (`simpleSchemaCC.xsd`) is added to the cache and associated with the default namespace, by entering `""` as the target namespace:

```
    var nsTarget="";
    oSchemaCache.add(nsTarget,"simpleSchemaCC.xsd");
```

After this has been done, we call the getSchema() method with the relevant namespace (the default one in this case) to return the Schema as an object:

```
var oSchema = oSchemaCache.getSchema(nsTarget);
```

We then define a constant – a simple type is identified by the type identifier "8704" – and then get a reference to the collection of top-level simple and complex types via the types property, which returns an ISchemaItemCollection:

```
var SOMITEM_SIMPLETYPE=8704;
var oEls = oSchema.types;
```

We proceed to iterate through each type and when we find a simple type, we call the user-defined method WalkItem(), passing the simpleType object as a parameter. This is discussed below:

```
var i=0;
while (i<oEls.length)
{
        if (oEls[i].itemType==SOMITEM_SIMPLETYPE)
                WalkItem(oEls[i]);

        i++;
}

return;
}
```

The WalkItem() method walks through the simple type and determines the base types of the object, which are returned as an ISchemaItemCollection.

```
function WalkItem(obj)
{
   var SOMITEM_DATATYPE_INTEGER=8468;

  strName = obj.name;

  //Gets ISchemaItem Collection of base Types
  var objBaseTypes = obj.baseTypes;
```

We then walk through each base type of the simple type, getting the itemType (code for the type of the item) of the attribute – an ISchemaType object. If this type is an integer, the DisplayRange() method is called (although this could clearly be extended) passing the simpleType object as an argument and the name of the simple type.

```
var k=0;
while (k<objBaseTypes.length)
{
        //Stores the reference to the ISchemaType Interface
        var strType = objBaseTypes(k).itemType;

        if (strType==SOMITEM_DATATYPE_INTEGER)
                DisplayRange(obj,strName);

        k++;
}
```

Within the `DisplayRange()` method, the restrictions can be accessed from the `ISchemaType` object and so we can get the `minInclusive` and `maxInclusive` values directly:

```
//Takes an ISchemaItem object
function DisplayRange(obj,strName)
{
        var intMinVal = obj.minInclusive;
        var intMaxVal = obj.maxInclusive;
        var strInput = "";
```

Finally, we can create the HTML and insert it into the `DIV` defined as "expr" in the form in our document, dynamically creating some validation JavaScript code to ensure the entered value meets the constraints defined in the Schema:

```
        strInput += "<b>"+strName+"</b><br>";
        strInput += " <input type=\"text\" name=\"" +  strName + "\"";
        strInput += " onkeyup=\"if (isNaN(parseInt(this.value)) ||
                (parseInt(this.value)>" + intMaxVal + " ||
                parseInt(this.value)<" + intMinVal + ")) ";

        strInput += "alert('Range for " + strName + " is " +
                intMinVal + " to " + intMaxVal + "')\">";

        document.all("expr").insertAdjacentHTML("beforeEnd",strInput);
        }
//--></SCRIPT>
    </HEAD>
    <BODY>
        <FORM ID="Form1">
            <H3>
                Author details
            </H3>
            <DIV ID="expr">
            </DIV>
            <P>
            <INPUT TYPE="button" VALUE="CreateHTML" ONCLICK="CreateHTML()" />
            </P>
        </FORM>
    </BODY>
</HTML>
```

When the user enters a `PersonsAge`, the validation rules that have been dynamically created from the XSD are run. Furthermore, all web pages that make use of this Schema, or even the `PersonsAge` simple type of this Schema (although it is more likely this validation would be done based on some element the `PersonsAge` simple type had been applied to in its `type` attribute), can be validated against new constraints by simply updating the central Schema.

This completes our look at the SOM; but have a look at the MSXML SDK for further information. As an exercise, try to create documentation for a Schema using the SOM.

Summary

We have looked in detail at the schema support available in the MSXML 4.0 parser, and you will know by now that XSD and XDR are the prime schema methods used in MSXML for validating your documents. Both are extremely useful and, although in the longer term the move will be towards XSD, XDR is important for certain aspects of schema validation. Part of this is due to the historic usage of XDR and another is the future usage in IE 6, which uses the MSXML 3.0 parser – no support for client-side validation of XSD Schemas without some hefty downloads.

Although relatively new, XSD is already being adopted and introduced into many products inside and outside of Microsoft – that is the main advantage of XSD over other schemas. As it follows global specifications, it enables diverse product ranges to send Schemas between one another – something very important in e-commerce and business-to-business scenarios.

In particular, SQL Server 2000 uses XSD Schemas (albeit an earlier version to the recommendation), the .NET Framework heavily uses XSD Schemas, as does Visual Studio .NET. SOAP, a platform-independent technology for enabling web services, uses XSD Schema, as do other products such as IBM's WebSphere.

Look for XSD to become a part of your development process in almost any application environment you are part of in the future.

XML Application Development with MSXML 4.0
SOAP
XHTML
XML Schemas DTDs XPath CSS
XML Namespaces
XML 1.0
MSXML

XPath in MSXML

The XML Path Language, **XPath**, is an important part of the XML family in that it allows selected and filtered access to data within XML documents. In this chapter we will look at XPath as a separate language, but it is always used in combination with some other XML technology, such as the Document Object Model (DOM), Extensible Stylesheet Language Transformations (XSLT), the XML Pointer Language (XPointer), the XML Query Language (XQuery), and potentially many others.

Prior versions of MSXML supported a syntax called XSL Patterns that was a precursor to XPath 1.0. MSXML 2.6 supports a significant amount of the XPath 1.0 specification. MSXML 3.0 and above fully support the XPath 1.0 standard and this is the basis of the examples in the chapter. As an example of the differences between the two languages, consider the following.

This first example uses XSL Patterns to get the first node in a node-set:

```
somenodeset[0]
somenodeset [index() = 0]
```

In contrast, using XPath you would have the following:

```
somenodeset[1]
somenodeset[position() = 1]
```

Similarly, to get all nodes in a node-list before the fourth node, XSL Patterns uses the following comparison:

```
somenodeset[index() $le$ 2]
```

Whereas in XPath both the position indicator and the operator are different:

```
somenodeset[position() &lt; 2]
```

These are just some simple examples to illustrate the two versions are very incompatible and you can see this yourself if you have a look at the MSXML 2.5 SDK and compare the XSL Patterns reference with the XPath reference in MSXML 4.0.

MSXML 4.0 has implemented full support for XPath version 1.0 and even adds a few extensions. The chapter will first look at the XPath 1.0 W3C specification as it is implemented in MSXML 4.0 and following this will consider the XPath extensions added by Microsoft. XPath expressions can use an unabbreviated form, which we will look at, but there is also an abbreviated form that allows us to dramatically shorten the expressions. The chapter will then demonstrate a sample application, which will use many of the expressions discussed, including the Microsoft extensions, and we will conclude the chapter with some practical examples of working with XPath.

XPath Overview

XPath enables the addressing of, or navigation to, chosen parts of an XML document, providing a number of functions for the manipulation of strings, numbers, Booleans, and node-sets. When navigating an XML document, using XPath, a starting point is used, which is defined as the **context node**. A destination is arrived at via a series of **location steps**. A **location path** is a particular type of XPath expression that is used to select a set of nodes relative to the starting node, and consists of a series of location steps. A location step has a direction known as an **axis**. XPath has thirteen axes (we will discuss each of them later in the chapter). Additionally, a location step contains a **node test**, which specifies the type of node selected and, if applicable, its expanded name. There are seven types of node, which we'll also discuss later. Finally, a location step can have zero or more **predicates**, which are arbitrary expressions used to further filter and refine the set of nodes selected by the location step.

Let's look at a simple example to clarify the terminology. XPath uses both abbreviated and unabbreviated syntaxes, which we will look at in more detail later. The full unabbreviated syntax for a location step is the axis name, followed by a double colon (`::`), plus the node test, followed by zero or more predicates within square brackets. So, consider the expression `child::para[position()=last()]`. This expression selects the last child `para` element of the context element. `child` is the name of the axis, followed by the double colon, and then `para` is the node test, with the predicate in square brackets. Here, the predicate expression is `position()=last()` which uses the XPath `position()` function to return the position of a node within a node-set, and the XPath, `last()` function that returns the index of the last node in a node-set. Hence, this returns `true` when the chosen child node in the location step is the last in the node-set.

XPath Data Model

Rather than working directly on the XML document, XPath works on an abstract tree view of the document. This structure is called the **XPath data model**. The W3C has also defined an XML Infoset which will attempt to share common terms and data models between the various specifications that are produced – it is expected that XPath version 2.0 will share a common data model with XSLT 2.0 and XQuery 1.0 where possible.

In fact, everything in the XML document is modeled as a **node** in the XPath data model. For example, a node can be the root element, some child element, or the text within a given element.

XPath Tree Structure

To illustrate how the XPath data model works, we will look at a simple XML document and then a diagram showing its XPath model. Consider the following document:

```
<xml version="1.0" encoding="utf-8">
<weather>
    <city temp="26">Santiago</city>
    <city temp="22">Rancagua</city>
</weather>
```

We can now draw a model diagram of this document as seen by XPath:

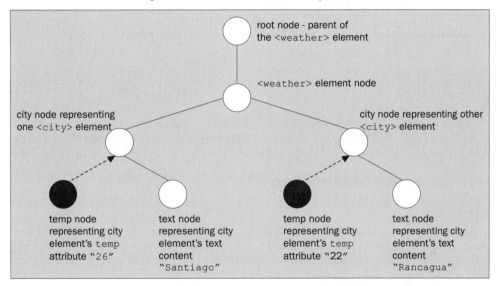

This is a fairly simple example, but you will already notice that the nodes are sometimes not as obvious as you may think – many don't appear directly as distinct items of the serialized document. For example, the root node is not a visible element in the actual XML document, like the document node in the DOM.

In fact, there are seven node types in the XPath model, which we will now look at.

XPath Node Types

In XPath, the data model defines the following types of nodes:

- ❑   Root node
- ❑   Element nodes
- ❑   Attribute nodes
- ❑   Namespace nodes
- ❑   Processing Instruction nodes
- ❑   Comment nodes
- ❑   Text nodes

Some of these node types use the concept of an **expanded name**. This is based on namespaces, where the local-part is some string, and the namespace is either null or a string. Two expanded names can be considered equal if they have the same local-part, and either both have a null namespace or both have the same namespace URI.

XPath also uses the concept of **document order**, where a node is ordered after its preceding siblings and then after their parent node. Note that the order of attribute nodes, namespace nodes, and nodes from external sources is not specified and should not be relied upon. Root nodes and element nodes have their children in the order they appear in the document, with every node having exactly one parent element node, except the root node, which has no parent. The node descendants of a node are its children and the children of its children (called grandchild nodes) and so on. To illustrate these concepts, consider the following XML document.

```
<?xml version="1.0"?>
<championship>
    <group name="e">
        <team rank="1">Celtic</team>
    </group>
</championship>
```

The `<championship>` element node is the root element node (distinct from the document root, which is its parent and not visible). The `<group>` element node is the first (and in fact only) child element of the root element and the `<team>` element node is the grandchild node of the `<championship>` root element node.

Let's now consider each of the XPath node types.

Root Node

The root node is the root of the XPath tree. It occurs only once within the document, and has as children a processing instruction node and any comment nodes that appear before and after the document element. The string value of the root node is the concatenation of all text node descendants, in document order. The root node does not have an expanded name.

Element Nodes

An element node exists for every element within the XML document. It has an expanded name, obtained by expanding the QName (or Qualified Name), in other words the element name plus prefix. This expanded name of an element node is null if there is no prefix or associated namespace.

The children of a given element node are the element nodes, comment nodes, processing instruction nodes, and text nodes for its content. Note that the attribute nodes are not regarded as child nodes in XPath – this is highlighted in the diagram with the dashed lines and a pointer to the parent element node. Internal and external entity references are expanded and any character references are resolved.

Attribute Nodes

Attribute nodes are associated with an element node, which may have zero or more attributes. An element node is the parent of an attribute, but an attribute is *not* the child of its parent element. This may seem strange, but it allows the elements and attributes to be selected using different XPath axes, which we look at shortly. An attribute node also has an expanded name and value, the first being similar to an element expanded name, and the latter conforming to the normal rules of XML, as well as allowing an empty string.

Namespace Nodes

Every element has an associated set of namespace nodes, one for each distinct namespace prefix that is in scope for that element. This includes the `xml` prefix, implicitly declared by the XML Namespaces Recommendation, as well as one for the default namespace in scope. In a similar way to attributes, the element is the parent of these namespace nodes, but they are not children of the element. Elements never share namespace nodes.

So an element will have a namespace node for the following conditions:

❑ For every attribute on the element whose name starts with `xmlns:`

❑ For every attribute on an ancestor element whose name starts with `xmlns:` (unless the element itself or a closer ancestor re-declares the prefix).

❑ For an `xmlns` attribute, if the element or some ancestor has an `xmlns` attribute, and the value of the `xmlns` attribute for the nearest such element is non-empty.

❑ For every namespace bound using the DOM `SelectionNamespaces` property.

> Note that an **xmlns=""** undeclares the default namespace.

Processing Instruction Nodes

A processing instruction node exists for every processing instruction (PI), except for those processing instructions that occur within the Document Type Declaration. A common mistake is to view the XML declaration as a processing instruction – it is not. MSXML, however, treats this differently from the specification and you can actually access the XML declaration in this way. You should avoid using such non-standard methods, though, to prevent problems in the future.

The PI has an expanded name; the local part being the PI's target and the namespace URI being null. Another, often confusing, aspect is that the string value of the PI is in fact the part following the target, excluding the "?>" at the end of course. The string value often contains multiple attributes, but they are not treated in the same way as attribute nodes and are in fact treated as a simple string.

Consider the following processing instruction for associating an XML document with a stylesheet:

```
<?xml-stylesheet href="someURI.xsl" type="text/xsl"?>
```

The value of this PI node is `href="someURI.xsl" type="text/xsl"` and you cannot access the `href` and `type` as separate attributes – both the `href` and `type` attributes are treated as one string and so if you were to set the value of this PI, the value would be the string `"href="someURI.xsl"type="text/xsl"` as opposed to setting the values of the `href` and `type` attributes separately.

Comment Nodes

There is a comment node for every comment in the XML source (except for the Document Type Declaration) and they do not have an expanded name. The value of the comment node is simply the text between the opening `<!--` and closing `-->` characters.

In the following comment node, the value of the comment is `"List of Product Categories"`:

```
<!--List of Product Categories-->
```

Text Nodes

Character data is grouped into text nodes, does not have an expanded name, and you can never have two immediately adjacent sibling text nodes. The actual value of a text node, which must contain at least one character, is simply the character data. Each character within a CDATA section is treated as though the `<![CDATA[` and `]]>` were removed, and every occurrence of < and & is replaced by < and & respectively.

Characters inside comments, processing instructions, and attribute values do not produce text nodes. Line-endings in external entities are normalized to #xA as specified in the XML Recommendation.

So, consider the following:

```
<![CDATA[Number of products < 50 & cost < 85 dollars]]>
```

This would be treated as the following text node value:

```
Number of products &lt; 50 &amp; cost &lt; 85 dollars
```

Context in XPath

An important aspect of evaluating XPath statements is the context, which comprises six parts:

- ❑ Context node-set which defines the node-set that is currently being processed. This will generally be the node-set selected by the template match. In the case of `for-each`, the `select` attribute defines a new set of nodes that will be the context node-set for processing within the `for-each` element.

- ❑ The context node, which is of prime importance as it represents the node that XPath expressions are defined in relationship to.

- ❑ The context position and context size, which define the current position within the context node-set, which is always less than or equal to the context size.

- ❑ A set of variable bindings, mapping the names of variables to their values.

- ❑ A function library, mapping function names to functions. There is a core XPath function library that must be implemented.

- ❑ A set of namespace declarations for the expression in scope, which map prefixes to URIs.

In MSXML, which follows the W3C Recommendation, context is evaluated differently for the DOM as opposed to XSLT.

> Note that in the examples, we explicitly use MSXML 4.0 – the latest version of the MSXML parser at the time of writing. This uses the ProgID for a **DOMDocument** object as "**Msxml2.DOMDocument.4.0**". You can equally use other versions of the parser by replacing this with for example "**Msxml2.DOMDocument.3.0**".

How MSXML Determines Context

Understanding the context in DOM is simpler than in XSLT, as it is more directly defined by the developer using `selectNodes()` methods, whereas in XSLT the context is often less visible to the creators of XSLT stylesheets who just use templates to match particular patterns. Consider the following simple XML document to illustrate these concepts – although it would be handy to understand some basic DOM and XSLT, the sample is fairly simple and should be understood without it. The code files are available in the book's code download from http://www.wrox.com/.

The sample XML file, `results1.xml`, looks like this:

```xml
<?xml version="1.0" encoding="utf-8" ?>
<championship>
    <group name="e">
        <team rank="1">Celtic</team>
        <team rank="2">Juventus</team>
        <team rank="3">Porto</team>
        <team rank="4">Rosenburg</team>
    </group>
    <group name="g">
        <team rank="1">Deportivo la Coruna</team>
        <team rank="2">Lille</team>
        <team rank="3">Manchester United</team>
        <team rank="4">Olympiakos</team>
    </group>
</championship>
```

The code of `results1.htm` is discussed below:

```html
<html>
    <head>
        <title>Results</title>
        <script language="javascript">
          <!--
```

There are two main functions in this sample to illustrate how the context node is evaluated in DOM and XSLT. Both methods use a global variable containing the parsed `results1.xml` document:

```javascript
var xmlDoc = new ActiveXObject("Msxml2.DOMDocument.4.0");
xmlDoc.async = false;
xmlDoc.setProperty("SelectionLanguage", "XPath");
xmlDoc.load("results1.xml");
```

Notice that we have to set the `SelectionLanguage` property to `XPath` – in MSXML 4.0 this is the default and so not really required, however in earlier MSXML versions (which you may be using) the default is `XSLPattern`, which is a much simpler query language used primarily by older versions of MSXML.

The first method is `domContextNode()`. This creates an empty variable and another variable referencing the document element node (the child of the root node as we discussed above):

```javascript
function domContextNode()
{
   var strDisplayText="";
   var objDocEl = xmlDoc.documentElement;
```

Next, a `selectNodes()` method is used to return all the `<team>` element nodes from each group. At this point, the select is being performed from the `documentElement`, which makes the `<championship>` node the context node – in other words, the select is applied within this node. This information is stored in a variable:

```
//Context node is "championship" element
var objTeamNodes = objDocEl.selectNodes("group/team");
strDisplayText += "Getting teams - '" + objDocEl.nodeName
    + "' is context node<br>";
```

Following this, a `for` loop is used to iterate through the node-list:

```
for (var objTeam = objTeamNodes.nextNode(); objTeam;
    objTeam = objTeamNodes.nextNode())
```

The `objTeamNodes` variable stores a node-list of `<team>` elements and the iterator initially points to a position just before the first node, so the call to `nextNode()` initially points to the first node. The iterator moves through each node while one exists. As it does this, it uses the currently iterated node as the context element. You can see this in the code as it accesses the `parentNode` of the context node (held in `objTeam`), which is the `<group>` element, and returns the `name` attribute. The final result is written to the screen:

```
{
//Context node is one of the "group" elements
strDisplayText+="Accessing teams - '" +
            objTeam.parentNode.nodeName
        + " " + objTeam.parentNode.getAttribute("name")
        + "' is parent of context node<br>"
document.all("text").innerHTML=strDisplayText;
}
}
```

You can see in the following figure that the context node changes from `championship` to each of the `team` elements, shown by the variation in the group name:

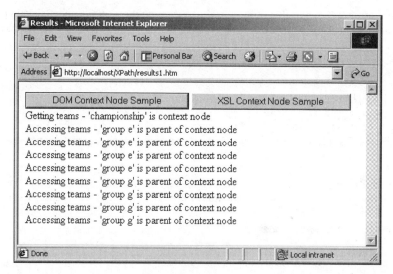

In comparison, `xslContextNode()` uses an XSL stylesheet to create the same output in a similar manner. Within this function, the XSL transform file, `results1.xsl`, is loaded and the `transformNode()` method is used to return the transformed output, which is then written to the output:

```
function xslContextNode()
{
    var xslDoc = new ActiveXObject("Msxml2.DOMDocument.4.0");
    xslDoc.async = false;
    xslDoc.load("results1.xsl");

    strDisplayText = xmlDoc.transformNode(xslDoc);
    document.all("text").innerHTML=strDisplayText;
}
```

The remainder of the page, including how the functions above are initiated on the button events, is shown below.

```
//--></script>
</head>
<body>
    <form ID="Form1">
        <input type="button" value="DOM Context Node Sample"
                onclick="domContextNode()" />
        <input type="button" value="XSL Context Node Sample"
                onclick="xslContextNode()" />
        <div id="text">
        </div>
    </form>
</body>
</html>
```

The XSL file, `results1.xsl`, is listed below – as you can see it is fairly simple:

```
<?xml version="1.0" ?>
<xsl:stylesheet version="1.0"
                xmlns:xsl="http://www.w3.org/1999/XSL/Transform">
    <xsl:template match="championship">
        Getting teams - championship is context node.<br />
        <xsl:for-each select="group/team">
            Accessing teams - group
            <xsl:value-of select="parent::node()/attribute::name" />
            is parent of context node.<br />
        </xsl:for-each>
    </xsl:template>
</xsl:stylesheet>
```

Stylesheets are considered in detail in the next chapter, but we will discuss this one briefly so you can have some understanding of how XPath is used. All stylesheets must contain an XSL processing instruction with a `version` attribute, and a reference to the XSL namespace (`http://www.w3.org/1999/XSL/Transform`). The `<xsl:template>` element contains a `match` attribute, which contains a pattern that, when found within the source XML document, will invoke the template. In our case we want to match on the `championship` document element:

```
<xsl:template match="championship">
```

When this is matched, the championship element node becomes the context node – any XPath expressions that occur within the template are done in reference to this node. Some detail is then written to the output about the context node. Next is an interesting effect of context nodes that is similar to the way the context node changes in the DOM, when an <xsl:for-each> element is used in XSLT:

```
<xsl:for-each select="group/team">
   Accessing teams - group
      <xsl:value-of select="parent::node()/attribute::name" />
   is parent of context node.<br />
</xsl:for-each>
```

The context node changes within the xsl:for-each loop from the championship node to a team node in scope in the loop. So, the context node is basically the node in the node-set that is in scope for the loop, where the node-set is determined by the select expression (and it is relative of course to the context node that was in scope prior to the xsl:for-each element).

Clicking the **XSL Context Node Sample** button gives the same output as when we used the DOM.

Now you should have a good understanding of the context node in XPath. Let's look at the other aspects of context – the above code will be an important basis for many of the examples below.

We will modify the XSLT file to illustrate the changing context position. The context position tells us where we are within a node-set – remember the node-set may contain just one node. We have updated the XSLT file now (and renamed it to results2.xsl) to include this code:

```
...
<xsl:for-each select="group/team">
   Accessing teams - group
   <xsl:value-of select=" parent::node()/attribute::name" />
      is parent of context node.<br />
      Context Position : <xsl:value-of select="position()" /><br />
</xsl:for-each>
...
```

This outputs the context position. In the case of the championship node being the context node, this will output 1 as it is a single node node-set. In the case of <xsl:for-each>, however, the node-set is made up of all the team nodes and so the context position will go from 1 to the context size, which is 8.

We have also modified the HTML page (now called results2.htm) to add a third button and the corresponding function:

```
function xslContextPosition()

        var xslDoc = new ActiveXObject("Msxml2.DOMDocument.4.0");
        xslDoc.async = false;
        xslDoc.load("results2.xsl");

        str = xmlDoc.transformNode(xslDoc)
        document.all("text").innerHTML=str;
    }
```

Clicking on the XSL Context Position Sample button to see the context position gives the output shown below:

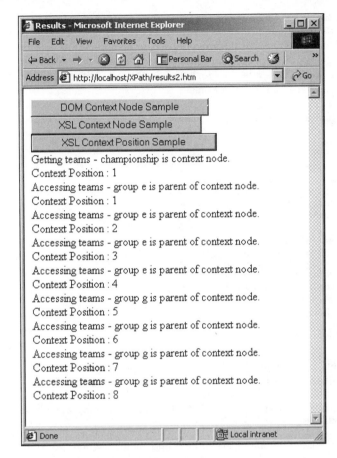

You should now have an understanding of how to work with context in XPath, so let's look at how we select information relative to the context, with location paths.

Location Paths and Location Steps

As we mentioned earlier, a location path is a particular type of XPath expression that is used to select a set of nodes relative to the starting node. It consists of a series of location steps, each composed of the following:

- ❑ An axis, of which there are thirteen (which we'll look at in a moment).

- ❑ A node test, which specifies the type of node selected and, if applicable, its expanded name. There are seven types of node, which we'll discuss later.

- ❑ Zero or more optional predicates, which are arbitrary expressions used to further filter and refine the set of nodes selected by the location step.

Let's start by looking at the thirteen axes of XPath.

Axes

An XPath axis is either a **forward axis** or a **reverse axis**. A forward axis only contains the context node or nodes that are after the context node in document order. The reverse axis only contains the context node with nodes that are before it in document order, or just the nodes before the context node. The return value of the `position()` function is interpreted depending on the axis. For a forward axis, it is the relative position within the node-set – for a reverse axis, it is the position from the end of the node-set (opposite of the forward axis, for example).

For the following discussions, we will again use the `results1.xml` file, shown below:

```xml
<?xml version="1.0" encoding="utf-8" ?>
<championship>
    <group name="e">
        <team rank="1">Celtic</team>
        <team rank="2">Juventus</team>
        <team rank="3">Porto</team>
        <team rank="4">Rosenburg</team>
    </group>
    <group name="g">
        <team rank="1">Deportivo la Coruna</team>
        <team rank="2">Lille</team>
        <team rank="3">Manchester United</team>
        <team rank="4">Olympiakos</team>
    </group>
</championship>
```

Let's first look at the forward axes:

❑ `child` – this axis contains the children of the context node. Remember that attribute nodes and namespace nodes are *not* children or element nodes, and so the `child` axis never returns attributes or namespace nodes in the returned node-set. To access these attribute and namespace nodes, you can use the `child` axes in combination with one of these other axes (for example, `child::node()/attribute::name`).

Looking at our sample file, if the context node is the element `<group>` with the attribute `name` with a value `"e"` then the `child` axis will contain the four `<team>` element nodes.

❑ `parent` – the `parent` axis contains the node that is the parent of the context node. Note however that the root node has no parent node.

Looking at our sample file, if the context node is the element `<group name="e">` then the `parent` axis will be the `<championship>` element node.

❑ `descendant` – this axis will contain the descendants of the context node, in other words, the context node's children, their grandchildren, and so on. Like the `child` axis, the `descendant` axis never contains attribute nor namespace nodes.

Looking at our sample file, if the context node is the element `<group name="e">` then the `descendant` axis will contain the four `team` element nodes.

❑ `descendant-or-self` – this axis includes the nodes on the `descendant` axis as well as the context node itself.

So, looking at our sample file, if the context node is the element `<group name="e">` then the `descendant-or-self` axis will contain the `<group>` element node with the `name` attribute with value `"e"`, as well as four `<team>` element nodes.

❑ following-sibling – this axis contains all the following sibling nodes of the context node. This axis is always empty if the context node is an attribute node or namespace node.

So, looking at our sample file, if the context node is the element <team rank="1"> then the following-sibling axis will contain three element nodes each with a rank attribute of 2, 3, and 4 respectively.

❑ following – the following axis contains all nodes that appear in document order after the context node, excluding any descendants, attribute nodes, and namespace nodes.

So, looking at our sample file, if the context node is the element <group name="e"> then the following axis will contain the group node with the attribute name with the value "g", as well as four child nodes of this group node.

❑ attribute – the attribute axis contains the attributes of the context node and will be empty unless the context node is an element.

In our sample, if the context node is the element <group name="e"> then the attribute axis will contain the name attribute node with the value "e".

❑ namespace – the namespace axis will contain any namespace node of the context node and, like the attribute axis, will be empty unless the context node is an element.

❑ self – this axis contains only the context node.

The reverse axes are as follows:

❑ ancestor – the ancestor axis is the opposite of the descendant axis and contains the ancestors of the context node. This is the context node's parent and its grandparent and so on. This will always include the root node unless the context node is the root node.

Looking at our sample file, if the context node is the element <group name="e"> then the ancestor axis will contain the championship element node and root node.

❑ ancestor-or-self – this axis contains the ancestor axis as well as the context node.

Looking at our sample file, if the context node is the element <group name="e"> then the ancestor axis will contain the championship element node and root node as well as the context node group.

❑ preceding-sibling – this axis contains all the preceding sibling nodes of the context element and is the opposite of the following-sibling axis. When the context node is an attribute node or a namespace node, this axis will always be empty (like the following-sibling axis).

Looking at our sample file, if the context node is the championship element then the XPath expression group[2]/team[@rank='4']/preceding-sibling::team using the preceding-sibling axis will contain the three team element nodes in the second group each with a rank attribute of 1, 2, and 3 respectively.

❑ preceding – the preceding axis contains all nodes before the context node in document order. This includes all nodes that appear before the context element.

Looking at our sample file, if the context node is the element <group name="g"> then the preceding axis will contain the previous group element as well as four team element nodes (the children of the name="e" group).

Let's now look at how we can use the axes, in a couple of simple examples. These examples can be found in the `results3.htm` file. We will cover only the two new functions, as much of the file is the same as the previous `results1.htm` and `results2.htm` files. We are going to demonstrate the `descendant` and `ancestor` axes – working with the others is much the same.

Clicking on the Descendant Axes Sample invokes a function called `descendant()`, which is shown below:

```
function descendant()
{
   var str="";
   var objDocEl = xmlDoc.documentElement;

   //Context node is "championship" element
   var objTeamNodes = objDocEl.selectNodes("descendant::team");

   for (i=0; i<objTeamNodes.length; i++)
   {
      str+="Descendant node:" +
      objTeamNodes[i].nodeName +
      objTeamNodes[i].getAttribute("rank") + "<br>";
   }

   document.all("text").innerHTML=str;
}
```

You will notice from the top of the function that the context node is set to the document element `<championship>` node. From this context node, we use the `selectNodes()` DOM method to return a node-set based on the XPath expression parameter we set. In our case, we use the `descendant` axis and ask for all `team` nodes on this axis – this is done by separating the `descendant` keyword and node name by two colons:

```
var objTeamNodes = objDocEl.selectNodes("descendant::team");
```

This is powerful as it returns a node-set containing all the team nodes (which we then iterate through in a `for` loop) and simply outputs some information to clarify that it is `team` nodes we have in our node-list. The output is shown below:

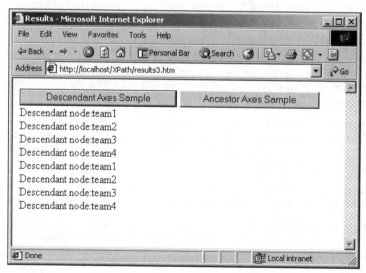

In contrast, another function does an XPath query on the ancestor axis by calling the ancestor() function when the **Ancestor Axes Sample** button is clicked:

```
function ancestor()
{
   var str="";
   var objStartEl = xmlDoc.documentElement.childNodes[0].childNodes[3];

   //Context node is "championship" element
   var objGroupNodes = objStartEl.selectNodes("ancestor::group");

   for (i=0;i<objGroupNodes.length;i++)
   {
      str+="Ancestor group node : " +
      objGroupNodes[i].nodeName + " " +
      objGroupNodes[i].getAttribute("name")+ "<br>";
   }

   document.all("text").innerHTML=str;
}
```

You should first notice that the context element is set to be the fourth child (because DOM counts from zero) of the first child of the document element, in other words, the element <team rank="4">Rosenburg</team>. The node-set query is done with an XPath expression on the ancestor axes for group element nodes:

```
var objGroupNodes = objStartEl.selectNodes("ancestor::group");
```

Of course, this will return a one node node-set as there is only one ancestor group element node, which is in fact its parent element node. Therefore, the output from this would be:

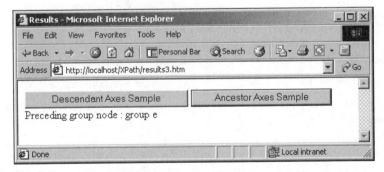

When we looked at our XPath expressions above, we considered the axis we were working on. In addition to the axis, there was another part, separated by double colon characters. This part, to the right of the "::" in our samples, is called a **node test** and is very flexible. We will look at XPath node tests now.

Node Tests

A node test is used on an axis to filter the node-set along the axis on which we are working. The node test specifies the node type and expanded name on which to filter the axis node-set.

In MSXML there are really two types of node tests – the first is a **name test** and the second a **node type test**. A name test is the most common method you will use for selecting nodes in your XPath expressions. A name test can be based on either all nodes of the principal node type, the QName of the node, or the NCName of the node. The NCName is an XML name that does not contain a colon.

In the first case the principal node type is of prime importance, although it is important for all name tests. The principal node type is based on the axis that is being evaluated. So, for the `attribute` axis, the principal node type is "attribute"; for the `namespace` axis it is "namespace", and for all other axes the principal node type is "element".

An asterisk (*) is used to select all nodes of a given type based on the principal node type. So, looking back to our sample XML file, if the context node is the first `group` element, then the XPath expression `attribute::*` would return the `name` attribute (as well as any others that may be added in the future to the `group` element). With the same context node, the expression `following-sibling::*` would return the second `group` element node. Similarly, the expression `child::*` would return all four `team` elements that are children of the `<group name="e">` element.

The second type of XPath name test is based on a QName, or qualified name. We saw this kind of expression in our examples above, but these examples never highlighted that the expanded names must match. In other words, if the node has a namespace, then this must also match the node in the XPath query, in order to test `true`. So, in our example, we used `ancestor::group`. If the `group` had been associated with some namespace, however, we could have had a similar expression such as `ancestor::wrox:group`. The prefix is first expanded based on namespace declarations in the context document, before it is compared to the source nodes – this therefore means that the prefix used is irrelevant because it is the URIs that must match.

The final type of XPath name test is based on an NCName, where the prefix is expanded the same way as a QName, but the nodes are selected according to the principal node type. The matching of nodes is based on the same expanded namespace URI, and the local name is irrelevant.

XPath expressions can also have node type tests, which allow you to override the principal node type and select from other axes. MSXML has four node type tests:

- ❑ `comment()` – this can be used to select comment node types from a document.

- ❑ `node()` – this can be used to select any type of node from the source document.

- ❑ `processing-instruction()` – this can be used to select processing-instruction nodes in the document.

- ❑ `text()` – this returns text nodes in the document.

So, looking back to our sample XML file, if the context node is one of the `team` element nodes, then `child::text()` would return the data within that node – "Celtic" or "Juventus", for example.

So far we can access a particular axis and get back a node-set based on a particular principal axis (or even from other axes), but XPath allows further filtering using predicates, which allow you to create another node-set based on a filtered initial node-set. For example, you may wish to filter the node-set of teams in our example to only those who came first in the group. Let's now look at predicates.

Predicates

> Note that XSLT provides a range of functions that useful in evaluating expressions –
> these are discussed later in the chapter.

A predicate can be applied to an XPath expression to further filter a node-set on a given axis to produce
a new node-set – similar on the way a WHERE clause is used in a SQL statement to filter the rows
selected. The predicate is enclosed within square brackets after the node test and returns either a
number or a Boolean value. If a number is returned then it is evaluated based on the context position of
the context node. If the context position and the evaluated number are equal, then the expression is
evaluated to a Boolean true and it is included in the result node-set, otherwise it is excluded.

So, looking back at our sample XML file, if the context node is the championship document element
node, then a predicate could be used to retain the first group element node using the XPath expression:

```
child::group[position()=1]
```

Furthermore, the last group could be selected by the following expression:

```
child::group[position()=last()]
```

The first selects the group elements on the child axis and then uses a predicate to get the last group
element node in the node-set. You can even build your XPath expression using multiple location steps,
so that the following XPath expression would return all team element nodes after the second team
node of the second group element node:

```
child::group[position()=2]/child::team[position()>2]
```

If this is used in an XML document, we must replace the ">" with its named entity equivalent ">".
More commonly, a Boolean value will be generated – or at least a value that can be converted to a
Boolean value. In this case the predicates, or predicate, are evaluated and those that evaluate to true
are included in the result node-set, while those that evaluate to false are excluded.

Considering the examples above, rather than finding the group element node by index, it can be done
based on its attribute value:

```
child::group[attribute::name='e']
```

The above expression would also select the first <group> element node. The following, and more
complicated, expression would select the second (because XPath counts from 1) element node of the
first group if it has a value "Juventus":

```
child::group[position()=1]/child::team[position()=2][self::team='Juventus']
```

Think of this as being like the "AND" keyword in SQL where the condition is that "team='Juventus'"
– XPath also has the "and" keyword to do a similar thing. As you can imagine there are a number of
possibilities and we will be exploring some of these later.

Finally, imagine we altered our sample XML document so that one of the node were repeated in the second group – for example, the text of fourth node in the second group "Olympiakos" was changed to "Celtic". The following expression would return any values in the first group that also appear in the second group:

```
group[1]/team[.=//group[2]/team]
```

If no text nodes appear in both groups, then an empty node-set is returned – however in the case of the modified sample, a node with the text value "Celtic" will be returned.

XPath Syntax

XPath defines some variations on syntax that can be used when creating expressions, such as relative and absolute location paths, as well as abbreviated and unabbreviated syntax. Let's now take a look at these.

Relative and Absolute Location Paths

XPath expressions are based on either a relative location path or an absolute location path.

A **relative location path** is constructed from a series of **location steps**, each separated by a "/" character. Each location step selects a node-set relative to a context node, which is initialized to some starting context node. Following context nodes are set to each node in the new node-set for the following location step. The set of nodes identified in this following step are unioned together to create a new node-set, and so on. So, consider the following expression:

```
child::group[position()=1]/child::team[position()=2]
```

There are location steps here; the first selects the first child <group> element relative to the context node. This location step sets the context for the next location step – in other words the context node is now the first child <group> element of the initial context node. The second location step now selects the second child <team> element node from the context <group> element node.

An **absolute location path**, however, starts with "/" followed by some relative location path. This therefore selects the root node of the context document, and location steps are done relative to this root path, in the same way as for the relative location path. So the above expression may be re-written as follows:

```
/child::group[position()=1]/child::team[position()=2]
```

This expression is in fact exactly the same as the one above because the championship element is in fact the document root element and it only has child group elements. In other cases, the absolute location path may be something completely different!

Unabbreviated and Abbreviated Syntax

After working through the examples, it becomes apparent that we need some way to shorten the XPath expressions, as working with many axes in a given expression could make it very long. Fortunately, XPath supports an **abbreviated syntax** – both syntaxes are generally interchangeable and you can replace some unabbreviated expression with an abbreviated one and vice-versa. The syntax we have been using so far is known as **unabbreviated syntax**, and it is very important that we understand how this works before using the abbreviated syntax. In fact, sometimes we may need to revert to the unabbreviated syntax when the abbreviated form doesn't allow us to do something, such as along the ancestor axis.

For example, the following is an XPath expression we saw earlier, in unabbreviated form:

```
child::group[position()=1]/child::team[position()=2][self::team="Juventus"]
```

In abbreviated format, we could write this as:

```
group[1]/team[2][.="Juventus"]
```

You can see how much shorter this is and arguably easier to follow for most people. Still, without understanding the unabbreviated format you may get lost in the abbreviated syntax. For example, in the unabbreviated format use of the child axis is implicit, so (as you can see in the expression) you do not have to state you are using that axis – in the unabbreviated format you must state the axis. Without knowing this, you will likely get lost on where you are in your expression, or even what axis you are on.

We have discussed the unabbreviated format in some detail – let's now briefly look at some examples of how the abbreviated format can be used instead of the longer unabbreviated format, illustrating the differences between the two. Further on in the chapter we'll look at an extensive sample section comparing the various syntaxes.

The unabbreviated expression `child::team` can be abbreviated as `team` to locate the `<team>` child of the context node – this is because the child node is implicit in the abbreviated syntax. Similarly, if the context node is the first `group` element node, then the unabbreviated expression `attribute::name` could be abbreviated as `@name`. As a final example, if the root node is the context node, then the unabbreviated syntax `descendant-or-self::team` will select all the `<team>` nodes in the document. The abbreviated form would be `//team`.

Operations and Expressions

When using XPath (abbreviated or unabbreviated), there are a number of operators and special characters that can be applied to expressions, which we'll take a look at now.

Operators and Patterns

The following patterns are used in XPath as operators to create expressions to select XPath nodes:

❑   `//` is the abbreviated syntax operator equivalent to the `descendant-or-self` unabbreviated expression when started from the root node. It starts from the root node and selects all descendant nodes. No matter what depth the operator is used at, it always starts from the root node. We must therefore always be careful when using this as it can be very resource intensive and very slow for large documents. As an example, `//team` would select all `<team>` elements in the entire document.

❑   `/` is the same as the unabbreviated `child` axis expression and selects the immediate children of the element node on the left of the operator. For example, `group[1]/team` would select all `<team>` children of the first `<group>` element.

❑   `.` indicates the current context and is the same as the unabbreviated `self` axis. So, if the context node was `<championship>`, the `.` would select the `<championship>` node.

❑   `*` is a wildcard operator and selects all elements regardless of their name (but not as a wildcard for a match on a sub-string). It is used in both abbreviated and unabbreviated expressions. For example, if a `<group>` element in our example is the context node, then the expressions (unabbreviated) `child::*` and (abbreviated) `./*` would both select all `<team>` child nodes.

❑ @ selects an attribute of a given node and is the abbreviated expression of the unabbreviated `attribute`. So, if `<group>` is the context node, then `@name` and `attribute::name` would both return the `name` attribute node.

❑ `@*` is similar to the above operator, but as you would expect, returns all attributes of the context node regardless of their name. So, if `<group>` is the context node, then `@*` and `attribute::*` would both return the `name` attribute node as well as any other attributes that may be present on the `<group>` node.

❑ `:` is a namespace separator and is equivalent in both abbreviated and unabbreviated XPath expressions. Therefore, the expressions `/wrox:group` and `child::wrox:group` are equivalent if `wrox` has the same namespace URI in both cases.

❑ `[]` is used to enclose filter expressions or predicates.

In addition to these operators, there are some operators that are associated more with numeric/arithmetic operations:

❑ `[]` is used to hold an index to an item within a collection. An example would be when `<championship>` is the context element, `//group[1]` which would select the first `<group>` element anywhere in the document – in other words the first of any descendant `<group>` elements. In unabbreviated syntax this would be written `//group[position()=1]`.

❑ `+` performs addition. So, the following expression would select the next node if the context node is a `<team>` node. In unabbreviated form it would be `child::team[position()+1]` while the abbreviated form would be `./team[position()+1]`.

❑ `-` performs subtraction. Similar to the above, the following unabbreviated expression returns the penultimate `<team>` element node `child::team[position()=last()-1]` and the following does the same in abbreviated syntax: `./team[position()=last()-1]`.

❑ `div` performs floating-point division such as `//group[count(//group) div 2]` which returns the first group node, because count(`//group`) counts the number of group nodes in the document (which is two) and divides this number by two (which gives one) and returns the node at this position in the selected node-set (that is the first one).

❑ `*` performs multiplication, for example, `//group[(count(//group) div 2) * 2]`, which returns the second group node, because count(`//group`) counts the number of group nodes in the document (which is two) and divides this number by two (which gives one) and this result is multiplied by two and returns the node at this position in the selected node-set (that is the second one).

❑ `mod` returns the integer remainder from a truncating division. So, we could get every second node element with the unabbreviated expression `child::team[position() mod 2 = 0]` or the abbreviated expression `./team[position() mod 2 = 0]`.

`()` is used to group operations so that precedence is established.

Comparison and Union

In addition to the operators we looked at above, XPath provides Boolean and comparison operators that can be used in unabbreviated and abbreviated expressions:

❑ and performs logical AND operations. So, the following example could be used to select all `<group>` nodes that have a name attribute and at least one `<team>` child element. With `<championship>` as the context node, the unabbreviated form would be `child::group[attribute::name and child::team]` while the abbreviated form would be `./group[@name and team]`. In comparison, the expression `./group[@name][team]` first selects all group nodes with a name attribute and then tests whether each has any team child elements. The and operator works from left to right and converts each result to a Boolean value and exits if one is `false`. A similar but very different method of multiple predicates is based on repeatedly filtering node-sets, which is very different from evaluating tests to a Boolean `true`/`false`. In particular this would make a difference in the expression `./group[count(team)>4 and position()=1]` because there are no `<group>` elements with more than four team nodes and hence the expression immediately returns `false`. The multiple predicate expression `./group[1][count(team)=4]`, which first returns the first group node and **then** filters this to select where there are four child `<team>` elements. In contrast `./group [count(team)=4][1]` first returns all `<group>` nodes with four child `<team>` elements and then selects the first of these. It is possible the two results could be different.

❑ or performs logical OR operations. So, the following example could be used to select all `<group>` nodes that have a name attribute or at least one `<team>` child element. With `<championship>` as the context node, the unabbreviated form would be `child::group[attribute::name or child::team]` while the abbreviated form would be `./group[@name or team]`.

❑ `not()` provides negation of the value of an expression. The following example could be used to select all group nodes that have a name attribute, but not a `<team>` child element – in other words, a `<group>` element with no children. With `<championship>` as the context node, the unabbreviated form would be `child::group[attribute::name and not(child::team)]` while the abbreviated form would be `./group[@name and not(team)]`.

❑ = is an equality operator.

❑ != is an inequality operator and evaluates whether two expressions are equal as opposed to `not()` which negates the expression (so if the value is `true`, `not(expression)` returns `false`). So, with group as the context node, to get all the nodes except the last one, the unabbreviated form would be `child::team[position()!=last()]` while the abbreviated form would be `./team[position()!=last()]`.

❑ < is a less-than operator. So, another way to get all the nodes except the last one, with `<group>` as the context node, would be to use the unabbreviated form `child::team[position() &lt; last()]` or the abbreviated form `./team[position()&lt; last()]`. Note that when working directly with the DOM, you can use the "<" character rather than its entity declaration <, which must be used in serialized XML documents.

❑ <= is a less than-or-equal-to-operator. So, to get the first two team nodes, with `<group>` as the context node, the unabbreviated form would be `child::team[position() &lt;= 2]` while the abbreviated form would be `./team[position()&lt;= 2]`. Note that when working directly with the DOM, you can use the "<=" characters rather than the entity declaration <=, which must be used in serialized XML documents.

❑ > is a greater-than operator. So, another way to get all the nodes except the first two, with `<group>` as the context node, would be to use the unabbreviated form `child::team[position() &gt; 2]` or the abbreviated form `./team[position() &gt; 2]`. Note that you can also use the ">" character rather than its entity declaration >.

❑ >= is a greater-than-or-equal-to operator. So, another way to get all the nodes except the first node, with <group> as the context node, would be to use the unabbreviated form `child::team[position() &gt;= 2]` or the abbreviated form `./team[position()&gt;= 2]`. Note that you can also use the ">=" characters rather than with the entity declaration >=.

❑ | is called a set operator and returns the union of two sets of nodes. This can be extremely useful for joining two diverse node-sets into one node-set. So, for example, consider the situation that also the <group> element contained not only <team> child nodes, but in fact various child elements such as <fixtures> and <results>. To get a node-set containing both <team> and <fixtures> element nodes, but not <results> element nodes, we could use the following syntax (with a <championship> element node as the context element). The unabbreviated form is `child::group[child::team | child::fixtures]` while the abbreviated form would be `./group[team | fixtures]`.

Note that all union queries must have the same sub-tree and root node, so you cannot just branch off to other parents or children and so on, in a single union.

We now have enough understanding about how to create XPath expressions, but XPath offers even further functionality via XPath functions, which we'll look at now.

XPath Functions

XPath functions are made up of node-set functions, string functions, Boolean functions, and number functions; and MSXML 4.0 even adds its own set of extension functions to enhance the possibilities available to us.

Node-Set Functions

The node-set functions in XPath can be used to return information about a particular node or node-set.

count(node-set)

The `count()` function takes a node-set as its parameter and returns the number of nodes in the node-set.

id(object)

The `id()` function returns a node-set containing the node or nodes with a given ID attribute. If the argument object is not a node-set then the argument is converted to a string and the resulting string treated as a whitespace-delimited list of tokens, each of which is then used as candidate ID value.

If the argument is a node-set then each node in turn within this node-set is converted into a string and the resulting string is treated as a whitespace-delimited list of tokens, each of which is then used as a candidate ID value.

So, consider the following XML document (championship.xml) with validating inline DTD:

```
<?xml version="1.0" encoding="utf-8" ?>
<!DOCTYPE championship
[
<!ELEMENT championship (group+)>
<!ELEMENT group   (team+)>
<!ATTLIST group
    id ID #IMPLIED
```

```
    name CDATA #REQUIRED>
<!ELEMENT team (#PCDATA)>
<!ATTLIST team
    id ID #IMPLIED
    rank CDATA  #REQUIRED>
]>
<championship>
    <group id="groupID" name="e">
        <team rank="1">Celtic</team>
        <team rank="2">Juventus</team>
        <team rank="3">Porto</team>
        <team rank="4">Rosenburg</team>
    </group>
    <group id="groupID" name="g">
        <team id="dla" rank="1">Deportivo la Coruna</team>
        <team rank="2">Lille</team>
        <team rank="3">Manchester United</team>
        <team rank="4">Olympiakos</team>
    </group>
</championship>
```

Interestingly, in MSXML, if `validateOnParse` is set to `true` (which is the default in MSXML) then this document won't validate because there is two identical `id` attributes – each `<group>` element has an `id` attribute with the value `groupID` assigned. However, if we set the `validateOnParse` property of the `DOMDocument` object to `false` (or are using a parser in non-validating mode), then this will parse. If the `id` attributes are unique (as is recommended) then it can be validated as normal.

In this case, calling `selectNodes("id('groupID')")` will return the first element with an `id` attribute with a value of `groupID` in document order – namely the first `<group>` element. However, selecting a node-set and evaluating the `id` returns a set of nodes with the given id, so `selectNodes(//group[id ('groupID')])` returns two nodes – both `<group>` element nodes. Finally, we can pass in multiple `id` values to the `id()` function and so the following returns two elements – the first `<group>` element and the first `<team>` element of the second `<group>` element – `selectNodes(id('test dla'))`.

last()

The `last()` function returns the value of the context size, which is the number of nodes in the selected node-set. Within XSLT, when `last()` is used within an `<xsl:template>`, it returns the number of nodes selected by the relevant `<xsl:apply-templates>` expression. When used within an `<xsl:for-each>` expression, it returns the number of nodes selected by the relevant `<xsl:for-each>` expression.

For example, the following expression selects the last `para` child element:

```
chapter/para[last()]
```

and the following selects all elements except the last:

```
chapter/para[position()!=last()]
```

local-name(node-set)

The `local-name()` function returns the local part of the expanded name of a node. In other words, if there is a namespace prefix then it returns the name after the colon. If there is no namespace, then simply the name is returned.

If a node-set is passed as part of the argument, then it returns the name of the first node in document order (because it is possible that more than one node may be present in the node-set). If the node-set passed is empty then an empty string is returned. If no node-set is passed (the most common scenario in XSLT) then the context node is evaluated according to the same rules.

So, if a node-set (passed as a parameter or the context node) had a node representing a `<paragraph>` element then the `local-name()` function would return `paragraph`. If the same element was `<wrox:paragraph>` then the `local-name()` function would still return `paragraph`.

Equally, in the sample document we have been working with, the expression:

```
//@*[local-name(.)='rank']) | (//*[local-name(.)='group']
```

returns the first `<group>` element node, then the four `rank` attribute nodes (which are attributes of the `<team>` child nodes of the first `<group>`) and so on for the second `<group>`.

name(node-set)

The `name()` function returns a QName (qualified name) that represents the name of a node. This will usually be the name of the node as it is in the XML document, including any namespace prefix.

If a node-set is passed as part of the argument, then it returns the name of the first node in document order (because it is possible that more than one node may be present in the node-set). If the node-set passed is empty then an empty string is returned. If no node-set if passed (the most common scenario in XSLT) then the context node is evaluated according to the same rules.

So, if a node-set (passed as a parameter or the context node) had a node representing a `<paragraph>` element then the `name()` function would return `paragraph`. If the same element was `<wrox:paragraph>` then the `name()` function would now return `wrox:paragraph`.

namespace-uri(node-set)

The `namespace-uri()` function returns a string representing the namespace URI in the expanded name of the node.

If a node-set is passed as part of the argument, then it returns the namespace URI of the first node in document order (because it is possible that more than one node may be present in the node-set). If the node-set passed is empty then an empty string is returned. If no node-set is passed (the most common scenario in XSLT) then the context node is evaluated according to the same rules.

Consider the case where we have a typical XSLT document with the default namespace `"http://www.w3.org/1999/XSL/Transform"` and another namespace with the prefix `wrox` associated to `"http://www.wrox.com"`. If a node-set (passed as a parameter or the context node) had a `<paragraph>` element node then the `namespace-uri()` function would return `http://www.w3.org/1999/XSL/Transform`. If the same element was `<wrox:paragraph>` then the `namespace-uri()` function would now return `http://www.wrox.com`.

position()

This function returns the value of the context position, typically the number of the current node relative to its parent. Note that the first node is numbered 1 (rather than index 0 as in many programming languages). The `position()` function is evaluated in a very similar way to the `last()` function discussed above.

So, the following XPath expression selects the second child node of the context element:

```
chapter/para[position()=2]
```

and the following selects the last:

```
chapter/para[position()=last()]
```

String Functions

There are a number of XPath native string functions that perform evaluations, concatenations, and comparisons of objects and strings in XPath.

concat(string1, string2, ..., stringN)

The `concat()` function takes any number of arguments, which it converts to strings before concatenating them and returning the resultant string.

So the expression `concat("sku","562","B")` would return the string `sku562B`.

contains(string, substring)

The `contains()` function returns `true` if `string` contains `substring`; otherwise `false`.

For example, the expression `contains("sku562B","B")` would return `true`, whereas the call `contains("sku562B","598")` would return `false`.

normalize-space(string)

The `normalize-space()` function removes leading and trailing whitespace characters and replaces sequences of whitespace characters within the `string` with a single whitespace character. If a string is passed, then this is the string that the `normalize-space` applies to, otherwise if no argument string is passed, then it is the value of the context node that is evaluated.

It is important to note that the XML Recommendation defines a whitespace character as #x9, a tab, #xA, a newline, #xD, a carriage return; or #20, a space.

So, consider the following string:

```
<somestring>¿Quien es

                          Chile?
      ¡O'Higgens de Rancagua!
</somestring>
```

If we pass the text of the `<somestring>` element to the `normalize-space()` function the result would be:

```
¿Quien es Chile? ¡O'Higgens de Rancagua!
```

starts-with(string, substring)

This function returns `true` if `string` starts with `substring`, otherwise it returns `false`. If either of the arguments is not a string, then it is first converted to a string before evaluation.

151

For example, the expression starts-with("Blue Jersey, Extra Large", "Blue") returns true, whereas the expression starts-with("Blue Jersey, Extra Large", "Red") returns false.

string(object)

This function converts the relevant object to a string. A node-set is converted by taking the string value of the first node in document order, and if the node-set is empty then an empty string is returned. If no object is passed, the context element is evaluated according to these rules.

A number is converted as follows:

❑ NaN is converted to the string NaN.

❑ Positive zero and negative zero are represented as the string 0.

❑ Positive infinity is converted to Infinity and negative infinity to -Infinity.

❑ If the number is an integer represented in decimal form then the result is the integer with no decimal point or leading zeros. The number is preceded by a negative sign (-) if it is less than zero. For example, string(1.00) is converted to 1.

Any other number will be represented in a decimal form with at least one digit before the decimal point and one digit after. There can be no leading zeros, except immediately before the decimal point. After the decimal point as many digits as necessary are permitted to distinguish from other IEEE 754 numeric values.

The Boolean value false is converted to the string false, and the value true is converted to the string true.

Some examples of conversions using the string() function are:

❑ string(98.00) returns 98

❑ string(-098.70) returns -98.7

❑ string(true) returns true

string-length(string)

This function returns the number of characters in the string. If no string is passed as a parameter, then the context node is evaluated. If the parameter is not a string type, it is first converted to a string before it is evaluated.

For example:

❑ string-length("hello") returns 5

❑ string-length(98.00) returns 2 (because it is first converted to a string, as above)

Remember that it is the number of characters in the string that are counted and not the number of characters in the source document. So, & is regarded as a single (ampersand) character and Unicode surrogate pairs are regarded as a single character.

> Note that the string functions do a normalization from the XML document – so the
> & entity reference in an XML document is converted to "&" prior to evaluation
> by a string function (so just typing "&" as a fixed value within string function will
> return a string length of 5!). Therefore in the examples below assume the value is
> retrieved from an XML document.

Some examples of the use of this function are shown below:

❑   string-length("www.wrox.com") returns 12

❑   string-length("") returns 0

❑   string-length("𠀀") returns 1

substring(string, startPos, length)

This function returns a substring (shorter string that is part of the larger string) of the parameter
string, starting at the integer startPos and ending after length characters. The length parameter
is optional and if it is not specified, then the substring is from startPos to the end of the string. Note
that the first position is 1 (and not index 0 as in many programming languages).

Remember that, as above, it is the number of characters in the string that is counted and not the number of
characters in the source document. So, & is regarded as a single (ampersand) character and Unicode
surrogate pairs are regarded as a single character. Furthermore, the startPos and length values are
rounded according to the XPath round() function. So 1.4 is rounded down to 1 and 1.5 rounded up to 2.

Below are some examples of the function in use:

❑   substring("www.wrox.com",0,4) returns www.

❑   substring("www.wrox.com",4,5) returns wrox.

❑   substring("S & L",3,3) returns & L (this is the XML output – the output in
    the text will be "& L").

substring-after(string, substring)

This function returns the portion of string that follows the occurrence of substring. If any of the
parameters are not a string, they are first converted prior to evaluation.

For example, the call substring-after("price=$26.99","=") returns $26.99.

substring-before(string, substring)

This function returns the portion of string that precedes the occurrence of substring. If any of the
parameters are not a string, they are first converted prior to evaluation.

For example, the call substring-before("price=$26.99","=") returns price.

translate(string, repString, subString)

This function returns a string where all the occurrences of any character in repString within string
are replaced by the corresponding character from subString (where corresponding means at the same
position in both subString and repString). It is commonly used to convert characters from lower
case to upper case and vice versa.

Note that if a character at a given position in repString does not have a corresponding character at the same position in subString, then it will be omitted from string. So, if subString is an empty string then all occurrences of repString characters are removed from string.

This is best illustrated with some examples:

- ❑ translate("12","12","34") returns 34 (1 is replaced with 3, and 2 is replaced with 4)
- ❑ translate("12","21","34") returns 43 (2 is replaced with 3, and 1 is replaced with 4)
- ❑ translate("12","12","5") returns 5 (1 is replaced with 5, and 2 is omitted)
- ❑ translate("chile","c","C") returns Chile (c is replaced with C)
- ❑ translate("US$45.98","$US","€") returns €45.98 ($ is replaced with €, and U and S are omitted)
- ❑ translate("chile","c","") returns hile (c is removed)

Note that the characters are XML characters rather than Unicode characters and so the text 𠀀 is treated as a single character and NOT individual characters.

Boolean Functions

XPath has a number of Boolean functions that are used to return strings or numbers.

boolean(object)

This converts the object parameter to a Boolean if possible. Numbers are true if the number is non-zero and not NaN. Node-sets are true only if they are non-empty. A string that is of non-zero length is true.

Some examples of its use are as follows:

- ❑ boolean(0) returns false
- ❑ boolean(1) returns true
- ❑ boolean(-2) returns true
- ❑ boolean("string") returns true
- ❑ boolean("") returns false

false()

This function returns the Boolean value false and is used because XPath has no Boolean constants available.

lang(string)

This function returns true if the context node is the same as, or a sub-language of, the language being tested.

The language of the context node is determined by the xml:lang attribute on the context node, or if there is no xml:lang attribute, by the xml:lang attribute of the nearest ancestor node, such as parent's parent, etc. If there is no such attribute, false is returned. If xml:lang exists, then case is ignored, as is any suffix starting with "-" (defining a sub-code of the language, such as "en-us").

So, the following examples show the return value of a call to lang():

❑   For <para xml:lang="es"/> the call lang("es") returns true

❑   For <para xml:lang="it"/> the call lang("es") returns false

❑   For <para xml:lang="en-us"/> the call lang("en") returns true

not(boolean)

The not() function returns the negation of its argument, so that not(false()) will return true and not(true()) will return false. For example, not(position()=last()) will return true for all nodes but the last node in a given node-set.

true()

This function returns the Boolean value true and is used because XPath has no Boolean constants available.

Number Functions

XPath has several functions that are used to return numbers.

ceiling(number)

This function returns the smallest integer value that is greater than or equal to the numeric value of the argument. If the argument is not a number, it is first converted to a number using the rules for the number() function. For example:

❑   ceiling(2.0) returns 2

❑   ceiling(2.2) returns 3

❑   ceiling(2.6) returns 3

❑   ceiling(-0.1) returns 0

floor(number)

This function returns the largest integer value that is less than or equal to the numeric value of the argument. If the argument is not a number, it is first converted to a number using the rules for the number() function. This is unlike what you may be used to in traditional arithmetic, whereby numbers up to X.5 (where X represents some arbitrary integer) are rounded down to X and the numbers X.5 and above are rounded up to X+1. For example:

❑   floor(2.0) returns 2

❑   floor(2.2) returns 2

❑   floor(2.6) returns 2

❑   floor(-0.1) returns -1

number(object)

This function converts the object to a number according to the following rules. If no object is passed, then the context node is evaluated.

If the `object` argument is a string then leading and trailing whitespace characters are removed and the string, with an optional minus sign followed by some number, is evaluated to the nearest IEEE 754 number; any other string is converted to `NaN`.

The Boolean `true` is evaluated to `1` and `false` is converted to `0`. A node-set is converted to a string and then evaluated as a string. Some examples of using the number function are:

❑ `number(5.92)` returns `5.92`

❑ `number(-5.92)` returns `-5.92`

❑ `number("5.92")` returns `5.92`

❑ `number(false())` returns `0.0`

❑ `number("")` returns `NaN`

round(number)

The `round()` function returns the integer that is closest to the argument value. Values are returned unchanged (`NaN` returns `NaN`, for example) except for the following cases:

❑ For positive values, where the part after the decimal point is greater than .0 and less than .5, the result is the integer value before the decimal point. Where the part after the decimal point is equal to or greater than .5 then the result is the integer value before the decimal point plus 1.

❑ For negative values, where the part after the decimal point is greater than .0 and less than or equal to .5, the result is the integer value before the decimal point. Where the part after the decimal point is greater than .5 then the result is the integer value before the decimal point minus 1.

The following show the return values from calls to the `round()` function:

❑ `round(1.1)` returns `1.0`

❑ `round(1.5)` returns `2.0`

❑ `round(1.6)` returns `2.0`

❑ `round(-1.1)` returns `-1.0`

❑ `round(-1.5)` returns `-1.0`

❑ `round(-1.6)` returns `-2.0`

sum(node-set)

The `sum()` function returns the sum of all the numeric nodes in the node-set, where non-numeric values are first converted to a number, according to the `number()` function, before evaluation.

Hence, if we pass the following XML fragment as the node-set to the `sum()` method, such as `sum(//num)`, then the result is `90`:

```
<randomNums>
    <num>45</num>
    <num>23</num>
    <num>22</num>
</randomNums>
```

XPath Extension Functions (MSXML 4-Specific)

There are a number of operations that it is either difficult or impossible to do with the XPath 1.0 Recommendation, hence the MSXML 4.0 parser provides a number of functions to evaluate nodes based on their data type. Although specific to MSXML 4.0, this is a perfectly common practice among various processors (within XSLT, for example) and provides fall-back methods when a given parser does not support an extension. These extensions are associated with a namespace specific to the parser so they can be ignored by parsers not supporting the given namespace (and hence functionality). Additionally, XSLT provides the `<fallback>` element, which allows you to tell the parser what to do when it doesn't support a given extension.

These extensions can be divided into two broad sections. The first provides support for the XML Schemas Recommendation (XSD), and the second covers some miscellaneous functions for working with data types.

Whatever functions you are using, they must use a qualified name. You are free to declare the prefix yourself, but the value of the namespace is fixed as `"urn:schemas-microsoft-com:xslt"`. So, a namespace declaration could be `xmlns:ms="urn:schemas-microsoft-com:xslt"`.

In a stylesheet this would be defined as follows:

```
<xsl:stylesheet xmlns:xsl="http://www.w3.org/1999/XSL/Transform"
                xmlns:ms="urn:schemas-microsoft-com:xslt"
                version="1.0">
```

Alternatively, when used in the DOM, this would be declared as follows:

```
objDoc.setProperty("SelectionNamespaces", "xmlns:ms='urn:schemas-microsoft-
                com:xslt'")
```

Firstly, those targeting XSD are as follows.

ms:type-is(URI, local-name)

This extension function compares the data type of the current node with the XSD data type specified in the arguments. The URI specifies the namespace URI for the data type and the local-name is the name excluding the prefix of the data type.

Note also that not only will a match occur on a given data type, but also any XSD-derived types from that type. So a match on a `string` type will also match `normalizedString`, `token`, and other types derived from `string`. The same applies for other types.

So, the following example will match any node that is an integer type or any XSD type derived from `integer`, such as `nonPositiveInteger`:

```
ms:type-is("www.w3.org/2001/XMLSchema","integer")
```

The following will match only `nonPositiveInteger` types (or types derived thereof), but not all integer types:

```
ms:type-is("www.w3.org/2001/XMLSchema","nonPositiveInteger")
```

ms:type-local-name([node-set])

This method returns the unqualified XSD type of the current node or first node in document order in the `node-set` argument. If no argument is provided, then the context node is evaluated.

This function will return the XSD type for simple types, such as integer, string, and ID. More complex types that use the `name` attribute in defining the XSD class will return the name of the class.

The following expression would return all child nodes of the context node that are defined as a `nonNegativeInteger` XSD type:

```
"./*[ms:type-local-name()='nonNegativeInteger']"
```

ms:type-namespace-uri([node-set])

This method complements the `ms:type-local-name()` function and returns the namespace URI of the current node or first node in document order in the `node-set` argument. If no argument is provided, then the context node is evaluated.

This function will return an empty string for simple types, such as integer, string, and ID. More complex types that use the `name` attribute in defining the XSD class will return the URI that they are defined in.

The following expression would return all child nodes of the context node that have been defined as custom user types in the namespace "`http://www.deltabis.com/xsd-types`":

```
"./*[ms:type-namespace-uri()='http://www.deltabis.com/xsd-types']"
```

ms:schema-info-available()

This function simply returns `true` if the XSD type information is available for the current node. You may have an instance with an associated XSD Schema in a given namespace. If you then add another namespace to the instance document and create elements, but don't associate an XSD Schema with this namespace, then this would return `false` for `ms:schema-info-available()` whereas the default namespace associated with the XSD Schema will return `true`.

Several miscellaneous functions (in other words not targeted specifically at XSLT or Schemas) are discussed below.

ms:string-compare(string1, string2, language, options)

This function compares two strings lexicographically, that is, in the order in which they would normally appear in a dictionary.

It compares `string1` and `string2` (non-string values are converted to strings before evaluation) based on the sort order as the strings would appear in the `language` parameter ("en-us", for example) – if this parameter is empty then it defaults to the system environment language.

There are two `options`. The first, "u", changes the default of case-sensitive with lowercase first to case-sensitive with uppercase first. The second option, "i", performs a case-insensitive comparison, with the order not affected by the case.

If `string1` is before `string2` then it returns –1. If `string1` is lexicographically equal to `string2` then it returns 0. Finally, if `string1` is after `string2` then the value 1 is returned. For example, consider the following results:

- ❏   `ms:string-compare("10","11","en-US")` returns –1

- ❏   `ms:string-compare("11","11","en-US")` returns 0

- ❏   `ms:string-compare("11","10","en-US")` returns 1

- ❏   `ms:string-compare("a","a","en-US")` returns 0

- ❏   `ms:string-compare("a","A","en-US")` returns –1

- ❏   `ms:string-compare("a","A","en-US","u")` returns 1

- ❏   `ms:string-compare("a","A","en-US","i")` returns 0

- ❏   `ms:string-compare("ç","Ç","es","i")` returns 0

- ❏   `ms:string-compare("ç","Ç","es","u")` returns 1

ms:utc(string)

This function is used to convert date and time values into coordinated universal time, UTC, which can be sorted and compared lexicographically using the `ms:string-compare()` function.

The `string` parameter should be a time-related XSD type and is then converted, with the UTC date time returned as:

```
CCYY-MO-DDTHH:MM:SS:mmm
```

This is an ISO 8601 abbreviated date where CC is the century, YY is the years, MO the month, DD the day, T is a separator, HH is the hours, MM the minutes, SS the seconds, and finally mmm the milliseconds, with optional time part and time zone. For example, "2001-09-25T07:27:59-11:00" which means that the time given (after T) is 11 hours behind Universal Coordinated time (UTC). You can also write this as "2001-09-24T18:27:59Z" where the Z indicates the time is with respect to UTC and so the 11 hours difference defined above is taken away from the local time (just after the T).

ms:namespace-uri(string)

This takes a qualified string and returns the URI of the prefix.

So, if the following namespace had been defined in the source document:

```
xmlns:ns="http://www.citix.com/ns"
```

when the qualified element `<ns:myElement/>` was passed to the `ms:namespace()` function, it would return `http://www.citix.com/ns`.

ms:local-name(string)

This returns the non-qualified (without prefix or namespace qualification) name of the XSD type of the current node or the first node in document order in the provided node-set.

So to return all node-types with the built-in XSD type `integer` and any other types that have an unqualified representation as `integer` you would have the following:

```
//*[ms:type-local-name()='integer')]"
```

Similarly, the following would return all elements in the document with the custom type (simple or complex) that has the qualified name "mytype:postcode":

```
//*[ms:type-local-name()='postcode')]"
```

ms:number(string)

This function takes an XSD number and converts it to an XPath number. It is very similar to the XPath `number()` function, but consider the following differences.

Firstly, the XPath `number()` function works as follows:

- ❑   `number(5.92)` returns `5.92`
- ❑   `number(-5.92)` returns `-5.92`
- ❑   `number("5.92")` returns `5.92`
- ❑   `number("5.9e5")` returns `NaN`
- ❑   `number("5.9e-5")` returns `NaN`
- ❑   `number("")` returns `NaN`

Whereas the MSXML extension `number()` function can convert mathematical notation into numbers rather than `NaN`. It works as follows:

- ❑   `ms:number(5.92)` returns `5.92`
- ❑   `ms:number(-5.92)` returns `-5.92`
- ❑   `ms:number("5.92")` returns `5.92`
- ❑   `ms:number("5.9e5")` returns `5.9e5`
- ❑   `ms:number("5.9e-5")` returns `5.9e-5`
- ❑   `ms:number("")` returns `NaN`

ms:format-date(datetime, format, locale)

This function takes an XSD date-related value in the parameter `datetime` and converts it to the format defined in `format`. The restriction on the format parameter is as defined in the Win32 API `GetDateFormat()` function. Finally, the optional `locale` parameter defines the locale to use for formatting the date, "EN_us", for example.

> *The `GetDateFormat()` function is discussed at the following URL:*
> http://msdn.microsoft.com/library/default.asp?url=/library/en-us/dnintl/html/s24b4_a.asp

So, to convert the date "2000-09-25" to the format "Tue, Sep 25 01" you would use this function as follows:

```
ms:format-date("2000-09-25", "ddd",' MMM dd yy","en_us")
```

ms:format-time(datetime, format, locale)

This function works in a similar way to the one above, but converts XSD-related times to a given format. The restriction on the format parameter is as defined in the Win32 API GetTimeFormat() function. Finally, the optional locale parameter defines the locale to use for formatting the date, such as "en_us" and defaults to the system locale.

So, to convert the time "14:27:02" to the format "2:27:02 PM" you would use this function as follows:

```
ms:format-time("14:27:02", "hh':'mm':'ss tt","en_us")
```

Worked Example XPath Expressions

This section is going to look at worked examples using XPath. These samples are based on MSXML 4.0 and so use version-dependent ProgIDs ("Msxml2.DOMDocument.4.0") – however, you can change this to work with other versions of MSXML down to MSXML version 2.6; although note that with the exception of msxsl:script, the extension functions are part of MSXML 4.0 and above only.

The worked examples are provided via a sample application that is included with the download files for this chapter, so let's first look at that.

The Sample Application

A fragment of the XML source document, catalog.xml, is shown below. It details a simple catalog of items available from a business:

```
<?xml version="1.0" ?>
<CatalogFamily xmlns="http://tempuri.org/catalog.xsd"
               xmlns:xsi="http://www.w3.org/2001/XMLSchema-instance"
               xsi:schemaLocation="
                             http://tempuri.org/catalog.xsd catalog.xsd">
   <Company email="info@sightkeys.org"
            buyersURI="http://www.sightkeys.org/buyers/" sellerAuth="322" />
   <ProductFamily familyID="pftops" LastUpdate="2001-08-26T18:39:09"
                  buyersURI="http://www.sightkeys.org/buyers/tops">
      <Product ProductID="CFC3" items="34">
         <colour>green</colour>
         <size>M</size>
         <price>31.99</price>
         <colour>green</colour>
         <size>L</size>
         <price>45.99</price>
      </Product>
      <Product ProductID="CFC4">
         <colour>black</colour>
         <size>L</size>
```

```
            <price>32.99</price>
        </Product>
    </ProductFamily>

    ...other ProductFamily elements
</CatalogFamily>
```

You can see that this references the XSD Schema file `catalog.xsd` and has the default namespace of `"http://tempuri.org/catalog.xsd"`. We don't discuss the XSD Schema in any detail in this chapter as the intention is to focus on XPath – it is a good idea, however, that you read and understand it with the knowledge you gained in the Schemas chapter. We will be discussing the parts of the Schema that are important to the examples when we look at them below.

Another important file to look at is `expressions.xml` – this contains all of the XPath expressions we are going to work with and dynamically populates the user interface page. A fragment of this file is shown below:

```xml
<?xml version="1.0" encoding="utf-8" ?>
<expr>
    <ex id="1">
        <context>/</context>
        <desc>
            Selects the child node of the root,
            which is the CatalogFamily element node
        </desc>
        <abb>./*</abb>
        <unabb>child::*</unabb>
    </ex>
    <ex id="2">
        <context>/ns:CatalogFamily</context>
        <desc>
            Selects the three ProductFamily
            child nodes of the document element
        </desc>
        <abb>./ns:ProductFamily</abb>
        <unabb>child::ns:ProductFamily</unabb>
    </ex>
    ...
</expr>
```

The document element `<expr>` element contains twelve `<ex>` child nodes, which are the expressions, each numbered sequentially with the `id` attribute. Each child node contains a `<context>` element containing an XPath expression that will set the context for the example, a `<desc>` node with a description of the sample, an `<abb>` element that contains the abbreviated form of the example, and finally an `<unabb>` element containing the unabbreviated format of the expression.

Finally, the user interface brings all of these files together as a DOM implementation using JavaScript. The full source for this file, `catalog.htm`, is shown below and then discussed.

The key to the population of the page is in the `onload()` function, which calls the `LoadVals()` method to retrieve the XPath expressions from the example file `expressions.xml`:

```
<body onload="LoadVals()">
```

```
<html>
    <head>
        <title>Catalog</title>
```

The `LoadVals()` method loads and parses the `expressions.xml` file and sets its `SelectionLanguage` property to "XPath". This is not necessary in MSXML 4.0 as XPath is the default, but it makes it easier for you to run the sample on lower versions of MSXML, which use the default XSL Patterns syntax.

```javascript
<script language="javascript">
    <!--
function LoadVals()
{
   var xmlDoc1 = new ActiveXObject("Msxml2.DOMDocument.4.0");
   xmlDoc1.async = false;
   xmlDoc1.setProperty("SelectionLanguage","XPath");
   bol = xmlDoc1.load("expressions.xml");
```

Next, the `<ex>` element nodes are selected using the XPath expression "`//ex`":

```javascript
   var strExp="";
   var objNodes=xmlDoc1.selectNodes("//ex");
```

We then iterate through the nodes of this node-set and create a string containing the value of the `<context>`, `<abb>`, and `<unabb>` elements, delimited by the "`$`" character:

```javascript
   for (i=0;i<objNodes.length;i++)
   {
      strExp=objNodes[i].childNodes[0].text
         + "$" + objNodes[i].childNodes[3].text
         + "$" + objNodes[i].childNodes[2].text;
```

Finally, an `<option>` element is created and added to the **XPath Expression** drop-down list. Its display value is composed of the ID number assigned to the expression and its description. Its value is the dollar-delimited string we created above:

```javascript
      var oOption = document.createElement("option");
      document.all("XPathVals").add(oOption);
      oOption.innerText = objNodes[i].getAttribute("id")
                        + ". " + objNodes[i].childNodes[1].text;
      oOption.value = strExp;
   }
}
```

Now, the user can interact with the interface and does so by choosing the appropriate XPath expression from the drop-down list. This change triggers a screen update by calling the method `PopXPath()`, shown below. This method first gets the value of the XPath query selected and puts it into an array. It then sets the "context" textbox with the context expression and determines whether to set the abbreviated or unabbreviated XPath expression depending on whether the checkbox is checked:

```javascript
function PopXPath()
{
   document.all("results").innerHTML="";
   var val = document.all("XPathVals").value;

   var arrVals = val.split("$");
   document.all("context").value=arrVals[0];
```

```
        if (document.all("AbbCheck").checked==false)
            document.all("xpath").value=arrVals[1];
        else
            document.all("xpath").value=arrVals[2];
    }
```

Following this, the query is executed by clicking the **Query** button, which invokes the method XPathQuery(). This method first retrieves the file, XPath query, and XPath context expression from the page:

```
function XPathQuery()
{
    var strXMLFile = document.all("xpathfile").value;
    var strXML = document.all("xpath").value;
    var strContext=document.all("context").value;
```

Next, the catalog.xml source file is loaded and parsed into the DOM:

```
    var xmlDoc = new ActiveXObject("Msxml2.DOMDocument.4.0");
    xmlDoc.async = false;
    xmlDoc.validateOnParse=true;
    strXMLxmlDoc.load(strXMLFile);
```

After XPath has been set as the selection language, we also have to set the SelectionNamespaces property so that we can qualify our XPath selections with the namespaces in the source document. In our case, we associate the prefix "ns" with the source document default namespace of http://tempuri.org/catalog.xsd. To use the MSXML 4.0 extension functions, we must also associate the prefix "ms" with the URI urn:schemas-microsoft-com:xslt.

```
    xmlDoc.setProperty("SelectionLanguage","XPath");
    xmlDoc.setProperty("SelectionNamespaces",
                    "xmlns:ns='http://tempuri.org/catalog.xsd'
                    xmlns:ms='urn:schemas-microsoft-com:xslt'");
```

Next, we first set the context node by executing the "context" XPath expression, which returns a single node. Following this, we use this as the context to execute the XPath query on the document:

```
    var objContext = xmlDoc.documentElement;
    objContext = objContext.selectSingleNode(strContext);
    var objNodes = objContext.selectNodes(strXML);

    document.all("results").innerHTML="";
```

Finally, we iterate through each of the nodes returned in the node-set and call the Display() method, discussed next:

```
    for (i=0;i<objNodes.length;i++)
        Display(objNodes[i]);
    }
```

The Display() method gets the XML from the node, and the XML is appended to the existing content for display to the user:

```
      function Display(objNode)
      {
         var strXML = objNode.xml;

         document.all("results").text += strXML + "\n";
      }

   //--></script>
      </head>
      <body onload="LoadVals()">
      ...
      </body>
   </html>
```

The resulting application is shown below:

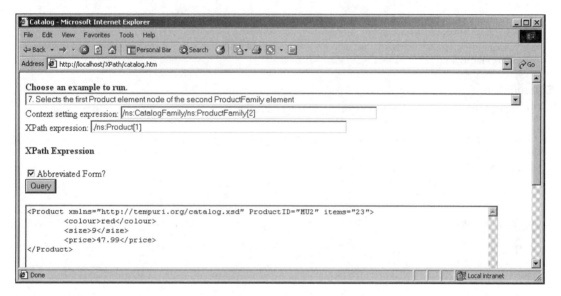

To use the application, select an example from the drop-down list – the context setting and XPath expressions will appear in the textboxes beneath. You can choose to view them in abbreviated form, and see the result by pressing the Query button.

We have now discussed the application, which itself makes significant use of XPath. Let's move on with the XPath examples.

XPath Examples

Each of the examples below is numbered the same as in the drop-down box. We won't write out the results here as some are lengthy, but running the application will allow you to modify the expressions to see how XPath works for yourself.

Example 1

Selects the child node of the root, which is the CatalogFamily element node.

Context: /

Abbreviated Syntax: ./*

Unabbreviated Syntax: child::*

Example 2

Selects the three ProductFamily child nodes of the document element.

Context: /ns:CatalogFamily

Abbreviated Syntax: ./ns:ProductFamily

Unabbreviated Syntax: child::ns:ProductFamily

Example 3

Selects all product element nodes in the first ProductFamily.

Context: /ns:CatalogFamily/ns:ProductFamily[1]

Abbreviated Syntax: .//ns:Product

Unabbreviated Syntax: descendant-or-self::ns:Product

Example 4

Selects all text nodes of the colour element first Product element node, which should return the color "green".

Context: /ns:CatalogFamily/ns:ProductFamily[1]/ns:Product[1]/ns:colour

Abbreviated Syntax: ./text()

Unabbreviated Syntax: child::text()

Example 5

Returns a three node node-set containing the familyID attributes of all the ProductFamily element nodes.

Context: /ns:CatalogFamily

Abbreviated Syntax: ns:ProductFamily/@familyID

Unabbreviated Syntax: child::ns:ProductFamily/attribute::familyID

Example 6

Selects the last `Product` element node of the first `ProductFamily` element.

Context: `/ns:CatalogFamily/ns:ProductFamily[1]`

Abbreviated Syntax: `./ns:Product[position()=last()]`

Unabbreviated Syntax: `child::ns:Product[position()=last()]`

Example 7

Selects the first `Product` element node of the second `ProductFamily` element.

Context: `/ns:CatalogFamily/ns:ProductFamily[2]`

Abbreviated Syntax: `./ns:Product[1]`

Unabbreviated Syntax: `child::ns:Product[position()=1]`

Example 8

Selects the `LastUpdate` attribute of the `colour` context node.

Context: `/ns:CatalogFamily/ns:ProductFamily[3]/ns:Product[1]/ns:colour`

Abbreviated Syntax: `../../../ns:ProductFamily[3]/@LastUpdate`

Unabbreviated Syntax: `ancestor::ns:ProductFamily/attribute::LastUpdate`

Example 9

Selects a particular `productID` sub-family (two) elements based on the product ID name starting with "`MU`" from the entire document.

Context: `/ns:CatalogFamily`

Abbreviated Syntax: `.//ns:Product[starts-with(@ProductID,"MU")]`

Unabbreviated Syntax: `descendant-or-self::ns:Product[starts-with(attribute::ProductID,"MU")]`

Example 10

This returns the `ProductFamily` elements that have less than 50 items in their inventory.

Context: `/ns:CatalogFamily`

Abbreviated Syntax: `./ns:ProductFamily[sum(Product/@items)<50]`

Unabbreviated Syntax: `ns:ProductFamily[sum(child::Product/attribute::items)<50]`

Example 11

Returns all elements in the document that are derived from the XSD string type.

Context: /

Abbreviated Syntax: `//*[ms:type-is('http://www.w3.org/2001/XMLSchema','string')]`

Unabbreviated Syntax: `descendant-or-self::*[ms:type-is('http://www.w3.org/2001/XMLSchema','string')]`

This will return an individual `<size>` element – to understand where this comes from, examine the `<size>` element as in the XSD (`catalog.xsd`) as follows:

```
<xsd:element name="size" type="maxsizes" />
```

The `maxsizes` type is defined as follows:

```
<xsd:simpleType name="maxsizes">
    <xsd:restriction base="xsd:string">
        <xsd:minLength value="1" />
        <xsd:maxLength value="2" />
    </xsd:restriction>
</xsd:simpleType>
```

As you can see, this type is based on the built-in XSD `string` type and hence the `size` element will also be based on this type.

Example 12

Returns all element and attribute nodes in the source that are associated with the XSD Schema namespace "`http://tempuri.org/catalog.xsd`".

Context: /

Abbreviated Syntax: `//*[ms:namespace-uri(.)='http://tempuri.org/catalog.xsd']` | `//@*[ms:namespace-uri(.)='http://tempuri.org/catalog.xsd']`

Unabbreviated Syntax: `descendant-or-self::*[ms:namespace-uri(self::node())='http://tempuri.org/catalog.xsd']` | `descendant-or-self::attribute[ms:namespace-uri(self::node())='http://tempuri.org/catalog.xsd']`

In this sample, this is not an essential function because we explicitly defined the namespace in our `SelectionNamespaces` property. However, if this had not been done, then this method would be the only way of getting the namespace association for a node.

Example 13

Returns all attribute nodes that are based on the `dateTime` XSD type and are on the "23 November, 2001".

Context: /

Abbreviated Syntax:
`//@*[ms:type-is('http://www.w3.org/2001/XMLSchema','dateTime') and (ms:format-date(., 'dd MMMM, yyyy')='23 November, 2001')]`

Unabbreviated Syntax:
`descendant::node()/attribute::*[ms:type-is('http://www.w3.org/2001/XMLSchema','dateTime') and (ms:format-date(self::node(), 'dd MMMM, yyyy')='23 November, 2001')]`

This will return an individual `LastUpdate` attribute. This is because the `LastUpdate` attribute is the only attribute based on the `dateTime` built-in XSD data datatype:

```
<xsd:attribute name="LastUpdate" type="xsd:dateTime" use="required" />
```

Therefore the first test is that attributes are of this type and as most of them are not, the boolean "and" stops at the first evaluation. When it is of type `dateTime`, the context node, which has it's date and time in XSD standard format "2001-11-26T18:39:09" is re-formatted using the `ms:format-date` function and compared against the string "23 November, 2001". This is true for only one node and so this is the only one returned.

Dynamic Form Generation

> The sample code for this application can be found in the "`Form`" directory of the download for this chapter. You will need access to a web server to run the ASP page, although otherwise this isn't necessary.

One of the most mundane tasks for writing web applications is often the creaton of the user and administrator input pages where the application data is initially entered – how many web applications have beautiful user interfaces and impossible (if not manual) administrator and maintenance interfaces! It is very common to have almost no client validation and a lot of server validation hence putting stress on the server or vice-versa making for ineffective business rules on the server. Usually this is due to time and resource constraints and often one is chosen over the other based on preferred skills. It would be ideal if we could see the benefits of XML Schema, which will be at the heart of almost all data-oriented XML applications to also generate much of the web page creation and business rule validation that takes us 80% of the time to create. With the power of XML Schemas and the flexibility of XPath combined with the DOM, we can generate much of this work on either the client of the server.

In this final practical example of working with XPath, we are going to show how it can be combined with the other XML technologies such as DOM and XML Schema to dynamically create an HTML input form with validation checks when the user enter values. We will demonstrate how it is relatively simple to use this practice client- or server-side with almost no change in the code to successfully use XML Schema, XPath, and DOM as front- or back-end technology for dynamic web applications.

Although we will primarily look at the client, a server-side example is also provided and there is no reason why much of the business rules in server-side scripting couldn't be dynamically generated too. Please remember this is an example of what can be done and not "Wrox XPath Generator 2001", hence it would need quite a bit of work to deal with many real-world applications. However the techniques used here can easily be built upon to create a very effective framework.

A description of the files making up the example form is shown below (note that the catalog XML Schema used for this sample is a simpler version of catalog.xsd we worked with earlier):

❑ catalog.xsd – XML Schema file containing constraints for catalog XML instances.

❑ newcatalog.xsd – advanced XML Schema file containing constraints for catalog XML instances.

❑ catalog.htm – user interface based on DHTML.

❑ catalog.asp – user interface based on ASP.

❑ formgen.inc – core functions for dynamic generation on the client and server.

How does it Work?

To run the client-side form generation program, run the file catalog.htm from the Form directory. A drop-down list shows the samples for this chapter; so leave this as the default **Example1** and click the **Create Latest Form** button, which will dynamically generate a list of input boxes (three in this case). Each input has validation assigned to it automatically, and you can see this if you click in the **CompanyName** box and then move from it without entering any information – you will get the error message: **You must have a value for CompanyName**. Now, enter the following values into the form – note that after each you may get a message box indicating that the value you have entered is invalid (don't enter the quotes!).

❑ CompanyName – "Panda Productions"
❑ email – "steven@deltabis.com"
❑ buyersID – "ID672"

You will now have some errors. The first value will enter fine, but the e-mail address causes problems as the workers at this fictitious company use their NT logon IDs as well as stating whether they are internal or corporate ("internal" or "corp") users and then the fictional domain name "catcorp" and then finally their location (".com" or ".co.uk"). The value given didn't fit this, so you get an error – if you tried this more than three times we apologize, and although you may hate us, at least you have seen an example of sophisticated dynamic validation!

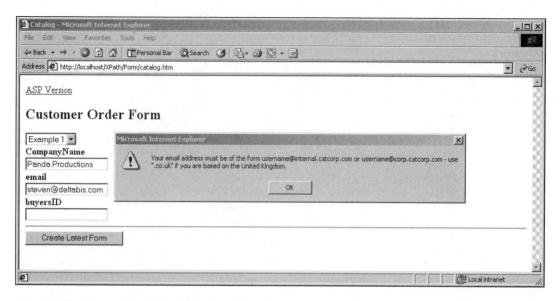

Finally, the buyersID will also have failed because policy has it that these must be integer values and so "ID" causes a validation error. Let's look at the code to see what is going on in the background.

Code Behind

The XML Schema file catalog.xsd stores the constraints for any XML Schema that is to be created for a catalog within the business. It effectively contains the business rules for the data types and data constraints that can be used. This file is shown below:

```
<?xml version="1.0" encoding="utf-8" ?>
<xsd:schema targetNamespace="http://tempuri.org/catalog.xsd"
            elementFormDefault="qualified"
            xmlns="http://tempuri.org/catalog.xsd"
            xmlns:xsd="http://www.w3.org/2001/XMLSchema">
    <xsd:element name="CatalogFamily">
        <xsd:complexType>
            <xsd:sequence>
                <xsd:element ref="Company"/>
            </xsd:sequence>
        </xsd:complexType>
    </xsd:element>
    <xsd:element name="Company">
        <xsd:complexType>
            <xsd:sequence>
                <xsd:element name="CompanyName" type="xsd:string" />
                <xsd:element name="email" type="emailAddress" />
            </xsd:sequence>
            <xsd:attribute name="buyersID" type="xsd:integer" />
        </xsd:complexType>
    </xsd:element>
    <xsd:simpleType name="emailAddress">
        <xsd:restriction base="xsd:string">
            <xsd:pattern value="[A-Za-z]{5}@((internal)|(corp))
                                \.catcorp\.((com)|(co.uk))" />
```

```
            <xsd:annotation>
                <xsd:appinfo>
                    Your email address must be of the form
                    username@internal.catcorp.com or
                    username@corp.catcorp.com - use \".co.uk\" if you are
                    based on the United Kingdom.
                </xsd:appinfo>
            </xsd:annotation>
        </xsd:restriction>
    </xsd:simpleType>
</xsd:schema>
```

It is a fairly simple schema with a root <CatalogFamily> element, which currently contains a single child reference to a <Company> element. The global definition of the <Company> element has an anonymous complex type child, which is composed of a sequence of two elements and an attribute. The first element is <CompanyName> where valid data type is a built-in string type and the second element is <email> whose type is the custom emailAddress simpleType definition; the attribute is buyersID, which must be an integer type. Finally the <emailAddress> simpleType is based on the restriction of a string type, and uses a regular expression pattern to limit the valid values for the type (as was discussed above). Additionally there is an annotation and appInfo definition with some information that is used by the application, as we will see shortly.

The user interface page catalog.htm is discussed below and is not overly complex either. The global variable strResult is used to hold the HTML that is written out to the screen and is gradually built up during the script.

```
<html>
    <head>
        <title>Catalog</title>
        <script language="javascript">
                var strResult="";
```

The only method explicitly declared within the document is the UpdateDisplay() method, which performs client interface updates. The submit event is first canceled as we handle updates using DHTML directly. There are two directions after this – if a display update has been passed in strNewDisplay, then this is inserted into the xsdForm <div> element and the global variable set to empty again. Otherwise, we are assuming the user has just clicked to create the interface and so the <div> is cleared of the previous form creation and the LoadXSD() method called, which is discussed below and is included by the JavaScript script element including the formgen.inc file.

```
        function UpdateDisplay(strNewDisplay)
        {
            window.event.returnValue=false;
            if (strNewDisplay!="")
            {
                document.all("xsdForm").insertAdjacentHTML(
                    "beforeEnd",strNewDisplay);
                strResult="";
            }
            else
            {
                var XSDFile = document.all("xsdfile").value;
                document.all("xsdForm").innerHTML="";
```

```
            LoadXSD(XSDFile);
        }
    }
    </script>
    <script language="javascript" src="formgen.inc"></script>
</head>
```

Finally, the `<form>` itself consists of a title, `<select>` element containing the examples available, the `xsdForm` `<div>` element where the interface is created, and finally a `submit` button with an `onclick` handler. The `onclick` actually uses a 'try...catch' statement – this is not strictly necessary in the client-side version, but we want this code to work server side with limited code changes and because there is no `onclick` event handler in the server-side version, the call to `UpdateDisplay()` would cause an error without the `try...catch` around it.

```
<body>
    <a href="catalog.asp">ASP Version</a>
    <form ID="orderform">
        <h2>
            Customer Order Form
        </h2>
        <select id="XSDfile" name="xsdfile">
            <option value="catalog.xsd">
                Example 1</option>
            <option value="newcatalog.xsd">
                Example 2</option></select>
        <div id="xsdForm">
        </div>
        <hr>
        <input type="submit"
                onclick="try {UpdateDisplay('')} catch(e){};"
                value="Create Latest Form" />
    </form>
</body>
</html>
```

The core functionality is provided by the JavaScript include file and the important parts of this file are discussed below. The `LoadXSD()` method initially loads the XSD file that is passed in (from the `<select>`) and sets the `SelectionNamespaces` property to use the `ns` prefix for the document namespace, the `xsd` prefix for the XML Schema namespace, and the *ms* prefix for the Microsoft extension functions prefix. Next from the `documentElement` a `selectNodes` is called with the `xsd:element` XPath expression returning the immediate `xsd:element` child nodes. Finally each element child node is iterated through and the `ProcessChild()` method is called passing in the immediate child node of the `xsd:element` definition.

```
var xmlDoc = "";
function LoadXSD(XSDFilePath)
{
    xmlDoc = new ActiveXObject("Msxml2.DOMDocument.4.0");
    xmlDoc.async = false;
    xmlDoc.validateOnParse=true;
    bol = xmlDoc.load(XSDFilePath);

    xmlDoc.setProperty("SelectionLanguage","XPath");
    xmlDoc.setProperty("SelectionNamespaces",
                "xmlns:ns='http://tempuri.org/catalog.xsd'
```

173

```
                              xmlns:xsd='http://www.w3.org/2001/XMLSchema'
                              xmlns:ms='urn:schemas-microsoft-com:xslt'");

         var xmlDocEl = xmlDoc.documentElement;
         //Global Element Declarations
         var objGlobalEls = xmlDocEl.selectNodes("xsd:element");

         for (i=0;i<objGlobalEls.length;i++)
         {
            if (objGlobalEls[i].hasChildNodes())
               ProcessChild(objGlobalEls[i].childNodes[0]);
         }
      }
```

The `ProcessChild()` method processes this child node that has been passed in and determines the `baseName` property to route the processing to the appropriate handler.

```
function ProcessChild(objNode)
{
   switch (objNode.baseName)
   {
      case "element" : ProcessElement(objNode);break;
      case "attribute" : ProcessAttribute(objNode);break;
      case "complexType" : ProcessComplexType(objNode);break;
      case "sequence" :   ProcessSequence(objNode);break;
      case "restriction" : ProcessRestriction(objNode);break;
      case "pattern" : ProcessPattern(objNode);break;
   }
}
```

We won't discuss all of the handlers here as you can look at these in the code. The first of these is `ProcessElement()`, which sets the `strScript` global variable to empty – this is useful because it allows multiple validation parts to be inserted into the final code.

```
function ProcessElement(objNode)
{
   //Reset this global variable
   strScript="";
```

The first test checks if the element definition is a reference definition to some global element by checking the `ref` attribute value. If this is set, then an XPath expression returns the global element definition with the name of the reference attribute and the node is selected and the `ProcessElement()` method is called again to process this global element definition.

```
         //Is it a reference node?
         if (objNode.getAttribute("ref")!=null)
         {
            strXPath = "xsd:element[@name='"
                    + objNode.getAttribute("ref") + "']";
            var objNewNode = xmlDoc.documentElement.selectSingleNode(strXPath);
            ProcessElement(objNewNode);
            return;
         }
```

If however the `type` attribute is defined then the element is processed directly with the name of the element stored in the `strName` variable, later used to give the `<form>` element a name in the user interface. A test is then done to see if it is a built-in type (starts with the `xsd` prefix) or whether it a custom type. In the first case, the `GetFormElement()` method is called to get back the HTML element for this data type (such as `<text>` for `xsd:string`) and then the `InsertValidation()` method is called to associate some validation with the HTML element (such as validate a value has been entered). One this is done, any child elements (such as anonymous `complexType` definitions) are again processed.

```
if (objNode.getAttribute("type")!=null)
{
    strName = objNode.getAttribute("name");

    //Is built-in type
    if (objNode.getAttribute("type").indexOf("xsd:")>-1)
    {
        var strHTMLEl = GetFormElement(objNode.getAttribute("type"));
        InsertValidation("<b>"  + strName + "</b><br>"
                            + strHTMLEl,strName);

        //Are there more sibling element nodes?
        if (objNode.nextSibling!=null)
            ProcessElement(objNode.nextSibling)
    }
```

If the type is a custom type, then this is retrieved via an XPath statement (currently works only for `simpleType` elements) and the `ProcessSimpleType()` method is called.

```
    else
    {
        strXPath = "xsd:simpleType[@name='"
                    + objNode.getAttribute("type") + "']";
        var objNewNode = xmlDoc.documentElement.
                        selectSingleNode(strXPath);
        ProcessSimpleType(objNewNode);
    }
}

return;
}
```

The `GetFormElement()` is a useful method that creates an HTML element for a given XSD base type and also associates some validation with this element. This is currently implemented for the built-in `string` and `integer` types, but is easily extensible.

```
function GetFormElement(strType)
{
    var strHTMLEl;

    switch (strType)
    {
        case "xsd:string" :
        {
            strHTMLEl="<input type=\"text\" name=\"" + strName
                    + "\" onblur=\"validate_" + strName + "(this)\">";
            strScript += "if (obj.value=='') alert('You must have
```

```
                                 a value for " + strName + ".');";
                strScript += "\n";
                break;
            }
            case "xsd:integer" :
            {
                strHTMLEl="<input type=\"text\" name=\"" + strName
                            + "\" onblur=\"validate_" + strName + "(this)\">";
                strScript += "if (isNaN(obj.value)) alert('The value
                            for " + strName + " must be an integer.');";
                strScript += "\n";
                break;
            }
        }

        return strHTMLEl;
    }
```

The `ProcessPattern()` method is invoked whenever an `<xsd:pattern>` element is found in the Schema. This defines a regular expression and so some script is dynamically created to generate a regular expression object with the matching pattern entered from the value attribute of the `<xsd:pattern>` element. Furthermore, if the `<xsd:annotation>` element is the next sibling element then we have decided to put the pattern validation information in here so it can be displayed to the user – this is better than some generic error message. The error message is actually stored in the `<xsd:appinfo>` element. Finally, the appropriate HTML element is created using the `GetFormElement()` method using the parent base type and the appropriate validation information inserted.

```
function ProcessPattern(objNode)
{
    strScript += "var re = new RegExp('"
                    + objNode.getAttribute("value") + "');\n";
    strScript += "var r = (obj.value).match(re);\n";

    if (objNode.nextSibling.baseName=="annotation")
        strErrorMessage = objNode.nextSibling.text;

    strScript += "if (r==null) alert('" + strErrorMessage + "');";
    strScript += "\n";

    var strHTMLEl = GetFormElement(objNode.parentNode
                                    .getAttribute("base"));
    InsertValidation("<b>"  + strName + "</b><br>"
                    + strHTMLEl,strName);
}
```

The final method we have to look at is the `InsertValidation()` method, which dynamically inserts JavaScript into the output. Note that because this script is dynamically inserted into the HTML document, the `defer` attribute must be used. Each validation function is given the name `"validate_"` plus the name of the element or attribute that is being validated (for example, `"validate_CompanyName"`). When this is complete, the entire HTML with the associated script is passed to the `UpdateDisplay()` method, which we discussed above.

```
function InsertValidation(strHTML, strFName)
{
    var sScript='SCRIPT defer>'
```

```
          sScript = sScript + 'function validate_' + strFName
                   + '(obj){' +strScript + ' }'
          sScript = sScript + '</script' + '>';

          strResult += strHTML + "<br><" + sScript;
          UpdateDisplay(strResult)
     }
```

An example of the HTML code produced by this process is shown below; specifically the code for the e-mail validation is shown.

```
<html>
<head>
   <title>Catalog</title>
</head>
<body>
   ...
<b>email</b>
<br>
<input type="text" name="email" onblur="validate_email(this)" >
<br>
<script defer>
   function validate_email(obj)
   { var re = new
     RegExp('[A-Za-z]{5}@((internal)|(corp))\.catcorp\.((com)|(co.uk))');
     var r = (obj.value).match(re);

     if (r==null)
        alert('Your email address must be of the
                form username@internal.catcorp.com
                or username@corp.catcorp.com - use \".co.uk\"
                if you are based on the United Kingdom.');

        if (obj.value=='')
           alert('You must have a value for email.');
   }
</script>
   ...
</html>
```

You will see that in the **SELECT** drop-down box, there is a reference to **Example 2**; this is simply a slightly more complex XML Schema that adds an element and attribute definition to the `catalog.xsd` Schema and runs it through the above script to dynamically generate the output. This is simply to demonstrate the reusability of the script.

Furthermore, a server-side implementation is available by clicking on the **ASP Version** `catalog.asp` link at the top of the page and does all the work with XML on the server to provide better cross-browser compatibility. There are almost no changes required to the original DHTML version to make this work server-side.

Firstly, some server-side script is added to get the name of the XSD file to work with, posted by the SELECT item, and the server-side `UpdateDisplay()` method is called.

```
<%@Language="JScript"%>
<%
   var strResult="";
   if (Request.QueryString.Count>0)
      UpdateDisplay("");
%>
```

The server-side version of UpdateDisplay() is almost identical to the client-version, but a runat="server" attribute is assed to the <script> element and the XSD file is obtained from the QueryString and then the Server.MapPath() method passed the full physical path to the LoadXSD() method.

```
<script language="JScript" runat="server">
    function UpdateDisplay(strNewDisplay)
    {
        if (strNewDisplay!="")
            strResult=strNewDisplay;
        else
        {
            var XSDFile = Request.QueryString("XSDfile");
            strResult="";

            LoadXSD(Server.MapPath(XSDFile));
        }
    }
</script>
```

From there, the only difference is in the HTML <div> section, which simply outputs the value of the strResult server side global variable.

```
...
<div id="xsdForm">
    <%=strResult%>
</div>
...
```

Now we have server-side process create the input and validation using the exact same process as described above.

You should try running your own schemas through this script and also build on it to allow for the slightly more complex conditions you may have. Also, have a look at the Schema Object Model (SOM), which is discussed in Chapter 3, "*Schemas in MSXML*", and acts as an API to access the schema (combining this with the above method allows you to create a better dynamic validation model) albeit that the SOM is new and proprietary to MSXML 4.0.

Summary

This chapter has discussed XPath in much detail, as it relates to MSXML 2.6 and above. Because certain useful functions have been identified that aren't included in the XPath standard, later versions of MSXML use non-standards extension functions.

MSXML 4.0 has implemented full support for XPath version 1.0 and even adds a few extensions. The chapter first looked at the XPath 1.0 W3C standard as it is implemented in MSXML 4.0. XPath expressions can use an unabbreviated form which we looked at in detail, but there is also an abbreviated form that allows us to dramatically shorten the expressions and we demonstrated how these can be used to good effect.

Te looked at the various axes were looked at as well as examples of location steps and location paths and how these can be used with predicate expressions to intelligently filter the selected nodes. All of the XPath functions, including the Microsoft extension functions were also considered.

We then went on to demonstrate a sample application which used many of the expressions discussed, including the Microsoft extensions and we concluded the chapter with some practical examples of working with XPath.

Finally the chapter showed a real-world sample application of how Schemas, XPath, and the DOM can be combined to create dynamic user interfaces with complex validation.

You should take a look at the W3C web site and the work in progress on XPath 2.0, to keep up to date with what's happening.

XML Application Development with MSXML 4.0
SOAP
XHTML
XML Schemas DTDs XPath CSS
XML Namespaces
XML 1.0
MSXML

5

XSLT in MSXML

The **Extensible Stylesheet Language** (**XSL**) is a styling and transformation language within the XML family of technologies. XSL has two constituent technologies known as **XSL-Formatting Objects** (**XSL-FO**) and **XSL Transformations** (**XSLT**). XSL-FO, found at http://www.w3.org/TR/xsl, is a formatting language primarily intended for the visual presentation of XML. XSLT, found at http://www.w3.org/TR/xslt, is used to transform the structure of XML to another structure – such as is often needed for e-business applications. XSLT currently finds most use in styling XML for browser presentation, and data transformation when passing XML between applications.

> *MSXML currently offers no support for XSL-FO. For more information on XSL-FO and how it can be used, see "Professional XSL" (Wrox Press, ISBN 1-861003-57-9).*

Within the world of MSXML, there are two main types of XSLT you are likely to come across: Microsoft's pre-standards XSL implementation, and the official W3C XSLT language. There are major differences between the two implementations, and although Microsoft has moved on and adopted the official language, the parsers continue to support the older implementation for backwards compatibility. This will be discussed further below.

Within the chapter we will look at both versions of XSL as provided by MSXML, but focus mainly on the W3C version. We will study the syntax of the elements and functions, as well as their usage. For most elements we'll provide a full working example of practical XSLT, which you can modify and reuse in your own developments.

What is XSLT?

XSLT allows the transformation of XML documents from an **input structure** into a different **output structure**. It does this by selecting **match patterns** in the input and using **templates** to format the output according to the required output structure. The match patterns are specified using XPath expressions or the XPath subset XSL Patterns. XSLT is unlike most (if not all) languages you have used before. It is not procedural – it is declarative, and does not modify the structure of the XML document. In fact, a close parallel could be drawn between XSLT and SQL, where an XPath expression is equivalent to a SQL SELECT statement. Of course, XSLT is much more sophisticated than this (hence the existence of this chapter!) and can in fact use procedural languages through extensions and make use of some procedural features such as if and when statements and for loops, or inherit from other stylesheets.

The best way to start is with a practical illustration of XSLT in action. We are going to look at a simple example that will demonstrate both the older and more recent implementations by taking an XML file and transforming it into HTML so that it can be viewed in the browser.

> **In order to view the newer (or official) XSLT implementation directly in your web browser, you must be running MSXML 3.0 or higher in replace mode or have Internet Explorer 5.5 or higher – the older implementation will also still work.**

You will need the files simple.xml, simple.xsl, simpleIE5.xml, and simpleIE5.xsl to try this example. All of the files are available in the code download.

Consider the following XML data (simpleIE5.xml):

```
<?xml version="1.0" encoding="utf-8" ?>
<?xml-stylesheet type="text/xsl" href="simpleIE5.xsl" ?>
<html>
    <head></head>
    <body>
        <p>hello world</p>
    </body>
</html>
```

It is fairly simple XML, but you may notice the new processing instruction used within the XML file to indicate which stylesheet should be used to transform the data. The type attribute should have a value of text/xsl and in this case the href attribute points to the Internet Explorer 5 XSL file (simpleIE5.xsl), shown below.

> **The xsl namespace is http://www.w3.org/TR/WD-xsl and is interpreted only by MSXML to indicate that the language is based on Microsoft's pre-standard XSL syntax. Many problems are attributable to the incorrect use of this single namespace declaration.**

```
<?xml version="1.0" ?>
<xsl:stylesheet xmlns:xsl="http://www.w3.org/TR/WD-xsl">
    <xsl:template>
        <HTML>
            <HEAD></HEAD>
            <BODY>
```

```
                <xsl:apply-templates />
            </BODY>
        </HTML>
    </xsl:template>
    <xsl:template match="p">
        The message is <xsl:value-of select="." />.
    </xsl:template>
</xsl:stylesheet>
```

The output from this transformation is shown below the output is the same for simple.xml and simple IE5.xml:

A very important point to note is the xsl namespace used within this file. Also, notice the use of templates – the template with no match template first matches the document root (<html> element) of the stylesheet and will match all nodes. For any nodes that are explicitly mentioned (such as the <p> element in our case),, it displays a simple message to the user placing the content of the <p> element in the place where the apply-templates comes. The value of the match attribute on the <template> elements is in fact a subset of that available to you in XPath – it is called an XSL Pattern. We'll come back to this later in the chapter.

Contrast this example with a stylesheet created to conform to the W3C XSLT Recommendation (you will notice that Microsoft calls the older version "XSL" and refers to the newer standard as "XSLT"). First the XML file (simple.xml) shows how the processing instruction is slightly different:

```
<?xml version="1.0" encoding="utf-8" ?>
<?xml-stylesheet type="text/xsl" href="simple.xsl" ?>
<html>
    <head></head>
    <body>
        <p>hello world</p>
    </body>
</html>
```

Notice that the only thing that has changed in the XML file is the reference to the new stylesheet, simple.xsl. The stylesheet is shown below:

```
<?xml version="1.0" ?>
<xsl:stylesheet version="1.0"
    xmlns:xsl="http://www.w3.org/1999/XSL/Transform">
    <xsl:template match="p">
        <HTML>
            <HEAD></HEAD>
            <BODY>
                The message is <xsl:value-of select="." />.
```

```
        </BODY>
      </HTML>
    </xsl:template>
  </xsl:stylesheet>
```

You should first notice that the namespace used within this stylesheet is different from the previous one and references the URI defined for the W3C Recommendation – namely http://www.w3.org/1999/XSL/Transform. You will also see that the <p> element can be directly matched in the standard implementation, whereas in the older implementation an extra template is required to match the document element and use apply-templates to invoke further processing. Apart from that this simple example doesn't illustrate too much of a difference, (the output from this is exactly the same as before), but there *are* other significant differences, which we'll discuss later.

Before we look at the details of the two implementations supported, let's consider what support is available in each MSXML version.

Support in MSXML

MSXML 2.5 (which comes withIE 5) and previous versions support the pre-standard Microsoft XSL implementation defined by the namespace http://www.w3.org/TR/WD-xsl. IE 4 never supported direct browsing of XML documents and use of XSL, soIE 5.0 was the first opportunity to work with XSL in the browser.

MSXML 2.6 and later versions support both implementations: the IE 4 andIE 5 pre-standard Microsoft XSL implementation, defined by the namespace http://www.w3.org/TR/WD-xsl, and the W3C standard implementation, defined by http://www.w3.org/1999/XSL/Transform.

You will already know that XSLT is heavily dependent on XPath and so the updates mentioned within the XPath chapter also apply to this chapter, such as the full XPath support provided as of MSXML 2.6 and above as well as the new extension functions within MSXML 4.0.

Another point worth noting, due to the many uses of XSLT in the presentation layer, is browser support. IE 4 does not directly support rendering of XML based on stylesheets, but this *is* supported inIE 5 and beyond, although this is of course based on the older XSL implementation. However, as of IE 6, the parser shipped is MSXML 3.0 so you will be able to use standards-compliant stylesheets in your developments. This parser is also the default parser shipped with Windows XP.

There are full working examples for almost all of the elements discussed below. These are available in the code download for this chapter. You may want to launch the file xslt.htm, which has two dropdowns and a text area. The dropdown on the left chooses the file you will be working with and defaults to Example XML File (which is sampleAll.xml, the XML file used in most examples). The second dropdown lists all of the elements or sample names. You simply choose the sample to run, click transform, and the result will be displayed for you to examine.

Note that these examples use the MSXML 3.0 parser. We could have easily used the MSXML 4.0 parser, but only for the W3C example. MSXML 4.0 does not support the loading and parsing of the older XSL version and hence if we used this we would have to switch between parser versions; so instead we stay with version 3.0 (and assume it is the default browser satisfied by the following conditions).

To run the examples you must satisfy one of the following conditions:

❑ Have IE 6.0 installed.

❑ Have another version of Internet Explorer installed, with MSXML 3.0 installed in replace mode.

Rather than list the entire code here for `sampleAll.xml`, the following screenshot gives an indication of its contents and structure:

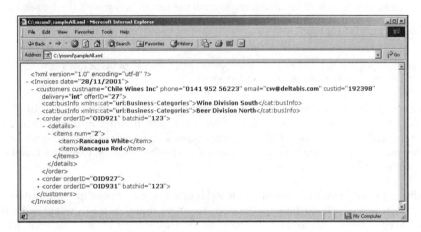

Microsoft XSL Implementation

> **To run these examples, choose the IE 5 Sample XML file entry from the sample page dropdown.**

We are going to start by taking a quick look at the pre-standard implementation that Microsoft introduced back in 1998, which is an implementation of the W3C's December 1998 Working Draft. The working draft implementation was introduced in MSXML before XSLT became a W3C Recommendation so that developers could get used to using, and gain the benefits of, such a language until the W3C released the full Recommendation – although Microsoft made it clear from early on that it would support the Recommendation as and when it was released. Earlier adopters of XML technologies on a Microsoft platform still commonly use the MSXML 1998 implementation today. However, standards-based implementation is the way forward, so we are not going to dwell too long on the 1998 implementation. It is included to give you an understanding for the times when you come up against old stylesheets.

A good source of examples when working with IE 5 is http://www.xml101.com/examples/.

The MSXML December 1998 implementation, found at http://www.w3.org/TR/1998/WD-xsl-19981216, consists of elements, functions, and patterns. Some of these are similar to what exists in the XSLT standard, but many don't exist or are implemented in a different fashion. Although the future of work with XSLT will use the official W3C Recommendation, it is very important you understand what came before it so you can upgrade any older implementations you come across (and this is very common).

XSL Elements

A discussion and example of each element is shown below in alphabetical order.

xsl:apply-templates

This element tells the processor to apply the appropriate template based on the XSL Pattern expression and node context. It selects a node-set comprising all the nodes that match the `select` attribute – when there's no `select` expression, all children are selected. Where multiple templates are matched, the last one in the document is selected.

```
<xsl:apply-templates order-by="sort criteria" select="expression"
    mode="QName"> </xsl:apply-templates>
```

The `order-by` attribute is an optional attribute that takes a semi-colon separated list of sorting expressions. These are relative to the `select` expression, which indicates the context the template should be executed within, and sorts the resulting output accordingly. Finally, the `mode` attribute allows the same template to appear multiple times within the stylesheet and be executed based on the `mode` attribute specified in the `<apply-templates>` element.

So, the following example selects a template matching "customers/order" and orders the selected node-set by the `itemSetID` attribute on the `order` context node. As a secondary order (if there are two nodes that have the same `itemSetID`), it orders by the text of the `<items>` element, which is a child of the `<details>` element.

```
<xsl:apply-templates select="customers/order"
    order-by="@itemSetID;details/items" mode="summary"/>
```

apply-templates from the 1998 implementation differs quite significantly from the W3C implementation. As we will see later, in the W3C implementation, sorting is handled differently and there is also support for passing parameters to templates.

xsl:attribute

The `<attribute>` element creates attribute nodes, which are sent to the output. You will typically use this when outputting another XML format, such as XHTML for web browser display or WML for mobile devices.

```
<xsl:attribute name="attribute-name"></xsl:attribute>
```

The `name` attribute is required and specifies the name of the attribute to be created in the output.

The example below is creating XHTML output for display in a browser. It outputs an anchor element with an `href` attribute, part of which is fixed and part of which contains the value specified in the "ordered" attribute of whichever `<order>` element is the context node:

```
<A>
    <xsl:attribute name="href">
        http://www.someuri.com/
            order.asp?orderid=<xsl:value-of select="@orderID" />
    </xsl:attribute>
</A>
```

xsl:choose

The `<xsl:choose>` element provides conditional processing using `<xsl:when>` and `<xsl:otherwise>` elements.

```
<xsl:choose>
</xsl:choose>
```

This element is a parent for `<xsl:when>` and `<xsl:otherwise>` elements which are used to perform conditional testing. It is very much like the procedural select statement (in C or Visual Basic), but does not require an explicit break or exit.

Further details can be found in the discussions below on xsl:otherwise and xsl:when (which also shows an implementation).

xsl:comment

This element generates an HTML-type comment in the output.

```
<xsl:comment>
</xsl:comment>
```

This causes any text generated from children of this node to be enclosed within HTML style comments in the output, in other words `<!-- some comments -->`.

Considering our example, `commentIE5.xsl`, if the `<customers>` element is the context node then the following will generate an output comment containing the customer name, `<!--Chile Wines Inc-->`:

```
<xsl:comment><xsl:value-of select="@custname" /></xsl:comment>
```

xsl:copy

The `<xsl:copy>` element copies the current node from the source to the output with the same name, namespace, and type as the source node. Note that it doesn't copy attributes and children automatically and so you must select these nodes through templates as shown in the example below.

```
<xsl:copy>
</xsl:copy>
```

With the `<xsl:copy>` element, it is possible to transform source XML documents to some other format.

The following example (`copyIE5.xsl` in the download) copies the `<order>` elements and attributes to the output to generate a simple list of all the orders within the source document:

```
<?xml version="1.0" ?>
<xsl:stylesheet xmlns:xsl="http://www.w3.org/TR/WD-xsl">
   <xsl:template>
      <xsl:apply-templates />
   </xsl:template>
   <xsl:template match="order">
      <xsl:copy>
```

```
        <xsl:apply-templates select="@*" />
    </xsl:copy>
</xsl:template>
<xsl:template match="@*">
    <xsl:copy>
        <xsl:value-of select="." />
    </xsl:copy>
</xsl:template>
</xsl:stylesheet>
```

The first template matches all nodes and initializes the processing of the stylesheet. Remember we want to use templates to filter out the nodes we wish to work with. So, we first want to match the `<order>` element by setting the `match` attribute value on an `<xsl:template>`. Within this template, we use the `<xsl:copy>` element to copy the current `order` node to the output and then use a further `apply-templates` to match all attribute nodes of this node – the `"@*"` expression does this. Then we need a template to match this pattern, and this is the final template we have. It does the fairly simple job of copying the name and value of the attribute to the output.

xsl:element

The `<xsl:element>` element creates an element in the output with the name specified in the `name` attribute. If you omit the `name` attribute, an element called `null` is created in the output – it is however mandatory in the full specification, so it is not a good idea to start omitting it now (and what benefit would you get?).

```
<xsl:element name="element name">
</xsl:element>
```

You may use this element to output, for example, an XHTML element such as an anchor. You could of course do this by simply using an `<A>` element with the appropriate XSL within it. However, in more complex cases the element may be dynamic. For example, imagine transforming an XML document for an e-commerce site. You display either an image of the product or a description depending on what is available in the source document – in this case, rather than `xsl:choose` statements, you are better off just dynamically creating the element name based on the source element name.

The following example (`elementIE5.xsl` in the download) creates in the output an anchor element with an `href` attribute with the value `"customers.asp?custid=192398"`:

```
<?xml version="1.0" ?>
<xsl:stylesheet xmlns:xsl="http://www.w3.org/TR/WD-xsl">
    <xsl:template>
        <xsl:apply-templates />
    </xsl:template>
    <xsl:template match="customers">
        <xsl:element name="a">
            <xsl:attribute name="href">
                customers.asp?custid=<xsl:value-of select="@custid" />
            </xsl:attribute>
        </xsl:element>
    </xsl:template>
</xsl:stylesheet>
```

The template matches any `<customers>` element nodes and within this template the `<xsl:element>` element creates an `<a>` element. Within this an attribute called `href` is created with a value of the `custID` source attribute. This is an important place to notice the implications of whitespace. The values within the `<xsl:attribute>` element must not be separated by any whitespace (including carriage returns) or this will appear in the output. Whitespace is discussed later in the chapter.

The output would be something like:

`<a href="customers.asp?custid=192398"/>`

xsl:eval

This element evaluates a script expression and outputs a string.

```
<xsl:eval language="language name">
</xsl:eval>
```

The `language` attribute defaults to JScript, but other languages can be specified – the most common other settings here are JavaScript or VBScript and less common languages such as PerlScript may also be used. The expressions that can be contained in this element are quite flexible, including calls to script functions declared within the stylesheet. You can use the XML reserved characters <, >, and &. Also, any functions must be placed within an `xsl:script` section (discussed below) and enclosed within a CDATA section. Accessing values within the source is done in the same way as you would use the DOM to work with nodes. For example, you can use `selectSingleNode()`, `getAttribute()`, and the other functions normally available.

The following example, `evalIE5.xsl`, illustrates how the `<xsl:eval>` element can be used to generate output that is dynamically calculated from the source:

```
<?xml version="1.0" ?>
<xsl:stylesheet xmlns:xsl="http://www.w3.org/TR/WD-xsl">
    <xsl:template>
        <xsl:apply-templates />
    </xsl:template>
    <xsl:template match="items">
        Current Total Number of items:<xsl:eval>totalItems(this);</xsl:eval>
    </xsl:template>
    <xsl:script><![CDATA[
    var items=0;

    function totalItems(obj)
    {
        var strMess = "Free Shipping";
        var ret="";

        items += parseInt(obj.getAttribute("num"));
        ret=items;

        if (items<10)
            ret+=" #No " + strMess;
        else
            ret+=" #" + strMess;

        return ret;
    }
    ]]></xsl:script>
</xsl:stylesheet>
```

The context for the `<xsl:eval>` element is the `<items>` element, which is matched by the template. The function called by `xsl:eval` is `totalItems()` and the current node is also passed using the JavaScript `this` keyword. The `totalItems()` function relies on a previously defined global variable called `items`, which contains the total number of items currently calculated. The function proceeds to get the `num` attribute of the context node by using the `getAttribute()` function. Additionally, if the number of items has reached a set threshold (and therefore qualifies for free shipping), then the message sent to the user changes, and this is also reflected in the code in the `strMess` variable. Finally, the return value from this function, the value of the `ret` variable, is the output from the `xsl:eval` call and is displayed.

The output from this would be something like the following:

```
Current Total Number of items:2 #No Free Shipping
Current Total Number of items:7 #No Free Shipping
Current Total Number of items:13 #Free Shipping
```

Note that although very popular in many current XSL stylesheets, the `<xsl:eval>` element does not exist in the W3C Recommendation and is replaced by `msxsl:script` in the MSXML implementations, so using it will just add to the conversions you need to make when upgrading your XSL files to conform to the W3C Recommendation. The W3C Recommendation allows extension functions to be added and associated with namespaces to provide better suitability for working in XML.

xsl:for-each

This element repeatedly iterates through the context node-set because otherwise only the first node in document order would be selected from the nodeset.

```
<xsl:for-each order-by="sort criteria" select="expression">
</xsl:for-each>
```

The node-set is selected by the expression given by the value of the `select` attribute and is ordered as specified by the `order-by` attribute. The `order-by` attribute is optional (defaulting to document order) and takes a semi-colon separated list of sorting expressions relative to the `select` expression (which itself indicates the context that the template should be executed within).

The example below, `foreachIE5.xsl`, shows how we could display in alphabetical order all of the wines that have been purchased:

```
<?xml version="1.0" ?>
<xsl:stylesheet xmlns:xsl="http://www.w3.org/TR/WD-xsl">
    <xsl:template>
        <xsl:apply-templates />
    </xsl:template>
    <xsl:template match="customers">
        <TABLE>
            <xsl:for-each select="order/details/items/item" order-by=".">
                <TR>
                    <TD>
                        <xsl:value-of select="." />
                    </TD>
                </TR>
            </xsl:for-each>
        </TABLE>
    </xsl:template>
</xsl:stylesheet>
```

The template matches the `<customers>` element – this is so we can later access *all* of the `<item>` elements within a single node-set. We output an HTML `<TABLE>` element and then move into our `<xsl:for-each>` element. The `select` attribute here selects all `<item>` elements within our source document into a single node-set – further to this, the `order-by` attribute is set to order by the context node within that selection, which would of course be the `<item>` element itself! This function orders alphabetically, but a minus sign in front of this (-.) would order in reverse alphabetical order (for whatever reason you might want to do that). Within this it is all pretty simple – a standard table is written out with the names of the wine listed.

The output will be something like the following. This is just a fragment – run the sample to see the whole output:

```
<TABLE>
<TR>
<TD>
Chillan Red
</TD>
</TR>
<TR>
<TD>
Chillan Red
</TD>
</TR>
<TR>
<TD>
Northern Sweet White
</TD>
</TR>
<TR>
<TD>
Rancagua Red
</TD>
</TR>

</TABLE>
```

xsl:if

The `<xsl:if>` element allows conditional constructs within your stylesheet.

```
<xsl:if test="expression" expr="script" language="language">
</xsl:if>
```

The `test` attribute is required and returns `true` or `false` depending on the outcome of its expression. For example, you may test if you are at a certain position in the context or if a given node contains a certain value or even whether the node exists at all. If this is the only attribute and it evaluates to `true`, then the content within the element is invoked. However, you can also use the `expr` attribute to have some script evaluate and return a Boolean value (the script language is defined by the value of the `<xsl:if>` `language` attribute). We won't go into the details of the `expr` attribute – it is pretty much the same as the `<xsl:eval>` element, but in this case it *must* return either `true` or `false`. If the value is `true` and the resulting value of the `test` attribute is `true`, then the net result is `true` and the content of the `<xsl:if>` element is entered into. If either, or both, are `false`, then the net result is `false` and the content of the `<xsl:if>` element is ignored.

To show how `xsl:if` can be used, the following example (`ifIE5.xsl`) demonstrates using the `test` attribute alone, as well as in combination with some scripting, to produce conditional output:

```
<?xml version="1.0" ?>
<xsl:stylesheet xmlns:xsl="http://www.w3.org/TR/WD-xsl">
    <xsl:template>
        <xsl:apply-templates />
    </xsl:template>
    <xsl:template match="customers">
        <xsl:if test=".[@delivery='int']">International Delivery.</xsl:if>
        <xsl:if test="@offerID" language="JavaScript"
            expr="GetDiscount(this.getAttribute('offerID'))">
        You are entitled to a <xsl:eval>ShowDiscount()</xsl:eval> discount.
        </xsl:if>
    </xsl:template>
    <xsl:script><![CDATA[
    var discount="0%";

    function GetDiscount(intOfferID)
    {
        var ret=true;

        if (intOfferID<5)
            ret=false;
        else if (intOfferID>5 && intOfferID<=15)
            discount="5%";
        else if (intOfferID>15 && intOfferID<=25)
            discount="8%";
        else if (intOfferID>25 && intOfferID<=35)
            discount="12%";
        else
            discount="5%";

        return ret;

    }

    function ShowDiscount ()
    {
var dis = "";

dis = discount;
discount="0%";

return dis;
    }
    ]]></xsl:script>
</xsl:stylesheet>
```

With the template match on the `<customers>` element, the first `<xsl:if>` element has a `test` attribute that checks if the `delivery` attribute of the context (`customers`) element is equal to the value `"int"`, indicating an international delivery customer. If it returns `true`, then some simple text is added to the output to indicate "International Delivery", otherwise this part is left blank.

The second `<xsl:if>` element does a more complex test. The `test` attribute first checks whether the context element has an `offerID` attribute and also performs some script evaluation via the `expr` attribute. This calls the `GetDiscount()` function, passing the value of the offered attribute as a parameter. The `GetDiscount()` function initializes the return value to `true` using the `ret` variable. It then performs a series of `"if... else..."` statements to determine the boundary of the `intOfferID` attribute value – within certain boundaries, the discount available changes. In our case, the value of the attribute is "27" and so the discount will be "12%". The discount value is actually stored in a global variable called `discount`. This is because we can only return a Boolean value, but we want to indicate the value of the discount in the text of the output. Storing this as a global variable allows us to use `<xsl:eval>` to retrieve this value immediately within the `<xsl:if>` element. Indeed this is what we do, invoking the function `ShowDiscount()`. We could actually just have placed the variable name `discount` within the `<xsl:eval>` element, but we use the function call instead so that we can re-initialize the global variable value to "0%" once we have used it. We re-initialize this for good practice rather than have any problems that may occur.

The output will be something like the following:

International Delivery.
You are entitled to a 12% discount.

Note that the W3C implementation of `xsl:if` is nowhere near as powerful as the one defined in the Microsoft XSL implementation. In fact, it only has the `test` attribute. This makes the `<xsl:if>` element in the old XSL implementation more powerful. However, the W3C XSLT in MSXML implements very powerful procedural scripting functionality like the `expr` attribute, with the `<msxsl:script>` element, which you would use instead of the `<xsl:if>` element.

xsl:otherwise

The `<xsl:otherwise>` element provides conditional processing using `<xsl:choose>` and `<xsl:when>` elements.

```
<xsl:otherwise>
</xsl:otherwise>
```

This element is a child of `<xsl:choose>` and sibling of one or more `<xsl:when>` elements, all of which are used to perform conditional testing. The optional `<xsl:otherwise>` element is like the default item in the procedural select statement (in C or Visual Basic) as it is the value that is used if all other tests are false.

Further details can be found in the discussions of `xsl:when` (which also shows an implementation) and `xsl:choose`.

xsl:pi

This element creates a processing instruction in the output such as an XSL stylesheet processing instruction, which would be useful when transforming one XML document to another format that should once again be transformed.

```
<xsl:pi name="processing instruction name">
</xsl:pi>
```

The only attribute expected here is the `name` of the processing instruction you are to create – the actual text of the processing instruction should be the content of the element.

193

So, the example below (piIE5.xsl) shows how an xml-stylesheet processing instruction can be created in the output:

```
<?xml version="1.0" ?>
<xsl:stylesheet xmlns:xsl="http://www.w3.org/TR/WD-xsl">
    <xsl:template match="/">
        <xsl:pi name="xml-stylesheet">type="text/xsl" href="piIE.xsl"</xsl:pi>
    </xsl:template>
</xsl:stylesheet>
```

The output from this template would be like the following:

```
<?xml-stylesheet type="text/xsl" href="piIE.xsl"?>
```

xsl:script

This element allows you to insert procedural code, for example defining global variables and functions within the stylesheet itself.

```
<xsl:script language="language">
</xsl:script>
```

The only attribute expected here is the language your script will be created in. The <xsl:script> element's contents are enclosed within a CDATA section – this is to escape any reserved characters (<, &, etc.) that are used in XML and may be processed as XML characters causing the stylesheet to fail while parsing.

The following fragment is taken from the <xsl:if> element description above, so to see the full stylesheet, you should look back at that element:

```
...
    <xsl:script><![CDATA[
    var discount="0%";

    function GetDiscount(intOfferID)
    {
        var ret=true;

        if (intOfferID<5)
            ret=false;
        else if (intOfferID>5 && intOfferID<=15)
            discount="5%";
        else if (intOfferID>15 && intOfferID<=25)
            discount="8%";
        else if (intOfferID>25 && intOfferID<=35)
            discount="12%";
        else
            discount="5%";

        return ret;

    }

    function ShowDiscount()
    {
```

```
    var dis = "";

    dis = discount;
    discount="0%";

    return dis;
      }
     ]]></xsl:script>
...
```

We won't discuss the functionality of the procedural code – it is outlined in the `xsl:if` example. However, you can see how the contents of the `<xsl:script>` element are enclosed within a CDATA section.

To call the function, we could write (as shown in the `xsl:if` example):

```
<xsl:if test="@offerID" language="JavaScript"
   expr="GetDiscount(this.getAttribute('offerID'))">...</xsl:if>
```

The `expr` attribute *must* return a Boolean value that is evaluated with the test – no other return type is permitted here – any other type results in a type mismatch error and will cause your transform to fail. Alternatively, we can use the `xsl:eval` function, which can return any text value:

```
<xsl:eval>ShowDiscount()</xsl:eval>
```

Note that in this case, the `language` attribute is not specified in the `<xsl:script>` tag, so the language is assumed to be JScript, though you can specify your choice, with JavaScript and VBScript the other alternatives.

Also, because the `<xsl:script>` block defines a global variable called `discount` within its code block, we can write this to the output as follows:

```
<xsl:eval>discount</xsl:eval>
```

The output from this template, fully defined in the `xsl:if` example, would be like the following:

International Delivery.
You are entitled to a 12% discount.

A further interesting note is that you can also instantiate COM objects as of IE 5.01. However, this is of course dependent on the environment allowing you the privileges to do so – whether that's client-side or server-side! If your application runs through a browser, then you will be very limited in the objects you can create client-side because otherwise anyone could randomly create objects on your computer and wreak havoc with your system. On the server the same limitations often apply, although because it is on the server, it is assumed that it was put there after carrying out testing and putting security measures in place. A COM object is very useful for encapsulating your code (as opposed to scripting where the source is available) and is often used to connect to data sources or perform complex business logic. Furthermore, many applications on your system (client or server) can be accessed via COM interfaces and hence provide advanced functionality to your stylesheet processing.

Note that in the W3C implementation, the `<xsl:script>` element *does not exist*. Microsoft has accomplished this functionality through extension functions, which is an officially recommended way of adding functionality. However, although it is a standard way, the actual extension `msxsl:script` is not implemented across all XML parsers – in other words, the script will work only when using MSXML and no other parser (unless of course, it provides support for it).

xsl:stylesheet

This element is perhaps the most significant element as it is the root stylesheet element containing the `<xsl:template>` and `<xsl:script>` elements.

```
<xsl:stylesheet default-space="default" indent-result="yes"
    language="language" result-ns="value">
</xsl:stylesheet>
```

The `default-space` attribute can only be set to `default` and indicates that whitespace should be preserved in the source document. If the stylesheet specifies `indent-result="yes"` (the default and *only* value is `yes`, so you don't have much choice here), this tells the processor to preserve in the output any whitespace that appears in the stylesheet and furthermore that the XSL processor may add whitespace to the result tree (possibly based on whitespace stripped from either the source document or the stylesheet) in order to indent the result nicely. The `language` attribute defines the procedural language that will be used as default within the stylesheet – typical values here are `JScript`, `VBScript`, or `JavaScript`. Finally, we have `result-ns` whose value must be a namespace prefix. If this attribute is specified, all result elements must belong to the namespace identified by this prefix (the result namespace). If there is a namespace declared as the default namespace, then an empty string may be used as the value to specify that the default namespace is the result namespace.

The following example shows how you can use MSXML to output elements according to XSL-Formatting Objects as defined by the namespace `http://www.w3.org/TR/WD-xsl/FO`. Although MSXML does not support XSL-FO we can still use this technique to output them, perhaps for interpretation by some processor that does offer XSL-FO support.

```
<?xml version="1.0" ?>
<xsl:stylesheet
    xmlns:xsl="http://www.w3.org/TR/WD-xsl"
    default-space="default"
    indent-result="yes"
    language="VBScript"
    xmlns:fo="http://www.w3.org/TR/WD-xsl/FO"
    result-ns="fo">

    <xsl:template>
        <xsl:apply-templates />
    </xsl:template>
    <xsl:template match="customers/order[0]/details/items/item[1]">
        <fo:block font-size="10pt" space-before="12pt">
            <xsl:value-of select="." />
        </fo:block>
    </xsl:template>
</xsl:stylesheet>
```

Notice that the element within the template that is matched by a slightly more complex XPath expression is qualified with the `fo` prefix (`fo:block`). You will also see that the default language has been set to `VBScript`, and if no `language` attribute is set on the `<xsl:script>` elements, then this would be the default for those as well.

The output from this template would be like the following:

```
<fo:block font-size="10pt" space-before="12pt">
Rancagua Red
</fo:block>
```

Note that the WC3 implementation is dramatically different from this version of the
`<xsl:stylesheet>` element, and none of the attributes on this 1998 implementation appear on the
official W3C version.

xsl:template

The `<xsl:template>` element is used to create a reusable template for generating output for particular
node types and context.

```
<xsl:template language="language" name="QName" match="pattern"
    priority="number" mode="QName">
</xsl:template>
```

The `language` attribute defines the name of the language used in the template (in `<xsl:eval>`
elements) and the usual values are `VBScript`, `JScript`, or `JavaScript`. The name attribute is a
qualified name (QName – a combination of a prefix associated with a namespace and a local name),
which is expanded to a full namespace qualified name, and those with prefixes are expanded based on
the namespace declarations in effect at that point. The `match` attribute contains an XSL Pattern
expression (a subset of XPath) that determines the node-set and context the template will operate on.

The `priority` attribute would allow matching templates to be ordered by a given priority. The non-
standard implementation does not implement priority and so the `priority` attribute has no effect.
However, it is worth discussing why it exists to understand the implementation better and lead you
towards the standard implementation. The more specific templates are given a higher priority by default
than those that are less specific. The default priorities are calculated according to the following:

❑ Patterns such as `node()`, `text()`, and `*` are not frequently selected and so have a low default
priority of `-0.5`.

❑ Patterns of a name or attribute are very common and have a default priority of `-0.25`.

❑ Qualified patterns match only on given namespace axes and so are more specific than the
others. They have a default priority of `0.0`.

❑ Other specific patterns are given default priorities of `0.5`. An example would be
`customers/order[0]/details[2]`, which is a more specific expression.

❑ You can of course assign your own priorities to templates as a real number from `-9` to `+9`.

The final `<xsl:template>` attribute is mode, another of the items not implemented in this non-standard
version. This is a QName with an optional prefix, which theoretically allows a template to be run multiple
times for a given pattern. This is discussed in detail in the W3C implementation section of the chapter.

The relatively simple example overleaf shows how a template matching the `<customers>` element can
be used with some simple scripting:

```
<?xml version="1.0" ?>
<xsl:stylesheet xmlns:xsl="http://www.w3.org/TR/WD-xsl">
   <xsl:template>
      <xsl:apply-templates />
   </xsl:template>
   <xsl:template name="CustDateMatch" match="customers" language="VBScript">
      <xsl:comment>
         <xsl:eval>Date &amp; " at " &amp; Time</xsl:eval>
      </xsl:comment>
   </xsl:template>
</xsl:stylesheet>
```

The content of the `<xsl:eval>` element is evaluated as VBScript rather than the default JScript and we must escape the & character with the XML `&amp;` entity.

The output from this template would be like the following:

```
<!--10/5/2001 at 1:30:56 AM-->
```

xsl:value-of

This element inserts the value of the selected node as a text string.

```
<xsl:value-of select="Expression">
</xsl:value-of>
```

The `select` attribute must be present and should contain an XSL Pattern expression that is evaluated against the current context. If a node-set is returned, then the text value output is the value of the first node in this node-set.

You can see this element in action in almost all of the examples, so a short example is shown here using one of the available XSLT functions (which we'll look at later in the chapter):

```
<?xml version="1.0" ?>
<xsl:stylesheet xmlns:xsl="http://www.w3.org/TR/WD-xsl">
   <xsl:template>
      <xsl:apply-templates />
   </xsl:template>
   <xsl:template match="Invoices">
      <xsl:value-of select="@date[date(.) &gt; date('2001-11-27')]" />
   </xsl:template>
</xsl:stylesheet>
```

The template matches the `<Invoices>` document element and its only content is an `<xsl:value-of>` element that writes out the date attribute of the `<Invoices>` element if it is greater than the date in the code. In this case, the `@date` attribute is selected – any test on this node should be done within the square brackets. Within this, we match the current node, converting the value of "." (which is the current node – the `date` attribute) to a date using the `date()` function and see if it is greater than the date given in the other `date` function. Note how the ">" sign must be escaped with `&gt;`. The value will only be written out if the date is greater, otherwise it will be ignored.

The output from this template would be like the following:

```
28/11/2001
```

xsl:when

The `<xsl:when>` element provides conditional processing using `<xsl:choose>` and `<xsl:otherwise>` elements.

```
<xsl:when test="boolean expression" expr="boolean script"
   language="language">
</xsl:when>
```

This element will be the child element of an `<xsl:choose>` element and may occur multiple times.

The `test` attribute is required and returns `true` or `false` depending on the outcome of its expression. You may test if you are at a certain position in the context or if a given node contains a certain value. If this is the only attribute and it evaluates to `true`, then the content within the element is invoked. However, you can also use the `expr` attribute to have some script evaluate and return a Boolean value. The script language is defined by the value of the `language` attribute. We won't go into the details of the `expr` attribute – it is pretty much the same as the `<xsl:eval>` element, but in this case it *must always* return either `true` or `false`. If the value is `true` and the resulting value of the `test` attribute is `true`, then the net result is `true` and the content of the `<xsl:when>` element is entered into. If either, or both, are `false`, then the net result is `false` and the content of the `<xsl:when>` element is ignored.

When one of these tests has completed its processing, the `<xsl:choose>` is exited and processing continues with the next element. If none of the `<xsl:when>` elements are `true` then the `<xsl:otherwise>` element is processed, if it exists otherwise, the `<xsl:choose>` is just bypassed.

The following example shows how `<xsl:when>` can be used in conjunction with `<xsl:choose>` and `<xsl:otherwise>` to output some text indicating whether the number of items is sufficient for the order level: small (3 items), medium (6 items), and large (10 items):

```
<?xml version="1.0" ?>
<xsl:stylesheet xmlns:xsl="http://www.w3.org/TR/WD-xsl">
   <xsl:template>
      <xsl:apply-templates />
   </xsl:template>
   <xsl:template match="order">
      <xsl:choose>
         <xsl:when test="details/items[@num $lt$ 3]">
Order <xsl:value-of select="@orderID" /> needs <xsl:eval>3 -
this.childNodes[0].childNodes[0].getAttribute("num")</xsl:eval> more items to be a
Small Order.</xsl:when>
         <xsl:when test="details/items[@num $lt$ 6]">
Order <xsl:value-of select="@orderID" /> needs <xsl:eval>6 -
this.childNodes[0].childNodes[0].getAttribute("num")</xsl:eval> more items to be a
Medium Order.</xsl:when>
         <xsl:otherwise>
Order <xsl:value-of select="@orderID" /> needs <xsl:eval>10 -
this.childNodes[0].childNodes[0].getAttribute("num")</xsl:eval> more items to be a
Large Order.</xsl:otherwise>
      </xsl:choose>
      <xsl:apply-templates />
   </xsl:template>
</xsl:stylesheet>
```

The first template will match the document root and uses an `apply-templates` to process the other templates. The template matches the `<order>` elements and the child of this template is an `<xsl:choose>` element. Within this element are two `<xsl:when>` elements and an `<xsl:otherwise>` element. The first `<xsl:when>` has a `test` attribute that is `true` when the num attribute of the `<items>` element descendent is less than the value 3. When it is, it simply writes out some text, with a short calculation using `<xsl:eval>` to determine how many items are required to satisfy the order. The second `<xsl:when>` also has a `test` attribute that is `true` when the num attribute of the `<items>` element descendent is less than the value 6. When it is, it simply writes out some text, with a short calculation using `<xsl:eval>` to determine how many items are required to satisfy the order. The `<xsl:otherwise>` is a catch-all test and will write out similar information for any elements not caught by the first two `<xsl:when>` elements. Note that in this example, the whitespace is relevant and so the format is exactly as it appears in the stylesheet.

The output from this template would be like the following:

```
Order OID921 needs 1 more items to be a Small Order.
Order OID927 needs 1 more items to be a Medium Order.
Order OID931 needs 4 more items to be a Large Order.
```

XSL Functions

The 1998 Microsoft implementation has a few functions for counting and data formatting. We will describe them briefly first and then see them in action in an example at the end of the section. For more information on these functions, you should look at the MSXML SDK version 2.5 or less.

> You can download the MSXML 2.5 SDK SP1 from http://msdn.microsoft.com/downloads/sample.asp?url=/MSDN-FILES/027/001/439/msdncompositedoc.xml

- ❑ `absoluteChildNumber(node)` – this returns the number (starting from 1) of the node relative to all siblings. The parameter is the node you are querying.

- ❑ `ancestorChildNumber(nodename, node)` – this returns the number (starting from 1) of the nearest ancestor of a node with the requested node name. The parameters are the name of the node you are interested in and the node identifying where to start the search.

- ❑ `childNumber(node)` – this returns the number of the node relative to its siblings (starting from 1). The parameter is the node that contains the child you are interested in.

- ❑ `depth(node)` – this returns the depth within the document tree at which the specified node appears (starting from 1). The parameter is the node you are interested in.

- ❑ `formatDate(varDate, bstrFormat)` – formats the supplied date. The varDate parameter is the one you are formatting and the bstrFormat is based on the formats defined by the Win32 API call, `GetDateFormat()`, which gives information on the many possible ways of formatting the date. The `GetDateFormat()` function is discussed at the following URL: http://msdn.microsoft.com/library/default.asp?url=/library/en-us/dnintl/html/s24b4_a.asp.

- ❏ formatIndex(index, bstrFormat) – formats the supplied integer (index) using the specified numerical system (bstrFormat). The bstrFormat can be one of the following:

  - ❏ "1" – Standard numbering system.
  - ❏ "01" – Standard numbering with leading zeros.
  - ❏ "A" – Uppercase sequence: A–Z, AA–ZZ.
  - ❏ "a" – Lowercase sequence: a–z, aa–zz.
  - ❏ "I" – Uppercase Roman numerals: I, II, III, IV, …
  - ❏ "i" – Lowercase Roman numerals: i, ii, iii, iv, …

- ❏ formatNumber(dblNumber, bstrFormat) – this formats the supplied number (dblNumber) using the specified format (bstrFormat). The bstrFormat can be one of the following:

  - ❏ "#" – Display only significant digits.
  - ❏ "0" – Display insignificant zeros if a number has fewer digits than there are zeros in the format.
  - ❏ "?" – Add spaces for insignificant zeros on either side of the decimal point so that decimal points align with a fixed-point font.
  - ❏ "." – Indicate the placement of the decimal point within the format.
  - ❏ "," – Display a comma as a thousands separator, or scale a number by a multiple of one thousand.
  - ❏ "%" – Display a number as a percentage of 100.
  - ❏ "E-" – Display a number in scientific format (exponential notation).
  - ❏ "E+" – Place a minus sign by negative exponents and a plus sign by positive exponents.

- ❏ formatTime(varTime, bstrFormat) – formats the supplied time. The varTime parameter is the one you are formatting and the bstrFormat is derived from the Win32 API call, GetTimeFormat.

- ❏ uniqueID(node) – returns the unique identifier for the supplied node within the node-set (like generate-id() in the W3C XSLT Reccomendation). The parameter is the node for which the unique identifier is to be returned.

The following example is called methods.xsl and illustrates some of the above, based on our sample XML document, sampleAll.xml:

```
<?xml version="1.0" ?>
<xsl:stylesheet xmlns:xsl="http://www.w3.org/TR/WD-xsl">
   <xsl:template>
      <xsl:apply-templates />
   </xsl:template>
   <xsl:template match="order[1]" language="JavaScript">
      <xsl:eval>absoluteChildNumber(this)</xsl:eval>
      <xsl:eval>ancestorChildNumber("Invoices",this)</xsl:eval>
      <xsl:eval>childNumber(this)</xsl:eval>
      <xsl:eval>depth(this.parentNode)</xsl:eval>
```

```
            <xsl:eval>formatIndex(9, "i")</xsl:eval>
            <xsl:eval>formatNumber(10.00, "00.000")</xsl:eval>
            <xsl:eval>uniqueID(this)</xsl:eval>
        </xsl:template>
    </xsl:stylesheet>
```

The output from this will be something like the following:

```
3
1
2
2
ix
10.000
209035104
```

When the second template is matched, the context node will be the second (zero-based index) `order` element child of the `<customers>` element. Looking at the output, the first line is equal to 3 because this order element has two previous siblings – the first `<order>` element node and the `<busInfo>` element node. The second line (`ancestorChildNumber` equal to 1) is because the `<Invoices>` element is the first relative to its sibling nodes. The third line showing the `childNumber` will return the value 2 because it is the second child of the name `order` in document order. The next line returns the `depth` of the parent element of the `<order>` element – this is the `<customers>` element and it is two steps from the document root. Following this, the Roman numerals `ix` are converted from the number 9 using `formatIndex()`. Then the 10.00 is passed to `formatNumber()` function, ensuring there are two positions prior to the decimal point and three after for the given number. Finally, the `uniqueID()` function will be different every time as it returns a unique ID for the node.

Creating Stylesheets

So far we have seen how to create XML documents and XSL documents that can style them, but we have used the DOM to do the transforms. We may also browse the XML pages directly and have them styled or transformed to be presented to clients on a web browser capable of displaying XML (such as IE 5+ or to a lesser extent, Netscape 6.0+), transforming on the server into HTML format to display on any web browser or via other applications.

This section will look at creating an XML document and using XSLT to transform it to HTML format, using CSS to style the documents.

A Basic Stylesheet

To associate an XML document with an XSL document, you simply add a processing instruction to the XML document in the form:

```
<?xml-stylesheet type="text/xsl" href="url of stylesheet"?>
```

This should be added immediately after the XML declaration or `<!DOCTYTPE>` declaration. So if we had the XSL stylesheet `sampleIE5Display.xsl` then we would have the declaration:

```
<?xml-stylesheet type="text/xsl" href="sampleIE5Display.xsl"?>
```

MSXML will notice only the first XML `<?xml-stylesheet?>` declaration where the `type` is `"text/xsl"`. However, IE can directly browse XML files styled with cascading stylesheets and any number of these may be available:

```
<?xml-stylesheet type="text/css" href="style1.css"?>
<?xml-stylesheet type="text/css" href="style2.css"?>
```

These will be merged together by IE on processing and applied directly to the XML documents, with any duplicate definitions in later CSS files overriding earlier definitions.

So, consider the following simple XML document (`direct.xml`):

```
<?xml version="1.0" encoding="utf-8" ?>
<?xml-stylesheet type="text/css" href="directstyle1.css" ?>
<?xml-stylesheet type="text/css" href="directstyle2.css" ?>
<Invoices date="28/11/2001">
    <customers custname="Chile Wines Inc">
        <contact>
            <address>
                <street>7272 Argyle Street</street>
                <city>Glasgow</city>
                <country>Scotland</country>
            </address>
            <phone>141-020-2929292</phone>
        </contact>
        <order orderID="OID921" batchid="123">
            <details>
                <items num="2">
                    <item>Rancagua White</item>
                    <item>Rancagua Red</item>
                </items>
            </details>
        </order>
    </customers>
</Invoices>
```

The first simple stylesheet (`directstyle1.css`) is as follows and defines items appropriate to the invoice:

```
Invoices    { display: block; }
customers   { display: block; }
items       { display: block; background-color:green;}
item {display: block; font-weight:bold; font-family:Arial}
```

The second simple stylesheet (`directstyle2.css`) is more oriented towards defining `<contact>` element details and is as follows:

```
contact {display: block;background-color:Silver;}
street {display: block; font-weight:lighter;font-family=Arial}
city {display: block; font-weight:bold;font-family=Arial}
country {display: block; font-weight:bolder;font-family=Arial}
phone {display: block; color:Red;font-weight:normal;font-family=Arial}
```

The stylesheets will work through the XML document and display the items met according to the styles defined in the stylesheets. So, when the `<contact>` element is met, it is created as a separate block with a silver background color. As its sub-elements are parsed, they are styled within this section, with their local styles taking precedence. So when the `<phone>` element is matched, the color of the text is changed to red – some of the other styles of the elements are also changed according to their definition in the appropriate stylesheet.

The output from this is as follows:

However, we can do much better and more sophisticated processing when we combine XML, XSL, and CSS to generate output.

Integrating Cascading Stylesheets (CSS) and Client Scripting

We have many options when using cascading stylesheets with XML and XSL documents to style output HTML documents. In fact, we have all the options already available to us, such as external stylesheets, global styles, and localized styles. You can also include client-side scripting to create the HTML page as you normally would.

The following example uses the files `sampleIE5Display.xml` (which you should browse directly to see the results), `sampleIE5Display.xsl`, and `samplestyle.css` to demonstrate an example of these working together. The XML file `sampleIE5Display.xml` is the same as the `sampleAll.xml` file we have been working with, but has the following processing instruction added:

```
<?xml-stylesheet type="text/xsl" href="sampleIE5Display.xsl" ?>
```

The transform that creates the HTML output is performed by the following XSL stylesheet, `sampleIE5Display.xsl`:

```
<?xml version="1.0" ?>
<xsl:stylesheet xmlns:xsl="http://www.w3.org/TR/WD-xsl">
    <xsl:template>
        <xsl:apply-templates />
    </xsl:template>
    <xsl:template match="/">
        <HTML>
            <HEAD>
                <style>
                        h2 {background-color:darkblue;}
                        DIV {cursor:hand;}
                </style>
                <link rel="stylesheet" type="text/css"
```

```
                    href="samplestyle.css" />
                <SCRIPT LANGUAGE="Jscript">
                    <xsl:comment><![CDATA[
          function mouseover()
          {
            e = window.event.srcElement;
            if (e.style.backgroundColor != 'white')
              e.style.backgroundColor = 'white';
            else
              e.style.backgroundColor = 'lightblue';
          }

          function mouseout()
          {
            e = window.event.srcElement;
            if (e.style.backgroundColor != 'lightblue')
              e.style.backgroundColor = 'lightblue';
            else
              e.style.backgroundColor = 'white';
          }
       ]]></xsl:comment>
                </SCRIPT>
            </HEAD>
            <BODY>
                <xsl:apply-templates />
            </BODY>
        </HTML>
    </xsl:template>
    <xsl:template match="customers">
        <h2>
            <xsl:attribute name="style">color:yellow</xsl:attribute>
            <xsl:value-of select="@custname" />
        </h2>
        <xsl:element name="a">
            <xsl:attribute name="href">mailto:
            <xsl:value-of select="@email" /></xsl:attribute>
            <xsl:attribute name="class">email</xsl:attribute>
            <xsl:value-of select="@email" />
        </xsl:element>
        <p>
            <font class="subheader">Wines</font>
            <xsl:apply-templates />
        </p>
    </xsl:template>
    <xsl:template match="order">
        <DIV class="orders">
            <b>Order
            <xsl:value-of select="@orderID" />
            </b>
        </DIV>
        <xsl:apply-templates />
    </xsl:template>
    <xsl:template match="items/item">
        <DIV STYLE="background-color:white;color:darkblue;"
            onmouseover="mouseover()" onmouseout="mouseout()">
            <xsl:value-of select="." />
        </DIV>
    </xsl:template>
</xsl:stylesheet>
```

205

The first template will match the root element and causes templates to be applied. Therefore, the next template will match the document root, which also causes the other templates to be processed. The `apply-templates` within the document root will initially match the `customers` template and the output from this template will be placed here. Within the `customers` template, the `orders` template and `apply-templates` will cause the order template to be matched and finally within here, each item of the `items` node-set will be processed. Let's now look at how we create the HTML. We can embed most of the HTML elements we want to use within the root template and call the other templates within this to generate the other HTML fragments such as tables, paragraphs, and others. There is a globally defined `<STYLE>` element within the stylesheet, which should appear within the `<HEAD>` element as in usual HTML:

```
<style>    h2 {background-color:darkblue;}
      DIV {cursor:hand;}
</style>
```

This is a fairly simple CSS and just defines the style of any `<h2>` or `<DIV>` elements within the document. Following this, there is a link to an external CSS document, which must be within the HTML content and not as a processing instruction because MSXML will not associate the CSS style defined by a PI with the HTML document automatically – the HTML parser should do this instead. So, `samplestyle.css` defines three classes and a style for any bold, `<b>`, tags. This file is as follows:

```
.subheader {font-weight:bold;font-family=Arial}
.orders {background-color:lightgreen;color:darkgreen;cursor:auto;}
.email {color:green;}
b {text-decoration:underline}
```

Following global and external style definitions, we can also define them as normal on any element within the XSL document, as we do in the `items/item` template for the `<DIV>` element:

```
<DIV STYLE="background-color:white;color:darkblue;" >
...
    <xsl:value-of select="." />
</DIV>
```

Finally, we can dynamically create the `style` attribute and apply our own styles to this using our previous CSS definitions, as well as any we wish to add. This is how we create the anchor element for the e-mail address:

```
<xsl:element name="a">
    <xsl:attribute name="href">mailto:<xsl:value-of select="@email" />
    </xsl:attribute>
    <xsl:attribute name="class">email</xsl:attribute>
    <xsl:value-of select="@email" />
</xsl:element>
```

So, having considered all of the style options we have, we can also see that `SCRIPT` blocks can be dynamically inserted into the HTML `<HEAD>` elements, keeping in mind that it is best to enclose any script within CDATA sections to escape any XML special characters. We use these in the HTML document as we normally would, and the style of the `<DIV>` element is dynamically changed by calling methods when the mouse pointer moves over and out of the element:

```
<DIV STYLE="background-color:white;color:darkblue;"
          onmouseover="mouseover()" onmouseout="mouseout()">
   <xsl:value-of select="." />
</DIV>
```

The output HTML generated is shown here:

MSXML has moved on and as of MSXML 2.6, from its initial position as an early adopter of the XSL specifications, Microsoft has started to become gradually more standardized and adopt the global W3C XSLT Recommendation. This is the future of work with XSLT, although it is very important we understand what came before it so we can upgrade any older implementations we come across.

Let's now look at the W3C XSLT implementation.

W3C XSLT Implementation

The following section will work through the elements and functions available to us in XSLT. You can treat it as a reference section if you wish, but its purpose is not a complete reference on each item – it is intended to complement the SDK documents available with MSXML. Rather, we intend to look at some of the more important and complex conditions that occur when using XSLT with MSXML in the real world, with full working examples as we go.

When working through the examples we have tried to ensure that the output is readable and have not relied on any particular output format, such as HTML. This allows us to understand the output better and concentrate on XSLT itself. This approach brings us into the world of whitespace in XML, where whitespace is very significant. So where there is a new line in our XSLT, this new line will appear in the output, as will spaces, etc. There is a section later that discusses whitespace in XML. The best way to understand whitespace is to play around with the examples after you have completed this chapter.

These examples will work only using MSXML 3.0 or MSXML 4.0 – if you followed the instructions at the start of the chapter to ensure you have the correct software installed then you will have no problems.

XSLT Elements

A discussion and example of each element is shown below in alphabetical order.

xsl:apply-imports

This element allows templates from imported stylesheets to be invoked while working within the current template. This does not override the current template, but rather it *adds* to the processing of the current template.

```
<xsl:apply-imports />
```

When you match a template with a pattern using the `<xsl:template>` element, you process the contents of the current template. However, XSLT allows you to import stylesheets into the current template, but the templates defined in the current template have higher precedence.

> In other words, if a particular `match` expression is true for two templates, one in the main stylesheet and another in an imported stylesheet, then the main stylesheet template will be used.

However, it may be the case that we still want to use some functionality of an imported template, but add this functionality to the template defined in the importing stylesheet. Often this would be the case where we want to avoid duplicating content within the templates.

The following example, `apply-imports.xsl`, shows how `xsl:apply-imports` can be used to output different information for the same pattern match based on a global variable (which could for example be passed into the stylesheet):

```
<?xml version="1.0" ?>
<xsl:stylesheet version="1.0"
   xmlns:xsl="http://www.w3.org/1999/XSL/Transform">
   <xsl:import href="apply-imports2.xsl" />
   <xsl:param name="type" select="'detail'" />
   <xsl:output indent="yes" omit-xml-declaration="yes" />
   <xsl:template match="customers">
      <div>
      <xsl:choose>
         <xsl:when test="$type='detail'">
            <xsl:apply-imports />
         </xsl:when>
         <xsl:otherwise>
            Company Name: <xsl:value-of select="@custname" />
         </xsl:otherwise>
      </xsl:choose>
      </div>
   </xsl:template>
</xsl:stylesheet>
```

xsl:import is discussed later, but must come as a direct child of the <xsl:stylesheet> element and refers to the other XSL stylesheet discussed below. We then define a simple parameter – just for illustration in this example – and set its value to detail. Imagine that the parameter here could be passed in from some external application – it is empty by default or is set to detail for detailed information to be sent to the output. Notice that an <xsl:output> element is used (common through all examples), which instructs the processor about certain details for the output. Two attributes are set – the first, indent="yes", simply instructs the processor to include additional whitespace to neatly display the element output. The second attribute omit-xml-declaration instructs the processor *not* to output the XML declaration that comes at the top of an XML file. The template matches the <customers> element, defines a containing <DIV> tag, and then uses an <xsl:choose> element to determine the output. If the type parameter is set to detail then it processes the <xsl:apply-imports> element, otherwise it displays the company name. When the <xsl:apply-imports> element is processed, MSXML will look in any imported stylesheets for a template that matches the current one. In our case, it looks into the apply-imports2.xsl stylesheet for any template matching the expression customer. Of course, we have defined one that matches (or the example would be useless). This is shown below; the apply-imports2.xsl stylesheet is a fairly simple stylesheet outputting detailed company information:

```
<?xml version="1.0" ?>
<xsl:stylesheet version="1.0"
    xmlns:xsl="http://www.w3.org/1999/XSL/Transform">
    <xsl:output indent="yes" omit-xml-declaration="yes" />
    <xsl:template match="customers">
        Company Details : <xsl:value-of select="@custname" />
        Company Phone : <xsl:value-of select="@phone" />
        Company Email : <xsl:value-of select="@email" />
    </xsl:template>
</xsl:stylesheet>
```

An interesting note is that the customers template from the main stylesheet is not replaced – you can see this as the <DIV> tags appear in the output – rather it is supplemented with the information from the xsl:apply-imports matching template.

The output will be something like the following:

```
<div>
  Company Details : Chile Wines Inc
  Company Phone : 0141 952 56223
  Company Email : cw@deltabis.com
</div>
```

xsl:apply-templates

This element tells the processor to apply the appropriate template based on the XPath expression and node context. It selects a node-set based on the select expression, which is a valid XPath expression. When there is no select expression, all children of the context node are selected. Where multiple templates are found, the last one in the document is selected.

```
<xsl:apply-templates select="expression" mode="Expression">
    <xsl:with-param />
    <xsl:sort />
</xsl:apply-templates>
```

The mode attribute allows the template called to be invoked multiple times depending on the mode, which must be a qualified name (namespace plus local name). The <xsl:with-param> and <xsl:sort> child elements are optional.

The <xsl:sort> element can occur many times and states the nodes that should be ordered in the node-set that is selected. This ordered node-set is then used by the matching template. If no sort order is provided, then document order is used.

The <xsl:with-param> element is used to pass parameters to the matching template. However, the parameter will only be passed to the template if a <param> element with the same name is defined within the matching template. Otherwise, the parameter will be ignored.

The following example, apply-templates.xsl, shows how a simple invoice display stylesheet may use the <apply-templates> element to output some summary information at the top of the page, followed by detailed invoice information. The first mode, summary, would invoke a simple template to output some content about the context <order> element, and the second template with no mode attribute would output more detailed information about the same context <order> element:

```
<?xml version="1.0" ?>
<xsl:stylesheet version="1.0"
   xmlns:xsl="http://www.w3.org/1999/XSL/Transform">
   <xsl:output indent="yes" omit-xml-declaration="yes" />
   <xsl:template match="Invoices">
=============
ORDER SUMMARY (ordered by largest orders)
=============<xsl:text></xsl:text>
      <xsl:apply-templates select="customers/order" mode="summary">
         <xsl:sort select="details/items/@num"
                          data-type="number" order="descending" />
      </xsl:apply-templates>

=============
ORDER DETAILS
=============<xsl:text></xsl:text>
      <xsl:apply-templates select="customers/order">
         <xsl:sort select="details/items/@num" order="descending" />
         <xsl:with-param name="GenerationTime" select="'18:57PM'" />
      </xsl:apply-templates>
   </xsl:template>
   <xsl:template match="customers/order" mode="summary">
Order<xsl:value-of select="@orderID" />
   </xsl:template>
   <xsl:template match="customers/order">
   <xsl:param name="GenerationTime" />
<xsl:if test="position()=1">
Generated at <xsl:value-of select="$GenerationTime" />
</xsl:if>
For <xsl:value-of select="@orderID" /> there is <xsl:text></xsl:text>
<xsl:value-of select="details/items/@num" /> items.<xsl:text></xsl:text>
   </xsl:template>
</xsl:stylesheet>
```

The first `<xsl:apply-templates>` element in the `match="Invoices"` template will select a template matching the `customers/order` pattern in "summary" mode and the resulting node-set from a query on the source document will be sorted first by the number of items, using the child `<xsl:sort>` element with the sort expression `details/items/@num` relative to the context. The sort is based on numbers by setting the `data-type` attribute appropriately, which can have a number, text or a QName as its value. There is more on the `<xsl:sort>` element later in the chapter. The `<xsl:apply-templates>` matches one template and displays some summary order information, with the orders with the most items at the top. Notice the use of the `<xsl:text>` element, which is used a lot in the examples and which converts new lines into a single line and removes leading and trailing spaces.

The second `<apply-templates>` element is very similar, but operates with no mode attribute and also passes in a `GenerationTime` parameter to indicate the time the invoice was created. To allow it to be passed through there must be an `<xsl:param>` element declared as a direct child of this `<xsl:template>` with the same name as the parameter passed from the `xsl:apply-templates`. Notice that it then uses the XPath expression with the `<xsl:if>` element to output the time only if the current node is the first node. This parameter could of course be a global variable, but as in procedural languages, you want to limit the creation of global variables – particularly if you are thinking about modularizing your templates.

The output generated will be something like the following:

```
=============
ORDER SUMMARY (ordered by largest orders)
=============
OrderOID931
OrderOID927
OrderOID921


=============
ORDER DETAILS
=============
Generated at 18:57PM
For OID931 there is 6 items.
For OID927 there is 5 items.
For OID921 there is 2 items.
```

xsl:attribute

The `<attribute>` element creates attribute nodes that are sent to the output. We typically use this when outputting another XML file, or a format such as XHTML for display on some sort of web browser.

```
<xsl:attribute name="attribute-name" namespace="uri"></xsl:attribute>
```

The `name` attribute is required and specifies the name of the attribute to be created in the output. This name attribute can be dynamically assigned, with its value being a set of curly braces, `{ }`, with some expression inside – as with `<xsl:value-of>` elements. For example:

```
<xsl:attribute name="{@itemName}" namespace="uri"></xsl:attribute>
```

The `namespace` attribute specifies the namespace that the value of the `name` attribute should be bound to.

The example below will create XHTML output for display in a browser. The output will include a qualified anchor element with an `href` attribute with the value specified in the `<ordered>` element of the context `<order>` element:

```
<wrox:a>
   <xsl:attribute name="href" namespace="wrox">
   http://www.someuri.com/ order.asp?orderid=
      <xsl:value-of select="@orderID" />
   </xsl:attribute>
</wrox:a>
```

For further examples, see the section on `<xsl:element>`.

xsl:attribute-set

The `xsl:attribute-set` of attributes allows us to group attributes that are commonly used throughout the document and that can be reused and apply groups of attributes to elements, rather than creating multiple `xsl:attribute` definitions.

```
<xsl:attribute-set name="QName" use-attribute-sets="QNames">
</xsl:attribute-set>
```

The `name` attribute is required and specifies the name of the `attribute-set` to be created in the output – it can also contain a prefix to define it in a particular namespace. The `use-attribute-sets` attribute allows inheritance from other defined `<attribute-set>` elements, the name of each `attribute-set` being written separated by whitespace.

This element is used on `<xsl:element>`, `<xsl:copy>`, and `<xsl:attribute-set>` elements, and the same functionality could also be achieved using the `<xsl:attribute>` element. However, you will find this method to be particularly useful when you are repeatedly defining common combinations of attributes – the values can be dynamically determined using normal XSLT techniques. Furthermore, your common attributes could be imported or included from an external file and therefore you can standardize which attributes and values are being used. You can override attributes defined in an `attribute-set` by setting attributes locally on the element, using `<xsl:attribute>`.

The following example, `attribute-set.xsl`, shows how an `attribute-set` can be used when working with the `<xsl:copy>` element, which is discussed further below, to modify the `<order>` element:

```
<?xml version="1.0" ?>
<xsl:stylesheet version="1.0"
   xmlns:xsl="http://www.w3.org/1999/XSL/Transform">
   <xsl:output indent="yes" omit-xml-declaration="yes" />
   <xsl:template match="order">
      <xsl:copy use-attribute-sets="FurtherInfo">
         <xsl:attribute name="manager">Loreto</xsl:attribute>
         <xsl:apply-templates select="@*" />
      </xsl:copy>
   </xsl:template>
   <xsl:template match="@*">
      <xsl:copy>
         <xsl:value-of select="." />
      </xsl:copy>
   </xsl:template>
```

```
      <xsl:attribute-set name="FurtherInfo">
         <xsl:attribute name="delivered">yes</xsl:attribute>
         <xsl:attribute name="manager">Steven</xsl:attribute>
      </xsl:attribute-set>
      <xsl:template match="text()" />
   </xsl:stylesheet>
```

The first template matches the `<order>` elements and within this, the `<xsl:copy>` element is applied to the `<order>` element. It has a `use-attribute-sets` attribute with the value `FurtherInfo`, which is defined in an `<xsl:attribute-set>` element at the bottom of the stylesheet. This means that the attributes `delivered` and `manager`, with the values `"yes"` and `"Steven"` respectively, will also be appended to the output copy of the `<order>` element. However, within this `<xsl:copy>`, there is a local `<xsl:attribute>` element, which has its name attribute set to `manager`, with the value `"Loreto"`. As this `manager` attribute was already defined by the `<FurtherInfo>` element, it already exists on the `<order>` element (with the value `"Steven"`). However, as this is a local attribute declaration, it overrides this and so the new value of the attribute is `"Loreto"`. Beyond this, an `<xsl:apply-templates>` element is used to copy all attributes that currently exist on the `<order>` element.

The output will be something like the following:

```
<order delivered="yes" manager="Loreto" orderID="OID921" batchid="123" />
<order delivered="yes" manager="Loreto" orderID="OID927" />
<order delivered="yes" manager="Loreto" orderID="OID931" batchid="123" />
```

xsl:call-template

This element allows you to invoke a template directly by calling it by its name, which is particularly useful when encapsulating commonly used pieces of XSLT. For example, if we commonly write out a table in our XSLT, (or wish to do so in more XSLTs) we can create a generic implementation inside a `<call-template>` element and then when required, simply invoke the `call-template` to generate the output, passing in parameter as desired.

```
   <xsl:call-template name="QName">
   </xsl:call-template>
```

The `name` attribute of this template is the name of the `xsl:template` we want to invoke. The template we are calling does not need to have a `match` attribute, but it can if desired. When calling the template using `xsl:call-template`, the `match` attribute is ignored, so we can even have both a `name` and `match` for two separate purposes. The context is *not* changed as a result of using this (unlike `xsl:apply-templates`), so the context is the same in the template as it was when the `xsl:call-template` was processed. Also, this element can contain multiple `<xsl:with-param>` child elements to pass values into the template.

The example below, `call-template.xsl`, demonstrates all of the above features of calling templates to provide an odd/even output rotation system – much like the way many HTML tables rotate colors for odd/even table rows. However, we will just use characters rather than unnecessary HTML elements.

```
   <?xml version="1.0" ?>
   <xsl:stylesheet version="1.0"
      xmlns:xsl="http://www.w3.org/1999/XSL/Transform">
      <xsl:output indent="yes" omit-xml-declaration="yes" />
      <xsl:template name="rotate" match="*[local-name()='busInfo']">
```

```
        <xsl:param name="even" select="'*'" />
        <xsl:param name="odd" select="'-'" />
        <xsl:choose>
            <xsl:when test="position() mod 2 = 0">
                <xsl:value-of select="$even" />
                <xsl:apply-templates />
            </xsl:when>
            <xsl:otherwise>
                <xsl:value-of select="$odd" />
                <xsl:apply-templates />
            </xsl:otherwise>
        </xsl:choose>
    </xsl:template>
    <xsl:template match="item">
        <xsl:call-template name="rotate">
            <xsl:with-param name="even" select="'='" />
            <xsl:with-param name="odd" select="'$'" />
        </xsl:call-template>
    </xsl:template>
    <xsl:template match="text()">
        <xsl:value-of select="." />
        <xsl:text>&#xA;</xsl:text>
    </xsl:template>
</xsl:stylesheet>
```

The first template, rotate, is the most complex as the template matches any element that has the local-name() busInfo (because this has a namespace associated with it, so we can exclude the namespace with the local-name() XPath function), which matches two elements within our source document. Within this, two parameters called even and odd are defined and initialized with the values "*" and "-" respectively. In HTML this could be the colors of odd and even rows. After this, an <xsl:choose> element selects even nodes and outputs the value of the even parameter ("*") and then the value of the respective element. Otherwise, for odd nodes it outputs the value of the odd parameter ("-") and then the value of the respective element.

The second template matches any <item> elements (of which there are many) and uses the <xsl:call-template> element to use the functionality defined earlier for the <busInfo> element. We can call the template named rotate to output generic odd and even type lines, simply by using it as the value of the name parameter on the <xsl:call-template> element. Further to this, because we defined the parameters odd and even in the rotate template, we can pass in our own values for these from within the <xsl:call-template> element – we do this and pass even as "=" and odd as "$" (although in HTML this could again be colors). The <item> element remains the context element and so this is the value that is output.

One other point worth mentioning is that the match="text()" template will match any text nodes and output their value as well as a new line. This is best done by enclosing the newline special character reference
 within an <xsl:text> element.

The output will be something like the following fragment:

-Wine Division South
$Rancagua White
=Rancagua Red
$Chillan Red
=Rancagua White
$Santiago Red
=Rancagua White
$Rancagua Red
$Southern Fruity Red

xsl:choose

This element doesn't differ from the 1998 implementation. Further details can be found in the `xsl:when` discussion below.

xsl:comment

This element doesn't differ from the 1998 implementation.

xsl:copy

The `<xsl:copy>` element copies the current node from the source to the output with the same name, namespace, and type as the source node. Note that it doesn't copy attributes and children automatically.

```
<xsl:copy use-attribute-sets="QName List">
</xsl:copy>
```

With the `<xsl:copy>` element, transformation of source XML documents to some other format is possible.

The following example (`copy.xsl`) copies the `<order>` elements and attributes to the output to generate a simple list of all the orders within the source document:

```
<?xml version="1.0" ?>
<xsl:stylesheet version="1.0"
    xmlns:xsl="http://www.w3.org/1999/XSL/Transform">
    <xsl:output indent="yes" omit-xml-declaration="yes" />
    <xsl:template match="order">
        <xsl:copy use-attribute-sets="FurtherInfo">
            <xsl:apply-templates select="@*" />
        </xsl:copy>
    </xsl:template>
    <xsl:template match="@*">
        <xsl:copy>
            <xsl:value-of select="." />
        </xsl:copy>
    </xsl:template>
    <xsl:attribute-set name="FurtherInfo">
        <xsl:attribute name="delivered">yes</xsl:attribute>
        <xsl:attribute name="manager">Steven</xsl:attribute>
    </xsl:attribute-set>
    <xsl:template match="text()" />
</xsl:stylesheet>
```

Notice that an `<xsl:output>` element is used, which instructs the processor about certain details for the output. Two attributes are set – the first, `indent="yes"`, simply instructs the processor to include additional whitespace to neatly display the element output. The second attribute, `omit-xml-declaration`, instructs the processor *not* to output the XML declaration that comes at the top of an XML file. The first template matches all nodes and initializes the processing of the stylesheet. Remember we want to use templates to filter out the nodes we wish to work with so we first want to match the `<order>` element by setting the `match` attribute value on an `<xsl:template>`. Within this template, we use the `<xsl:copy>` element to copy the current "order" node to the output and use the new `use-attribute-sets` attribute to tell the processor to add the attributes defined in the `FurtherInfo` attribute-set to the output `<order>` element. We will look at this more later. We then use a further `apply-templates` to match all attribute nodes of this node – the "`@*`" expression does this. The final template matches this pattern, and does the fairly simple job of copying the name and value of the attribute to the output.

The output will be something like the following:

```
<order delivered="yes" manager="Steven" orderID="OID921" batchid="123" />
<order delivered="yes" manager="Steven" orderID="OID927" />
<order delivered="yes" manager="Steven" orderID="OID931" batchid="123" />
```

Note that the `<xsl:copy>` element of the W3C implementation has been improved to support attribute sets.

xsl:copy-of

The `<xsl:copy-of>` element copies the current node and all children from the source to the output with the same name, namespace, and type as the source node, copying attributes and children automatically.

```
<xsl:copy-of select="expression" />
```

The `select` attribute simply determines the nodes to be copied to the output. You may commonly use in conjunction with temporaryfragments when you want to write the same collection of nodes to the output in more than one place, or to deep copy an element and all of its descendent nodes. It cannot have any child elements.

The following example illustrates both of these uses. It uses both a temporary fragment to output some information as well as deep copying all of the order information:

```
<?xml version="1.0" ?>
<xsl:stylesheet version="1.0"
    xmlns:xsl="http://www.w3.org/1999/XSL/Transform">
    <xsl:output indent="yes" omit-xml-declaration="yes" />
    <xsl:variable name="header">
        <xsl:text>A list of the current orders is shown below.&#xA;</xsl:text>
    </xsl:variable>
    <xsl:template match="customers">
        <xsl:copy-of select="$header" />
        <xsl:apply-templates />
    </xsl:template>
    <xsl:template match="order">
        <xsl:copy-of select="."></xsl:copy-of>
    </xsl:template>
    <xsl:template match="text()" />
</xsl:stylesheet>
```

A variable called `header` is created, which stores a temporary fragment of some header text followed by a newline character. The first template matches the `<customers>` element and uses the `<xsl:copy-of>` element to copy the content of the `header` variable to the output. It uses an `apply-templates` and then has a template that matches the `<order>` elements, which also uses the `<xsl:copy-of>` element to copy the context `<order>` element and all of its descendent nodes to the output.

The output from this stylesheet would be:

```
 A list of the current orders is shown below.
<order orderID="OID921" batchid="123">
<details>
<items num="2">
<item>Rancagua White</item>
<item>Rancagua Red</item>
```

```
</items>
</details>
</order>
<order orderID="OID927">
<details>
<items num="5">
<item>Chillan Red</item>
<item>Rancagua White</item>
<item>Santiago Red</item>
<item>Rancagua White</item>
<item>Rancagua Red</item>
</items>
</details>
</order>
<order orderID="OID931" batchid="123">
<details>
<items num="6">
<item>Southern Fruity Red</item>
<item>Rancagua White</item>
<item>Rancagua Red</item>
<item>Rancagua White</item>
<item>Chillan Red</item>
<item>Northern Sweet White</item>
</items>
</details>
</order>
```

xsl:decimal-format

The `<xsl:decimal-format>` element is used to define the interpretation of a format pattern used by the `format-number()` function. It applies exclusively to `format-number()` and does not affect any other elements or functions.

```
<xsl:decimal-format name="QName" decimal-separator="char"
    grouping-separator="char" infinity="string" minus-sign="char"
    NaN ="string" percent="char" per-mille="char" zero-digit="char"
    digit="char" pattern-separator="char">
</xsl:decimal-format>
```

This element should be defined as a child of the `<xsl:stylesheet>` or `<xsl:transform>` elements only. All attributes are optional. The `name` attribute defines the name by which the `format-number()` function will refer to the formatting provided by a given `<xsl:decimal-format>` element. If no name is assigned, then this will become the default decimal format (only one may exist). The `decimal-separator` attribute (default ".") is the character separating the integer and fraction part of a real number. The `grouping-separator` attribute (default ",") is the character separating groups of digits, such as thousands (for example 1,000). The `infinity` attribute (default "Infinity") is the string representing infinity. The `minus-sign` attribute (default "-") is the character representing the minus sign. The `NaN` attribute (default "NaN") is the character representing the "Not a Number" string. The `percent` attribute (default "%") is the character representing the percentage character. The `per-mille` attribute (default "‰" – character #x2030) is the character representing the per-thousand character. The `zero-digit` attribute (default "0") is the character representing the digit zero. The `digit` attribute (default "#") is used to indicate where a leading zero digit can occur. The `pattern-separator` attribute (default ";") separates the sub-pattern for positive numbers from that of negative numbers in the `format-number()` function.

One important point to note is that this element does not affect the formatting of the number – this is handled by the format pattern of the `format-number()` function – it affects the display that is output.

The example below, `decimal-format.xsl`, demonstrates the use of this element in various formatting patterns:

```
<?xml version="1.0" ?>
<xsl:stylesheet version="1.0"
   xmlns:xsl="http://www.w3.org/1999/XSL/Transform">
   <xsl:output indent="yes" omit-xml-declaration="yes" />

   <xsl:decimal-format name="scotland" decimal-separator=','
      grouping-separator='.' />
    <xsl:decimal-format name="us" decimal-separator='.'
      grouping-separator=',' />
   <xsl:decimal-format name="esp" infinity='Infinito' NaN="No es Numero" />

   <xsl:template match="order[@batchid][1]">
   <xsl:value-of select="format-number(@batchid, '###,###.00')" />
   <xsl:text>&#xA;</xsl:text>
   <xsl:value-of select="format-number(@batchid, '###.###,00',
      'scotland')" />
   <xsl:text>&#xA;</xsl:text>
   <xsl:value-of select="format-number(-@batchid, '###.###,00',
      'scotland')" />
   <xsl:text>&#xA;</xsl:text>
   <xsl:value-of select="format-number(@batchid, '###,###.00', 'us')" />
   <xsl:text>&#xA;</xsl:text>
   <xsl:value-of select="format-number(@batchid div 0, '###,###.00')" />
   <xsl:text>&#xA;</xsl:text>
   <xsl:value-of select="format-number(@batchid div 0, '###,###.00',
      'esp')" />
   <xsl:text>&#xA;</xsl:text>
   <xsl:value-of select="format-number(@batchid*@orderID,
      '###,###.00','esp')" />
   <xsl:text>&#xA;</xsl:text>
   <xsl:value-of select="format-number(@batchid,
      '###,###.00;(###,###.00)')" />
   <xsl:text>&#xA;</xsl:text>
   <xsl:value-of select="format-number(-@batchid,
      '###,###.00;(###,###.00)')" />
   <xsl:text>&#xA;</xsl:text>
   </xsl:template>

   <xsl:template match="text()" />
</xsl:stylesheet>
```

The example defines three formats, `scotland`, `us`, and `esp` – the first two simply showing how the separators can be defined. The final one shows how translation of the output can be done for Spanish using this element. The template matches the first `batchid` – simply a number that will be used in the examples. The third parameter of the `format-number()` function takes the name of the `<xsl:decimal-format>` element that will output the appropriate display. The first `format-number()` uses the default decimal format – it has no third parameter. The others take the name of an `<xsl:decimal-format>` element to display the number in the required format.

The output would be something like the following:

```
123.00
123,00
-123,00
123.00
Infinity
Infinito
No es Numero
123.00
(123.00)
```

xsl:element

The `<xsl:element>` element creates an element in the output with the name specified with a namespace defined in the optional `namespace` attribute. It is also possible to apply sets of pre-defined attributes to any element created this way.

```
<xsl:element name="element name" namespace="uri-reference"
    use-attribute-sets="QName">
</xsl:element>
```

We may use this element to output some XHTML element such as an anchor tag. We could of course do this by simply using an `<A>` element with the appropriate XSL within it, but in more complex cases the element may be dynamic. An example of this is given for the MSXML 1998 implementation described above and it isn't difficult to modify this to the W3C implementation. So, let's consider a more complex example to illustrate the improved features of the W3C definition.

The following example (`element.xsl`) creates a set of `dispatch` elements describing orders that have been completed. Note that any whitespace here is just for presentation – we will see ways of working with this later on.

```
<?xml version="1.0" ?>
<xsl:stylesheet version="1.0"
    xmlns:xsl="http://www.w3.org/1999/XSL/Transform">

    <xsl:output indent="yes" omit-xml-declaration="yes" />

    <xsl:template match="order">
    <xsl:element name="wrox:dispatch" namespace="uri:wroxOrders"
        use-attribute-sets="FurtherInfo">
        <xsl:attribute name="wrox:Custhref" namespace="uri:wroxOrders">
            customers.asp?custid=<xsl:value-of select="../@custid" />
        </xsl:attribute>
        <xsl:attribute name="wrox:Orderhref" namespace="uri:wroxOrders">
            customers.asp?custid=<xsl:value-of select="@orderID" />
        </xsl:attribute>
    </xsl:element>
    </xsl:template>

    <xsl:attribute-set name="FurtherInfo">
    <xsl:attribute name="audit:delivered" namespace="uri:wroxAudit">
        yes
    </xsl:attribute>
```

```
         <xsl:attribute name="audit:manager" namespace="uri:wroxAudit">
            Steven
         </xsl:attribute>
   </xsl:attribute-set>
   <xsl:template match="text()" />
</xsl:stylesheet>
```

This example has a template that matches the `<order>` element and within this creates the `<dispatch>` element. Notice that the `name` attribute, which informs the processor what to call the outputted element, has a `wrox` prefix. Unless you have defined this prefix to be associated with some namespace within your XSLT document, you must associate this with a namespace using the namespace attribute (who would have guessed?). In our case, we assign the value `uri:wroxOrders` to the namespace attribute. Finally, this attribute has its `use-attribute-sets` attribute set to the value `FurtherInfo`. This references an `xsl:attribute-set` defined in the stylesheet and appends the attributes defined within this element to the `<dispatch>` element – as though they have been appended with multiple `xsl:attribute` statements. These attributes are also qualified, but with an `audit` prefix which is associated with the namespace `uri:wroxAudit`. For further discussion on this, see the description of `xsl:attribute-set`. Carrying on with the `<dispatch>` element, two attributes are defined that are attached to this element – `Custhref` and `Orderhref`, which are also qualified.

The output would be something like the following:

```
<wrox:dispatch audit:delivered="yes" audit:manager="Steven"
wrox:Custhref="customers.asp?custid=192398" wrox:Orderhref="customers.asp?custid=OID921"
xmlns:wrox="uri:wroxOrders" xmlns:audit="uri:wroxAudit" />

<wrox:dispatch audit:delivered="yes" audit:manager="Steven"
wrox:Custhref="customers.asp?custid=192398" wrox:Orderhref="customers.asp?custid=OID927"
xmlns:wrox="uri:wroxOrders" xmlns:audit="uri:wroxAudit" />

<wrox:dispatch audit:delivered="yes" audit:manager="Steven"
wrox:Custhref="customers.asp?custid=192398" wrox:Orderhref="customers.asp?custid=OID931"
xmlns:wrox="uri:wroxOrders" xmlns:audit="uri:wroxAudit" />
```

xsl:fallback

This element allows you to build in capability to provide back-up functionality if the element cannot be handled by the parser. For example, this may occur when the element is part of a newer version of XSL or an unsupported extension function. This is common when we have used extension functions of a given parser and some other parser parses our stylesheet.

```
<xsl:fallback>
</xsl:fallback>
```

This element should be a child of the element that you are providing fallback for. If the `version` attribute of the `<xsl:stylesheet>` element is greater than that known to the parser, then when an unknown XSLT element is encountered, the `xsl:fallback` mechanism will be invoked. In the case of extension functions (see `<msxsl:script>` element), if the namespace is unknown or not supported by the parser, then when an element is encountered that uses this namespace, the `<xsl:fallback>` element will be processed. These `<xsl:fallback>` elements can be chained together as siblings to provide backup functionality for each other. In other words, if the fallback itself is not supported, then the next fallback is processed.

The example below, `fallback.xsl`, shows how a future stylesheet might be designed to work with a hypothetical XSLT version 5.0, which has introduced (theoretically of course) the new element `<xsl:replace>`, which replaces all occurrences of one string with some other string:

```
<?xml version="1.0" ?>
<xsl:stylesheet version="5.0"
    xmlns:xsl="http://www.w3.org/1999/XSL/Transform">
    <xsl:output indent="yes" omit-xml-declaration="yes" />
    <xsl:template match="Invoices">
        <xsl:replace match="-" replace="/">
            <xsl:value-of select="." />
            <xsl:fallback>
                <xsl:value-of select="translate(@date,'/','-')" />
            </xsl:fallback>
        </xsl:replace>
    </xsl:template>
</xsl:stylesheet>
```

In this example, the `<xsl:stylesheet>` element's `version` attribute has been set to `5.0`, which is some future XSLT standard. All that the template of this stylesheet does is change the format of the input date from "28/11/2001" to the preferred format "28-11-2001". This format change is done by wrapping the new `<xsl:replace>` element around any of the text that is to be changed. However, if you try to use this in your stylesheet it will throw an error because the functionality is not supported and you haven't told it what to do in such a case. To cope with this, the `<xsl:fallback>` element can be used to tell it to do something else. In this example, we accomplish our goal using the XSLT `translate()` function, although other cases may be more complex.

The output would be something like the following:

28-11-2001

This output is caused because the `translate()` function takes the date in the original format with slashes ("/") and replaces each slash character with a dash ("-").

xsl:for-each

This element iterates through the context node-set determined by the `select` expression.

```
<xsl:for-each select="expression">
</xsl:for-each>
```

The node-set is selected by the expression given by the value of the `select` attribute, and the node-set is returned. Each source element selected as you work through the node-set becomes the new context for any expressions within the `<xsl:for-each>` element.

The example below, `for-each.xsl`, shows how we could display all of the wines that have been ordered in alphabetical order:

```
<?xml version="1.0" ?>
<xsl:stylesheet version="1.0"
    xmlns:xsl="http://www.w3.org/1999/XSL/Transform">
    <xsl:output indent="yes" omit-xml-declaration="yes" />
    <xsl:template match="customers">
```

```
    <TABLE>
        <xsl:for-each select="order/details/items/item">
            <xsl:sort select="." order="ascending" />
            <TR>
                <TD>
                    <xsl:value-of select="." />
                </TD>
            </TR>
        </xsl:for-each>
    </TABLE>
  </xsl:template>
</xsl:stylesheet>
```

The template matches the <customers> element – this is so we can later access all of the <item> elements within a single node-set. We output an HTML <TABLE> element and then move into our <xsl:for-each> element. The select attribute here selects all <item> elements within our source document into a single node-set. Further to this, the <xsl:sort> child element attribute is set to order by the context node within that selection, which would of course be the <item> element itself! This function orders alphabetically (ascending). After this it is all pretty simple – a standard table is written out with the names of the wine listed.

The output will be something like the following fragment.

```
<TABLE>
<TR>
<TD>
Chillan Red
</TD>
</TR>
<TR>
<TD>
Chillan Red
</TD>
</TR>
<TR>
<TD>
Northern Sweet White
</TD>
</TR>
<TR>
<TD>
Rancagua Red
</TD>
</TR>
.
</TABLE>
```

xsl:if

The <xsl:if> element allows conditional constructs within your stylesheet.

```
<xsl:if test="expression">
</xsl:if>
```

The `test` attribute is required and returns `true` or `false` depending on the outcome of its expression. You may test if you are at a certain position in the context or if a given node contains a certain value. If this attribute evaluates to `true`, then the content within the element is invoked.

To demonstrate `xsl:if`, the following example shows how you can use the `test` attribute alone as well as in combination with some scripting to produce conditional output:

```
<?xml version="1.0" ?>
<xsl:stylesheet version="1.0"
    xmlns:xsl="http://www.w3.org/1999/XSL/Transform"
    xmlns:msxsl="urn:schemas-microsoft-com:xslt"
    xmlns:wrox="uri:wroxbooks">

    <msxsl:script language="JScript" implements-prefix="wrox"><![CDATA[
    function GetDiscount(intOfferID)
    {
        var discount="0%";

        if (intOfferID<5)
            discount="0%";
        else if (intOfferID>5 && intOfferID<=15)
            discount="5%";
        else if (intOfferID>15 && intOfferID<=25)
            discount="8%";
        else if (intOfferID>25 && intOfferID<=35)
            discount="12%";
        else
            discount="5%";

        return discount;
    }
    ]]></msxsl:script>

    <xsl:output indent="yes" omit-xml-declaration="yes" />

    <xsl:template match="customers">
        <xsl:if test="@delivery='int'">International Delivery.</xsl:if>
        <xsl:if test="@offerID">
          You are entitled to a
          <xsl:value-of select="wrox:GetDiscount(number(@offerID))" />
          discount.
        </xsl:if>
    </xsl:template>
</xsl:stylesheet>
```

With the template match on the `<customers>` element, the first `<xsl:if>` element has a `test` attribute that checks if the `delivery` attribute of the context (`customers`) element is equal to the value "`int`", indicating an international delivery customer. If it returns `true`, then some simple text is added to the output to indicate "International Delivery", otherwise this part is left blank.

The second `<xsl:if>` element offers a more complex test. The `test` attribute first checks if the context element has an `offerID` attribute and if so, the internal content is evaluated. This contains some text, but the main feature is an `<xsl:value-of>` element whose value is dependent on an internal function call. We won't be going into detail on how this works as it is covered in the `<msxsl:script>` element section further below. However, in brief, the `wrox` namespace is defined at the top of the stylesheet as a prefix for extension functions. When we wish to call a method defined within the `<msxsl:script>` element in the document, we simply append this prefix to the front of the method (like a qualified element) and pass in the relevant parameter(s). In our case, the parameter is the `offerID` attribute, which can be passed in normal XPath syntax. However, as we are going to be performing mathematical comparisons with the value, we use the XPath `number` function to convert it to a number type. The method simply returns a discount amount based on an `"if... else..."` series of tests, and the resulting value is returned as the output to the `<xsl:value-of>` element and written to the output. In our case, the value of the attribute is "27" and so the discount will be "12%".

The output will be something like the following. This is just a fragment – run the sample to see the whole output:

International Delivery.
You are entitled to a 12% discount.

xsl:import

The `<xsl:import>` element allows you to import a stylesheet along with its definitions and templates into the importing stylesheet.

```
<xsl:import href="uri" />
```

This is a top-level element and so must be a direct child of the `<xsl:stylesheet>` or `<xsl:transform>` element and must precede all other children. The `href` attribute specifies the URI of the stylesheet file to be imported into the current stylesheet. An important distinction between `include` and `import` is that stylesheets imported by the `<xsl:import>` element are given less precedence than the stylesheet that imports them – the main stylesheet.

However, we can have the situation where multiple imports are done by the main stylesheet, and even imports within these imported stylesheets. In the case of the main or importing stylesheet, those stylesheets that are imported further down in the stylesheet are given precedence over those imported higher up in the stylesheet. Furthermore, any stylesheets that are imported within these imported stylesheets are given higher precedence than those that are next down in the document. So, if stylesheet A imports stylesheet B and C, and B itself imports stylesheet D, then the overall precedence would be A, B, D, and then C.

You can see an example of importing stylesheets in the discussion of the `<xsl:apply-imports>` element earlier in this section of the chapter.

xsl:include

This element allows you to include another stylesheet within the including stylesheet.

```
<xsl:include href="uri" />
```

This is a top-level element and so must be a child of the <xsl:stylesheet> or <xsl:transform> element but can appear anywhere at this level in the stylesheet. The href attribute specifies the URI of the stylesheet file to be included within the current stylesheet. An important distinction between include and import is that stylesheets included by the <xsl:include> element are given exactly the same precedence as the stylesheet that includes them – the main stylesheet. In other words, it's as if the definitions in the included stylesheet were written in the including stylesheet in the first place.

As an example, the following is the principal stylesheet, which uses the <xsl:include> element to output some invoice information:

```
<?xml version="1.0" ?>
<xsl:stylesheet version="1.0"
    xmlns:xsl="http://www.w3.org/1999/XSL/Transform">
    <xsl:output indent="yes" omit-xml-declaration="yes" />
    <xsl:template match="Invoices">
        <xsl:text>Invoice at date </xsl:text>
        <xsl:value-of select="@date" />
        <xsl:text>.</xsl:text>
        <xsl:apply-templates />
    </xsl:template>
    <xsl:include href="include2.xsl" />
</xsl:stylesheet>
```

This is deliberately simple to demonstrate the concept – it has one template, which matches the <Invoices> element, writes out some information, then calls <xsl:apply-templates> to process the rest of the nodes. Near the end of the stylesheet there is an <xsl:include> element, which includes the XSLT file include2.xsl, shown below:

```
<?xml version="1.0" ?>
<xsl:stylesheet version="1.0"
    xmlns:xsl="http://www.w3.org/1999/XSL/Transform">
    <xsl:output indent="yes" omit-xml-declaration="yes" />
    <xsl:template match="customers">
        <xsl:text>&#xA;Customer </xsl:text>
        <xsl:value-of select="@custname" />
    </xsl:template>
</xsl:stylesheet>
```

Again, it is simple XSLT that matches the <customers> elements and writes out the customer name. The net effect is that the <customers> template is included in the principal stylesheet and processed as though it was originally part of it.

The output will be like the following:

Invoice at date 28/11/2001.
Customer Chile Wines Inc

xsl:key

This element declares a named key for use with the XPath key() function in expressions to provide a much simpler way of accessing complex documents and improving access performance.

```
<xsl:key name="QName" match="Pattern" use="expression">
</xsl:key>
```

This is a top-level element and so it must appear as a child of the `<xsl:stylesheet>` or `<xsl:transform>` element. The name attribute is the name that the `<xsl:key>` element will be referenced by in any `key()` function. The `match` attribute specifies a pattern matching expression that will define the nodes to which the key is applicable. This is the same as how you would define a match expression for a template. The `use` attribute contains an expression that identifies a node within the matching node that provides a value for the node.

Once the key or keys have been determined for a given stylesheet, they can be referenced by the XPath `key()` function as follows:

```
nodeset = key('key name', 'key value')
```

A node-set of the nodes for the given key matching the "`key value`" is returned.

Thorough examples of using the `<xsl:key>` element can be found in the "*XSLT Keys*" section later in the chapter.

xsl:message

This element sends a text message. It can stop the processing and pass this message to the environment or some message buffer, and can raise a system-level error that can be trapped and handled. It is commonly used to debug XSLT stylesheets under development, although **future** MSXML implementations will also allow debug information to be sent to a log file.

```
<xsl:message terminate="yes | no" >
</xsl:message>"
```

The `terminate` attribute indicates to the stylesheet whether the processing of the XSLT should terminate upon emitting this message – `yes` means terminate and `no` means continue processing. Compare this to compilation of some procedural language – `yes` is like an that is unrecoverable and stops compilation; `no` is like a warning where compilation still occurs and you are given the warning messages that were received. The slight difference is that you get to determine the context of the messages. Often messages can be used as the simple business rules of stylesheets.

With MSXML 3.0, the `terminate="no"` attribute is ignored and no message is reported. With `terminate="yes"`, the error message is raised to the environment and can be handled using the usual JavaScript or VBScript error handling capabilities.

The following example uses the `<xsl:message>` element to output an error message, identifying any element that does not contain a `batchid`:

```
<?xml version="1.0" ?>
<xsl:stylesheet version="1.0"
   xmlns:xsl="http://www.w3.org/1999/XSL/Transform">
   <xsl:output indent="yes" omit-xml-declaration="yes" />
   <xsl:template match="order">
      <xsl:if test="not(@batchid)">
         <xsl:message terminate="yes">
            The batchid for <xsl:value-of select="@orderID" /> was not
               provided.
         </xsl:message>
      </xsl:if>
   </xsl:template>
</xsl:stylesheet>
```

The `test` of the `<xsl:if>` element will return `false` if the `batchid` attribute does not exist, so the `not()` function returns `true` for this condition to the `test` attribute and processes the contents. In this case, there is a child `<xsl:message>` element that stops processing and outputs a message to the environment.

The output message in this case is:

The batchid for OID927 was not provided.

xsl:namespace-alias

This element can be used to replace the specified prefix with another namespace or prefix.

```
<xsl:namespace-alias stylesheet-prefix="NCName" result-prefix="NCName" />
```

This element should have no child elements and must occur as a child of the `<xsl:stylesheet>` or `<xsl:transform>` element, but may occur multiple times. The `stylesheet-prefix` attribute should contain the text of the prefix as declared in the XSLT – that is, the one being used. The `result-prefix` attribute should then contain the text of the prefix that should be generated for this namespace in the output.

The main purpose of this is to enable the transformation of one XSLT stylesheet to another, although there may be other uses. Generating a stylesheet would require `<xsl:template>` elements to be output, though these would be interpreted by the first stylesheet and not be output. However, if the prefix points to a namespace not recognizable by the XSLT processor then it will not be parsed and can then be output, having its namespace in the output qualified as an XSLT element.

Consider the following example to illustrate how this works. It generates only part of a stylesheet, but the concept could easily be expanded upon to produce more complex stylesheets:

```
<?xml version="1.0" ?>
<xsl:stylesheet version="1.0"
    xmlns:xsl="http://www.w3.org/1999/XSL/Transform"
    xmlns:dxsl="uri:DynamicXSL">

    <xsl:output indent="yes" omit-xml-declaration="yes" />
    <xsl:namespace-alias stylesheet-prefix="dxsl" result-prefix="xsl" />
    <xsl:template match="customers">
        <xsl:comment>
            This generates a dynamic XSLT customers template.
        </xsl:comment>
        <dxsl:template match="customers">
            <dxsl:comment>
                This XSLT customers template was dynamically generated.
            </dxsl:comment>
        </dxsl:template>
    </xsl:template>
</xsl:stylesheet>
```

An extra namespace is declared with the prefix `dxsl`, which identifies dynamic XSL elements – those XSL elements we don't want parsed on the initial pass through. We also have an `<xsl:namespace-alias>` element telling the processor that any elements with the prefix `dxsl` should be associated with the `xsl` prefix (and hence namespace) when output. Within the template, there is another template defined using the `dxsl` prefix (so as not to be processed) and on output, this is changed to use the XSL prefix associated with the XSLT namespace.

The output message in this case is:

```
<!--This generates a dynamic XSLT customers template.-->
<xsl:template match="customers" xmlns:xsl="http://www.w3.org/1999/XSL/Transform">
<xsl:comment>This XSLT customers template was dynamically generated.</xsl:comment>
</xsl:template>
```

xsl:number

The `<xsl:number>` element inserts a formatted number into the result tree based on a range of attributes that can be set on the element.

```
<xsl:number level="single | multiple | any" count="Pattern" from="Pattern"
value="number expression" format="string" lang="nmtoken"
letter-value="alphabetic | traditional" grouping-separator="char"
grouping-size="number" />
```

The `level` attribute determines what levels of the tree should be considered and what kind of sequencing should be applied. The `count` attribute specifies which nodes should be counted to determine a sequence at this level. The `from` attribute will state where this counting should start. The `value` attribute is an expression that should be converted to a number – a sequence number determined by the context position is given. The `format` attribute says how the sequence should be numbered – it takes the same values as the `formatIndex()` function in the XSL 1998 implementation discussed above. The `lang` attribute specifies the language to be used, which defaults to the system language. The `letter-value` attribute distinguishes the numbering schemes used in a given language. The `grouping-separator` attribute is the character that separates groups of digits (such as ","), and the `grouping-size` attribute is the number of digits within a group.

The example below demonstrates how to output a list of the wines in each order as a numbered list:

```
<?xml version="1.0" ?>
<xsl:stylesheet version="1.0"
    xmlns:xsl="http://www.w3.org/1999/XSL/Transform">
    <xsl:output indent="yes" omit-xml-declaration="yes" />
    <xsl:template match="customers">
        <xsl:apply-templates select="//items" />
    </xsl:template>
    <xsl:template match="items">
        <xsl:number level="single" value="position()" format="1." />
        <xsl:text>&#xA;</xsl:text>
        <xsl:apply-templates select="item" />
    </xsl:template>
    <xsl:template match="item">
        <xsl:text>&#x9;</xsl:text>
        <xsl:number level="single" value="position()" format="I." />
        <xsl:value-of select="." />
        <xsl:text>&#xA;</xsl:text>
    </xsl:template>
    <xsl:template match="text()" />
</xsl:stylesheet>
```

The `customers` template invokes an `<xsl:apply-templates>` to process a node-list of the `items` in the source document. The `items` template then uses an `<xsl:number>` element to output the context position in a numerical format followed by a period. A newline character is added and `xsl:apply-templates` is called to process further children. It uses another template, which matches `<item>` elements, and outputs a space character followed by a Roman numeral list of the wines requested in order.

The output message in this case is:

1.
   I.Rancagua White
   II.Rancagua Red
2.
   I.Chillan Red
   II.Rancagua White
   III.Santiago Red
   IV.Rancagua White
   V.Rancagua Red
3.
   I.Southern Fruity Red
   II.Rancagua White
   III.Rancagua Red
   IV.Rancagua White
   V.Chillan Red
   VI.Northern Sweet White

xsl:otherwise

This element doesn't differ from the 1998 implementation. Further details can be found in the discussions of `xsl:when` (which also shows an implementation).

xsl:output

This element sets a series of options for use in the serialization of the result tree, such as determining the output encoding, omitting the XML declaration that is output by default, and determining whether the XML should be formatted with indents and document type declarations.

```
<xsl:output method = "xml | html | text | QName" version="nmtoken"
  encoding="string" omit-xml-declaration="yes | no" standalone="yes | no"
  doctype-public="string" doctype-system="string"
  cdata-section-elements="QNames" indent="yes | no" media-type="string" />
```

The `method` attribute determines the result tree type and defaults to `xml`. The `version` attribute refers to the XML version, which is currently "`1.0`". The `encoding` attribute specifies the encoding to use for the output. The `omit-xml-declaration` attribute states whether the XML declaration should appear in the output, which it does by default – this is used in the examples. The `standalone` attribute states whether a standalone declaration should be output. The `doctype-public` attribute specifies if a public identifier is to be used in the DTD, and the `doctype-system` attribute specifies if a system identifier is to be used in the DTD. The `cdata-section-elements` attribute identifies those elements that contain text nodes that should be output using CDATA sections. Finally, the `indent` attribute says whether additional whitespace should be used for formatting in the output, and the `media-type` attribute specifies the MIME content type for the output.

The example below, `output.xsl`, shows how a simple XHTML document can be output:

```
<?xml version="1.0" ?>
<xsl:stylesheet version="1.0"
    xmlns:xsl="http://www.w3.org/1999/XSL/Transform">
    <xsl:output method="html"
        doctype-public="-//W3C//DTD XHTML 1.0 Transitional//EN"/>
```

```
    <xsl:template match="customers">
       <html xmlns="http://www.w3.org/1999/xhtml" lang="en-US">
          <head></head>
          <body>
             <b>
                <xsl:value-of select="@custname" />
             </b>
          </body>
       </html>
    </xsl:template>
</xsl:stylesheet>
```

The `<xsl:output>` element is instructed to output HTML (therefore no XML declaration will be output) and the `doctype` is set to transitional XHTML. The output from this example is shown below:

```
<!DOCTYPE html PUBLIC "-//W3C//DTD XHTML 1.0 Transitional//EN">
<html lang="en-US" xmlns="http://www.w3.org/1999/xhtml">
<head></head>
<body>
<b>Chile Wines Inc</b>
</body>
</html>
```

xsl:param

This element declares a named parameter for use within an `<xsl:stylesheet>` or `<xsl:template>` and allows a default value to be set.

```
<xsl:param name="QName" select="Expression">
</xsl:param>
```

The `name` attribute sets the name by which the parameter will be referenced and the expression sets the parameter, the value of which can be a simple text value or tree fragment. The `<xsl:param>` element must appear as a direct child of the `<xsl:stylesheet>`, `<xsl:transform>`, or `<xsl:template>` element and inherits the value of any parameter passed to one of these if the passed parameter has the same name. If not, it uses the default value, and if there is no default value it contains an empty string.

Examples of the `<xsl:param>` element can be seen in the `xsl:apply-imports` and `xsl:call-template` element discussions above.

xsl:preserve-space

This element preserves whitespace in whitespace-only text nodes in a document. This includes characters such as – `&#32;` (space), `&#13;` (carriage return), `&#9;` (tab) and `&#10;` (newline), which are present in most documents and can radically effect your output.

```
<xsl:preserve-space elements="tokens" />
```

This must be a direct child of an `<xsl:stylesheet>` or `<xsl:transform>` element. The `elements` attribute takes a list of qualified names that should have their whitespace preserved. The default action is to preserve these text nodes, but an `<xsl:strip-space>` element may remove these nodes, so it may be necessary to mention specific nodes that should ignore the `<xsl:strip-space>` and preserve whitespace.

Consider the following string:

```
<name><first>Steven</first> <second>Livingstone</second></name>
```

The whitespace-only text node between `</first>` and `<second>` is significant as it separates the first and second name. With it, the name reads "Steven Livingstone", and without, it reads "StevenLivingstone". In this case we would wish to preserve the whitespace-only text node.

Examples and further discussion can be found in the "*Controlling Whitespace*" section later in this.

xsl:processing-instruction

This element creates a processing instruction in the output.

```
<xsl:processing-instruction name="processing instruction name">
</xsl:processing-instruction>
```

The only attribute expected here is the `name` of the processing instruction you are to create – the actual text of the processing instruction should be the content of the element.

The example below, `pi.xsl`, shows how an `xml-stylesheet` processing instruction can be created in the output:

```
<?xml version="1.0" ?>
<xsl:stylesheet version="1.0"
    xmlns:xsl="http://www.w3.org/1999/XSL/Transform">
    <xsl:output indent="yes" omit-xml-declaration="yes" />
    <xsl:template match="/">
        <xsl:processing-instruction name="xml-stylesheet">
            <xsl:text>type="text/xsl" href="piIE.xsl"</xsl:text>
        </xsl:processing-instruction>
    </xsl:template>
</xsl:stylesheet>
```

Notice that we make use of the `<xsl:text>` element within the template. Although discussed later, it's worth mentioning that this merges adjacent text nodes and strips spaces. So, the two carriage returns (one before the opening `<xsl:text>` tag and one after it closes) are removed and the contents of the PI run on one line.

The output from this template would be like the following:

```
<?xml-stylesheet type="text/xsl" href="piIE.xsl"?>
```

msxsl:script

The `<msxsl:script>` element allows global variables and methods to be declared within, and externally from, the stylesheet, and to be invoked directly in the templates.

```
<msxsl:script language="language" implements-prefix="namespace prefix">
</msxsl:script>
```

The `language` attribute defaults to JScript, but other languages can be specified – the most common other settings here are JavaScript or VBScript; this is the language that your procedural script is written in. The `implements-prefix` attribute declares a prefix that has been associated with a namespace in the namespace declarations of the XSLT document. This prefix is then associated with the relevant script block and hence is qualified by a namespace within the stylesheet.

To show how `msxsl:script` can be used we'll look again at an example that we used earlier to illustrate the `<xsl:if>` element. This section will focus on how the `<msxsl:script>` element works.

```xml
<?xml version="1.0" ?>
<xsl:stylesheet version="1.0"
    xmlns:xsl="http://www.w3.org/1999/XSL/Transform"
    xmlns:msxsl="urn:schemas-microsoft-com:xslt"
    xmlns:wrox="uri:wroxbooks">

    <msxsl:script language="JScript" implements-prefix="wrox"><![CDATA[
    function GetDiscount(intOfferID)
    {
        var discount="0%";

        if (intOfferID<5)
            discount="0%"
        else if (intOfferID>5 && intOfferID<=15)
            discount="5%";
        else if (intOfferID>15 && intOfferID<=25)
            discount="8%";
        else if (intOfferID>25 && intOfferID<=35)
            discount="12%";
        else
            discount="5%";

        return discount;
    }
    ]]></msxsl:script>

    <xsl:output indent="yes" omit-xml-declaration="yes" />

    <xsl:template match="customers">
        <xsl:if test="@delivery='int'">International Delivery.</xsl:if>
        <xsl:if test="@offerID">
            You are entitled to a
            <xsl:value-of select="wrox:GetDiscount(number(@offerID))" />
            discount.
        </xsl:if>
    </xsl:template>
</xsl:stylesheet>
```

The first thing to notice is the two new namespace declarations on the `<xsl:stylesheet>` element. The first is mandatory when working with extension functions – `xmlns:msxsl="urn:schemas-microsoft-com:xslt"` (you can of course change the prefix as long as you are consistent in its implementation). The second defines our own custom namespace, which will be used to reference our script functions – `xmlns:wrox="uri:wroxbooks"`. We define our own prefix and assign our own namespace to it. Now, we can define an `<msxsl:script>` element with JScript as our implementation language and tell it to use our `wrox` prefix to qualify the methods. It is wise to enclose any script in this element in a CDATA section in case you have special characters that would cause an error when parsing the document. The function declared is straightforward, so we won't discuss it here.

We want to invoke the method as part of an `<xsl:value-of>` element, so we do this as the expression within the `select` attribute. The function call should be qualified by our namespace prefix so it is associated with the script block it is described in – so in this case the expression starts with the `wrox:` prefix. The method we are calling is `GetDiscount()`, which takes a numerical value as its argument (actually a variant type, but we work with it as a number, so we convert it to a number first using the XPath `number()` function). The parameter that is converted to the number is the `offerID` attribute on the context `<customers>` element. The value returned from this method call is the discount the user will get and is displayed in the output.

The output will be like the following fragment:

International Delivery.
You are entitled to a 12% discount.

xsl:sort

The `<xsl:sort>` element provides sorting criteria for node-sets that are selected by `<xsl:apply-templates>` or `<xsl:for-each>` elements.

```
<xsl:sort select="expression" lang="nmtoken" data-type="text | number | QName"
order="ascending | descending" case-order="upper-first | lower-first" />
```

The `select` attribute determines the sort key for the node and defaults to the context node. The `lang` attribute determines the language alphabet to be used for sorting, and defaults to the environment language alphabet – this could be used to sort Chinese strings, for example. The `data-type` attribute specifies the type of the key that is to be sorted – this can be as text, converted and sorted numerically, or some qualified name, where the expanded namespace determines the data type. The `order` attribute should be `ascending` (the default) or `descending`, and finally the `case-order` attribute specifies uppercase first (the default) or lowercase first.

The `<xsl:sort>` element is demonstrated in the examples for the `<xsl:apply-templates>` and `<xsl:for-each>` elements.

xsl:strip-space

This element strips whitespace from whitespace-only text nodes in a document.

```
<xsl:strip-space elements="tokens" />
```

This must be a direct child of an `<xsl:stylesheet>` or `<xsl:transform>` element. The `elements` attribute takes a list of qualified names that should have their whitespace stripped. The default action is to preserve these text nodes, but an `<xsl:strip-space>` element may override this default behavior and remove these nodes, so it may also be necessary to **explicitly** specify specific nodes that should ignore the `<xsl:strip-space>` and not have their whitespace stripped using the `<xsl:preserve-space>` element discussed above.

In the string `"<birth><century>19</century> <year>74</year></birth>"`, the whitespace-only text node between `"</century>"` and `"<year>"` is not significant as it separates the century and year, which are normally read together. With it, the data reads "19 74" and without, it reads "1974". In this case we would wish to strip the whitespace-only text node.

Examples and further discussion can be found in the "*Controlling Whitespace*" section later in this chapter.

xsl:stylesheet

This element is perhaps the most significant element as it is the root stylesheet element containing all other XSLT elements. Note that a synonym for this is `<xsl:transform>`.

```
<xsl:stylesheet id="id" version="number"
        extension-element-prefixes="NCNames"
        exclude-result-prefixes="NCNames">
</xsl:stylesheet>
```

This element will contain at least one namespace declaration, which in the case of the W3C implementation within MSXML will be `xmlns:xsl="http://www.w3.org/1999/XSL/Transform"` – although the prefix can be anything we want, as long as we are consistent throughout the document. The `id` attribute is used to uniquely identify the node within the document, which allows embedding of multiple XSLT documents. The `version` attribute of this corresponds to the version of XSLT being used, which is 1.0 in the W3C implementations within MSXML. The `extension-element-prefixes` attribute is a whitespace-separated set of prefixes that have been associated with namespaces that are associated with extension implementations (such as other processors). The `exclude-result-prefixes` attribute is used to prevent a specified namespace from being output. Based on the prefix supplied here, it will be suppressed in the output. However, it is the namespace declaration that is suppressed – it does not remove the prefixes belonging to any elements associated with this namespace that are output.

The example that follows will find the `<busInfo>` element that describes some business classification information. In our example we will get the business category and output this value within a new element in the output – a common scenario when transforming XML to other formats. Furthermore, the `<busInfo>` element is actually qualified with a category namespace within the document:

```
<?xml version="1.0" ?>
<xsl:stylesheet version="1.0"
      xmlns:xsl=http://www.w3.org/1999/XSL/Transform
      xmlns:oracle="http://www.oracle.com/XSL/Transform/java"
      xmlns:saxon="http://www.icl.com/saxon"
      extension-element-prefixes="oracle saxon"
      xmlns:cat="uri:Business-Categories"
      exclude-result-prefixes="cat oracle saxon">

   <xsl:output indent="yes" omit-xml-declaration="yes" />

   <xsl:template match="cat:busInfo">
      <Classification>
         <xsl:value-of select="." />
      </Classification>
   </xsl:template>

   <xsl:template match="text()" />
</xsl:stylesheet>
```

Looking at the `<stylesheet>` element, we come across two less familiar namespaces –
`xmlns:oracle="http://www.oracle.com/XSL/Transform/java"` and
`xmlns:saxon="http://www.icl.com/saxon"`, which refer to the Oracle and Saxon parsers
respectively. We may use these so that any extension functions we build would work across multiple parsers
– look in the `<xsl:fallback>` element section for further information on why we might do this. The
`extension-element-prefixes` attribute defines the namespaces that refer to both of these parsers for
working with any extension functionality they may provide. After this there is a namespace declaration, with
the prefix `cat` being associated with the namespace URI `uri:Business-Categories`. The final attribute,
`exclude-result-prefixes`, tells the processor to suppress any namespace declaration associated with
`cat`, `oracle`, or `saxon` in the output. Why do we do this? Well, we qualify the `<busInfo>` element as the
XPath expression on the template within the stylesheet, within this we create our `<Classification>`
element, and within this write out the value within this `<busInfo>` element. However, if we do not exclude
the `cat` prefix, then the namespace declaration associated with the `cat` prefix will be written as an attribute
on the `Classification` element. Excluding the `cat` prefix means that this unwanted effect is ignored and
the namespace associated with the `cat` prefix is not written out.

The output from this template would be like the following:

`<Classification>Wine Division South</Classification>`

The output from this template without excluding the `cat` prefix would be like the following:

`<Classification xmlns:cat="uri:Business-Categories">Wine Division South</Classification>`

Note that this WC3 implementation is dramatically different from the 1998 version of the
`<xsl:stylesheet>` element and none of the attributes on the 1998 implementation appear on this version.

xsl:template

The `<xsl:template>` element is used to create a reusable template for generating output for particular
node types and context.

```
<xsl:template name="QName" match="pattern" priority="number" mode="QName">
</xsl:template>
```

The `name` attribute is a qualified name that is expanded, and those with prefixes are expanded based on
the namespace declarations in effect at that point. The `match` attribute contains an XPath pattern
expression that determines the node-set and context that the template will operate on.

The `priority` attribute allows matching templates to be ordered by priority. The more specific
templates are given a higher priority by default than those that are less specific. The default priorities
are calculated according to the following:

❑   Patterns such as `node()`, `text()`, and `*` are not very commonly selected and so have a low
    default priority of `-0.5`.

❑   Patterns of a name or attribute are very common and have a default priority of `-0.25`.

❑   Qualified patterns match only on given namespace axes and so are more specific than the
    others. They have a default priority of `0.0`.

❑　Other specific patterns are given default priorities of 0.5; an example would be customers/order[0]/details[2].

❑　You can of course assign your own priorities to templates as a real number from -9 to +9. At least this is what we are told in the MSXML SDKs, but the W3C Recommendation does not define a limit on this number as such, and when working with MSXML we will find that we can use any real number to define our priorities! If the priority is important in our implementation, then it is better to assign our own rather than rely on the default ones so as to optimize the performance of our stylesheet.

The final xsl:template attribute is mode, which is a QName with an optional prefix. It allows a template to be run multiple times for a given pattern. This basically means that we can match a given expression pattern for multiple templates, but the one with the selected mode is the only one executed. The default has no mode. So, we could use xsl:apply-templates to match a node twice. In the first case we can specify no mode on the <xsl:apply-templates> element and so the default template will be used – the same way we have been doing in all our examples thus far. In the second case, we can add the attribute mode to another <xsl:apply-templates> element with the value equal to that of some mode attribute on an <xsl:template> element further on in the stylesheet, matching the same pattern. The result is that the same node is processed twice, but different outputs are given.

The following example illustrates all the concepts we have just discussed. The delivery is dependent on certain occurrences within the stylesheet and uses priorities depending on what occurs. Furthermore, some customer information is also output and this comes at both the start and end of the output, so modes are used to implement this:

```
<?xml version="1.0" ?>
<xsl:stylesheet version="1.0"
    xmlns:xsl="http://www.w3.org/1999/XSL/Transform">
    <xsl:output indent="yes" omit-xml-declaration="yes" />

    <xsl:template match="/">
       <xsl:apply-templates />
       <xsl:apply-templates select="//order" />
       <xsl:apply-templates mode="index" />
    </xsl:template>

    <xsl:template match="customers">
       <xsl:text>Order Details of customer "</xsl:text>
       <xsl:value-of select="@custname" />
       <xsl:text>".

</xsl:text>
    </xsl:template>

    <xsl:template match="customers" mode="index">
<xsl:text disable-output-escaping="yes">
&lt;Customer Details&gt;
=================
</xsl:text>Customer name : <xsl:value-of select="@custname" />
Phone No : <xsl:value-of select="@phone" />
Email : <xsl:value-of select="@email" />
    </xsl:template>

    <xsl:template match="order[details/items[@num&lt;5]]" priority="6">
       <xsl:text>
```

```
    * Status for Order ID "</xsl:text>
        <xsl:value-of select="@orderID" />
        <xsl:text>" - too few items to be delivered.
        </xsl:text>
    </xsl:template>

    <xsl:template match="order[@batchid]" priority="5">
        <xsl:text>
    * Status for Order ID "</xsl:text>
        <xsl:value-of select="@orderID" />
        <xsl:text>" - batch id assigned, so can be delivered.
        </xsl:text>
    </xsl:template>

    <xsl:template match="order">
        <xsl:text>
    * Status for Order ID "</xsl:text>
        <xsl:value-of select="@orderID" />
        <xsl:text>" - no batch id so must first be assigned one.
        </xsl:text>
    </xsl:template>
</xsl:stylesheet>
```

We use the `<xsl:text>` element a lot in this example to control how our whitespace affects the output. We will be exploring the effects of whitespace on this example in the "*Controlling Whitespace*" section of this chapter. For now, let's concentrate on how the `<xsl:template>` element affects this example.

Look at the first `<xsl:template>` at the top of the stylesheet, which has three `<xsl:apply-templates>` elements. The first selects all nodes (no `match` attribute), so we then need a template that will first match the `<customers>` element in the source, as we want some header information. This is a relatively simple template much like what we have used before, and outputs some text. The second `<xsl:apply-templates>` element selects all `<order>` elements in the entire document and this can match three templates. The first possible match occurs when the `order` attribute has a `batchid` attribute defined. The second match is for those `<order>` elements whose descendent `<items>` elements have a `num` attribute that is less than the integer 5. The final match is for any `<order>` element at all. If these were run without any `priority` attributes, then the first match would be the first `<order>` element in the sample XML document. Although it will match the `match="order"` template, the rules for priority tell us that if there is a more specific match (narrowing the scope of the match more), then that template will be executed instead. On this first `<order>` element in fact both other order-based templates will match – one because this element indeed has a `batchid` attribute and so the `match="order[@batchid]"` expression will be `true`, and the other because its descendent `<items>` element has a `num` attribute that is less than 5, matching the expression `match="order[details/items[@num<5]]"`. Looking at the XSLT code, the `match="order[@batchid]"` is first from the bottom up, and according to the way XSLT matches templates it will be matched first, and so the contents of this would be invoked first. However, some predefined "business rules" state that it is more important to tell the output that there are not enough items than that there is no `batchid`. This is mainly because whatever application generates the invoices XML document, a `batchid` will not be assigned to an order with less than 5 items, although an order with less than 5 items can still be given a `batchid`. To accomplish this, we can use the `xsl:template priority` attribute.

In this example, we give the `match="order[@batchid]"` template a priority of 5 and the `match="order[details/items[@num<5]]"` a priority of 6, which means that in the case where both of these templates are true (such as the case we just described), then the higher priority template will be executed. Hence, the `match="order[details/items[@num<5]]"` template is actually executed and its content processed. Look at the others on your own to understand how priorities determine the order they are executed.

The final `<xsl:apply-templates>` in the top `<xsl:template>` element has no `select` attribute, but does have a `mode` attribute. What this means is that all nodes will once again be selected, like in the first `<xsl:apply-templates>` we discussed. However, the `mode` attribute states that only templates with a `mode` attribute with the same value, `index` in this case, will be matched. Indeed, we once again match the `<customers>` element and as this has the appropriate `mode` attribute, some contact information about the company is given.

The output from this template would be like the following:

Order Details of customer "Chile Wines Inc".

_____

* Status for Order ID "OID921" - too few items to be delivered.

* Status for Order ID "OID927" - no batch id so must first be assigned one.

* Status for Order ID "OID931" - batch id assigned, so can be delivered.

```
<Customer Details>
==================
Customer name : Chile Wines Inc
Phone No : 0141 952 56223
Email : cw@deltabis.com
```

We will be exploring the effects of whitespace later, again using this example, in the "*Controlling Whitespace*" section.

xsl:text

The example below shows how the `<xsl:text>` element can be used to create an `xml-stylesheet` processing instruction in the output:

```
<?xml version="1.0" ?>
<xsl:stylesheet version="1.0"
    xmlns:xsl="http://www.w3.org/1999/XSL/Transform">
    <xsl:output indent="yes" omit-xml-declaration="yes" />
    <xsl:template match="/">
        <xsl:processing-instruction name="xml-stylesheet">
            <xsl:text>type="text/xsl" href="piIE.xsl"</xsl:text>
        </xsl:processing-instruction>
    </xsl:template>
</xsl:stylesheet>
```

Notice that we make use of the `<xsl:text>` element within the template. With the `<xsl:text>` element, the two carriage returns (one before the opening `xsl:text` and one after it closes) are removed, so the contents of the PI runs on one line.

With no `<xsl:text>` elements, the output would look something like the following:

```
<?xml-stylesheet
  type="text/xsl" href="piIE.xsl"
  ?>
```

With the `<xsl:text>` elements, the output from this template would be like the following:

```
<?xml-stylesheet type="text/xsl" href="piIE.xsl"?>
```

xsl:transform

This element is a synonym for the `<xsl:stylesheet>` element and has the same functionality. The main reason it exists is to illustrate XSLT's capability to act as a processor to transform data formats as well as style output.

See the discussion on `xsl:stylesheet` for more details.

xsl:value-of

The `<xsl:value-of>` element outputs the value of the selected node as a text value.

```
<xsl:value-of select="expression" disable-output-escaping="yes | no" />
```

The `select` attribute selects a node based on the context node and any returned node-set is converted to a string using the XPath function – this also implies that if a node-set is returned, then the output will be the string value of the first node in document order. The `disable-output-escaping` attribute is used to control output escaping and defaults to `no`. For example, if the value of the selected node is `&lt;` and if the `disable-output-escaping` is set to "no", then it will be escaped and the output value will be `&lt;`. However, if `disable-output-escaping` is set to "yes", then it will not be escaped and so it will be parsed, and the output will be the "<" character.

The `<xsl:value-of>` element is used in other examples in this chapter, so refer to these for examples of implementation.

xsl:variable

This element declares a local or global named variable for use within an `<xsl:stylesheet>` or `<xsl:template>` and allows a value to be set.

```
<xsl:variable name="QName" select="Expression">
</xsl:variable>
```

The `name` attribute sets the name by which the variable will be referenced. The `select` attribute is an expression that will determine the value of the variable – this is optional and if it is omitted, the contents of this element will determine the value of the variable.

If we want to assign a string value to this, then we must assign quotes around the value:

```
<xsl:variable name="book" select="'Professional XML'">
```

We don't need to do this if it is a number we are assigning:

```
<xsl:variable name="age" select="27">
```

We can also use XPath expressions and other variables to determine the value of the variable:

```
<xsl:variable name="totalorders" select="sum(//items/@num)">
```

Finally, the value of the variable can be an XML fragment:

```
<xsl:variable name="winelist">
   <xsl:for-each select="//item">
      <wine><xsl:value-of select="." /></wine>
   </xsl:for-each>
</xsl:variable>
```

Examples of the `<xsl:variable>` element can be seen in the `<xsl:copy-of>` element discussion above.

xsl:when

The `<xsl:when>` element provides conditional processing using `<xsl:choose>` and `<xsl:otherwise>` elements.

```
<xsl:when test="boolean expression">
</xsl:when>
```

This element will be the child element of an `<xsl:choose>` element and may occur multiple times. The `test` attribute is required and returns `true` or `false` depending on the outcome of its expression. You may test if you are at a certain position in the context or if a given node contains a certain value. If this is the only attribute and it evaluates to `true`, then the content within the element is invoked.

When the processing for an `<xsl:when>` element that tested `true` has completed its processing, the `<xsl:choose>` is exited and processing continues with the next element. If none of the `<xsl:when>` elements are `true` then the `<xsl:otherwise>` element is processed – if it exists.

The following example shows how `<xsl:when>` can be used in conjunction with `<xsl:choose>` and `<xsl:otherwise>` to output some text indicating whether the order level is small, medium, or large:

```
<?xml version="1.0" ?>
<xsl:stylesheet version="1.0"
   xmlns:xsl="http://www.w3.org/1999/XSL/Transform">
   <xsl:output indent="yes" omit-xml-declaration="yes" />
   <xsl:template match="order">
      <xsl:choose>
         <xsl:when test="details/items[@num &lt; 3]">
           <xsl:value-of select="@orderID" /> : Small Order.</xsl:when>
         <xsl:when test="details/items[@num &lt; 6]">
           <xsl:value-of select="@orderID" /> : Medium Order.</xsl:when>
         <xsl:otherwise>
           <xsl:value-of select="@orderID" /> : Large Order.</xsl:otherwise>
      </xsl:choose>
      <xsl:text>&#xA;</xsl:text>
      <xsl:apply-templates />
   </xsl:template>
   <xsl:template match="text()" />
</xsl:stylesheet>
```

The template matches the <order> elements and the child of this template is an <xsl:choose> element. Within this element are two <xsl:when> elements and an <xsl:otherwise> element. The first <xsl:when> has a test attribute that is true when the num attribute of the <items> element descendent is less than the value 3. When it is, it simply writes out some text. The second <xsl:when> also has a test attribute that is true when the num attribute of the <items> element descendent is less than the value 6, and when it is, it simply writes out some text. The <xsl:otherwise> is a catch-all test and will write out similar information for any elements not caught by the first two <xsl:when> elements.

The output from this template would be like the following:

OID921 : Small Order.
OID927 : Medium Order.
OID931 : Large Order.

xsl:with-param

The <xsl:with-param> element outputs the value of the selected node as a text value.

```
<xsl:with-param name="QName" select="expression" />
```

This can only be the child of <xsl:call-template> or <xsl:apply-templates> elements. It passes the parameter with the name given in the name attribute and the value given by the select expression. The passing of the parameter is successful only when the <xsl:template> that is used has a top-level <xsl:param> element with the same name as the parameter in the <xsl:with-param> element.

The <xsl:with-param> can been seen in practice in the <xsl:call-template> or <xsl:apply-templates> examples earlier in the section.

XSLT Functions

In the last chapter we worked through an extensive number of XPath functions that are available to XSLT and the DOM. There are some functions more exclusive to working with XSLT and these are outlined briefly below:

❑ current() – this function returns a node-set that has the current node as its only member. This is not always equal to the context node when working with predicates in your expression.

❑ document(object, node-set) – this function allows you to access external XML resources. If you provide a single string then it is treated as a URI and the XML document at that URI is retrieved as a node-set. If the single argument is a node-set then it treats each node as a string URI, retrives the XML document at each URI and returns a union of these documents. If there are two arguments, then the first is treated as before, but the second argument is a node-set indicating the base URL, which the contents of the first argument are relative to. If the parameter list is empty then the result is the XML source of the XSLT itself.

❑ element-available(string) – this function returns true if a particular instruction or extension element is available for use. So, for MSXML, element-available("xsl:text") returns true, while element-available("saxon:doctype") returns false.

- ❑ format-number(number, string, string) – this function converts numbers for human reading. The first parameter is the number to convert, the second the format pattern, and the last is optional, describing the decimal format. See the discussion of the <xsl:decimal-format> element for more detail on the available options.

- ❑ function-available(string) – this function tests the parser for function availability and returns true if the function is available in the function library, so function-available("format-number") returns true.

- ❑ generate-id(node-set) – this returns a string of ASCII alphanumeric characters that uniquely identifies the node in the node-set in document order. If there is no argument, the context node is used. There is also no guarantee that the unique ID created here will not be the same as the ID attribute on an element (although it is unlikely).

- ❑ key(name, value) – this function retrieves the key defined by an <xsl:key> element with the specified name and value. Keys are discussed further below.

- ❑ msxsl:node-set(string) – this allows you to convert tree fragments into a node-set.

- ❑ system-property(string) – this allows you to access environment properties and the parameter must be a valid system property. The current values are xsl:version, xsl:vendor, xsl:vendor-url, and msxsl:version.

- ❑ unparsed-entity-uri(string) – this function provides access to declarations of unparsed entities in the DTD of the source document. It returns the URI of the unparsed entity – for example, the URI to a JPG image.

Controlling Whitespace

When working through the examples you will have no doubt discovered the important part that whitespace plays in XML. When we talk of whitespace, we mean those invisible characters that are part of any XML document we create and have an effect on its output. You may wonder why this seems like a new issue! Well, it's not – when using HTML. However, we barely noticed their effects because many rules that are part of HTML ensure that whitespace is kept to a minimum. For example, two consecutive spaces are made into one space in HTML, new lines are ignored (hence why we need a <br> tag) and so we can ignore any effects of whitespace. In XML we cannot – the invisible characters (space),  (carriage return), 	 (tab) and
 (newline) are present in most documents and can radically affect our output. The XML attribute xml:space allows us to control space to some extent within the source document. This will always override any whitespace handling in the XSLT document.

An important thing to understand is that when we talk about whitespace, we often mean those characters that are regarded as whitespace characters (discussed above) that occur between element nodes – in other words, whitespace text nodes. This does not necessarily include text within these elements. So, consider the following string "<a> <b>hello </b></a>" – the whitespace between <a> and <b> is a whitespace text node and may or may not be significant – MSXML will strip this to a single space. However, the whitespace after the text "hello" is part of the text and is not a whitespace text node.

One way of controlling the whitespace in our output, used a lot in the examples, is the <xsl:text> element, which sends literal text to the output and so the whitespace within this is retained. However, we must watch out for interference with the development tool we are working with – many have been created to work with HTML and so whitespace is sometimes ignored or modified. For example, in the Visual Studio 7 (Beta 2) product, the line "<xsl:text>   </xsl:text>", which has three spaces, is converted when saved to "<xsl:text></xsl:text>" with no spaces. To keep the spacing we can use something like Notepad, which does not cause this side effect. Alternatively, we can use character references to explicitly put in whitespace characters – in this case, we could write "<xsl:text>   </xsl:text>", where   is the entity reference for a space, and will be preserved in all browsers. See the section on <xsl:template> element for more information.

We have already discussed the <xsl:preserve-space> and <xsl:strip-space> elements, which allow explicit definition of the nodes that should have their whitespace preserved or removed. Commonly these are used in combination to remove all space from all elements, with exceptions specified in the <xsl:preserve-space> element. However, there is a catch you may not be aware of – MSXML 3.0 and 4.0 strip the whitespace characters from the source XML document before the XSLT even sees them. You can put a whole page of tabs in your source and these will all be stripped! Multiple spaces are trimmed to a single space. The only way to preserve these is by using the previously discussed xml:space attribute in the source XML document.

The following example (strippreserve.xml, listed as **Strip/Preserve Sample** in the drop-down box, and strippreserve.xsl) demonstrates how we can work with whitespace. The following XML document contains some whitespace text nodes, notably between the <city>Milan</city> and <country>Italy</country> elements and the </century> and <year> elements:

```
<?xml version="1.0" encoding="utf-8" ?>
<wineslists>
   <wine id="292">Made in <city>Milan</city> <country>Italy</country> in
<fullyear><century>19</century>

<year>87</year></fullyear> this is an intense, opaque color in the    glass, with
an        opulent nose of exotic Asian <ing>  spices</ing>, <ing>cedar</ing>,
<ing>violets</ing>, <ing>dark ripe fruits</ing>, and   <ing>mocha.</ing>  </wine>

</wineslists>
```

We can then use the following XSLT to demonstrate how whitespace can be handled to output a paragraph:

```
<?xml version="1.0" ?>
<xsl:stylesheet version="1.0"
   xmlns:xsl="http://www.w3.org/1999/XSL/Transform">
   <xsl:output omit-xml-declaration="yes" />
   <xsl:preserve-space elements="*" />
   <xsl:strip-space elements="fullyear" />
   <xsl:template match="winelists">
      <xsl:apply-templates />
   </xsl:template>
   <xsl:template match="wine">
      <xsl:value-of select="." />
   </xsl:template>
   <xsl:template match="text()" />
</xsl:stylesheet>
```

The `<xsl:preserve-space>` element is used to tell the processor to keep all text nodes in the elements in the document. Then the `<xsl:strip-space>` element is used to indicate that the contents of the `fullyear` element should be the exception to this and spaces should be stripped – this removes a space between `</century>` and `<year>` and also removes the newline character. The latter is removed by the MSXML processor anyway, but the space will be preserved – that is why we want to remove it so the date runs together properly in the output.

The output with no whitespace handling would be:

Made in Milan Italy in 19 87 this is an intense, opaque color in the   glass,
with an   opulent nose of exotic Asian   spices, cedar, violets, dark
ripe fruits, and   mocha.

The output when the stylesheet is applied as discussed above would be:

Made in Milan Italy in 1987 this is an intense, opaque color in the   glass,
with an   opulent nose of exotic Asian   spices, cedar, violets, dark
ripe fruits, and   mocha.

So what do we do when there is space in the actual text of the element that is not a whitespace text node, but we still want to remove it? This is where the `normalize-space()` function can be used to strip whitespace characters into a single whitespace. This was discussed in detail in the last chapter – essentially it takes a node that is converted to a string and whitespace is trimmed to a single space.

In our example we can change the `wine` template as follows:

```
<xsl:template match="wine">
    <xsl:value-of select="normalize-space(.)" />
</xsl:template>
```

The output when the stylesheet is applied would be:

Made in Milan Italy in 1987 this is an intense, opaque color in the glass, with an opulent nose of exotic Asian spices, cedar, violets, dark ripe fruits, and mocha.

XSLT Keys

The `<xsl:key>` element was briefly mentioned above when we said it "declares a named key for use with the XPath `key()` function in expressions to provide a much simpler way of accessing complex documents and improving access performance".

As an example, consider the following document, which lists all the order IDs for orders which have a "Rancagua Red" `item` grandchild; see the xsl:key [Example A] example entry in the sample file dropdown.

```
<?xml version="1.0" ?>
<xsl:stylesheet version="1.0"
  xmlns:xsl="http://www.w3.org/1999/XSL/Transform">
    <xsl:output indent="yes" omit-xml-declaration="yes" />
    <xsl:key name="order-search" match="order" use="./details/items/item" />
```

```
        <xsl:template match="/">
        <xsl:text />The ID's of the orders for "Rancagua Red" are:<xsl:text />
        <xsl:for-each    select="//order[./details/items/item='Rancagua Red']">
           <xsl:text>&#xA;</xsl:text>
           <xsl:value-of select="@orderID" />
        </xsl:for-each>
        <xsl:text>&#xA;</xsl:text>
        <xsl:text />The ID's of the orders for "Chillan Red" are:<xsl:text />
        <xsl:for-each select="//order[./details/items/item='Chillan Red']">
           <xsl:text>&#xA;</xsl:text>
           <xsl:value-of select="@orderID" />
        </xsl:for-each>
        </xsl:template>
        <xsl:template match="text()" />
    </xsl:stylesheet>
```

The XPath expressions `//order[./details/items/item='Rancagua Red']` and `//order[./details/items/item='Chillan Red']` do a full scan of all decendants twice and select the orders element nodes which isn't very efficient. Using keys in XSLT we can improve this efficiency as shown below; see the xsl:key [Example B] example entry in the sample file dropdown.

```
    <?xml version="1.0" ?>
    <xsl:stylesheet version="1.0"
        xmlns:xsl="http://www.w3.org/1999/XSL/Transform">
           <xsl:output indent="yes" omit-xml-declaration="yes" />

        <xsl:key name="item-search" match="order" use="./details/items/item" />
         <xsl:template match="/">
        <xsl:text />The ID's of the orders for "Rancagua Red" are:<xsl:text />
           <xsl:for-each select="key('item-search', 'Rancagua Red')">
              <xsl:text>&#xA;</xsl:text>
              <xsl:value-of select="@orderID" />
           </xsl:for-each>
        <xsl:text />The ID's of the orders for "Rancagua Red" are:<xsl:text />
           <xsl:for-each select="key('item-search', 'Chillan Red')">
              <xsl:text>&#xA;</xsl:text>
              <xsl:value-of select="@orderID" />
           </xsl:for-each>
        </xsl:template>
        <xsl:template match="text()" />
    </xsl:stylesheet>
```

The first updated line shows how the `<xsl:key>` element can be used to group the item elements together – this is better than the first example where we repeatedly used a similar XPath expression with a simple change in the predicate to evaluate the text of the element node. Now we perform one operation and all elements are grouped, using `"item-search"` as the name of the index, and the match XPath expression will match the `<order>` element nodes and the use attribute specifies that it is the `<item>` grandchild element that we want to create the index with. Remember the index created isn't necessarily of unique elements (there are multiple `"Chillan Red"` text nodes), but rather grouped. The key values retrieved by the use attribute will be individual values required to retrieve each selected node.

Following this, within the templates we can directly retrieve the nodes using the key() function, passing the first parameter as the name of the key and the second parameter the value of the key – very much like the SELECT statement in SQL, without the DISTINCT keyword being used. We do this for two lists, but the same key is used both times giving a dramatic performance improvement, especially for larger documents. A node-set is returned from the key() function and so we can do anything we would normally do with a node-set, and in our case we loop through each of the nodes and output the ordered attribute.

If we knew we just wanted to create a list of order IDs of all the items with the value "Rancagua Red", we could make our key more specific as follows; see the xsl:key [Example C] example entry in the sample file dropdown.

```
<?xml version="1.0" ?>
<xsl:stylesheet version="1.0"
    xmlns:xsl="http://www.w3.org/1999/XSL/Transform">
    <xsl:output indent="yes" omit-xml-declaration="yes" />
    <xsl:key name="item-search" match="order"
        use="./details/items/item[.='Rancagua Red']" />
    <xsl:template match="/">
    <xsl:text />The ID's of the orders for "Rancagua Red" are:<xsl:text />
        <xsl:for-each select="key('item-search', 'Rancagua Red')">
            <xsl:text>&#xA;</xsl:text>
            <xsl:value-of select="@orderID" />
        </xsl:for-each>
    </xsl:template>
    <xsl:template match="text()" />
</xsl:stylesheet>
```

In this case, we can avoid indexing nodes that are not of interest – this again would be most useful in a larger document where we wanted to find out information on a specific set of items. In fact, we can even use this method to link documents together much like a foreign key in a database. Consider where the details on the manager of a given order containing a certain item are required (in other words, who manages orders for this wine?). The actual manager information is stored in a separate file called keyref.xml and is shown below:

```
<?xml version="1.0" encoding="utf-8" ?>
<managersOrders>
    <manager name="Steven">
        <order orderID="OID921" />
        <order orderID="OID931" />
    </manager>
    <manager name="Loreto">
        <order orderID="OID927" />
    </manager>
</managersOrders>
```

This file simply stores the manager's name and associated orders as children of the <manager> element node. The actual XSLT that generates our output is shown below:

```
<?xml version="1.0" ?>
<xsl:stylesheet version="1.0"
    xmlns:xsl="http://www.w3.org/1999/XSL/Transform">
    <xsl:output indent="yes" omit-xml-declaration="yes" />
    <xsl:variable name="doc"
        select="document('keyRef.xml')/managersOrders" />

    <xsl:key name="item-search" match="order"
        use="./details/items/item" />

    <xsl:key name="orderRef" match="manager" use="order/@orderID" />
    <xsl:template match="/">
    <xsl:text />The ID's of the orders for Rancagua Red are:<xsl:text />
        <xsl:for-each select="key('item-search', 'Rancagua Red')">
            <xsl:variable name="item" select="@orderID" />
```

```
         <xsl:for-each select="$doc">
            <xsl:text>&#xA;</xsl:text>
            <xsl:text />Manager of order <xsl:value-of
               select="$item" /> is <xsl:text />
            <xsl:value-of select="key('orderRef', $item)/@name" />
         </xsl:for-each>
      </xsl:for-each>
   </xsl:template>
   <xsl:template match="text()" />
</xsl:stylesheet>
```

A variable is defined called doc, which used the document() function to get a node-set from the keyref.xml external document we defined above and selects the child nodes of the <managerOrders> document element. This is to prevent accessing the external document repeatedly later on and just access the stored variable. Next we have the XSLT key we have been working with previously. Finally, there is another XSLT key called keyRef that matched the <manager> element in the external document – we will soon see how this works.

Within the template and after the header information, an iteration is done through each of the nodes in our key that have the text "Rancagua Red". Also, a variable is defined that holds the orderID – this is going to act as the foreign key in the external document, but since we are going to use a for-each in the external document, we will change context and consequently lose access to the elements within the primary document. So, storing the information in a variable will allow us to access the node within the loop. Next, as was mentioned, we use a for-each loop. This is not used in the traditional manner; it is actually used to change context to the external document (because context is changed in a for-each loop) so no "looping" actually goes on, but it allows us to use the key() function a little later. First, some text is written out indicating the order that is being looked at. and then the key() function is used as follows:

```
<xsl:value-of select="key('orderRef', $item)/@name" />
```

This was repeated here because is it quite tricky to understand. The orderRef key was defined in the primary document, but we can still access it here – it used the orderID attribute of the order child element of each <manager> element node. We then pass as a second parameter the $item variable that was defined in the primary document to hold the orderID – and so the two orderIDs can be mapped. Finally, the <manager> element node is returned from the key() function and so we just get its name attribute, which is the manager's name.

The output from this transformation is shown below:

Orders details for Rancagua Red are:
Manager of order OID921 is Steven
Manager of order OID927 is Loreto
Manager of order OID931 is Steven

Summary

We have covered a lot of material in this chapter and by now we should have a good understanding of XSLT and its elements, attributes, and functions, along with a good insight into how it is practically implemented in the real world.

We learned about the original implementation from Microsoft, which is essential to anyone developing on a Microsoft platform and targeting Internet Explorer. We also learned about the W3C standard implementation, which is part of MSXML 3.0 (and therefore comes with IE 6) and MSXML 4.0.

Finally, we looked through some significant issues, such as whitespace, which are important to understand when working with XML – especially when using it for application interoperation.

This is by no means the end – the scope of XSLT is huge and its potential applications even larger. XSLT can be employed within enterprises and applied in areas from e-commerce to application and database integration. We'll be using XSLT much more throughout the rest of the book.

XML Application Development with MSXML 4.0
SOAP
XHTML
XML Schemas DTDs XPath CSS
XML Namespaces
XML 1.0
MSXML

6

Simple API for XML (SAX) in MSXML

The Microsoft support web site has an interesting knowledge-base article, Q266228 *"PRB: Loading large XML files into the XML DOM drains system resources"*, which describes how, if we are processing large XML files, the Document Object Model (DOM) API is not very helpful. This behavior is by design, and we'll notice such behavior with any DOM-based XML parser, not just with MSXML. The reason being, with DOM, the parser will read the XML document character-by-character and load it completely into memory before processing can take place. On an average, the memory requirement of the DOM API is double the size of the actual XML document. Hence, to process a 50MB XML document with the DOM, you may need 100MB of memory, and you'll also have to wait until the entire document is loaded into memory and ready to be processed. In addition, we might notice an additional slowdown in application performance while such a large XML document is being unloaded from memory.

In this chapter we'll look at the **Simple API for XML**, or **SAX**, which is an excellent lightweight alternative to the DOM, and see how it can result in best performance in certain scenarios, for example while working with large XML documents. The chapter begins with a quick introduction to SAX: its origin, evolution, benefits, and limitations. The rest of chapter is devoted to programming SAX version 2 with MSXML 4.0. More specifically, this chapter covers the following topics:

- ❑ Introduction to SAX 2.
- ❑ Basics of SAX programming with MSXML.
- ❑ Namespaces and SAX.
- ❑ XSD validation with SAX.

❑   Using MXXMLWriter to create XML documents using SAX.

❑   XSLT and SAX.

❑   Using the SAX AppWizard to rapidly build SAX applications using Visual C++.

Note that this chapter does not cover SAX version 1.0, as MSXML never supported it. Starting with MSXML 3, Microsoft added support for SAX 2. Almost all the examples in this chapter are written using MSXML 4.0, which fully supports SAX version 2.0.

SAX, the Simple API for XML

On Saturday, December 13, 1997, Prof. Peter Murray-Rust, the creator of the XML-DEV mailing list and author of the first Java-based XML browser (JUMBO), initiated a discussion on having a standard API for XML parsing. David Megginson, author of the Ælfred XML parser, led that discussion and made regular postings to XML-DEV on SAX design questions, often with his own view of the pros and cons of each choice. The goal was to have an event-based (discussed later) standard API for fast XML parsing. David continued coordinating the discussion and wrote the proposal for the interface, together with its Java implementation. About a month later, in January 1998, the first draft interface for SAX was released and was very well received by XML-DEV members. Over several months the discussion continued, various members identified shortcomings and suggested changes, and finally on Monday, May 11, 1998, SAX 1.0 was released, along with its Java implementation. SAX was developed with Java in mind, but today's implementations support various other languages including Python, C++, Perl, and Visual Basic. SAX 1.0 was superseded in May 2000 by SAX 2.0, which introduced support for XML Namespaces and proprietary extensions.

SAX, like the DOM, defines an abstract API to process XML documents. Unlike the DOM, which is created and sanctioned by the W3C, SAX does not belong to any standards body and is the creation of a group of developers on the XML-DEV mailing list.

XML-DEV is an open, unmoderated list supporting XML implementation and development, and it is hosted by OASIS. More information can be found at http://www.xml.org/xml/xmldev.shtml. SAX has recently switched over to the SourceForge project infrastructure, which now holds the official SAX package and documentation. The best place to find more information about SAX and track its progress is http://sax.sourceforge.net.

Another important distinction between DOM and SAX is the difference between their technical approaches. DOM is a tree-based API that loads the document into memory and then allows an application to navigate that tree; however SAX is an event-based API that simply reads the stream of the input XML document and reports parsing events to the application. A SAX-based XML parser simply reads the input XML document stream and generates different events based on the current context, such as start of a document, start of an element, character data, end of an element, end of a document, and so on. The application using the SAX parser implements a pre-defined interface(s), which has methods to handle such events generated by the parser.

SAX Versus DOM

At first glance SAX and DOM may seem wildly different, but in reality each of them is simply a different projection of the XML Infoset onto programming types. It's very much possible to use SAX to build DOM trees or portions of DOM trees, and conversely it's possible to traverse the DOM trees and emit SAX streams and events. This synergy between SAX and DOM leads to various interesting possibilities.

Both SAX and DOM are very well suited for particular kinds of applications, so deciding which to use depends on the performance and design requirements. SAX is a better option when:

❑ You have a very large XML document to process.

❑ You do not need to change the contents of the document.

❑ You do not need random-access to the XML document data. (Random-access to the XML document data refers to the ability to directly access specific portions of the XML document, or to resolve internal cross-references such as ID and IDREFs.)

❑ You need to abort the parsing at any time during the processing.

❑ You need to retrieve small chunks of data from an XML document.

❑ You need to build the XML document and serialize/transmit it, and do not necessarily need it in memory.

❑ You want to process the XML document data immediately, without waiting for the entire document to be loaded into memory.

❑ You don't want to be restricted to a tree-like hierarchical view of XML, as in the DOM. Since the SAX parser reads the input XML stream and sends the parsing notifications to the application, the application can easily then build and utilize any data structure implementation (such as stacks, queues, hashes, etc.), instead of just restricting itself to the.

These benefits do not come for free – the event-based push model makes application-side programming more complex. For instance, using the DOM is just a matter of instantiating objects and calling methods or accessing properties, while using SAX requires the application to implement certain interfaces and register them with the parser. In addition, in most cases, SAX also requires applications to maintain the state. For instance, if an application is working on an XML document that contains elements with the same name, but have different meaning depending on the parent node, the application will need to maintain state or remember who the parent is. Finally, it is important to remember that since the SAX parser just streams the document through, without caching it, SAX parsing only supports a forward-only, read-only approach.

The DOM enjoys the following benefits:

❑ It has a much simpler programming model.

❑ It facilitates editing of XML document data and structure.

❑ It supports random access to XML data.

❑ Is better integrated with XPath and XSLT.

❑ Is better suited for performing complex searches and data retrieval.

❑ Starting with version 4.0, Internet Explorer supported DOM. However, to date, no browser supports SAX.

In summary, DOM and SAX each have their own strengths and weaknesses – deciding which to use depends on the task to be accomplished.

Event-Driven XML Processing

The **event-based** interface is based on a **push model**, in which the application registers with a parser and gives it a document to process. The parser then sends messages to the application, telling it about the items it encounters as it processes the document. Examples of such message notifications include "start tag", "end tag", "character data", etc. The parser reads the stream of the input XML document without caching the entire document in memory or secondary storage. The application event handler simply responds to events and updates its state.

Consider the following XML document:

```
<?xml version="1.0" ?>
<Teacher>
    <Name>Great Lake Music</Name>
    <Phone>566-6606</Phone>
</Teacher>
```

When the above XML document is given to an event-based XML parser, it reads the input XML stream, generates the following events, and sends them to the application event handler:

```
Start Document

Start Element (Teacher)

Start Element (Name)
Characters (Great Lake Music)
End Element (Name)

Start Element (Phone)
Characters (566-6606)
End Element (Phone)

End Element (Teacher)

End Document
```

The following diagram illustrates how event-driven parsing works:

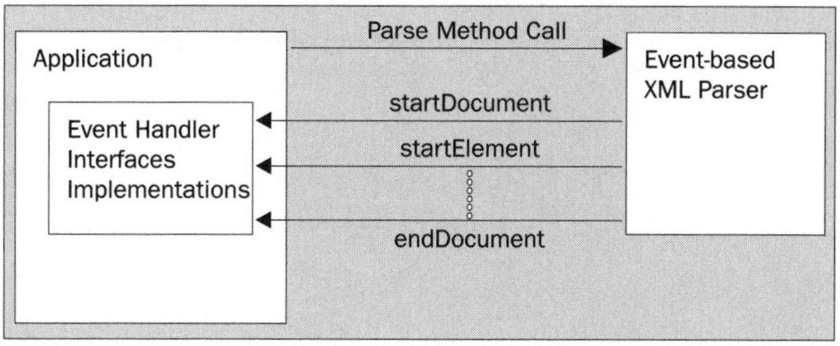

To summarize, the actual control flow of an event-driven parsing application consists of the following steps:

1. The application creates a new parser instance.

2. The application registers the event handler (interface implementation) class with the parser.

3. The application requests the parser to start parsing a particular document.

4. The parser goes through the document stream sequentially, and for each construct (tag, character data, etc.) it sends events to (in other words, calls methods of) the application's handler class.

5. The application receives the data (as parameters of its handler functions) and uses it at will.

SAX is the most important attempt to standardize an interface for event-driven XML parsing. SAX defines various handler interfaces, which an application may implement and register with the parser. The SAX parser then simply calls these application-implemented interface methods, passing the relevant parsing information.

The primary interface of SAX is ContentHandler. Most SAX applications implement this interface and the parser uses this interface to report basic logical content of a document, like the start and end of elements and character data.

All the interfaces and methods are discussed in greater detail later in the chapter, however, here is a quick table summarizing the main SAX interfaces. The first column lists the name of the native Java interface as defined by the SAX documentation, while the next two columns list the MSXML (C++/COM and Visual Basic) interface names defined by Microsoft:

Java Interface	MSXML C++/COM	MSXML Visual Basic	Description
Content Handler	ISAXContent Handler	IVBSAXContent Handler	The main interface used to report basic document content events, for example, start and end of elements, character data, etc.
Error Handler	ISAXError Handler	IVBSAXError Handler	The parser reports all fatal errors, errors, and warnings through this interface.
XMLReader	ISAXXML Reader	IVBSAXXML Reader	The parser implements this interface allowing applications to register event handlers for document processing, to initiate a document parse, and to query and set features and properties in the parser.
DTD Handler	ISAXDTD Handler	IVBSAXDTD Handler	The parser uses this interface to report notation and unparsed entity declarations to the application.
Decl Handler	ISAXDecl Handler	IVBSAXDecl Handler	The parser uses this interface to report DTD element and attribute declarations.
Lexical Handler	ISAX Lexical Handler	IVBSAXLexical Handler	The parser uses this interface to report lexical information such as comments and CDATA.
Attributes	ISAX Attributes	IVBSAX Attributes	The parser implements this interface allowing access to attribute collections.
Locator	ISAX Locator	IVBSAX Locator	The parser implements this interface in order to provide location information, such as line number, character position, etc.
Entity Resolver	ISAXEntityRe solver	IVBSAXEntity Resolver	The application may implement this interface to provide customized handling of external entities.
XMLFilter	ISAXXML Filter	IVBSAXXML Filter	An XMLFilter is like an XMLReader, except that it obtains its events from another XML reader rather than a primary source like an XML document. Filters can modify a stream of events as they pass them on to the final application.

With this understanding of SAX, let's now move forward and see how MSXML supports SAX 2.0.

Basics of SAX in MSXML

The May 2000 preview release of MSXML 3.0 first introduced support for SAX 2.0. However, this release just supported the C++/COM SAX interfaces. Two months later the second preview release of MSXML 3.0 added support for Visual Basic SAX interfaces. The names of the MSXML interfaces are the same as they are in the Java language, only prefixed with ISAX for C++/COM and IVBSAX for Visual Basic.

The September 2001 release of MSXML 4.0 further enhances the SAX 2 functionality and adds lots of cool features including:

❑ XSD validation with SAX.

❑ Complete support for XML namespaces and tracking of namespace declarations.

❑ Ability to generate XML as well as HTML output.

❑ XSLT processor integration with SAX.

❑ Ability to generate SAX events from a DOM tree and likewise build a DOM tree out of SAX events – allowing better integration of DOM and SAX in an application.

❑ Support for SAX filters.

All these features are discussed, with illustrations, in the rest of the chapter.

MSXML SAX Programming Examples

In this section we'll discuss the SAX programming model with MSXML. Let's start with a very basic example of parsing an input XML document using SAX.

Counting Element Nodes

We'll write this application (available in the code download as BasicSaxParsing.vbp) in Visual Basic 6.0 using MSXML 4.0. Let's first look at the input XML document, which we'll assume is saved as c:\SAX\broadband.xml:

```
<?xml version="1.0" ?>
<DSLProviders ZipCode="60195">
   <Provider ID="1" Name="EarthLink" Rate="49.99"/>
   <Provider ID="2" Name="Ameritech" Rate="49.99"/>
   <Provider ID="3" Name="AT&amp;T @Home" Rate="19.99"/>
   <Provider ID="4" Name="DirectTV DSL" Rate="49.99"/>
</DSLProviders>
```

Next, start Visual Basic 6.0 and open a new **Standard EXE** project. Click on **Project | References...** and add the reference for **Microsoft XML, v4.0**.

The goal of this application is to parse the broadband.xml file and count the number of <Provider> elements. As described earlier, a SAX parser uses the ContentHandler interface to report basic document content events, such as start and end of elements, etc.; we'll implement this interface and increment the element count variable when the endElement() method is called with Provider as the element name.

Let's first implement the `ContentHandler` interface. Add a class module and rename it as `ContentHandlerImpl`. This is the class where we'll implement the `IVBSAXContentHandler` interface methods:

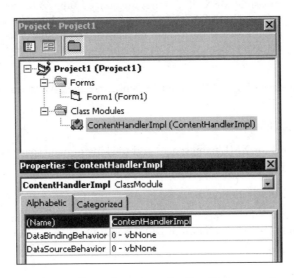

In the ContentHandlerImpl class code window write the first line as:

```
Implements IVBSAXContentHandler
```

It's now time to implement all the methods inside the `IVBSAXContentHandler` interface. To do this, select the **IVBSAXContentHandler** entry from the classes/interfaces combo box and Visual Basic will automatically add the method definition for one of the methods of the `IVBSAXContentHandler` interface:

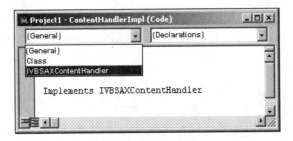

Next, click on each **IVBSAXContentHandler** method from the declarations combo box, to have Visual Basic add the declaration:

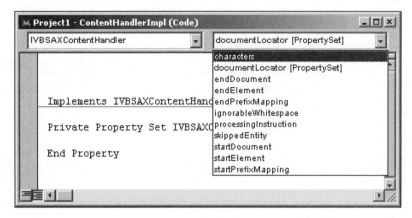

We'll declare an integer variable in this class to hold the count of <Provider> elements. The variable will be initialized to 0 in the startDocument() implementation, and we'll increment its value by 1 in the endElement() implementation, if the element name is Provider:

```
Implements IVBSAXContentHandler

Public intElemCount As Integer

Private Sub IVBSAXContentHandler_startDocument()

    intElemCount = 0

End Sub

Private Sub IVBSAXContentHandler_endElement(strNamespaceURI As String,
strLocalName As String, strQName As String)

    If strLocalName = "Provider" Then
        intElemCount = intElemCount + 1
    End If

End Sub

'Rest of the interface methods go here with blank implementation
```

When the parser reads the XML document it sends notifications to our event handler implementation by calling its methods. It passes the context information as the method parameters. For instance, when it encounters an end element tag, it calls the endElement() method of the ContentHandler implementation and passes the namespace URI, local name, and the qualified name of that element. Since we are not using namespaces yet, the strNamespaceURI parameter will be blank, and both the strLocalName and strQName parameters will contain the element name.

For this application there is no need to implement the rest of the IVBSAXContentHandler methods, so we'll leave them all with blank implementations. Our ContentHandler interface implementation is ready; let's now look at the rest of the application code, which actually starts the parsing.

In the form code window add the following under the Form_Load method:

```
Private Sub Form_Load()
    'An instance of SAX Parser object
    Dim ReaderObj As New SAXXMLReader40

    'An instance of ContentHandler interface implementation class
    Dim CHImplObj As New ContentHandlerImpl

    'Register the above class instance with the parser
    Set ReaderObj.contentHandler = CHImplObj

    'Start the parsing
    ReaderObj.parseURL "c:\SAX\broadband.xml"

    MsgBox CHImplObj.intElemCount & " Provider elements found!"

    Unload Me
End Sub
```

MSXML 4.0 provides the SAXXMLReader40 co-class that implements the ISAXXMLReader/ IVBSAXXMLReader interface, and which can be used by an application to set and query various SAX parsing behaviors, register event handling classes with the parser, and initiate the parsing of an XML document.

The above lines of code:

1. Create an instance of the SAXXMLReader40 SAX parser class.

2. Create an instance of our class that implements the ContentHandler interface.

3. Register the interface implementation class instance with the parser by setting SAXXMLReader40's contentHandler property.

4. Initiate the parsing of the XML document c:\SAX\broadband.xml by calling SAXXMLReader40's parseURL method. Remember to update the path if you have placed the XML file in some different folder. The parser then scans through the XML document in serial fashion, and generates and sends various events to the registered ContentHandler implementation class. In the ContentHandler implementation we count the number of <Provider> elements, by incrementing a count for each endElement call with Provider as the element name.

5. Then display the element count value and end the application.

Save the project as BasicSAXParsing.vbp, the form file as form1.frm, and the class implementation file as ContentHandlerImpl.cls. When you run the project you should see the following:

Instead of pressing F5 *and running the application, it would be nice to step into the program execution by pressing* F8 *or by clicking on the* **Debug | Step Into** *menu item. You'll notice how the call to the* `parseURL` *method leads to a sequence of event method calls in the* `ContentHandler` *implementation class.*

Importing XML into a Database

It is very common today to exchange data in XML format, either in real time or as a batch operation. Consider a scenario where Company A wants to send some complex data to its clients, Company B, C, and D on a monthly basis. Company A already has the data to be sent in its database (let's say in Oracle 9.0.1 for SUN Solaris 7), and when the client companies receives that data they need to import it into their databases (let's say SQL Server 2000 running on Microsoft Windows 2000), and let's assume that the only way to send the data is to FTP it. In addition, each client requires just a few fields from the source data. The easiest and most convenient solution would be for Company A to export its database data as an XML file (that contains data and metadata or schema) and upload that onto the FTP sites of client companies, who could then run a batch program to import that data into their databases. The import process would simply involve processing the XML document and running insert/update SQL statements on the database tables. If the XML data file to be imported is huge (let's say 200MB), DOM would not be a good choice here; however, a SAX application will work like a charm!

Let's look at another SAX example application, available in the code download as `XML2DB.vbp`. Once again, we'll use MSXML 4.0 and Visual Basic 6.0. Here is the input XML document to be imported, which we'll assume is saved as `c:\SAX\sales.xml`:

```xml
<?xml version="1.0"?>
<Sales month="November" year="2001">
   <Product ID="1">
      <Quantity>230</Quantity>
      <Price>27.99</Price>
   </Product>
   <Product ID="2">
      <Quantity>680</Quantity>
      <Price>14.99</Price>
   </Product>
</Sales>
```

Our SAX application should parse this XML document, create a table named `November2001` (based on the `<Sales>` element attributes), and then insert a row for each `<Product>` sub-element.

Once again, start Visual Basic 6.0 and create a new **Standard EXE** project. Add the reference for **Microsoft XML, v4.0**. Add the class module and rename it as `ContentHandlerImpl`. Write the following line in the class code window:

```
Implements IVBSAXContentHandler
```

Now, add the blank implementation of each `IVBSAXContentHandler` interface method, as described in the previous example. This time we'll again just implement the `ContentHandler` interface; later in the chapter we'll see examples of implementing other SAX interfaces.

In this `ContentHandler` implementation we'll respond to `characters`, `endElement`, and `startElement` interface method calls. Other interface methods will have blank implementations. Let's look at the implementation of these three methods, followed by an explanation of what we are doing here:

```
Implements IVBSAXContentHandler

Dim ProductId As String
Dim Quantity As String
Dim Price As String
Dim TempString As String
Dim TableName As String

Private Sub IVBSAXContentHandler_startElement(strNamespaceURI As String _
                    , strLocalName As String, strQName As String _
                    , ByVal oAttributes As MSXML2.IVBSAXAttributes)

    Select Case strQName
        Case "Product"
            ProductId = oAttributes.getValueFromQName("ID")

        Case "Sales"
            TableName = oAttributes.getValueFromQName("month") & _
                        oAttributes.getValueFromQName("year")

            SQLStmt = "create table " & TableName & " (ProdID int, " & _
                "Qty int, Price decimal(10,2))"
            MsgBox SQLStmt
    End Select

    TempString = ""

End Sub

Private Sub IVBSAXContentHandler_characters(strChars As String)

    TempString = TempString + strChars

End Sub

Private Sub IVBSAXContentHandler_endElement(strNamespaceURI As String _
                    , strLocalName As String, strQName As String)

    Select Case strQName
        Case "Quantity"
            Quantity = TempString
        Case "Price"
            Price = TempString
        Case "Product"
            SQLStmt = "insert into " & TableName & " values (" & _
                    ProductId & "," & Quantity & "," & Price & ")"
            MsgBox SQLStmt
    End Select

    TempString = ""

End Sub

'Rest of the interface methods go here with blank implementation
```

In the input XML document the <Sales> element has month and year attributes – we would like to build the table name by joining the values of these attributes; and the <Product> node has an ID attribute, needed while inserting that data row into the table.

When the SAX parser encounters the beginning of any element it calls startElement() in the ContentHandler implementation, passing the element information (namespace URI, local name, and qualified name), along with the IVBSAXAttributes interface, which allows access to that element's attributes.

In our startElement() method we simply access the IVBSAXAttributes instance to get the attribute values. If it's a <Product> element, we save the value of the ID attribute in the ProductID class variable, and if it is a <Sales> element, we build the TableName variable by combining the attribute values for month and year. We then MsgBox the "Create Table..." statement (in reality we would connect to the database and execute this statement). TempString is used as a variable to hold the element data value (the string between <element> and </element>) temporarily, and its value is copied into the respective class variable in the endElement() implementation.

> *It's important to remember that the parser is free to call the characters() interface method multiple times, even for a data value between a single <element> and </element>. This is the reason why we are adding the strChars input value to TempString, instead of just assigning strChars to it.*

In the endElement() method implementation, if the current element being ended is <Quantity> or <Price>, we simply save the TempString variable's value into the respective class data member (Quantity or Price in this case). However, if it's an endElement for <Product>, we build an insert into... SQL statement and show it using a message box (in reality, we would execute this SQL statement). Finally, we reinitialize the TempString variable, which holds the data between any <element> and matching </element>.

That's pretty much it for the ContentHandler implementation. Let's now look at the main application code that fires the parsing, after registering the content handler interface class with the parser. This code is similar to the application code in our first example; the only difference is that we now tell it to parse a different XML document (c:\SAX\sales.xml).

Write the following lines of code in the Form_Load() method for the form:

```
Private Sub Form_Load()
    'An instance of SAX Parser object
    Dim ReaderObj As New SAXXMLReader40

    'An instance of ContentHandler interface implementation class
    Dim CHImplObj As New ContentHandlerImpl

    'Register the above class instance with the parser
    Set ReaderObj.contentHandler = CHImplObj

    'Start the parsing
    ReaderObj.parseURL "c:\SAX\sales.xml"

    MsgBox "Done"

    Unload Me
End Sub
```

Save the class file as `ContentHandlerImpl.cls`, the form file as `form1.frm`, and the project as `XML2DB.vbp` (in a different folder if you don't want to overwrite the files from the previous example). Run the application, and you should see the following four message boxes:

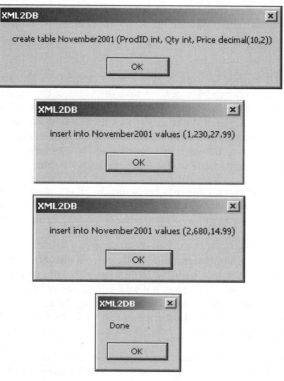

After the parsing is over, the "Done" message box is displayed and the call "Unload Me" ends the application.

Aborting the Parsing

Let's now look at an example of aborting the parsing when some condition is met. Remember that with the DOM, once parsing is started it's not possible to abort the operation; however, with SAX it is possible to abort, suspend, and resume the XML parsing.

> For some reason the MSXML 4.0 RTM release does not provide support for the **IMXReaderControl** interface, which is available in previous releases. This interface provides the ability to abort, suspend, and resume SAX parsing operations. If you look at the MSXML 4.0 type library (using tools like OLE/COM Object Viewer), you'll notice that **SAXXMLReader30** does implement **IMXReaderControl** interface, but **SAXXMLReader40** does not. Hence in the following examples, whenever we need to abort SAX parsing we'll be using the **SAXXMLReader30** class instead of **SAXXMLReader40**, but will still add a reference to MSXML 4.0 DLL. However, it is important to remember that the interface **IMXReaderControl** is non-standard and it would be difficult (or impossible) to migrate applications to other SAX implementations.

For this example we'll again use the c:\SAX\broadband.xml file from the first example. We'll parse the XML document until we get a provider whose rate is less than $49. Therefore, once we find a `<Provider>` element whose `Rate` attribute value is less than $49, we'll abort the parsing.

The project is available in the code download as `TestAbort.vbp`. It is a Visual Basic 6.0 Standard EXE project, with a reference to MSXML 4.0, and a class module called `ContentHandlerImpl`. Again we are implementing just the `IVBSAXContentHandler` interface. For this example we'll only have to respond to the `startElement()` method call – all other interface methods still exist but will have blank implementations.

Here is the `IVBSAXContentHandler` implementation class code:

```
Implements IVBSAXContentHandler

Public ReaderCtrl As IMXReaderControl

Private Sub IVBSAXContentHandler_startElement(strNamespaceURI As String _
                   , strLocalName As String, strQName As String _
                   , ByVal oAttributes As MSXML2.IVBSAXAttributes)

    If strQName = "Provider" Then
        RateVal = oAttributes.getValueFromQName("Rate")
        NameVal = oAttributes.getValueFromQName("Name")

        If CInt(RateVal) < 49 Then
            MsgBox "Found! " & NameVal & " ($" & RateVal & ")"
            ReaderCtrl.abort
        Else
            Debug.Print "Ignoring " & NameVal & " ($" & RateVal & ")"
        End If

    End If

End Sub

Private Sub IVBSAXContentHandler_characters(strChars As String)
End Sub

'Rest of the interface methods go here with blank implementation
```

The above declares a class variable of type `IMXReaderControl`, whose value will be initialized from the main application code with the `SAXXMLReader30` object.

Inside the `startElement()` method implementation code, we check if it's for a `<Provider>` element; if yes, then we get the values of the `Rate` and `Name` attributes. If the rate is less than 49, then we show that using a message box and abort the SAX parsing, otherwise we just print the "ignoring..." message in Visual Basic's immediate window using `Debug.Print`.

Double-click on the form and write the following lines of code under the `Form_Load()` method:

```
Private Sub Form_Load()

    Dim ReaderObj As New SAXXMLReader30
    Dim CHImplObj As New ContentHandlerImpl

    'Register the Content Handler
    Set ReaderObj.contentHandler = CHImplObj

    'Initialize the IMXReaderControl object
    Set CHImplObj.ReaderCtrl = ReaderObj

    'Start the parsing
    ReaderObj.parseURL "c:\SAX\broadband.xml"

    'End the application
    Unload Me

End Sub
```

Debug trace through the code (*F8*) and you'll notice two important points here: first, you'll never see the "ignoring..." message for the last record ("DirectTV DSL"), because we call abort before that (on the "AT&T @Home" record). Moreover, even though we call abort, the startElement() function processing continues; it's only when this function returns that the parsing stops.

Locating a Record in a Large XML File: DOM versus SAX

This is a very interesting example. It shows how SAX can be a lifesaver while working with very large XML documents. The aim is to search for a record based on some attribute-matching condition. This search will be performed on a very large XML document and then we'll compare the time taken by SAX and DOM to locate a particular record.

The large file we will be using in this example was generated using a Visual Basic helper application (BuildHugeXMLDoc.vbp). It simply loops 1,000,001 times and writes a <row> element line in the output text file. This <row> element has an ID attribute, which is nothing but the value of the index (hence, a value from 0 to 1,000,000), and each element has some test text. The output file, which we'll assume is stored as c:\sax\hugefile.xml, is approximately 58MB in size.

Let's now create the application that parses the above XML document to locate a record, using SAX and DOM. It is available in the code download as DomVsSAX.vbp. It is a Visual Basic 6.0 Standard EXE project, with a reference to MSXML 4.0, and a class module that implements the IVBSAXContentHandler interface:

```
Implements IVBSAXContentHandler

Public ReaderCtrl As IMXReaderControl

Private Sub IVBSAXContentHandler_startElement(strNamespaceURI As String _
                    , strLocalName As String, strQName As String _
                    , ByVal oAttributes As MSXML2.IVBSAXAttributes)

    If strQName = "row" Then
        If oAttributes.getValueFromQName("ID") = Form1.txtFindID.Text Then
            ReaderCtrl.abort
```

```
          End If
      End If

End Sub

'Rest of the interface methods go here with blank implementation
```

This time we just add the implementation for the startElement() method; all other interface method implementations are left blank. Inside the startElement() implementation we check if the current element is "row" and if its ID attribute's value matches the value specified on the form. If it does, we call abort, which stops the parsing.

Let's now look at the application code. The application form looks like this:

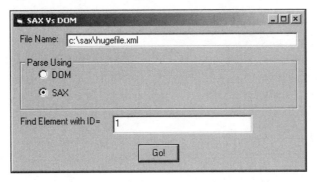

Let's first look at the SAX processing code:

```
Private Sub ProcessUsingSAX()
    'An instance of SAX Parser object
    Dim ReaderObj As New SAXXMLReader30

    'An instance of ContentHandler interface implementation class
    Dim CHImplObj As New ContentHandlerImpl

    'Register the above class instance with the parser
    Set ReaderObj.contentHandler = CHImplObj

    Set CHImplObj.ReaderCtrl = ReaderObj

    StartTime = Timer
    Form1.MousePointer = vbHourglass

    'Start the parsing
    ReaderObj.parseURL txtFileName.Text

    Form1.MousePointer = vbNormal
    lblTimeTaken.Caption = "Time taken: " & Timer - StartTime & " Secs."

End Sub
```

The above code is not very different from the earlier examples – the only difference is that before parsing, it changes the mouse pointer and records the start time. When `parseURL()` returns (either `abort` is called when an element is found, or the entire document is processed and the element was not found), it resets the mouse pointer and calculates the time taken by the SAX parsing.

The DOM parsing code looks like this:

```
Private Sub ProcessUsingDOM()
    Dim XMLDocObj As New MSXML2.DOMDocument40
    Dim MatchingNode As MSXML2.IXMLDOMNode

    StartTime = Timer
    Form1.MousePointer = vbHourglass

    XMLDocObj.Load txtFileName.Text
    XMLDocObj.setProperty "SelectionLanguage", "XPath"

    Set MatchingNode = XMLDocObj.selectSingleNode("/Data/row[@ID='" & _
                        txtFindID.Text & "']")

    Form1.MousePointer = vbNormal
    lblTimeTaken.Caption = "Time taken: " & Timer - StartTime & " Secs."

    On Error Resume Next
    MsgBox MatchingNode.xml

End Sub
```

The above code uses the DOM to load the entire document into memory and then applies the XPath expression to perform the search. MSXML DOM is covered in greater detail in Chapter 2, while XPath programming with MSXML is covered in Chapter 4.

Here comes the interesting part – the parsing results. We'll keep changing the search criteria and see how SAX and DOM respond.

When searching for an element with ID = 0 (the very first element), SAX returned almost immediately (less than 1 second), while DOM took about 52 seconds (on the author's laptop with 320 MB RAM, Pentium III, 750 MHz.).

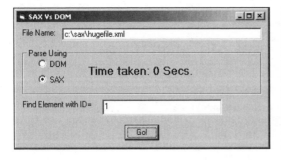
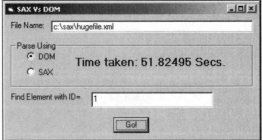

While parsing with DOM, the CPU usage spikes to more than 90% during building the in-memory DOM tree and the memory usage continuously goes up. With SAX also, you may notice the high CPU usage, but for a lesser period; and also the memory count will remain constant, it will not go up with SAX.

These are the statistics after changing the search criteria several times:

Find Element with ID=	SAX	DOM
1	Immediately (< 0.1 seconds)	52 seconds
10000	0.41 seconds	44 seconds
100000	4 seconds	43 seconds
500000	20 seconds	44 seconds
999999	42 seconds	46 seconds
-1 (non-matching entry)	42 seconds	47 seconds

Note that the time taken by DOM is nearly constant – the reason being that the majority of time goes into building the in-memory tree. While with SAX, the time taken changes with the amount of data read, if the matching record is found at the beginning of the input XML stream the result comes back almost immediately, however, if the matching record is towards the end of the XML stream, the time taken is longer – but note that it still does not demand any extra memory.

It is important to remember that the above statistics are achieved via an ability to abort the parsing using a non-standard SAX interface (IMXReaderControl) available with MSXML 3.0 and not with MSXML 4.0.

Implementing Error Handler

The SAX2 API defines an interface, ErrorHandler, which an application may implement in order to handle recoverable and/or fatal errors while parsing. If the application does not implement this interface (like all the samples above), and if some errors occur, the parser does not report such parsing errors and unexpected behavior can occur.

Let's see an example of implementing an error handler. To test, we'll use the copy of c:\SAX\broadband.xml from the first example, and make a slight change (mismatched attribute quotes) to violate the well-formedness constraint of the document. Save the new document as c:\SAX\broadband2.xml:

```
<?xml version="1.0" ?>
<DSLProviders ZipCode="60195">
    <Provider ID='1" Name="EarthLink" Rate="49.99" />
    <Provider ID="2" Name="Ameritech" Rate="49.99"/>
    <Provider ID="3" Name="AT&amp;T @Home" Rate="19.99"/>
    <Provider ID="4" Name="DirectTV DSL" Rate="49.99"/>
</DSLProviders>
```

Once again we'll look at a Visual Basic project, available in the code download as `TestErrHandling.vbp`, which has a reference to MSXML 4.0, and a class module (`ContentHandlerImpl`) to implement the `ContentHandler` interface. We could use the same class to implement `IVBSAXErrorHandler`, but instead have added another class module named `ErrorHandlerImpl` to implement the error-handling interface.

The `IVBSAXErrorHandler` interface defines three methods:

❑ `error`: through this method the parser reports any recoverable error. Later in the chapter we'll see how the XSD schema errors are reported using this method.

❑ `fatalError`: through this method the parser reports any error that corresponds to the definition of a fatal error in section 1.2 of the W3C XML 1.0 Recommendation. Examples of this include anything that violates the well-formedness of the XML document.

❑ `ignorableWarning`: the current implementation of SAX 2 in MSXML does not use this method yet. However, future releases of the parser may use this method to report warnings or any errors not defined by the W3C XML 1.0 Recommendation.

For this example all the `ContentHandler` methods will have a blank implementation (it's also possible to completely skip the `ContentHandler` implementation and then not set the SAXReader's `contentHandler` property). Add a new class module and blank implementations for the `IVBSAXContentHandler` interface. Then add another class module to implement `IVBSAXErrorHandler` as shown below:

```
Implements IVBSAXErrorHandler

Private Sub IVBSAXErrorHandler_fatalError( _
                ByVal oLocator As MSXML2.IVBSAXLocator _
                , strErrorMessage As String _
                , ByVal nErrorCode As Long)

    MsgBox "Error occurred at line " & oLocator.lineNumber & _
           ", Character " & oLocator.columnNumber & " while parsing " & _
           oLocator.systemId & vbNewLine & vbNewLine & strErrorMessage & _
           vbNewLine & "Error Code: " & nErrorCode
End Sub


'Rest of the interface methods go here with blank implementation
```

We simply implement the `fatalError()` method. When the parser reports any errors, it passes the relevant information (such as line number, column number, error text, source file, etc.) as input parameters. In our `fatalError` implementation we just `MsgBox` this information.

Now that we've implemented the error-handling interface, we need to register it with the parser so that the parser can use it and call methods on it in case of any errors. Write the following code in the `Form_Load()` method:

```
Private Sub Form_Load()
    'An instance of SAX Parser object
    Dim ReaderObj As New SAXXMLReader40

    'An instance of ContentHandler interface implementation class
    Dim CHImplObj As New ContentHandlerImpl
```

```
                'An instance of ErrorHandler interface implementation class
                Dim EHImplObj As New ErrorHandlerImpl

                'Register the above class instances with the parser
                Set ReaderObj.contentHandler = CHImplObj
                Set ReaderObj.errorHandler = EHImplObj

                On Error Resume Next

                'Start the parsing
                ReaderObj.parseURL "c:\SAX\broadband2.xml"

                Unload Me
        End Sub
```

When you run this application you should see the following:

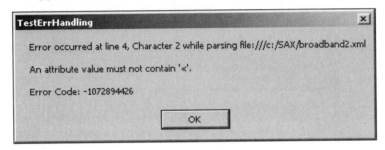

LexicalHandler and EntityResolver Interfaces

In addition to the standard content events (start document, start element, end document, etc.), MSXML SAX 2 implementation can also generate information about *lexical* elements in an XML document. Lexical elements refer to constructs such as comments, DTD declarations, CDATA, etc.

Let's look at one final example before moving on to the next section. This example will show two things:

- ❏ First, how to receive the lexical information (CDATA, comments, DTD declarations, start and end of an entity) notifications from the parser.

- ❏ Second, how to implement an interface that the parser will call before opening any external entities (such as external entities referenced within a document).

The first task is achieved by implementing the LexicalHandler interface, while the latter is solved by implementing the EntityResolver interface. Let's first look at the test XML file, which we'll assume is saved as c:\SAX\prodinfo.xml:

```
<?xml version="1.0"?>
<!DOCTYPE services SYSTEM "test.dtd" [
]>
<!-- Test Document -->
<service>
    <plan ID="1">
        <product>&ProductName;</product>
```

```
        <contact>12</contact >
        <![CDATA[
                <<
                Promotional plan & valid
                till 31st December 2001.
                >>
        ]]>
    </plan>
</service>
```

This XML file has a comment line, a CDATA section, and refers to an external DTD file (test.dtd). The test.dtd file resides in the same directory as the XML file and has just one line, defining the &ProductName; entity used in the XML document:

```
<!ENTITY ProductName "MAXSpeed DSL">
```

If you open the prodinfo.xml file in Internet Explorer, you should see the following:

Let's now create a new Visual Basic 6.0 Standard EXE project, add a reference to MSXML 4.0, and add a class module named EventsImpl. (The project is available in the code download as OtherEvents.vbp.) Write the first two Implements lines in the EventsImpl class code window, and then select all methods for both the interfaces from the drop-down combo box as described earlier. The full code is as follows:

```
Implements IVBSAXLexicalHandler
Implements IVBSAXEntityResolver

Private Sub IVBSAXLexicalHandler_startDTD(strName As String _
        , strPublicId As String, strSystemId As String)
```

```
        Debug.Print "LexicalHandler: StartDTD=>" & strName & " " & _
                strPublicId & " " & strSystemId & vbNewLine
End Sub

Private Sub IVBSAXLexicalHandler_endDTD()
    Debug.Print "LexicalHandler: endDTD " & vbNewLine
End Sub

Private Sub IVBSAXLexicalHandler_comment(strChars As String)
    Debug.Print "LexicalHandler: comment=>" & strChars & vbNewLine
End Sub

Private Sub IVBSAXLexicalHandler_startCDATA()
    Debug.Print "LexicalHandler: startCDATA" & vbNewLine
End Sub

Private Sub IVBSAXLexicalHandler_endCDATA()
    Debug.Print "LexicalHandler: endCDATA" & vbNewLine
End Sub

Private Sub IVBSAXLexicalHandler_startEntity(strName As String)
    Debug.Print "LexicalHandler: startEntity=>" & strName & vbNewLine
End Sub

Private Sub IVBSAXLexicalHandler_endEntity(strName As String)
    Debug.Print "LexicalHandler: endEntity=>" & strName & vbNewLine
End Sub

'The only IVBSAXEntityResolver method
Private Function IVBSAXEntityResolver_resolveEntity( _
        strPublicId As String _
        , strSystemId As String) As Variant

    Debug.Print "EntityResolver: resolveEntity=>" & strPublicId & " " & _
                strSystemId & vbNewLine
End Function
```

This time the interface method implementation is pretty straightforward. For each method we just print the method name along with the parameter values in the Visual Basic immediate window, using `Debug.Print` statements.

Now, to register these events with the parser, write the following code in the application's `Form_Load()` method:

```
Private Sub Form_Load()
    'An instance of SAX Parser object
    Dim ReaderObj As New SAXXMLReader40

    'An instance of class that implements
    'LexicalHandler and EntityResolver interfaces
    Dim EvntsImpl As New EventsImpl
```

```
      ReaderObj.putFeature _
      "http://xml.org/sax/features/external-parameter-entities", True

      'Register the entity resolver
      Set ReaderObj.entityResolver = EvntsImpl

      'Register the LexicalHandler
      ReaderObj.putProperty _
          "http://xml.org/sax/properties/lexical-handler", EvntsImpl

      'Start the parsing
      ReaderObj.parseURL "c:\SAX\prodinfo.xml"

  End Sub
```

The above code starts with a standard line for creating a SAXXMLReader40 object. It then creates an instance of the class that implements the LexicalHandler and EntityResolver interfaces. It then registers this object as the EntityResolver handler by setting the reader's entityResolver property. However, prior to that, it makes a call to the reader's putFeature() method. We'll discuss this in the next section, for now you can assume that the call to putFeature() is required in order to enable the EntityResolver interface.

Also note how the LexicalHandler implementation class is registered with the reader object – we call the reader's putProperty() method to set the callback interface for lexical parsing events. We'll also discuss putProperty() in the next section, for now just see how we register the lexical event handler with the parser.

You can set the breakpoint at the End Sub line above, and when you execute the above application, you should see the following lines in Visual Basic's immediate window:

```
LexicalHandler: StartDTD=>services  file:///c:/SAX/test.dtd
EntityResolver: resolveEntity=> file:///c:/SAX/test.dtd
LexicalHandler: startEntity=>[dtd]
LexicalHandler: endEntity=>[dtd]
LexicalHandler: endDTD
LexicalHandler: comment=> Test Document
LexicalHandler: startEntity=>ProductName
LexicalHandler: endEntity=>ProductName
LexicalHandler: startCDATA
LexicalHandler: endCDATA
```

Note how the parser notifies the application of various parsing and lexical analysis events. The actual content of the CDATA section is returned as part of ContentHandler's characters() method call. Since we did not implement that interface, we are just seeing the call to startCDATA() followed by endCDATA(), without the actual CDATA content.

Starting with MSXML4, the parser does not support DTD validation. It just supports schema validation for XML documents. Let's now look at some examples of validating XML while parsing it using SAX.

XSD Schema Validation with SAX

XML Schema Definition, or XSD for short, refers to the W3C's Schema Recommendation, an XML-based grammar for describing the structure of XML documents. A schema-aware validating parser, such as MSXML 4.0, can validate an XML document against an XSD Schema and report any discrepancies. Apart from the XML validation, schemas have many other benefits. However, for our discussion we'll just focus on validating an XML document against an XSD Schema, while parsing the document with SAX. MSXML 4.0 support for schemas is covered in greater depth in Chapter 3.

> *To learn more about the XML Schema W3C specification, which is divided into three parts, you should visit the W3C web site. The three parts are: XML Schema Part 0: Primer (http://www.w3.org/TR/xmlschema-0/), XML Schema Part 1: Structures (http://www.w3.org/TR/xmlschema-1/), and XML Schema Part 2: Datatypes (http://www.w3.org/TR/xmlschema-2/). Another resource for learning about Schemas is "Professional XML Schemas" from Wrox Press (ISBN: 1-861005-47-4).*

Before looking at the XSD validation functionality with SAX, let's first look at an important aspect of customizing or extending SAX parsers through features and properties.

Features and Properties

SAX 2 introduced the concepts of **features** and **properties**, which can be used to observe and control the parser behavior. They also allow parser writers to add custom extensions that an application can query for, and use if available.

The XMLReader interface was chosen to have getFeature()/putFeature() and getProperty()/putProperty() method pairs that allow applications to query and set feature flags and property values. The feature flags are always Boolean (true or false), while the property values are arbitrary objects. The MSXML implementation of XMLReader (SAXXMLReader40) implements these methods and we may call them to set and query features and properties. For instance, before calling parseURL() on a SAXXMLReader40 parser object, we may call putFeature() on it, with schema-validation as the feature name and true as the value, and tell the parser to validate the XML document while parsing.

We saw an example of putProperty() and putFeature() earlier, during the LexicalHandler / EntityResolver example:

```
ReaderObj.putProperty _
    "http://xml.org/sax/properties/lexical-handler", EvntsImpl
```

According to SAX 2, LexicalHandler is an optional extension interface, and a parser may support it to send lexical event notifications (CDATA, comments, etc.) to the application. As this is an optional extension interface, MSXML supports registering a LexicalHandler class with the parser through the above putProperty() method call. In the above example, ReaderObj is a SAXXMLReader40 instance, while EvntsImpl is an instance of a class that implements IVBSAXLexicalHandler.

```
ReaderObj.putFeature _
    "http://xml.org/sax/features/external-parameter-entities", True
```

*DTDs provide a mechanism to declare content that we can just declare once, and use later at various places in the XML document. These are called **entities** and they work in a very similar way to #define in C programming. These entities can be defined either in the inline DTD or in external DTDs. During the LexicalHandler/EntityResolver example we saw an example of an external entity (ProductName). If we want the MSXML SAX parser to notify our application when it tries to resolve such external entities, we should implement the IVBSAXEntityResolver interface and enable its external-parameter-entities feature by calling the above putFeature() method.*

A Simple Validation Example

XSD validation with SAX basically requires the following steps before parsing begins:

❑ Implement at least the error handler interface, to capture errors when the document is invalid. If we do not implement this interface, the parser will fail with unexpected results when the document is invalid.

❑ Create an instance of the XMLSchemaCache40 class and load a schema XSD file into it, by calling the Add() method on the instance.

❑ Enable the schema-validation feature for SAXXMLReader40 by calling its putFeature() method.

❑ Set the previously created XMLSchemaCache40 object as the value of the schemas property for SAXXMLReader by calling its putProperty() method.

Let's now look at an example of this. Here is the input XML document (c:\sax\music.xml) to be parsed and validated:

```
<?xml version="1.0" ?>
<MusicTeachers>
    <Teacher>
        <Name>Murphys Music Inc</Name>
        <Address>103 Diane Drive</Address>
        <Phone>(999)999-9999</Phone>
        <Email>some@teacher.org</Email>
        <Type>Private Teacher</Type>
        <Teaches>Guitar, Bass Guitar</Teaches>
        <Style>Pop Rock</Style>
        <Rates>$12 per 1/2 Hour</Rates>
    </Teacher>
</MusicTeachers>
```

The above XML document adheres to the following music.xsd schema:

```
<?xml version="1.0"?>
<xsd:schema xmlns:xsd="http://www.w3.org/2001/XMLSchema">
    <xsd:element name="MusicTeachers">
        <xsd:complexType>
            <xsd:sequence>
                <xsd:element name="Teacher" minOccurs="0"
                        maxOccurs="unbounded" >
                    <xsd:complexType>
                        <xsd:sequence>
```

```
                        <xsd:element name="Name" type="xsd:string" />
                        <xsd:element name="Address" type="xsd:string" />
                        <xsd:element name="Phone" type="xsd:string" />
                        <xsd:element name="Email" type="xsd:string" />
                        <xsd:element name="Type" type="xsd:string" />
                        <xsd:element name="Teaches" type="xsd:string" />
                        <xsd:element name="Style" type="xsd:string" />
                        <xsd:element name="Rates" type="xsd:string" />
                    </xsd:sequence>
                </xsd:complexType>
            </xsd:element>
        </xsd:sequence>
    </xsd:complexType>
  </xsd:element>
</xsd:schema>
```

The above schema file (which we'll assume is saved as `c:\sax\music.xsd`) defines the structure for `MusicTeachers` records.

Create a new Visual Basic Standard EXE project, add a reference to MSXML 4.0, and add a class module named `ErrorHandlerImpl`. Add the code in this class module to implement `IVBSAXErrorHandler`:

```
Implements IVBSAXErrorHandler

Private Sub IVBSAXErrorHandler_error( _
          ByVal oLocator As MSXML2.IVBSAXLocator _
        , strErrorMessage As String _
        , ByVal nErrorCode As Long)

    MsgBox "Error (" & CStr(nErrorCode) & ")" & vbNewLine & _
          strErrorMessage & vbNewLine & "At line " & _
          oLocator.lineNumber & " character " & _
          oLocator.columnNumber
End Sub

'Rest of ErrorHandler methods with blank implementation
```

For simplicity we only implement the `error()` method; the other two methods have blank implementations. If the parser encounters any violation of the XSD schema it calls the `ErrorHandler`'s `error()` method, passing the error information, such as the position in the XML document where the error occurred, the error message, and the error code. Save the class module as `ErrorHandlerImpl.cls`.

Double-click on the form and add the following code within the `Form_Load()` method:

```
Private Sub Form_Load()
    'An instance of SAX Parser object
    Dim ReaderObj As New SAXXMLReader40

    'An instance of ErrorHandler interface implementation class
    Dim ErrHandImpl As New ErrorHandlerImpl
```

```
            'Object to hold the Schema
            Dim SchemaObj As New MSXML2.XMLSchemaCache40

            'Register the above class instance with the parser
            Set ReaderObj.ErrorHandler = ErrHandImpl

            SchemaObj.Add "", "c:\sax\music.xsd"

            'Configure the SAX reader to enable validation
            ReaderObj.putFeature "schema-validation", True
            ReaderObj.putProperty "schemas", SchemaObj

            On Error Resume Next
            'Start the parsing
            ReaderObj.parseURL "c:\SAX\music.xml"

            If Err.Number = 0 Then
                MsgBox "Document is valid according to schema"
            End If

        Unload Me
    End Sub
```

The above lines of code simply load the schema file (c:\sax\music.xsd) in an XMLSchemaCache40 object and set this object as the schemas property for the XMLReader. Also, we enable the schema-validation feature by calling the putFeature() method on XMLReader.

When we now run the code, when the XML file is valid with respect to the XSD schema, we see the following:

Now go ahead and change something (alter an element name, or add/remove an element, etc.) in the c:\SAX\music.xml file to make it invalid (however, keeping it well-formed!) and then run the program again – it should report the validation error this time. For instance, we changed the name for the Teacher element to Teacher1 and got the following message:

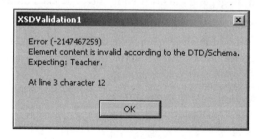

Note that as soon as the parser sees the inconsistency, it reports it via a call to `ErrorHandler`'s error method, and aborts the parsing. However, if we want to continue the parsing and possibly get all the XSD validation errors, just add one line to the above code to enable the **exhaustive-errors** feature:

```
ReaderObj.putFeature "schema-validation", True
ReaderObj.putProperty "schemas", SchemaObj
ReaderObj.putFeature "exhaustive-errors", True
```

In this case, we also need to comment out or remove the code that produces the message that the document is valid according to the schema.

Now the parser won't stop at the first validation error, it will continue to parse the entire document, reporting further validation inconsistencies, if any.

Also, if we want to get the **schema information** about the element being parsed (such as the values of `minOccurs` and `maxOccurs` attributes for that element in the XSD schema), we may implement the interface `IMXSchemaDeclHandler`, create an instance of a class that implements this interface, and register the instance with the parser reader object, as below:

```
ReaderObj.putProperty "schema-declaration-handler", SchDeclHandlerObj
```

Let's see an example of this. For this example also, we'll use the `music.xml` and `music.xsd` files mentioned above.

Create a Visual Basic 6.0 Standard EXE project (available in the code download as `SchemaInfo.vbp`), add a reference to MSXML 4.0, add a class module, and name it `SchemaDeclHandler`. In this class module, we'll implement the `IMXSchemaDeclHandler` interface:

```
Implements IMXSchemaDeclHandler

Private Sub IMXSchemaDeclHandler_schemaElementDecl(ByVal oSchemaElement _
        As MSXML2.ISchemaElement)
    Debug.Print oSchemaElement.Name & " (" & _
            oSchemaElement.minOccurs & ", " & _
            oSchemaElement.maxOccurs & " )"
End Sub
```

Next, double-click on the form and write the following code under the `Form_Load()` method:

```
Private Sub Form_Load()
    Dim ReaderObj As New SAXXMLReader40
    Dim SchemaObj As New MSXML2.XMLSchemaCache40

    Dim SchDeclHandlerObj As New SchemaDeclHandler


    SchemaObj.Add "", "C:\sax\music.xsd"

    ReaderObj.putFeature "schema-validation", True
    ReaderObj.putProperty "schemas", SchemaObj
    ReaderObj.putProperty "schema-declaration-handler", SchDeclHandlerObj

    On Error Resume Next
```

279

```
        ReaderObj.parseURL "C:\SAX\music.xml"

        Unload Me
End Sub
```

Debug trace (*F8*) through the application and we see the following text in the immediate window:

MusicTeachers (1, 1)
Teacher (0, -1)
Name (1, 1)
Address (1, 1)
...
...

The above output specifies that according to the schema the <MusicTeachers> element can (and should) appear just once in the XML document, the <Teacher> element may occur zero or more times, and so on.

SAX2 and Namespaces Support

XML Namespaces provide a simple method for qualifying element and attribute names used in XML documents by associating them with a namespace identified by a URI. XML Namespaces are the solution to the problem of ambiguity and name collisions. Namespaces are generally associated with prefixes that serve as the shorthand of the URI.

> *To learn more about XML Namespace, visit the W3C site at http://www.w3.org/TR/REC-xml-names/. Another great resource to learn Namespaces is "Professional XML 2nd edition" (Wrox Press, ISBN 1-861005-05-9). Microsoft Developer's Network (MSDN) web site also has a good article on Namespaces (http://msdn.microsoft.com/msdnmag/issues/01/07/xml/xml0107.asp).*

SAX 2 adds support for XML Namespaces. If the XML document uses namespaces, then SAX 2-enabled parsers, such as MSXML 4.0, provide the namespace information (URI, prefix, etc.) along with the other information, while calling ContentHandler interface methods such as startElement(), endElement(), etc. We may then use this namespace information in our application as desired.

Let's look at a small example illustrating namespace support in MSXML SAX parsing. In the following example, we'll perform different processing based on the namespace which the XML is from. Let's look at our input XML document, which we'll assume is saved as c:\SAX\namespace.xml. Note that the namespace is declared for each <AChannel> element below:

```
<?xml version="1.0" ?>
<SalesChannels>
    <uk:AChannel xmlns:uk="http://uk.sales">
        <uk:Name>ABCD</uk:Name>
        <uk:Amount>3000</uk:Amount>
    </uk:AChannel>

    <us:AChannel xmlns:us="http://us.sales">
```

```
        <us:Name>ABCD</us:Name>
        <us:Amount>900</us:Amount>
    </us:AChannel>

</SalesChannels>
```

The document contains two AChannel records with the same name (ABCD), but each belongs to a different namespace. Let's look at the SAX parsing code that processes this XML document.

Create a Visual Basic 6.0 Standard EXE project (available in the code download as NamespaceEx.vbp), add a reference to MSXML 4.0, add a class module and name it ContentHandlerImpl, and finally add the interface method implementation declarations for IVBSAXContentHandler:

```
Implements IVBSAXContentHandler
Dim AmountVal As String

Private Sub IVBSAXContentHandler_endElement( _
      strNamespaceURI As String, strLocalName As String, strQName As String)

   If strLocalName = "Amount" And strNamespaceURI = "http://uk.sales" Then
    Debug.Print "Do UK specific processing on amount: " & AmountVal
   Else
    If strLocalName = "Amount" And strNamespaceURI = "http://us.sales" Then
       Debug.Print "Do US specific processing on amount: " & AmountVal
    End If
   End If

End Sub

Private Sub IVBSAXContentHandler_startElement( _
      strNamespaceURI As String, strLocalName As String, _
      strQName As String, ByVal oAttributes As MSXML2.IVBSAXAttributes)

    AmountVal = ""

End Sub

Private Sub IVBSAXContentHandler_characters(strChars As String)
    AmountVal = AmountVal + strChars
End Sub

Private Sub IVBSAXContentHandler_startPrefixMapping( _
                 strPrefix As String, strURI As String)

   Debug.Print "startPrefix: " & strPrefix & " (" & strURI & ")"
End Sub

Private Sub IVBSAXContentHandler_endPrefixMapping(strPrefix As String)
    Debug.Print "endPrefix: " & strPrefix
End Sub

'Rest of the interface methods go here with blank implementation
```

We handle a few methods from the `ContentHandler` interface, the rest of the methods have blank implementations and are not shown here. The above code is pretty self-explanatory; it basically makes use of the information passed to it as parameters.

The application code that actually starts the parsing is contained in the form; write the following code under the `Form_Load()` method:

```
'An instance of SAX Parser object
Dim ReaderObj As New SAXXMLReader40

'An instance of ContentHandler interface implementation class
Dim CHImplObj As New ContentHandlerImpl

'Register the above class instance with the parser
Set ReaderObj.contentHandler = CHImplObj

'Start the parsing
ReaderObj.parseURL "c:\SAX\namespace.xml"

Unload Me
```

The above lines simply create the `SAXXMLReader40` and `ContentHandler` implementation class instances, register the `ContentHandler` interface, and start the parsing. If we set the breakpoint on the last line in the above code and then run the program, we see the following output lines in the Visual Basic's immediate window:

```
startPrefix: uk (http://uk.sales)
Do UK specific processing on amount: 3000
endPrefix: uk
startPrefix: us (http://us.sales)
Do US specific processing on amount: 900
endPrefix: us
```

The `startPrefixMapping()` method call indicates the beginning of the prefix-URI namespace mapping, while the `endPrefixMapping()` method is called when the scope of `prefix-URI` ends. The methods like `startElement()`, `endElement()`, etc., now get the namespace URI value and, in our code, we are simply showing a different text for different namespaces.

The namespace reporting feature is by default turned on. If we wish to, we can disable the namespace support by adding following line:

```
ReaderObj.putFeature "http://xml.org/sax/features/namespaces", False
```

Once we add this line, before the `parseURL()` method call, we notice that the `startElement()`, `endElement()`, etc., methods do not get any value for namespace URI and local name parameters.

Also, if we need to know the mapping between prefixes and namespace URIs, we may add the following line:

```
ReaderObj.putFeature "http://xml.org/sax/features/namespace-prefixes", True
```

When the `"http://xml.org/sax/features/namespace-prefixes"` is enabled, the parser sends the namespace prefix and URI mapping information as part of the attributes collection parameter during the `startElement()` method call.

Creating XML Documents Using SAX

Let's say we are writing some application that connects to the database, gets the data from some tables, builds XML out of that data, and then needs to stream that XML to some client application, possibly running over the Internet. In this case, we don't need to cache the XML or hold it in memory (as in DOM) on the server, we just need to build and stream it to the client immediately.

Let's now look at SAX from a different angle and learn to *create* XML documents using SAX.

The MXXMLWriter Class

In this section we'll learn about `MXXMLWriter`, a very interesting class that provides support for handling the output generated by SAX events, and which can be used to generate XML documents. This generated XML document output can appear in three forms: as a string, as a stream, or as a DOM object. Hence, it provides interesting opportunities for working with SAX and DOM together, apart from building XML strings and streaming the XML output.

The `MXXMLWriter` class implements `ISAXContentHandler`, `IVBSAXContentHandler`, `ISAXErrorHandler`, `IVBSAXErrorHandler`, etc. and it can easily be used as the event target for SAX parsing. In addition to these SAX interfaces, it also implements `IMXWriter` interface, which helps generate XML or DOM output.

That means we can connect the `MXXMLWriter` class with `SAXXMLReader`, and when `SAXXMLReader` generates SAX events, `MXXMLWriter` will accumulate data passed by the events, and automatically build XML documents that can be accessed as a string, a stream, or a DOM document. Let's look at an example of this, which will clarify the concept further.

Output as a String

In this example we'll build an XML document by manually calling methods of the SAX event handler. We'll create an instance of `MXXMLWriter40` class (remember it implements the `IVBSAXContentHandler` interface). We'll then typecast this object to type `IVBSAXContentHandler` interface and then call this interface's methods such as `startDocument()`, `startElement()`, and so on. When we do this, `MXXMLWriter40` internally builds the XML document in response to the event method calls, and the resultant XML document can be accessed using its `output` property.

The code for this project is available in the download as `XMLWriter1.vbp`. It is a Visual Basic 6.0 Standard EXE project, with reference to MSXML 4.0, and the following lines of code in the `Form_Load()` method:

```
Private Sub Form_Load()
    Dim WriterObj As New MXXMLWriter40
    Dim AttrsObj As New SAXAttributes40
```

```
         Dim ContHandler As IVBSAXContentHandler

         WriterObj.indent = True
         WriterObj.standalone = True

         'Typecasting so that we can call ContentHandler SAX events
         Set ContHandler = WriterObj

      ContHandler.startDocument

      AttrsObj.addAttribute "", "", "ID", "", "1"

      ContHandler.startElement "", "", "Employee", AttrsObj
      AttrsObj.Clear

      ContHandler.startElement "", "", "Name", AttrsObj

      ContHandler.startElement "", "", "FirstName", AttrsObj
      ContHandler.characters "Tyler"
      ContHandler.endElement "", "", "FirstName"

      ContHandler.startElement "", "", "LastName", AttrsObj
      ContHandler.characters "Sheffield"
      ContHandler.endElement "", "", "LastName"

      ContHandler.endElement "", "", "Name"
      ContHandler.endElement "", "", "Employee"
      ContHandler.endDocument

      MsgBox WriterObj.output

         Unload Me
   End Sub
```

We start by creating an instance of class `MXXMLWriter40`, and set its `indent` property to `true` to get pretty XML output, and set its `standalone` property to `true`, which sets the `standalone` attribute to "yes" in the resulting XML.

As mentioned earlier, the `MXXMLWriter40` class implements various interfaces including `IVBSAXContentHandler`, `IVBSAXDTDHandler`, `IMXWriter`, etc. The default interface for `MXXMLWriter40` is `IMXWriter`, which facilitates generating the XML document as a string, a stream, or DOM document, and is also used for controlling various properties such as `indent`, `encoding`, etc. It's possible to typecast the `MXXMLWriter40` instance to any other SAX events interface, and when we manually fire events, the `MXXMLWriter40` object responds to them and internally builds an XML document. That's what we are doing in the above code. We are typecasting the `MXXMLWriter40` instance to `IVBSAXContentHandler` and then firing various `ContentHandler` events, such as `startDocument()`, `startElement()`, etc., on it. Now, using the `output` property of the `MXXMLWriter40`, we can access the resultant XML, and later we'll see how to use this property to control the format (string, stream, or DOM object) of the resultant XML.

When we run the above application, we see the following:

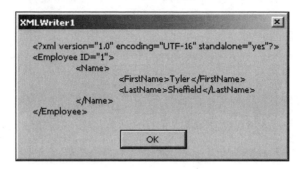

Let's now look at a little variation of this example. In the following example, instead of manually firing the events we'll use the SAXXMLReader40 object to parse some XML file, and we'll set this reader's contentHandler property as an MXXMLWriter40 instance. When the parsing finishes, we'll have the same XML document that we parsed, available through the MXXMLWriter40 instance. This can be very handy in scenarios where, let's say on a web server, we have some data stored in XML files that needs to be streamed to the client in response to some requests, and we don't want to take the overhead of loading the entire XML document in memory, we just need to read and stream the data to the client. We can set the output property of MXXMLWriter40 to the ASP Response object, which will then directly stream the XML to the client. We'll see an example of this very soon, but first let's see how to get the XML text from a file, without implementing any event handler, but by using only the MXXMLWriter40.

This project is available as XMLWriter2.vbp. It has a reference to MSXML 4.0, and the following code in the Form_Load() method:

```
Private Sub Form_Load()
    Dim WriterObj As New MXXMLWriter40
    Dim ReaderObj As New SAXXMLReader40

    Set ReaderObj.contentHandler = WriterObj

    ReaderObj.parseURL "c:\sax\sales.xml"

    MsgBox WriterObj.output
    Unload Me

End Sub
```

We first create instances of MXXMLWriter40 and SAXXMLReader40 and then the MXXMLWriter40 instance is set as the contentHandler for the reader object – this is possible because the MXXMLWriter class implements the IVBSAXContentHandler interface. Next, we call the reader to parse c:\sax\sales.xml, which leads to the reader generating parsing events and sending them to the MXXMLWriter40 object, which internally builds the same XML document again, in response to the SAX events. When we run the above code, we see the following:

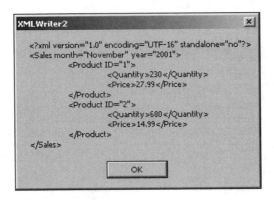

Output as a Response Stream

Let's now see an ASP equivalent (`WriterTest.asp`) of the above example:

```
<%@ Language=VBScript %>
<%
    Response.ContentType = "text/xml"
    Set writer = Server.CreateObject("Msxml2.MXXMLWriter.4.0")
    Set reader = Server.CreateObject("Msxml2.SAXXMLReader.4.0")

    Set reader.contentHandler = writer
      writer.output = Response

    reader.parseURL Server.MapPath("sales.xml")
%>
```

Once again, we create an instance of `MXXMLWriter` and `SAXXMLReader`, and set the reader's `contentHandler` as an `MXXMLWriter` object. This time we are asking the writer to send the output to an ASP `Response` stream (and hence to the client). When we then call `parseURL()`, the SAX parser generates events, which are received by `MXXMLWriter`, whose implementation generates XML in response to those events and then streams that XML to the ASP `Response` stream.

Output as a DOM Document Object

Finally, let's look at an example of how to work with SAX and DOM together in one application. In this example we'll develop an ASP application, which will connect to a database and generate XML using SAX, while setting the `MXXMLWriter`'s `output` property to a DOM document object. This way, the XML is available in MSXML DOM and we can, for instance, apply a stylesheet to search or update the XML data.

In our ASP page (`SAX2DOM.asp`), we first we connect to the `Northwind` database and get data from the `employees` table (note you need to provide the connection string details specific to your machine):

```
Response.ContentType = "text/xml"
ConnStr = "PROVIDER=SQLOLEDB;SERVER=.;UID=sa;PWD=;DATABASE=Northwind"
Set conn = Server.CreateObject("ADODB.Connection")
Set rs = Server.CreateObject ("ADODB.Recordset")
```

```
conn.Open ConnStr
set rs.ActiveConnection = conn

rs.Open "select LastName, FirstName, Title from employees"
```

Next, we create the required MSXML objects and set the writer properties:

```
Set writer = Server.CreateObject("Msxml2.MXXMLWriter.4.0")
set reader = Server.CreateObject("Msxml2.SAXXMLReader.4.0")
set atrs = Server.CreateObject("Msxml2.SAXAttributes.4.0")
set XmlDOMObj = Server.CreateObject("Msxml2.DOMDocument.4.0")

writer.omitXMLDeclaration = true
writer.indent = true
```

The next line is important as it sets the writer output as a DOM document object:

```
writer.output = XmlDOMObj
```

Next, we set the writer as the content handler for the reader object, then iterate over database records and generate SAX events:

```
set reader.contentHandler = writer

reader.contentHandler.startDocument
reader.contentHandler.startElement "","","Employees", atrs

while not rs.EOF
  atrs.Clear
  set objFields = rs.Fields
  For intLoop = 0 To (objFields.Count - 1)
    atrs.addAttribute "", "", objFields.Item(intLoop).Name, "" _
                  , objFields.Item(intLoop).Value
  Next

  reader.contentHandler.startElement "", "", "rec", atrs
  reader.contentHandler.endElement "", "", "rec"

  rs.Movenext
wend

reader.contentHandler.endElement "","","Employees"
reader.contentHandler.endDocument
```

Finally, we close the database connection and recordset and send the response as the value of the DOM document's xml property. As the XML is now available as a DOM document we have various options to use it however we wish, for example applying a stylesheet, using it as a data island, etc. In this example, for simplicity, we are sending the XML straight to the client:

```
rs.Close
conn.Close
```

```
set rs= nothing
set conn= nothing

Response.write XmlDOMObj.xml
```

When we call this ASP page, this is what the output looks like:

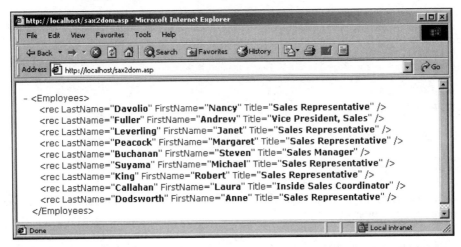

While we are talking about SAX and DOM integration, let's look at one more example before we move on to the next section looking at XSLT with SAX.

DOM to SAX

The previous example illustrated how to get a DOM document from SAX events; let's now look at how to generate SAX events if we already have an XML document loaded in the DOM. As an example of this, let's say we have an XML DOM document available, and we need to save its content into a database; it would be easier to generate SAX events for the XML document and write into the database using event handlers.

We'll be using Visual Basic again for this example, and our project is called DOM2SAXEx.vbp. To generate SAX events from a DOM document, the only thing we have to do differently is parse the DOM document object to the parse() method of SAXXMLReader40. The SAXXMLReader40 then parses the DOM document and sends events to our content handlers:

```
Private Sub Form_Load()
    Dim XmlDOMObj As New MSXML2.DOMDocument40
    Dim CHImpl As New ContentHandlerImp
    Dim ReaderObj As New SAXXMLReader40

    Set ReaderObj.contentHandler = CHImpl

    XmlDOMObj.Load "c:\SAX\sales.xml"

    ReaderObj.parse XmlDOMObj
End Sub
```

XSLT and SAX

MSXML supports an interface named IXSLProcessor, which can be used as an efficient way of applying stylesheets. MSXML 4.0 enhanced this interface to accept the objects that implement SAX interfaces, allowing SAX-based applications to capture and respond to transformation events. Let's look at an example of this, available in the download as XSLTAndSax.vbp. You will also need to place a copy of the broadband.xsl stylesheet in the c:\sax folder.

This is a Visual Basic 6.0 Standard EXE project, with a reference to MSXML 4.0, and a class module (ContentHandlerImpl) containing interface and method declarations for IVBSAXContentHandler. The code for the Form_Load() method of the form looks like this:

```
Dim XMLDocObj As New MSXML2.DOMDocument40
Dim StyleDocObj As New MSXML2.FreeThreadedDOMDocument40
Dim XSLTemplateObj As New MSXML2.XSLTemplate40
Dim XSLProc As MSXML2.IXSLProcessor
Dim CHImpl As New ContentHandlerImpl

'Load the style sheet
StyleDocObj.Load "c:\sax\broadband.xsl"

'Initialize the template object
Set XSLTemplateObj.stylesheet = StyleDocObj

'Get the IXSLProcessor interface from the template
Set XSLProc = XSLTemplateObj.createProcessor

'Load the input XML file
XMLDocObj.Load "c:\sax\broadband.xml"

XSLProc.input = XMLDocObj

'Send the XSLT transformation events to our ContentHandler
XSLProc.output = CHImpl

XSLProc.Transform
```

The above code uses the XSLTemplate40 class and IXSLProcessor interface to do the transformation. The important line is the one that sets the output property of IXSLProcessor to our ContentHandler implementation, which causes SAX events to be fired when MSXML applies the transformation. When the project is run the output is as follows:

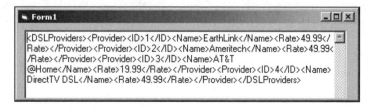

Using SAX AppWizard

All the examples above were written either using Visual Basic or VBScript (for ASP). If you are a C++ developer and would like to use SAX in your Visual C++ applications, we have good news for you!

Microsoft provides an **AppWizard** that we can use from the Visual C++ development environment to quickly build SAX applications. You can read about the SAX Win32 AppWizard at the Microsoft support site at http://support.microsoft.com/support/kb/articles/Q276/5/05.ASP. The link to the download page is http://support.microsoft.com/default.aspx?scid=http://download.microsoft.com/download/xml/samole/3.0/W9X2K/EN-US/SAXAppWizard.exe. Once you have the file downloaded, open it, and extract all the files onto your hard disk. Copy the SAXAppWizard.awx file to the MSDev Template folder, which by default is located at c:\Program Files\Microsoft Visual Studio\Common\MSDev98\Template. Start Visual C++ 6.0, and you should see the SAX Win32 AppWizard listed under the Projects tab:

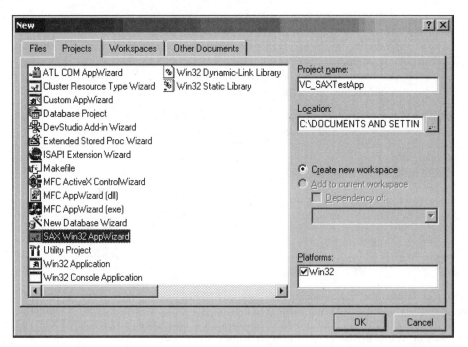

Create a new project, of type SAX Win32AppWizard, name the project VC_SAXTestApp, and click OK. The next screen will offer you the chance to add the interface and methods that you would like to implement:

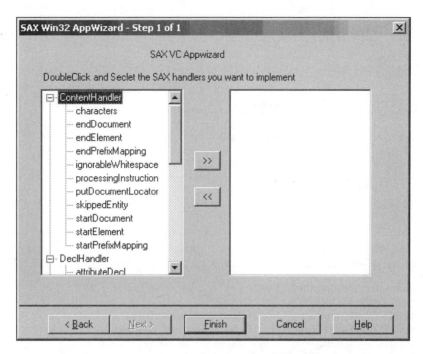

Select all the methods under **ContentHandler** and click **Finish**. The wizard generates the interface wrapper class files and a few supporting methods, such as `prt` for displaying the output. Check the `main()` function implementation in the file `VC_SAXTestApp.cpp`. The wizard adds the code to:

❑ Create a `SAXXMLReader` object.

❑ Create an instance of the class that implements `ISAXContentHandler`. This class is actually derived from a wrapper class created by the wizard, which actually implements all the methods for the `ISAXContentHandler` interface. This allows the flexibility to choose the methods you would like to implement; the rest will be already implemented in the base class.

❑ Call `putContentHandler()` to register the `ContentHandler`.

❑ Call the `parseURL()` method on the reader.

In the following example we'll simply print all the elements along with their attributes and the character data from the XML document file specified as the command line parameter. Open the file `VC_SAXTestAppContentHandler.cpp` and add the following code under the `startElement()` method:

```
prt (L"<%s", pwchLocalName, cchLocalName);
int lAttr;
pAttributes->getLength(&lAttr);
for(int i=0; i<lAttr; i++)
{
    wchar_t * ln, * vl; int lnl, vll;
    pAttributes->getQName(i,&ln,&lnl);
    prt(L" %s=", ln, lnl);
```

```
        pAttributes->getValue(i,&vl,&vll);
        prt(L"\"%s\"", vl, vll);
    }
    printf(">");
    return S_OK;
```

Add the following code under the `endElement()` method:

```
    prt(L"</%s>",pwchLocalName,cchLocalName);
    return S_OK;
```

Add the following code under the `characters()` method:

```
    prt(L"%s", pwchChars, cchChars);
    return S_OK;
```

Build the project and execute it with `c:\sax\broadband.xml` as the command-line parameter – the results should be as follows:

Parsing document: c:\sax\broadband.xml
<DSLProviders ZipCode="60195">
    <Provider ID="1" Name="EarthLink" Rate="49.99"></Provider>
    <Provider ID="2" Name="Ameritech" Rate="49.99"></Provider>
    <Provider ID="3" Name="AT&T @Home" Rate="19.99"></Provider>
    <Provider ID="4" Name="DirectTV DSL" Rate="49.99"></Provider>
</DSLProviders>
Parse result code: 00000000

MSXML 4.0 SAX 2 Reference

As we have seen, SAX (Simple API for XML) 2.0 defines a set of abstract interfaces that can be used to process XML documents, as well as to build XML documents. The MSXML SAX implementation provides support for both C++ and Visual Basic, and this reference section presents a useful guide to SAX 2 implementation in MSXML 4.0. In the tables that follow, where two names are given for methods, the first is for C/C++/COM and the second is for Visual Basic.

ContentHandler Interface

`ContentHandler` is the primary SAX interface that is used to process XML documents using SAX. The application can implement this interface to receive the core information and logical content of an XML document. On the other hand, an application can call `ContentHandler` methods to build an XML document.

C/C++/COM	Visual Basic
ISAXContentHandler	IVBSAXContentHandler

Members

Member	Description
startDocument	Indicates the beginning of a document.
endDocument	Indicates the end of a document.
startElement	Indicates the beginning of an element. Element's namespace identifier, a local name, a qualified name, and a collection of attributes are passed as parameters to this method. Qualified name or QName refers to the element name including the prefix, if any.
endElement	Indicates the end of an element.
characters	Indicates character data. Remember that parser may call characters just one time and pass all the character data once; or call this method multiple times and pass the element character data in chunks.
startPrefix Mapping	Just before calling startElement, the parser calls this method to indicate a namespace declaration entering scope.
endPrefix Mapping	Just after calling endElement, the parser calls this method to indicate a namespace declaration leaving scope.
ignorable Whitespace	This method is called only for element-only content models when a DTD/Schema is present. This method indicates an ignorable whitespace in element content. MSXML SAX 2 current implementation is non-validating, and hence it does not call this method.
skippedEntity	The parser calls this method whenever an entity is skipped. It is also called in the case of an external DTD declaration. Depending on the feature settings, the parser might call this method for external entities.
processing Instruction	The parser calls this method for each processing instruction found in the source XML document.
putDocument Locator document Locator	The parser calls this method before invoking any other method; and passes the ISAXLocator (IVBSAXLocator for Visual Basic) interface, which an application can cache and use later to get the contextual information (such as line number, column number) about the source XML document.

ErrorHandler Interface

The parser uses this interface to report all fatal errors (well-formedness errors), non-fatal errors (validation errors), and warnings.

C/C++/COM	Visual Basic
ISAXContentHandler	IVBSAXContentHandler

Members

Member	Description
error	Indicates an XML 1.0 non-fatal error. Parser uses this method to report recoverable errors such as validation errors, XML version mismatches, etc.
fatalError	Indicates an XML 1.0 fatal error. Parser uses this method to report non-recoverable errors such as violation of well-formedness constraint, encountering an unrecognized character encoding, etc.
ignorable Warning	Indicates conditions that are less serious than errors or fatal errors. MSXML 4.0 SAX implementation does not call this method.

XMLReader Interface

The parser implements this interface allowing applications to register event handlers for document processing, to initiate a document parse, and to query and set features and properties in the parser.

C/C++/COM	Visual Basic
ISAXXMLReader	IVBSAXXMLReader

MSXML 4.0 provides a co-class named SAXXMLReader40 that implements the XMLReader interface.

ProgID	GUID
Msxml2.SAXXMLReader.4.0	{7c6e29bc-8b8b-4c3d-859e-af6cd158be0f}

Members

Member	Description
putContentHandler contentHandler	Registers a ContentHandler implementation with the reader.
getContentHandler contentHandler	Returns the current ContentHandler implementation or null if one hasn't been registered yet.
putDTDHandler dtdHandler	Registers a DTDHandler implementation with the reader.
getDTDHandler dtdHandler	Returns the current DTDHandler implementation or null if one hasn't been registered yet.
putEntityResolver entityResolver	Registers an EntityResolver implementation with the reader.
getEntityResolver entityResolver	Returns the current EntityResolver implementation or null if one hasn't been registered yet.
putErrorHandler errorHandler	Registers an ErrorHandler implementation with the reader.
getErrorHandler errorHandler	Returns the current ErrorHandler implementation or null if one hasn't been registered yet.
putBaseURL baseURL	Sets the base URL for the document that is used to resolve relative links.
getBaseURL baseURL	Returns the base URL for the document.
putSecureBaseURL secureBaseURL	Sets the secure base URL for the document.
getSecureBaseURL secureBaseURL	Returns the secure base URL for the document.
putProperty	Sets the value of a property.
getProperty	Returns the specified property's value.
putFeature	Allows an application to control the reader behavior by setting the state of features.

Table continued on following page

Member	Description
getFeature	Returns the specified feature's state (true/false).
parseURL	Instructs an XMLReader implementation to initiate the parsing of an XML document specified by a system identifier (URI).
parse	Instructs an XMLReader implementation to initiate the parsing of an XML document specified by the input source, where the input source can be a URI, a DOMDocument, or a character or byte stream.

Locator Interface

The parser implements this interface and passes a reference to this interface to the application before calling any other method during the parsing. The application can then cache this interface and use it later to discover context information (such as line number, column number, etc.) when an event method is called.

C/C++/COM	Visual Basic
ISAXLocator	IVBSAXLocator

Members

Member	Description
getLineNumber lineNumber	Returns the 1-based line number where the current serialization event ends.
getColumnNumber columnNumber	Returns the 1-based column number where the current serialization event ends.
getPublicId publicId	Returns the public identifier of the entity that is currently being processed.
getSystemId systemId	Returns the system identifier of the entity that is currently being processed.

DTDHandler Interface

The parser uses this interface to report notation and unparsed entity declarations to the application.

C/C++/COM	Visual Basic
ISAXDTDHandler	IVBSAXDTDHandler

Members

Member	Description
notationDecl	Indicates a notation declaration.
unparsedEntityDecl	Indicates an unparsed entity declaration.

DeclHandler Interface

An application can implement this extension handler to receive the information about DTD element and attribute declarations in the source XML document.

C/C++/COM	Visual Basic
ISAXDeclHandler	IVBSAXDeclHandler

Members

Member	Description
attributeDecl	Indicates an attribute type declaration.
elementDecl	Indicates an element type declaration.
externalEntityDecl	Indicates a parsed external entity declaration.
internalEntityDecl	Indicates a parsed internal entity declaration.

LexicalHandler Interface

An application can implement this extension interface to receive notifications about the lexical information (such as comments and CDATA) inside the source XML document.

C/C++/COM	Visual Basic
ISAXLexicalHandler	IVBSAXLexicalHandler

Members

Member	Description
comment	Indicates XML comments.
startCDATA	Indicates the beginning of a CDATA section. The content of the CDATA section are reported using the characters() method.
endCDATA	Indicates the end of a CDATA section.
startEntity	Indicates that the parser has started processing internal or external entity.
endEntity	Indicates that the parser has finished processing internal or external entity.
startDTD	Indicates the beginning of a DTD.
endDTD	Indicates the end of a DTD.

EntityResolver Interface

An application can implement this interface to provide custom resolution of external entities. The XMLReader will call the resolveEntity() method in the application's EntityResolver implementation before resolving the public or system identifiers.

C/C++/COM	Visual Basic
ISAXEntityResolver	IVBSAXEntityResolver

Members

Member	Description
resolveEntity	Returns a variant data type value representing the entity or null to indicate systemId should be used as the URI.

XMLFilter Interface

This interface facilitates pipeline-style processing by allowing multiple ContentHandler implementations to be chained together. An XMLFilter is like an XMLReader, except that it obtains its events from another XML reader rather than a primary source like an XML document. Filters can modify a stream of events as they pass them on to the final application.

C/C++/COM	Visual Basic
ISAXXMLFilter	IVBSAXXMLFilter

Members

Member	Description
putParent getParent parent	Sets or gets a reference to the instance of the XMLReader interface.

Attributes Interface

The parser implements this interface allowing access to attribute collections. Attributes are generally exposed as an unordered property bag that can be traversed by name or position.

C/C++/COM	Visual Basic
ISAXAttributes	IVBSAXAttributes

Members

Member	Description
getLength length	Returns the number of attributes for an element.
getURI	Gets the attribute's namespace URI by index.
getLocalName	Gets the attribute's local name by index.
getQName	Gets the attribute's qualified name by index.
getIndexFromQName	Finds an attribute by qualified name and returns the zero-based index of the matching attribute.
getIndexFromName	Finds an attribute by name and returns the zero-based index of the matching attribute.
getTypeFromQName	Searches the attributes by qualified name and returns the matching attribute's type as specified in DTD or schema. The return value is CDATA if DTD/schema is not found.
getTypeFromName	Searches the attributes by name and returns the matching attribute's type as specified in DTD or schema.
getType	Finds an attribute by index and returns the matching attribute's type as specified in DTD or schema.
getValue	Returns the value of the attribute by index.
getValueFromName	Finds an attribute by namespace name and returns the matching attribute's value.
getValueFromQName	Finds an attribute by qualified name and returns the matching attribute's value.

IMXAttributes Interface

This interface defines methods that allow creating or editing attribute collection. MSXML 4.0 provides an implementation of this class via a co-class named `SAXAttributes40`.

ProgID	GUID
Msxml2.SAX Attributes.4.0	{88d969ca-f192-11d4-a65f-0040963251e5}

Members

Member	Description
addAttribute	To add an attribute to the end of the attribute collection.
addAttribute FromIndex	To add an attribute to the end of the attribute collection and set its value the same as the value of attribute whose index is passed as parameter.
removeAttribute	To remove an attribute from the collection.
setAttribute	To set an attribute in the list.
setAttributes	To copy all existing attributes to the specified object.
setLocalName	To set the local name of an attribute.
setQName	To set the qualified name of an attribute.
setType	To set the type of an attribute.
setURI	To set the namespace URI for an attribute.
setValue	To set the attribute's value.
clear	To clear the attribute collection; however, this does not free up the space immediately, as the collection items are kept for reuse.

IMXSchemaDeclHandler Interface

An application may implement this interface to receive schema information about the element being parsed. The application can then register the implemented interface with the reader by setting the `schema-declaration-handler` property using the `putProperty()` method call.

Members

Member	Description
schema ElementDecl	The validating parser generates a call to this method before calling `startElement()`, and passes the `ISchemaElement` interface. The application can then use the `ISchemaElement` interface to get the schema information about the current element.

IMXWriter Interface

This interface can be used to produce XML or HTML documents using SAX. MSXML 4.0 provides two co-classes that implement this interface. The class MXXMLWriter is used to build XML documents, while the class MXHTMLWriter is used to generate HTML documents by firing the SAX events. The generated document can be accessed either using an IStream object, or as a DOMDocument object, or simply as a string. The output property on the IMXWriter interface facilitates access to generated document.

ProgID	GUID
Msxml2.MXXMLWriter.4.0	{88d969c8-f192-11d4-a65f-0040963251e5}
Msxml2.MXHTMLWriter.4.0	{88d969c9-f192-11d4-a65f-0040963251e5}

Members

Member	Description
indent	Set it to true to build a "pretty printed" (indented) resultant document.
omitXMLDeclaration	Set it to true to skip the XML declaration line in the output document.
disableOutputEscaping	Set this property to true to avoid escaping of special characters (such as ampersand, &).
encoding	Use this property to get or set the encoding for the output.
standalone	Used to control the value of the standalone attribute in the XML declaration line.
version	Used to specify the value of the version attribute in the XML declaration line.
byteOrderMark	Set this to true to tell the writer to output Byte Order Mark (BOM) for appropriate encoding as per XML 1.0 specification.
flush	Used to flush the object's internal buffer to its target IStream/string.
output	By default, the generated document is available as a string. Use this property to get the output either as a DOMDocument object or as an IStream interface.

Features and Properties

The XMLReader interface has four methods to observe and control the parser behavior. These methods include getFeature(), putFeature(), getProperty(), and putProperty(). The feature flags are always Boolean (true or false), while the property values are arbitrary objects.

Features

The following table shows the features that can be accessed using the getFeature() and putFeature() methods:

Name	Description
exhaustive-errors	During SAX XSD validation, if this feature is set to true, the parser reports all validation errors instead of aborting at the first validation error.
schema-validation	Set this feature to true to enable SAX XSD validation.
server-http-request	By default, the parseURL() method uses the WinInet component. Set this feature to true to use the server-safe ServerXMLHTTP component when the parseURL() method is called on the XMLReader.

The following feature names should be prefixed using http://xml.org/sax/features/ (for example: http://xml.org/sax/features/external-general-entities).

Name	Description
external-general-entities	Set this feature to true to include external text entities.
external-parameter-entities	Set this feature to true to include the external parameter entities (such as external DTD subset).
lexical-handler/parameter-entities	Set this feature to false to disable the firing of lexical events.
namespaces	The default value of true for this feature makes namespace URIs and local names available during various event callbacks.
namespace-prefixes	If the namespaces feature is set to true, this feature controls if the namespace-prefixes are treated as other attributes (and hence generating events for them).
preserve-system-identifiers	The default value of false for this feature leads to resolving all the system identifiers reported by the reader.

Properties

Name	Description
schema-declaration-handler	Used to register the IMXSchemaDeclHandler implementation handler with the XMLReader.
schemas	Used to register a schema with the XMLReader.
charset	Used to externally define the encoding for the documents being parsed using the parse method.

Name	Description
xmldecl-encoding	Used to get the encoding declared in the XML header of the currently parsed document.
xmldecl-version	Used to get the XML version declared in the XML header of the currently parsed document.
xmldecl-standalone	Used to get the value of the standalone attribute in the XML header of the currently parsed document.

The following feature names should be prefixed using http://xml.org/sax/properties/ (for example: http://xml.org/sax/properties/declaration-handler)

Name	Description
declaration-handler	Used to register the DeclHandler implementation with the XMLReader.
lexical-handler	Used to register the LexicalHandler implementation with the XMLReader.
dom-node	Used to get the source DOM node for the current SAX event, during SAX parsing using the parse() method, where SAX events are generated from an IXMLDOMNode object.
xml-string	Used to get the characters in the XML source for the current SAX event.

Summary

The Simple API for XML, or SAX, is an excellent alternative to DOM, especially for efficiently parsing large XML documents. SAX is designed around the event-based push model. In this approach, the parser reads the input stream of the XML document and sends notifications to the application about the parsing events, along with necessary information as part of method parameters.

In this chapter we started with a discussion of what SAX is; it's history, evolution, and comparison with DOM. We then looked at a few simple SAX parsing examples using MSXML 4.0. We saw how to search using SAX and abort the parsing.

Then we looked at some of the features that MSXML 4.0 introduced, including XSD validation and namespace support. Then we looked at the MXXMLWriter class to build an XML document from SAX events. We saw how to build the XML string, and send the output to a stream or an XML DOM document. Here we learned about some interesting possibilities that arise from integrating SAX and DOM. Next, we looked at the XSLT support with SAX that was introduced in MSXML 4.0, before looking at the SAX Win32 AppWizard, a tool to help Visual C++ developers to quickly build SAX applications. Finally we presented a guide to SAX 2 implementation in MSXML 4.0.

The following chapter looks at styling XML content, including using CSS and IE behaviors.

XML Application Development with MSXML 4.0
SOAP
XHTML
XML Schemas DTDs XPath CSS
XML Namespaces
XML 1.0
MSXML

7

Styling XML Content

We mentioned earlier in the book that the two main uses of XML and XSLT are presentation and application interchange. By presentation we mean display to an end user, such as displaying an input form or the user interface of a web page; by application interchange, we mean creating or altering the format of an XML document to pass the XML to some other application that expects a given XML format. In this chapter we are going to concentrate on presenting XML data to users, with familiar technologies such as CSS and XSLT as well as those that may be less familiar, such as behaviors, VML, and SVG.

The aspects we will look at show how MSXML is used on both the client and the server, as a separate product and directly with Internet Explorer.

The chapter looks at:

- ❑ Integrating CSS with XSLT.
- ❑ Practical development with CSS.
- ❑ Attached behaviors and element behaviors.
- ❑ Graphical XML with VML and SVG.

The XML-related technologies discussed in this chapter have been improved with the release of new browser versions. In fact, Internet Explorer 6 alone has a series of CSS updates. For a reference on Internet Explorer and other browser features, see "HTML 4.01 Programmer's Reference" (ISBN 1-861005-33-4). This chapter will show you what you can do with MSXML to work with these features.

For each example we will tell you which version of Internet Explorer is being used, but your implementation is a design decision. Exactly what you decide to use will be initially based on whether you are targeting a web browser or some pervasive device (such as a mobile phone). This will likely determine whether you use CSS or behaviors at all as many of the newer standards (WML, for example) are XML-based and use their own formats for display. XSLT will almost always be used in this case to generate the appropriate XML. If you are only targeting browsers and are looking at output to all browser types then you will always use CSS, and maybe even XSLT, but the behaviors and vector graphics would not be used: that is, unless you choose to create output specific files for these browser types and detect the incoming browser and output the appropriate file – this is discussed in detail in Chapter 10, "*Transformations on the Server*". The cool thing about XML is that you can do server transforms to target the browsers of your choice, allowing you to give the rich environment where it is supported!

This last point is very important when using XML and its technologies with clients where you have limited or no control. Developers have previously been put off developing an HTML page that uses a set of technologies only supported by one browser because of the need to develop different HTML pages for different browsers, languages, and devices. With XML, although never seamless, it is a lot easier. You can write stylesheets that can transform HTML on the server for clients not supporting XSLT directly. If certain browsers do not support particular technologies, then during the transform you can use a different template or an imported stylesheet to generate appropriate output for it. Of course, you still have to develop the replacement functionality, but with the XML technologies it is a lot easier to plug in components. Even better, because of the ability to separate different parts of functionality you will find re-usable parts improving more and more – a good example is some of the schema and XSLT libraries already available. Examples of these can be found at the following URLs:

- ❑ http://www.schema.net/
- ❑ http://www.biztalk.org/
- ❑ http://www.oasis-open.org/
- ❑ http://www.xslt.com/

Integrating Cascading Style Sheets (CSS)

This section intends to give you some indication as to how CSS is developed and used in HTML and XML, concentrating on how CSS is implemented rather than the properties, values, and features available. If you are unfamiliar with Cascading Style Sheets, you can find out more in "HTML 4.01 Programmer's Reference" (ISBN 1-861005-33-4).

Overview

Cascading Style Sheets is a W3C standard that provides control over how a page is displayed through a user agent such as a browser. Primarily for HTML, it is increasingly being applied to XML and related technologies, because it is simple, proven, and already very well supported in the industry. You will likely have used it when creating HTML pages for any kind of browser and this will have been based upon the CSS Level 1.0 Recommendation (http://www.w3.org/TR/REC-CSS1) or some version of it. The creation of CSS Level 3.0 (http://www.w3.org/TR/css3-roadmap/) is currently under development, although IE 6 has already introduced the concept of CSS 3.0 custom cursors, which allows the modification of the cursor's appearance on a web page in relation to the page's content. Let's now consider some of the basic important concepts of CSS to refresh your mind.

CSS can be used internally or externally from the data (HTML, XML) document and can be applied to individual elements, elements of the same type, or elements of the same group. To apply some style to an individual element, we simply set the `style` attribute on the element and insert the appropriate name-value pairs as shown below. Unlike XML, the name-value pairs are not case sensitive. This example will create a `<div>` element with the properties that its background color is white and the color of any text is dark blue.

```
<div style="background-color:white;color:darkblue;">Some Text</div>
```

If this were the intended style for all of the `<div>` tags, it would become repetitive. To avoid this, we can use the `<style>` element as a child of the `<head>` element to provide a page-level style definition for `<div>` elements – **element styles**. So, the above example could be rewritten as:

```
<html>
    <head>
        <style>
            div {background-color:white;color:darkblue;};
        </style>
    </head>
    <div>Some Text</div>
</html>
```

This method would have the same effect as the above method and so all `<div>` elements will have their background color white and the color of any text dark blue.

While that's useful, especially with a document using `<div>` elements, the same style applied to all elements can be very restricting, especially if we want to apply different styles on certain `<div>` elements. There are two alternatives to this that maintain the key idea of re-use – in other words, that don't require us to define the style on the tags themselves. The first of these is through unique `id` attributes, while the latter is based on classes. In fact, they may even be combined, although it is not advisable to have two elements with the same ID.

The **unique ID** method works using the `id` attribute that can be applied to an HTML element. Once again this should be defined within a `<style>` element and uses a hash symbol (#) to uniquely identify the element, as we do in the code snippet below with `DocumentTitle` and `Copyright`.

```
<html>
    <head>
        <style>
            #DocumentTitle {background-color:white;color:darkblue;};
            #Copyright {background-color:grey;color:black;};
        </style>
    </head>
    <div>Some Text</div>
</html>
```

We may want to define a style that can be applied to multiple elements that are the same type. To do this we define a **class**, which is indicated by a period (.) followed by the name. The example below defines a class (`para`) and uses it on two elements:

```
<html>
   <head>
      <style>
         .para {background-color:lightblue;color:darkblue;};
      </style>
   </head>
   <div class="para">
      Style class "para".
   </div>
   <table>
      <tr>
         <td class="para">
            Style class "para".
         </td>
      </tr>
   </table>
</html>
```

We can also use combinations of these, such as locally overriding the color of a font while inheriting the properties of a given class. In fact, when we combine these and there are two that conflict, there is a **precedence order**. So, if our class and ID type both define a color, then the class property takes precedence. An example is shown below, but the precedence order is:

❑   Locally declared properties have highest precedence.

❑   Class styles.

❑   ID styles.

❑   Element styles.

If we use external stylesheets (discussed below), then it is just as though these were directly included in the file where the <link> element is included. If there is a conflict between an internally and externally defined style, then the one that takes precedence is the one that was defined last in the document order when the external file has been included.

Creating an external stylesheet is simple. We just create a text document with the extension .css and its contents are in the same format as the contents of a <style> element as we discussed above. To include it in the HTML document, we just use a <link> element within the <head> element as follows:

```
<link rel="stylesheet" type="text/css" href="filename.css" />
```

To demonstrate all that we have discussed above, consider the following HTML and CSS files (css1.htm and css1.css). First the HTML file:

```
<html>
   <head>
      <style>
         div {font-family:Arial;background-color:red;color:darkblue;};
         #DocumentTitle {background-color:white;color:darkblue;};
         #Copyright {background-color:gray;color:white;};
         .para {background-color:lightblue;color:darkblue;};
      </style>
   <link rel="stylesheet" type="text/css" href="css1.css" />
   </head>
```

```
<body>
    <div style="background-color:white;color:blue;">
        Style applied directly on element.
    </div>
    <div>
        Style applied on global element.
    </div>
    <div id="DocumentTitle">
        Style ID "DocumentTitle".
    </div>
    <div id="Copyright" class="para">
        Class style overrides ID style.
    </div>
    <div class="para">
        Style class "para".
    </div>
    <table border="2" class="para">
        <tr>
            <td>
                Style class "para".
            </td>
        </tr>
    </table>
    <div class="para" style="color:green;">
        Style class "para".
    </div>
</body>
</html>
```

The external CSS file (css1.css) is defined as follows:

```
td    {font-weight:bold;background-color:yellow;};
para  {background-color:lightblue;color:blue;};
```

Note that the external CSS is linked to *after* the <style> element, so the para class defined in the external document will override the internally defined one. Running this example will generate the following page:

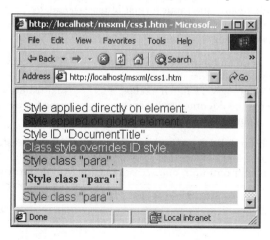

What we have discussed thus far may be as far as you have taken CSS, but it has a bright future despite the rising popularity of XSLT. There is currently no support planned in MSXML for the other XSL standard, XSL-FO (XSL-Formatting Objects). So, it seems that XML will be used for data, XSLT will order and select the data to be displayed and the format in which to display it, while CSS will be used for coloring, positioning, and similar features.

> *XSL became a W3C Recommendation on October 15 2001. You can find out more at http://www.w3.org/TR/2001/REC-xsl-20011015/.*

It is common to use CSS with HTML, but what about with XML? Well, we can directly browse an XML document in IE 5+, which can be formatted directly with a Cascading Style Sheet – distinct from the styling available with XSLT. Let's look at this now.

Comparison of CSS and XSLT

The following table summarizes when CSS or XSLT can be used and the relative advantages and disadvantages of each:

	CSS	XSLT
Ordering	Can't reorder elements, perform comparisons, or work with other XML documents.	Allows extensive reordering, generated text, and calculations, and can incorporate other XSLT documents.
Display	Provides very effective method of displaying the XML documents when reordering isn't necessary.	Used by itself and without XSL Formatting Objects (which is not available in MSXML), there is very limited styling without CSS (which is why it is almost always used in combination).
Input	Unable to alter the input format other than to change how it is viewed in terms of styling.	Can generate a different XML output format from the input XML format.
Output	Very good and extremely easy to do for report-type documents that don't involve doing very much except showing the document with some basic styling.	Allows generation of sophisticated tables, HTML fragments, and access to attribute values, and so can be used for any kind of output.
Compatibility	CSS is not fully supported by all browsers and devices and so not suitable for output in many cases.	Allow transformation of input format to suitable output format depending on the browser or device being used.

	CSS	XSLT
Uses	CSS itself would be used for a word processing document, reporting, or XML fragments that are saved as files or in a database that just need to be displayed as is, with some simple styling. Additionally, it is most suited to XML files that are mainly element-based, although we will see how you can also display data from attributes in this chapter.	Very good for dynamic interface applications or applications that feed into other applications. Most interactive applications would use XSLT with some CSS for style.

CSS with XML

When we talk of browsing XML using CSS, we are talking of creating a display that will simply color and position the XML. CSS doesn't have the power of XSLT and can't reorder elements, perform comparisons, or work with other XML documents, but it does provide a very effective method of displaying the XML documents when this isn't necessary. CSS will be mainly used when the XML document will be displayed in the order that elements appear in the document. CSS is already moving towards Level 3 though, which offers more advanced XSLT-like functionality.

So what are the instances when we would use CSS? Well, a word processing document is perhaps an obvious one, but consider a set of XML fragments that are saved as files or in a database. These may contain information on an invoice which doesn't necessarily need the functionality of XSLT, because it simply needs to be displayed to be read by a user. Even the results of a dynamically created XML fragment may well just need to be formatted for display. The advantages of XSLT over CSS are that XSLT allows extensive reordering, generated text, and calculations, as well as the generation of sophisticated tables and access to attribute values, but this is often not necessary. Basically, using CSS with XML is very useful and extremely easy to do for report-type documents that don't involve doing very much except showing the document.

Let's look at an example of how we could display our invoice example using just CSS. The XML document is fairly complex and so there will be some things that don't fit well with CSS. This example will help us get a good idea of the limitations when using XML and CSS together.

We will use a document called `sample.xml`, as below:

```xml
<?xml version="1.0" encoding="utf-8" ?>
<?xml-stylesheet type="text/css" href="1b.css" ?>
<Invoices date="28/11/2001" xmlns:cat="uri:Business-Categories">
    <customers custname="Chile Wines Inc" phone="0141 952 56223"
               email="cw@deltabis.com" custid="192398"
               delivery="international" offerID="27">
        <cat:busInfo>Wine Division South</cat:busInfo>
        <cat:busInfo>Beer Division North</cat:busInfo>
        <order orderID="OID921" batchid="123">
            <details>
                <items num="2">
                    <item>Rancagua White</item>
                    <item>Rancagua Red</item>
                </items>
```

```
            </details>
        </order>
        <order orderID="OID927">
            <details>
                <items num="5">
                    <item>Chillan Red</item>
                    <item>Rancagua White</item>
                    <item>Santiago Red</item>
                    <item>Rancagua White</item>
                    <item>Rancagua Red</item>
                </items>
            </details>
        </order>
        <order orderID="OID931" batchid="123">
            <details>
                <items num="6">
                    <item>Southern Fruity Red</item>
                    <item>Rancagua White</item>
                    <item>Rancagua Red</item>
                    <item>Rancagua White</item>
                    <item>Chillan Red</item>
                    <item>Northern Sweet White</item>
                </items>
            </details>
        </order>
    </customers>
</Invoices>
```

Before we start, what does the document look like with no stylesheet applied? This is shown in the following screenshot:

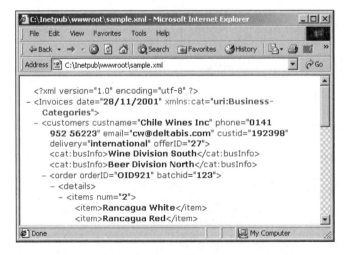

Internet Explorer has an internal XSLT stylesheet that provides this display using CSS within it. We can see it by entering res://msxml.dll/DEFAULTSS.xsl. It's not a very pretty format, even to someone who just wants to view some brief details. So how can CSS with XML be used to improve this?

The first thing to do is to create a CSS text document with a set of page sections reflecting the main parts of the XML document. The way this was done in the sample document was to look at those elements that contain many child elements – this typically indicates a standalone section, a new section or sub-section. In this case, the <Invoices> element refers to the entire document, the <busInfo> element contains some separate business information, and <customers> refers to a given customer, containing a series of <order> elements. Each "order" section contains one or more "details" sections and each "details" section contains a series of "items" sub-sections that contain the <item> elements. The CSS file is called 1a.css and looks like this:

```
Invoices        { display: block;}
cat\:busInfo    { display: block;}
customers       { display: block;}
order           { display: block;}
details         { display: block;}
items           { display: block;}
items item      { display: block;}
```

To associate an XML document with a CSS document, we simply add a processing instruction to the XML document in the form:

```
<?xml-stylesheet type="text/xsl" href="url of stylesheet"?>
```

This should be added immediately after the XML declaration or <!DOCTYTPE> declaration. So if we had the CSS stylesheet style1.css then we would have the following declaration:

```
<?xml version="1.0" encoding="utf-8" ?>
<?xml-stylesheet type="text/css" href="style1.css"?>
```

MSXML will notice only the first XML <?xml-stylesheet> declaration where the type attribute is "text/css". However, IE can directly browse XML files styled with Cascading Style Sheets and any number of these may be available:

```
<?xml-stylesheet type="text/css" href="style1.css"?>
<?xml-stylesheet type="text/css" href="style2.css"?>
```

These will be merged together by IE on processing and applied directly to the XML documents. This kind of usage is very good when we want to separate our styles into separate files so that combinations of style fragments can be used throughout our application simply by including the appropriate processing instruction.

Within the sample.xml document, we have to tell it to use the particular stylesheet to display the details, and we do this via an XSL processing instruction at the top of the page, as follows:

```
<?xml version="1.0" encoding="utf-8" ?>
<?xml-stylesheet type="text/css" href="1a.css" ?>
<Invoices date="28/11/2001" xmlns:cat="uri:Business-Categories">
    <!--Item information goes here -->
</Invoices>
```

Using the stylesheet (`1a.css`), `sample.xml` will look like this:

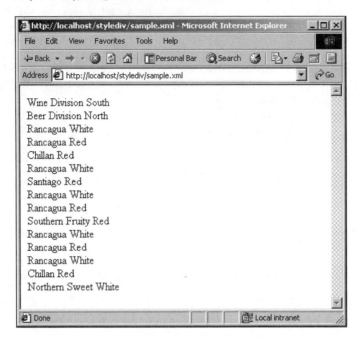

While it is not very visually exciting, we have at least formatted the data within the elements of the XML document and no longer see all the namespaces, tags, and attributes that could confuse some users. While the XML document is parsed, it uses the CSS to format any element if there is a style by that element name. `<Invoices>` is the document element and there is also a stylesheet style entry called `Invoices`, which says to block display it – display it on its own line. Most of the styles are fairly obvious, but there are two interesting ones.

The `cat\:busInfo` is different from the others and this is based on how CSS deals with namespaces in XML documents, which is looked at in more detail below. The `cat` is a prefix we used to associate the `style` attribute with some namespace defined in the XML document; the slash ("`\`") escapes the colon, which is already part of CSS, and the name of the style attribute is `busInfo`. While parsing, if we just use `busInfo`, the element will not be noticed as it uses the default namespace to associate the CSS styles with the element names. In CSS, namespaces can be supported, but it's not as obvious as we may wish.

> **The namespace declaration for any qualified element must be on the document element – so we must declare all xmlns declarations on the document element no matter where or how often they are used in the XML document.**

This is a limitation, but one which might be updated in the future. In our case, this means that the `xmlns:cat="uri:Business-Categories"` declaration must be on the `<Invoices>` element:

```
<Invoices date="28/11/2001" xmlns:cat="uri:Business-Categories">
```

If we declare it anywhere else, CSS will not recognize it and our data belonging to elements qualified by this namespace will not be styled. When creating styles for prefixed elements, we have to use the prefix in the document, as well as escaping the colon before the local name – this stops it being recognized as a CSS sub-class, which we'll look at in a moment. This is why we use `cat\:busInfo` rather than `cat:busInfo`. We can style for as many namespace declarations as we wish if we choose to work this way.

The second important thing to know is that CSS is pretty intelligent in styling based on the structure of our document. Imagine we have the following XML:

```
<Employee>
    <name>Roberto Perez</name>
</Employee>
<Company>
    <name>Scottish Translations Incorporated</name>
</Company>
```

If we create a style for <name>, it will be matched in two element instances. However, CSS allows the <name> elements to be defined as sub-classes of their respective parent elements and the styles applied to them independently. So, we could write CSS for these as follows:

```
Employee:name { color:red ;}

Company:name { color:green ;}
```

In fact, this can be iterated as `class:sub-class:sub-class` and so on, like the `parent:child:child` XML relationship. We have used this to display each <item> child of the <items> element on a separate line (otherwise each <item> of a given <items> element would be treated as one text node and shown on one line). One thing you will not notice is styles for attributes. That is because direct browsing of XML with CSS doesn't natively "see" attributes, so they are ignored – this is a limitation for many XML documents, and hence this method is very much suited to "document" type information such as reports, articles, and books. We will see a simple way around this limitation later on.

Now that the basics are understood, we can apply some style to the document to make it slightly more readable, using the following CSS (`1b.css`):

```
Invoices
{
    display: block;
    background-color: gray;
    color: yellow;
    font-family: Arial;
    font-style: italic;
    text-align: right;
    font-size: large;
}

cat\:busInfo
{
    display: block;
    background-color: green;
}

customers
{
```

```
        display: block;
        background-color: red;
}

order      { display: block;}
details    { display: block;}

items
{
        display: block;
        border: 2px solid black;
}

items item
{
        display: block;
        color:darkblue;
        font-size: 14px;
        background-color: orange;
        font-family: Arial;
        font-style: normal;
        text-align: left;
        cursor:hand;
}
```

This is mainly CSS combined with some of the principles we outlined above. The result is an improved display, shown in the following screenshot:

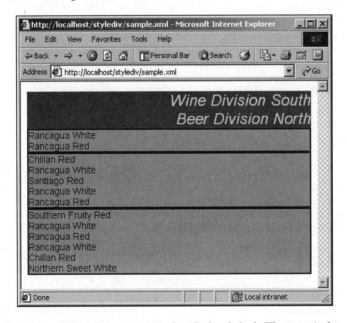

This is a vast improvement from where we started with the default IE view. At least now we can see some division of information, with each order divided into sections separated by borders and some coloring. To improve on this we can use HTML in the source document and the HTML namespace in our CSS, which we'll look at next.

CSS and Namespaces

We have already seen how custom namespaces are treated differently when working with CSS in that we have to explicitly use the prefix associated with the style. MSXML also treats the HTML namespace specially when directly browsing XML files with CSS. Like the custom namespaces we discussed above, the HTML namespace must be declared on the document element – in our case, that is the <Invoices> element as follows, with the other namespace declarations of our document:

```
<Invoices date="28/11/2001"
          xmlns:HTML="http://www.w3.org/Profiles/XHTML-transitional"
          xmlns:cat="uri:Business-Categories">
```

With this declared, we can use many of the HTML elements within our XML source to mark up the document. You may see this as limiting your document because it is based on HTML, but with the HTML elements simply embedded in the source and associated with the HTML namespace, it is a simple XSLT transform (using the copying techniques discussed in Chapter 5) to remove all elements associated with this namespace and hence leave us with the pure XML document! Accordingly, this is a valid technique for documents that will be simply displayed pretty much as they are, but with some display formatting using HTML as an advanced formatting on top of CSS.

We have created an example of our sample source document being designed to use HTML elements. This improves the control we have over the display and the use of images and tables. Each of our HTML elements must be prefixed with the HTML prefix we defined earlier so that they can be recognized as mark up. A fragment of the example source XML document (invoiceHTML.xml) is shown below:

```
<?xml version="1.0" encoding="utf-8" ?>
<?xml-stylesheet type="text/css" href="1c.css" ?>

<Invoices date="28/11/2001"
          xmlns:HTML="http://www.w3.org/Profiles/XHTML-transitional"
          xmlns:cat="uri:Business-Categories">

    <customers custname="Chile Wines Inc" phone="0141 952 56223"
               email="cw@deltabis.com" custid="192398"
               delivery="international"
               offerID="27">

    <HTML:IMG src="invoices.jpg" height="35"
              width="170" alt="Invoices Online" />

    <cat:busInfo>
       <HTML:span>Wine Division South</HTML:span>
    </cat:busInfo>
    <cat:busInfo>
       <HTML:span>Beer Division North</HTML:span>
    </cat:busInfo>

    <order orderID="OID921" batchid="123">
       <details>
          <items num="2">
          <HTML:table>
             <item>
                <HTML:tr>
                   <HTML:td>Rancagua Red</HTML:td>
                </HTML:tr>
             </item>
```

```
                <item>
                    <HTML:tr>
                        <HTML:td>Rancagua White</HTML:td>
                    </HTML:tr>
                </item>
            </HTML:table>
            </items>
        </details>
    </order>
    </customers>
</Invoices>
```

We discussed the namespace declaration earlier, so the first new thing we will see is:

```
<HTML:IMG src="invoices.jpg" height="35"
         width="170" alt="Invoices Online" />
```

There is nothing too complicated going on here – an HTML image (`<img>`) element is qualified using the HTML prefix and will simply display an image when processed. Further down the document, you can see the use of the `<span>` element to wrap the busInfo data, as well as an embedded `<HTML:table>` to contain the `<item>` elements that are part of each order. These are all straightforward, so we will avoid explanation of them here.

Notice we now reference the style sheet `1c.css`, which is where things get a little more interesting. The style sheet is shown below:

```
Invoices
{
    display: block;
    background-color: gray;
    color: yellow;
    font-family: Arial;
    font-style: italic;
    text-align: right;
    font-size: large;
}

customers
{
    display: block;
    background-color: white;
}

cat\:busInfo
{
    display: block;
    background-color: maroon;
}

order      { display: block;}
details    { display: block;}

items
{
    display: block;
    border: 2px solid black;
    text-align: left;
}
```

```
HTML\:IMG
{
    border: 2px solid black;
}

HTML\:A:visited HTML\:IMG
{
    border-color: grey;
}

HTML\:A:active HTML\:IMG
{
    border-color: red;
}

HTML\:A:link HTML\:IMG
{
    border-color: blue;
}

HTML\:TABLE
{
    table-layout:fixed;
    background-color: red;
}

HTML\:TR
{
    background-color: orange;
}

HTML\:TD
{
    display: block;
    color: darkblue;
    font-size: 14px;
    font-family: Arial;
    font-style: normal;
    text-align: left;
    cursor: hand;
}

HTML\:SPAN
{
    text-decoration:underline;
}

HTML\:b
{
    color:blue;
}
```

In the styling you may notice some differences from what was used earlier, such as color or font size – these are just to improve the display and are not really part of an MSXML discussion. However, you will notice that we no longer use the item style, because it is within a table cell instead. In fact, to style any of the HTML elements we have defined, we have to use the prefix/namespace method we discussed earlier. For example, the table cells are styled as follows:

```
HTML\:TD
{
    display: block;
    color: darkblue;
    font-size: 14px;
    font-family: Arial;
    font-style: normal;
    text-align: left;
    cursor: hand;
}
```

This similar method is repeated for all appropriate elements. We *cannot* use the `items item` sub-class relationship when we have other elements from a different namespace as child elements splitting them up. In other words, `items HTML\:table item` does not work. The resulting display is as shown:

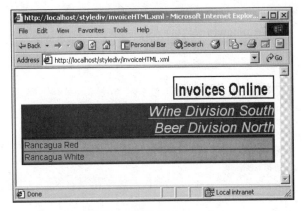

We mentioned that directly viewing XML with CSS means that we cannot see the attributes of the document. We are next going to look at how we can use scripting to overcome this limitation and allow XML/CSS to be used for a much wider scope of document.

Overcoming CSS Limitations

As we mentioned above, CSS does not display the attributes when browsing an XML document. However, it does allow us to use the HTML namespace and some scripting to accomplish our goal. The idea of this section is not to demonstrate the "be all and end all" of doing this – we will demonstrate an effective reusable technique to correct this problem.

The first part of the resolution is to add some scripting to the XML document we discussed above. This is no different from working with the other HTML elements. In the example we have included this as a child of the document element (`<Invoices>`) as shown in the following fragment (`HTMLScriptSample.xml`):

```
<?xml version="1.0" encoding="utf-8" ?>
<?xml-stylesheet type="text/css" href="1d.css" ?>
<Invoices date="28/11/2001"
          xmlns:HTML="http://www.w3.org/Profiles/XHTML-transitional"
          xmlns:cat="uri:Business-Categories">

  <HTML:SCRIPT language="JavaScript"> <!--

  function document.onreadystatechange()
```

```
    {
        if (document.readyState=="complete")
        ShowInfo();
    }

    function ShowInfo()
     {
     var strValidAtts="date custname phone email cusid delivery orderID
        batchid num offerID";

     var obj = document.body.getElementsByTagName("*");

     for (j=0;j<obj.length;j++)
     {
        var strName = obj[j].nodeName;
        var oAttrib = obj(j).attributes;

           for (var i=0;i<oAttrib.length;i++)
        {
            if (oAttrib[i].specified)
            {
                if (strValidAtts.indexOf(oAttrib[i].nodeName)!=-1)
                {
                var strDisp = strName + "_" + oAttrib[i].nodeName;

                var newEl= "<span" + " class='"+strDisp+"'>";
                newEl+= oAttrib[i].nodeValue;
                newEl+= "</span>";

                obj[j].insertAdjacentHTML("afterBegin",newEl);
                }
            }
        }
     }

return;
}
    --></HTML:SCRIPT>
</Invoices>
```

Let's look at the script to understand what's going on. The `document.onreadystatechange()` event handler invokes the `ShowInfo()` method when the `readyState` property is set to complete (that is, the document is fully ready) and this method is used to do the work – this is because we don't necessarily want to have anything clicked to invoke the action, as it should already be there when the user gets to the page. Also, the use of the `<HTML:body>` element is overridden by the HTML `<body>` template built into the parser (there is an outline of an HTML document used when working with this method – `<html>`, `<title>`, `<head>`, and `<body>` tags are present).

The first thing the method does is use a variable containing the names of the attributes we want to display – the main reason for this is that we can't access the namespaces of the elements from within the HTML document object model so it doesn't allow us to ignore elements in the HTML namespace, which would be the preferred technique. This means that when we ask for the attributes collection of a given element we don't just get the attributes defined in the XML document – we also get a series of "possible" attributes from the HTML DOM – such as onclick, id, etc. Many of these can be filtered out because they are null or empty, but some are not because they are assigned default values (such as hidefocus=false, etc). Consequently, the simplest technique is to have a series of allowed attributes, and as long as they are in the variable strValidAtts, they can be processed to the output.

The next step is a call to getElementsByTagName() with the XPath expression "*", which returns all elements within the document body.

> Note that we must specify the **<body>** of the document to return the elements we have created in our XML document – the others are the HTML template elements we mentioned above, such as **<html>** and **<title>**.

Next, we step through all of the elements of the collection and find those attributes for each element which have been specified (that is, some value has been set) and using the JavaScript indexOf() method, the attribute name is found in our variable string of allowable attributes. At this point we have a valid attribute. The indexOf() method returns the position of the sub-string x within the string y in the positionofX = y.indexOf(x) expression. It is -1 if it does not appear at all.

Finally, our script creates a document name using the name of the element, concatenated with an underscore and then the attribute name. A <span> element is created which has a CSS class name set to this newly created name – the content of the <span> element is the data of the attribute. Finally, this text is appended immediately after the element in which the attribute(s) occurred and becomes part of the HTML document.

Before returning to look at the CSS part, it is worth clearing up why we used the element name, underscore, and attribute combination for a class name rather than just insert the attribute as an XML element or use a HTML element which has its style set. Well, when done dynamically, the style is not reflected unless we use the class name – in other words, if we just define an element style in the CSS and then dynamically create a new element to represent an attribute the style is *not* applied – we *must* set the className attribute of the new XML element. So, simply adding a new XML element for the attribute would cause it to inherit the style of the element defined above it – something we don't always want to happen. By using a class name, we can have any style applied to this dynamically-created element.

The CSS document (1d.css) is slightly unique in that it follows the elementname_attributename pattern to define classes of styles. The document is shown below, though the first part of the document is the same as 1c.css, so it has been omitted from the fragment to save space.

```
Invoices
{
  display: block;
  background-color: gray;

    . . .
    . . .

HTML\:b
{
```

```
      color:blue;
   }
   .Invoices_date
   {
       display: block;
       color:darkgray;
       text-decoration:none;
       background-color:white;
       font-style: normal;
       font-weight:bold;
       text-align: right;
       font-size: large;
       text-decoration:none;
   }

   .customers_custname
   {
       display: block;
       text-decoration:none;
       background-color:gray;
       font-style: italic;
       text-align: right;
       font-size: medium;
   }

   .customers_phone
   {
       display: block;
       text-decoration:none;
       background-color:gray;
       font-style: italic;
       text-align: right;
       font-size: medium;
   }

   .customers_email
   {
       display: block;
       color:darkblue;
       text-decoration:none;
       background-color:gray;
       font-style: italic;
       text-align: right;
       font-size: medium;
       cursor:hand;
   }

   .customers_cusid
   {
       display: block;
       text-decoration:none;
       background-color:green;
   }

   .customers_delivery
   {
       display: block;
       background-color:black;
       text-decoration:none;
       font-style:normal;
```

```
}

.customers_offerID
{
    display: none;
}

.order_orderID
{
    display:block;
    background-color:green;
    text-align:left;
    font-size:smaller;
    text-decoration:none;
    font-style:normal;
}

.order_batchid
{
    display: block;
    background-color:red;
    text-align:left;
    font-size:smaller;
    text-decoration:none;
    font-style:normal;
}

.items_num
{
    display:none;
}
```

We won't analyze all the combinations because they are all similar in execution. For each element that had an attribute we had in the XML document, we have created a class name to reflect this. The <Invoices> element has a date attribute, so we have a class name of .Invoices_date, which matches the same class name that was created in the JavaScript portion of the XML source. Now we can repeat this method and style for each class that we want to display. We decided that the num attribute of the <items> element doesn't look good in the display because it is just a number in the middle of the order with no context or meaning, so we set its display to none and it is not shown in the display. The result is shown in the following screenshot:

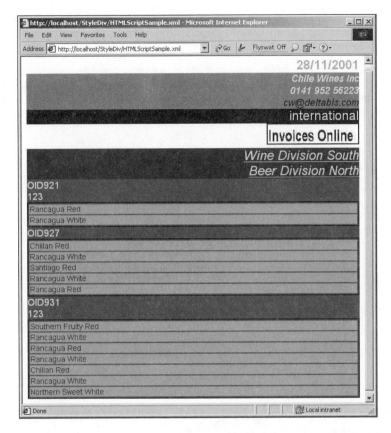

This is much more effective than the cluttered, basic XML document we started with. It is pretty limited though, and while it's useful for getting the point across and effective for more experienced readers, some of the context is difficult to follow (we may know what the order is, but not everyone would!). It also lacks a more powerful structure and there are likely to be some calculations and numbering we would like to have added. This is where we can use XSLT. It is much more powerful and when we are looking for a more advanced document, then it's the clear winner. Nevertheless, CSS/XML is still very good and extremely easy to do for report type documents.

Let's now see how XSLT with the help of CSS allows us to create more powerful presentation pages.

CSS and XSLT

While working through the last few sections, you will have seen applications where just using the simplicity of browsing XML with CSS would be ideal and would save creating complex XSLT documents. However, you will also have recognized that this method would be ineffective in many other applications that require more flexibility in their display. CSS can then work with XSLT to provide maximum flexibility.

Let's look at how CSS can be used with the different versions of MSXML. We will look at the two implementations discussed in the XSLT chapter – the Microsoft XSL 1998 implementation and the XSLT W3C Recommendation. Although the two technologies have many similar aspects, when there are differences these will be noted and demonstrated.

CSS and XSLT are complementary to each other. We can forge a powerful combination through using XSLT to perform reordering and advanced functionalities, while CSS is used to manage display, such as colors and fonts.

> The worked examples in this section will revert back to our original XML document, **sample.xml**. It is assumed you have read the chapter on XSLT (Chapter 5) or have a good knowledge of XSLT.

Element-level Styling in XSLT

When using CSS to style elements of an XSLT-generated document, the simplest method we can use is to directly set the style on the element in question, within its style attribute. In XSLT there are two ways to accomplish this – **directly** or **dynamically**. Using the direct method we simply specify the style attribute with its name-value pairs as follows:

```
<xsl:template match="item">
   <div style="background-color:white;color:darkblue;">
      <xsl:value-of select="." />
   </div>
</xsl:template>
```

This simply creates a <div> element with a white background color and dark blue colored text. However, we can also dynamically assign the style attribute using the <xsl:attribute> element.

```
<xsl:template match="customers">
   <xsl:element name="a">
   <xsl:attribute name="href">
      mailto:<xsl:value-of select="@email"/>
   </xsl:attribute>
   <xsl:attribute name="style">
      text-decoration:none; font-weight:bold;
   </xsl:attribute>

   <xsl:value-of select="@email" />
   </xsl:element>
</xsl:template>
```

This will create the following output:

```
<a href="mail:tocw@deltabis.com"
   style=" text-decoration:none; font-weight:bold;">
   cw@deltabis.com
</a>
```

Using the XSLT Recommendation that was first supported in MSXML 3, we can also use attribute sets to group attributes. This is particularly useful when there are multiple attributes that should be applied to a given element, not necessarily using CSS. A good example is the HTML <table> element that is commonly used in web pages:

```
<xsl:template match="customers">
   <xsl:element name="table" xsl:use-attribute-sets="address-table">
      <xsl:element name="tr">
         <xsl:element name="td">
            Customer Name
         </xsl:element>
         <xsl:element name="td">
            <xsl:value-of select="@custname"/>
         </xsl:element>
      </xsl:element>
      <xsl:element name="tr">
         <xsl:element name="td">
            Telephone
         </xsl:element>
         <xsl:element name="td">
            <xsl:value-of select="@phone"/>
         </xsl:element>
      </xsl:element>
      <xsl:element name="tr">
         <xsl:element name="td">
            Email
         </xsl:element>
         <xsl:element name="td">
            <xsl:value-of select="@email"/>
         </xsl:element>
      </xsl:element>
   </xsl:element>
</xsl:template>

<xsl:attribute-set name="address-table">
   <xsl:attribute name="rows">3</xsl:attribute>
   <xsl:attribute name="cols">2</xsl:attribute>
   <xsl:attribute name="style">
      text-decoration:none; font-weight:bold;
   </xsl:attribute>
</xsl:attribute-set>
```

The `<xsl:attribute-set>` element is used to contain the elements that can be applied to all address tables in the document. This outputs the following HTML fragment:

```
<table rows="3" cols="2" style=" text-decoration:none; font-weight:bold;">
   <tr>
      <td>Customer Name</td>
      <td>Chile Wines Inc</td>
   </tr>
   <tr>
      <td>Telephone</td>
      <td>0141 952 56223</td>
   </tr>
   <tr>
      <td>Email</td>
      <td>cw@deltabis.com</td>
   </tr>
</table>
```

However, we're still likely to want to go a step further and at least style the elements from a page-level view using element styles, IDs, or classes – in other words be able to define a global style in a `style` section in the `<head>` of an html page. This is fairly simple to do in XSLT, but for completeness we should address this method.

Page-level Styling with XSLT

Creating page-level styling for HTML display is really not much different to that for a normal HTML document. Within the `<head>` section, we create a `<style>` element that contains the definitions for our element styles. The following section illustrates how this could be done for displaying in IE 5+ browsers (or any browser if the transform is done server-side) using the MSXML XSL 1998 implementation. This is `InternalCSSIE5.xsl` in the code download and is demonstrated with `InternalCSSIE5.xml`:

```
<?xml version="1.0" ?>
<xsl:stylesheet xmlns:xsl="http://www.w3.org/TR/WD-xsl">
   <xsl:template>
      <xsl:apply-templates />
   </xsl:template>
   <xsl:template match="customers">
   <html>
      <head>
         <style>
            h2 {background-color:darkblue;color:white;}
            .info {cursor:hand;}
         </style>
      </head>
      <body>
         <h2>
            <xsl:value-of select="@custname" /> .
         </h2>
         <div class="info">Customer Name :
            <xsl:value-of select="@phone" /></DIV>
         <div class="info">Email Address :
            <xsl:value-of select="@email" /></DIV>
         <xsl:apply-templates />
      </body>
   </html>
   </xsl:template>
</xsl:stylesheet>
```

The W3C version of this is shown below. This is `InternalCSS.xsl` in the code download and is demonstrated with `InternalCSS.xml`.

```
<?xml version="1.0" ?>
<xsl:stylesheet version="1.0" xmlns:xsl="http://www.w3.org/1999/XSL/Transform">
   <xsl:template match="customers">
      <html>
         <head>
            <style>
               h2 {background-color:darkblue;color:white;}
               .info {cursor:hand;}
            </style>
         </head>
         <body>
            <h2>
               <xsl:value-of select="@custname" />
            </h2>
```

```
                <div class="info">Customer Name :
                    <xsl:value-of select="@phone" /></div>
                <div class="info">Email Address :
                    <xsl:value-of select="@email" /></div>
                <xsl:apply-templates />
            </body>
        </html>
    </xsl:template>
    <xsl:template match="text()" />
</xsl:stylesheet>
```

Both stylesheets are quite similar. You can see that the `<style>` element is embedded within the `<head>` element and contains an element style for the HTML `<h2>` element and a class style called `info`. These styles then apply to the appropriate elements within the entire XSLT. So, the `<h2>` element that contains the customer name is styled by the `<h2>` element style, and the two `<div>` elements that have their `class` attribute set to `info` are also styled appropriately. This applies not only in the initial template, but all templates within the XSLT or those included (because it really applies to the HTML output of these.)

The two stylesheets produce the same output, as shown:

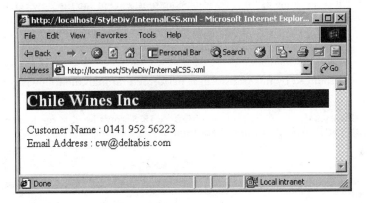

An alternative option is to use external stylesheets. It is likely that we will need to reuse stylesheets and this is why we use external stylesheets, which we'll look at next.

Using External Stylesheets

We can also use an external stylesheet to include styles, which is achieved by including the following line in the head section of the HTML document:

```
<link rel="stylesheet" type="text/css" href="style.css" />
```

We can use this technique to separate all of the CSS presentation information from the XSLT – this is probably the best way to use them together as it follows the principles of separating the technologies (data, presentation, and display). All of the principles of CSS we discussed above can be used when working with CSS/XSLT. We can even use script within our XSLT to allow DHTML in the HTML.

Generating DHTML

We saw in Chapter 5, "*XSLT in MSXML*", that we can use script in the XSLT document, but what happens when we don't want this script to be parsed by the XSLT processor and want it to be used by the HTML document instead? We wrap the `<script>` element firstly in an `<xsl:comment>` element and enclose it in a CDATA section to escape any special XML characters, as shown below:

```
<script language="Jscript"><xsl:comment>

<![CDATA[function function()
    {
        alert("I am a function.");
    }
]]></xsl:comment></script>
```

The following example demonstrates how to use imported stylesheets as well as HTML scripting to create a more interactive interface for the user. This can be found in the code download as `scriptCSS.xml`, `scriptCSS.xsl`, and `samplestyle.css`.

The XML document is the same as our previous examples, except the file now references the XSL document rather than a CSS document.

```
<?xml-stylesheet type="text/xsl" href="ScriptCSS.xsl" ?>
```

The HTML output produced by this transform is performed through the following XSL stylesheet.

> **Note that this uses the W3C Recommendation so IE 5 won't be able to view this unless you run MSXML 3.0 or above in replace mode.**

```
<?xml version="1.0" ?>
<xsl:stylesheet version="1.0" xmlns:xsl="http://www.w3.org/1999/XSL/Transform">
    <xsl:template match="customers">
        <html>
            <head>
                <style>
                    h2 {background-color:darkblue;color:white;}
                    .info {cursor:hand;
                        background-color:lightgreen;
                        color:darkgreen;}
                </style>

                <link rel="stylesheet" type="text/css" href="samplestyle.css" />

            <script language="Jscript"><xsl:comment>
            <![CDATA[function mouseover()
                {
                    e = window.event.srcElement;
                    if (e.style.backgroundColor != 'white')
                    e.style.backgroundColor = 'white';
                    else
                    e.style.backgroundColor = 'lightblue';
                }
```

```
            function mouseout()
            {
                e = window.event.srcElement;
                if (e.style.backgroundColor != 'lightblue')
                e.style.backgroundColor = 'lightblue';
                else
                e.style.backgroundColor = 'white';
            }
        ]]></xsl:comment></script>

        </head>

        <body>
            <h2>
                <xsl:attribute name="style">color:yellow</xsl:attribute>
                <xsl:value-of select="@custname" />
            </h2>
                <xsl:element name="a">
                <xsl:attribute name="href">mailto:
                <xsl:value-of select="@email" />
                </xsl:attribute>

                <xsl:attribute name="class">email</xsl:attribute>
                <xsl:value-of select="@email" />
                </xsl:element>
                <p>
                    <font class="subheader">Wines</font>
                    <xsl:apply-templates />
                </p>
        </body>
    </html>

</xsl:template>
    <xsl:template match="order">
    <div class="info">
        <b>Order
            <xsl:value-of select="@orderID" />
        </b>
    </div>
        <xsl:apply-templates />
        </xsl:template>
        <xsl:template match="items/item">
    <div style="background-color:white;color:darkblue;"
        onmouseover="mouseover()" onmouseout="mouseout()">
        <xsl:value-of select="." />
    </div>
    </xsl:template>

    <xsl:template match="text()" />
</xsl:stylesheet>
```

You should have a good understanding of how the template works, so let's look at how we create the HTML. We can embed most of the HTML elements we want to use within the root template and call the other templates within this to generate the other HTML fragments, such as tables, paragraphs, and others. There is a globally defined `<style>` element defined within the stylesheet, which should appear within the `<head>` element as in ordinary HTML:

```
<style>
   h2 {background-color:darkblue;color:white;}
   .info {cursor:hand;background-color:lightgreen;color:darkgreen;}
</style>
```

This is fairly simple CSS and just defines the style of any `<h2>` or `.info` class elements within the document. Following this, there is a link to an external CSS document (`samplestyle.css`), which defines two classes and a style for any `<b>` tags. The file looks like this:

```
.subheader {font-weight:bold;font-family=Arial}
.email {color:green;}
b {text-decoration:underline}
```

So, having considered all of the style options we have, we can also see that `<script>` blocks can be dynamically inserted into the HTML `<head>` elements, keeping in mind it is best to enclose any script within CDATA sections to escape any XML special characters. We use these in the HTML document as we normally would. To improve the visibility of the `<div>` element, we have done the following:

```
<div style="background-color:white;color:darkblue;"
             onmouseover="mouseover()" onmouseout="mouseout()">
   <xsl:value-of select="." />
</div>
```

The HTML output that is generated is shown here:

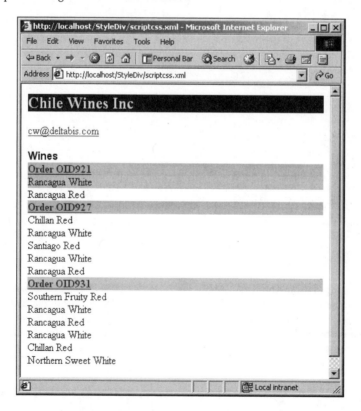

With the techniques displayed in this chapter combined with those in the XSLT chapter, we are now able to present information to web browsers. If you are considering presenting to browsers that do not support XML directly, you should look at Chapters 9 to 11 which deal with using MSXML as a server-side component.

Working with XSLT and Script

XSLT and scripting can be used in combination, either directly as part of a web page or separately as part of an XSLT transform. The following sections of this book deal in detail with CSS and XSLT:

❑ Data islands – Chapter 12, "*Working with Data on the Client*".

❑ XSLT parameters and styling – Chapter 10, "*Transformations on the Server*".

Element Behaviors

If you have done much work on client-side development with IE and MSXML, you will likely have heard of, or even worked with, scripting component technologies such as scriptlets and behaviors. The architecture of these is shown in the following diagram:

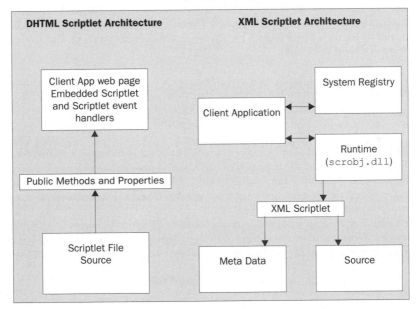

Scriptlets were introduced with IE 4 in an attempt to provide a means to separate and re-use client-side scripting. It was fairly successful in that it was a move onwards from the previous technologies available, such as basic VBScript and JavaScript within the HTML page itself. However, it was recognized that it also had some failings. It was necessary to put a great deal of code into the hosting HTML page in order to handle events and program the scriptlets. It also broke browser compatibility. DHTML **behaviors** were introduced with IE 5 and they allow function-based components to be attached to elements in the HTML page based on namespaces – this form of DHTML behaviors is commonly referred to as **attached behaviors**.

Let's look at this kind of behavior briefly in order to understand the general concepts of behaviors, as our topic of element behaviors is simply an extension of these concepts.

Behaviors Overview

The DHTML behaviors introduced with IE 5 were later renamed to attached behaviors. This is because these kinds of behaviors are like components that can be applied to any element, so an attached behavior could change the color an anchor link of an HTML page when we move over it. What this is saying is that a behavior can be attached to an element. In other words, we could attach a `mouseover` color change behavior to an `<a>` element, a `<div>` element, and in fact any HTML or other element we choose to assign it to. We will look at an example below.

While powerful, there is a slight problem when assigning these to elements. When we create an `<img>` element, we expect an exact result – an image displayed, perhaps with a border and maybe some alternative text. If we want it to react when we move the mouse over it, we can attach a behavior such as the one discussed above.

We do not expect the `<img>` tag to have a text value attribute that is dynamically shown as a `.jpg` when rendered in the browser (although it may be useful!). If we wanted this, we would use some other component or scripting.

So what are we getting at? Well, the elements we have used for years in HTML have a consistent, predetermined, and known result. The effects these elements produce cannot be altered in any way without using scripting and external functionality. Therefore, when we use a `<textarea>`, we always get an exact result as we do when we use an `<H1>` tag. In IE 5.5 this concept was applied to behaviors and the result was **element behaviors**.

Element behaviors are very similar to attached behaviors, except element behaviors have a known and consistent effect. We cannot dynamically change how they work – they will always offer certain basic functionality. Unlike attached behaviors, we cannot detach the behavior from an element and assign it a new behavior.

This may sound like a limitation of attached behaviors, but imagine the situation where working with elements in XSLT resulted in the functionality of the XSLT element changing as we used it, or even being completely different. Of course, the functionality could change if we start modifying the actual source code, but the idea is that the element behavior is encapsulated and exhibits a consistent, clear approach.

The discussion above should now have clearly shown the difference between attached behaviors and element behaviors. While they are very much different, there is no reason why an element behavior could not use an attached behavior –in just the same way a `<div>` tag can have a behavior attached.

Let's now look at these in action, starting with an attached behavior.

Attached Behaviors

An attached behavior is assigned to an element using a stylesheet style, and works with namespaces to allow us to define a qualified element. Let's first look at how we create a component that will allow us to show a login form on a web page.

The first task we have to do is create an **HTML Component (HTC)** file that will contain the script that will provide the behavior. Look in the `behav` folder of the code download for `LoginAttach.htc`, shown here:

```
<PUBLIC:HTC URN="login">
   <PUBLIC:ATTACH EVENT="ondocumentready" ONEVENT="DoInit()" />
   <PUBLIC:PROPERTY NAME="email" />
   <PUBLIC:PROPERTY NAME="password" />
   <PUBLIC:PROPERTY NAME="postTo" />
   <script language="jscript">

function DoInit()
{
   LoginDefaults();
   CreateLogin();
}

function LoginDefaults()
{
   if (email == null)
      email = "you@domain.com";

   if (password == null)
      password = "";

   if (postTo == null)
      postTo = "http://www.wrox.com/handler.asp";
}

function CreateLogin()
{
   var htmTxt="";
   htmTxt += "<form id='' name='' method='post' action='" + postTo + "'>"
   htmTxt += "<label id='' for=''>Email Address</label><br />"
   htmTxt += "<input type='text' id='' name='email' value='" + email + "'>
               </input>"
   htmTxt += "<br />"
   htmTxt += "<label id='' for=''>Password</label><br />"
   htmTxt += "<input type='password' id='' name='' value='" + password + "'>
               </input><br />"
   htmTxt += "<input type='submit' value='submit'></input>"
   htmTxt += "</form>"

   element.innerHTML = htmTxt;
}

   </script>
</PUBLIC:HTC>
```

An attached behavior component must use a <PUBLIC:HTC> element to contain the script and can also have a URN attribute identifying the component. Within this, we can then define the events that should be linked to, as well as properties and methods that should be available to the host document. The example first attaches to the ondocumentready event in the host HTML document as specified in the EVENT attribute, which fires when the document has been completely parsed and built. This is linked to an internal event handler called DoInit() via the ONEVENT attribute.

```
<PUBLIC:ATTACH EVENT="ondocumentready" ONEVENT="DoInit()" />
```

Following this, three public properties are declared which are accessible by the host document. These are declared as follows:

```
<PUBLIC:PROPERTY NAME="email" />
<PUBLIC:PROPERTY NAME="password" />
<PUBLIC:PROPERTY NAME="postTo" />
```

This effectively creates three global variables (`email`, `password`, and `postTo`), which are available to the script and allow parameters to be passed in. Similarly, methods can also be exposed to the host document with the syntax `<PUBLIC:METHOD NAME="somemethod" />`. Finally, the `<script>` element can be added, which contains the script that implements the behavior. This is just as we would create a script block in HTML. The first of the methods in the sample document is the one we earlier linked to the `ondocumentready` event and invokes two methods, the first setting the default values for the behavior and the other actually implementing the behavior. The names of these methods can be anything we wish – the names used here are not compulsory.

In the `CreateLogin()` method of the sample, the form is actually created and some text boxes are inserted. Note that the public properties accessed as variables are usually used to insert values in to the HTML that is created. Finally, the resulting HTML is output to the hosting document. This is very simple, because the element that invoked the behavior is accessible as an object via an element. This means we can just use its `innerHTML` property (like with a `<div>` tag) to display the result.

So how do we actually attach our behavior? Well, there are three things we have to do in the HTML document to actually use the behavior. The first is to define a namespace that will allow us to identify our elements within the document. The fairly odd usage can only be used on the root `<html>` element and so it will look something like this, with `wrox` the name of the namespace:

```
<html xmlns:wrox>
```

Next, we actually create an element qualified with this namespace. This is important, because if we don't associate the namespace, IE (5.0 and above for attached behaviors) will just ignore the element. To create our own elements in attached behaviors, we simply use the following syntax:

```
<namespace:elementName property1="value1" property2="value2"/>
```

The final thing we have to do is associate the attached behavior with the elements and this is done via a style definition. Associating the behavior is much like we did earlier when browsing XML directly with CSS using the HTML namespace. A `<style>` element can be used in the `<head>` element. The specific element is styled by escaping the namespace, appending the name of the element, and finally identifying the behavior that should be associated with it, using the following syntax:

```
namespace\:elementName {behavior:url(behaviorFile.htc);}
```

Let's look at how this is implemented in `LoginAttach.htm`, below:

```
<html xmlns:wrox xmlns:wrox2>
  <head>
    <style>
      wrox\:login {behavior:url(LoginAttach.htc);}
      wrox2\:login {behavior:url(LoginAttach2.htc);}
      wrox2\:register {behavior:url(LoginAttach2.htc);}
    </style>
    <link rel="stylesheet" type="text/css" href="css1.css" />
  </head>
```

```
    <body>
        <wrox:login email="steven" password="steven"
                    postTo="http://www.deltabis.com/enter.asp" />
        <wrox2:login email="steven@wrox.com" password="wrox"
                    postTo="http://www.deltabis.com/enter.asp" />
        <wrox2:register email="loreto@steven.com" password="lola"
                    postTo="http://www.deltabis.com/go.asp" />
        <input type="button" value="ShowHTML"
                onclick="alert(document.documentElement.outerHTML)"/>
    </body>
</html>
```

You can see this document actually uses two namespace definitions:

```
<html xmlns:wrox xmlns:wrox2>
```

Like an actual XML document, we can create as many namespace definitions as we wish in order to separate our element definitions. In the case of this sample, it is wrox and wrox2. Next, the <head> tag contains three style definitions; one is for the element <wrox:login> that uses the behavior LoginAttach.htc, and the last two are for the elements <wrox2:login> and <wrox2:register>, and use the behavior LoginAttach.htc. We will see what these mean below. Further on in the document, we have three elements defined that contain initial parameters to pass to the respective behaviors:

```
<wrox:login email="steven" password="steven"
            postTo="http://deltabis.com/enter.asp" />
<wrox2:login email="steven@wrox.com" password="wrox"
            postTo="http://deltabis.com/enter.asp" />
<wrox2:register email="loreto@steven.com" password="lola"
            postTo="http://deltabis.com/go.asp" />
```

We create three elements to show the positive and negative side effects of the flexibility of attached behaviors. The first element shows how the behavior can be used and its output is defined by the CSS style we defined with the same element name earlier. The second was to show how element behavior could be completely changed within a new namespace. The local name of the element is the same as the first but a new namespace is used and the associated style uses a slightly different behavior. (To keep it simple, the "new" behavior only adds some text to the labels on the output.) This could be tricky for a designer who is unaware of namespaces and is using each of these behaviors expecting the same result – each namespace qualifies an element that may implement different functionality! To further show how it can be more of a problem, the <wrox:register> element and <wrox:login> element actually are exactly the same and produce the same output. This is likely to confuse any designers creating web pages, and then there are the developers using script to dynamically attach and detach behaviors on the element. This makes creating libraries of functionality extremely difficult and potentially confusing – hence we need element behaviors.

Incidentally, notice that we can use a link to an external stylesheet and any content inserted from the behavior will have the appropriate style applied. We can click the ShowHTML button to view the HTML for the page – we'll see the significance of this shortly. The output from this page is shown in the following screenshot:

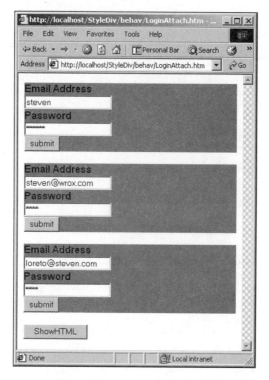

As we discussed earlier, however, there are good reasons why creating element behaviors is more advantageous. Let's now create a more stabilized element definition using element behaviors.

Creating an Element Behavior

Element behaviors are fairly similar to attached behaviors, so we won't have to repeat the entire discussion of the behavior file, though there are some important differences we will highlight and discuss.

The HTC file is called LoginElement.htc (in the behav folder of the download) and is listed below (the modified lines are highlighted and the unchanged code omitted for brevity):

```
<PUBLIC:COMPONENT tagName="login">
    ...
function CreateLogin()
{
    ...
    htmTxt += "<input type='submit' value='submit'></input>"
    htmTxt += "</form>"

    element.innerHTML = element.innerHTML + htmTxt;
}

</script>
</PUBLIC:COMPONENT>
```

This file has two significant differences from the attached behavior file discussed above. The first is its root – instead of the <PUBLIC:HTC> element, the behavior is wrapped in the element:

```
<PUBLIC:COMPONENT tagName="login">
```

The tagName attribute is now very important and is the name of the element that uses this behavior in the HTML document. The second important difference is the change to the following line of the CreateLogin() method:

```
element.innerHTML = element.innerHTML + htmTxt;
```

As mentioned above, the element keyword gives access to the element as an object, where the tag is used in the HTML document. So, this line sets the innerHTML property of the element to its current value combined with the HTML the function just created.

The HTML page that hosts element behaviors below (LoginElement.htm) is a bit different from the attached behaviors discussed above.

```
<html xmlns:wrox>
   <head>
      <?import namespace="wrox" implementation="LoginElement.htc" >
      <link rel="stylesheet" type="text/css" href="css1.css" />
   </head>
   <body>
      <wrox:login email="steven" password="steven"
                  postTo="http://www.deltabis.com/enter.asp">
         <h3>
            Username and Password Entry
         </h3>
      </wrox:login>
         <input type="button" value="ShowHTML"
                onclick="alert(document.documentElement.outerHTML)"/>
   </body>
   <textarea id="oop"></textarea>
</html>
```

As usual, a namespace is defined to qualify the elements we create. However, CSS in the <head> element is not used to assign element behaviors. Instead, we use a mechanism that looks like the start of a processing instruction and import the behavior into the document, with the specified namespace and implementation at the given file location. The namespace attribute of the <import> tag should match that defined on the <html> root tag. This is because we can use multiple namespaces as before, and may want to directly associate an imported behavior with one of these namespaces.

We can then specify the <login> element that we want to display. This name must match that of the tagName attribute in the behavior and must be qualified with the namespace associated with this behavior in the import statement. As with attached behaviors, we pass the starting property values as attributes. However, unlike the attached behavior, we can specify some child text. If we look back at the CreateLogin() function, we see that this is read and output with the display. The result is as shown (LoginElement.htm):

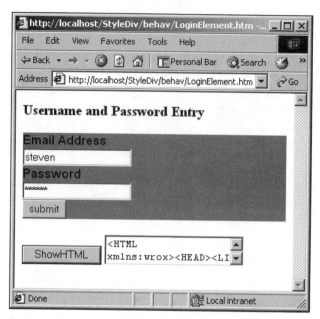

There are two important things worth mentioning just now because they will be contrasted with the next example. An external stylesheet can be used and any HTML elements inserted by the behavior will inherit the style specifications defined in the stylesheet. In addition, the **ShowHTML** button will display the entire HTML output for the document (as shown below) in the `textarea` box:

```
<html xmlns:wrox>
   <head>
      <link href="css1.css" type="text/css" rel="stylesheet">
   </head>
   <body>
      <?import namespace=wrox
               implementation="http://localhost/test/ProXML/StyleDiv
                                /behav/LoginElement.htc" />

      <wrox:login email="steven" password="steven"
                     postTo="http://www.deltabis.com/enter.asp">
         <H3>
            Username and Password Entry
         </H3>
         <form id="" name="" action="http://www.deltabis.com/enter.asp"
               method="post">

            <label id="Label1" for="">Email Address</LABEL>
            <br />
            <input id="Text1" value="steven" name="email"></INPUT>
            <br />
            <label id="Label2" for="">Password</LABEL>
            <br />
            <input id="Password1" type="password" value="" name="">
            <br />
            <input type="submit" value="submit" ID="Submit1"
                  NAME="Submit1"></INPUT>
         </form>
      </wrox:login>
```

```
        <input id="Button1" onclick="alert(document.documentElement.outerHTML)"
               type="button" value="ShowHTML" name="Button1">
        <textarea id="oop"></textarea>
    </body>
</html>
```

Although this may seem obvious, it displays the resulting HTML and allows us to access the elements and attributes created by the behavior using scripting from within the containing HTML document. Let's look now at how the `viewLinkContent` attribute can be employed and how it changes things slightly.

Further Customization with viewLinkContent

The last point of the previous section is an interesting one – what if we want to just give the result as a single result of the element behavior and not allow the HTML page to change this? We may not want the HTML page messing around with the action of the form and other settings – that's why we expose properties. To solve this, the `viewLinkContent` attribute can be set to `True` using the following syntax:

```
<PUBLIC:DEFAULTS viewLinkContent="True" />
```

If we say that the example above (`LoginElement.htc`) embedded the result of the behavior in the HTML document, then using the `viewLinkContent` attribute links the content. It is not a hyperlink of any kind, as the content from the behavior is displayed, but the actual HTML of the behavior content is not accessible or viewable. This allows much better encapsulation of our element behavior – after all, we don't see any more from an `<img>` tag than the `tagname` and properties we can set.

This is one change from the element behavior HTC document we discussed above. The other is that we no longer use the `element` object to insert the result in the source and instead use `document.body`. The code from the sample (`LoginElementView.htc`) is shown below:

```
<PUBLIC:COMPONENT tagName="login">
    <PUBLIC:DEFAULTS viewLinkContent="True" />
    <PUBLIC:ATTACH EVENT="ondocumentready" ONEVENT="DoInit()" />
    <PUBLIC:PROPERTY NAME="email" />
    <PUBLIC:PROPERTY NAME="password" />
    <PUBLIC:PROPERTY NAME="postTo" />
    <PUBLIC:PROPERTY NAME="stylefile" />
    <SCRIPT LANGUAGE="jscript">

    ...

function CreateLogin()
{
    var htmTxt="";
    htmTxt += "<link rel='stylesheet' type='text/css'
                    href='" + stylefile + "' />"
    htmTxt += "<form id='' name='' method='post' action='" + postTo + "'>"
    htmTxt += "<label id='' for=''>Email Address</label><br />"
    htmTxt += "<input type='text' id='' name='email' value='" + email + "'>
        </input>"
    htmTxt += "<br />"
    htmTxt += "<label id='' for=''>Password</label><br />"
    htmTxt += "<input type='password' id='' name='' value='" + password + "'>
        </input><br />"
```

```
        htmTxt += "<input type='submit' value='submit'></input>"
        htmTxt += "</form>"

    document.body.innerHTML = element.innerHTML + htmTxt;
}
</script>
</PUBLIC:COMPONENT>
```

The new line in the `CreateLogin()` method now sets the display of the result of the behavior and this cannot be accessed within the hosting page – unlike the previous example. The HTML, when clicking the ShowHTML button in `LogonElementView.htm`, is shown below:

```
<html xmlns:wrox>
    <head>
    </head>
    <body>
        <?import namespace=wrox implementation="LoginElementView.htc" />
        <wrox:login email="steven" password="steven"
            postTo="http://www.deltabis.com/enter.asp" stylefile="css1.css">
            <h3>
                Username and Password Entry
            </h3>
        </wrox:login>

        <input id="Button1"
                onclick="alert(document.documentElement.outerHTML)"
                type="button" value="ShowHTML" name="Button1">
    </body>
</html>
```

Notice that the resulting HTML does not display in the output of this kind of behavior – we only see the display, not the HTML. So, the result of the behavior cannot be tampered with and the result is completely encapsulated within the component. This means that in an internal or external development environment we can be assured that our code will function cleanly and do its task without interference from the host document – for example a developer of a web page could assume that a `getElementsByTagName()` or `getElementsByID()` call will not return parts of the included behavior and hence cause havoc with the code, and that the document object model doesn't change with the inclusion of some behavior.

What you will also notice is that when using `viewLinkContent`, the stylesheet in the host document no longer has any effect on the results generated from our behavior (because it is linked, not embedded). To use the stylesheet, we must embed it within the component itself. However, this is not as restrictive as you may think because of the properties that can be used. In fact, if you look at the `.htc` file there is a new global property called `stylefile` and you can also see this being set in the source HTML page when the attribute is created. This is simply used to dynamically create a link to an external stylesheet in the behavior. The result is as shown:

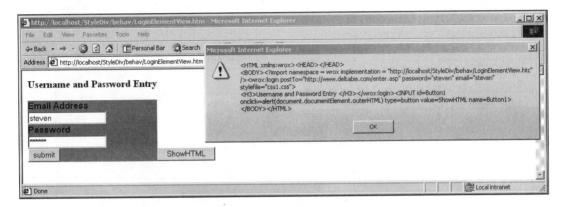

One final thing to note about element behaviors is the use of the `literalContent` attribute. This states that the content should not be parsed and inserted directly as HTML into the containing document, but should be available through scripting – like an XML data island. This of course doesn't work when we have set `viewLinkContent` to `true` because this doesn't embed the result. We could use this to contain things such as XML results from the element behavior.

Try using these element behaviors in your web pages – they are very powerful and an extensive library of behaviors can be built up. They don't cause browser incompatibilities as they are just ignored by incompatible browsers, although any literal content within them is written out – so care must be taken.

Graphical XML

The use of graphics on the Web has twisted and turned over the years, from GIFs to JPGs to PNG and Flash, as well as others. Arguably, Flash is now seeing the most success. Based mainly on its use of vector graphics at its core, it is in general able to have much smaller file sizes than its counterparts, even when working with animation. However, it is difficult to program something to produce a Flash output. Something similar to Flash is happening in the XML world in the form of **SVG** or **Scalable Vector Graphics**. SVG is a W3C Recommendation and you can find out more at http://www.w3.org/TR/SVG/.

SVG is an open standard, defined by the W3C, and improves on **VML** (**Vector Markup Language**) by offering full DOM support and even some of its own custom methods, so it is fully scriptable using many of the methods you have learned in this book. It is also *very* powerful at generating graphics and is far more accomplished in this sense than VML. Currently, however, it has very little support in products – although we will see an example later.

A comparison of VML and SVG can be found here:
http://www.grapl.com/vmlnotes/introduction/vml_and_svg_compared.htm. You can find
more information about SVG at http://www.adobe.com/svg/indepth/faq.html.

SVG is definitely the way forward, but Microsoft has already invested heavily in VML, which is built in to IE 5+ and is a large part of the Office products and related applications. It is simple, effective, and has proven itself in many products.

Some very good examples of VML in practice are available at
http://www.vmlsource.com/demos.htm.

The graph in the following screenshot was generated using Microsoft Excel and makes heavy use of VML, giving a good example of its power:

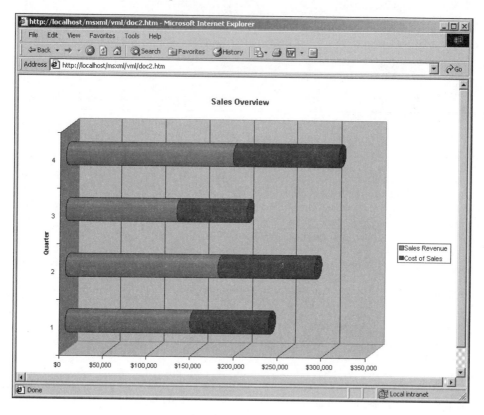

Vector Graphics for the Web

Vector Markup Language is used in Microsoft Office 2000, Visio, and Internet Explorer 5.0+ when working with web pages. It is not a W3C initiative so it is not compatible on most other browsers. Although SVG is the future of XML vector graphics, as of IE 6 there is no real support for it and so VML will be around for a quite some time. However, as VML is also XML, it is only a transform away from SVG. It is possible that products will become available to do this because manual transforms would be very difficult due to the size and scope of SVG (it is *much* larger than VML), as well as the complex creation of vector graphics (you don't want to have to translate the coordinates of shapes by hand!).

With VML we can create various types of shapes, such as rectangles, ovals, circles, triangles, clouds, trapezoids, text, and much more. As we work through the examples, we will start to see that complex graphics would only be written directly by a developer who was either insane, a genius, or the usual combination of the two. In fact, vector graphics (in VML or SVG) will typically be created using a GUI, so the exact details are not essential and can be looked up in a VML reference, although an understanding is needed. If you plan on dynamically generating vector graphics from your application, there is an extensive reference section at http://msdn.microsoft.com/workshop/author/vml/default.asp.

VML Technical Overview

One cool thing about VML is that it uses something we already understand pretty well – attached behaviors; based on our recent discussion of attached behaviors, some of the following HTML should look familiar:

```
<html xmlns:vml="urn:schemas-microsoft-com:vml"
      xmlns="http://www.w3.org/TR/REC-html40">

   <head>
      <style>
         vml\:* {behavior:url(#default#VML);}
      </style>
   </head>
   <body>
      <vml:element property1="value1" property2="value2" property3="value3">
      </vml:element>
   </body>
</html>
```

The vml prefix is used to identify those elements which are related to VML and are qualified by the namespace urn:schemas-microsoft-com:vml, and as we know, this must be declared on the HTML root element. The vml prefix can be any name we choose, as long as it is unique in the document.

A style section should be declared which specifies a style with an associated behavior applied to any element in the vml namespace (indicated by the "*"). The behavior is a default behavior that ships with IE, so we specify the file URI as #default#VML.

Finally, the <vml> elements are defined in the HTML body with the appropriate properties to define how it should be displayed.

The basic element of VML is the <shape> element, which is some closed curve in two dimensions. Basically, all elements and other shapes we will work with in VML are in some way derived from the <shape> element. The function of the <shape> element is actually pretty obvious – let's illustrate it with an example, simple.htm, which draws a square on a web page, as shown:

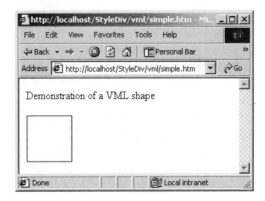

If we view the source of this web page we see the following:

```
<html xmlns:vml="urn:schemas-microsoft-com:vml"
    xmlns="http://www.w3.org/TR/REC-html40">
  <head>
    <style>
        vml\:* {behavior:url(#default#VML);}
    </style>
  </head>
  <body>
    Demonstration of a VML shape
  <p>
    <vml:shape style='width:500pt;height:500pt'
              path="M 0,0 L 0,100, 100,100, 100,0, X E">
    </vml:shape>
  </p>
  </body>
</html>
```

We have discussed the rest of this page, so let's look at the `<vml:shape>` element. The `height` and `width` values of the `style` attribute, and the `path` attribute are the minimum required to draw the shape – the first two being fairly obvious and defining the relative dimensions of how the shape should be drawn. The `path` attribute requires some analysis. At first this looks a bit cryptic, but it's actually quite straightforward. The `M` that starts the value means "move" and takes the "pen" from the current position (which could be anywhere initially) to the coordinates given as an `(x,y)` pair – x being the horizontal axis and y the vertical. Remember that when drawing computer graphics, the x moves to the *right* and the y moves *downwords*.

Following this, we have an `L` character which then uses a series of `(x,y)` coordinates to draw from the current position (initialized by the "move") to the given coordinates. So, the first value says `0,100`, meaning that a line should be drawn from the initialized position of `0,0` to `0,100`. After the line is drawn, the pen stays at the end coordinates of the last action – `0,100` in our case. The next value is `100,100`, which draws a line from `0,100` to `100,100`, and finally the last pair is from `100,100` to `100,0`. This draws three of the lines of the square. The `X` simply means draw a line from the current position to the start position, and hence the top of the square is drawn. The `E` indicates that the path is complete and the drawing is terminated.

The `<shape>` element can have a number of attributes assigned, such as the fill color, the line color, alternate text, and many others. Below is a quick reference to the shapes and elements available to help us understand what VML can do for us.

VML Shapes

VML consists of a number of predefined shapes such as lines, circles, and rectangles, with the aim of making VML more usable for common displays. We will use some of these in the examples below. The available shapes are:

❑   `vml:rect` – creates a rectangle.

❑   `vml:roundrect` – creates a rectangle that is rounded at the corners.

❑   `vml:line` – draws a line between two coordinates.

❑   `vml:polyline` – draws a line between a series of points.

❑   `vml:oval` – creates an oval.

❑   `vml:image` – creates an image, much like the HTML `<img>` element.

❑   `vml:curve` – creates a curve between specified points.

❑   `vml:arc` – creates a pre-defined arc shape.

To gain further information, refer to the URL at the beginning of this section, which details a number of shape attributes and shape sub-elements that can create extremely complex outputs. For now, however, let's look at some examples of VML in action.

An Oval Shape

The following example creates an oval shape:

```
<html xmlns:vml="urn:schemas-microsoft-com:vml"
      xmlns="http://www.w3.org/TR/REC-html40">
   <head>
      <style>
         vml\:* {behavior:url(#default#VML);}
      </style>
   </head>
   <body>
      Demonstration of a VML Oval shape
      <p>
         <vml:oval fillcolor="red" style="width:200;height:100" />
      </p>
   </body>
</html>
```

Creating an oval is quite simple – we use the vml namespace and <oval> element. We must specify width and height for the vector, but fillcolor is optional, though here we have set it to red. The output is as shown:

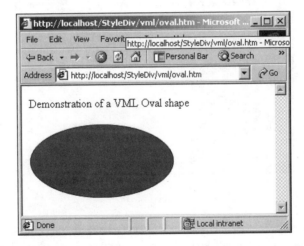

Gradient and Shadow

We can also apply gradients and shadows to VML elements, as is illustrated in the following example, which creates a rectangle with a yellow to green color and an embossed shadow:

```
<html xmlns:vml="urn:schemas-microsoft-com:vml"
      xmlns="http://www.w3.org/TR/REC-html40">
   <head>
      <style>
         vml\:* {behavior:url(#default#VML);}
      </style>
```

```
        </head>
        <body>
            Demonstration of a VML Shadow and Gradient
            <p>
                <vml:rect style="height:100px;WIDTH:100px" fillcolor="yellow"
                        strokecolor="green">
                <vml:shadow on="true" type="emboss" offset="5pt,5pt"/>
                <vml:fill type="gradient" color2="green" angle="90"/>
                </vml:rect>
            </p>
        </body>
    </html>
```

Here we use the `<vml:rect>` element with the mandatory `width` and `height` properties set and a fill color of `yellow`. The `strokecolour` determines the color that the shape should be outlined in, which we have specified here as `green`. The `<vml:shadow>` element should be a child element of the `<shape>` element it applies to, and we specify it should be embossed. The `offset` attribute takes an (x,y) coordinate saying how far on from the coordinates of the parent shape the shadow will be drawn. Also, the `<fill>` element must be a child of the element it applies to – in this case we set its `type` to be a `gradient` change to the `color2` attribute at a right angle of 90 degrees to the coordinates. The output is as shown:

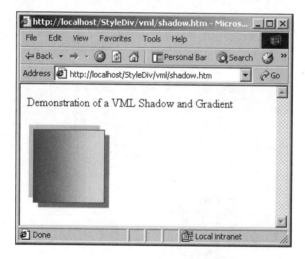

Logo Example

The following example shows how an advanced logo could be created using only VML. It makes use of several VML elements and properties to illustrate how advanced graphics can be created. The output is as shown:

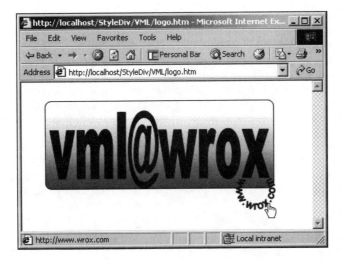

Some text is displayed on a background with more text at the bottom right, which also functions as a link to a specified URL. It is created by the code in `logo.htm`, below:

```html
<html xmlns:vml="urn:schemas-microsoft-com:vml"
      xmlns="http://www.w3.org/TR/REC-html40">
   <head>
      <style>
         vml\:* {behavior:url(#default#VML);}
      </style>
   </head>
   <body>
      <p>
      <vml:roundrect fillcolor="white"
                     style='position:absolute; margin-left:17.85pt;
                           margin-top:9pt;width:250pt; height:95pt'>
         <vml:fill type="gradient" color2="green" angle="180" />
      </vml:roundrect>
      <vml:shape fillcolor="black"
                 style='position:relative; margin-left:22pt;
                       margin-top:19pt;width:240pt;height:100pt'
                 coordsize="21600,21600"
                 path="m0,0l21600,0m0,21600l21600,21600e">
         <vml:path textpathok="true" />
         <vml:textpath on="true" fitpath="true" fitshape="true"
                       style='font-family:"Arial Black";'
                       string="vml@wrox" />
      </vml:shape>

      <vml:oval fillcolor="green"
                style='position:absolute;
                      left:238pt;top:100pt;width:35pt;height:35pt'
                href="http://www.wrox.com" target="_new">
         <vml:path textpathok="true" />
         <vml:textpath on="true" style='font-family:"Arial";'
                       string="www.wrox.com" />
      </vml:oval>
      </p>
   </body>
</html>
```

349

A rounded rectangle is initially created in document order, which means it will sit at the back of the display. It is given a `fillcolor` of `black` and uses absolute positioning. A child element uses a gradient `green` fill to gradually change from black to green at 180 degrees to the initial position (from top to bottom). Next is a `<vml:shape>` element which is actually used to create the text, and a `<vml:path>` element, which has to be a child element, is used to state that the `textpath` that will display the text is to be shown. The `<vml:textpath>` element is used to render the text in the `string` attribute (`vml@wrox` in our case). The `fitpath` and `fitshape` attributes tell IE whether the text should be rendered exactly within the shape or whether it can overlap the boundaries if necessary.

Finally, an `<oval>` element is defined. It has an `href` attribute with a target of `"_new"`, which will open a new browser window at the specified URI when clicked (like an HTML anchor tag). We can then specify that a text string should be used in the shape of the oval – this effectively replaces a basic oval shape with the specified string, `"www.wrox.com"`, taking the form of an oval.

We have touched on VML and in fact this subject could be a book itself. If you are interested in using vector graphics, then make sure you follow what is happening with Microsoft at http://msdn.microsoft.com/workshop/author/vml/default.asp and more widely at http://www.w3c.org/svg.

Scalable Vector Graphics

> **To run this example, you must download and install the Adobe SVG Viewer version 3.0 from http://www.adobe.com/svg/viewer/install/main.html.**

We aren't going to discuss SVG in detail within this chapter mainly because it's not directly supported by any browsers yet. However, it will become very important and so we will demonstrate how it can be used with a short example. The example demonstrates the fictional Wrox homepage for Scalable Vector Graphics.

The SVG file is shown below (`wrox.svg` in the code download):

```
<?xml version="1.0"?>
<?xml-stylesheet href="svg.css" type="text/css" ?>
<!DOCTYPE svg PUBLIC "-//W3C//DTD SVG 20001102//EN"
                     "http://www.w3.org/TR/2000/03/WD-SVG-20000303/DTD/svg-
                      20000303-stylable.dtd">
<svg width="400" height="300">
   <rect class="sidebar" x="0" y="0" width="20" height="300"/>
   <rect class="topbar" x="0" y="0" width="400" height="60" />
   <g>
   <ellipse class="logobackground" cx="55" cy="25" rx="140" ry="70" />
   <text class="logo" x="0" y="50">svg@wrox</text>
   <text class="logolink">
      <a xlink:href="http://www.wrox.com">
      <text x="50" y="70">www.wrox.com</text></a>
   </text>
   </g>
   <g>
   <rect class="displaycenter" x="100" y="100" width="200" height="150"/>
   <text class="maintext" x="110" y="110" dy="1.5em">
   <tspan x="110" style="stroke:white;">
   Welcome to the Wrox SVG site.
```

```
      </tspan>
      <tspan x="110" dy="2em">
      We provide great articles on SVG
      </tspan>
      <tspan x="110" dy="1em">
      graphics, as well as VML.
      </tspan>
      <tspan x="110" dy="2em">
      So make sure you visit
      </tspan>
      <tspan x="110" dy="1em">
      graphics, so make sure you visit
      </tspan>
      <tspan x="110" dy="1em">
      us at <a xlink:href="http://www.wrox.com">http://www.wrox.com</a>
      </tspan>
      </text>
      <rect x="110" y="220" width="180" height="20" style="fill:darkblue;"/>
      <text class="subtext" x="145" y="235">www.wrox.com</text>
      </g>
   </svg>
```

The DOCTYPE declaration should be used to indicate to the parser that this is an SVG compliant document:

```
<!DOCTYPE svg PUBLIC "-//W3C//DTD SVG 20001102//EN"
                "http://www.w3.org/TR/2000/03/WD-SVG-20000303/DTD/svg-
                20000303-stylable.dtd">
```

The <svg> root element should define the width and height of the canvas that the SVG will be placed onto – an example is width="800" and height="600" for an 800x600 size screen.

```
<svg width="400" height="300">
```

The <rect> element allows the definition of a rectangle (like the <rect> element in VML) and we need to define the x and y coordinates of where this should be placed – it is also useful to define the width and height attributes if we want to strictly control the rectangle (rather than it just using the remainder of the available canvas).

```
<rect class="sidebar" x="0" y="0" width="20" height="300"/>
```

The <g> element is commonly used to group a set of element definitions into one set, similar to how a <div> tag works in HTML.

```
<g>
<ellipse class="logobackground" cx="55" cy="25" rx="140" ry="70" />
<text class="logo" x="0" y="50">svg@wrox</text>
<text class="logolink">
    <a xlink:href="http://www.wrox.com">
    <text x="50" y="70">www.wrox.com</text></a>
</text>
</g>
```

In the above fragment, we can also see an example of an `<ellipse>` definition (like a VML `<oval>` element) and a `<text>` element. The `<text>` element is very common and can contain other `<text>` elements. In the example above, a link is also placed in the page – SVG uses XLink mechanisms, but this isn't dramatically different from a normal HTML anchor tag.

Within the text element, it is very important to use the `<tspan>` element. When text is added, it starts at the coordinates of the parent `<text>` element. When using the `tspan` element, we can generate multiple lines of text using the `dy` attribute, which is the "y differential" – that is, how much to add to the previous `tspan` y position. The example above shows how to create multiple lines of text within a formatted SVG rectangle using the `<rect>`, `<text>`, and `<tspan>` elements.

This SVG file actually uses a CSS file for styling it (as you can see in the processing instruction for the element) and this is shown below. Notice how we use the combination of the XML element tag name and then a period (".") followed by the class name as defined in the XML document, to apply the relevant styling (`svg.css` in the code download):

```
text.logo {font-size:30;fill:green;stroke:green;}

text.logolink {font-size:15;fill:green;stroke:red;}

rect.displaycenter {fill:blue;stroke:black;stroke-width:3;}

text.maintext {font-size:12;fill:green;stroke:black;font-weight:normal;
    font-family: Arial,sans-serif}

ellipse.logobackground {stroke:green; fill:black;}

rect.sidebar {fill:grey;}

rect.topbar {fill:green;}

text.subtext {font-size:15;stroke:yellow;}
```

Notice how the `stroke` and `fill` attributes are used to determine the color and background of the SVG elements. Finally, the output is shown below – remember the entire content of the SVG is from XML, so an XSLT stylesheet could be applied to generate this output where desired.

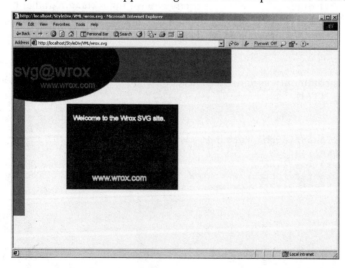

Summary

We have covered quite a few subjects in this chapter. We first looked at how Cascading Style Sheets can be integrated into an application, with a comparison of their advantages and disadvantages against XSLT. We considered when each may or may not be chosen over the other. You will have learned from this that it is very common to integrate them both.

The ability to integrate CSS directly with XML was discussed and demonstrated and you will have learned how to use the HTML namespace and how to overcome CSS limitations with client scripting. This led to a discussion of how CSS can be integrated with XSLT to produce sophisticated output for web applications. We covered element-level, page-level, and external CSS integration, as well as how DHTML can be generated in the XSLT output.

Element behaviors are a *very* useful client-side addition, and we discussed how code can be encapsulated using these and then used within web pages. We also discussed DHTML behaviors and how viewLinkContent can be used to prevent our element behaviors from being dynamically modified.

Finally, we saw how these behaviors are used within the Vector Markup Language to produce fast downloading and dynamic graphics. Some basic examples were demonstrated using VML, and there was a brief introduction to what can be done with Scalable Vector Graphics, which is the future for web graphics.

In the next chapter we'll meet a couple of other technologies which are still at a very early stage of development, and show how to emulate some of their functionality with MSXML.

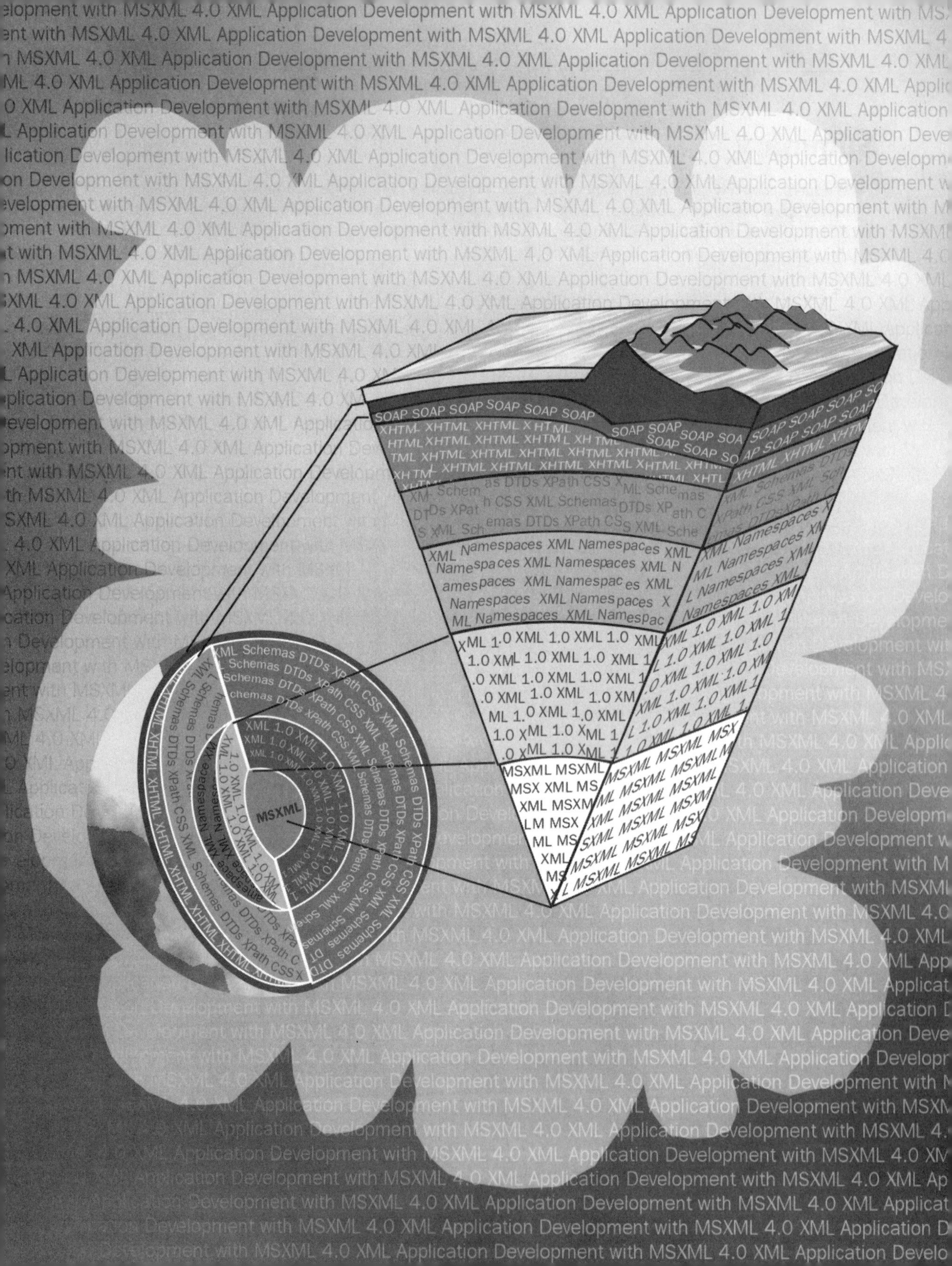
XML Application Development with MSXML 4.0
SOAP
XHTML
XML Schemas DTDs XPath CSS
XML Namespaces
XML 1.0
MSXML

8

Linking and Pointing

In this chapter we shall be looking at some of the technologies that allow us to define links between XML documents and to identify arbitrary parts of XML documents. More accurately, we will be looking at the specifications of technologies that will *one day* allow us to perform these operations, as the technologies we'll be looking at are at the cutting edge of web development, and though there are reasonably solid specifications for these technologies, implementations are few and far between.

The technologies in question are XLink and XPointer, and we will briefly be looking at RDF as well. This is a practical book, and so rather than having just a rehash of the specifications, we begin by reviewing each to get a picture of the ideas behind it. We then have a look at some scripts showing how we can emulate the functionality of these, as yet unsupported, specifications in MSXML.

The code presented in this chapter is that of an exploratory prototype, which approximates some of the functionality of a web annotation system developed by the W3C. The intention is not to present a complete application, with polished code, but to suggest how some of the ideas of linking and pointing might be approached to create novel applications using MSXML.

Introduction to Linking and Pointing Technologies

In this section we'll briefly describe the aims of each of the technologies currently under development, and show what kinds of functionality they will eventually offer. At present they are not supported in MSXML but, as we'll see later, we can achieve some of the same goals using those technologies that *are* supported.

Extending XPath: XPointer

A **pointer**, in the context of XML, is a means of locating a place in a document. If we have two pointers, we can identify a specific section of a document. We saw in Chapter 2 how the DOM could be addressed programmatically to locate a particular part of a document, and in Chapters 4 and 5 we saw how XPath could do the same. Both approaches even allow us to pick out a series of sections based on various criteria – directly coded using DOM methods, or through XPath within XSLT.DOM and XPath are extremely useful, but have limitations. Probably the most significant of these is the level of granularity available. Let's look at what is meant by this.

What Your Browser Doesn't Understand

The Document Object Model is found within most browsers and, augmented with XPath facilities supplied by tools like MSXML, provides a versatile, reasonably consistent, and straightforward system for manipulating documents. Take a piece of XHTML source:

```
<p>It will be necessary to identify <i>fragments</i> of the document, with more
detail than may be specified using XPath.</p>
```

Viewed in a browser we see:

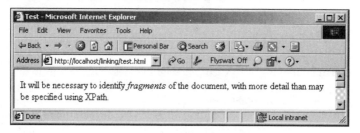

The way the DOM sees this is:

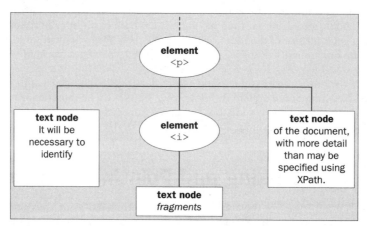

We can pick up the text in italics either by means of node objects, for instance along the lines of:

```
nodesInParagraph = pNode.childNodes;
for(var i = 0; i< nodesInParagraph.length; i++){
    if(nodesInParagraph.item(i).nodeName == "i") break;
}
var text = node.text;
```

or by using XPath; again with JScript, we could simply use:

```
var node = pNode.selectSingleNode("/i");
var text = node.text;
```

However, say we want to pick up the part of the text highlighted in bold below:

It will be necessary **to identify** *frag*ments of the document, with more detail than may be specified using XPath.

Using just XPath on its own we can't. As we will see later on, there is at least one way of hacking this requirement using DOM and XPath, together with additional script. However, this is a general limitation of XPath and so it makes sense to look for a *general* solution. The general solution takes the form of another Specification, XPointer.

Points, Ranges, and Locations

Points, ranges, and locations are three terms that form the foundations of **XPointer**. In the interests of formality, the W3C specifications base their definitions on extreme cross-reference, and making sense of their documentation can often be difficult. In actual fact, treated informally the concepts are perfectly straightforward.

A **point** is a place in a document before or after a particular character. We might have a space between two words in a sentence, but to manipulate the text it is useful to differentiate between the place after the last letter in the first word (before the space) and the place before the second word in the sentence (the point after the space). Most word processors show the cursor as a vertical line between character locations; that cursor refers to a point.

The document model deals with nodes, and so the place immediately before or after a node can also be described as a point. The specification actually talks about a point being the 'gap', the place between two characters (a **character point**) or between two nodes (a **node point**).

A **range** is the 'stuff' between two points, and it doesn't matter where those points are within a document – the stuff doesn't have to make well-formed sense. There are a couple of essential criteria for a range though – the start and end points have to be in the same document and the start point *must* come before the end point. These criteria shouldn't be too difficult to uphold, as in practice most of the time we deal with one document at a time, and a rule of thumb in reality is that the end generally comes after the start!

The third key definition is that of a **location**. XPointer builds on the ideas of XPath, and within XPath there are the following nodes:

- ❏ root nodes
- ❏ element nodes
- ❏ text nodes

- ❏ attribute nodes
- ❏ namespace nodes
- ❏ processing instruction nodes
- ❏ comment nodes

An XPointer location is one of the above *or* one of these:

- ❏ points
- ❏ ranges

Following through from this, XPointer also has the notion of a **location-set**, which is like the node-set we might get back from running an XPath expression over a document, but could also include points and ranges.

Beyond the Hyperlink: XLink

The **XML Linking Language** (**XLink**) became a W3C Recommendation in June 2001. The comparatively recent arrival of this specification is a little ironic, as the basic characteristics of XLink date back to the origins of hypertext. What the specification describes is a generalization and formalization of document linking, providing a framework that features flexibility far beyond that of HTML hyperlinks. We are all used to a link being a thing that sits behind a piece of text or an image on a web page, waiting humbly for someone to browse along and click on it to visit another page. An XLink is not so shy – it doesn't have to go in one direction, because it has a more versatile role than that of an HTML link. An XLink can describe a link between resources, be they documents, nodes, elements, or pretty much anything that is identifiable. It isn't limited to one resource at either end either.

Linking and Pointing in Practice

So far we have been discussing specifications that have been developed for pointing and linking; now we will consider a practical application, which incorporates some of these ideas. We will look at one particular system and see how we might start to emulate some of its functionality with JScript and MSXML.

Annotation: An Application of Linking

One of the major drawbacks of the Web as it stands is that the information it presents is predominantly read-only. Even so, it is relatively straightforward to add content – there are tools available to hide the technicalities of HTML and FTP, so designing and uploading material only requires basic computer literacy. Nevertheless, content isn't everything – there is also structure to consider. To some extent structure can be written in the form of hyperlinks specified inside pages, but this still means working within narrow boundaries of how information can be represented and presented. What if you come across page X that states categorically something that you know to be false? Of course it would be possible for you to write and publish your own page, providing the evidence that unquestionably refutes page X's suggestions, but then how would anyone reading page X know about the existence of your rock-solid arguments? One answer is **annotations**.

We will now look at an existing annotation system and then go on to see how we might create our own.

Annotea and Amaya

Annotea (`http://www.w3.org/2001/Annotea/`) is a project that forms part of the W3C's efforts to take the Web to its next level of evolution – the "Semantic Web". The semantics in question will appear in the form of meta data, and linking technologies can supply meta data describing the relationships between entities on the Web. An Annotea implementation will consist of clients, usually web browsers, and one or more servers that act primarily as link databases. The client will allow the user to identify a particular area of a web page and enter their annotation. This information will be sent to an Annotea server, which will record the identified page area and the annotation. At present Annotea is fairly experimental, but it is clear that this kind of collaborative facility has a lot of potential wherever people need to discuss documents, be it on the web or on a company's local intranet.

For reasons we shall see soon enough, there are very few browsers which support annotations. Not surprisingly, the browser developed by the W3C for testing new technologies, **Amaya**, has this support (free download from `http://www.w3.org/Amaya/`). In the view below, the word 'XPath' has had an annotation attached, signified by the pencil icon:

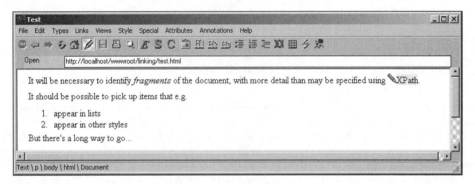

This is done by selecting the text with the mouse in the usual fashion, clicking the Annotations menu, and selecting Annotate selection. When this option is selected, a window with a box in it appears, like this:

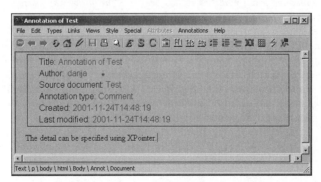

The box in the window contains information about the annotation, and the note itself: "The detail can be specified using XPointer" has been added by the user. When this annotation is saved (using File I Save), the information will either be stored locally or posted to a remote Annotea server, depending on the configuration.

The information that the system deals with is shown in this diagram:

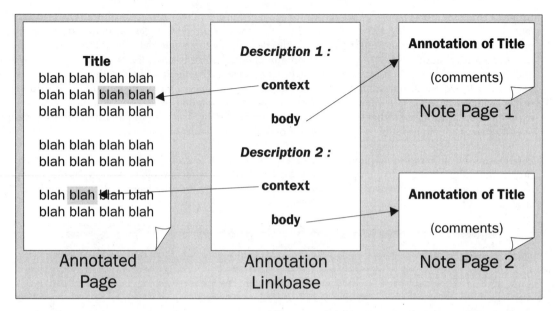

Here two annotations have been added to the page on the left, the text of which is contained in two separate pages on the right. The meta data that links the original page and the annotations is maintained in another location, labeled Annotation Linkbase above. The links are not given in-line in the page, as we usually see in web pages, instead they are held out-of-line in a completely separate document. The key parts of the meta data are the **context** and **body** of each annotation. The body refers to the note itself, containing whatever the user chose to type. The context is the location of the data that is being annotated, that is, the area that was selected on the original document.

The page that is annotated is not modified in this process – one of the major benefits of this kind of system is that notes can refer to existing, read-only documents.

To view existing annotations with Amaya, you begin by navigating to the page of interest in the normal fashion. Selecting Load annotations from the Annotations menu will then pick up any annotations recorded on the servers for which Amaya is configured. Pencil icons will appear on screen, corresponding to the annotations, and clicking on an individual pencil will highlight the text to which the annotation refers, in the same fashion as shown in the first screenshot above. Double-clicking on the pencil icon will bring up a separate window containing the note:

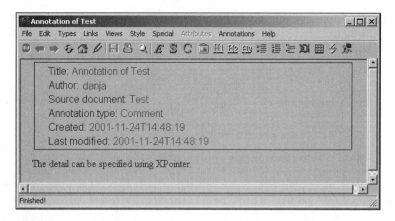

Linking Meta Data

When the annotation was added for the screenshots above, because Amaya was configured to store annotations locally (the default), two files were created in the Amaya user directory (<*windir*>/profiles/<*username*>/amaya). One of these files simply contains the note itself, wrapped in HTML. The other contains the linking information, wrapped in RDF/XML. Before we take a look at the link file, we will have a quick review of its format.

RDF

The **Resource Description Framework** (**RDF**) is another W3C creation, and is the focus of the "Semantic Web" vision. Unfortunately RDF has gained something of a reputation for being complicated. To a small extent this reputation is deserved, as the framework attempts to bridge the canyon between the theoretical world of mathematical logic and the 'real' world of web protocols and languages, and in the process often bewilders people on either side of the gap. However, like most technologies, RDF can be used on a need-to-know basis, and for the purposes of this chapter a few paragraphs will be enough to see how the linking information of Annotea is expressed.

> *RDF is covered extensively in the Wrox Press book "Professional XML Meta Data" (ISBN 1-861004-51-6) and the specifications and many other documents can be found on the Web, linked from http://www.w3.org/RDF.*

The key to RDF is the concept of a **resource**. A resource is anything that can be identified by means of a **URI** (**Uniform Resource Identifier**). A URI can be seen as a more general case of the URL in which the identifier doesn't necessarily refer to the access mechanism (such as HTTP). In other words it doesn't have to be a real address as it is only used for unique identification. Thus a resource can be virtually anything: a web page, a book, a person, a company, a place, a time, or even a process. As long as a suitable means is available to uniquely identify something, it can be a resource.

The descriptions of the Resource Description Framework are made up of **subject-predicate-object statements,** where the subject is the resource being described, the predicate is a *property* of the resource, and the object is the *value* of that property. The first example in the RDF Specifications (in the "Model and Syntax" Recommendation) is the sentence:

"Ora Lassila is the creator of the resource http://www.w3.org/Home/Lassila".

In this statement the subject is the resource "`http://www.w3.org/Home/Lassila`", the predicate/property is "`creator`", and the object is "`Ora Lassila`". The primary syntax of RDF uses XML, and the above could be expressed in RDF/XML as follows:

```
<rdf:RDF>
    <rdf:Description about="http://www.w3.org/Home/Lassila">
        <dc:creator>Ora Lassila</dc:creator>
    </rdf:Description>
</rdf:RDF>
```

The RDF XML syntax isn't intended for human consumption, but it is reasonably clear in this example that the resource the description is about is "`http://www.w3.org/Home/Lassila`", and the creator is specified in the child element. The `rdf:` and `dc:` prefixes refer to XML namespace declarations which we'll come to in a moment, omitted here for clarity. This example is in fact a slightly special case, where the name "Ora Lassila" is given literally. The subject of an RDF statement will always be an identified resource, whereas the object may either be an RDF literal, a primitive XML datatype (in this case a string), or more commonly another RDF resource. We might, for example, prefer to refer to `Ora` by using the URL of his online biography as a URI, and replace the nested element above with something like:

```
<dc:creator rdf:resource="http://www.w3.org/Home/Lassila/biography.html"/>
```

If we are able to make a statement like "*Ora Lassila is the creator of the resource http://www.w3.org/Home/Lassila*", then we have the information needed to answer queries like: "*Who is the creator of the resource http://www.w3.org/Home/Lassila?*" and "*What has Ora Lassila created?*" Of course, as humans we are in a good position to know what is meant by terms such as "creator" and can guess that "Ora Lassila" is probably the name of a person, quite possibly of Finnish descent. If we see two sentences including the same term we can usually tell from the context whether or not the term has the same meaning in each, so we could tell that, for example, in a religious book the word "Creator" would have rather different connotations than those above.

The terms used in an RDF document are qualified using XML namespaces, so for instance the term "creator" can be found in the Dublin Core namespace, and the example above should contain a declaration for this, along with the other namespace used, the RDF namespace. So the first line of the example becomes:

```
<rdf:RDF xmlns:rdf="http://www.w3.org/1999/02/22-rdf-syntax-ns#"
         xmlns:dc="http://purl.org/dc/elements/1.1/ ">
```

Namespaces in RDF are used as identifiers, so there is no reason to expect that typing the URI into a browser will bring up anything particularly interesting, or even anything at all. As it happens, there is a URL: http://purl.org/dc/elements/1.0/, which refers to a page containing the following information:

Label: Creator
The person or organization primarily responsible for creating the intellectual content of the resource. For example, authors in the case of written documents, artists, photographers, or illustrators in the case of visual resources.

The Dublin Core vocabulary in fact defines terms that are primarily used in bibliographical databases – other terms include "title", "subject", and "publisher", though the Dublin Core Metadata Initiative itself (http://dublincore.org/) goes further, aiming to promote meta data standards to facilitate more intelligent information systems.

The human definition of "creator" in Dublin Core is quite clear, but human language is often ambiguous, and ideally we want our vocabularies in a form that machines will feel comfortable with. The W3C addressed these issues by providing an extensible mechanism for defining vocabularies of standard terms. This mechanism is described in the RDF Schema Specification.

RDF Schemas, as described in the W3C Recommendation at http://www.w3.org/TR/rdf-schema, should not be confused with XML Schemas, described in Chapter 3 of this book.

RDF Schemas are themselves defined using RDF (Dublin Core's is at http://dublincore.org/documents/dcq-rdf-xml/); here is a snippet from the W3C's RDF Schema for annotations:

```
<rdf:Property rdf:about="http://www.w3.org/2000/10/annotation-ns#annotates">
    <rdfs:label xml:lang="en">annotates</rdfs:label>
    <rdfs:comment>Relates an Annotation to the resource to which the
                 Annotation applies. The inverse relation is
                 'hasAnnotation'
    </rdfs:comment>
    <rdfs:isDefinedBy resource="http://www.w3.org/2000/10/annotation-ns#"/>
</rdf:Property>
```

It's tempting to start believing that RDF really *is* complicated, but the concepts in this snippet are straightforward, only obscured somewhat by an indigestible syntax. The first line tells us that we are talking about "`http://www.w3.org/2000/10/annotation-ns#annotates`", which is an `rdf:Property`. An `rdf:Property` is defined in the RDF Model and Syntax Recommendation (hence the `rdf:` prefix) and is simply a resource that is also a property. The contained elements here come from the RDF Schemas namespace, and are used to define properties of this resource. The first is a human-readable label for the resource (`rdfs:label`), with an attribute qualifying the (human) language, then we have a human-readable comment (`rdfs:comment`). Both of these are defined as RDF literals, in other words XML elements with text content. The property `rdfs:isDefinedBy` refers to a resource (strictly speaking, the attribute `resource` should be namespace qualified, that is `rdf:resource`). This rather reflexive property explicitly states where the namespace, in which this term is defined, is located.

The annotations RDF Schema contains a dozen or so terms, each defined in a similar manner to the above snippet. A major benefit of defining terms in this fashion is that when such a term is used elsewhere, it is tied to a single point. There can be little doubt that two documents that refer to "`http://www.w3.org/2000/10/annotation-ns#annotates`" are talking about the same thing. As the term has associated meaning, computers can describe and reason about resources using reasonably unambiguous semantics.

The phrase "need-to-know" was used a couple of pages ago, and we are now in danger of overstepping the mark. Before looking at the annotations file, there is one more idea we need from the RDF model: *anonymous* resources. To minimize the risk of further darkening RDF's reputation, here is a fairytale analogy. When the Three bears returned home, Mother Bear exclaimed: "Someone's been eating my porridge!" Father Bear also exclaimed: "Someone's been eating my porridge!" Based on the bears' statements, we know we are talking about two resources, which we can refer to using a unique naming scheme such as `bearfood://mothers/porridge` and `bearfood://fathers/porridge`. We know that something ate them, and conveniently the property `ate` is defined in the (made up) `tb` vocabulary. We also know that *someone* ate these resources, and there is a class `person` defined in the `foaf` vocabulary (made up elsewhere) that we can use within an RDF statement to express this fact. So, loosely transcribing this information into RDF/XML we have:

```
<rdf:Description>
    <tb:ate rdf:resource="bearfood://mothers/porridge" />
    <tb:ate rdf:resource="bearfood://fathers/porridge" />
    <rdf:type resource="http://xmlns.com/foaf/0.1#person" />
</rdf:Description>
```

The *someone* described here is an anonymous resource. In the fairytale world of the Semantic Web, the information here may be logically combined with facts from another source (for example: http://www.hiyah.com/library/goldilocks.html) that describes a young girl who is fond of porridge, to yield an RDF statement beginning:

```
<rdf:Description rdf:about="Goldilocks">
```

At present systems to provide this kind of functionality are generally at an experimental stage, but techniques for logical reasoning with computers have been around for decades, and it is only a matter of time before these are assimilated into the web environment.

Annotations Link File

When an annotation was added to a document, as seen in the screenshots earlier, an XML file was generated by Amaya. It begins with the standard XML processing instruction, then the namespace declarations:

```
<?xml version="1.0" ?>
<r:RDF xmlns:r="http://www.w3.org/1999/02/22-rdf-syntax-ns#"
       xmlns:a="http://www.w3.org/2000/10/annotation-ns#"
       xmlns:http="http://www.w3.org/1999/xx/http#"
       xmlns:d="http://purl.org/dc/elements/1.0/">
```

In this document the r: prefix will refer to the RDF namespace, which contains the basic terms that are likely to be needed in an RDF representation (usually the prefix rdf: is used instead, but the meaning is the same). The a: prefix will refer to terms in the W3C annotations vocabulary, http: to the eponymous vocabulary from the W3C (which isn't actually used in the file listed here), and d: to the Dublin Core vocabulary we encountered before the bears.

The 'meaningful' body of the file is contained in an <r:Description> element without an about attribute – the annotation is an anonymous resource. Though it is likely that any processor that will use this information in a sophisticated, semantic fashion will ascribe an ID or temporary name to the resource, the nature of the annotation is carried by the resources to which it relates, and no explicit identification is required.

```
<r:Description>
<r:type resource="http://www.w3.org/2000/10/annotation-ns#Annotation" />
<r:type resource="http://www.w3.org/2000/10/annotationType#Comment" />
```

The first two elements come from RDF core – they state that this resource is in the class of resources identified as Annotation in the annotations space, and also that it is in the class of Comment in another space. The benefits of the way the information is carried in the latter is debatable; arguably this would be better expressed giving a property of annotationType and a value of Comment. The next element leaves no doubt:

```
<a:annotates r:resource="file://C:\Inetpub\wwwroot\linking\test.xml" />
```

We saw the RDF Schema definition of annotates earlier. Here it is used to say that the thing that is being annotated by this resource can be identified as "file://C:\Inetpub\wwwroot\linking\test.xml", and this identifier happens to be usable on a Windows machine to locate a particular file.

Now things start getting really interesting:

```
<a:context>file://C:\Inetpub\wwwroot\linking\test.xml#xpointer(string-
            range(/html[1]/body[1]/p[1],"",106,5))
</a:context>
```

The context refers to the thing being annotated – specifically the five characters reading from character number 106 into the first paragraph in the body of the HTML document `test.xml`. Referring back to the Amaya screenshots, this is the piece of highlighted text, the word 'XPath'. The excitement of the last element was a little premature, as the next few lines are rather dull:

```
<d:title>Annotation of Test</d:title>
<d:creator>danja</d:creator>
<a:created>2001-11-24T14:48:19</a:created>
<d:date>2001-11-24T15:12:11</d:date>
```

The `d:` prefix refers to Dublin Core, and using this vocabulary we have literals giving the title of this (anonymous) resource, the creator/author of the annotation, and the date/time when this annotation was last edited. The `a:created` element contains the date/time at which the annotation was first created.

The last piece of information about the annotation resource gives the location of the HTML file containing the note itself. Because of the configuration settings used with Amaya this again is on the local file system, the filename having been decided by the Amaya application when the note was created:

```
<a:body r:resource= "file://E:\WINNT\profiles\danny\amaya\
                     annotations\annots1h4.2.html"/>
```

To wrap things up, we have the closing tags for this description element and the RDF document:

```
</r:Description>
</r:RDF>
```

Re-engineering with MSXML

The aim in this section will be to see how to develop a system that can provide the same kind of annotation functionality as Amaya but using a standard browser such as IE on the client-side and ASP plus MSXML on the server-side. If we use the W3C's annotation implementation as a model, then anything we come up with will stand a good chance of being interoperable with standard systems later on. So, we have seen the user interface and the kind of link information file that Amaya uses. From this we can derive a requirements specification for an annotation system of our own. We need to:

❑   Provide a mechanism by which the user can identify specific text in a document.

❑   Provide a mechanism by which the user can enter the text of their note.

❑   Generate an HTML page containing the text of the note.

❑   Generate a file containing the linking information.

❑   Provide a means of viewing annotations on a page.

The second item on the list should be trivial – getting text off the user is a common requirement in web-based systems. Though it's relatively easy to build and save a text file, from what we've seen of MSXML the third item will certainly be trivial if we use XHTML for the note file, so we can build and save the document using a DOM object. At first sight the fourth item might seem daunting if we are to use the same format as Amaya – after all, *RDF is complicated*. However, if we view RDF as simply being a particular XML format in which we are going to store the information, the task appears a lot more straightforward – all we need to do is build an XML file with the same structure as those used by Amaya. The fact that the end result will be RDF is fairly irrelevant, we only need to deal with the semantics contained in the RDF model as it directly relates to our application. We are only using the file to store a handful of simple pieces of data which our application will generate (and later read), so in other words all we need to do is build an arbitrary DOM tree. The first and final items on the list are rather more demanding.

Existing Clients

At the time of writing, the W3C site lists four client systems that are compatible with Annotea, and to get a handle on how others have approached the task of providing such systems it is worth having a quick review of these. The first client listed is Amaya, a browser designed and built from scratch by the W3C. The others are:

❑   **Annozilla** (http://annozilla.mozdev.org/) – a project to give the Mozilla browser (on which Netscape is based) an annotation facility. The functionality will be built in at a native level.

❑   **Snufkin** browser (http://jibbering.com/snufkin.html) – essentially a package of scripts that extend the functionality of Internet Explorer 5, which uses a third-party ActiveX component to receive native browser events. In other words, IE is extended at an application level.

❑   **Interfacing Annotea Via JavaScript** (document level) (http://www.w3.org/2001/Annotea/Bookmarklet/Annotea-JavaScript.html) – rather than being a client as such, this is an experimental interface with Annotea, designed to allow annotations to be used with any standard JavaScript-capable browser. First impressions might be that this is exactly what we are thinking of building here. As it happens, this system has two quite significant drawbacks – only document-level annotations are possible, and the system uses a Java servlet to interface between the browser and the Annotea server.

Effectively then, either existing clients are browsers "souped-up" at an internal application level, or they only provide limited capabilities (and still require additional external interfacing).

A Prototype Annotation System

We have restricted ourselves to a standard browser and whatever scripting MSXML can offer us, so returning to the first item on our list of requirements, how on earth can we provide a mechanism by which the user can identify specific text in a document? When we have someone else's web page in our browser window, our actions are quite limited – we can select text from the screen and paste it into another application, we can click on links which will take us to wherever has been preordained, but that's about it.

A good place to start is to pull the content of the web page into a space where we have some control, and in the context of MSXML the best place is an in-memory DOM tree. Once we have grabbed the data there is nothing to stop us manipulating the tree to make elements in the tree more interactive in the browser. We could just deal with the tree in a local browser, and if we want a collaborative system, upload the annotation data to a shared server. However, MSXML scripting is just as straightforward on the server-side as on the client-side, and usually it's easier to share things from a server than from a client so for this prototype application we'll locate pretty much everything on a server.

If we take another look at the 'difficult' example we saw in the section describing linking technologies, we will see that things aren't as straightforward as they seem:

It will be necessary **to identify** *fragm*ents of the document, with more detail than may be specified using XPath.

Let's say we need to write code that will give us something interactive in the browser window. This interactive device would allow us to identify the highlighted area above. We can make areas of the text generate events, such as onClick and onMouseOver, but these areas have to be 'primed' to be able to generate these events – they have to be hyperlinks. So one approach might be to make everything on the screen capable of generating events, and as we want to be able to make selections down to the character level, this means making every character an individual hyperlink. Of course this wouldn't be too difficult to do with a script, though getting the right kind of behavior might take some time. This approach might potentially lead to a system as user-friendly as Amaya, but here we will take a much simpler approach based around HTML forms. The application is a demonstration of what can be done, and is just a prototype. Although it's fine for the purposes of the chapter it would need a lot more tweaking before it could be used seriously.

User Interface

An annotation system has two functional parts, one to allow the addition of annotations to a page and another to allow the viewing of the page and its annotations. In Amaya these are tightly integrated, but here we aren't delving into the internals of a browser and the result is that two parts are more distinct in the code. This is reflected in the user interface of the prototype system, and though it would be relatively straightforward to create a more unified UI it will be easier to understand the underlying operation with the creation and viewing of annotations kept separate.

In this system all the work will be done server-side, and the user interacts with the system using standard HTML forms and hyperlinked pages, most of which will be generated dynamically.

For the first functional part of the system (creating annotations) we begin by getting some initial information into the system. We need the location of the page we wish to annotate, the file in which we wish to store the annotation linking information, and as a little icing we will add the name of the person making the annotation. The initial form (first.htm) looks like this:

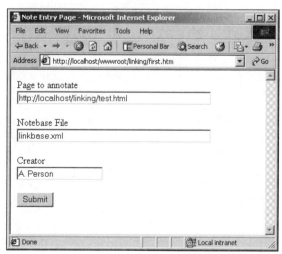

This page contains just a simple HTML form. Clicking on the button will submit the data to the server, which will respond by presenting the main user interface for adding annotations:

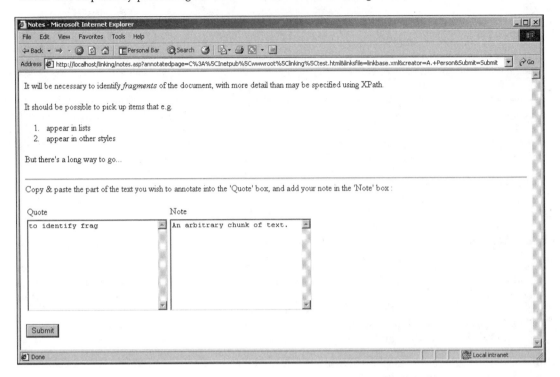

The material on this page above the horizontal line is the content of the file specified in the form above (`http://localhost/wwwroot/linking/test.html`), which is the page to be annotated. The source page has been loaded into an MSXML DOM object and pushed out using the `xml` property. The instructions immediately below the line explain how this minimally interactive way of specifying a particular section of text operates. The words "to identify *frag*" were selected out of the content displayed at the top of the window using the mouse, and copied and pasted into the form text area, which was marginally easier than typing them in, though this would have had the same end result. The right-hand text area contains the text that will be this user's annotation of the particular piece of text entered in the left-hand box. Clicking on the Submit button will cause the Quote and the Note to be read and recorded by the system, which will usually re-present this same view – source document on top, form below. If however the user had entered/pasted a piece of text that appears more than once in the document, there is a problem – how to tell which occurrence of the text the user wishes to annotate. The system deals with this by presenting another page, in effect asking the user to be more specific. Say for example the user wished to add a note to the word "appear" in the second list item. They will enter this word in the Quote box and their corresponding note in the Note box and then press the Submit button. The word appears twice, so the user would be presented with this view in the browser window:

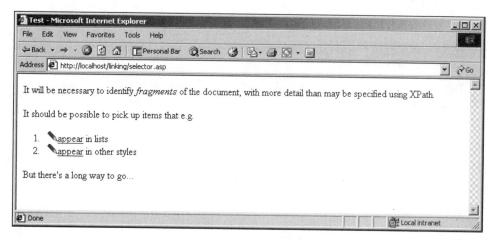

Here the two occurrences of the text are presented as hyperlinks (with a little pencil icon). Clicking on the required link will notify the system as to which occurrence of the word the user wants to add the note they entered in the preceding **Note** box. After clicking the link the user will again be presented with the main **Note** entry view as above – source document on top, form below.

The second part of the system deals with viewing a document that has been annotated. To get started a couple pieces of information are needed, so as before the prototype system uses a simple HTML (`browse.htm`) form to get this information off the user:

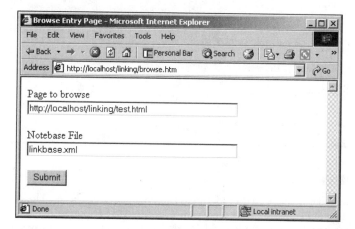

Clicking the button will take the user to a view of the annotated page:

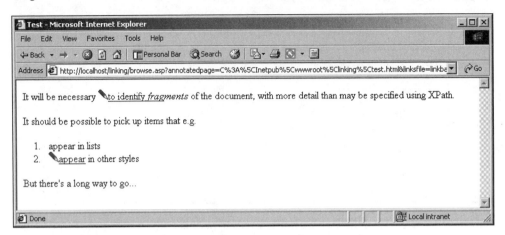

In this view any text that has associated annotations is delivered as a hyperlink. Clicking on a hyperlink will take the user to the annotation, so clicking on "to identify *frag*" will show the user the following in their browser window:

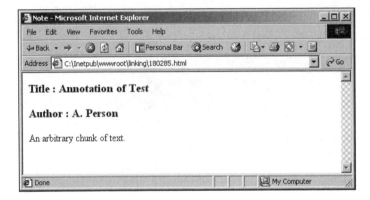

Code Overview

This prototype system has been written in JScript to run on an IIS web server. The code uses some operations (greedy regular expressions) that only appeared in MS Scripting Engine 5.5 (downloadable from http://www.microsoft.com/msdownload/vbscript/scripting.asp), so this must be available on the server, in addition to MSXML of course. There is quite a lot of script, and to prevent this getting out of hand (and also to facilitate reuse), most functionality is wrapped up into JScript objects. Though the operations for adding annotations to a page and viewing the annotations can be considered separate, there is actually a fair amount of code overlap. This is most notable where the annotation creation part displays a view of the source document with hyperlinks on multiple occurrences of a piece of text – the script at the core of this (markeddoc.asp) is exactly that at the core of the document viewing part of the application.

It is stressed that the system is presented only as an early prototype – significant parts of the functionality have been skipped in the interests of getting a feel for what is possible, rather than trying to create a complete, robust implementation.

The code used in this prototype application is contained in the files listed below. There are a lot of files, but most of these are fairly short scripts, each more or less handling a single piece of functionality:

- ❑ `first.htm` – HTML form used to get into the annotation-creation part of the system.

- ❑ `notes.asp` – Page for adding annotations to a document.

- ❑ `locator.asp` – Finds the occurrences of a text snippet (quote) in a DOM document, the locations expressed as XPointers.

- ❑ `selector.asp` – Displays repeated occurrences of a piece of text in a document as hyperlinks (clicking on a hyperlink identifies a particular occurrence).

- ❑ `makepointer.asp` – Functions for constructing simple XPointer expressions.

- ❑ `markeddoc.asp` – Creates an object that contains a DOM tree into which hyperlinks can be inserted according to XPointer expressions.

- ❑ `notenode.asp` – Represents a <Description> element in an RDF linkbase.

- ❑ `notewriter.asp` – Creates a linkbase file and allows the addition of annotation data.

- ❑ `textdoc.asp` – Contains two utility objects: `TextDocument` provides helper methods for accessing the text content of a DOM document and `TextBlock` for aligning pointers within a document fragment.

- ❑ `browse.htm` – HTML form used to get into the annotation page view part of the system.

- ❑ `browse.asp` – Presents an annotated page with items hyperlinked to the annotations.

- ❑ `pointexpr.asp` – Parses simple XPointer expressions.

- ❑ `notereader.asp` – Used for loading an annotations linkbase from disk.

- ❑ `tidygrab.asp` – Pulls an HTML file off the web and converts it into a local MSXML-readable XML file.

We will first look at the code used to create annotations, then the scripts used for browsing annotated documents, and finally the `tidygrab.asp` script which can be used for pre processing HTML documents.

Running the Application

To run the basic application all that is required is a standard IIS server with Scripting Engine 5.5 and MSXML installed, and any standard browser. Additional requirements for `tidygrab.asp` are given in the section at the end of this chapter which describes this script.

If the files listed above (available for download from http://www.wrox.com/) are placed in a subdirectory of the web server's root called \linking, then pointing a local browser at http://localhost/linking/first.htm will allow the creation of annotations and http://localhost/linking/browse.htm will allow the viewing of annotations.

Creating Annotations

The core code that is used to create annotations is found in four scripts, and the relationships between these files can be seen in the following diagram. As well as the ASP files, we have the page containing the form to get us into the system (first.htm). The page being annotated will have come from the Web (although in the discussion here it's on a local host for convenience). The main user interface, notes.asp, will pass information back to notewriter.asp, which will generate the file containing the linking information and the individual note files, shown shaded here. The script notenode.asp contains the code that will create an object representing one particular annotation.

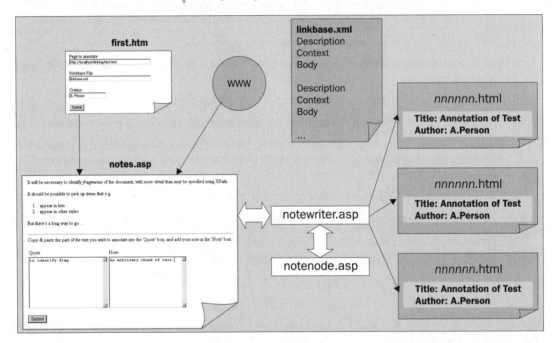

Several other scripts are involved in this part of the application (such as the code to handle multiple text occurrences in a document), but we will leave these for a moment in the interests of clarity.

Before we start on the scripts, we will set up a means of getting some initial information into the system. We need the location of the page we wish to annotate, the file in which we wish to store the annotation linking information, and the name of the person making the annotation. This is the initial form we saw earlier:

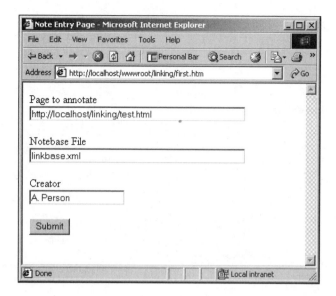

The code (`first.htm`) is straightforward:

```html
<html>
   <head>
      <title>Note Entry Page</title>
   </head>
   <body bgcolor="#FFFFFF" text="#000000">
      <form name="sourceForm" method="get" action="notes.asp">
         Page to annotate
         <br>
         <input type="text" name="annotatedpage"
                value="http://localhost/linking/test.html" size="50">
         <p>
            Notebase File
            <br>
            <input type="text" name="linksfile" value="linkbase.xml"
                   size="50">
         <p>
            Creator
            <br>
            <input type="text" name="creator" value="A. Person" size="20">
         <p>
            <input type="submit" name="Submit" value="Submit">
      </form>
   </body>
</html>
```

Note that for each text field we are supplying a default value – during development this makes life a lot easier.

We will now have a look at the source of `notes.asp` – the user interface for creating annotations, the code which displays the window we saw earlier with the source document on top, and Note and Quote boxes below. The code for `notes.asp` is in three main blocks – the first block reads the information supplied from the HTML entry form above. These details are loaded into the `Session` object provided by ASP, to maintain this information as long as a particular user is adding annotations.

```
<%@ LANGUAGE=JScript %>
<!-- #INCLUDE FILE="notewriter.asp" -->
<!-- #INCLUDE FILE="locator.asp" -->
<%
var sourceDoc;

if(!Session("initialized")){
   var strAnnotatedPageUrl =
      new String(Request.QueryString("annotatedpage"));
   sourceDoc = Server.CreateObject("MSXML2.DOMDocument.4.0");
   sourceDoc.async = false;
   sourceDoc.setProperty("ServerHTTPRequest", true);
   sourceDoc.load(unescape(strAnnotatedPageUrl));

   var linksFilename = Request.QueryString("linksfile");
   var noteWriter = new NoteWriter(linksFilename);
   noteWriter.setCreator(Request.QueryString("creator"));
   noteWriter.setAnnotatedPageUrl(strAnnotatedPageUrl);
   var titleNode = sourceDoc.documentElement.selectSingleNode(
                  "/html/head/title/text()");
   if(titleNode != null)
   noteWriter.setTitle(titleNode.nodeValue);

   Session("sourceDoc") = sourceDoc;
   Session("noteWriter") = noteWriter;
}
```

The variable `sourceDoc` is the `DOMDocument` object used to retain the page being annotated. A check is made to see if the `Session` object contains an entry for `"initialized"`; if so this block of code has been visited before and is skipped.

The name of the file to be annotated is picked up by `strAnnotatedPageUrl` from the data sent using the POST method in the initial entry form, and the `DOMDocument` is loaded from this location. The name of the file that will be used to hold link data is used to construct a `noteWriter` object (we'll be looking at this shortly). This object will be responsible for recording the annotations, and so the data passed from the initial entry form is passed into this object.

The `titleNode` variable picks up the contents of the <title> tags in the document being annotated, using an XPath expression. Once this has been passed to the `noteWriter` object, the `sourceDoc` DOM and `noteWriter` objects are placed in the `Session` object for safekeeping.

After its first loading, when the user has entered information in the Note and Quote boxes, `notes.asp` will call itself. The second section of `notes.asp` looks after this information, calling on methods in `notewriter.asp` to record the annotations:

```
else { // session already initialized
   var xpointer;
   var strNote;
   var oldNoteWriter = Session("noteWriter");
   noteWriter = new NoteWriter(oldNoteWriter.strLinkFilename);

   noteWriter.strAnnotatedPageUrl = oldNoteWriter.strAnnotatedPageUrl;
   noteWriter.strTitle = oldNoteWriter.strTitle;
   noteWriter.strCreator = oldNoteWriter.strCreator;

   if(Session("selecting") != true){ // normal circumstances
      var strQuote = new String(Request.Form("quote"));
```

```
        strNote = new String(Request.Form("note"));
        var locator = new Locator(Session("sourceDoc"));
        var xpointers = locator.getLocations(strQuote);
```

The previous `noteWriter` is retrieved from the `Session` object, and a new `noteWriter` is created. This construction and the following lines, which copy properties from `oldNoteWriter`, are needed to work around a limitation of the `Session` object in JScript. We can pass objects into the `Session` object and when we retrieve them access their properties directly, but unfortunately their methods will no longer work.

The session variable `"selecting"` will be true if this page has been called from the page that handles multiple occurrences of the **Quote** text in the document. We will see how that part of the system operates later.

Whatever the user has entered in the **Quote** and **Note** boxes is placed in two new strings – `Request.Form("something")` is actually a reference, and further down the line we would hear complaints if these were passed instead of proper strings. The `getLocations` function in `location.asp` is called on to generate an array of XPointer (string) expressions using the source document and the **Quote** box string. If the **Quote** box text only appears once in the source document then this array will only contain one element, and that will be the pointer of interest. If there were more than one occurrence, then another script is used to narrow this down. If this is the case then the `xpointers` array and the **Note** box text are stored in `Session` objects and control is handed to `selector.asp`:

```
        // selected text is unique in document
    if(xpointers.length == 1){
        xpointer = xpointers[0];
    } else { // need to select individual xpointer
        Session("xpointers") = xpointers;
        Session("note") = strNote;
        Session("selecting") = true;
        Response.Redirect("selector.asp");
    }
```

If it was necessary to narrow down a selection, then the details will now be found in session variables:

```
    } else { // selecting is true
        xpointer = Request.QueryString("xpointer");
        strNote = new String(Session("note"));
        Session("selecting") = false;
    }
```

The `noteWriter` object has been reconstructed, and we now use it to record the current annotation by calling the `addNote()` method, with the particular XPointer expression and **Note** box text as parameters:

```
        noteWriter.addNote(xpointer, strNote);
    }
    Session("initialized") = true;
%>
```

The last section of `notes.asp` has the HTML responsible for showing the `<form>` elements for user input, and displays the source page (from a DOM object):

```
<html>
    <head>
        <title>Notes</title>
    </head>
    <body bgcolor="#FFFFFF" text="#000000">
```

```
<!-- Output the original document -->
    <%
        Response.Write(Session("sourceDoc").xml);
    %>
    <hr>
        Copy & paste the part of the text you wish to annotate into the
        'Quote' box, and add your note in the 'Note' box:
    <form name="notesForm" method="post" action="notes.asp">
        <table>
            <tr>
                <td>Quote</td>
                <td>Note</td>
            </tr>
            <tr>
                <td>
                    <textarea name="quote" cols="30" rows="10"></textarea>
                </td>
                <td>
                    <textarea name="note" cols="30" rows="10"></textarea>
                </td>
            </tr>
        </table>
        <p>
            <input type="submit" name="Submit" value="Submit">
            <input type="hidden" name="source" value="notes">
        </p>
    </form>
</body>
</html>
```

Generating an XPointer Expression

We now come to an attempt at emulating a new technology, the code that will take the text quoted from the document the user is annotating, together with a quote from that page, and build an XPointer expression which describes the quote's location on the page. To fully implement the facilities described in XPointer to a level where it could be used in a similar manner to the way we can now use XPath would take an awful lot of programmer-hours, and a corresponding forest's worth of pages to describe. However, all we need to worry about here is a tiny (but very useful) subset of the specification, which follows most of that currently used in the Amaya system. At the time of writing, the specification is only at the W3C's Candidate Recommendation stage, so some leeway in interpretation of the specification is excusable, and here we are following some of the interpretation taken by the developers of Amaya. Essentially we only need to consider two expression forms, and the first of these describes the block of text highlighted in bold here:

It will be **necessary** to identify *fragments* of the document, with more detail than may be specified using XPath.

This first scenario is where the beginning and end points within the document lie within the same element within a document. The XPointer expression that corresponds to this is:

```
xpointer(string-range(/html[1]/body[1]/p[1],"",12,9))
```

The section is described using a `string-range` function, beginning with an XPath expression pointing to the first `<p>` element within a `<body>` element within an `<html>` element (it happens to be in the first paragraph of a web page). The next parameter in the `string-range` function is a string for which the function will search in the specified region; here an empty string is given, as we aren't interested in searching. The first number gives the index within this region of the first character of interest, and the second number gives the number of characters (including the first) onwards to which we are referring.

The second scenario is slightly more complex as we have the selection crossing node boundaries:

It will be necessary to identify *frag*ments of the document, with more detail than may be specified using XPath.

Here we begin with a pair of `string-range` functions, as above, but this time they are each only one character long. These are wrapped in `start-point` and `end-point` functions, which in turn provide parameters for a `range-to` function:

```
xpointer(start-point(xpointer(string-range(/html[1]/body[1]/p[1],"",22,
1))))/range-to(end-point(string-range(/html[1]/body[1]/p[1]/i[1],"",4, 1))))
```

Though the syntax of this second expression appears rather cumbersome, the fact that it is based around two functions that are essentially the same as the simpler expression above means that the actual coding needed to deal with these kinds of expressions is far less demanding than first impressions would suggest.

So how do we get this kind of expression from our quote and document data? From one angle we can look at the text on the page as a flat series of characters, from another we can see the page as a bunch of XML nodes. If we put these views together, we can get to the answer.

The page in the earlier screenshots (`test.html`) obviously included markup; in fact it has the following HTML in its body:

```
<p>It will be necessary to identify <i>fragments</i> of the document, with
more detail than may be specified using XPath.</p>

<p>It should be possible to pick up items that e.g.</p>
<ol>
    <li>appear in lists</li>
    <li>appear in other styles</li>
</ol>

<p>But there's a long way to go...</p>
```

We can easily (as demonstrated below) convert the source document into a node-list, and run through that list pulling the text out of each node. What we get is this:

Node	Length	Content
0	33	It will be necessary to identify
1	10	fragments
2	69	of the document, with more detail than may be specified using XPath.
3	49	It should be possible to pick up items that e.g.
4	16	appear in lists
5	23	appear in other styles
6	32	But there's a long way to go...

We have also noted the number of character in the text content of each node. This is useful information. Taking the page to be annotated as plain text we get this:

It will be necessary to identify fragments of the document, with more detail than may be specified using XPath. It should be possible to pick up items that e.g. appear in lists appear in other styles But there's a long way to go...

Let's assume the user has entered the piece of text highlighted in the 'difficult' example above, so the quote is "to identify frag". Assume for now that we've picked up the index of the quote in the text. This happens to have the value 21, and we can compare this figure alongside the sum of the lengths of the nodes, until we find the number of the node in which this quote appears. We know the number of characters in the quote, so we can find which node the end of the quote appears in too.

We will use JScript regular expressions to find the occurrences of a string in a block of text, and this operation together with those needed to get the page as plain text are found in the file textdoc.asp:

```
<%
function TextDocument(xmlDoc){

    this.xmlDoc = xmlDoc;

    this.textNodeList =
        xmlDoc.documentElement.selectNodes("/html/body//text()");

    this.textNodeCount = this.textNodeList.length;
    this.indexArr = new Array(this.textNodeCount);
    this.strWholeText  = "";

    for(var i = 0;i < this.textNodeCount;i++){
        this.strWholeText  += this.textNodeList.item(i).text+" ";
        this.indexArr[i] =  this.textNodeList.item(i).text.length+1;
    }
    this.getNodesBetween = getNodesBetween;
    this.getTextMatches = getTextMatches;
}
```

Here we have selected all the text nodes in the supplied DOM document and accumulated the text in a string, strWholeText. At the same time we have placed the length of the text in each text node in an array, indexArr. This block of code is the constructor of a TextDocument object, and two class methods are declared at the end of this constructor. The regular expression operation is found in one of these methods:

```
function getTextMatches(strTest){
    var arrMatches = new Array();
    var i = 0;
    var regexp = new RegExp(strTest, "g");
    var arr;
    while((arr = regexp.exec(this.strWholeText)) != null){
        arrMatches[i++] = arr.index;
    }
    return arrMatches;
}
```

The method is supplied with the string to find, and an array to contain the indexes of the matches is created. The regular expression object is constructed using the test string, with the global flag set because we want it to locate every occurrence of the string in the block of text. Calls on the regular expression object's exec() method are made, which will step through the text being examined. As long as the value returned is non-null (in fact an array) the index property of this value is placed in the array of matches. The array of integers containing the indexes is then returned. The TextDocument class contains another utility method, which we will use later on:

```
function getNodesBetween(startNode, endNode){
    var allElements = this.xmlDoc.documentElement.selectNodes("//*");
    var nodeArray = new Array();
    var i=0;
    var j=0;

    while(allElements.nextNode() != startNode);
    while(allElements.nextNode() != endNode){
        nodeArray[j++] = allElements.nextNode();
    }
    return nodeArray;
}
```

All this method does is select the elements found between startNode and endNode and load them into an array, which is returned.

The script that calls on the method above is locator.asp, which obtains the occurrences of a text snippet (quote) in a DOM document and returns the locations expressed as XPointers. This script will construct a Locator object, which has five methods that are declared in the constructor. It uses the matching method of a TextDocument object, and one of these is created in the constructor from the supplied DOM document. The rest of the constructor initializes a handful of variables:

```
<!-- #INCLUDE FILE="makepointer.asp" -->
<!-- #INCLUDE FILE="textdoc.asp" -->
<%
function Locator(xmlDoc){

    this.textDoc = new TextDocument(xmlDoc);
    this.setStartCharIndex = setStartCharIndex;
    this.setEndCharIndex = setEndCharIndex;
    this.getStartCharPos = getStartCharPos;
    this.getEndCharPos = getEndCharPos;
    this.getLocations = getLocations;

    this.startCharIndex = 0;
    this.endCharIndex = 0;
    this.startCharPos = -1;
    this.endCharPos = -1;
    this.startNodeIndex = -1;
    this.endNodeIndex = -1;
    this.startNode = null;
    this.endNode = null;
}
```

Assume for a moment that the index of a string within a block of text has been obtained. We saw earlier how we can compare such a figure with the sum of the lengths of the nodes, until we find the number of the node in which this quote appears. The following two methods carry out this operation for the start and end indexes of a string found within a block of text. Not only do we want to find the node in which the points appear, we also want to know how many characters into the text content of the node the points are. These values (startCharPos and endCharPos) can be obtained at the same time. Setting the values of the start and end indexes of the quote string within a block of plain text by calling the following methods will then locate the nodes and the character positions within the document from which the text was extracted. These values are held in member variables of the Locator object.

```
function setStartCharIndex(intIndex){
    this.startCharIndex = intIndex;
     var acc = 0;
    for(var i = 0;i<this.textDoc.indexArr.length;i++){
        if(acc+this.textDoc.indexArr[i] > this.startCharIndex){
            this.startNodeIndex = i;
            this.startCharPos = this.startCharIndex - acc;
            break;
            }
        acc += this.textDoc.indexArr[i];
    }
    this.startNode = this.textDoc.textNodeList.item(this.startNodeIndex);
}

function setEndCharIndex(intIndex){
    this.endCharIndex = intIndex;
    var acc = 0;
    for(var i = 0;i<this.textDoc.indexArr.length;i++){
        if(acc + this.textDoc.indexArr[i] >= this.endCharIndex){ // =
            this.endNodeIndex = i;
            this.endCharPos = this.endCharIndex - acc;
            break;
            }
        acc += this.textDoc.indexArr[i];
    }
    this.endNode = this.textDoc.textNodeList.item(this.endNodeIndex);
}
```

Of course to be able to set the values by calling the methods above we have to know what the character indexes are, and the following method contains the call to TextDocument.getTextMatches(str) that finds these values. The method begins with a couple of regular expression operations to clean up the quote string it has received. The array of indexes is then obtained and the methods above are called using these values.

```
function getLocations(strQuote){

    var regexp = /(\r\n)+/g; // replace newlines with a space
    strQuote = strQuote.replace(regexp, " ");

    var regexp = /\s+$/; // trim spaces off end
    strQuote = strQuote.replace(regexp, "");

    var matches = this.textDoc.getTextMatches(strQuote);
    var xpointers = new Array();
    for(var i = 0;i < matches.length;i++){
        this.setStartCharIndex(matches[i]);
        this.setEndCharIndex(matches[i] + strQuote.length);
```

The `TextBlock` object is created in another part of the `textdoc.asp` script and we'll be looking at that next. Essentially here the value of `startCharPos` is modified to use the same referencing system as XPointer. Once this has happened a call to the `getXPointer` function will create the corresponding XPointer expression, which is placed into an array element. Once all the matches have been handled, an array of XPointer expressions is returned.

```
        var textBlock = new TextBlock(this.startNode, this.startCharPos);
        this.startCharPos = textBlock.positionLeft();            .

        textBlock = new TextBlock(this.endNode, this.endCharPos);
        this.endCharPos = textBlock.positionLeft();
        xpointers[i] = getXPointer(this.startNode, this.startCharPos,
            this.startNode.text.length, this.endNode, this.endCharPos);
        }
        return xpointers;
    }
```

The script ends with a couple of accessor methods used to get the start and end indexes of a particular location:

```
function getStartCharPos(){
    return this.startCharPos;
}

function getEndCharPos(){
    return this.endCharPos;
}
%>
```

If we take another look at the DOM view of a document, we can see the purpose of the `TextBlock` object we used above:

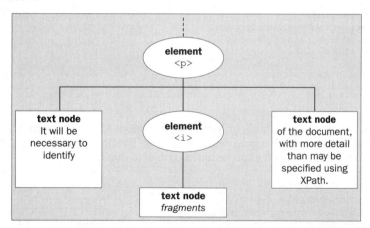

The indexes obtained by the regular expression matching process allow us to identify a specific node and the position within that node at which a quoted string occurs. Therefore, we might know for instance that the word detail is in the text node at the right of the diagram, so many characters in. The XPointer expression we need, however, will be looking at this text relative to the whole block, that is the contents of the paragraph element at the top. The `positionLeft` method of a `TextBlock` object allows us to shift the frame of reference back to the start of the left-hand text node, adding the lengths of the text in the intervening text nodes. The `TextBlock` code is found later in the `textdoc.asp` script. The constructor begins by copying the node and (character) position values into member variables, and then the object's two methods are declared.

```
function TextBlock(node, position){
    this.node = node;
    this.position = position;
    this.positionLeft = positionLeft;
    this.positionRight = positionRight;
}
```

The `positionLeft` method works by simply moving sibling-to-sibling to the left of the starting node, accumulating the length of the text found along the way. It would be possible for this loop to step into other nodes at the same level of the DOM tree, so a check is made to ensure that every node has the same parent:

```
function positionLeft(){
    var swapNode = this.node.previousSibling;
    var parNode = this.node.parentNode;

    while((swapNode != null) && (swapNode.parentNode == parNode)){
        this.position += swapNode.text.length+1;
        swapNode = swapNode.previousSibling;
    }
    return this.position;
}
```

The second method we won't be using for a while, but its operation is essentially the inverse of `positionLeft` – it shifts the frame of reference along to the right:

```
function positionRight(){
        nodeLength = this.node.text.length;
        var nodesPassed = 0;
    while(nodeLength <= this.position){
        nodesPassed++;
        this.position -= nodeLength;
        this.node = this.node.nextSibling;
        nodeLength = this.node.text.length;
        }
        return this.position;
}
%>
```

The other script used in the generation of XPointer expressions to identify parts of a document contains the functions that build the actual expressions themselves. The first function of `makepointer.asp` is given a node and returns an XPath expression that points to that node:

```
<%
function getXPath(targetNode){
    var currentNode = targetNode.parentNode;
    var strXPath = "";
    var sibling;
    var tag;
    var twinNumber;
for(;currentNode.nodeName != "#document";currentNode =
    currentNode.parentNode){
        tag = currentNode.nodeName;
        twinNumber = 0;
        sibling = currentNode;
        for(;sibling != null;sibling = sibling.previousSibling){
```

```
            if(sibling.nodeName == tag) twinNumber++;
        }
    strXPath = "/"+currentNode.nodeName+ "["+(twinNumber)+"]" + strXPath;
    }
return strXPath;
}
```

The function uses two loops, one nested inside the other. However, before doing anything else it takes as its starting point the parent of the node it has received. The outer loop will step up through the hierarchy of ancestors from this node until the name of the node given is "#document", which refers to the node at the top level of the hierarchy, above such nodes as <html>. The inner loop steps back through nodes on each level in the tree, checking to see if the name of the node matches that of the node in question. If the node sent to this function had for an ancestor the third <p> element in a document, then this loop would acknowledge the preceding <p> elements by incrementing the twinNumber counter. The string strXPath accumulates the names of the ancestors that loops pass through, together with the index of the ancestor from which the node in question is descended. The result is a string in XPath syntax, for instance /html[1]/body[1]/p[3].

The getXPointer function makes up the rest of makepointer.asp and does little more than wrap the location information it has received in XPointer syntax. There are two alternatives to consider; in the simpler case the identified text all lies in the same node, and the string-range numbers refer to the start character and the number of characters:

```
function getXPointer(startNode, startCharPos, startNodeLength, endNode,
        endCharPos){

    var strStartRange;
    if(startNode == endNode){ // In same text block, e.g.
        // xpointer(string-range(/html[1]/body[1]/p[1],"",4,8)

        strStartRange = "string-range("
            + getXPath(startNode)
            +",\"\","+(startCharPos+1)
            +",";
        strStartRange =
            "xpointer("
                + strStartRange
                + (endCharPos-startCharPos)
                + "))";
        return strStartRange;

    } else {    // not in same text block
```

In the second case two string-range functions are required, the first pointing to the single character at the beginning of the identified area and the second pointing to the character at the end of the area, for example:

```
xpointer(start-point(string-range(/html[1]/body[1]/p[1]/a[2],"",0,1))
/range-to(end-point(string-range(/html[1]/body[1]/h1[1],"",7,1)))))
```

This again is merely a matter of concatenating strings:

```
        strStartRange = "string-range("
            + getXPath(startNode)
            +",\"\","+(startCharPos+1)
            +", 1";
```

```
            strStartRange = "xpointer("
            + strStartRange + "))";
        }
        var strEndRange = "string-range("
                + getXPath(endNode)
                +",\"\","+endCharPos+", 1)";

        return "xpointer(start-point("
        +strStartRange+")/range-to(end-point("
            +strEndRange+")))";
    }
%>
```

Creating a Linkbase

So far we have seen the code for `notes.asp`, which acts as the user interface, and the code used to generate XPointer expressions. We will now look at the files that take care of saving the annotation data to disk. Two files look after this responsibility: `notewriter.asp`, which constructs the files that hold the annotation information, and `notenode.asp`, which models an individual annotation's linking information. We will now look at how this latter script operates.

The linking model we are using is based around the RDF format used by Amaya. The linking details and other meta data relating to an individual annotation will be contained within a description block, which will be created as an element in a DOM tree. Here is an example of such an element:

```
<rdf:Description>
    <rdf:type resource="http://www.w3.org/2000/10/
                        annotation-ns#Annotation" />
    <rdf:type resource="http://www.w3.org/2000/10/annotationType#Comment" />
    <ann:annotates rdf:resource="http://localhost/linking/test.html" />
    <ann:context>http://localhost/linking/test.html#xpointer(string-
                range(/html[1]/body[1]/p[1],"",44,2))</ann:context>
    <dc:title>Annotation of Test</dc:title>
    <dc:creator>A. Person</dc:creator>
    <ann:body rdf:resource="C:\inetpub\wwwroot\linking\756598.html" />
    <dc:date>2001-11-26T12:59:39</dc:date>
    <ann:created>2001-11-26T12:59:39</ann:created>
</rdf:Description>
```

The model is an object containing a node representing the parent `rdf:Description` element, and most of the code in `notenode.asp` consists of methods to set and get the values of the child nodes of this element. The listing begins with a constructor merely containing declarations for each of the methods that will be available to manipulate the object:

```
<%
function NoteNode(){
    this.createNode = createNode;
    this.setNoteNode = setNoteNode;
    this.getNoteNode = getNoteNode;
    this.initCommonNodes = initCommonNodes;

    this.getNoteAnnotatedFilename = getNoteAnnotedFilename;
    this.getNoteContext = getNoteContext;
    this.getNoteTitle = getNoteTitle;
    this.getNoteCreator = getNoteCreator;
    this.getNoteDate = getNoteDate;
```

```
        this.getNoteFilename = getNoteFilename;

        this.setNoteAnnotatedFilename = setNoteAnnotatedFilename;
        this.setNoteContext = setNoteContext;
        this.setNoteTitle = setNoteTitle;
        this.setNoteCreator = setNoteCreator;
        this.setNoteFilename = setNoteFilename;
        this.setNoteDate = setNoteDate;
        this.setNoteCreated = setNoteCreated;

        this.updateNode = updateNode;
    }
```

The first four methods act on the parent `rdf:Description` node, the first method actually creating it. The `initCommonNodes` method sets up the elements common to all annotation descriptions in this format. The following `getXxx` methods get individual child nodes from the parent, and the `setXxx` methods set the appropriate part of the child node that will contain the data. Let's look at the code for each of these methods.

The method that creates the node is supplied with the DOM document object that will contain the descriptions, and a locally accessible reference to this object is made. The node will be the parent of all the data nodes, so it is called `parentNode`. A namespace-qualified element is created (the '1' parameter refers to note-type elements) and appended to the container document, and a local reference is created. Later on we are going to be querying the description node with XPath expressions, and to be able to use these with qualified element names it is necessary to inform the container document in advance of the namespace prefixes, hence the `property` setting. The other two methods are included to allow convenient access to the whole node object:

```
function createNode(linkDoc){
    // <rdf:Description>
    this.linkDoc = linkDoc;
    var parentNode = this.linkDoc.createNode(1, "rdf:Description",
        "http://www.w3.org/1999/02/22-rdf-syntax-ns");
    this.linkDoc.documentElement.appendChild(parentNode);

    this.linkDoc.setProperty("SelectionNamespaces",
        "xmlns:rdf = 'http://www.w3.org/1999/02/22-rdf-syntax-ns#'"
        +" xmlns:dc = 'http://purl.org/dc/elements/1.0/'"
        +" xmlns:ann = 'http://www.w3.org/2000/10/annotation-ns#'"
        +" xmlns:http = 'http://www.w3.org/1999/xx/http#'");

    this.parentNode = parentNode;
}

function setNoteNode(parentNode){
    this.parentNode = parentNode;
}

function getNoteNode(){
    return this.parentNode;
}
```

The next method initializes the nodes common to all description elements, which when serialized look like this:

```
<rdf:type resource="http://www.w3.org/2000/10/annotation-ns#Annotation" />
<rdf:type resource="http://www.w3.org/2000/10/annotationType#Comment" />
```

First each (namespace-qualified) element is created, then its attribute (the resource reference) is set, and finally each element is appended to the parent (description) node:

```
function initCommonNodes(){
    var type1Element = this.linkDoc.createNode(1, "rdf:type",
            "http://www.w3.org/1999/02/22-rdf-syntax-ns");
    type1Element.setAttribute("resource",
        "http://www.w3.org/2000/10/annotation-ns#Annotation");
    this.parentNode.appendChild(type1Element);

    var type2Element = this.linkDoc.createNode(1, "rdf:type",
            "http://www.w3.org/1999/02/22-rdf-syntax-ns");
    type2Element.setAttribute("resource",
        "http://www.w3.org/2000/10/annotationType#Comment");
    this.parentNode.appendChild(type2Element);
}
```

We will now see the first of the setter methods, which will create an element of this form:

```
<ann:annotates rdf:resource="http://annotatedfile.html" />
```

This begins by following the same simple pattern as in the `initCommonNodes()` method, but it is possible that there will already be a node representing the 'annotates' information in the DOM tree, so rather than simply append the new node we call a method that will either add the node if it doesn't already exist or replace the node if it does:

```
function setNoteAnnotatedFilename(strAnnotatedFilename){
    var annotatesElement = this.linkDoc.createNode(1, "ann:annotates",
        "http://www.w3.org/2000/10/annotation-ns#");
    annotatesElement.setAttribute("rdf:resource", strAnnotatedFilename);
    this.updateNode("/ann:annotates", annotatesElement);
}
```

The `updateNode()` method is used by all setter methods of this type, so it is generalized to take the XPath expression pointing to the node of interest as one argument and the new/replacement node as the other. Depending on whether or not the node exists, a new node is created or the old node replaced:

```
function updateNode(strPath, newElement){

    var oldElement = this.parentNode.selectSingleNode(strPath);
    if(oldElement == null){
      this.parentNode.appendChild(newElement);
    } else {
        this.parentNode.replaceChild(newElement, oldElement);
    }
}
```

The next method is another setter, this time to push data into an element like this:

```
<ann:context>http://something.html#xpointer(expression)</ann:context>
```

Following the Amaya/Annotea format, the data is contained as element content rather than as an attribute as in the previous setter method, so all this means is that we have to create a text node and append it:

```
function setNoteContext(strContext){
    var contextElement = this.linkDoc.createNode(1, "ann:context",
            "http://www.w3.org/2000/10/annotation-ns#");
```

```
      var contextTextNode = this.linkDoc.createTextNode(strContext);
      contextElement.appendChild(contextTextNode);
      this.updateNode("/ann:context", contextElement);
   }
```

The rest of the setter methods, follow the pattern above, where the data is placed in a contained text node, or place it into an attribute:

```
      // <dc:title>Annotation of A Page</dc:title>
   function setNoteTitle(strTitle){
      var titleElement = this.linkDoc.createNode(1, "dc:title",
            "http://purl.org/dc/elements/1.0/");
      var titleTextNode = this.linkDoc.createTextNode(strTitle);
      titleElement.appendChild(titleTextNode);
      this.updateNode("/dc:title", titleElement);
   }

      // <dc:creator>A. Person</dc:creator>
   function setNoteCreator(strCreator){
      var creatorElement = this.linkDoc.createNode(1, "dc:creator",
            "http://purl.org/dc/elements/1.0/");
      var creatorTextNode = this.linkDoc.createTextNode(strCreator);
      creatorElement.appendChild(creatorTextNode);
      this.updateNode("/dc:creator", creatorElement);
   }

      // <ann:body rdf:resource="http://notefile.html" />
   function setNoteFilename(strNoteFilename){
      var bodyElement = this.linkDoc.createNode(1, "ann:body",
            "http://www.w3.org/2000/10/annotation-ns#");
      bodyElement.setAttribute("rdf:resource", strNoteFilename);
      this.updateNode("ann:body", bodyElement);
   }

      // <dc:date>2001-11-15T17:36:41</dc:date>
   function setNoteDate(strDate){
      var dateElement = this.linkDoc.createNode(1, "dc:date",
            "http://purl.org/dc/elements/1.0/");
      var dateTextNode = this.linkDoc.createTextNode(strDate);
      dateElement.appendChild(dateTextNode);
      this.updateNode("dc:date", dateElement);
   }

      // <ann:created>2001-11-15T17:36:38</ann:created>
   function setNoteCreated(strCtreated){
      var createdElement = this.linkDoc.createNode(1, "ann:created",
            "http://www.w3.org/2000/10/annotation-ns#");
      var createdTextNode = this.linkDoc.createTextNode(getDate());
      createdElement.appendChild(createdTextNode);
      this.updateNode("ann:created", createdElement);
   }
```

The remainder of notenode.asp is a series of getter methods that correspond to the setters above. Again there are two different forms, depending on whether the data is contained in an attribute or as text content. Either way, the node in question is first addressed using an XPath expression. The responsibility for handling a query on a non-existent node is passed onto the caller, which is more likely to know why such a query was made. If the data is in an attribute, the information is returned following a call to getAttribute on the addressed node; if the data is in textual content, then this is simply obtained using the node's .text property:

387

```
function getNoteAnnotedFilename(){
    var node = this.parentNode.selectSingleNode("ann:annotates");
    if(node == null) return null;
    return node.getAttribute("rdf:resource");
}

function getNoteContext(){
    var node = this.parentNode.selectSingleNode("ann:context");
        if(node == null) return null;
    return node.text;
}

function getNoteTitle(){
    var node = this.parentNode.selectSingleNode("dc:title");
        if(node == null) return null;
    return node.text;
}

function getNoteCreator(){
    var node = this.parentNode.selectSingleNode("dc:creator");
        if(node == null) return null;
    return node.text;
}

function getNoteDate(){
    var node = this.parentNode.selectSingleNode("dc:date");
        if(node == null) return null;
    return node.text;
}

function getNoteFilename(){
    var node = this.parentNode.selectSingleNode("ann:body");
        if(node == null) return null;
    return node.getAttribute("rdf:resource");
}
%>
```

The last file in this part of the application is the script responsible for persisting the annotation information, generated from user input from notes.asp. This script glues the application together, and is contained in notewriter.asp. It operates by allowing the creation of a NoteWriter object, which contains a DOM representation of the link file data. It has methods for creating and writing the file, together with a method for generating an XHTML file from the user's annotation comments. So here we have notewriter.asp, which begins with the NoteWriter object constructor, and a prototype for the linking information DOM object:

```
<!-- #INCLUDE FILE="notenode.asp" -->
<%

function NoteWriter(strLinkFilename){
    this.strLinkFilename = strLinkFilename;
    this.linkDoc.async = false;
    this.getXml = getXml;
    this.setAnnotatedFilename = setAnnotatedFilename;
    this.setTitle = setTitle;
    this.setCreator = setCreator;
    this.createLinkFile = createLinkFile;
    this.createNoteFile = createNoteFile;
    this.loadLinkFile = loadLinkFile;
```

```
      this.addNote = addNote;
  }
  NoteWriter.prototype.linkDoc =
     Server.createObject("Msxml2.DOMDocument.4.0");
```

The constructor takes one argument, the name of the file into which the link data will be written, the body of the constructor being little more than a series of method declarations.

The first three methods receive items of information that will remain constant during an annotation session – the location of the page being annotated, the title of this page, and the creator, which is a string containing the name of the author of the annotations.

```
  function setAnnotatedFilename(strAnnotatedFilename){
     this.strAnnotatedFilename = strAnnotatedFilename;
  }

  function setTitle(strTitle){
     this.strTitle = "Annotation of "+strTitle;
  }

  function setCreator(strCreator){
     this.strCreator = strCreator;
  }
```

Next we have a method that will return an XML string representation of the link file, followed by a method that will attempt to load the named XML file from disk into the `linkDoc` DOM document. If the call to `load` has left a null `documentElement`, then the file does not yet exist and a method is called (coming next) to create such a file:

```
  function getXml(){
     return this.linkDoc.xml;
  }

  function loadLinkFile(){
     this.linkDoc.load(Server.MapPath(this.strLinkFilename));
        if(this.linkDoc.documentElement == null){
           this.createLinkFile(this.strLinkFilename);
        }
  }
```

The link file is modeled on the format used by Amaya, which is in RDF/XML syntax. The XML declaration is inserted right at the start of the document; the standard line that says that what follows is XML. Next the document root element (`rdf:RDF`) is created, complete with the namespace declarations:

```
  function createLinkFile(){
     var pi = this.linkDoc.createProcessingInstruction("xml",
              "version=\"1.0\"");
     this.linkDoc.insertBefore(pi, this.linkDoc.childNodes.item(0));

     rootElement = this.linkDoc.createNode(1, "rdf:RDF",
                  "http://www.w3.org/1999/02/22-rdf-syntax-ns");

     this.linkDoc.documentElement = rootElement;
     rootElement.setAttribute("xmlns:dc", "http://purl.org/dc/elements/1.0/");
```

```
        rootElement.setAttribute("xmlns:ann",
                                 "http://www.w3.org/2000/10/annotation-ns#");
        rootElement.setAttribute("xmlns:http",
            "http://www.w3.org/1999/xx/http#");

        this.linkDoc.save(Server.MapPath(this.strLinkFilename));
    }
```

The result of calling this method will be a new file on disk with text content much like this:

```
<?xml version="1.0" ?>
<rdf:RDF xmlns:rdf="http://www.w3.org/1999/02/22-rdf-syntax-ns"
         xmlns:dc="http://purl.org/dc/elements/1.0/"
         xmlns:ann="http://www.w3.org/2000/10/annotation-ns#"
         xmlns:http="http://www.w3.org/1999/xx/http#"/>
```

The next method is called whenever a new description element (that is, a new annotation) is required. It takes one parameter, strContext, which will be an XPointer expression. If the link document hasn't already been loaded it will be loaded. The internals of the description element are handled by a NoteNode object, which is created and initialized here. The location of the file being annotated and the context (the XPointer to the identified text, prefixed by the file URI) are passed into this object, a value is sent for the date, and elements are created using a method below. As this prototype application doesn't contain any facilities for modifying the annotations, both the values are set to the current time. The node as built by this call is retrieved from the NoteNode object and added to the link document, which is then saved.

```
    function addNote(strContext){

        if(this.linkDoc.documentElement == null) this.loadLinkFile();

        var noteNode = new NoteNode();
        noteNode.createNode(this.linkDoc);
        noteNode.initCommonNodes();

        noteNode.setNoteAnnotatedFilename(this.strAnnotatedFilename);
        noteNode.setNoteContext(this.strAnnotatedFilename+"#"+strContext);
        noteNode.setNoteTitle(this.strTitle);
        noteNode.setNoteCreator(this.strCreator);

        var strNoteFilename = this.createNoteFile(strNote);
        noteNode.setNoteFilename(strNoteFilename);
        noteNode.setNoteDate(getDate());
        noteNode.setNoteCreated(getDate());

        this.linkDoc.documentElement.appendChild(noteNode.getNoteNode());

        this.linkDoc.save(Server.MapPath(this.strLinkFilename));
    }
```

The next method will receive the comment text as entered by the user and create an XHTML file in which to store it. The name of the file will be a random 6-digit number with an .html extension. There is potential for naming the file based on parameters like the date, time, and author, but as the data is only intended to be machine-readable unique identifiers are adequate. The while loop here ensures that there isn't already a file of that name, by attempting to load it:

```
    function createNoteFile(strNote){
        var rnd;
        var rndname;
```

```
    var filename;
    var exists = true;
    var xmlDoc = Server.CreateObject("MSXML2.DOMDocument.4.0");

    do{
        rnd = Math.random();
        rndname = (new String(rnd)).slice(3,9)+".html";
        filename = Server.MapPath(rndname);
        xmlDoc = Server.CreateObject("MSXML2.DOMDocument.4.0");
        exists = xmlDoc.load(filename);
    }while(exists);
```

The next two lines build the outer elements of a simple XHTML document by loading a string directly into the DOM object.

```
    var htmlShell = "<html xmlns=\"http://www.w3.org/1999/xhtml\">"
            +"<head><title>Note</title></head></html>";

    xmlDoc.loadXML(htmlShell);
```

A <body> element is created, and then a couple of <h3> elements that will display the author and the title of the annotation. Once these have been appended to the DOM object the note itself is added as a bare text node:

```
    var bodyNode = xmlDoc.createElement("body");

    var hNode = xmlDoc.createElement("h3");
    var textNode = xmlDoc.createTextNode("Title : "+this.strTitle);
    hNode.appendChild(textNode);
    bodyNode.appendChild(hNode);

    hNode = xmlDoc.createElement("h3");
    var textNode = xmlDoc.createTextNode("Author : "+this.strCreator);
    hNode.appendChild(textNode);
    bodyNode.appendChild(hNode);

  textNode = xmlDoc.createTextNode(strNote);
    bodyNode.appendChild(textNode);
    xmlDoc.documentElement.appendChild(bodyNode);
    xmlDoc.save(filename);
    return filename;
}
```

The result of calling this method will be a file which, when viewed in a browser, will look something like this:

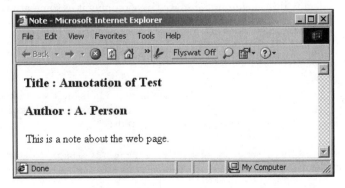

The last method in `notewriter.asp` simply takes the current date and time and formats it in the same manner as found in Amaya annotations:

```
function getDate(){
   var strDate = "";
   var objDate = new Date();
   strDate += objDate.getYear()+"-";
      strDate += (objDate.getMonth() + 1) + "-";
      strDate += objDate.getDate() + "T";
      strDate += objDate.getHours() + ":";
      strDate += objDate.getMinutes() + ":";
      strDate += objDate.getSeconds();
      return(strDate);
}
%>
```

The string returned by this method will look something like this:

```
2001-11-26T17:39:58
```

Interpreting XPointer Expressions

We have seen how it is possible to create simple XPointer expressions that are good enough to allow us to create the linking data needed in the annotation application. We can now turn to the other side of the coin, which is viewing an annotated document. Let's examine the central problem. Let's say we want to somehow highlight the part of our document described by the following XPointer expression:

```
xpointer(start-point(string-range(/html[1]/body[1]/p[1],"",22,1))/
range-to(end-point(string-range(/html[1]/body[1]/p[1]/i[1],"",4,1))))
```

which corresponds to the section of text highlighted in bold here:

It will be necessary **to identify** *frag*ments of the document, beyond what may be specified using XPath.

which will correspond to the following section of source HTML:

```
<p>It will be necessary to identify <i>frag</i>ments</i> of the document, beyond what
may be specified using XPath.</p>
```

If we naively try to identify this section in the source by wrapping it in some arbitrary tags, we can see a complication:

```
<p>It will be necessary <tag>to identify <i>frag</tag>ments</i> of the document,
beyond what may be specified using XPath.</p>
```

The source is no longer well-formed. Intuitively it seems a good idea to try and keep the block of text we are interested in within the same grouping, and on first examination, it looks like we may be able to work around the problem by chopping up the document thus:

```
<p>It will be necessary <tag>to identify <i>frag</i></tag><i>ments</i> of the
document, beyond what may be specified using XPath.</p>
```

Here our arbitrary tags legally delimit the area in which we are interested, but unfortunately we have introduced another complication. Though it won't make any difference here with the italic tags, the view in a browser produced by one continuous, for example, `<h1>`, block will be very different than that produced by two such blocks, even if they are adjacent. Another option loses the 'unity' of our arbitrary tags, but is less likely to disrupt existing document formatting:

```
<p>It will be necessary <tag>to identify</tag><i><tag>frag</tag>ments</i> of the
document, beyond what may be specified using XPath.</p>
```

We'll shortly take a look at the script that will carry out this transformation for us, but first we have to get the information out of existing XPointer expressions. We are only going to be considering two different forms of XPointer expression, and as far as this prototype is concerned this means we can take a stylistic liberty and focus on extracting the information from these in as simple a way as possible.

The context elements in the link file have their XPointer expressions prefixed with the location of the page being annotated, with a rather convenient # delimiter, thus:

```
http://localhost/query/test.html#xpointer(string-
range(/html[1]/body[1]/p[3],"",15,4))
```

It is trivial to strip off the prefix, so let's see the two examples again:

```
xpointer(string-range(/html[1]/body[1]/p[1],"",12,9))
```

```
xpointer(start-point(xpointer(string-range(/html[1]/body[1]/p[1],"",22,
1)))/range-to(end-point(string-range(/html[1]/body[1]/p[1]/i[1],"",4, 1))))
```

We know that whatever we encounter will be in one of these forms, so given an arbitrary expression (after stripping the prefix URI) our first job will be to determine which type it is. The second form has the string `range-to` in the middle of it, which we can use to tell which category the expression falls in. Not only that, if the expression is in the second category then the location of `range-to` also gives us a marker in the string between the `start-point` and `end-point` expressions.

The code that will extract values from an expression is based around an object called `PointExpr`, and the script `pointexpr.asp` begins with the constructor, which starts with a string containing the XPointer expression:

```
<%
function PointExpr(strXPointer){
    // split the string at the # sign
    var hash = strXPointer.indexOf("#");
    var strDoc = strXPointer.substring(0, hash);
    var strLoc = strXPointer.substring(hash);

    var strRight;

    this.arrRange1 = splitRange(strLoc);
```

We've chopped the document URI part of the string off, and have passed the remainder to the `splitRange` function below. That returns an array containing the parameters of the first `string-range` function in the string supplied. In other words, if we send:

```
xpointer(string-range(/html[1]/body[1]/p[1],"",12,9))
```

`splitRange()` will return the four-element array of strings:

```
{"/html[1]/body[1]/p[1]", "", "12", "9"}
```

The array returned is stored in the object variable `this.arrRange1` for future access. Now we move on to see which of the two forms the expression is in by trying to find a substring match for `"range-to"`.

```
var intMiddle = strLoc.indexOf("range-to");
this.nRanges = 1;
if(intMiddle != -1){ // there are two ranges
    this.nRanges = 2;
    strRight = strLoc.substring(intMiddle);
    this.arrRange2 = splitRange(strRight);
}
```

If the substring was found, then the material to the right of this (containing the `end-point` expression) gets run through the `splitRange()` function as well. The `nRanges` member variable records the number of ranges found in the expression.

Despite the neat little array it returns, `splitRange()` is a very unsophisticated function. It finds the position of the first substring that matches the string `"string-range"`, and the first `")"` character after this point, and using these gets the contents of the parentheses. Here we take advantage of a nifty JScript string method: `split()`. This will chop the string on which it is called into separate tokens according to whatever we tell it to use as a separator. The method returns an array of these tokens. In this case we use a comma as a separator, and call the method on a string containing the comma-separated list of function parameters, and this gives us our neat array of values:

```
function splitRange(str){
    var intRangeStart = str.indexOf("string-range");
    var intRangeEnd = str.indexOf(")", intRangeStart-1);
    var range = str.substring(intRangeStart+13, intRangeEnd);
    var arrSplit = range.split(",");
    return arrSplit;
}
```

The rest of the constructor declares a series of methods that will allow us to access the values in the XPointer expression that the object exposes:

```
    this.getLeftPath = getLeftPath;
    this.getRightPath = getRightPath;
    this.getLeftRangeStart = getLeftRangeStart;
    this.getLeftRangeLength = getLeftRangeLength;
    this.getRightRangeStart = getRightRangeStart;
    this.getRightRangeLength = getRightRangeLength;
    this.getDocUrl = getDocUrl;
}
PointExpr.prototype.arrRange1 = null;
PointExpr.prototype.arrRange2 = null;

function getDocUrl(){
    return this.strDoc;
}
```

The accessor methods each contain a little code to pull the appropriate element out of the appropriate array:

```
function getLeftPath(){
    return this.arrRange1[0];
}

function getRightPath(){
    return this.arrRange2[0]
}

function getLeftRangeStart(){
    return parseInt(this.arrRange1[2])-1;
}

function getLeftRangeLength(){
    return parseInt(this.arrRange1[3]);
}

function getRightRangeStart(){
    return parseInt(this.arrRange2[2]);
}

function getRightRangeLength(){
    return parseInt(this.arrRange2[3]);
}
%>
```

Just to clarify what this script will do: if we construct a `pointExpr` object using an expression of the kind found in the `<context>` element of an annotation description, we can then access the parameters contained in that expression by calling the `getRangeX` methods, which will return an array containing those values. There are two forms of expression we are dealing with. If the expression is of the second type, in other words it runs over node boundaries, `arrRange1` will contain the details of the left-hand position and `arrRange2` will contain those of the right-hand position. The accessor methods deliver the particular value in the expression that the caller has requested.

The script we've just seen falls squarely into the quick-and-dirty category, but there are two mitigating circumstances – firstly we have decided to work in a very limited domain, so there is no real need for the script to be any more comprehensive than it is. Secondly, this functionality has been pulled out to stand in its own script. When a full-featured XPointer parser becomes available, we will be able to replace this script with an adapter, without affecting any of the rest of the code.

Now we can get the values out of an expression, we can take a look at how we can create the transformed document we discussed earlier. The source for this is in the file `markeddoc.asp` and basically it creates an object that contains a DOM tree into which hyperlinks can be inserted according to XPointer expressions. Again the script is object-oriented, and here a `MarkedDoc` object is created from a DOM document. There are only four methods, and only one of these will we be calling from outside of this script – `addMark(pointExpr, href)` will insert a hyperlink into the document at a place determined by an XPointer expression, with the aid of the other three methods.

```
<!-- #INCLUDE FILE="pointexpr.asp" -->
<!-- #INCLUDE FILE="textdoc.asp" -->
<%
function MarkedDoc(xmlDoc){
    this.xmlDoc = xmlDoc;

    this.addMark = addMark;
    this.tagNode = tagNode;
```

```
      this.tagNodePart = tagNodePart;
      this.createNodeTag = createNodeTag;
}
```

The `createNodeTag` (pencil) method creates an XML node of the following form:

```
<a href = "xxxx"/>
```

If the Boolean pencil variable is `true`, then a child element is added to the node, giving the following form:

```
<a href = "xxxx"><img src = "pencil.gif" border = "0"></a>
```

Of course this XML node will be equivalent to HTML code when it's serialized out: a hyperlink to the value contained in the member variable `href`, with or without a pencil icon.

```
function createNodeTag(pencil){
    var nodeTag = this.xmlDoc.createElement("a");
    nodeTag.setAttribute("href", this.href);
    if(pencil){
        var imgElement = this.xmlDoc.createElement("img");
        imgElement.setAttribute("src", "pencil.gif");
        imgElement.setAttribute("border", "0");
        nodeTag.appendChild(imgElement);
    }
    return nodeTag;
}
```

The next method receives as its arguments a text node and a node as created by the last method. It uses a `DOMDocumentFragment` as a temporary holder. The fragment object is created and the `nodeTag` appended as a child. This fragment is then inserted into the DOM tree just before the text node. The text node is then removed from the tree and added as a child to the `nodeTag` node. The `nodeTag` node has been inserted immediately above the text node, and the effect is that when the DOM object is serialized, the text node will appear as a hyperlink.

```
function tagNode(textNode, nodeTag){
    var docFragment = this.xmlDoc.createDocumentFragment();
    docFragment.appendChild(nodeTag);
    textNode.parentNode.insertBefore(docFragment, textNode);
    textNode.parentNode.removeChild(textNode);
    nodeTag.appendChild(textNode);
}
```

The next method carries out an operation very similar to that of the method above, except here we want to add a hyperlink to text that might start part way through a text node, or finish before the end of the node. A fragment object is again created, and if the start of the selection is part way through the node, the text to the left of the selection is taken and a completely new text node made from this, which is appended to the fragment:

```
function tagNodePart(textNode, intSelStart, intSelLength, nodeTag){
    var docFragment = this.xmlDoc.createDocumentFragment();

    var text = textNode.text;
    if(intSelStart > 0){ // unselected text on left?
        leftNode =
```

```
    this.xmlDoc.createTextNode(text.substring(0, intSelStart));
       docFragment.appendChild(leftNode);
    }
```

We now deal with the section that is going to get the hyperlink. Another text node is created from this and appended to the fragment:

```
    subNode =
 this.xmlDoc.createTextNode(text.substring(intSelStart,
                            intSelStart+intSelLength));
    nodeTag.appendChild(subNode);
    docFragment.appendChild(nodeTag);
```

Now the text to the right of the selected area (if there is any) is put into a third node and this too is appended to the fragment. The fragment is then appended to the document in place of the text node:

```
    // where to start + how many characters
    rightPointer = intSelStart + intSelLength;

    if(rightPointer < text.length){ // unselected text on right?
       rightNode = his.xmlDoc.createTextNode(text.substring(
                                        rightPointer));
    docFragment.appendChild(rightNode);
    }
 textNode.parentNode.insertBefore(docFragment, textNode); // new, ref
 textNode.parentNode.removeChild(textNode);
}
```

The following method uses the two methods above to insert a hyperlink into the document in the required position. The operation is a little different dependent on whether or not the text that will be hyperlinked falls within one node or crosses node boundaries. In the first case, the method locates the text node in question using the getLeftPath() method of the pointExpr object provided. It then creates a new hyperlink node using createNodeTag() and passes this and the other values obtained from the pointExpr object to the tagNodePart() method we have just seen:

```
function addMark(pointExpr, href){
   this.href = href;

   var textBlock;
   if(pointExpr.nRanges == 1){

      intSelStart = pointExpr.getLeftRangeStart();
      leftNode = this.xmlDoc.selectSingleNode(pointExpr.getLeftPath()
                                       +"/text()");
      textBlock = new TextBlock(leftNode, intSelStart);
      intSelStart = textBlock.positionRight();
      leftNode = textBlock.node;

      intSelLength = pointExpr.getLeftRangeLength();
      leftTagNode = this.createNodeTag(true);
   this.tagNodePart(leftNode, intSelStart, intSelLength, leftTagNode);
```

If the text does stretch across nodes, things are a little more complicated. Let's say that the text "identify fragments of the doc" has been selected. First we deal with the piece of text contained in the left-hand text node, highlighted here:

<p>It will be necessary to **identify**<i>fragments</i> of the document, beyond what may be specified using XPath.</p>

First of all the node is located, and then the piece of text of interest is found. Here we are using the character pointers as used in XPointer expressions (counting from the start of the text block), so first we have to change the frame of reference to the individual node. The `TextBlock.positionRight()` method from `textblock.asp` is used for this purpose.

```
} else { // 2 ranges, i.e. selection crosses node boundaries

// left-hand fragment
leftNode = this.xmlDoc.selectSingleNode(pointExpr.getLeftPath()
                                    +"/text()");

intSelStart = pointExpr.getLeftRangeStart();
intSelLength = leftNode.text.length;
textBlock = new TextBlock(leftNode, intSelStart);
intSelStart = textBlock.positionRight();
leftNode = textBlock.node;

leftTagNode = this.createNodeTag(true);
this.tagNodePart(leftNode, intSelStart, intSelLength, leftTagNode);
```

Now the same operation is carried out for the right-hand fragment, in the example:

<p>It will be necessary to identify<i>fragments</i> **of the docu**ment, beyond what may be specified using XPath.</p>

As this side begins at the start of the characters, the selection start parameter is passed as zero:

```
// right-hand fragment
intSelEnd = pointExpr.getRightRangeStart();

rightNode = this.xmlDoc.selectSingleNode(pointExpr.getRightPath()
                                     +"/text()");
textBlock = new TextBlock(rightNode, intSelEnd);
intSelLength = textBlock.positionRight();
rightNode = textBlock.node;

rightTagNode = this.createNodeTag(false);
this.tagNodePart(rightNode, 0, intSelLength, rightTagNode);
```

Note the nodes in-between the endpoints need the same treatment, for example:

<p>It will be necessary to identify<i>**fragments**</i> of the document, beyond what may be specified using XPath.</p>

This operation is carried out with the help of the `TextDocument.getNodesBetween()` method (in `textdoc.asp`) we saw earlier, which supplies an array containing the nodes found between the two nodes used as arguments. Each of these nodes is passed to the `tagNode()` method, along with a new node to provide the hyperlink:

```
    // between
        var textDoc = new TextDocument(this.xmlDoc);
        var betweenNodes = textDoc.getNodesBetween(leftTagNode, rightTagNode);
        for(var i=0; i < betweenNodes.length;i++){
            currentNode = betweenNodes[i];
            this.tagNode(betweenNodes[i],this.createNodeTag(false));
            }
        }
    }
%>
```

The `MarkedDocument` class is used for two purposes in the application, firstly in the creation of annotations, where it allows the user to select the individual piece of text they wish to annotate, if the text appears more than once. We'll now have a look at the script that controls this. The class is also used in the viewing of an annotated document, which we will see shortly.

Referring back to the annotation entry form page we saw earlier (`notes.asp`), when an array containing more than one XPointer expression is returned by the `Locator` object the following piece of script will run:

```
Session("xpointers") = xpointers;
Session("note") = strNote;
Session("selecting") = true;
Response.Redirect("selector.asp");
```

The following is the content of `selector.asp`, the target of the redirection:

```
<%@ LANGUAGE=JScript %>
<!-- #INCLUDE FILE="pointexpr.asp" -->
<!-- #INCLUDE FILE="markeddoc.asp" -->
<%
    var doc = Session("sourceDoc").cloneNode(true);
    var markedDoc = new MarkedDoc(doc);
    var xpointers = Session("xpointers");
    var strQuote = Session("quote");
    var pointexpr;
    var href = "notes.asp?xpointer=";

    for(var i=0;i<xpointers.length;i++){
        pointexpr = new PointExpr(xpointers[i]);
        markedDoc.addMark(pointexpr, href+xpointers[i]);
    }
    Response.Write(doc.xml);
    Response.End();
%>
```

The code starts by making a copy of the DOM document that is being annotated – the methods of a `MarkedDocument` object modify the DOM tree, which is a side effect we don't want here. Like the DOM document, the array of XPointer strings and the quote text were passed into session variables in `notes.asp`, and here they are retrieved. The XPointer array is stepped through, and for each expression a corresponding hyperlink is added to DOM document `doc` using `markedDoc.addMark`. The target of the hyperlink is `notes.asp`, but an additional piece of data will be passed along to identify the particular XPointer expression that has been chosen. If we revisit the example we saw earlier, the second occurrence of the word "appear" was higlighted like this:

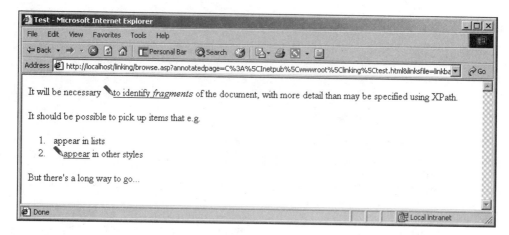

The HTML source behind this line (generated by `selector.asp`) is as follows:

```
<li>
<a href="notes.asp?xpointer=xpointer(string-range(/html[1]/body[1]/ol[1]
                                /li[2],&quot;&quot;,1,6))">
   <img src="pencil.gif" border="0"/>
   appear
</a>
in other styles
</li>
```

Before the redirection was made to `selector.asp` in `notes.asp`, a flag was set to indicate that a selection was to take place (`Session("selecting") = true`). When `notes.asp` is reloaded, after a link on the generated page has been clicked, the `"selecting"` flag will cause the following code (in `notes.asp`) to run:

```
        xpointer = Request.QueryString("xpointer");
        strNote = new String(Session("note"));
        Session("selecting") = false;
```

The value given in the hyperlink (`notes.asp?xpointer=`xxx) will thus be delivered to the `xpointer` variable. The value that was passed into `Session("note")` by `notes.asp`, that is, the text of the annotation, is also retrieved and these two values are used to create the new annotation through the call to :

```
   noteWriter.addNote(xpointer, strNote);
```

We have now covered all the code used to create the annotations, so it's time to move on to the other side of the prototype application.

Viewing the Annotated Document

Opposite is a block diagram of the key parts of the viewer. We start at `browse.htm`, which is used to enter the locations of the annotated document and the linkbase file. This brings up `browse.asp`, which builds a page based on the source document and the linking information found in the linkbase, which is read using `notereader.asp`. A `MarkedDocument` object is used to insert the hyperlinks into the source document. The links on the page will point to the individual annotations.

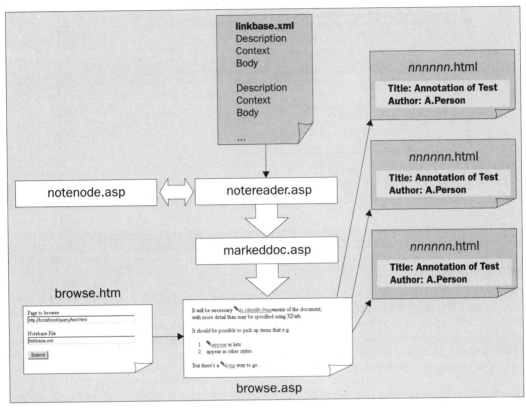

To get into a position where we can view an annotated page we have another simple form-based entry page (browse.htm):

```html
<html>
   <head>
      <title>Browse Entry Page</title>
   </head>
   <body bgcolor="#FFFFFF" text="#000000">
      <form name="sourceForm" method="get" action="browse.asp">
         Page to browse
         <br>
         <input type="text" name="annotatedpage"
               value="http://localhost/linking/test.xml" size="50">
         <p>
         Notebase File
         <br>
         <input type="text" name="linksfile" value="linkbase.xml" size="50">
         <p>
         <input type="submit" name="Submit" value="Submit">
      </form>
   </body>
</html>
```

Once again for testing purposes we have set the default text. In a browser window, the form looks like this:

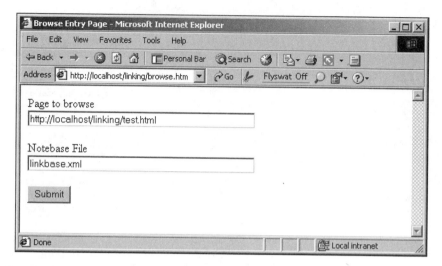

Reading the RDF

The ASP page this information will be POSTed to is `browse.asp`, and we'll come to that in a moment. First we have the script that will load the link data into the system, `notereader.asp`. This constructs an object, which acts as an interface between the contents of the link data file and `browse.asp`. The constructor simply loads the named XML file in an in-memory DOM object. Its only method uses XPath, so once again we have to set the document's `SelectionNamespaces` property for it to be able to interpret element names with prefixes.

```
<!-- #INCLUDE FILE="notenode.asp" -->
<%
function NoteReader(strLinkFilename){

    this.linkDoc = Server.CreateObject("MSXML2.DOMDocument.4.0");
    this.linkDoc.async = false;
    this.linkDoc.load(unescape(Server.MapPath(strLinkFilename)));
    this.getDescriptionNodes = getDescriptionNodes;

    this.linkDoc.setProperty("SelectionNamespaces",
        "xmlns:rdf = 'http://www.w3.org/1999/02/22-rdf-syntax-ns#'"
    +" xmlns:dc = 'http://purl.org/dc/elements/1.0/'"
    +" xmlns:ann = 'http://www.w3.org/2000/10/annotation-ns#'"
    +" xmlns:http = 'http://www.w3.org/1999/xx/http#'");
}
```

The sole method loads all the `<rdf:Description>` elements (complete with children) from the link file into a node-list, which the method then iterates through, creating a `NoteNode` object for each description block. These are loaded into an array, which the method returns. The `NoteNode` objects of course will have all their `getXxx` and `setXxx` methods available, which means that the data is now in a very usable form.

```
function getDescriptionNodes(){

    var descriptions = this.linkDoc.documentElement.selectNodes("*");
    var notes = new Array(descriptions.length);
    var note;
    for(var i = 0;i<descriptions.length;i++){
```

```
        note = new NoteNode();
        note.setNoteNode(descriptions.item(i));
        notes[i] = note;
    }
    return notes;
}
%>
```

The page that builds the annotated document view (browse.asp) is as follows:

```
<%@ LANGUAGE=JScript %>
<!-- #INCLUDE FILE="notereader.asp" -->
<!-- #INCLUDE FILE="pointexpr.asp" -->
<!-- #INCLUDE FILE="markeddoc.asp" -->
<%
    var annotatedDoc = Server.CreateObject("MSXML2.DOMDocument.4.0");
    annotatedDoc.async = false;
    annotatedDoc.load(unescape(Request.QueryString("annotatedpage")));
    annotatedDoc.preserveWhiteSpace = true;

    // read in linkbase file
    var noteReader = new NoteReader(Request.QueryString("linksfile"));

    var notes = noteReader.getDescriptionNodes();

    var markedDoc = new MarkedDoc(annotatedDoc);

for(var i=0;i<notes.length;i++){
    filename = notes[i].getNoteFilename();
    pointExpr = new PointExpr(notes[i].getNoteContext());
    markedDoc.addMark(pointExpr, filename);
}

Response.Write(annotatedDoc.xml);
Response.End();
%>
```

There isn't much to this script, as most of the work is done elsewhere in code we have already seen. The document that has been annotated is loaded first of all, then a NoteReader object is called upon to load the information contained in the linkbase file. A MarkedDocument object is created, and the hyperlinks are then added, each based on a Description entry in the linkbase file.

What this script will do (with the aid of other objects) is transform the page that has been annotated by wrapping every identified piece of the page with tags in the manner we saw earlier, and what we will be wrapping these pieces with are hypertext links pointing to the XHTML files containing the comments the user entered, so if the selected text was "a long way" in the original document, and the annotation text was saved in 013720.htm the result would be:

```
<p>But there's <a href="C:\inetpub\wwwroot\linking\013720.html"><img
src="pencil.gif" border="0"/>a long way </a>to go...</p>
```

After adding a few annotations to a document using the earlier part of the application, we can pick it up in the browser:

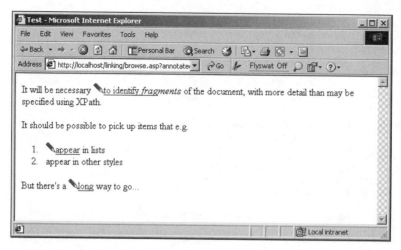

We have the sections clearly identified, and clicking on one of the links will bring up the page created from the user's comment:

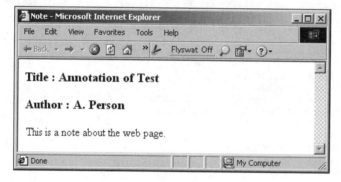

As a first prototype the system isn't too bad, though it is worth pointing out some of the more glaring holes. Most obviously there are parts of the Amaya annotation system that haven't even been attempted, such as the ability to modify and delete annotations. Another significant omission is the facility to post annotation information to remote servers. Though it hasn't really been mentioned, the application as it stands will only annotate XML documents, though there is something that can be done about this, which we'll be seeing in the next few pages.

Converting HTML to XML

At the start of this chapter we made the assumption that the source page we would be dealing with would be XML. For an annotation tool to be much use on the Web, it would have to deal with the format of pages found there, and in general this certainly isn't XML. Though use of XHTML is growing, this is only found on a tiny proportion of the Web; more generally pages are found in various versions of HTML. Or rather purporting to be HTML – a significant proportion of pages fall far short of any HTML standard, and it is only due to the forgiving nature of most browsers that these can be viewed at all. So how do we get this stuff found on the Web into a form that MSXML can use? Fortunately help is at hand, thanks to a rather magical tool from Dave Raggett of the W3C, "HTML Tidy". We will now see how this tool (wrapped as a COM object) can be used in a script to make a HTML to XML preprocessor for the annotation tool.

HTML Tidy

There isn't space here to describe HTML Tidy beyond the essentials we need in the context of MSXML, but basically it is a utility that fixes mistakes in HTML. For instance, given something like:

```
<h1>heading
<h2>subheading</h3>
```

Tidy will correct to:

```
<h1>heading</h1>
<h2>subheading</h2>
```

HTML Tidy offers a very wide range of options for cleaning and formatting HTML, and the one we're interested in here is its ability to reformat HTML into XML. The regular version is a command-line tool, available for virtually any platform from http://www.w3.org/People/Raggett/tidy/ (it's "postcardware", so don't forget the stamp). Several GUI and HTML editors have been built around the same base code, as well as a COM component, and this latter is what we'll be using here.

TidyCOM

TidyCOM is a free component by André Blavier, which adds most of the functionality of HTML Tidy to Windows programming languages. It is available as a DLL from http://perso.wanadoo.fr/ablavier/TidyCOM/ and installation is simply a matter of registering the DLL. For example, from the same directory as TidyCOM.dll type the following at the command prompt:

>regsvr32 TidyCOM.dll

To use this component in a script, it is necessary to create an instance of it, and working with server-side JScript this calls for a line like this:

```
var objTidy = Server.CreateObject("TidyCOM.TidyObject");
```

The fixing and formatting behavior of HTML Tidy can either be specified in command-line options (several dozen are available) or using a configuration file. Similarly, the behavior of a TidyCOM object can be loaded from a text file or specified through its Options property. So if for example we want to use the object to make all the tags in an HTML file upper-case, we could say:

```
objTidy.Options.UppercaseTags = true;
```

The TidyCOM interface offers three methods to carry out the transformation:

❑ TidyToMem() – applies Tidy to a file and returns tidied content as a string.

❑ TidyToFile() – applies Tidy to a file and saves the result as another file (can be same file).

❑ TidyMemToMem() – applies Tidy to a string and returns a string.

In the preprocessor for our annotation application, we'll be using the TidyToFile() method. The part of the script that will carry out this part of the preprocessing is as follows:

405

```
var objTidy = Server.CreateObject("TidyCOM.TidyObject");

    // Convert to XHTML
objTidy.Options.OutputXhtml = true;

    // Add XML declaration (pi)
objTidy.Options.AddXmlDecl = true;

    // Convert non-XML named entities to numeric form
objTidy.Options.NumericEntities = true;

    // Remove any DOCTYPE declaration
objTidy.Options.Doctype = "omit";

    // Apply Tidy to strSourceFile, result in strTargetFile
objTidy.TidyToFile(strSourceFile, strTargetFile);
```

The options chosen here are those, that provide an end result that is likely to be suitable for use with MSXML. Among the available options for `TidyCOM` there is `OutputXml`, which might have seemed a more appropriate choice than `OutputXhtml` as used here. However, this does not allow the removal of the `DOCTYPE` declaration. If this declaration is left in, then MSXML will attempt to validate the document against the given DTD, and in practice a lot of the time it will be found that there are things on the web page that are not covered by the DTD. This workaround raises another issue, in that MSXML may balk at entities that might have been declared in associated character entity sets (for example: ` `). To get around this, the `NumericEntities` option is set to `true` so these are replaced by numeric equivalents (` ` becomes ` `), which will now pass happily through the XML parser.

Using HTML Tidy can be something of an eye-opener. When it cleans a file, it produces an informational list of warnings, for example:

line 8 column 2 - Warning: discarding unexpected </span>
line 16 column 1 - Warning: <table> lacks "summary" attribute
line 19 column 1 - Warning: <tr> unknown attribute value "middle"
line 21 column 1 - Warning: <table> lacks "summary" attribute
line 36 column 1 - Warning: <table> lacks "summary" attribute
line 39 column 5 - Warning: img lacks "alt" attribute
...

The list includes details of the changes it has made, as well as recommendations on how the HTML can be improved. These recommendations include suggestions for making the page more accessible, an important consideration for all web content providers. More information on this can be found at http://www.w3.org/WAI/Resources/. If Tidy encounters something it doesn't recognize, and so can't fix the problem, this will be recorded in a list of errors. `TidyCOM` provides access to the warnings and errors through the following properties:

- ❑ `TotalWarnings` – number of warning messages.

- ❑ `Warning(i)` – ith warning message.

- ❑ `TotalErrors` – number of error messages.

- ❑ `Error(i)` – ith error message.

These warnings and errors can be very useful when trying to get HTML pages into a form usable by MSXML, so in the HTML preprocessor code we are about to see there is script to get these into a form that is convenient for server-side activities.

HTML to MSXML Preprocessor

The facilities offered by HTML Tidy through `TidyCOM` go a long way towards getting web-style HTML into MSXML, but there is still one common problem that needs to be resolved. Some of the character sequences that occur in scripts embedded in HTML pages are not friendly. For instance, let's say the following appears in the head of a HTML document:

```
<script type="text/javascript" language="JavaScript">
    var x = 123 && 345;
</script>
```

Perfectly reasonable script as far as most browsers are concerned, but if we leave this in an otherwise acceptable XML document and try and load it into a MSXML DOM document, it will cause the error: "A name was started with an invalid character". What the parser doesn't like here is the sequence "&&". It is probable that the main reason for loading a web page into an XML DOM tree would be to do things with the page content, rather than anything relating to scripts in the page. Because of this, a brute force solution is offered here – strip out `<script>` blocks altogether. This is pretty straightforward to achieve using JScript's regular expressions facilities, as we will see in a moment. First though, an overview of the preprocessing script. The script (`tidygrab.asp`) will be provided with the URL of the page we want to make MSXML-friendly. It will construct a `TidyGrab` object which will tie together most of the operations needed.

This script uses the `WinHTTP` component, which needs to be installed – see Chapter 16.

There are many potential errors that might occur along the way, so fairly thorough error logging is carried out. The script is in no way tied to the annotation application, and is likely to be useful in other applications; an example of its use (commented out) is given first:

```
<%@ LANGUAGE=JScript %>
<%
/* sample usage
 var tg = new TidyGrab("http://microsoft.com");
 var xmlDoc = tg.getXmlDoc();
 Response.Write(xmlDoc.xml);
 Response.Write(tg.getErrors());
 Response.End();
 */
```

A `TidyGrab` object is created with the source URL being supplied. A call to the `getXmlDoc()` method will return a DOM document containing the cleaned XML version of the page at the URL. The XML is displayed, followed by all the warnings and errors generated by the script. Using the Microsoft site as a source, the result is a reasonably legible view of the page, followed by 30 or so warnings from HTML Tidy, primarily regarding the page's accessibility failings. Note that images won't be displayed – the page shown in the browser will be local, and so any relative links to images will thus be broken. The start of the code proper is the `TidyGrab()` object constructor. This retains the URL supplied, and then declares the methods of the class. Three empty strings are created to hold any error messages generated in different parts of the script. The strings `htmlFilename` and `xmlFilename` hold the (local) locations for the HTML page grabbed and the cleaned XML version respectively.

```
function TidyGrab(strUrl){
    this.strUrl = strUrl;
```

```
   this.getPage = getPage;
   this.saveStrToFile = saveStrToFile;
   this.tidyToXml = tidyToXml;
   this.getXmlDoc = getXmlDoc;
   this.getErrors = getErrors;

   this.strHttpErrors = "";
   this.strXmlDocErrors = "";
   this.strTidyErrors = "";
   this.htmlFilename = "local.html";
   this.xmlFilename = "local.xml";
}
```

The method that will effect the preprocessing for us is getXmlDoc(), which calls the other methods and functions. Calling this method (after constructing a TidyGrab object) will cause the following to happen, through calls to other methods in the object:

❑   The page at the supplied URL will be pulled off the Web into a string (getPage).

❑   The string will have all <script> blocks removed (stripScripts).

❑   The string will be saved to disk locally (saveStrToFile).

❑   An HTML Tidy transformation will be applied to this local file, and the result saved (tidyToXml).

Once the local XML file has been created, an MSXML DOM document is created from the cleaned file. If the DomDocument.load() method returns false, then the operation has failed, and the error details are collected in a string, with HTML tags added to make it easy to view the error through a Response.Write call.

```
function getXmlDoc(){

   var htmlText = this.getPage();
   htmlText = stripScripts(htmlText);
   this.saveStrToFile(htmlText, Server.MapPath(this.htmlFilename));
   var tidyObj = this.tidyToXml(Server.MapPath(this.htmlFilename),
                               Server.MapPath(this.xmlFilename));

   var xmlDoc = Server.CreateObject("Msxml2.DOMDocument.4.0");
   xmlDoc.async = false;

   var success = xmlDoc.load(Server.MapPath(this.xmlFilename));
   if(success == false){
      this.strXmlDocErrors = "<p/> XML Document load error : "
      + "<br/>"+xmlDoc.parseError.reason
      +"<br/>line "+xmlDoc.parseError.line
      +", position "+xmlDoc.parseError.linepos
      +"<br/>"+xmlDoc.parseError.srcText;
   }
   return xmlDoc;
}
```

The getPage() method uses a WinHTTPRequest object to pull the page from the URL specified. Should this operation fail, the exception is caught and the error details placed in a string, again formatted for easy display:

```
function getPage(){
   var strResult;
   try{
```

```
        // Create the WinHTTPRequest object
    var WinHttpReq = Server.CreateObject("WinHttp.WinHttpRequest.5");

        //  Create a HTTP request
        var temp = WinHttpReq.Open("GET", this.strUrl, false);

        //  Send the HTTP request
        WinHttpReq.Send();

        //  Retrieve the response text
        strResult = WinHttpReq.ResponseText;
    }catch(objError){
        this.strHttpErrors = "<p/>WinHttp Error :"
    + "<br/>" + objError
    + "<br/>" + (objError.number & 0xFFFF).toString()
    + "<br/>"+objError.description;
    }

        //  Return the response text
        return strResult;
    }
```

The `saveStrToFile` uses a `FileSystemObject` to save the named string to the named file, overwriting if the file already exists (`FileSystemObject` is described in the JScript documentation):

```
function saveStrToFile(strText, strFilename){

    var objFileSystem = Server.CreateObject("Scripting.FileSystemObject");
    var textFile = objFileSystem.CreateTextFile(strFilename, true);
// overwrite flag is true
    textFile.Write (strText);
    textFile.Close();
}
```

The `tidyToXml()` method uses a `TidyCOM` object to clean and convert the file in `strSourceFile`, saving the result in `strTargetFile`, after setting the options we saw earlier:

```
function tidyToXml(strSourceFile, strTargetFile){

    // Create HTML Tidy COM object
    var objTidy = Server.CreateObject("TidyCOM.TidyObject");

    // Convert to XHTML option
    objTidy.Options.OutputXhtml = true;

    // Add XML declaration (pi) option
    objTidy.Options.AddXmlDecl = true;

    // Convert non-XML named entities to numeric form
    objTidy.Options.NumericEntities = true;

    // Remove any DOCTYPE declaration
    objTidy.Options.Doctype = "omit";

    // Apply Tidy to strSourceFile, result in strTargetFile
    objTidy.TidyToFile(strSourceFile, strTargetFile);
```

The latter part of the method uses the properties exposed by the `TidyCOM` interface to gather first the error messages then the warnings generated by the tidying process. These messages contain references to the HTML tags in the source document, so to allow display in a generated page the "<" and ">" characters found in the messages are escaped (to `&lt;` and `&gt;`) using a helper function listed later in the script:

```
    // Accumulate HTML Tidy error & warning messages
    this.strTidyErrors = "<p/> HTMLTidy Errors/Warnings";
    var i = 0;
    var strError;
    while(i<objTidy.TotalErrors){
        strError = objTidy.Error(i);
        strError = escapeTags(strError);
        this.strTidyErrors += "<br/>"+strError;
        i++;
    }
    while(i<objTidy.TotalWarnings){
        strError = objTidy.Warning(i);
        strError = escapeTags(strError);
        this.strTidyErrors += "<br/>"+strError;
        i++;
    }
}
```

The `getErrors()` method simply concatenates and returns the HTML-format errors messages generated by the previous methods:

```
function getErrors(){
    return this.strHttpErrors+this.strXmlDocErrors+this.strTidyErrors;
}
```

The following function uses the powerful regular expression capability of JScript to remove any `<script>...</script>` blocks found in the string it has been sent (the function uses a 'non-greedy' regexp; a good explanation of these can be found at http://www.4guysfromrolla.com/webtech/regularexpressions.shtml).

```
// Removes <script> blocks
function stripScripts(strText){
    var regexp = /<script(.|\n)+?<\/script>/gi;
    strText = strText.replace(regexp, "");
    return strText;
}
```

Finally the `escapeTags()` function replaces "<" and ">" so that a string containing these can be viewed literally in a browser:

```
function escapeTags(strSource){
    strSource = strSource.replace("<", "&lt;");
    strSource = strSource.replace(">", "&gt;");
    return strSource;
}
%>
```

Summary

XML 1.0 only reached the status of W3C Recommendation in February 1998 and a second edition (with fairly minor amendments) appeared in October 2000. There has been little talk of XML 2.0. The standard has been adopted globally by software developers in every corner of the market, and indeed by the academic world as well. The key to the success of XML is most likely its extensibility, its ability to play the role of a baseline language through which other technologies can communicate. Although most of the time we see the extensibility of XML demonstrated in 'yet another markup language', there are other areas in which this baseline has been extended to make more productive use of computers. A visit to the XML pages of the W3C will demonstrate that not all of the creative work is being done on top of XML but also underneath (XML Infoset) and at the sides. We have taken a look around some of these sides in this chapter – how one might point to particular pieces of text, or describe a link between two documents in a third document. These are things that aren't in the baseline XML, but add functionality alongside and in a tight relationship with what is described in the XML 1.0 Specification.

XML Application Development with MSXML 4.0
SOAP
XHTML
XML Schemas DTDs XPath CSS
XML Namespaces
XML 1.0
MSXML

9

Sending and Retrieving XML Data

The simplicity and flexibility of XML make it an ideal choice for moving data from one place to another. This is why the recent business-to-business (B2B) and application-integration initiatives like Web Services, BizTalk, ebXML, the .NET Framework, and RosettaNet rely heavily on XML. Since an XML document is simply a text format, it can be easily transmitted and utilized across platforms, across machines, and over the Internet. XML data can flow between, for example, a browser and web server, a database server and web server, various tiers of an n-tier application, or between two applications.

Using XML as the medium for "data-on-move", instead of traditional data transfer mechanisms (such as ADO recordsets, property bags, variant arrays, and field delimited text), offers interesting benefits and a lot of flexibility. Firstly, the data can move from one platform to another very easily, and any programming language can be used to access that data. Secondly, it does not suffer the overhead of marshaling ADO objects, and is a much cleaner and simpler interface when compared to property bags. We might think that passing XML strings can lead to performance issues, but in most cases we'll actually see better performance while passing XML strings as compared to passing ADO objects. In addition, XML compresses extremely well due to the repetitive nature of the tags used to describe data structure, and we can get better results by enabling the HTTP 1.1 compression feature while transmitting the XML data.

> *To learn more about using HTTP Compression with IIS, see Microsoft KB article Q255801 "How to Determine if HTTP Compression is in Use". Also see the article "Using HTTP Compression on Your IIS 5.0 Web Site" at*
> *http://www.microsoft.com/technet/prodtechnol/iis/maintain/featusability/httpcomp.asp.*

In this chapter we'll learn about generating XML data on the server or on the middle tier, sending it to the client, and also retrieving XML data posted by the client. We'll start by looking at various ways to generate XML and send it to the recipient; then we'll have a detailed look at `ServerXMLHTTP`, an important class to request or post HTTP data using MSXML. We'll also look at how to retrieve the XML data posted by the client. Finally we will consider data transmission in a distributed environment, and see how `ServerXMLHTTP` can help us when communicating with remote servers.

All of the sample files are included in the book code download available from the Wrox Press web site at http://www.wrox.com/.

Sending XML Data

Let's say we are developing a desktop application that needs to periodically update its content. To do this it calls an ASP page on our web server and gets the updated data. Next, we have to decide how we will send the updated data to the client desktop application.

The first approach would be to return data as delimited text. This is an old approach and has lots of limitations, such as if we were to send some binary data as part of the results. How would we validate the structure and contents of the result data on the client? The better approach would be to send the data to the client as an XML document. This will ensure that the data is self-describing, extensible, and human- and computer-readable so we can very easily parse and validate the contents on the client. In this section we'll look at various ways of generating the data on the server and sending it to the client.

Generating XML Manually

Let's start with a simple example to generate and send XML data to the client. The following ASP code, `TestSend1.asp`, manually generates the XML string and streams that to the `Response` object:

```
<%@ Language="VBScript" %>
<%
    Option Explicit
    Response.ContentType = "text/xml"

    Response.Write _
        "<?xml version='1.0' ?>" & _
        "<Personalization MemberID='10034'>" & _
        "<Name>Ann Garner</Name>" & _
        "<MyHome>/products/isd</MyHome>" & _
        "</Personalization>"
%>
```

The sample above is really straightforward. After setting the content type to `text/xml`, we simply spit out the XML using the `Response.Write` method call. With this method, it's our responsibility to make sure that the XML we are generating is at least well formed. When you run the above ASP page in the browser, you will see the following:

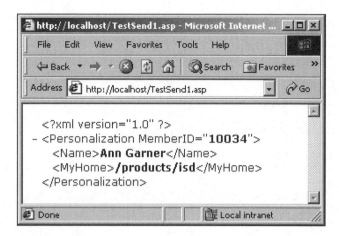

After setting the content type, we could even write the XML text as it is, instead of calling `Response.Write`, as in `TestSend1a.asp`:

```
<%@ Language="VBScript" %>
<%
    Response.ContentType = "text/xml"
%>

<?xml version='1.0' ?>

<Personalization MemberID='10034'>
<Name>Ann Garner</Name>
<MyHome>/products/isd</MyHome>
</Personalization>
```

Using DOM

So far we've dealt with very simple structured and textual XML data. What if we need to generate complex XML, which may also contain binary data (in some encoded form)? Let's also assume that we wanted to validate the generated XML before sending it to the client. The best option here would be to use MSXML DOM (Document Object Model) to dynamically build the XML documents.

Let's modify the above example to use the DOM to create the document instead of directly writing the XML text. For this and the rest of the examples we'll assume that MSXML 4.0 is installed on the server.

> *Prior to MSXML 4.0, it was possible to use version-independent ProgIDs and GUIDs, and by installing MSXML in replace mode it was possible to ensure that applications used the most recent parser. However, this approach leads to a lot of problems, making applications unstable because it was not the application that controlled which parser to use, but the settings and the mode in whichever parser was installed. MSXML 4.0 completely removes the support for version-independent ProgIDs/GUIDs and replace mode; it can be installed only in side-by-side mode. With this approach, now it's up to the application to choose which parser to use by specifying the version-dependent ProgIDs or GUIDs. This helps applications to work smoothly even if multiple versions of parsers are installed on a machine.*

In all the following examples, we'll use the version-dependent ProgIDs. The following code is `TestSendDOM.asp`:

```
<%@ Language="VBScript" %>
<%
    Option Explicit
    Response.ContentType = "text/xml"

    Dim objXMLDoc, objXMLDecl, objNode, objAttr, objChildNode

    Set objXMLDoc = Server.CreateObject("Msxml2.DOMDocument.4.0")

    Set objXMLDecl = _
    objXMLDoc.createProcessingInstruction("xml", "version='1.0'")

    objXMLDoc.appendChild objXMLDecl

    Set objNode = objXMLDoc.createElement("Personalization")
    objNode.setAttribute "MemberID", "10034"
    Set objXMLDoc.documentElement = objNode

    Set objChildNode = objXMLDoc.createElement("Name")
    objChildNode.nodeTypedValue = "Ann Garner"
    objNode.appendChild objChildNode

    Set objChildNode = objXMLDoc.createElement("MyHome")
    objChildNode.nodeTypedValue = "/products/isd"
    objNode.appendChild objChildNode

    Response.Write objXMLDoc.xml
%>
```

Like the first example, the above code also starts by setting the content type to `text/xml`. It then creates an XML `DOMDocument` object, and adds the XML declaration line using the `createProcessingInstruction()` and `appendChild()` method calls. We then create a `Personalization` element, add an attribute, and create `Name` and `MyHome` sub-elements. Finally we send the generated XML document to the response stream. The output is the same as before.

MSXML DOM interfaces are covered in greater detail in Chapter 2.

Using SAX

In some cases, when the data is not very dynamic, we might want to save the XML in a disk file on the server and then just send that XML file content whenever required, instead of generating XML every time the web page is called. Here, we may just want to read the file and stream the XML content, and do not necessarily need the full XML document loaded in memory, as happens with the DOM. In such scenarios, SAX (Simple API for XML) offers better performance and an efficient solution.

SAX programming with MSXML is covered in detail in Chapter 6.

Let's now look at an example (`TestSendSAX.asp`) of using SAX to read an XML file (`mySettings.xml`), parse it, and send the contents to the client:

```
<%@ Language="VBScript" %>
<%
    Option Explicit
    Response.ContentType = "text/xml"

    Dim writer, reader
    Set writer = Server.CreateObject("Msxml2.MXXMLWriter.4.0")
    set reader = Server.CreateObject("Msxml2.SAXXMLReader.4.0")

    Set reader.contentHandler = writer

    writer.output = Response

    reader.parseURL Server.MapPath("mySettings.xml")
%>
```

As we saw in Chapter 6, SAX is an event-based XML parsing API. It reads the XML document and generates parsing events. In the above example, we are using an MSXML-provided class, `MXXMLWriter`, as the `contentHandler` for SAX parsing. Hence, when the above code executes and starts parsing `mySettings.xml`, the MSXML SAX parser sends parsing event notifications to the `MXXMLWriter` object (`writer`), which in turn builds the XML document again. As we have specified the `output` property as the ASP `Response` object, it streams the resultant XML to the client, as shown:

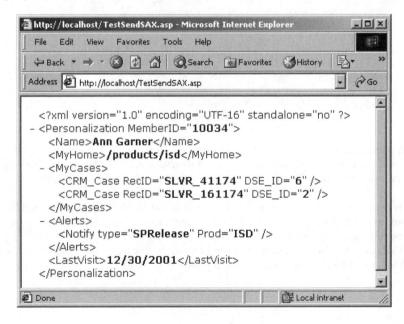

Using ADO

The above examples either manually created the XML document or used an XML file to read and send XML data to the client. Most of the time, though, we may want to read a database, build the XML, and send that to the client.

ADO (ActiveX Data Objects) is the primary data access API from Microsoft, and can be used to connect to just about any data source via OLE DB providers. ADO 2.1 first introduced support for XML persistence of ADO recordsets, then ADO 2.5 enhanced it by adding support for working with streams and also for hierarchical Recordset objects.

The following example, TestSendADO1.asp, connects to SQL Server 2000 and gets the data from the Customers table in the NorthWind sample database. It then uses the Save() method of the Recordset object to persist the data in XML format to the Response stream:

```
<%@ Language="VBScript" %>
<%
    Option Explicit
    Response.ContentType = "text/xml"

    Dim objADORS

    Set objADORS = Server.CreateObject("ADODB.RecordSet")

    objADORS.Open "SELECT CustomerId, ContactName FROM Customers", _
        "PROVIDER=SQLOLEDB; USER ID=sa; PASSWORD=;" & _
        "INITIAL CATALOG=NorthWind"

    objADORS.Save Response, 1 '1 stands for adPersistXML

    objADORS.Close

    Set objADORS = Nothing
%>
```

The second parameter to the Save() method is the enum value (1) for adPersistXML, which tells ADO to persist the data in XML format instead of its native ADTG (Advanced Data Tablegram) format. The persisted output contains the XML-Data schema followed by the actual data.

The ADO recordset can be persisted in XML format to a disk file, a stream, or an XML DOMDocument object, based on the first parameter passed to it. In the above example, we are passing the Response stream as the first parameter and hence the resultant XML is streamed to the client. To save the recordset XML as a disk file, we could pass the filename string as the first parameter, and to save the recordset XML to a DOM document, we could pass the MSXML DOMDocument object.

When we view `TestSendADO1.asp` in IE, the output looks like this:

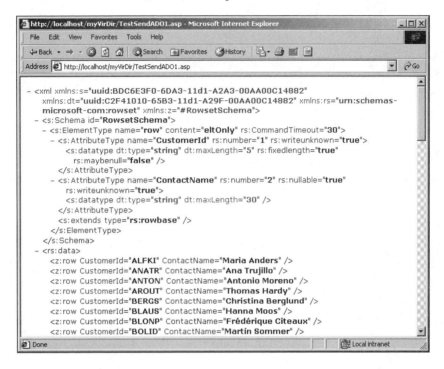

Using ADO and DOM

Using ADO's XML persistence support we can easily generate an XML document from the recordset. However, with this method we do not get much control over the output XML document. ADO generates an element (named `row`) per record, and an attribute for each column. Also, there is no way to omit the schema from the output XML.

The following example, `TestSendADOnDOM.asp`, illustrates using ADO and the DOM together – ADO to retrieve the database data and the DOM to generate the XML for that data.

We first set the content type to `text/xml`, then connect to the database and retrieve the recordset:

```
<%@ Language="VBScript" %>
<%
    Option Explicit
    Response.ContentType = "text/xml"

    Dim objADORS, objFields, objCurField
    Dim objXMLDoc, objXMLDecl, objNode, objAttr, objChildNode, objDataNode
    Dim iIndex

    Set objADORS = Server.CreateObject("ADODB.RecordSet")

    objADORS.Open "SELECT * FROM Authors", _
          "PROVIDER=SQLOLEDB; USER ID=sa; PASSWORD=;" & _
          "INITIAL CATALOG=Pubs"
```

Next, we create the XML DOM document object, the XML declaration line, and the root node:

```
Set objXMLDoc = Server.CreateObject("Msxml2.DOMDocument.4.0")

Set objXMLDecl = _
objXMLDoc.createProcessingInstruction("xml", "version='1.0'")

objXMLDoc.appendChild objXMLDecl

Set objNode = objXMLDoc.createElement("Authors")
Set objXMLDoc.documentElement = objNode
```

Next, we'll iterate over all the records to generate the rest of the XML document. For each record in the recordset, we'll create an element named `AnAuthor`, and then for each field in that record we'll create a sub-element under the `AnAuthor` element. The field sub-elements will have the same name as the field and the field's value will be used as the element content.

```
While not objADORS.EOF
    Set objFields = objADORS.Fields

    Set objChildNode = objXMLDoc.createElement("AnAuthor")
    objNode.appendChild objChildNode

    For iIndex = 0 to objFields.Count - 1
        Set objCurField = objFields.item(iIndex)

        Set objDataNode = _
            objXMLDoc.createElement(objCurField.Name)

        If not (IsNull(objCurField.value)) then
            objDataNode.nodeTypedValue = _
            trim(CStr(objCurField.value))
        End if
        objChildNode.appendChild objDataNode
    Next

    objADORS.MoveNext
Wend
```

Once the XML document is created we can do various things with it, including sending it to the client, and applying a stylesheet to transform it. In this example, we are just going to send the XML directly to the client:

```
Response.Write objXMLDoc.xml
objADORS.Close

Set objADORS = Nothing
%>
```

The above ASP page produces the following output:

Sending Binary Data

One of the reasons behind XML's success is its textual nature; XML documents are text documents and hence can travel from one platform to another without any compatibility issues. However, what if we were to send some binary data as part of the XML document, such as an image, or a Microsoft Word or PDF document?

In order to send the binary data as part of the XML document, it needs to be text encoded using the **base64** encoding.

> *Base64 encoding, specified in RFC 2045 – MIME (Multipurpose Internet Mail Extensions), uses a 64-character subset (A-Za-z0-9+/) to represent binary data and = for padding. Base64 processes data as 24-bit groups, mapping this data to four encoded characters. It is sometimes referred to as 3-to-4 encoding. Each 6 bits of the 24-bit group is used as an index into a mapping table (the base64 alphabet) to obtain a character for the encoded data. According to the MIME specification the encoded data has line lengths limited to 76 characters, but this line length restriction does not apply when transmitting base64-encoded binary XML data. For more information, go to http://www.ietf.org/rfc/rfc2045.txt. There is also further coverage of XML encoding issues with MSXML in Chapter 12, "Working with Data on the Client".*

Using MSXML DOM

MSXML DOM provides a convenient mechanism to encode binary data using base64 encoding. Let's look at an example of this.

The following ASP page, `TestSendBinary.asp`, accepts `EmployeeID` as a parameter and returns the employee details for that particular employee. The employee details also contain a `Photo` field, which is a SQL Server image data type field, and we'll send that field as base64-encoded text as part of our return XML.

The initial data-access code is similar to the code in the above example. We connect to the database and retrieve the `Employee` record. Then we create an XML `DOMdocument` object and create the root node. If a matching record is found, we add an element for each field:

```
<%@ Language="VBScript" %>
<%
    Option Explicit
    Response.ContentType = "text/xml"

    Dim objADORS, objFields, objCurField
    Dim objXMLDoc, objXMLDecl, objNode, objAttr, objDataNode
    Dim iIndex

    Set objADORS  = Server.CreateObject("ADODB.RecordSet")

    objADORS.Open "SELECT * FROM Employees WHERE EmployeeID = " & _
            Request.QueryString("EmployeeID"),  _
            "PROVIDER=SQLOLEDB; USER ID=sa; PASSWORD=;" & _
            "INITIAL CATALOG=Northwind"

    Set objXMLDoc = Server.CreateObject("Msxml2.DOMDocument.4.0")

    Set objXMLDecl = _
    objXMLDoc.createProcessingInstruction("xml", "version='1.0'")
    objXMLDoc.appendChild objXMLDecl

    Set objNode = objXMLDoc.createElement("EmpDetails")
    Set objXMLDoc.documentElement = objNode

    If not objADORS.EOF then

        Set objFields = objADORS.Fields

        For iIndex = 0 to objFields.Count - 1
            Set objCurField = objFields.item(iIndex)

            Set objDataNode = _
                objXMLDoc.createElement(objCurField.Name)
```

Next, we check if the field data type is binary (enum `205` for `adLongVarBinary`), and if so we set the DOM node data type as `bin.base64`, which in turn "auto-magically" converts binary field data to base64 format for us:

```
        If objCurField.Type = 205 then
            objDataNode.dataType = "bin.base64"
            objDataNode.nodeTypedValue = objCurField.value
        else
            If not (IsNull(objCurField.value)) then
                objDataNode.nodeTypedValue = _
                trim(CStr(objCurField.value))
            End if
        end if

        objNode.appendChild objDataNode

    Next

    End If

    Response.Write objXMLDoc.xml
    objADORS.Close

    Set objADORS = Nothing
%>
```

If you browse to the above ASP page in IE, the output will look like the following. The ASP page requires a `QueryString` parameter (`EmployeeID`), so make sure you include this in the URL.

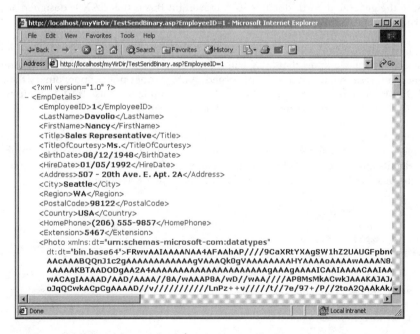

Note how the binary image field (`Photo`) is encoded using the base64 encoding by the MSXML DOM parser.

We can also send multiple binary files this way – if a database table has multiple binary fields, they will all be encoded using base64 in the final XML output.

> **The MSXML parser version 2.0a has a bug related to base64 encoding; it uses the asterisk (*) instead of the slash character (/) of the base64 character set. See KB article Q301356 for details, at http://support.microsoft.com/default.aspx?scid=kb;EN-US;q301356.**

In the above examples we used DOM in conjunction with ADO to build the XML document to be sent to the client. If we need to, we can update, query, or transform the document, since it's in memory as a DOM tree representation. If we don't need to further process the document on the server, and just need to stream the XML data to the client, we can use SAX and the MXXMLWriter class along with ADO as an efficient solution in such cases. Let's look at an example of this before moving on to the next section. In the following example we'll use ADO to fetch a record and we'll then build the XML document for that record, using SAX.

ADO, Binary Data, and SAX

In the earlier example, we learned about MSXML DOM's ability to work with binary data and convert it to base64 encoding. There is currently no such support in SAX, meaning that when we create XML documents using SAX, there is no way to convert binary data and output it in some encoded form (such as base64) in the generated XML document. A reason for this is that SAX is designed and well suited for simply reading the XML document.

However, in situations where we need to build large XML documents and do not need to process them, but simply send them, we know that SAX will score better when compared to DOM as far as performance and resource utilization is concerned. As SAX does not support binary data, we combine SAX and DOM and make the best use of both. In this example we'll use SAX to build the XML document, and use DOM to encode the binary field data into base64.

The following ASP page (TestSendADOnSAX.asp) accepts EmployeeID as a parameter and returns the employee details for that particular employee, like in the earlier example. Remember that the employee details also contain a Photo field, which is a SQL Server image (binary) data type field. We'll start with the usual code to set the content type and variable declarations:

```
<%@ Language="VBScript" %>
<%
    Option Explicit
    Response.ContentType = "text/xml"

    Dim objADORS, objFields, objField, strFieldName
    Dim objXMLDoc, objXMLElem

    Dim objWriter, objAttrib

    Set objADORS  = Server.CreateObject("ADODB.RecordSet")
    Set objWriter = Server.CreateObject("Msxml2.MXXMLWriter.4.0")
    Set objAttrib = Server.CreateObject("Msxml2.SAXAttributes.4.0")
```

Next, we fill the recordset:

```
objADORS.Open "select * from Employees where EmployeeID = " & _
        Request.QueryString("EmployeeID"),  _
        "PROVIDER=SQLOLEDB; USER ID=sa; PASSWORD=;" & _
        "INITIAL CATALOG=Northwind"
```

The MXXMLWriter class is used to fire the SAX events and create the XML document. The following lines of code set the properties to generate the formatted XML output and skip the XML declaration line from the output XML:

```
objWriter.indent = True
objWriter.omitXMLDeclaration = True
```

Next, we start actually building the document, by calling startDocument and creating the root element named EmpDetails, using the startElement method call:

```
objWriter.startDocument

objWriter.startElement "", "EmpDetails", "EmpDetails", objAttrib
```

For each field in the current record, we'll call startElement to generate the sub-element under the EmpDetails node:

```
If Not objADORS.EOF Then
   Set objFields = objADORS.Fields

   For Each objField In objFields
      strFieldName = objField.Name

      objWriter.startElement "", strFieldName, strFieldName, _
                    objAttrib
```

The next code block is at the heart of this example. If the field value is not NULL, we then check if the field data type is binary. If yes, we use MSXML DOM to build the XML document containing just one element for the binary field. We then fire the SAX characters event, passing the base64 encoded binary data using the Text property of the element just created. For other (non-binary) fields, we simply fire the SAX characters events passing the field value string.

```
If Not (IsNull(objField.value)) Then

    'adBinary=128, adLongVarBinary=205
    If objField.Type = 128 OR objField.Type = 205 Then

        Set objXMLDoc = _
            Server.CreateObject("Msxml2.DOMDocument.4.0")

        objXMLDoc.loadXML "<" & strFieldName & "/>"

        objXMLDoc.documentElement.dataType="bin.base64"
```

```
                    objXMLDoc.documentElement.nodeTypedValue = _
                        objField.Value

                    objWriter.characters _
                            objXMLDoc.documentElement.Text
            Else

                    objWriter.characters Trim(CStr(objField.Value))
                End If
            End If
```

We then end the field sub-element and at the end of the loop, we end the EmpDetails element. We finally end the document by calling the endDocument SAX event. The generated XML document is then sent to the client using Response.Write.

```
        objWriter.endElement "", strFieldName,strFieldName

    Next
    End If

    objWriter.endElement "", "EmpDetails", "EmpDetails"

    objWriter.endDocument

    Response.Write objWriter.output

    objADORS.Close
    Set objADORS = Nothing
%>
```

We access the generated XML document using the output property of the MXXMLWriter class. Again, add the QueryString parameter (EmployeeID) to your URL. Note that this is just a string containing XML text and not the in-memory tree representation of objects as happens with DOM. This example produces the same output as in the previous example.

With this example, let's now move forward to the next section and learn about using MSXML in conjunction with SQL Server 2000 XML features. The following example is one of the many ways to get SQL Server data in XML format over HTTP.

Using SQL Server 2000 Native XML Features

SQL Server 2000 introduced native support for XML. The FOR XML clause with the SELECT SQL statement allows direct access to relational data in XML format. SQL Server 2000 also introduced access to relation data in XML format directly over HTTP. A tool is provided to configure IIS virtual directories that point to a specific database in SQL Server. Once the virtual directory is configured, the data can be accessed either by writing SQL queries as part of a URL, or by saving queries in template files under the virtual directory and then accessing the template files. The results of queries are returned in XML format.

> To learn more about SQL Server 2000 XML features, see "Professional SQL Server 2000 XML" (ISBN 1-861005-46-6, Wrox Press).

In the following example, `TestSendSQL2K.asp`, we'll use ADO to connect to SQL Server 2000 and get `Authors` table data in XML format using SQL Server 2000's `FOR XML` clause. If no parameter is passed to the ASP page, the XML data is sent as it is to the client. However, if a parameter named `print` with a value of "Y" is passed to the ASP page, we load the returned XML text into a DOM document, apply a stylesheet (`authors.xsl`) to get HTML and send that to the client:

```
<%@ Language="VBScript" %>
<%
Option Explicit
Dim objConn, objADOComm, objADOStream
Dim objXMLDoc, objXSLDoc
Dim strXMLText

Set ObjConn      = Server.CreateObject("ADODB.Connection")
Set objADOComm   = Server.CreateObject("ADODB.Command")
Set objADOStream = Server.CreateObject("ADODB.Stream")

Set objXMLDoc    = Server.CreateObject("Msxml2.DOMDocument.4.0")

ObjConn.Open _
      "PROVIDER=SQLOLEDB; USER ID=sa; PASSWORD=;" & _
      "INITIAL CATALOG=Pubs"


objADOComm.CommandText = "select * from Authors FOR XML RAW"

Set objADOComm.ActiveConnection = ObjConn

objADOStream.Open

objADOComm.Properties("Output Stream").Value = objADOStream

objADOComm.Execute , , 1024 '1024 is enum for adExecuteStream
```

The above lines of code make a database connection, execute the `FOR XML` query and get the results in the `ADODB Stream` object.

The `FOR XML` query returns records in XML format without the root node. In other words, it returns an XML fragment instead of a well-formed document. Hence, we'll add the root node overselves before loading the XML text into the DOM document:

```
strXMLText = "<Authors>" & objADOStream.ReadText & "</Authors>"

If Request("print") = "Y" Then
   Response.ContentType = "text/html"

   objXMLDoc.loadXML strXMLText

   Set objXSLDoc    = Server.CreateObject("Msxml2.DOMDocument.4.0")
   objXSLDoc.load Server.MapPath("authors.xsl")

   Response.write objXMLDoc.transformNode(objXSLDoc)
Else
```

```
        Response.ContentType = "text/xml"
        Response.write strXMLText
    End If

    objADOStream.Close
    objConn.Close

    Set objADOStream = Nothing
    Set objConn = Nothing
%>
```

If the `print` parameter is passed to the ASP page, after loading the `Authors` XML data in a `DOMDocument` object, we load the XSL stylesheet, apply the transformation and send the resulting HTML to the client. The above page results in the following (notice "? print=Y" at the end of the URL):

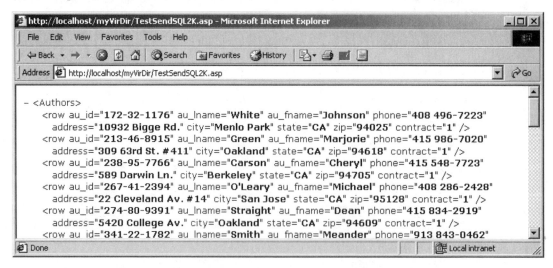

However, if no parameter is passed to the ASP page, we simply spit out the results of the FOR XML query and the output looks like this:

Passing XML Data from the Middle Tier

Let's now look at an example of passing XML data from a Visual Basic 6.0 COM component to an ASP page. The COM component will have just one class and a single method, GetAuthors, which connects to the Pubs sample SQL Server database and returns all the rows from the Authors table, in XML format.

The ASP page will then simply instantiate the COM object, call GetAuthors, which returns XML data as a string, and then either load this string into the XML DOM and process/transform it or directly stream the XML to the client. For simplicity, in this example, we'll just stream the returned XML string to illustrate the passing of XML data from one tier to another.

We first created a new Visual Basic 6.0 **ActiveX DLL** project, renaming the default class to PubsDBAccess, and saving the project as PubsDBAccessProj. References to MSXML 4.0 and Microsoft ActiveX Objects (ADO) 2.5 (or later) were added, as well as a public method called GetAuthors.

The implementation of this method is similar to the code in the previous ADO and DOM example, except here we have Visual Basic code instead of ASP VBScript code, and at the end we assign the DOM XML text to GetAuthors:

```
    GetAuthors = objXMLDoc.xml
End Function
```

For testing you will need to change the SQL Server connection parameters, then save and build the COM DLL.

Let's now look at the ASP code (TestSendComObj.asp), which accesses the above COM object:

```
<%@ Language="VBScript" %>
<%
    Option Explicit
    Response.ContentType = "text/xml"
    Dim objPubDBAcc

    Set objPubDBAcc = _
        Server.CreateObject("PubsDBAccessProj.PubsDBAccess")

    Response.Write objPubDBAcc.GetAuthors
%>
```

We first create an instance of our COM object and then call its GetAuthors method, which returns the Authors data as an XML string, and the ASP page simply streams that string to the Response object, producing exactly the same output as in the similar example described earlier:

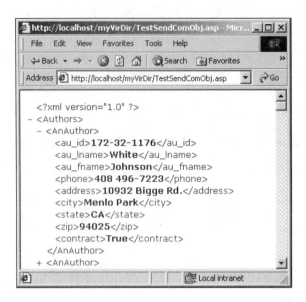

The alternative implementation of GetAuthors would be to return an IXMLDOMNode instead of a string. If we were to process the XML data again in the ASP page, in some cases it would have been better to return the IXMLDOMNode interface (when the document is very large and complex). However, returning a string generally results in better performance and gives us the freedom not to use MSXML on the client-side, and process the returned XML string as we wish. Another important point to remember is that when we return an interface pointer, each call to the property or method on the XML DOM object must go across the process/network boundaries, which might lead to performance/network-related issues.

All the examples above either generate the XML on the server or load a local XML file, but we might want to connect to a remote web site, get the XML, process it, and then send it to the client. For example, imagine that when our ASP page is called we need to get the XML from our partner's web site by sending an HTTP request for an XML file on their web site, process that XML, apply a transformation on it, and finally send the HTML to the client.

In the next section we'll learn how MSXML supports an excellent way to do HTTP-based communication. We'll continue to concentrate on the server/middle tier part of the programming – client-side HTTP communication using MSXML is covered later in Chapter 12, *"Working with Data on the Client"*.

ServerXMLHTTP

ServerXMLHTTP is a nice small class provided by MSXML (starting with version 3.0), to do **server-safe** HTTP communication. Before we go into the details of ServerXMLHTTP, let's briefly look at its history.

History

Microsoft IE relies on **WinInet** to do HTTP communication. WinInet is a low-level API provided by Microsoft that can be used by client applications (such as IE, Microsoft Office, etc.) to make HTTP calls.

MSXML 2 added a wrapper around WinInet and provided a class named XMLHTTP that can be used to access server XML data over HTTP. The XMLHTTP class implements the IXMLHTTPRequest interface defined by MSXML and has methods like open, setRequestHeader, and send, along with properties like status, responseXML, and responseText. For instance, in an HTML page, we can write some script code that instantiates XMLHTTP objects, loads XML from some remote server over HTTP and, let's say uses it to refresh the data on that web page.

XMLHTTP is designed for client-side HTTP access. It has the limitations of WinInet (is not thread-safe, limits the number of connections, and displays a user interface for some operations, such as collecting user credentials, etc.). It is best suited to be used from client applications and not on the server-side. There was a strong need to have a similar class to do server-side HTTP access – connecting to a remote server from an ASP page or a middle-tier COM component over HTTP.

With MSXML version 3.0, Microsoft introduced ServerXMLHTTP, a class similar to XMLHTTP, but thread-safe and designed for server-side HTTP access. The ServerXMLHTTP class implements the interface IServerXMLHTTPRequest, which is derived from IXMLHTTPRequest. It adds four methods: setTimeouts, waitForResponse, getOption, and setOption.

MSXML 4.0 further enhances the server-safe HTTP access by implementing IServerXMLHTTPRequest2 (which is derived from IServerXMLHTTPRequest), and adds two more methods (setProxy and setProxyCredentials) to control the proxy settings while using ServerXMLHTTP to access HTTP data through proxy servers.

The ServerXMLHTTP class does not use WinInet, but instead uses Microsoft Windows HTTP Services or **WinHTTP**, which is a new protocol stack specifically designed for server-side HTTP access.

WinHTTP

WinHTTP is a subset of WinInet, but is primarily designed to perform server-safe HTTP access. WinHTTP can be used in server applications (ASP pages, ISAPI extension DLLs, etc.) to connect to remote servers over HTTP and post and/or retrieve the data. It offers a thread-safe, reliable, and scalable HTTP access mechanism.

Like WinInet, WinHTTP is also available as a low-level API for C/C++ programmers, but unlike WinInet, WinHTTP is also accessible from scripts and Visual Basic as a COM object.

WinHTTP supports HTTP/1.0, HTTP/1.1, SSL, and server and proxy authentication. However, it doesn't support protocols other than HTTP, and it does not support autoproxy, autodialing, URL caching, etc. WinInet works on all the Microsoft platforms, but WinHTTP does not work on Windows 9x/Windows ME (and hence ServerXMLHTTP does not work on these platforms). WinInet uses some of the settings specified using IE, whereas no such thing is available with WinHTTP.

If a proxy is used to access the remote HTTP or HTTPS server, we need to inform WinHTTP about proxy settings. This can be done either using the proxy API provided by WinHTTP or the proxy configuration utility.

> **It is important to remember that WinHTTP proxy settings are separate from the proxy settings in IE. The -u parameter can be used with the `proxycfg` utility to import the current user's IE proxy settings; however, WinHTTP does not support auto-discovery and automatic configuration script-based proxy settings.**

As the `ServerXMLHTTP` component uses WinHTTP, the HTTP access using `ServerXMLHTTP` also depends on these proxy settings. Prior to MSXML 4.0, running the proxy configuration tool was the only way to set the proxy settings, but MSXML 4.0 now provides methods to specify proxy settings.

Proxy Configuration

The most common problem that developers face while working with `ServerXMLHTTP` is the error "Access Denied". This error may occur in either of two scenarios:

❑ The WinHTTP proxy settings are not configured correctly

❑ We are trying to access a site that requires integrated Windows authentication and the authentication information was either omitted or incorrect

We'll look at how to pass the NT authentication information later in the chapter. Let's now look at how to use the `proxycfg` tool to set the proxy settings for WinHTTP (and hence for `ServerXMLHTTP`).

The proxy configuration tool (`proxycfg.exe`) can be downloaded from http://msdn.microsoft.com/code/sample.asp?url=/msdn-files/027/001/468/msdncompositedoc.xml. Download the self-extracting EXE and unzip the files into an appropriate folder.

If we do not pass any parameters to the `proxycfg` utility, it will display the current WinHTTP proxy settings. The following are the command-line parameters available for use with the `proxycfg` utility:

Parameter	Description
-d	Specifies that all the HTTP and HTTPS servers should be accessed directly, without a proxy. We may use this switch if there is no proxy server.
-p	Used to list the proxy server for each protocol (HTTP or HTTPS). Also may be used to provide a list of servers that are accessed directly without a proxy.
-u	Specifies to use current user's IE proxy settings. However, remember that WinHTTP does not support automatic proxy detection and configuration script-based proxy detection.

> **The `proxycfg` tool updates the Registry and it is not possible to restore the previous settings. However, if required, we can remove the proxy configuration settings by deleting the `WinHttpSettings` key under \HKEY_LOCAL_MACHINE\SOFTWARE\Microsoft\Windows\CurrentVersion\Internet Settings\Connections.**

Let's look at some examples of using `proxycfg`. The following command displays the current WinHTTP proxy settings:

proxycfg

The following command tells `ServerXMLHTTP` (and all other WinHTTP applications) to directly access all the servers, without any proxy:

proxycfg -d

The next command specifies that all HTTP and HTTPS access should be done through the proxy server named `ISProxySvr`:

proxycfg –p ISProxySvr

The following command specifies that all HTTP and HTTPS access should be done through the proxy server named `ISProxySvr`, except any sites in `*.MyDomain.com`, which are accessed directly, bypassing the proxy:

proxycfg –p ISProxySvr "*.MyDomain.com"

The word `<local>` is the short form for any host names that do not contain a period (mostly intranet sites), and the following command specifies to use a proxy server for all HTTP and HTTPS access, except for local intranet servers, which are accessed directly:

proxycfg –p ISProxySvr "<local>"

Here we specify different proxies for HTTP and HTTPS access. Hence, all HTTP accesses (except local intranet sites) will go through `ISProxySvr` while all HTTPS requests will go through `SecISProxySvr`:

proxycfg –p "http=ISProxySvr https=SecISProxySvr" "<local>"

The next command is a special use of the `proxycfg` tool and can be used to access intranet web sites that require integrated Windows NT authentication where there is no proxy needed to access those servers. When you access the intranet web sites that are listed in the bypass list while configuring the proxy settings, if the proxy server is set (even if the server name is a string with one blank or any legal string value), WinHTTP will automatically pass the NTLM (NT LAN Manager) credentials to the server. Having said that, there is now no need to pass the user credentials to the `open` method to access such web sites using `ServerXMLHTTP`.

proxycfg –d –p " " "*"

Note the single space for the proxy server name (it's not a blank string, but has a single space), and that the bypass server list contains an asterisk (*), which means all server accesses.

> **Make sure to reset IIS (stop and restart) after running the proxy configuration utility. This is required since the utility updates the Registry.**

Having covered the basics, let's now look at the `ServerXMLHTTP` class and try out a few examples to see how it enables server-safe HTTP access.

Server-Safe HTTP Data Access

In this section we'll explore the `ServerXMLHTTP` class and see how it helps in performing server-to-server HTTP communication.

Loading Remote XML Documents

There are primarily two ways to access XML documents on a remote server: using the `setProperty` method of `DOMDocument` or directly, using `ServerXMLHTTP`.

Using DOMDocument

Let's look at the first method, which uses the standard DOM `load` method. Before we call `load`, however, we need to set the `ServerHTTPRequest` property to `true`. Consider the following code (`TestSXH1.asp`):

```
<%@ Language="VBScript" %>
<%
Option Explicit
Response.ContentType = "text/xml"

Dim objXMLDoc, objSelNode
Dim ProductID, SearchExp

ProductID = Request.QueryString("ProdID")
Set objXMLDoc = Server.CreateObject("Msxml2.DOMDocument.4.0")

objXMLDoc.setProperty "ServerHTTPRequest", true

objXMLDoc.async = false

objXMLDoc.load "http://MyRemoteServer/product.xml"

SearchExp = "/Product/row[@productid='" & ProductID & "']"

Set objSelNode = objXMLDoc.selectSingleNode (SearchExp)

Response.write objSelNode.xml
%>
```

The above ASP code accepts the `ProductID` as the parameter; it then loads an XML document from a remote web server, selects the record matching the input `ProductID`, and finally returns the XML details for that product to the client. Note that it is compulsory to set the `ServerHTTPRequest` property to `true`, otherwise the load will fail, because the `load` method does not support directly loading XML files over HTTP. More details on this can be found in the Microsoft KB article at http://support.microsoft.com/default.aspx?scid=kb;EN-US;q281142 (Q281142: PRB: Load Method Fails When Loading XML File over HTTP).

Behind the scenes, the DOMDocument uses the ServerXMLHTTP class to send an HTTP request for the remote XML document and loads the response XML into the DOM document. If the following call is made to the above ASP page:

http://localhost/MyVirDir/TestSXH1.asp?ProdID=AV-CB-01

The result is as follows:

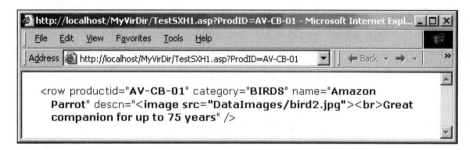

Using ServerXMLHTTP

We're finally ready to explore the flexibility and power of ServerXMLHTTP – let's now look at some examples of using it. The first example is the same as the previous one, but here we'll use ServerXMLHTTP directly, instead of using DOMDocument.

The following ASP code (TestSXH2.asp) produces exactly the same results as the preceding DOMDocument example, but it uses ServerXMLHTTP and directly sends a GET request for the remote XML document:

```
<%@ Language="VBScript" %>
<%
Option Explicit
Response.ContentType = "text/xml"

Dim objSXH, objSelNode
Dim ProductID, SearchExp

ProductID = Request.QueryString("ProdID")
Set objSXH = Server.CreateObject("Msxml2.ServerXMLHTTP.4.0")

objSXH.open "GET", "http://MyRemoteServer/product.xml", false

objSXH.send

SearchExp = "/Product/row[@productid='" & ProductID & "']"

Set objSelNode = objSXH.responseXML.selectSingleNode (SearchExp)

Response.write objSelNode.xml
%>
```

After creating the `ServerXMLHTTP` instance, we call its `open` method to initialize the HTTP request by specifying the method ("GET"), URL, and the behavior (synchronous). Then, using the `send` method, we actually send an HTTP request and receive the response. To process the response, we use the `responseXML` property, which contains the response of the `ServerXMLHTTP` request as an XML `DOMDocument`. We then select the `Product` node using the XPath expression. The matching row's XML text is then sent to the client using `Response.Write`. The output of this example is the same as the previous example when the following page is called:

http://localhost/MyVirDir/TestSXH2.asp?ProdID=AV-CB-01.

We just saw an example of loading a static XML file. It's very easy to update the above code to "GET" an ASP page instead of an XML document. When a "GET" or "POST" request is sent for the remote ASP page, that page can dynamically generate the XML and return that to us.

The following example (`TestSXH3.asp`) illustrates two things:

❑   How to call an ASP page and hence get dynamic XML

❑   How to trap HTTP errors when using `ServerXMLHTTP`

```
<%@ Language="VBScript" %>
<%
Option Explicit
Response.ContentType = "text/xml"

Dim objSXH

Set objSXH = Server.CreateObject("Msxml2.ServerXMLHTTP.4.0")

On Error Resume Next
objSXH.open "GET", "http://MyRemoteServer/tools.asp", false

objSXH.send

If Not Err.Number = 0 Then

    Response.Write "<Error type='Other' Code='" & Err.Number & "'>" &_
            Server.HTMLEncode(Err.Description) & "</Error>"
    Response.End
End If

If objSXH.status >= 400 AND objSXH.status <= 599 Then

    Response.Write "<Error type='HTTP' Code='" & objSXH.status & "'>" &_
            Server.HTMLEncode(objSXH.statusText) & "</Error>"
Else

    Response.Write objSXH.responseXML.xml
End If

%>
```

The above ASP code sends a "GET" HTTP request for a remote ASP page, which dynamically generates the XML from the database (not shown here).

We first do the standard script error handling by using On Error Resume Next and an Err object. However, this method will not capture any HTTP errors like "page not found", "authentication required", "server error", etc. For that, we examine the status and statusText properties of the ServerXMLHTTP object.

When the correct URL is specified, the HTTP call succeeds and we get the XML back:

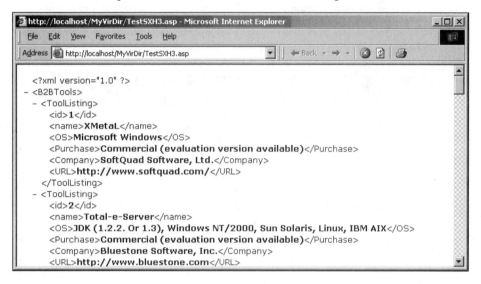

Try changing the URL to make it an invalid URL, refresh the page and you will see the details of an error message:

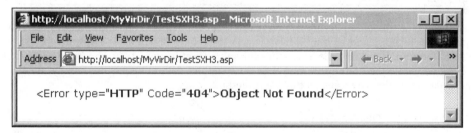

So far we have used ServerXMLHTTP to access XML data, but it can be used for any kind of HTTP access. Common uses include sending an HTTP request for a web page, getting HTML, and using regular expressions to extract some information (this process is called screen scraping). We can use it with SQL Server 2000 templates or updategram files to get/set SQL Server 2000 data. ServerXMLHTTP can also be used to POST requests. This leads to another interesting application – posting requests to SOAP servers or web services.

Let's see an example of doing an HTTP POST using ServerXMLHTTP.

Posting Requests Using ServerXMLHTTP

In the following example we'll post the data to a web service. This web service is used to get the sales rank and price for any book available on the Amazon or B&N web sites. This web service, known as SalesRankNPrice, is available at
http://www.PerfectXML.net/WebServices/SalesRankNPrice/BookService.asmx:

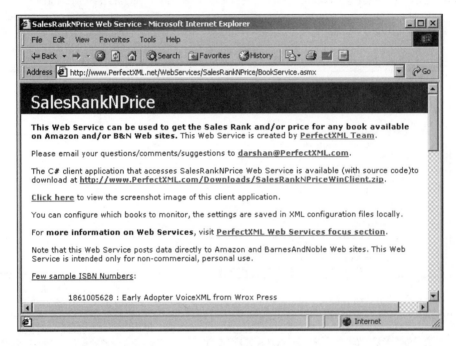

The ASP code for this example (TestSXH4.asp) is shown below. The open method will now have the first parameter as POST and next we'll have to add the request headers for Content-Type and Content-Length. The Content-Type header value is set to application/x-www-form-urlencoded, while the Content-Length is the length of data to be posted. Finally, the data to be posted is passed as the parameter to the send method.

```
<%@ Language="VBScript" %>
<%
Option Explicit
Response.ContentType = "text/xml"

Dim objSXH
Dim strPostText

Set objSXH = Server.CreateObject("Msxml2.ServerXMLHTTP.4.0")

objSXH.open _
"POST", "http://www.PerfectXML.net/WebServices/SalesRankNPrice/BookService.asmx/GetAll", _
false
```

```
strPostText = "ISBN=1861005466"


objSXH.setRequestHeader "Content-Type", "application/x-www-form-urlencoded"
objSXH.setRequestHeader "Content-Length", Len(strPostText)

objSXH.send strPostText

Response.Write objSXH.responseXML.xml
%>
```

The above code posts the string `"ISBN=1861005466"` to the web service, which returns the sales rank and price for that book as XML:

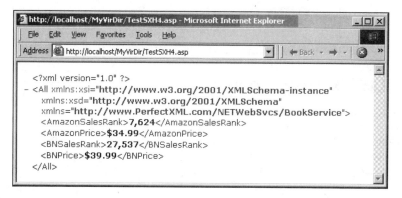

Sending Binary Data

Until now, we have been using the ResponseXML property of ServerXMLHTTP after the send method call. ServerXMLHTTP supports accessing the response in other formats as well, including text, stream, and an array of unsigned bytes, in addition to the XML DOMDocument response.

In this example (TestSXH5.asp) we'll learn how to retrieve and send binary data using ServerXMLHTTP:

```
<%@ Language=VBScript %>
<%
Response.ContentType = "image/gif"
Dim objSXH

Set objSXH = Server.CreateObject("Msxml2.ServerXMLHTTP.4.0")
objSXH.open "GET", _
            "http://www.wrox.com/Includes/images/newwroxlogo.gif", false

objSXH.send

Response.BinaryWrite objSXH.responseBody
%>
```

We first set the response content-type to image/gif. Then we create the ServerXMLHTTP object and do a GET on a remote image file. Once the send method returns, we'll have the image binary data in the responseBody member of ServerXMLHTTP as an array of unsigned bytes. We can then use ASP Response object's BinaryWrite method to send this binary data to the client. The output simply displays the Wrox logo:

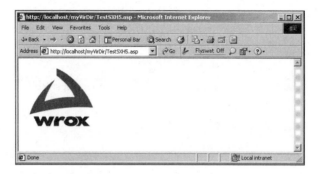

ServerXMLHTTP Reference

As we mentioned earlier, the ServerXMLHTTP40 class implements the interface IServerXMLHTTPRequest2, which is derived from IServerXMLHTTPRequest, which in turn extends the IXMLHTTPRequest interface. Note that both the XMLHTTP and ServerXMLHTTP classes implement the IXMLHTTPRequest interface. However, the XMLHTTP implementation uses WinInet and is well suited for client-side HTTP access, while ServerXMLHTTP uses WinHTTP and is designed for use as a server-safe HTTP access mechanism.

The ServerXMLHTTP40 class supports the following methods and properties:

Methods

Method	Description
open	This is the first method that is called on a ServerXMLHTTP instance, and initializes the HTTP request by specifying the request type (GET, PUT, POST, PROPFIND, etc.) and the URL. The third parameter is a Boolean value (default value is false) that indicates if the call is asynchronous. The final two parameters may be used to pass the user credentials for sites that require authentication.
setRequestHeader	This method can be used to set the HTTP request headers.
send	Actually establishes the HTTP connection, sends the requests and receives the response.
getResponseHeader	This method can be used to retrieve a particular HTTP response header.

Method	Description
getAllResponseHeaders	Retrieves all response headers as carriage return–line feed character separated name-value pairs.
setProxy	Introduced in MSXML 4.0, this method exactly maps to the functionality of the proxycfg utility and can be used to programmatically set the proxy settings.
setProxyCredentials	This method can be used to set the username and password for the proxy server.
setOption	Sets an option. The options include the escaping of the % character, URL redirection handling, etc.
getOption	Returns the value of an option. The options include the escaping of the % character, URL redirect handling, etc.
waitForResponse	Suspends execution for a specified number of seconds while waiting for an asynchronous send operation to complete.
abort	Cancels the current asynchronous HTTP request.
setTimeouts	This method allows specifying four separate timeout values (in milliseconds): timeout for resolving the domain name, connection time out, sending the data, and receiving the data timeout. The value of 0 means infinite timeout – keeps trying forever.

Properties

Properties	Description
status	This property can be accessed after the call to the send method to check the HTTP status code returned by the request.
statusText	This property is generally used in conjunction with status, to get the textual status.
responseText	After the send method, this property contains the response body as a string.
responseXML	If you know that the response is going to be XML, use this property to get DOM access to the HTTP response XML.
responseBody	The response as an array of unsigned bytes. Useful for working with binary data.
responseStream	This property provides access to the HTTP response as an IStream.
readyState	A four-byte integer property indicating the state of an asynchronous request. The values of readyState include 0 (uninitialized), 1 (Loading), 2 (Loaded), 3 (Interactive), and 4 (Completed).
onready statechange	This write-only property can be used by the scripting clients to specify an event handler to be invoked when the readyState property changes.

Retrieving Data

We saw that the `ServerXMLHTTP` class can be used to post data over HTTP. This brings interesting opportunities as far as server-to-server or between-tiers communication is concerned. For instance, we can post data to an ASP page from a middle-tier COM component, or post XML from one server to another, etc.

Let's look at a very simple example that adds two numbers. We'll pass the two numbers to the first ASP page, which will build XML with those two numbers and post it to another ASP page, residing on another virtual root (or possibly another web site). This ASP page will use the posted XML data and return the sum again as XML text.

Let's look at the first ASP page that accepts two numbers and posts them as XML to another ASP page (`TestPostXML.asp`):

```
<%@ Language="VBScript" %>
<%
Option Explicit
Response.ContentType = "text/xml"

Dim objSXH
Dim N1, N2, strPostText

Set objSXH = Server.CreateObject("Msxml2.ServerXMLHTTP.4.0")

objSXH.open "POST", "http://localhost/TestASP/TestDoAdd.asp", false

N1 = Request.QueryString("N1")
N2 = Request.QueryString("N2")

strPostText =    "<Add><Num1>" & N1 & "</Num1>" & _
         "<Num2>"& N2 & "</Num2></Add>"

objSXH.setRequestHeader "Content-Type", "application/x-www-form-urlencoded"
objSXH.setRequestHeader "Content-Length", Len(strPostText)

objSXH.send strPostText

Response.Write objSXH.responseXML.xml
%>
```

The above ASP code uses `ServerXMLHTTP` to POST data to `TestDoAdd.asp`, which is located in a different virtual root on the web server. It first builds the XML string containing two input numbers, sets the content-type and content-length and posts the XML to the ASP page. Finally, it simply sends the `responseXML` text (returned by `TestDoAdd.asp`) to the client.

> **Make sure that the two ASP pages reside on different virtual roots or Web sites, because if the ASP page to which the data was posted and the posting page reside on the same virtual root, you might experience some issues related to threading and hanging of IIS. To find more details about this, read Microsoft KB article Q290591 *"HOWTO: Submit Form Data by Using XMLHTTP or ServerXMLHTTP Object"* at http://support.microsoft.com/default.aspx?scid=kb;EN-US;q290591.**

Let's look at the page `TestDoAdd.asp`, where we'll receive the posted XML and process it (add two numbers):

```asp
<%@ Language="VBScript" %>
<%

Response.ContentType = "text/xml"

Dim objXMLDoc

Set objXMLDoc = Server.CreateObject("Msxml2.DOMDocument.4.0")

objXMLDoc.load Request

Num1 = CInt(objXMLDoc.selectSingleNode("/Add/Num1").nodeTypedValue )
Num2 = CInt(objXMLDoc.selectSingleNode("/Add/Num2").nodeTypedValue )

TotalSum = Num1 + Num2

Response.Write "<?xml version='1.0' ?>" & vbNewLine
Response.Write "<Sum>" & TotalSum & "</Sum>"
%>
```

The important point to note here is that the ASP page receives the data from the `Request` stream and directly loads `DOMDocument` from it. The rest of the code is straightforward; we select the `Num1` and `Num2` nodes, add them, generate the result `Sum` XML, and send it as the response.

The following is the result of passing `123` and `456` as querystring parameters to the `TestPostXML.asp` page:

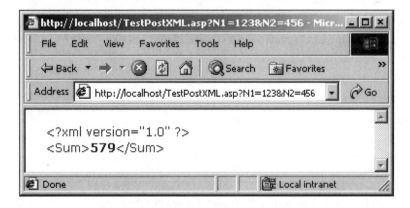

Working in a Distributed Environment

So far we've seen several examples of using `ServerXMLHTTP` to post and retrieve data between clients and servers. Let's look more specifically at its use in distributed computing. First we'll explain what we mean by distributed computing and then develop another example to show some of MSXML's useful helper classes in action.

In application development there are two paradigms that one can follow when architecting a solution. The first of these is the traditional client-server model in which the client is responsible for the user-interface and the server is responsible for delivering the application's functionality. In this model the client and server each have a fixed role and responsibility. This model can be expanded to an n-tier solution where the client is still responsible for the data presentation, a middle tier or business tier is responsible for business rules and logic, and a data tier is responsible for storing the data, but each machine still has a fixed role. If we needed to make this application more extensible we could adopt a **distributed** model. Distributed applications are those in which multiple, standalone applications share one another's features to offer more than they could on their own. Unlike the client-server model, where the roles are fixed, the distributed model allows the clients and servers to take on more dynamic roles.

A simple example of a distributed application is Microsoft's Office suite. For example, MS Word uses Outlook's e-mail functionality to add document delivery to its many features. Likewise, Outlook uses Word's word processing functionality for composing e-mail messages. An example of a distributed application in the e-commerce world would be a credit card processing service. Many e-commerce sites take advantage of third-party credit card processing companies. Instead of developing their own software or service, for a fee they can send a request to a remote service, that service will then process the credit card request, and then send back some sort of response. By using a standalone application, scalability and reliability can be increased. Since the application will run in its own process on a separate machine, if a fatal error occurs it won't bring down the system that called it. For scalability, by locating the service on another machine, more resources can be devoted to that particular process. Unlike the MS Office example, where the applications all reside on the same machine, this service could be, and usually is, hosted at a remote location.

The main problem when working in a distributed environment is marshaling data across the wire. In traditional Remote Procedure Calls (RPCs), one must create the necessary Interface Definition Language files, and serialize the parameters into a standard Network Data Representation (NDR) format to send them across the wire. Using SOAP and MSXML, the parameters can be marshaled using standard XML. This is much easier to develop (most RPCs are coded in C/C++).

Let's take a look how MSXML can be used in a distributed scenario. Although there is no dedicated functionality for working in distributed architectures, there are various features of MSXML that can be put to good use in such situations. We are going to focus on three helper objects that come with MSXML:

- ❑ ServerXMLHTTP
- ❑ XSLTemplate
- ❑ XSLProcessor

We've already seen ServerXMLHTTP in action; in a distributed scenario it will typically be used to:

- ❑ Receive XML from a remote web server/ASP page using HTTP GET.
- ❑ Post XML to a remote server/ASP page using HTTP POST.
- ❑ Post XML to a remote server/ASP page and then process the result returned in the Response object using HTTP POST.

We'll briefly take a look at the other two helper objects in the next sections, as they are both covered in greater detail in the next chapter. Then we'll see how, using these three objects, almost any communication task can be accomplished in a distributed application. We will build a simple application to illustrate these objects, somewhat based on the BizTalk Framework.

The BizTalk Framework is about application integration – getting applications to work together to accomplish more than they could by working alone, or combining multiple standalone applications, or parts thereof, into a new or greater "distributed" application. The BizTalk Framework was created to improve application integration and e-commerce through data-interchange standards based on XML. The bottom line is that application integration is accomplished through a loosely coupled system of exchanging messages. That is what our solution will illustrate. You can find more information on the BizTalk framework and its conceptual architecture at http://www.microsoft.com/BIZTALK/techinfo/framwork20.asp.

XSLTemplate

This object can be used to cache an XSLT template. Before the availability of the XSLTemplate object (prior to MSXML Release Candidate 2), transformNode and transformNodeToObject had to be used to invoke a transformation and the stylesheet had to be recompiled every time. This of course was very inefficient and not very scalable. Once an XSLTemplate has been created it doesn't have to be recompiled for each transform. It is free-threaded and stateless, thus suitable to be used in ASP page's application or session states.

It has one property, stylesheet, and one method, createProcessor(). The stylesheet property expects a DOMDocument as its only argument. Note, it must be a free-threaded DOMDocument (we'll see how to specify this in our example) or an error will result. The createProcessor() method creates a rental-threaded XSLProcessor object. Multiple processors can be created from a single template. For example, we could cache the XSLTemplate object in an application variable on a web site. Then, with each page request, instead of creating a new instance of the XSLTemplate object, we could just call the createProcessor() method of the already existing XSLT stylesheet. (There's a limit on how many simultaneous XSLProcessors per template can be created, but it is greater than 5000.) The template remains parsed and compiled, so that's one obvious performance gain.

The document passed in the stylesheet property becomes read-only until all references to templates and processors are released. Also, if the stylesheet property is modified, existing processors created from this template will not be affected by the change. The processor only takes a snapshot of the template when it is created, so the only way to update the processor is to create a new one.

XSLProcessor

This object can only be created using the createProcessor() method of an XSLTemplate object. Generally, two properties (input, output) and one method (transform()) will be used with this object. The input property specifies the XML document that is to be transformed. The output property is the result of that transformation. Finally, the transform() method performs an asynchronous transformation on the specified XML document using the XSL template that created this processor.

For more advanced operations the following methods can be used: `addObject()`, `addParameter()`, `reset()`, and `setStartMode()`. The `addObject()` method allows you to pass an object into the stylesheet. Properties of that object can then be retrieved inside the stylesheet. This allows your stylesheet to use things like `Dictionary` objects for more complex transformations. Also, you can pass an object in that contains business logic, and then execute methods of that object from inside your stylesheet. The `addParameter()` method allows you to pass parameters into your stylesheet much like the `addObject()` method. You can reset the state of the processor to the state it was in prior to calling `transform()` using the `reset()` method. This method, however, does not reset properties like `stylesheet` or `startMode`. Finally, the `setStartMode()` method allows you to specify subsets of large templates by passing in the name of the mode you want to execute. The mode is specified in the `mode` attribute of the `template` node inside your stylesheet. This allows you to execute different templates within a stylesheet, based upon business logic.

Now that we have a basic understanding of the objects we'll be using, let's take a look at the architecture our example is based upon.

> *You can find all the files for this application in the code download for this chapter; simply place the* `distributed` *folder and its contents in the root folder of your web server (or a virtual directory).*

Application Architecture

Our sample application will use ASP pages to simulate the workflow in the processing of a purchase request for customers in a B2B transaction. This solution will demonstrate how the three MSXML helper objects could be used in a distributed application. We will assume that three customers have submitted purchase requests but that they have not yet been processed. The user interface (UI) is an ASP page that allows us to choose one of the customers and submit their request to the system. Based on data contained in that request and some business logic on a remote server, an "approved/not approved" message will be returned, depending on whether the order can be fulfilled. (In this simple example we will hard-code a rule for this, but in a real application it would be likely that more complex business rules would have been defined, and stock levels would be checked in a database, for example.) The overall application is as shown in the diagram – we will discuss each stage in the following sections:

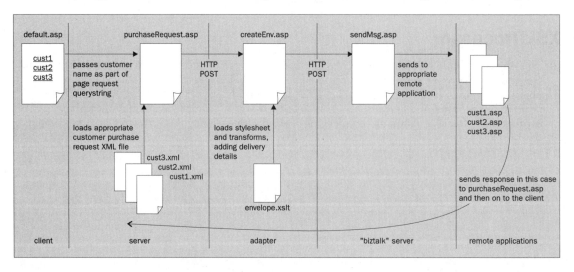

The first part of the workflow is as follows – the UI for our application will be a simple web page, `default.asp`, containing three hyperlinks. Directions at the top of the page will instruct the user to click on a hyperlink to submit a purchase request for the stated customer. Clicking on that link will transfer control to `PurchaseRequest.asp`, passing the customer name as part of the request, for example:

```
<a href="PurchaseRequest.asp?cust=Cust1.xml">Customer 1</a><br>
```

PurchaseRequest.asp

`PurchaseRequest.asp` first retrieves the name of the XML file that contains the purchase request for the specified customer from the `QueryString`. Next, a `DOMDocument` is created to load the XML file, and using the `setProperty()` method, we specify that `ServerHTTPRequest` should be used to load it. This implicitly creates the `ServerXMLHTTP` object in the background, and allows it to transparently load the XML document for us. (Remember, this is one of two ways `ServerXMLHTTP` can be created.)

```
set oXmlSend = Server.CreateObject("Msxml2.DOMDocument.4.0")
with oXmlSend
    .async = false
    .setProperty "ServerHTTPRequest",true
    .load Server.MapPath(sCustPath)
end with
```

The next step will be to explicitly create a `ServerXMLHTTP` object that will be used to send the `DOMDocument` we just loaded to the `createEnv.asp` page.

```
set oSrvHTTP = Server.CreateObject("MSXML2.ServerXMLHTTP.4.0")
oSrvHTTP.open "POST","http://localhost/msxml/createEnv.asp",false
```

We could have used this object to load the purchase request XML file too, specifying GET in the open() method, and then called the open() method again, this time specifying POST in the open() method. Instead we chose the other method to illustrate implicitly creating a ServerXMLHTTP object.

Finally, the `DOMDocument` is passed into the `send()` method and we simply `Response.Write` the `responseText` from our `ServerXMLHTTP` object to the page:

```
oSrvHTTP.send oXMLSend
Response.Write oSrvHTTP.responseText
```

After clicking on the Customer 1 link the page will simply look like the one displayed here:

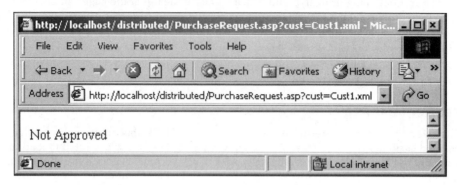

CreateEnv.asp

In the BizTalk world, this page would act as our "adapter". Using an `XSLTemplate` object that is cached on the ASP `Application` object, we transform the incoming purchase request. This transformation merely wraps an envelope around the purchase request, adding delivery information to our message. The process flow works by first loading a `DOMDocument` from the `Request` object.

```
dim oXmlReq, oXslProc, oSrvHTTP, startMode
set oXmlReq = Server.CreateObject("MSXML2.DOMDocument.4.0")
with oXmlReq
    .async = false
    .load Request
end with
```

The document is then queried using an XPath expression (see Chapter 4 for more information on XPath) and the `getAttribute()` method, which retrieves the value of an attribute of the specified node. The value that is returned will be used to specify the `startMode` of the XSLT that creates the envelope.

```
startMode = "Cust" & oXmlReq.selectSingleNode("//order").getAttribute
    ("cust_id")
```

An alternative would be to use the XPath expression `oXmlReq.selectSingleNode(//order/@cust_id).text`. Also, if working with a large XML document it would be better to avoid using the XPath "//", because it searches everywhere in the DOM tree, perhaps needlessly. If it is clear where the node is located in the XML document, then the entire path should be provided to avoid a performance hit.

The next step would be to create an `XSLProcessor` object. There is only one way to create this object, and that is through the `createProcessor()` method of an `XSLTemplate` object. We reference the template we have cached in the application state, and call its `createProcessor()` method like so:

```
set oXslProc = Application("oXslt").createProcessor()
```

Adding this `Application_OnStart` event to the `global.asa` file will cache the stylesheet in ASP's application state:

```
Sub Application_OnStart
    set oXslt = Server.CreateObject("Msxml2.XSLTemplate.4.0")
        set oXslDoc =
            Server.CreateObject("Msxml2.FreeThreadedDOMDocument.4.0")
            with oXslDoc
                .async = false
                .load Server.MapPath("envelope.xslt")
            end with

        set oXslt.stylesheet = oXslDoc
End Sub
```

Finally the `input` document and `startMode` are specified before calling the `transform()` method:

```
with oXslProc
    .input = oXmlReq
    .setStartMode startMode
    .transform()
end with
```

Now that our message has been wrapped with an envelope, it can be sent to the `sendMsg.asp` page to be delivered. To accomplish this, a `ServerXMLHTTP` object needs to be created. The `output` property of the `XSLProcessor` object returns a `DOMDocument` that will be sent to the `sendMsg.asp` page. Once again, the `responseText` property of the `ServerXMLHTTP` object is written to the page:

```
set oSrvHTTP = Server.CreateObject("MSXML2.ServerXMLHTTP.4.0")
oSrvHTTP.open "POST","http://localhost/msxml/sendMsg.asp",false
oSrvHTTP.send oXslProc.output
Response.Write oSrvHTTP.responseText
```

SendMsg.asp

This page will act as the pseudo "BizTalk server" in our application. Its main functions are to send and receive purchase requests to the proper customer. Once again, the `Request` object is loaded into a `DOMDocument`:

```
dim oXmlReq, oSrvHTTP, sDestination
set oXmlReq = Server.CreateObject("MSXML2.DOMDocument.4.0")
with oXmlReq
    .async = false
    .load Request
end with
```

From this document, the destination is extracted using an XPath expression:

```
sDestination = oXmlReq.selectSingleNode("//header").getAttribute("to")
```

Finally a `ServerXMLHTTP` object is used to transmit the document to the specified location. The response is then written to the page:

```
set oSrvHTTP = Server.CreateObject("MSXML2.ServerXMLHTTP.4.0")
oSrvHTTP.open "POST","http://localhost/msxml/" & sDestination,false
oSrvHTTP.send oXmlReq
Response.Write oSrvHTTP.responseText
```

This response gets passed back to `PurchaseRequest.asp`, and informs the user whether or not the request was approved.

Custn.asp

These pages (`cust1.asp`, `cust2.asp`, `cust3.asp`) act as the remote applications in our distributed application. The main function of these pages is to return a result to say whether the order could be fulfilled or not. To achieve this a `Request` object is loaded into a `DOMDocument`, and the document is queried for a quantity value, which is used to interrogate the business rules, in this case hard-coded into the page. Here is the code that achieves it:

```
dim oXmlReq, lQty
set oXmlReq = Server.CreateObject("MSXML2.DOMDocument.4.0")
with oXmlReq
    .async = false
    .load Request
end with

lQty = oXmlReq.selectSingleNode("//order").getAttribute("qty")

if lQty > 20 then
    Response.Write "Not Approved"
else
Response.Write "Approved"
end if
```

In a real-world example we would look the value up in a database, or process the values according to predefined business rules. Here we have hard-coded an evaluation of that value to simulate this. Each remote application would process the `DOMDocument` that is loaded from the `Request` object, perform business logic on that document, and then return a result. If, for example, this document were a credit card request, the application could process that request, charge the card whatever amount was specified, and return a confirmation of that result. By returning "Approved"/"Not Approved" we are simulating that confirmation. The main concept illustrated here is calling a remote application and receiving a result.

Although there is no real inherent support for distributed computing within MSXML, it offers an efficient, scalable solution to communicate between distributed applications. Not only can MSXML take care of message delivery and receipt over HTTP, it can also handle the parsing, validation, and transformation of those messages.

These capabilities can be extended even further using SOAP. With the availability of .NET and its built-in XML capabilities, we might wonder where MSXML will fit in. At the time of writing, MSXML/XSLT is faster than .NET's `System.Xml.Xslt` class, and MSXML will be necessary to integrate legacy COM applications into the .NET Framework, thus guaranteeing MSXML's longevity.

Summary

In this chapter we learned about a vital part of most web-based projects – sending and retrieving data. We saw how MSXML offers various solutions to generate XML on the server-side and pass the data across tiers.

This chapter focused on server-side data generation and transfer. We talked about `ServerXMLHTTP`, an important component inside MSXML to do server-safe HTTP access. We also learned how to work with binary data and tried out an example to post data to a server ASP page.

We also looked at an example of how MSXML can be used when working in a distributed environment. As you will recall, a distributed application combines multiple standalone applications into a greater "distributed" application. The idea is to allow multiple applications to accomplish more together than they could on their own.

Once we have data on the server, we might want to transform it to HTML or WML, etc., before sending it to the client. That's the focus of the next chapter – to show you how to efficiently do server-side transformations.

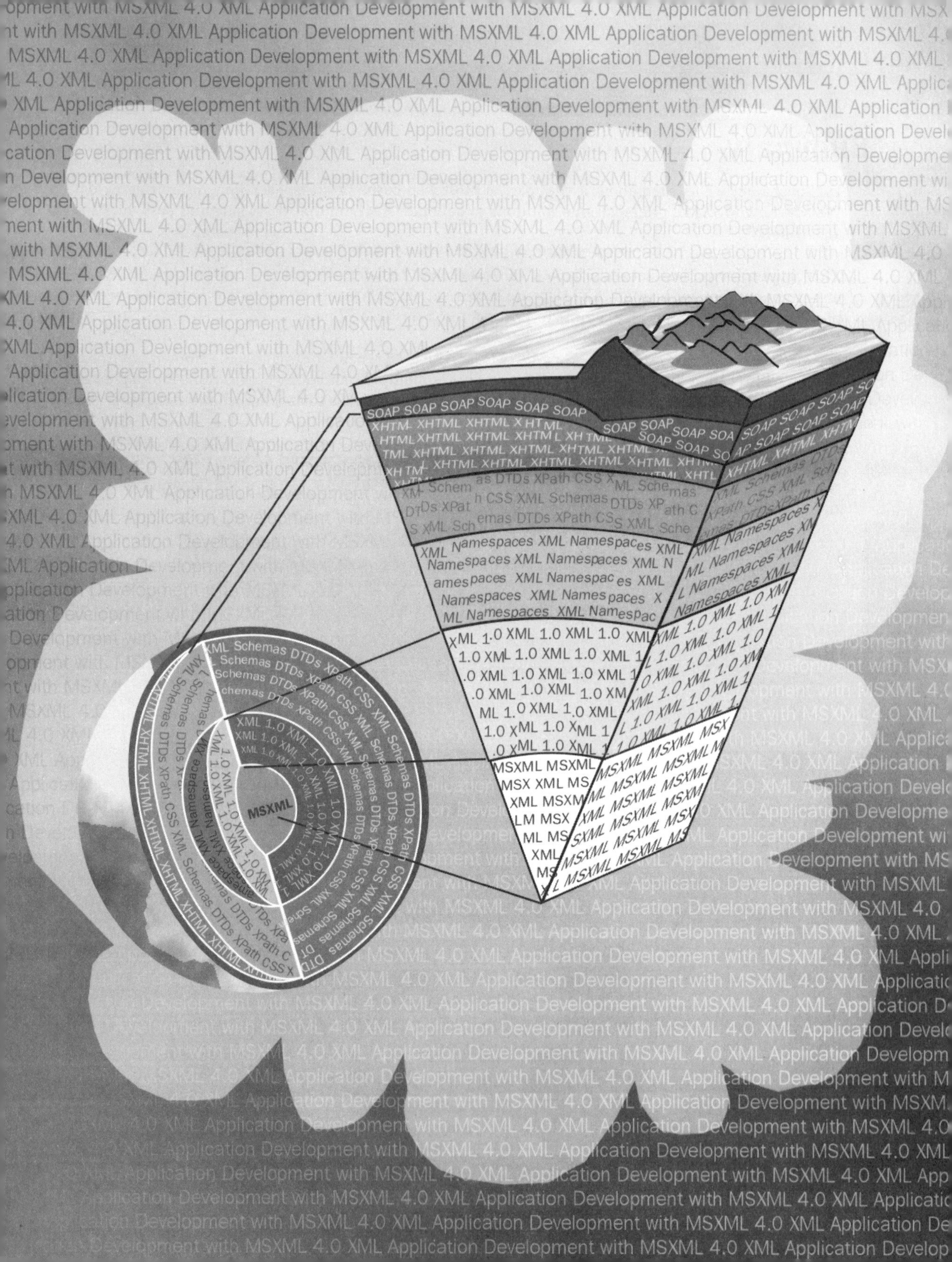

XML Application Development with MSXML 4.0
SOAP
XHTML
XML Schemas DTDs XPath CSS
XML Namespaces
XML 1.0
MSXML

10

Transformations on the Server

Internet Explorer is the only web browser available that provides good XML support. So, what happens when we want to target other browsers that do not have MSXML installed? In fact, what happens when we want to display pages on devices other than a desktop web browser, such as a mobile phone, PDA, or any other device, that don't use MSXML? This is where we can perform transformations on the server – one of the biggest advantages of working with MSXML.

From a developer's perspective, XML technologies are very good, but from a business point of view "to view this site you must have Internet Explorer 5.5 and above" is simply not an option and our XML adventure will be severely restricted if we rely on this kind of approach. In this chapter we'll look at how we can develop solutions for any kind of device, while not imposing any major restrictions on our use of XML.

Before we start, let's briefly consider the advantages and disadvantages of MSXML and XSLT on the server:

❑ The first advantage is that there are no fixed dependencies on client technologies such as browsers or devices.

❑ Another advantage is that it is simple to create dynamic XML and XSLT that can take input from other backend resources, such as databases and directory systems.

❑ One disadvantage to the user is that there is a potential impact on performance and response time (during very heavy load on the server) caused by doing all the transformations on the server, although this can be optimized and should not have much of an effect on the application.

❑ Another disadvantage is that a round-trip is required to change the XML for presentation. This can, however, sometimes be done on the client.

When working with XML on the server we can directly use any data source – columns from a database table can be marked up, and non-XML files can be parsed and marked up as XML. When this is done on the server, we can dynamically associate the XML that results with some stylesheet. It is possible to use such techniques even when sending data to the client, but working on the server allows a much more dynamic presentation, as we will see in this chapter.

One further advantage of working with XML on the server is that we can use additional validation and processing rules within our stylesheet, through scripting and extensions, or directly when working with the DOM.

Within this chapter we will look at the following:

❑ Non-XML data as well as XML, and how to access this information when posted from a web page.

❑ Detecting client browsers and devices, and serving up appropriate stylesheets.

❑ Interacting with remote servers and exchanging XML between servers.

❑ Advanced MSXML server concepts such as threading, and using the IXSLTemplate and IXSLProcessor objects to improve performance.

❑ Working with parameters and objects, including exposing COM object methods to our XSLT.

❑ The XSLISAPI filter.

❑ Command line batch (bulk) transforms.

❑ Suggestions on practices for working with XML server errors.

As we work through this chapter we will see that it is predominantly practical and code-based. However, there are examples embedded within the relevant sections that purely discuss the syntax of how to use the more important methods relevant to server transforms.

> **The downloaded sample code for this chapter contains a folder called `TransServer`. This should be referenced from an IIS virtual directory called `TransServer`.**
>
> **Note also that the WAP samples in the chapter use the WinWap WAP browser for Windows, which can be downloaded at http://www.winwap.org/winwap/download.html. The samples should work with any WML-compliant browser, but they have not been tested against any others and configuration issues are outside of the scope of this book.**

Receiving Data

Most applications receive data – either from a local web page or application, or from a remote system such as a business partner. Often we don't have control over the format that the data will be sent in and rely on the HTTP POST or HTTP GET methods of the <form> element. When posted using these methods, the data may be name-value pairs or non-XML data (for example, comma-delimited) posted in a hidden <form> element (a method commonly used in BizTalk Server).

Let's first consider the case where non-XML data is posted to the server. This is a relatively simple and widely available form, with no restrictions on HTML browsers or devices, and will therefore be the most commonly used method for getting data into our application.

The following examples will all be based on the same concepts, and the code used for each example will be fairly similar. The idea is to demonstrate how a simple, extensible, generic framework can be created to accept any kind of data document and use the DOM to create a server-side XML document. Following this, the same XSLT server transform will be used to show the user the values they entered in a common format. This will demonstrate the common solutions used in server-side XML.

Non-XML Data

The first case we are going to consider is the traditional method of using an HTML form to POST data to the server.

Data Posted from a Web Page

If you have used XML in any applications before, the following example should look fairly familiar to you, and will hopefully introduce some new techniques to improve productivity when developing XML applications. A web browser POSTs data to some URL – this is converted to XML on the server and processed. In this case we will show how this data can be posted, processed, and have a server-side stylesheet applied to write out the result.

The page displayed overleaf is the one that the user must enter the details into (postHTML.htm). The code for this page is just HTML, so we won't cover it here. We can see the basics of the invoice: a customer name, an e-mail address, a multiple selection of divisions the order is related to, the products that have been ordered (pretty basic in this case), an assigned batch ID, and finally, any comments that may be related to the delivery:

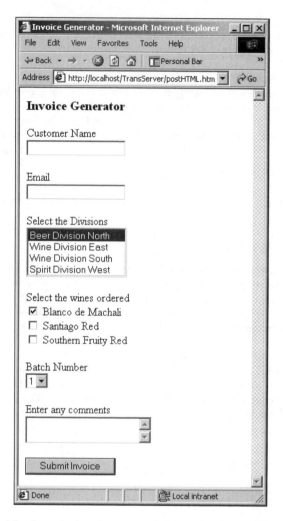

The action attribute of the form in the above page is DisplayInvoice.asp. This performs the processing: read in the posted data and output the result to the user. The code for DisplayInvoice.asp is listed below (using JScript):

```
<%@ Language="JScript"%>
<%
initServer();
var xmlDoc = BuildInvoice(Request.Form);

var xslDoc = Server.CreateObject("Msxml2.DOMDocument.4.0");
xslDoc.setProperty("NewParser", true );
xslDoc.async = false;
xslDoc.load(Server.MapPath("invoice.xsl"));

Response.Write(xmlDoc.transformNode(xslDoc));
%>
<!--#include file="postHTML.asp"-->
```

Early in this code, the `initServer()` method is invoked, which tells the code that will build the invoice that it should create a server-side instance of an MSXML 4.0 parser – this is because the same code is reused on the client later on. Next, the `BuildInvoice()` method is called with the collection of `POST`ed form data as its argument. This is discussed further below, but in short, it returns an XML `DOMDocument` of the invoice. The stylesheet is loaded in as an MSXML 4.0 `DOMDocument`, with the `NewParser` property set to `true`, which ensures that the better performance parser that comes with MSXML 4.0 is used. We also set the `async` property to `false` to indicate that it must process this before moving on – otherwise, it would be asynchronous and we would have to check the `readyState` property to determine when it was ready. However, this time the `load()` method of the `DOMDocument` is used.

When using MSXML prior to version 4.0 on the server there are serious limitations to what we can and should do with this method, that differ from usage on the client. Server-side, we should only load XML files (including XSLT and other files which are marked up as XML) that can be mapped through a drive letter (for example `"..\myfile\myxml.xml"`), as well as any object supporting `IStream` (such as ADO objects) and the `Request` object. Trying to load a full URL such as http://www.somwhere.com/file.xml will have unpredictable results and, more importantly, won't work. However, as of MSXML 4.0, we can use a special XML server object that allows us to safely use the `load()` method – we met this in Chapter 9 and will discuss it in detail later on, in the section on `ServerXMLHTTP`.

For the moment this doesn't cause us a problem because we can map to a file location for the XSLT we are going to work with. To do this, we use the `MapPath()` method of the `Server` object to resolve the file `invoice.xsl` to a full path. Finally, the `transformNode()` method of the `DOMDocument` transforms it using the stylesheet object passed as an argument.

The syntax for using the `transformNode()` method is as follows:

```
strOutput = objXMLDOMNode.transformNode(objXSL)
```

The output is a string output from the resulting transformation. `objXMLDOMNode` is the node that is to be transformed – typically this is a `documentElement` node, but other nodes can be used for document fragment transforms. For example, we may have three document sections in an XML document, as follows:

```
<xmlDoc>
    <Customers>...</Customers>
    <AccountManagers>...</AccountManagers>
    <Orders>...</Orders>
</xmlDoc>
```

We can then transform these three sections differently, like this:

```
strOutput1 = objXMLDOMNode.childNodes(0).transformNode(objXSL1)
strOutput2 = objXMLDOMNode.childNodes(1).transformNode(objXSL2)
strOutput3 = objXMLDOMNode.childNodes(2).transformNode(objXSL3)
```

In the case of our example, the result of the transformation is written to the `Response` object (the default `Server` object in this method) and then to the client.

This file also includes the ASP page `postHTML.asp` (discussed below), which is a library of routines used to take the posted data and create a valid XML string from it. In fact, exactly the same functions are also used client-side using JScript reflection in the example for posting XML data, which is the next example we will look at in this chapter. This way, we can get great reuse when we need to differentiate client and server operations.

The function library is initialized for use on the server through the method `initServer()`, which uses the previously declared global variable `objInvoiceXML` and instantiates an instance of the MSXML 4.0 DOM document. It is also set to use the new parser through the `setProperty()` method, and is set to do synchronous loading.

```
var objInvoiceXML = "";

function initServer()
{
    objInvoiceXML = Server.CreateObject("Msxml2.DOMDocument.4.0");
    objInvoiceXML.setProperty("NewParser", true );
    objInvoiceXML.async=false;
}
```

Following this, the main method is `BuildInvoice()`, which takes the request object as an argument (as noted above). The `BuildInvoice()` method builds up an XML DOM document and calls various methods, passing the relevant item or collection of items to the method. First, the XML declaration is created to specifically set the encoding to `ISO-8859-1`, which means that we can use special characters in languages using other Latin-based alphabets (such as **café** and **naïve**) – the `createProcessingInstruction()` method is used to do this.

```
function BuildInvoice(objReqForm)
{
    var objProcIns = objInvoiceXML.createProcessingInstruction("xml",
        "version='1.0' encoding='ISO-8859-1'");

    objInvoiceXML.appendChild(objProcIns);
```

The root `<Invoices>` element is created and its `date` attribute set using the `WriteDate()` method discussed below.

```
    var objElInvoice = objInvoiceXML.createElement("Invoices");
    objElInvoice.setAttribute("date",WriteDate());
```

The `<customers>` element is then created and has its `custname` and `email` attributes set to the relevant values from the form `POST`.

```
    var objElCust = objInvoiceXML.createElement("customers");
    objElCust.setAttribute("custname",objReqForm("custname"));
    objElCust.setAttribute("email",objReqForm("email"));
```

The `<customers>` element has immediate `<busInfo>` child elements, and a node-set containing these is returned from the `WriteDivisions()` method, which takes the `<busInfo>` form collection. Each node within the node-set is then iterated through and appended as a child element of the `<customers>` element created above. The `hasChildNodes()` method will return `true` when the `objbusInfoNodes` object still has children. The `appendChild()` adds each node as a child of the `objElCust` object and removes the node from the source `objbusInfoNodes` child nodes.

```
    var objbusInfoNodes = WriteDivisions(objReqForm("busInfo"));
    while (objbusInfoNodes.hasChildNodes())
        objElCust.appendChild(objbusInfoNodes.childNodes(0));
```

The <order> element is then created and the batchid attribute set from the value of the POSTed batchid item.

```
var objElOrder = objInvoiceXML.createElement("order");
objElOrder.setAttribute("batchid",objReqForm("batchid"));
```

The <items> element is also created with its num attribute set to the number of items selected in the WineGroup <select> element on the HTML page. Following this, the WriteItems() method is passed the multi-value WineGroup POSTed item and returns a node containing <item> child nodes, which is then iterated through. Each <item> is appended as a child node of the <items> element node created above. The hasChildNodes() method will return true when the objItemsNodes object still has children. The appendChild() adds each node as a child of the objElItems object and removes the node from the source objItemsNodes child nodes.

```
var objElItems = objInvoiceXML.createElement("items");
objElItems.setAttribute("num",objReqForm("WineGroup").Count);

var objItemsNodes = WriteItems(objReqForm("WineGroup"));
while (objItemsNodes.hasChildNodes())
   objElItems.appendChild(objItemsNodes.childNodes(0));
```

Next, the <details> element is created and the <items> element is appended as a child of this. The <comments> element is also created and the WriteComments() method is used to populate this.

```
var objElDetails = objInvoiceXML.createElement("details");
objElDetails.appendChild(objElItems);

var objElComments = objInvoiceXML.createElement("comments");
objElComments.appendChild(WriteComments(objReqForm("comments")));
```

The <details> element is appended as a child of the <order> element; the <comments> element is also appended as a child of the <order> element and then the <order> element itself (and children) is appended as a child of the <customers> element. The <customers> element is appended as a child of the <Invoices> document root element. Finally, the <Invoices> document element (objElInvoice) is appended to the DOM document root (objInvoiceXML) and the resulting DOM document is returned in the objInvoiceXML variable.

```
objElOrder.appendChild(objElDetails);
objElOrder.appendChild(objElComments);
objElCust.appendChild(objElOrder);
objElInvoice.appendChild(objElCust);

objInvoiceXML.appendChild(objElInvoice);

return objInvoiceXML;
}
```

The WriteDate() method returns the date and time of invoice creation and is used above as an attribute on the <Invoices> element.

```
function WriteDate()
{
   var dDate = new Date();
   return dDate.toString();
}
```

The `WriteDivisions()` method takes the `<busInfo>` parent element of the child `<items>` elements generated by the multiple `<select>` element on the input form. It then creates a wrapper element and iterates through each item in the posted multi-value item. The `createNode()` method is then used to create a new element node (the first parameter with the value "1" says it's an element node) with the name `<busInfo>` and prefix `cat`, which is qualified in the namespace `uri:Business-Categories`. The text of each newly created element node is set to the value of the posted item and the element is added as a new child of the wrapper element.

```
function WriteDivisions(objReqForm)
{
    var objbusInfoWrapper = objInvoiceXML.createElement("busInfoWrapper");

    for (var i=1;i<objReqForm.Count+1;i++)
    {
    var objbusInfo = objInvoiceXML.createNode(1,"cat:busInfo",
                                            "uri:Business-Categories");
        objbusInfo.text = objReqForm(i);
        objbusInfoWrapper.appendChild(objbusInfo);
    }

    return(objbusInfoWrapper);
}
```

The `WriteItems()` method does a very similar thing and takes the checkbox list of selected items in order and then returns a wrapper element containing a set of `<item>` child nodes.

```
function WriteItems(ReqItems)
{
    var objItemsWrapper = objInvoiceXML.createElement("itemsWrapper");

    for (var i=1;i<ReqItems.Count+1;i++)
    {
        var objItem = objInvoiceXML.createElement("item");
        objItem.text = ReqItems(i);
        objItemsWrapper.appendChild(objItem);
    }

    return(objItemsWrapper);
}
```

Finally, the `WriteComments()` method creates the comments section of the document. However, because this is freeform there is a chance that some invalid XML characters may be present, so the whole string is wrapped in a CDATA section:

```
function WriteComments(ReqComments)
{
    var objComments = objInvoiceXML.createCDATASection(ReqComments);

    return objComments;

}
```

The result is that `BuildInvoice()` returns a DOMDocument object containing XML, like the following (unformatted of course! – whitespace has been inserted to save your eyesight):

```
<?xml version="1.0" ?>
<Invoices date="Thu Oct 25 13:47:54 PDT 2001"
          xmlns:cat="uri:Business-Categories">
    <customers custname="Wine Online" email="wines@somewine.com">
        <cat:busInfo>Beer Division North</cat:busInfo>
        <cat:busInfo>Wine Division South</cat:busInfo>
        <order batchid="1">
            <details>
                <items num="1">
                    <item>Santiago Red</item>
                </items>
                <comments>
                    <![CDATA[Orders are < 5 so no discount for user]]>
                </comments>
            </details>
        </order>
    </customers>
</Invoices>
```

The output uses an XSLT transformation (`invoice.xsl`) and a CSS (`invoice.css`) to format the display – these are very similar to the examples we looked at in Chapter 7, "*Styling XML Content*", so to save repetition and concentrate only on the new bits, we won't discuss these here. The output of the above sample is as shown, which you can see by entering data into `postHTML.htm`:

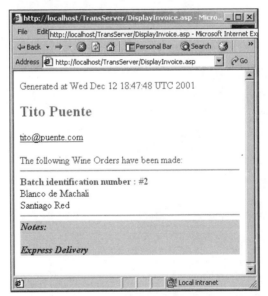

XML Data

Another increasingly common way of getting data from a client to the server is as XML. Apart from reducing load on the server, this also saves the server from knowing all the details of how to put the document together from its constituent parts. Remember that when we say "client" here, we may well mean some other server posting the data as well as a traditional client posting. In the example below we will improve on the basic POST model discussed above and the document that will be posted to the server will be an XML document.

You will need IE 5+ and MSXML 4.0 installed for this example to work. The input interface for the XML posting is the same as for the non-XML data discussed above. However, the client code underneath is significantly different. Below we show the script sections for postXML.htm – the rest of the page is HTML, which can be viewed in the file. This demonstrates how we can reuse the same code to create the XML document on both the client and server.

```javascript
<script language="javascript">
<!--
function Initialize()
{
   var custname = document.getElementsByName("custname")(0).value
   var email = document.getElementsByName("email")(0).value
   var busInfo = document.getElementsByName("busInfo")
   var batchid = document.getElementsByName("batchid")(0).value
   var WineGroup = document.getElementsByName("WineGroup")
   var comments = document.getElementsByName("comments")(0).value

   var req = new ActiveXObject("Scripting.Dictionary")

   req.Add("custname",custname);
   req.Add("email",email)

   //Create Divisions Collection
   var j=1;
   var objBusInfo = new ActiveXObject("Scripting.Dictionary")
   for (i=0; i<busInfo(0).options.length; i++)
      if (busInfo(0).options(i).selected.toString()=="true")
         objBusInfo.Add(j++,busInfo(0).options(i).text);

   req.Add("busInfo",objBusInfo);

   req("batchid")=batchid;

   //Create WineGroup Collection
   var j=1;
   var objWineGroup = new ActiveXObject("Scripting.Dictionary")
   for (i=0; i<WineGroup.length; i++)
      if (WineGroup(i).checked.toString()=="true")
         objWineGroup.Add(j++,WineGroup(i).value);

   req.Add("WineGroup",objWineGroup);
   req.Add("comments",comments);

   var xmlDoc = BuildInvoice(req)

   PostInvoice(xmlDoc)
}

function PostInvoice(objXML)
{
   var xmlhttp = new ActiveXObject("Msxml2.XMLHTTP.4.0");
   xmlhttp.Open("POST", "DisplayInvoiceXML.asp", false);
   xmlhttp.Send(objXML);

   alert(xmlhttp.responseText);
}
-->
</script>
```

The `Initialize()` routine performs most of the work and has the initial task of creating a collection that simulates the response object that is accessed on the server – this is to illustrate how easy it is to move between client-based and server-based applications. The first part of the function accesses the elements defined in the document by name and returns a collection of their values In fact, it does this even for a simple textbox element, so we must use an index of 0 to get the value of the first (and only) member. For multiple value elements, such as the `<select>` and checkboxes, the multiple values are returned as a simple collection.

Once these items have been stored in variables, we can then create a collection of items to simulate the `Request` object. To do this, we create an instance of the `Dictionary` object as follows:

```
var req = new ActiveXObject("Scripting.Dictionary")
```

With this, items can be added to the `Dictionary` object. Here we add the contents of the `custname` variable to the collection with a key identifier `"custname"` – in other words, we can directly access this element in the collection with the index name `"custname"`:

```
req.Add("custname",custname);
```

The same technique is used for all variables that were created earlier, but there are two notable variations with the `Divisions` and `WineGroup` collections. As these are multi-valued they must also be stored as their own collection – this is done by creating a separate instance of the `Dictionary` object for each, adding the appropriate values to this new dictionary instance, then adding the new dictionary instance as an item itself in the original collection. The example for `Divisions` is shown below:

```
//Create Divisions Collection
var j=1;
var objBusInfo = new ActiveXObject("Scripting.Dictionary")
for (i=0; i<busInfo(0).options.length; i++)
    if (busInfo(0).options(i).selected.toString()=="true")
        objBusInfo.Add(j++,busInfo(0).options(i).text);

req.Add("busInfo",objBusInfo);
```

After testing that a given item in the options of the `<select>` is in fact selected, it is added to the new instance of the `Dictionary` object (`objBusInfo`), with the iterative variable `j` as its identifier and the text of the option as the value. Once all options have been tested, the `objBusInfo` `Dictionary` object itself is added to the `req` `Dictionary` object instance as a new item. This allows us to simulate the `Request` object where a posted item has multiple values. A similar technique is used for the `WineGroup` variable.

Once the `req` `Dictionary` object has been created, the `BuildInvoice()` method we discussed above is used and the `req` object is its argument:

```
var XMLInvoice = BuildInvoice(req)
```

As we know, this returns an XML string, which we can then load as a `DOMDocument` using the `loadXML()` method. Finally, the data needs to get to the server. One common way of doing this is to store the XML in a hidden `<form>` element, `POST` the data to the server and use the `Request` object to extract the XML from the hidden field. Another way, and the way we are going to do it, is to work with the `XMLHTTP` object. As was briefly mentioned in the previous chapter, this is a client-side component that allows us to `POST` data directly to a web page without having to refresh the page.

In the example, the `PostInvoice()` method takes the `DOMDocument` as an argument:

```
var xmlhttp = new ActiveXObject("Msxml2.XMLHTTP");
xmlhttp.Open("POST", "DisplayInvoiceXML.asp", false);
xmlhttp.Send(objXML);
```

First, an instance of the `XMLHTTP` object is created and then the `open()` method of the `IXMLHTTPRequest` object is used to initialize it. The first parameter specifies that the data should be `POST`ed to the server, the second parameter is the URL for the data to be posted to, and the third parameter tells the object to wait until the processing is complete before returning.

The syntax for the `Open()` method is shown below:

```
objXMLHttpRequest.open(strMethod, strUrl, bolAsync, strUser, strPassword);
```

The first parameter specifies how the data should be sent to the server, and is one of `"POST"`,`"GET"`, `"PUT"` or `"PROPFIND"`.

The second parameter contains the URL to send the request to. It should be the name of the page in the directory that our script is in, an absolute URL (`http://...`), or relative URL (`/myfolder...`).

The third parameter tells the object whether it should use an asynchronous connection – it defaults to `true`, in which case we have to attach some method to the `onreadystatechange` property and have it do the work when the processing has been completed.

The final two parameters are the username and password (that will be sent over the network in plain text) and can be used as authorization for basic authentication.

So, continuing with the example, the `send()` method of the `XMLHTTP` request object must be called to invoke the request. This method should take the body of the message we want to send. In our case it is an XML object containing the invoice (`objXML`) and so the response will be encoded based on the encoding defined in our XML declaration, which is `ISO-8859-1` in this case.

You may be wondering how the invoice is built – well, the code uses JScript reflection to use the previous server-side code to output the client-side version, and calls the `initClient()` method to create a client-side instance of an MSXML 4.0 `DOMDocument`.

```
<script language="javascript">
  <!--
  var objInvoiceXML = "";
  initClient();

  <%
  Response.Write(initClient.toString());
  Response.Write(BuildInvoice.toString());
  Response.Write(WriteDate.toString());
  Response.Write(WriteDivisions.toString());
  Response.Write(WriteItems.toString());
  Response.Write(WriteComments.toString());
  %>
  //-->
</script>
<!--#include file="postHTML.asp"-->
```

When the server has completed processing, it returns some XML information in the `ResponseText` property and this is displayed to the user. Let's look server-side. The script on the server that receives the data is called `DisplayInvoiceXML.asp`:

```
<%@ Language="JScript"%>
<%
Response.CharSet = "ISO-8859-1";
var xmlDoc = new ActiveXObject("Msxml2.DOMDocument");
xmlDoc.async = false;
xmlDoc.load(Request);

//Do something else with XML Document...

Response.Write("The following XML document has been uploaded:\n\n" +
    xmlDoc.xml)
%>
```

The good thing about this is that the data that has been posted can be loaded directly into a `DOMDocument` by using the `load()` method with the `Request` object as the argument. That's all we really do in this example, although we would expect quite a lot more in a complex application. A message is returned to the user with details of the XML document that was uploaded, using `Response.Write` to send the data back as a response to the client request. This is the information that is available in the client-side `ResponseText` property, which we display using a JavaScript alert box. Note that the data being returned was pure XML, and so the `ResponseXML` property could have been used instead of the `ResponseText` property.

The result of this example is displayed here (you can view this using `postXML.asp`):

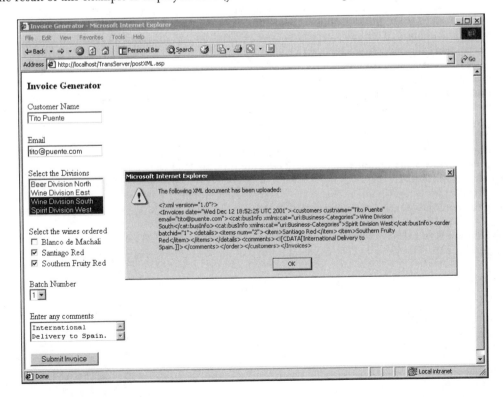

Notice that no refresh of the page is necessary, so you can maintain state on your data entry page and your applications can get a more sophisticated (and generally faster) interaction.

So far we have looked at the initial steps in XML-enabling our applications with MSXML. Often, however, some processing will be required, and transforms to generate the output will be based on detection of devices, browser types, and versions. Let's look at this now.

Processing Data

In this section we are going to look at how XML and XSLT can be used to interact with disparate clients. Of course, clients can be traditional clients such as users, or servers making requests to their peers.

We are first going to look at how to work with browser clients on the Web – currently the most common form of interaction, involving various desktop and mobile devices. Following this, we will look at how transformations are used when interacting with peer servers, which may well require the data in some other format.

Presenting Data to User Clients

To date, most users have interacted with web applications via desktop browsers such as Internet Explorer and Netscape Navigator, and this continues to be the dominant manner of interaction. This itself has presented us with many issues when creating web applications – mainly because the presentation of the applications was embedded within the pages themselves and, to avoid having multiple sets of business functionality across many versions of pages, most have stuck to a very basic common denominator. This gives very basic user interaction and dull web applications overall. However, many businesses can cope with such applications so long as they do the job required.

Applications are now being adopted on devices that were previously not much concern to organizations, such as mobile phones, personal digital assistants, and even voice and peer servers. This is making the process of creating corporate and public web applications much more complex, and various methods are being adopted to cope. Some say they won't support anything other than browsers – not a long-term option! Then there is the option of using a transcoder to dynamically convert your pages from HTML (or whatever) to a format appropriate for the end-point device. Although very useful for content-based sites, this is not a trustworthy option when you are creating sophisticated web applications. Over the next few years it is likely that XHTML is going to be the most common format across devices, so creating pages with XHTML mark up will mean that many devices can read and use them. However, this still lacks the fine grain control you may often need when creating your XML applications. So, what is the solution?

The solution is to use device detection techniques and device-specific stylesheets to produce output tailored for particular devices. The following diagram illustrates how this may work:

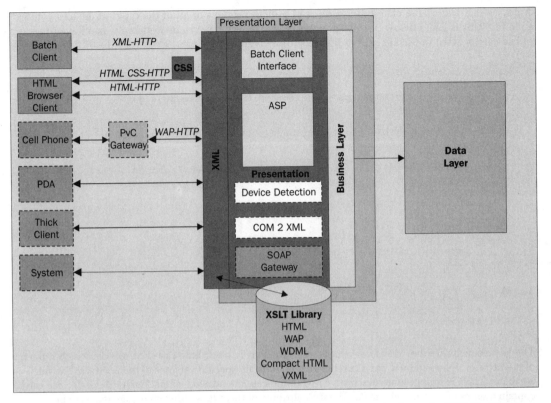

In this example portal architecture, all interaction goes over HTTP; whether it be HTML, WAP, or SOAP, HTTP is the basis for communication. A thin XML layer sits in front of the application and so communication is generally done via XML documents or fragments and, when something is not in XML format, it is converted into this in the presentation layer. The presentation layer itself talks to the backend data objects (components that communicate with backend devices such as databases and e-mail servers) and takes any results (for example, ADO recordsets) and converts them into an XML format, using a COM2XML process. Finally, a library of XSLT stylesheets is available and, after the presentation layer has performed device detection and has some results to display to the client, the relevant XSLT is selected and the XML transformed to present the response to the client.

The example below goes through one way of creating an XML-based system to support multiple devices and browsers – as would be expected there are many others and the exact details are based on your circumstances. However, what you should take away from this example is an understanding of some of the software architecture choices that need to be made and included in your design, as well as a basis for understanding the principles of developing applications for multiple devices.

The code for this application can be found in the `multidevice` *folder in the code download.*

Detecting Browsers and Devices

In this example we will illustrate how to detect and serve pages for three different types of device – an Internet Explorer 6.0 web browser, a Netscape Navigator 6.0 web browser, and a generic page for mobile devices based on the Wireless Markup Language. It is fully extensible and you can add any of your own devices if desired.

A device registration file called `devices.xml` contains details of all of the types of devices you want to style for. This is listed below (this is an example and would have to be updated if you have other types of browser or want to use specific stylesheets for a given browser):

```xml
<?xml version="1.0" ?>
<DisplayDevices>
    <device browser="Netscape" version="6" Name="Netscape 6.00">
        <page url="multi.asp" href="Netscape6.xsl" />
    </device>
    <device browser="Netscape" version="4.00" Name="Netscape 4.00">
        <page url="multi.asp" href="Netscape6.xsl" />
    </device>
    <device browser="IE" version="6.0" Name="Internet Explorer 6.0">
        <page url="multi.asp" href="IE60.xsl" />
    </device>
    <device browser="IE" version="5.0" Name="Internet Explorer 5.0">
        <page url="multi.asp" href="IE60.xsl" />
    </device>
    <device browser="IE" version="5.5" Name="Internet Explorer 5.5">
        <page url="multi.asp" href="IE60.xsl" />
    </device>
    <device browser="WAP" version="1" Name="WAP Browsers">
        <page url="multi.asp" href="WAP.xsl" />
    </device>
      <device default="IE60.xsl" />
</DisplayDevices>
```

The key elements are the `<device>` elements – these have an attribute called `browser`, which is the name of the browser, followed by a `version` attribute to indicate specific versions of the browser. The final attribute, `Name`, is simply some descriptive text to indicate the browser name. Each `<device>` tag can contain a series of `<page>` elements. The `url` attribute of these tags indicates a page that is to be transformed, followed by an `href` attribute defining the stylesheet to be used on this page for a given device.

In our case we are targeting the three specific devices shown. The page that will be doing the transforms is called `multi.asp`, and the XSLT stylesheets used are called `Netscape6.xsl`, `IE60.xsl`, and `WAP.xsl`. Obviously, this is a sample application and so the transforms are fairly limited – in a larger application you would have multiple `<page>` elements corresponding to individual pages and stylesheets.

The following script is one of the methods available in the `getxsl.asp` file, which is a common utility VBScript file we have created for detecting browsers and directing to the appropriate XSLT file (discussed further below). The first method is the `GetDeviceInfo()` function, which gets information on the browser type and version and stores it as a collection. It is currently limited to browser name and version, but could be expanded upon.

```vbscript
Dim objInfo
Set objInfo = Server.CreateObject("Scripting.Dictionary")

Function GetDeviceInfo()
    'If the browser is unknown then the following will be used
    strUserAgent = Request.ServerVariables("HTTP_USER_AGENT")
    If InStr(strUserAgent, "IE") Then
    objInfo.Add "browser","IE"

intVersion = CInt(Mid(strUserAgent, InStr(strUserAgent, "MSIE") + 5, 1))
    objInfo.Add "version",intVersion
```

```
        ElseIf InStr(strUserAgent, "Gecko") Then
    'Later Netscape Browser
        objInfo.Add "browser","Netscape"

        intVersion = CInt(Mid(strUserAgent, InStrRev(strUserAgent, "/")
            + 1, 2))
        objInfo.Add "version",intVersion
        ElseIf InStr(strUserAgent, "Mozilla") Then
    'A Netscape-compatible browser
        objInfo.Add "browser","Netscape"

        intVersion = CInt(Mid(strUserAgent, RevInStr(strUserAgent, "/")
            + 1, 1))
            objInfo.Add "version",intVersion
    Else
    'By default we will assume a WAP browser
        objInfo.Add "browser","WAP"
        objInfo.Add "version",1
    End If

    Set GetDeviceInfo = objInfo
End Function
```

Initially a global scripting object is created to contain the browser information so it is easily accessible by a key name. The function itself uses the HTTP header information to determine the browser information programmatically.

So, we can use code techniques to extract the browser and version information. This information is available as a string in the `HTTP_USER_AGENT` item of the `ServerVariables` collection:

```
strUserAgent = Request.ServerVariables("HTTP_USER_AGENT")
```

The string for Internet Explorer 6 is like the following:

```
Mozilla/4.0 (compatible; MSIE 6.0; Windows NT 5.0; .NET CLR 1.0.2914)
```

The code provides solutions to discover Microsoft browsers, older Netscape browsers, and the latest Gecko-based Netscape 6 browser, and it defaults to WAP output when it detects some other type of browser or device – this is something you would build on in a real application, or use a third-party component.

Once we have detected the device information, we can start to look at choosing a stylesheet to generate the output. This is what we are going to do now.

Choosing a Stylesheet

The method for selecting the appropriate stylesheet is called `GetStyleSheet()`. It uses the `GetDeviceInfo()` function and is also in the same utility file.

```
Function GetStyleSheet()
    Set objDictDevice = GetDeviceInfo()

    Set xmlDeviceDoc = Server.CreateObject("Msxml2.DOMDocument.4.0")
    xmlDeviceDoc.async = false
    xmlDeviceDoc.load(Server.MapPath("devices.xml"))
```

```
    strFullPageName = Request.ServerVariables("SCRIPT_NAME")
    strPage = mid(strFullPageName,InStrRev(strFullPageName,"/")
        +1,Len(strFullPageName))

    strXPath = "/DisplayDevices/device[@browser='" & _
                objDictDevice("browser") & "' and @version='" & _
                objDictDevice("version")& "']/page[@url='" & _
                strPage & "']/@href"

    Set objXSL = xmlDeviceDoc.selectSingleNode(strXPath)

    If typename(objXSL)<>"Nothing" Then
        strXSL = objXSL.text
        Else
        'is there ANY stylesheet for the browser
        strXPath = "/DisplayDevices/device[@browser='" & g_strBrowser &
                "']/page[@url='" & Lcase(strPage) & "']/@href"

        Set objXSL = xmlDeviceDoc.selectSingleNode(strXPath)
    End If

    If strXSL="" Then
        strXPath = "/DisplayDevices/device[@default]/@default"
        Set objXSL = xmlDeviceDoc.selectSingleNode(strXPath)
        strXSL = objXSL.text
    End If

    Set xslDoc = CreateObject("Msxml2.DOMDocument.4.0")
    xslDoc.async = false
    xslDoc.resolveExternals=false
    bol = xslDoc.load(server.MapPath(strXSL))

    Set GetStyleSheet = xslDoc
End Function
```

As mentioned above, this function first gets back the `Dictionary` object containing the browser and version information and then loads an instance of the `devices.xml` file we discussed earlier. It then uses the `SCRIPT_NAME` item of the `ServerVariables` collection and the `Mid()` function to get the name of the page that the method was invoked from. Note that for improved performance, at the expense of having to provide further developer configuration for reuse, we could declare the script name as a global constant rather than accessing the `ServerVariables` collection, which is slower.

```
    strFullPageName = Request.ServerVariables("SCRIPT_NAME")
    strPage = Mid(strFullPageName, InStrRev(strFullPageName,"/")+1,
            Len(strFullPageName))
```

Next, as we discussed above, we have to extract the name of the stylesheet to use from the `devices.xml` file. To do this, we create an XPath string (you can find out more about XPath in Chapter 4):

```
    strXPath = "/DisplayDevices/device[@browser='" & _
                objDictDevice("browser") & "' and @version='" & _
                objDictDevice("version")& "']/page[@url='" & _
                strPage & "']/@href"

    Set objXSL = xmlDeviceDoc.selectSingleNode(strXPath)
```

This uses a logical and operator to ensure that both the browser and version match, inserting the name of the browser and version from the `Dictionary` object. It also sets the `url` attribute equal to the `strPage` variable we worked out above, and finally returns the `href` attribute, which contains the name of the stylesheet.

If there is no stylesheet, then the default stylesheet is found in the `devices.xml` file as follows:

```
If strXSL="" Then
    strXPath = "/DisplayDevices/device[@default]/@default"
    Set objXSL = xmlDeviceDoc.selectSingleNode(strXPath)
    strXSL = objXSL.text
End If
```

Finally, the stylesheet is parsed, loaded into a `DOMDocument` object, and returned as a result. This is where the transformation and output is completed.

Performing the Transform

The actual transformation and hub of this example is the `multi.asp` page, shown below:

```
<%@ Language="JScript"%>
<%
if (Request.Form.Count>0){
    initServer();
    var xmlDoc = BuildInvoice(Request.Form);
}
else{
    var xmlDoc = Server.CreateObject("Msxml2.DOMDocument.4.0");
    var bol = xmlDoc.load(Server.MapPath("default.xml"));
}

var objXSL_L = GetStyleSheet()

Response.Write(xmlDoc.transformNodeToObject(objXSL_L,Response))
%>
<!--#include file="getxsl.asp"-->
<!--#include file="postHTML.asp"-->
```

As this example doesn't provide a form input page for the WAP example (detected because the number of items in the posted FORM collection will be zero), an XML file called `default.xml` contains a sample instance. Otherwise, data sent via the POST method of the FORM object is used. The stylesheet DOMDocument is returned and stored in the `objXSL_L` variable. Finally, the information is written to the output using the `transformNodeToObject()` function.

You will notice that both the common utility file `getxsl.xsl` and the XML creation file `postHTML.asp` are also included.

XSLT Output

The output for Internet Explorer and Netscape Navigator is quite similar, but significantly different from the mobile output. We won't be going into detail here about the contents of the stylesheets, as they are very similar to what we have been working with. So, to illustrate the difference, the stylesheet for Internet Explorer (`IE60.xsl`) uses the XMLHTTP object in client-side script to send the data to a queue and display a queue number:

```
function PrintInvoice(objXML){
    var xmlhttp = new ActiveXObject("Msxml2.XMLHTTP");
    xmlhttp.Open("POST", "printing.asp", false);
    xmlhttp.Send(objXML);

    alert(xmlhttp.responseText);
}
```

The output is displayed below. You can view this by submitting data from `postHTML.htm` (in the `multidevice` folder), which posts to `multi.asp`; or you can view `multi.asp` directly – this uses the file `default.xml` that contains some sample default values. The following example used the form values:

Customer Name: Wine Club
Email: steven@wineclub.com
Select the Divisions: Wine Division East
Wines Ordered: Blanco de Machali; Santiago Red
Batch Number: 2
Comments: Orders currently out of stock.

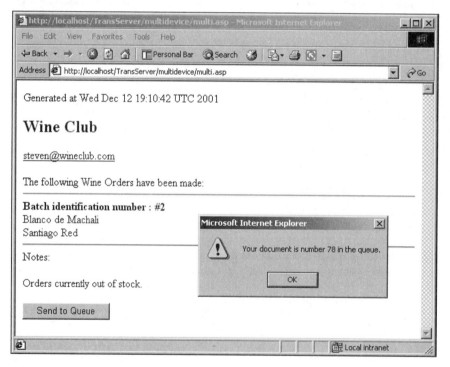

Netscape Navigator does not support the `XMLHTTP` object, so the Netscape stylesheet (`Netscape6.xsl`) generates code to use the traditional `GET` mechanism to request an `ID` from the printing queue (remote scripting, for example, could also be used).

```
<form action="printing.asp" method="get">
    <input type="submit" value="Send to Queue" />
    <input type="hidden" name="id" value="{//@batchid}" />
</form>
```

Incidentally, the page the information is sent to is called `printing.asp` and simply writes back that the invoice is in a printing queue. It generates the queue number randomly:

```
<%@ Language="JScript"%>
<%
Response.Write("Your document is number " + Math.round(Math.random()*100) +
            " in the queue.")
%>
```

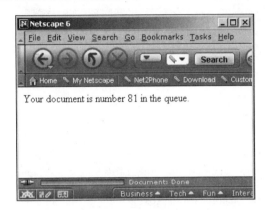

The Wireless Markup Language (WML), generated for the mobile devices is quite different from that above. A discussion of WAP and WML is outside the scope of this book, although you might like to reference *Professional WAP* (ISBN 1-861004-04-4), also published by Wrox Press, for more information. The stylesheet for WAP is called `WAP.xsl`.

Let's look at this WML stylesheet – one thing you will notice if you are new to WML is that although the entire page is generated and sent to the device, due to restrictions on size the information is broken into sections (called **cards**). These cards are much like bookmarks on inline anchor tags, but rather than jumping down the page in the way an HTML page does, with WML the section is redisplayed on the screen.

```
<?xml version="1.0" ?>
<xsl:stylesheet version="1.0"
              xmlns:xsl="http://www.w3.org/1999/XSL/Transform">
    <xsl:output omit-xml-declaration="yes" />
    <xsl:template match="Invoices">
```

The `xml` declaration should be omitted for WML documents. Devices expect WML documents to have the WML `DOCTYPE` declaration at the start of their documents. The easiest way to do this is to use the `<xsl:text>` element and set the value of the `disable-output-escaping` attribute to `"yes"` so that the `&lt;` will be interpreted as a < character:

```
<xsl:text disable-output-escaping="yes">
   &lt;!DOCTYPE wml PUBLIC "-//WAPFORUM//DTD WML 1.1//EN"
        "http://www.wapforum.org/DTD/wml_1.1.xml"&gt;
</xsl:text>
```

WML documents must have a `<wml>` root element. Notice that each card is given an `id` attribute, which can be used for jumping to that particular card using an inline `href` link. So we could jump to the `Main` card with the markup `<a href="Main">link</a>`. Here there are three links defined in addition to the `Main` card (which the other cards link back to):

```
<wml>
    <card id="Main" title="Main">
        Invoice Details for <h3>
            <xsl:value-of select="customers/@custname" />
        </h3>
        <a href="#general">General Details</a>
        <br />
        <a href="#orders">Orders</a>
        <br />
        <a href="#notes">Notes</a>
        <br />
    </card>
    <xsl:apply-templates />
</wml>
</xsl:template>
```

An `<xsl:apply-templates>` generates the other cards for the document. We won't go into great detail with this stylesheet – take a look at the source if you are interested. The only other part worth noting is that the link, like the HTML anchor tag, is used to provide a link to add the invoice to the queue:

```
<a href="http://localhost/test/ProXML/TransServer
        /multidevice/printing.asp?{//@batchid}">
    <b>Send to queue</b>
</a>
```

An example of the output is displayed below by navigating to `multi.asp` in the `server` folder:

```
<!DOCTYPE wml PUBLIC "-//WAPFORUM//DTD WML 1.1//EN"
                    "http://www.wapforum.org/DTD/wml_1.1.xml">
<wml>
    <card id="Main" title="Main">
        Invoice Details for <h3>Wine Club</h3>
        <a href="#general">General Details</a>
        <br />
        <a href="#orders">Orders</a><br /><a href="#notes">Notes</a><br />
    </card>
    <card id="general" title="Invoice">
        Generated at <br />
        <a href="http://localhost/test/ProXML/TransServer
                /multidevice/printing.asp?2">
            <b>Send to queue</b>
        </a>
        <br/>
        <big>Wine Club</big>
        <a href="mailto:steven@wineclub.com" class="email">
            steven@wineclub.com
        </a>
        <p><a href="#Main">back</a></p>
    </card>
    <card id="orders" title="Invoice">
        The following Wine Orders have been made:
        <p><b>BatchID: #2</b><br />
```

```
        Blanco de Machali<br />
        Santiago Red<br />
    </p>
    <p><a href="#Main">back</a></p>
  </card>
  <card id="notes" title="Invoice">
    Notes:
    <p>Orders currently out of stock.</p>
    <p><a href="#Main">back</a></p>
  </card>
</wml>
```

So, the front page when navigating to `multi.asp` in the `server` folder will be displayed as follows:

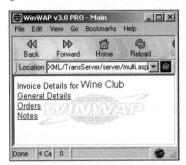

Clicking on the General Details link will display the following page:

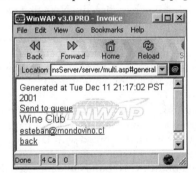

Clicking the back link and then the Orders link displays the list of orders in the batch:

Finally, clicking the back link and then the Notes link will show any attached comment:

That brings us to the end of looking at how the client interacts with the server. Taking it a step further we can look at how MSXML provides native support for interacting with servers as well.

Interacting with Other Servers

Let's take the example one step further. Consider the situation where we have to interact with a third-party server, an increasingly popular scenario. In this space there are many options open to us, such as SOAP, XML-RPC, and others. In fact, on the Windows platform, it is likely that any of these technologies will use the underlying MSXML parser anyway, so in certain circumstances it may be easier for us to just use the MSXML 4.0 parser directly. Note that we specify MSXML *4.0* here – prior to MSXML version 3.0 (specifically, prior to the `ServerXMLHTTP` component that ships with MSXML 3.0 and 4.0) there was no supported way of using MSXML on the server to interact with other servers – the `XMLHTTP` component does not support this (or more specifically, the `WinInet` component that it uses does not support this). In fact the Microsoft Windows HTTP Services (WinHTTP) 5.0 underlies this and is what is used by the `ServerXMLHTTP` component itself.

So, let's be completely clear about this. Using the `XMLHTTP` object on a desktop client works great and allows us to retrieve XML data from a remote web site without page refreshes, thus allowing richer and better integration of web applications when combined with DHTML (it will work only with Internet Explorer). Using `XMLHTTP` on the server will not work and has been a constant problem source in XML server-to-server applications based on MSXML builds to date – see the article on the limitations at the following address: http://support.microsoft.com/support/kb/articles/Q183/1/10.ASP.

On the contrary, `ServerXMLHTTP` should really only be used on the server (it will not work on Windows 95, 98, or WinME) and allows very similar functionality to that of the `XMLHTTP` object. It will no doubt become one of the most popular components of MSXML. We covered `ServerXMLHTTP` in detail in Chapter 9 but let's now look at it in conjunction with XSLT.

The ServerXMLHTTP Object

The methods and properties of the `ServerXMLHTTP` object were listed in detail in the previous chapter, "*Sending and Retrieving XML Data*", so they are only mentioned briefly here as a quick reminder. First the methods:

- ❏ abort()
- ❏ getAllResponseHeaders()
- ❏ getOption()
- ❏ getResponseHeader()
- ❏ open()
- ❏ send()
- ❏ setOption()
- ❏ setProxy()
- ❏ setProxyCredentials()
- ❏ setRequestHeader()
- ❏ setTimeouts()
- ❏ waitForResponse()

Then the properties:

- ❏ onreadystatechange
- ❏ readyState
- ❏ responseBody
- ❏ responseStream
- ❏ responseText
- ❏ responseXML
- ❏ status
- ❏ statusText

Using ServerXMLHTTP

To ensure this application works as intended, you need to go to the `server` folder in the download for this chapter.

> **Ensure you do the following for each sample as we work through the chapter!**

In `multi.asp`, change the values of the variables `strServerPath` and `strServerPathRoot` to the appropriate URL locations on your machine in the highlighted lines shown below:

```
...
//Get the delivery job ID
var strServerPath = "http:// yourserver/folder/server/remote1/jobid.asp"
objXMLHTTPSrv = Server.CreateObject ("MSXML2.ServerXMLHTTP.4.0");
objXMLHTTPSrv.open ("GET",strServerPath, false);
objXMLHTTPSrv.send ();
...
//Send to delivery and get the cost
```

477

```
var strServerPathRoot = "http://yourserver/folder/server
                                /remote2/deliveries.asp"
objXMLHTTPSrv2 = Server.CreateObject ("MSXML2.ServerXMLHTTP.4.0");
objXMLHTTPSrv2.onreadystatechange=handler;
objXMLHTTPSrv2.open ("POST",strServerPathRoot, false);
objXMLHTTPSrv2.send (xmlDoc);
...
```

> **This should also be done in future sections that use `multi.asp`!**

You will have to change the date attributes in the file `remote1/jobs.xml` (just follow the format illustrated in the file – DD/MM/YYYY – for example, 3/12/2001 for 3rd December 2001) depending on when you run the application. The dates should be today, tomorrow, and the day after relative to the system you are running the application on. Finally, ensure that the file `deliveries.xml` in the folder **remote2** can be written to. The easiest way in this example is to set the NTFS write privilege on the file to **EVERYONE** (because we need to give write access to the **IUSER_COMPUTERNAME** account that IIS will use when an anonymous user hits the web server) – we're not crazy enough to do this on a production system. On a production system ensure that you lock down write access to specific accounts!

The `ServerXMLHTTP` object can be used in two ways: indirectly with a `DOMDocument`, and directly. Earlier on in the chapter we used the `load()` method of the MSXML `DOMDocument` object to load an instance of an XML document stored on the local web server and used the `MapPath()` method of the `Server` object to get the full physical path to the file:

```
var xmlDoc = new ActiveXObject("Msxml2.DOMDocument.4.0");
xmlDoc.async = false;
xmlDoc.load(Server.MapPath("invoice.xml"));
```

It was stressed that this method should only be used with a desktop client browser and that using it on the server would give unpredictable results. However, we can indirectly use the `ServerXMLHTTP` object to allow loading of remote URL locations. To do this we simply use the `setProperty()` method of the `DOMDocument` and set the `ServerHTTPRequest` to `true`. So to make the above example server-safe to load some remote URL, we would do the following:

```
var xmlDoc = new ActiveXObject("Msxml2.DOMDocument.4.0");
xmlDoc.async = false;
xmlDoc.setProperty("ServerHTTPRequest",true);
xmlDoc.load("http://www.invoice-example.com/invoice.xml"));
```

When we use the above method, the `ServerXMLHTTP` object is actually used underneath the `DOMDocument` to perform the load of the URL – hence we have a server-safe way to load XML documents.

The alternative method is to use the `ServerXMLHTTP` object directly, which allows much more flexibility than using the `DOMDocument` method – we can use functionality much like that provided by the client `XMLHTTP` object. So, the following fragment would return the XML from a URL that returned XML documents for invoices:

```
objSrvHTTP = Server.CreateObject ("MSXML2.ServerXMLHTTP.4.0");
objSrvHTTP.open ("GET","http://www.invoice-example/ReturnInvoice.asp",
                    false);
```

```
objSrvHTTP.send ();
Response.ContentType = "text/xml";
Response.Write (objSrvHTTP.responseXML.xml);
```

In this example, having no data in the `send()` method will mean that the request will just return the result of the `ReturnInvoice.asp` page.

Let's look at an example of using the `ServerXMLHTTP` object directly to extend the example we have been working with thus far. A diagram of the sample scenario is shown:

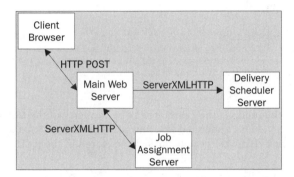

What we will now do is add some functionality that will first get the next delivery job ID number from the internal inventory server – there are a set number of deliverers per day who can do deliveries. Once these deliveries have been completed, some delivery management application closes the job ID and subsequent delivery requests have to find the next delivery job ID, which may be the following day.

Once this ID is retrieved the application sends it along with the details of the invoice to a third-party server, which creates a delivery document and cost. This is returned and displayed in the comments for the user – all happening seamlessly to the user.

> *This example uses MSXML 4.0 and the sample files for this example can be found in the* `server` *folder of the code download for this chapter.*

Within the `server` folder, changes (relative to the `multidevice` folder example we looked at above) have been made to `multi.asp` and two new folders, `remote1` and `remote2`, have been added. The `remote1` folder contains the file `jobid.asp`, which gets the next available delivery job ID, as well as `jobs.xml`, which contains the latest information on the delivery schedules and availability used by `jobid.asp`. The second folder, `remote2`, contains `deliveries.asp` to create a delivery and return the cost to the calling page, `deliveries.xml`, which stores the updated delivery information, and `convert.xsl`, which converts the posted invoice XML document to a format suitable for the `deliveries.xml` document. Let's first look at the updates to `multi.asp`, which makes extensive use of the `ServerXMLHTTP` object.

The main page, `multi.asp`, is shown below – this is the page that the user interface (`postHTML.htm`) will post to:

```
<%@ Language="JScript"%>
<%
var xmlDoc = new ActiveXObject("Msxml2.DOMDocument.4.0");
xmlDoc.async = false;
```

```
if (Request.Form.Count>0)
{
    str = BuildInvoice(Request.Form)
    xmlDoc.loadXML(str);
}
else
    var bol = xmlDoc.load(Server.MapPath("default.xml"));
```

The first instance of the ServerXMLHTTP object actually interacts with the first server and calls the page jobid.asp using the GET method. No information is passed with the send() method as it only expects an integer value to be returned:

```
//Get the delivery job ID
var strServerPath = "http://yourserver/folder/server/remote1/jobid.asp"
objXMLHTTPSrv = Server.CreateObject("MSXML2.ServerXMLHTTP.4.0");
objXMLHTTPSrv.open("GET",strServerPath, false);
objXMLHTTPSrv.send();
```

The result of the call is obtained via the responseText property of the ServerXMLHTTP object and stored in a variable. This value is appended as a new attribute called JobID to the <Invoice> element in the XML DOMDocument that was created earlier, and stored in the xmlDoc variable:

```
var lngJobID = objXMLHTTPSrv.responseText;
xmlDoc.documentElement.setAttribute("JobID",lngJobID);
```

The second instance of the ServerXMLHTTP object connects to the second remote server and calls deliveries.asp, discussed below. It is anticipated that there will be higher load at this site and so an immediate response may not be possible, so the event handler method handler() is assigned to the onreadystatechange property – this means that when the readyState property changes, this method will be called. The invoice XML DOMDocument is then POSTed to the ASP page as an argument to the send() method:

```
//Send to delivery and get the cost
var strDeliveryServerPath = "";
strServerPathRoot="http://yourserver/folder/server
                    /remote2/deliveries.asp";
objXMLHTTPSrv2 = Server.CreateObject("MSXML2.ServerXMLHTTP.4.0");
objXMLHTTPSrv2.onreadystatechange = handler;
objXMLHTTPSrv2.open("POST", strDeliveryServerPath, false);
objXMLHTTPSrv2.send(xmlDoc);

%>
<script language="javascript" runat="server">
```

The handler() method will be called four times (see the definition of readyState if you don't understand why) and when it has a value of 4, the processing will be complete and the result ready. When it is, the responseXML property is used to extract the updated XML DOMDocument and store it in the variable objUpdate. Next the stylesheet is obtained using the GetStyleSheet() method, and finally the output is written using the transformNode() method against the updated XML document, with the stylesheet as an argument:

```
function handler()
{
    if (objXMLHTTPSrv2.readyState == 4)
        {
            var objUpdate = objXMLHTTPSrv2.responseXML

            var objXSL_L = GetStyleSheet()

            Response.Write(objUpdate.transformNode(objXSL_L))
        }
}

</script>
<!--#include file="getxsl.asp"-->
<!--#include file="postHTML.asp"-->
```

We have seen how the main page collects the information, but let's look at what happens on the other servers. The first "server" in the folder is `remote1.asp` and this could be some server on our local network (in fact we have the job of setting the variable that points to the location of the server files, so it can be on Jupiter if we wish!). The delivery schedules and job IDs are stored in an XML file, `jobs.xml`, shown here:

```
<?xml version="1.0" encoding="utf-8" ?>
<jobs>
    <daily date="3/12/2001">
        <job UniqueID="24323445" DailyId="1" status="closed" />
        <job UniqueID ="32344456" DailyId="2" status="open" />
        <job UniqueID D="93343352" DailyId="3" status="open" />
    </daily>
    <daily date="4/12/2001">
        <job UniqueID ="24323445" DailyId="1" status="closed" />
        <job UniqueID ="32344456" DailyId="2" status="closed" />
        <job UniqueID ="93343352" DailyId="3" status="closed" />
    </daily>
    <daily date="5/12/2001">
        <job UniqueID ="24323445" DailyId="1" status="closed" />
        <job UniqueID ="32344456" DailyId="2" status="closed" />
        <job UniqueID="93343352" DailyId="3" status="closed" />
    </daily>
</jobs>
```

The company does delivery jobs daily and there are three per day. There are a maximum number of items that can be carried by any one job and, when this number is exceeded, the job status is set to `closed` – this is controlled by some external job management application. A company-wide unique ID is assigned to every job and is passed to the delivery company when assigning specific items to a particular delivery (see below).

The work on this server is done by the file `jobid.asp`, which is discussed below. There is one method in this file, which basically gets the next day based on the date in its argument – this is important when looking for a job ID, as we will see in a while.

```
<%@ Language="JScript"%>
<script language="JScript" runat="server">
function getNextDate(objCurrentDate)
{
    var Dtoday = objCurrentDate;
    var Dtomorrow = Dtoday.getDate() +1 ;
```

```
      Dtoday.setDate(Dtomorrow);
      return(Dtoday);
   }
   </script>
```

The XML file `jobs.xml` contains the available job IDs and so we need to load this file:

```
<%
var xmlDoc = Server.CreateObject("Msxml2.DOMDocument.4.0");
xmlDoc.async = false;
xmlDoc.load(Server.MapPath("jobs.xml"));
```

We then start with today's date and loop on a daily basis to find the `UniqueID` of a job that has its `status` set to open. This uses an XPath expression and the `selectSingleNode()` method to get a job ID. When a non-null node is found, the loop is exited and the text value is written to the output, and hence to the remote calling page `multi.asp`. Note that in case a valid date is not found within 100 days of the start date, a maximum of 100 attempts are made – after this, the loop will terminate and the job ID will be 0 (which in a real-world system would be flagged to the responsible manager!).

```
var objDate = new Date();
var strDate = "";

var intAttempts = 0;
while (objJobNode==null && intAttempts<100)
{
   strDate = objDate.getDate() + "/" + (objDate.getMonth()+1) + "/" +
             objDate.getFullYear();

   strXPath = "jobs/daily[@date='" + strDate +
             "']/job[@status='open']/@UnqiueID";

   var objJobNode = xmlDoc.selectSingleNode(strXPath);

   intAttempts++;
   objDate = getNextDate(objDate);
}

if (intAttempts==100)
   Response.Write("0");
else
   Response.Write(objJobNode.text);
%>
```

The second server corresponds to some delivery company that actually delivers the products for the company to the customer. The files for this are in the folder `remote2` and the work is done by the file `deliveries.asp`, which is discussed below. This file first loads the XML object that was posted by `multi.asp` in the second `ServerXMLHTTP` instance. This can be loaded directly via the `Request` object using the `load()` method.

```
<%@ Language="JScript"%>
<%
var xmlDoc = new ActiveXObject("Msxml2.DOMDocument.4.0");
xmlDoc.async = false;
xmlDoc.load(Request);
```

Following this, the conversion XSLT file, `convert.xsl`, is loaded – we discuss this more below.

```
var xslDoc = new ActiveXObject("Msxml2.DOMDocument.4.0");
xslDoc.async = false;
xslDoc.load(Server.MapPath("convert.xsl"));
```

Next is an interesting part of the application. We have to insert some data from the XML DOM document that was posted into the file `deliveries.xml` (discussed below). We of course have the option of using the DOM to extract the values needed from the `xmlDoc` document and dynamically create a fragment that can then be inserted into the `deliveries.xml` document. However, it is much easier to simply create an XSLT stylesheet that transforms the format of the XML from the source structure to the result structure using the `convert.xsl` XSLT. Further to this, we don't even need to get the result and then load it into a DOM document – we can do this directly using the `transformNodeToObject()` method. We simply need to create an empty instance of a DOM document (`objXMLOut` in our case) and then pass this as the second parameter to the `transformNodeToObject()` method, which stores the result of the transformation as a DOM document in the `objXMLOut` variable.

```
var objXMLOut = new ActiveXObject("Msxml2.DOMDocument.4.0");
objXMLOut.async = false;
xmlDoc.transformNodeToObject(xslDoc,objXMLOut)

var xmlDelivDoc = new ActiveXObject("Msxml2.DOMDocument.4.0");
xmlDelivDoc.async = false;
xmlDelivDoc.load(Server.MapPath("deliveries.xml"));
```

We want to use the cost later on and so we use `selectSingleNode()` to get this cost from the `objXMLOut` XML document – if we try to do this later on it will cause an error. It will cause an error because the following code appends the XML of the `objXMLOut` to the `deliveries.xml` DOM document instance, and when this is done, the appended node (the `documentElement` node in our case) is removed and no longer accessible in this object.

```
var strCost = objXMLOut.selectSingleNode("/Delivery/ItemSet/@cost").text;
xmlDelivDoc.documentElement.appendChild(objXMLOut.documentElement)
```

Note that this usage of appending a node is an extension from the W3C DOM specification – the `importNode()` method should be used instead, but isn't defined in MSXML 4.0. The updated delivery DOMDocument is then persisted using the `save()` method, with the physical path as an argument. Remember, we need to set the permissions on `deliveries.xml` so that everyone can write to the file.

```
xmlDelivDoc.save(Server.MapPath("deliveries.xml"));
```

The cost that we stored in `strCost` is then appended to the comments CDATA section of the `xmlDoc` DOM document invoice instance that was posted in the first place. Finally, the `ContentType` is set to `"text/xml"` so that the object that receives the response interprets the result as XML. The updated invoice document is written out and therefore is the result of the second `ServerXMLHTTP` instance in `multi.asp`.

```
xmlDoc.selectSingleNode("/Invoices/customers/order/comments")
                      .childNodes[0].text+=" The cost will be " +
                      strCost + " Pesos."

Response.ContentType = "text/xml"
Response.Write(xmlDoc.xml);
%>
```

Earlier we mentioned the file `convert.xsl` that takes the `POST`ed invoice DOM document instance and transforms it to a format valid for inserting into the `deliveries.xml` file.

The `<xsl:stylesheet>` root element has some interesting additions to what we normally see. The first is a namespace definition with the prefix `msxsl`, which is required when using scripting within the XSLT file (the prefix can be changed, but the namespace must be the same). Although it is recommended that you avoid script within your XSLT where possible, there are times where it can be very important, perhaps when some essential business logic or external resource is required. Also, we have to define a namespace for any methods that we are going to implement ourselves – in our case it is associated with the prefix `invoice`. Finally, we don't want any of these new namespaces appearing in the output, so we use the `exclude-result-prefixes` attribute to exclude the prefixes `msxsl` and `invoice`:

```
<?xml version="1.0" ?>
<xsl:stylesheet version="1.0"
                xmlns:xsl="http://www.w3.org/1999/XSL/Transform"
                xmlns:msxsl="urn:schemas-microsoft-com:xslt"
                xmlns:invoice="http://invoice-example.com/invoice"
                exclude-result-prefixes="msxsl invoice">

    <xsl:template match="Invoices">
       <Delivery jobid="{@JobID}">
          <xsl:apply-templates />
       </Delivery>
    </xsl:template>
```

Within the `customers` template, we invoke one of our user-defined functions called `GetCost()`, passing the number of `<item>` elements using the XPath `count()` function – this must be appended by our user-defined `invoice` namespace to qualify it as one of our defined methods. Remember that the curly braces are effectively the same as an `xsl:value-of` call, but can be embedded within the attributes.

```
    <xsl:template match="customers">
       <ItemSet customer="{@custname}"
                cost="{invoice:GetCost(count(order/details
                       /items/item))}">
          <xsl:apply-templates />
       </ItemSet>
    </xsl:template>
    <xsl:template match="items/item">
       <item>
          <xsl:value-of select="." />
       </item>
    </xsl:template>
    <xsl:template match="text()" />
```

Any functions that we wish to define and make available to the XSLT have to be defined within an `<msxsl:script>` block as shown below – we defined `GetCost()`. In this simple example, we don't need to define script within the XSLT, however, it is very possible that you may need to access some external data source to get the multiplier value for the cost. In order for this function to be qualified as one of our defined methods, you should set the `implements-prefix` attribute to the value of a prefix we created on the root `<xsl:stylesheet>` element – `invoice` in this case.

```
    <msxsl:script language="JScript" implements-prefix="invoice">
    function GetCost(intNumItems)
    {
```

```
            return intNumItems*100000;
        }
    </msxsl:script>
</xsl:stylesheet>
```

The file where the delivery information that is created by `convert.xsl` is stored is called `deliveries.xml`. This file is shown below and the node that is created with `convert.xsl` is highlighted:

```
<?xml version="1.0" encoding="utf-8" ?>
<Deliveries>
    <Delivery jobid="32344456">
        <ItemSet customer="Edward Scissorhands" cost="200000">
            <item>Blanco de Machali</item>
            <item>Southern Fruity Red</item>
        </ItemSet>
    </Delivery>
    <Delivery jobid="93343352">
        <ItemSet customer="Loreto Perez" cost="200000">
            <item>Blanco de Machali</item>
            <item>Southern Fruity Red</item>
        </ItemSet>
    </Delivery>
</Deliveries>
```

Example output, as displayed by Internet Explorer, of running this application from the `postHTML.htm` in the `server` folder is shown, where the following details were typed into the form:

Customer Name: Esteban Livingstone
Email: esteban@mondovino.cl
Select the Divisions: Wine Division East
Wines Ordered: Blanco de Machali; Southern Fruity Red
Batch Number: 3
Comments: *None*.

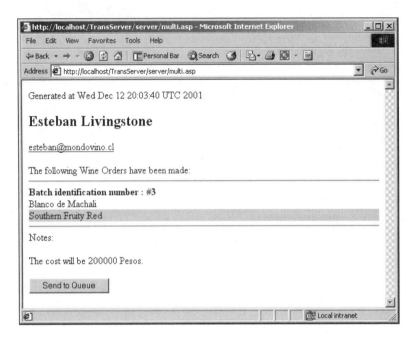

Let's continue by looking at some advanced concepts of working on the server and how we can improve the performance and functionality of stylesheets.

Advanced Server Concepts

Before we get into worked examples, we should take a step back and look at some of the theory behind the concepts of improving performance and functionality on the server. These are available as of MSXML 3.0 and above.

MSXML Threading Models

MSXML 3.0 and 4.0 have two threading versions and especially when working on the server it is essential that we fully understand the differences between the two and when to use them. The two models are **rental** and **free-threaded**. Those who've done work developing with ActiveX Server controls with ASP will know how important the distinction is.

> **The rental mode should only be used and released on a per page request for a user – or single-threaded access. Using it at session level will dramatically affect the performance for the user working with the application – using it at application level will affect the performance of the application for *all* users. In fact, IIS 5 and above prevents using rental mode in a session or application variable.**

The rental model is created like this in VBScript:

```
Set objXML = Server.CreateObject("MSXML2.DOMDocument.4.0")
```

or like this in JavaScript:

```
var objXML = Server.CreateObject("MSXML2.DOMDocument.4.0");
```

The rental model is generally used in a single web page when loading an XML document and/or XSLT document to perform a `transformNode()` or `transformNodeToObject()`. When completed, the XML and XSLT documents will be released and these instances will no longer be available until they are loaded again.

On the contrary, the free-threaded model is designed for multiple-thread access, which is common across sessions or applications in ASP. It is defined like this in VBScript:

```
Set Session("objXML") =
    server.CreateObject("MSXML2.FreeThreadedDOMDocument.4.0")
Set Application("objXML") =
    server.CreateObject("MSXML2.FreeThreadedDOMDocument.4.0")
```

or like this in JavaScript:

```
var Session("objXML") =
    Server.CreateObject("MSXML2.FreeThreadedDOMDocument.4.0");

var Application("objXML") =
    Server.CreateObject("MSXML2.FreeThreadedDOMDocument.4.0");
```

Notice that in this example we have used the Active Server Pages `Application` object to store the instance – we could equally have used the `Session` object, an object tag (for example: `<object runat=server id=objname>`), or even just an object variable in a web page.

We can, of course, use the free-threaded version in the same way we use the rental model, but there are performance gains when using the rental model, so when our application only needs a rental model, it is best to stick to it. However, the free-threaded object is required when loading stylesheets to be used with the `IXSLTemplate` object discussed below, or when we want to cache XML or XSLT objects for multi-threaded access in your application.

In Chapter 13, "*Performance, Scalability, and Security*", we will be looking at using `cloneNode()` to "replace" free-threaded models.

IXSLTemplate Object

Whenever we want to transform our XML document on the server using `transformNode()` or `transformNodeToObject()`, the stylesheet must be compiled into a DOM node and passed into the method to perform the transform. When a stylesheet is used often and doesn't change between uses, repeatedly recompiling it can be regarded as quite a performance hit – especially when there may be more complex stylesheets.

As was briefly covered in Chapter 9, the `XSLTemplate` object was introduced in MSXML 3.0 as an extension to the W3C DOM Recommendation (http://www.w3.org/TR/REC-DOM_Level_1/) to allow developers to avoid having to do this repeated compilation. In fact, it allows us to compile the stylesheet once and thereafter cache the compiled stylesheet and use it directly in future transforms. It can be used on the client or server, although here we will look at server-side usage.

The `IXSLTemplate` object has one method, the `createProcessor()` method. This creates a rental-mode `IXSLProcessor` object (see above discussion on threading models), which is basically a copy of the compiled cached stylesheet. The `IXSLTemplate` object also has one property, `stylesheet`. This allows us to assign a compiled stylesheet DOM node into the template and this stylesheet must be a `FreeThreadedDOMDocument`. Remember that this is a compiled and cached stylesheet, so changing the physical stylesheet will not affect the stylesheet in the template object.

So, the following example shows how to create an `XSLTemplate` object instance, cache a compiled stylesheet, and create an `XSLProcessor` object from it – this will be continued when we look at the `XSLProcessor` object next.

```
var xslFreeDoc = new ActiveXObject("Msxml2.FreeThreadedDOMDocument.4.0");
xslFreeDoc.async = false;
xslFreeDoc.load("convert.xsl");

var objXSLTemplate = Server.CreateObject("Msxml2.XSLTemplate.4.0");
objXSLTemplate.stylesheet = xslFreeDoc;

//Session("StyleCache") = objXSLTemplate

Application.Lock
Application("StyleCache") = objXSLTemplate
Application.UnLock

var xslProc = objXSLTemplate.createProcessor();
```

Looking at the code, the first thing that is done is to create an instance of the free-threaded DOM document, which must have the `async` property set to `false`. The target stylesheet is then compiled into a `DOMDocument` using the `load()` method.

Next, an `XMLTemplate` object is created and the stylesheet property is set to our free-threaded stylesheet we just loaded. We now have a cached and compiled version of the stylesheet and on the server we can store this in a session or application object based on your requirements.

Finally, when we want to actually get an instance of the compiled stylesheet to use in a transform, we must use the `createProcessor()` method, which will return an instance of an `XSLProcessor` object. We need to create an `XSLProcessor` object, using `createProcessor()`, for each instance of the compiled stylesheet we require to perform a transformation.

One other note – we can also use the `XSLTemplate` object to cache XML documents. This should generally not be done, because our XML changes a lot more often than stylesheets, and so the performance gain you see will likely be minimal and this procedure will potentially take up a lot of memory. However, it can be useful for caching some static, commonly-used XML data such as a look-up table.

IXSLProcessor Object

By now we have heard quite a bit about the `XSLProcessor` object, and briefly saw it in use at the end of the previous chapter. To recap, the `XSLProcessor` object uses an instance of a compiled stylesheet from an `XSLTemplate` object and is used to perform the transformations on some XML data. This object has quite a bit more to it than the `XSLTemplate` object, having five methods and seven properties, discussed below.

The following list shows the methods available to the `IXSLProcessor` object – examples of this will be demonstrated shortly:

❑   addObject(object, namespaceURI) – this can add object methods as extension functions to the compiled stylesheet. As arguments it takes the object and unique namespace to associate with the object extension functions in the stylesheet. If the object argument is null, the object previously associated with the namespaceURI parameter in the stylesheet will be released.

❑   addParameter(strName, varValue, namespaceURI) – adds the parameter with the name strName (which should be the name of a parameter defined in the stylesheet we want to set to the varValue argument). The varValue argument will be a string, number, DOMNode, or DOMNodeList. Finally, the namespaceURI is the URI to associate with this object. Passing a null value as varValue will result in any previously set parameter with the name strName being removed.

❑   reset() – this resets the XSLProcessor object to its original state; that is, the state of the XSLProcessor object when the createProcessor() method was called. So any object, parameters, etc., will be removed.

❑   setStartMode(strMode, namespaceURI) – this method allows us to specify the mode strMode in the URI namespaceURI that should be used when the stylesheet is initially executed. For more details on modes, see Chapter 5, "*XSLT in MSXML*".

❑   transform() – this method basically invokes the transform of the compiled stylesheet against the XML document specified using the input property, discussed below, and writes the result to the output.

The properties of IXSLProcessor are as follows:

❑   input – this property should be set to a DOMNode, which is the XML node to be transformed by the compiled stylesheet.

❑   output(objOutput) – this defines a custom output to write the result of the transformation. If no objOutput is provided, then a string is returned containing the text of the result encoded as Unicode (and any encoding on the xsl:output is ignored). The objects that can have the output written to them are those supporting IStream, IPersistStream, DOMDocument, the ASP IResponse object, ADODB.Stream, and the new IMXWriter that complements the SAX API.

❑   ownerTemplate – this returns the stylesheet template used to create this XSLProcessor object. This is still accessible when the template is released and so it may be different from the stylesheet property.

❑   readyState – returns the state of the processor and takes one of the values 1, 2, 3, or 4. It will be 4 when the request is complete.

❑   startMode – this returns the base name of the qualified start mode. It defaults to an empty string.

❑   startModeURI – this returns the URI part of the qualified start mode. It defaults to an empty string.

❑   stylesheet – this returns the stylesheet that was defined on the XSLTemplate object at the time this processor object was created.

XSLProcessor or transformNode()

At this point you may be interested to know why we would use the XSLProcessor object instead of transformNode() – some aspects may be obvious and others not:

❑ Improved scalability – the `XSLProcessor` object allows caching of XSLT and XML documents so they don't have to be parsed every time they are to be used.

❑ Improved performance – with the `XSLTemplate` object, compiled XSLT documents can offer much greater scalability than is offered by `transformNode()`, which uses newly-compiled stylesheets. In fact, we can use MTS to cache the `XSLTemplate` object to optimize across many sessions.

❑ Passing parameters – XSLT makes common use of parameters and so we can have much more dynamic and flexible stylesheets by using the `XSLProcessor` object's ability to pass external parameters to the compiled XSLT.

❑ Passing objects – similar to passing parameters, we can pass COM object methods as namespace extensions into our compiled stylesheets via the `XSLProcessor` object. Note that we don't actually pass the object itself in (we can't `TypeOf(objTheObjectIPassedIn)`), but rather the methods of the object are themselves available as extension functions.

Now that we understand some of the theory behind threading, templates, and processor objects, and the advantages of their use, let's look at how these can be used practically to enhance our distributed invoice application.

Extending and Improving Performance of Stylesheets

So, we can now enhance the application using the techniques we have learned. First let's look at how we can improve the performance of the application using the `XSLTemplate` and `XSLProcessor` objects, though it will probably be difficult to see a difference in performance with this simple application.

The XSLTemplate and XSLProcessor Objects

> Remember to set the appropriate access rights to files as discussed above (for example, `deliveries.xml`) to ensure the application works correctly. Also, this example will only work on IIS 5 as it uses the `IResponse` object not available in IIS 4.0.

We know that each user who uses the application will be assigned a stylesheet based on the browser and device they are using. It is obvious that for users repeatedly using the invoicing application, a performance improvement could be seen in caching the XSLT in the user's session and using the compiled version each time they use the application.

However, we know that the stylesheets must be free-threaded, so there is one change that we have to make in the file `getxsl.asp` in the `advanced` directory, and that is to create a free-threaded XSLT stylesheet instance, as shown:

```
Function GetStyleSheet()
...
    Set xslDoc = Server.CreateObject("Msxml2.FreeThreadedDOMDocument.4.0")
    xslDoc.async = false
    xslDoc.resolveExternals = false
    bol = xslDoc.load(server.MapPath(strXSL))

    Set GetStyleSheet = xslDoc
End Function
```

Now we can update `multi.asp`, and the updates to this are in the server script block. The `handler()` method has been updated to call two new methods – the `GetTemplate()` method, which returns an `XSLTemplate` object, and the `ShowResult()` method, which writes the result to the output.

```javascript
<script language="javascript" runat="server">
function handler()
{
    if (objXMLHTTPSrv2.readyState == 4)
    {
        var objUpdate = objXMLHTTPSrv2.responseXML

        objXSLTemplate = GetTemplate()

        ShowResult(objUpdate,objXSLTemplate)
    }
}
```

The `GetTemplate()` method returns an `XSLTemplate` object for the user, containing the compiled stylesheet that will be used to transform the invoice XML document. The `XSLTemplate` object's `stylesheet` property is set to the stylesheet returned from the `GetStyleSheet()` method discussed earlier. This template is then cached at application level so that this compiled stylesheet can be used directly from the `Application` object when the user re-executes the application.

```javascript
function GetTemplate()
{
    //Cache Stylesheet in Users Session
    if (Application("StyleSheet")==null)
    {
        var objXSL_L = GetStyleSheet()

        var objTemplate = new ActiveXObject("Msxml2.XSLTemplate.4.0");
        objTemplate.stylesheet = objXSL_L;

        Application("StyleSheet") = objTemplate
    }
    else
        var objTemplate = Application("StyleSheet")

    return(objTemplate);
}
```

The `ShowResult()` method takes the invoice XML object and the `XSLTemplate` object as arguments. It creates an `XSLProcessor` object instance and sets its input property to our invoice XML `DOMDocument`. The output is set to the ASP `IResponse` object, which means the results will be written directly to the output stream to create the web page. Finally, the transformation is invoked with the `transform()` method:

```javascript
function ShowResult(objXML,objTemplate)
{
    var xslProc = objTemplate.createProcessor();
    xslProc.input=objXML;
    xslProc.output=Response;
    xslProc.transform();
}

</script>
```

We won't show the output interface, as nothing has been changed in it. In fact, the application data is still exactly the same as it was in our last example, but we have now improved its performance and scalability.

Working with Parameters

Performance and scalability is not the only significant improvement with the XSLTemplate and XSLProcessor objects – they are also much more flexible and extensible. We now look at using parameters and objects to extend the functionality of the application.

Parameters can be used to add information to a stylesheet that isn't available internally. This may be because it is not in the XML document that will be transformed or cannot be accessed internally within the stylesheet, and can vary every time the stylesheet is processed.

In the example we are going to show how the logon name of the user and the location can be dynamically added to the output. This is information that typically wouldn't be available in an instance of the invoice XML document directly, because the logon happens separately. However, in our case and for simplicity, the username and location are stored as hidden form elements in the postHTML.htm page.

```
<html>
   <head>
      <title>Invoice Generator</title>
   </head>
   <body>
      <form action="multi.asp" method="post">
         ...
         <P>
         <input type="submit" value="Submit Invoice">
         </P>
         <input type="hidden" name="username" value="slivings">
         <input type="hidden" name="userlocation" value="Glasgow, Scotland">
      </form>
   </body>
</html>
```

Typically this kind of information may be obtained from an Active Directory store or database table.

Additionally, each XSLT stylesheet also has to be updated to accept the parameters and display them in the result. The following shows the changes made to IE60.xsl, but similar changes have been made to Netscape6.xsl and WAP.xsl.

```
<?xml version="1.0" ?>
<xsl:stylesheet version="1.0"
    xmlns:xsl="http://www.w3.org/1999/XSL/Transform">
   <xsl:param name="username" select="'unknown'" />
   <xsl:param name="userlocation" select="'unknown'" />
   <xsl:template match="Invoices">
      <html>
         <head>
         ...
         </head>
         <body>
            Generated at <xsl:value-of select="@date" /><br />
            By <xsl:value-of select="$username" /> from
            <xsl:value-of select="$userlocation" />.
            <xsl:apply-templates />
```

```
                    <input type="button" value="Send to Queue"
                           onclick="PrintInvoice()" />
            </body>
        </html>
    </xsl:template>
        ...
</xsl:stylesheet>
```

The two parameters, username and userlocation, have been defined as direct children of the <xsl:template> element and initialized with the values "unknown". This means that the text "unknown" will be displayed if any parameter does not have a parameter initialized.

To initialize the parameter, an external parameter with the same name as the parameter must be passed with some value. So, if we use the addParameter() method to add a parameter to the stylesheet called "wrox" with some value, if we want that value to be available within the stylesheet, then there must be an <xsl:param> element defined with the name attribute equal to "wrox". This is done in multi.asp, which now has a couple of updates, as shown:

```
<%@ Language="JScript"%>
...

if (Request.Form.Count>0)
{
    var strUsername = Request.Form("username").Item;
    var strUserLocation = Request.Form("userlocation").Item

    initServer();
    var xmlDoc = BuildInvoice(Request.Form);
}
...

function ShowResult(objXML, objTemplate)
{
    var xslProc = objTemplate.createProcessor();
    xslProc.input=objXML;
    xslProc.output=Response;

    xslProc.addParameter("username",strUsername);
    xslProc.addParameter("userlocation",strUserLocation);
    xslProc.transform();
}

...
```

As the username and userlocation really have nothing to do with the invoice itself, they are stored in two global variables, strUsername and strUserLocation, which store the values of these elements in the posted form. Also, these parameters are added to the compiled stylesheet using the addParameter() method – notice that each parameter that is added has the same name as one of the parameters in the stylesheet. Now this parameter within the stylesheet is assigned the relevant values.

Beyond parameters, we can also add object references to our stylesheet so it can implement validation rules within the stylesheets.

Transformation Business Rules with Object

The code examples for this section can all be found in the advanced directory.

> **If you don't already have the Windows Script Components you should download the latest version from** http://msdn.microsoft.com/downloads/sample.asp?url=/MSDN-FILES/027/001/733/msdncompositedoc.xml&frame=true.

The following component will be used to demonstrate how to use a COM object method within XSLT to work out the exchange rate for a given currency.

To enable this example to work, we have to register the Windows Script component named Wrox.wsc, available in the download. To do this, go to the DOS command line, navigate to the folder where Wrox.wsc resides (it is initially in the advanced folder of the download), and run the command:

>regsvr32 wrox.wsc

(or right-click on the file and select Register). You should see a message box indicating that the component has been successfully registered.

When working with scripting to generate web pages, it is very common to use COM components to provide the logic for our applications. What you should try to remember is that XSLT itself offers a lot of functionality and if it is possible to do something with XSLT itself then there is a significant enough performance difference to suggest doing so. Examples include string manipulation and the document function for getting external XML resources, as well as other functionalities. However, when we need to interact with a database or use some COM object or .NET functionality, then we can use external objects within our XSLT.

In our example there are two things that our object will need to do for us – the first is to get a unique internal ID and the second is to get the exchange rate for Dollars to Pesos. For simplicity, both of these are calculated and returned from the COM object itself, but more realistically the ID would be returned from a database table and the second could be the result of a web service call to some current exchange service provider.

The code for the Wrox.wsc COM object is shown below. We won't be discussing the details of Windows Scripting Components – if you are interested, visit http://msdn.microsoft.com/scripting for further information.

```xml
<?xml version="1.0"?>
<component>

<registration description="Wrox"
              progid="Wrox.WSC"
              version="1.00"
              classid="{220ca5ae-dded-4d25-b5a5-b43b71541944}">
</registration>

<public>
    <method name="GenerateInternalID">
        <PARAMETER name="batchid"/>
    </method>
    <property name="ExchangeRate">
        <get/>
    </property>
```

```
</public>

<implements type="ASP" id="ASP"/>

<script language="JScript">
<![CDATA[

var description = new Wrox;

function Wrox(){
   this.get_ExchangeRate = get_ExchangeRate;

   this.GenerateInternalID = GenerateInternalID;
}
```

The `GenerateInternalID()` method takes the assigned batch ID and uses some basic business rules to assign a fully unique ID. If the `batchid` is less than 3 it is regarded as a local customer, so some specific local customer code is returned (the value of the code is unimportant); if it is anything else it is regarded as a remote customer and some other code is assigned – this unique code is returned as the result of the call.

```
function GenerateInternalID(batchid){
   var lngInternalID="";
   var strSeparator=":";
   var strLocalCust="LC_";
   var strRemoteCust="RC_";

   if (batchid<3)
      lngInternalID=batchid.toString().concat(strSeparator,strLocalCust,
            Math.round(Math.random()*100000))
   else
      lngInternalID=batchid.toString().concat(strSeparator,strRemoteCust,
         Math.round(Math.random()*500000))

   return(lngInternalID);
}
```

The `ExchangeRate()` property is even simpler and just returns a string indicating the current exchange rate:

```
var ExchangeRate;

function get_ExchangeRate(){
   ExchangeRate = "1 $US = $1,000 Chilean Pesos";

   return ExchangeRate;
}

]]>
</script>

</component>
```

The code update to `multi.asp` to make use of this object is in fact extremely simple – the update in the `ShowResult()` method is shown overleaf. Note that the URL used in the `addObject()` method is simply a namespace identifier to uniquely identify our object methods as extension functions within the stylesheet – we must simply ensure that the namespace here and the one within the XSLT qualifying the function call are the same.

```
function ShowResult(objXML,objTemplate)
{
   var xslProc = objTemplate.createProcessor();
   xslProc.input=objXML;
   xslProc.output=Response;

   xslProc.addParameter("username",strUsername);
   xslProc.addParameter("userlocation",strUserLocation);

   var obj = Server.CreateObject("Wrox.WSC")
   xslProc.addObject(obj,"http://www.yoursite.com/businessrules");
   xslProc.transform();
}
```

We create an instance of the `Wrox.wsc` object, as is common with components, and then use the `XSLProcessor` object's `addObject()` method to add the object to the stylesheet. The first parameter is the object instance itself and the second parameter is some unique namespace that it can be identified from within the stylesheet.

Let's look at the updates to `IE60.xsl` – the changes to the other stylesheets are identical to this – have a look at the source if you are interested. The updates within `IE60.xsl` are highlighted below:

```
<?xml version="1.0" ?>
<xsl:stylesheet version="1.0"
                xmlns:xsl="http://www.w3.org/1999/XSL/Transform"
                xmlns:rules="http://www.yoursite.com/businessrules"
                exclude-result-prefixes="rules">
...
   <xsl:template match="order">
      <div class="info">
         <b>Batch identification number :
         #<xsl:value-of select="@batchid" />
         <br />
         Global Identification Number is
            "<xsl:value-of select="rules:GenerateInternalID
                                    (number(@batchid))" />"
         </b>
      </div>
      <xsl:apply-templates />
   </xsl:template>
...
   <xsl:template match="comments">
      <hr />
      <div class="notes">
         Notes:
         <p>
            <xsl:value-of select="." />
            <br />
            <xsl:value-of select="rules:get-ExchangeRate()" />
         </p>
      </div>
   </xsl:template>
   <xsl:template match="text()" />
</xsl:stylesheet>
```

The key to working with the object within XSLT is to add a namespace prefix and reference in the document root, in our case `xmlns:rules="http://www.yoursite.com/businessrules"` – notice this is the same as the input object namespace. We also don't want our custom object namespace in the output of the transform, so `exclude-result-prefixes="rules"` is used.

Now we can invoke methods and access properties on our object. We obtain the Global Identification Number as follows:

```
<xsl:value-of select="rules:GenerateInternalID(number(@batchid))" />
```

To invoke the method `GenerateInternalID()`, the object prefix `"rules"` must be used to qualify the method in the object namespace – as a parameter the `batchid` attribute of the `<order>` element is converted from a string to a number. This outputs an internal ID number, such as "4:RC_455008".

At the end of the comments section, the exchange rate information is written so the user can see it in the notes. When using properties, we have to prefix the property name with `"get-"` to return the value. So, in our case we have:

```
<xsl:value-of select="rules:get-ExchangeRate()" />
```

This will return the string "1 $US = $1,000 Chilean Pesos" which is added to the output, using the `Netscape.xsl` stylesheet (which is very similar to the IE 6 version, also available in the code download).

Using Netscape Navigator or Internet Explorer, enter the following values into `postHTML.htm` (in the advanced folder) and submit the form:

Customer Name: Glasgow Wine Club
Email: manager@winemp.co.uk
Select the Divisions: Wine Division East
Wines Ordered: Blanco de Machali; Santiago Red;
Batch Number: 4
Comments: <no comments>

The new output using Internet Explorer is shown overleaf:

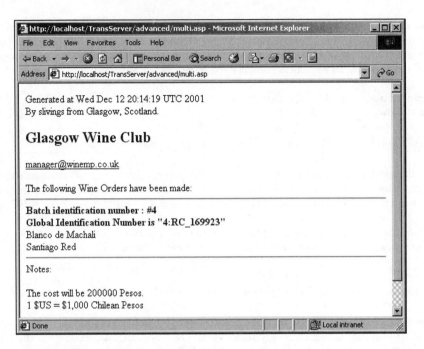

If you have any problems viewing this page in Netscape, check to ensure your coding is set to "Western ISO-8859-1 " – this is done via the View / Character Coding menu option.

We have now looked at many aspects of presenting information to users on multiple devices using distributed systems and how advanced transformations can be used to improve performance and flexibility. If we don't quite need this level of control then we can use the XSLISAPI component that is available from Microsoft, which we'll discuss in the next section.

Using XMLSchemaCache on the Server

The XMLSchemaCache object is a free-threaded object and is very useful as it allows us to cache XML Schema files that can at a later point validate one or more XML documents. Furthermore, because it is free-threaded, it can be cached in a similar way to the IXSLTemplate object and reused across our application.

We aren't going to look at this object here as it is discussed in detail in Chapter 11; however, it is an essential addition to working with XML and XSLT on the server!

XSLISAPI

XSLISAPI (XSL Internet Server Application Programming Interface) is a high-performance utility offered by Microsoft for circumstances where the information we wish to generate is much more straightforward. It simply takes some XML and XSL, and outputs the result. At the time of writing it is at version 2.1, and is available from http://msdn.microsoft.com/xml.

The current version states compatibility with MSXML 3.0 as well as MSXML 2.5 and MSXML 2.6 – it does run with MSXML 4.0 installed on the machine, however, there is no official word on compatibility with 4.0 as of yet, mainly due to the fact that, at the time of writing, MSXML 4.0 has just been released.

Beyond the simple combination of XML and XSLT to output the result, XSLISAPI uses the `XSLTemplate` object to improve efficiency, dynamically chooses a stylesheet based on browser and device characteristics, and allows for output encoding and character sets, and device customizable errors, as well as other features. Another great feature is the ability to combine XSL and ASP to produce dynamic output – a technique first looked at with IIS in *Professional Site Server 3.0* (ISBN 1-861002-50-5).

Configuration and Operation

> **At the time of writing, the basic installation requirements for version 2.1 can be found at the following URL: http://msdn.microsoft.com/library/en-us/dnxslgen/html/xslisapifilter.asp?frame=true.**

You should download the ISAPI filter from http://msdn.microsoft.com/xml, follow the installation steps, and verify that the installation is correctly working. These steps can be detailed and so Microsoft has provided a significant help document with the installation.

So how does it work? When you want a given XML file to use the ISAPI filter to dynamically use a stylesheet, in the `xml-stylesheet` processing instruction you specify a `server-config` attribute detailing the location of a file defining the stylesheet, like this:

```
<?xml-stylesheet type="text/xsl" server-config="myConfig.xml"
                href="style.xsl" ?>
```

It uses the browser and device characteristics specified in the `browscap.ini` file (`browscap.ini` is used to detect browser type and version and can be downloaded for free from http://www.cyscape.com/browscap/). It uses the file specified in `server-config` to determine the stylesheet to use for the transform. The configuration file is something like the following:

```
<?xml version="1.0" ?>
<server-styles-config>
   <device browser="Netscape" version="6.00">
      <stylesheet href="Netscape.xsl"/>
   </device>
   <!-- for WML 1.1 based browsers -->
   <device target-markup="WML1.1">
      <stylesheet href="WAP.xsl"/>
   </device>
   <!-- for IE 5 based browsers -->
   <device browser="IE" version="5.0">
      <stylesheet href="sampleA-IE5.xsl"/>
   </device>
</server-styles-config>
```

The filter then dynamically transforms the XML with the stylesheet and writes the result to the output.

Furthermore, when we mix ASP and XSL they are called **PASP files** and have the `.pasp` ending – these are limited to the server functionality of the MSXML version installed and so there is the limitation of working with remote URLs on the server that we discussed earlier.

There is a detailed document accompanying the filter download that explains the limitations and restrictions of working with the filter.

Example Implementation

This sample is available in the ISAPI directory of the code download – it is a starter example for you to build upon. It uses default.xml, which is an instance of our invoice XML document, as well as three stylesheets for IE 6, Netscape 6, and WAP.

We have seen these files before, but we must add the stylesheet processing instruction to the top of the XML document, as shown:

```
<?xml version="1.0" encoding="utf-8" ?>
<?xml-stylesheet type="text/xsl" server-config="Config.xml"?>
<Invoices date="Thu Oct 25 23:44:18 PDT 2001"
          xmlns:cat="uri:Business-Categories">
...
</Invoices>
```

This defines config.xml to contain the stylesheet associations, and looks like the following:

```
<?xml version="1.0" ?>
<server-styles-config>
    <device browser="Netscape" version="6.0">
        <stylesheet href="Netscape.xsl" />
    </device>
    <!-- for WML 1.1 based browsers -->
    <device target-markup="WML1.1">
        <stylesheet href="WAP.xsl" />
    </device>
    <!-- for IE 6 based browsers -->
    <device browser="IE" version="6.0">
        <stylesheet href="IE60.xsl" />
    </device>
</server-styles-config>
```

When run in Internet Explorer, the following output is given:

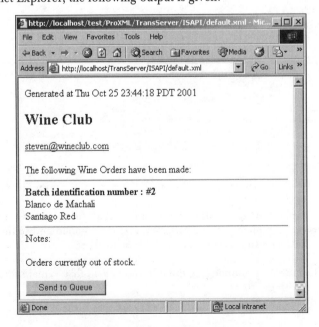

This output was dynamically created by the ISAPI filter using the `IE60.xsl` stylesheet. Assuming your `browscap.ini` files are up to date, the other transforms should display correctly in the appropriate browsers.

As a simple example of a PASP file, we could simply copy the `default.xml` file we used previously within the ISAPI directory and name the copy `default.pasp`.

> **You must also ensure that you copy the `global.asa` that came with the installation files into the root of the web site or the virtual directory of the application (that is, somewhere it will be executed). Ensure the file `Redirector.pasp` from the installation files is in the same ISAPI directory as the `default.pasp` we are now working with.**

Finally, ensure that the user who IIS impersonates will be in context when executing the application (whether that be IUSR_Computername or some other) and that they have write permissions to the directory where the PASP file resides – you only need to do this once, because the first time it actually creates an ASP file equivalent of your PASP file.

Note that you cannot set the encoding to UTF-8 when using the XML document with PASP files – this is because ASP outputs UTF-16 encoded data and does not allow switching the encoding in this way – so this was removed from the file.

The `default.pasp` file in the ISAPI directory is shown below. To illustrate the concept, we are simply going to append the IP address of the user who made the invoice "update" to the notes section. In a PASP file we can do pretty much anything we can do with ASP, but let's keep it simple.

```
<?xml version="1.0"?>
<?xml-stylesheet type="text/xsl" server-config="Config.xml"?>
<Invoices date="Thu Oct 25 23:44:18 PDT 2001"
          xmlns:cat="uri:Business-Categories">
    <customers custname="Wine Club" email="steven@wineclub.com">
        <cat:busInfo>Wine Division East</cat:busInfo>
        <cat:busInfo>Spirit Division West</cat:busInfo>
        <order batchid="2">
            <details>
                <items num="2">
                    <item>Blanco de Machali</item>
                    <item>Santiago Red</item>
                </items>
                <comments><![CDATA[Orders currently out of stock.
                    Update made by <%=Request.ServerVariables("REMOTE_ADDR")%>]]>
                </comments>
            </details>
        </order>
    </customers>
</Invoices>
```

This in fact creates a file called `__default.asp` in the same directory, which looks like the following:

```
<OBJECT RUNAT=server ID=XMLServDoc
PROGID="XSLISAPI.XMLServerDocument"></OBJECT>
<%
XMLServDoc.WriteLine "<?xml version=" & Chr(34) & "1.0" & Chr(34) & "?>"
XMLServDoc.WriteLine "<?xml-stylesheet type=" & Chr(34) & "text/xsl" & _
Chr(34) & "server-config=" & Chr(34) & _
```

```
"Config.xml" & Chr(34) & "?>"

XMLServDoc.WriteLine "<Invoices date=" & Chr(34) & _
"Thu Oct 25 23:44:18 PDT 2001" & Chr(34) & _
" xmlns:cat=" & Chr(34) & _
"uri:Business-Categories" & Chr(34) & ">"

XMLServDoc.WriteLine "    <customers custname=" & Chr(34) & "Wine Club" & _
Chr(34) & " email=" & Chr(34) & _
"steven@wineclub.com" & Chr(34) & ">"

XMLServDoc.WriteLine "    <cat:busInfo>Wine Division East</cat:busInfo>"
XMLServDoc.WriteLine "    <cat:busInfo>Spirit Division West</cat:busInfo>"
XMLServDoc.WriteLine "    <order batchid=" & Chr(34) & "2" & Chr(34) & ">"
XMLServDoc.WriteLine "      <details>"
XMLServDoc.WriteLine "        <items num=" & Chr(34) & "2" & Chr(34) & ">"
XMLServDoc.WriteLine "          <item>Blanco de Machali</item>"
XMLServDoc.WriteLine "          <item>Santiago Red</item>"
XMLServDoc.WriteLine "        </items>"
XMLServDoc.Write "        <comments><![CDATA[Orders currently out of
                          stock. Update made by "
XMLServDoc.Write Request.ServerVariables("REMOTE_ADDR")
XMLServDoc.WriteLine "]]></comments>"
XMLServDoc.WriteLine "      </details>"
XMLServDoc.WriteLine "    </order>"
XMLServDoc.WriteLine "</customers>"
XMLServDoc.WriteLine "</Invoices>"
XMLServDoc.URL = Request.ServerVariables("HTTP_SSXSLSRCFILE")
XMLServDoc.UserAgent = Request.ServerVariables("HTTP_USER_AGENT")
On Error Resume Next
XMLServDoc.Transform Response
If Err.Number <> 0 Then
    XMLServDoc.HandleError Response
End If
%>
```

We won't discuss this file, but it is obvious what has happened. The redirect file actually executes this file using the ISAPI filter to transform the output – pretty cool! The output is as follows:

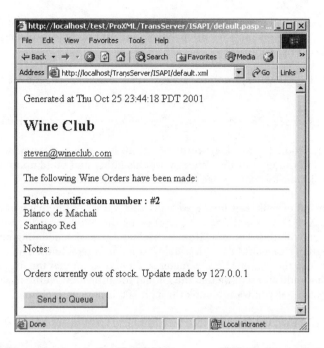

This has been a brief introduction to the ISAPI filter – you will find places where it may be useful and other places where it isn't too much use. However, for a quick and high-performance solution for presenting to multiple devices, it is a useful addition to our XML tools. Download the filter and work though the samples to see where it may be useful in your own applications.

Server Command Line and Batch Transforms

To date, it has been difficult to perform any kind of bulk transforms with MSXML because no utility was directly available to allow command-line processing. However, Microsoft now provides the MSXSL.exe utility available from http://msdn.microsoft.com/xml to allow command-line processing of XML documents. You can download either the source or just the executable; however, the source gives us the extra power of debugging. Note that, as the parser does not currently support references to extension functions, the XSLT used will not include references to any extension functions; but it will use parameters.

There is an extensive partner document that describes the functionality and switches of the utility, so rather than discuss these, let's create some examples to illustrate the utility in action.

First, create a directory called "invoice" – its location is unimportant. Next, copy all the files from the batch directory in the code download to this new invoice directory. Also copy the msxsl.exe file to this directory.

For the first example, open up the command-line console and navigate to the invoice directory. Type the following at the console:

```
>MSXSL default.xml ie60.xsl -o out.htm
```

This transforms the XML document default.xml using the stylesheet ie60.xsl and generates the HTML file out.htm.

503

As a second example, we will pass in the `username` and `userlocation` parameters from the command line – the parameters must be string values, and adding objects is not supported. The following code passes in the parameters:

>MSXSL default.xml ie60.xsl username="steven" userlocation="Glasgow,Scotland" >
out.htm

This has the parameters `username` and `userlocation` written to the output with the rest of the XSLT output.

There is a lot more functionality available through this utility, such as document validation control, whitespace control, and timing statistics. We can use this utility and build upon it if we want, however, to illustrate some bulk transformations, we will use MSXML 4.0 directly.

To illustrate the concept of bulk transforms, we will use a VBScript file that will create 100 HTML files by transforming the XML document `default.xml` using the `IE60.xsl` file. Although this is not going to change the world, it will illustrate how, from a command line or scheduling utility, we can invoke transforms to do anything we could do with usual web server interactions. The example will add the current index number to the `username` parameter as an indication that the files are individually transformed – another indicator will be that the Global Identification Number will also be different for every document created – if you want to look through 100 instances, feel free.

The VBScript code is shown below. First the `default.xml` document is loaded:

```
Set objXML = CreateObject("MSXML2.DomDocument.4.0")
objXML.async=false
objXML.load("default.xml")
```

An instance of the stylesheet is loaded into a free-threaded DOM document as we are going to use it with the `XSLProcessor` object:

```
Set objXSL = CreateObject("Msxml2.FreeThreadedDOMDocument.4.0")
objXSL.async=false
objXSL.load("IE60.xsl")
```

An `XSLTemplate` object is created to cache the compiled stylesheet:

```
Set objTemplate = CreateObject("Msxml2.XSLTemplate.4.0")
objTemplate.stylesheet = objXSL
```

The `createProcessor()` method creates an instance of an `XSLProcessor` object. Instances of the `Wrox.WSC` and `FileScripting` objects are created. The scripting object will be used to save the HTML files that are created.

```
Set xslProc = objTemplate.createProcessor()
xslProc.input=objXML

Set obj = CreateObject("Wrox.WSC")
set fso = CreateObject("Scripting.FileSystemObject")
```

Next, 100 iterations are done to create the files, with some simple variation in the parameters passed. Notice that we can still use parameters and pass objects to the stylesheet!

```
For i=0 To 100
    xslProc.addParameter "username","Steven" & i
    xslProc.addParameter "userlocation","Glasgow, Scotland"

    xslProc.addObject obj,"http://www.yoursite.com/businessrules"
    xslProc.transform()
```

Finally, each HTML file is saved to disk with the output of the transform as its contents:

```
    Set TextStream = FSO.CreateTextFile("transform" & i & ".htm")
    TextStream.Write(xslProc.output)
    TextStream.Close
Next
```

That now creates 100 individual HTML files. We used a very simple variation to vary the output, but it would be more likely that a commercial application would use many different XML input documents, such as invoices, and perhaps bulk XSLT transforms to dynamically create Excel documents for each invoice. Additionally, it may use SQL Server's XML functionality to update some database when the network is quiet – there are many opportunities in this area for you to explore.

Error Handling on the Server

It is essential that we know how to handle and prevent the errors that can occur when working with XML on the server. Particularly when working with the DOM, we should use the following techniques:

❑ Use the XMLSchemaCache to cache a valid XSD Schema that can later be used to validate an XML file.

❑ Use the validateOnParse property and set this to true, to validate against a DTD or Schema.

❑ Check the parseError property of the DOMDocument, which returns an IXMLDOMParseError object, which contains members to find out if an error occurred during parsing and what it was. Specifically the errorCode property will return the code of the last error while the reason property returns a more descriptive summary.

❑ Ensure that after calls to selectSingleNode, we check to ensure that the result is not null before attempting to use the result (for example, getting its text node value).

❑ Ensure that after calls to selectNodes(), we check to ensure that the result is not an empty node-set before attempting to use the result.

❑ When working with ServerXMLHTTP, check the status and statusText properties to ensure the page we have called exists and hasn't crashed.

❑ When using ServerXMLHTTP in asynchronous mode, set an appropriate value for the waitForReponse property.

❑ When working with ServerXMLHTTP, if the value from responseXML is not valid XML, then the responseBody will return a DOMDocument representing the error information, and we can access this information via the IXMLDOMParseError object itself.

This is an introduction to some of the techniques useful when working with XML on the server.

Summary

In this chapter we initially looked at how XML is commonly sent and received in today's applications, before looking at some techniques to improve productivity. We then moved on to see how we could interact with other servers to perform complex manipulation and transformation of source XML files.

We looked at some advanced MSXML concepts, such as the threading models available, the XSLTemplate and XSLProcessor objects, and how to use these in practice. Passing parameters and objects was discussed and illustrated in detail, and formed part of the invoice sample applications.

We worked through practical examples of detecting a client browser and serving up the appropriate stylesheet, as well as interacting with third-party servers. We looked at how a COM object can be created using Windows Scripting and its methods exposed within an XSLT stylesheet using extension functions. We also briefly discussed the XMLSchemaCache object used for caching XML Schema definitions.

Finally, we looked at some tools and efforts from Microsoft such as the ISAPI filter and MSXSL.exe tool. We ended the chapter by showing how MSXML can be used directly to perform bulk transforms, and also studied some error handling tactics. We used HTML documents, but the output could be any format you desire. In the following chapter we continue our look at working on the server and switch our attention to the use of XML Schemas.

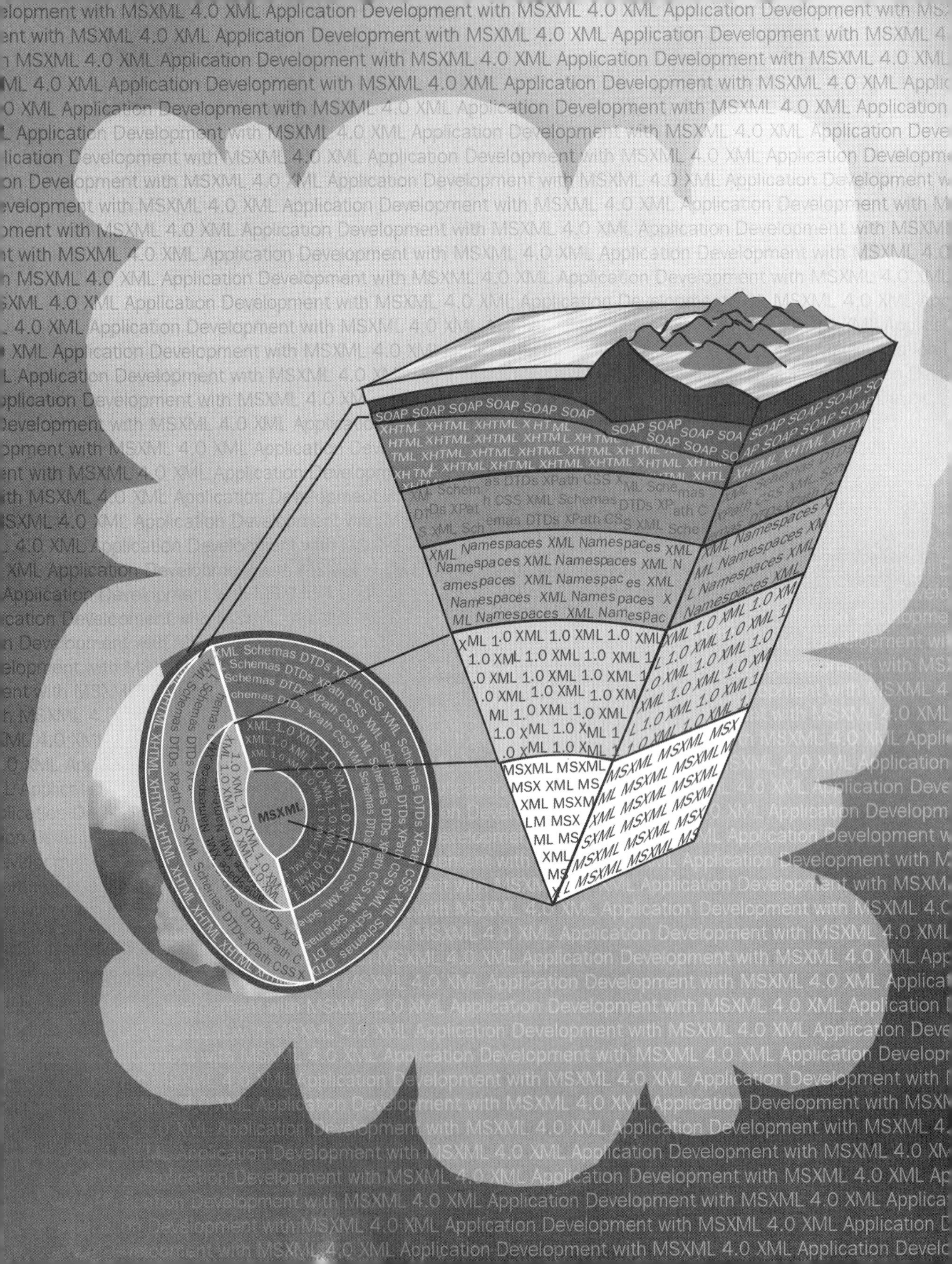
XML Application Development with MSXML 4.0
SOAP
XHTML
XML Schemas DTDs XPath CSS
XML Namespaces
XML 1.0
MSXML

11

Schemas on the Server

Server-side processing is an important area of use for MSXML. Early applications used its XSLT support to render content for browsers lacking native XML support, and the uses of MSXML on the server have expanded since then. Some applications that could be implemented client-side are implemented as server applications in order to avoid worrying about client platforms and which version of which XML processor, if any, is installed on the client. As applications are built that rely on the exchange of XML documents between client and server as a form of message passing, they must necessarily begin using XML processors like MSXML on the server. Business-to-business e-commerce applications increasingly fall into this category. An XML document summarizes some desired business exchange and its arrival at the server is intended to initiate some activity on the receiving partner's end. Obviously, the receiving partner must parse and process the document on their server.

Server-side use brings new challenges, not least of which is scalability. Optimizing MSXML for scalable server-side use quickly became a requirement for the Microsoft development team. Although optimization had been under consideration for some time, version 3.0 was the first to showcase a critical mass of performance features for server use. Some of these apply to all applications of MSXML; it is simply a more efficient XML processor. We're going to focus on a very specific optimization in this chapter – a pair of interfaces designed to speed up validation of XML documents on the server by caching schema files.

These interfaces will allow you to preload all the schemas your application requires and keep them in memory, parsed and ready for use, prior to receiving your first XML document. In addition, one of the interfaces offers an object model for inspecting W3C-style XML Schemas, so you will be able to efficiently inspect meta data as needed.

MSXML's developers spent considerable time pondering the performance issues of their component when used on the server. Since the schema caching interfaces are most useful on the server, you will necessarily have to consider issues that usually are only encountered on the server, such as multi-threading. In this chapter we will first look at the rationale for using MSXML and document validation on the server, then consider basic issues of using MSXML with ASP pages, before finally investigating schema caching. With that covered, we'll construct a simple application that illustrates schema caching. In particular, you will learn:

❑ Common scenarios for server-side XML document validation.

❑ MSXML threading models.

❑ Characteristics and use of the `IXMLDOMSchemaCollection` and `IXMLDOMSchemaCollection2` interfaces.

❑ How to implement efficient server-side validation with XML Schemas.

To begin, let's consider in general terms how MSXML validates a document, then see what complications are added when the server hosts the component. After we see what problems are encountered, we'll take up the issue of why you would still want to do server-side validation in spite of these problems.

Challenges of Server-Side Validation

Consider what happens when an XML instance document referencing a schema is loaded by MSXML. Upon detecting the reference to the schema (either through a namespace declaration beginning `x-schema:` for XDR schemas or the `schemaLocation` attribute for W3C XML Schemas), MSXML must locate the referenced schema file and load it. For local schemas, that requires making a trip to disk. For remote schemas referenced through an HTTP-based URL, MSXML makes an HTTP roundtrip to the remote server, which opens the schema on disk and returns its contents. Once MSXML has the schema file, it must parse it and initialize its internal structures. If the schema references other schemas, or the instance document contains other schema references, this process is repeated. As you can see, this is a potentially expensive undertaking in terms of performance:

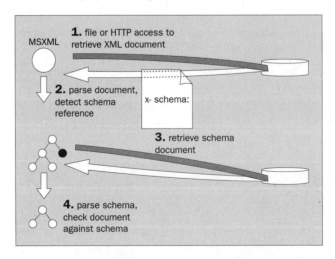

Now consider what happens when validation moves to the server. The problem scales in two ways. First, we may reasonably expect a server to have to handle *greater throughput* for XML documents than a client-side parser. A single server will typically be handling multiple concurrent clients. If the application is XML-based and requires validation, MSXML is going to get an intensive workout on the server. Second, it is likely that a production application requiring validation will involve *multiple schemas.* Unlike DTDs, schemas accommodate XML namespaces, prompting schema developers to use multiple schemas in an effort to modularize their meta data. Moreover, an application will be dealing with many sorts of documents, each described by a schema. As with so many other types of content, a cache mechanism is called for.

This is the point of the MSXML **schema cache interfaces**. It is far faster to maintain the internal structures of a loaded and parsed schema file in memory than to load and parse the schema each time. The overhead of maintaining one or more instances of the cache object in memory between requests is easily offset by the performance benefit gained through avoiding all the disk (or HTTP) accesses caused by loading schema files.

> *One account provided by Microsoft (http://msdn.microsoft.com/library/en-us/dnexxml/html/xml03202000.asp) claimed an 11% improvement in the initial release of the schema caching feature (MSXML v. 2.6) over the previous version using a loop that repeatedly loaded and validated an XML document on the server. Of course, the particular usage pattern of your application will modify performance, and there are as yet no published profilings of MSXML 4.0.*

You may wonder why we perform validation on the server if it proves to be such a bottleneck. In fact, many XML-based web applications bypass any sort of formal meta data entirely, choosing instead to rely on well-formed documents. In this case, although there is no formal, explicit schema, the programmer has something specific in mind and the code reflects this understanding. If the instance documents are generated by code written by the same team that wrote the receiving server-side code, that's perfectly OK. If the application is reliant on XSLT, the application will probably degrade gracefully for well-formed but invalid documents. (XSLT is a pattern-matching technology, so unrecognized patterns will be ignored.) If the application is simply a user interface, say an XSLT-styled newspaper, minor errors are generally tolerable. Certainly, though, it is better to use a formal schema that includes strict constraints on allowable values and explicit specification of the data types of elements and attributes.

The problem comes when you are dealing with clients that are not under your control, as is typical for business-to-business e-commerce. An implicit schema (in other words, understood but not written down as a formal document) leads to errors. If two or more teams are involved, two or more sets of interpretations result. Changes to the schema fail to get communicated. Even if all programmers involved have a perfect understanding of the schema, bugs in the client code can result in invalid documents. We would like to believe that the other party thoroughly tests their code or performs client-side validation, but we don't want to rely on that for a mission-critical application.

In this case, server-side validation acts as a sort of "**semantic firewall**". The XML vocabularies that your application uses are the interactions that enable client and server to communicate. The schemas are a formal description of the permissible interactions and so are a formal description of the application's behavior. A well-designed schema describes not only the content, but also the data types of that content. W3C XML Schemas additionally let us describe constraints on each information item, so we may formally describe field-level validity checks in the schema and have them enforced in MSXML. Prior to this capability, we generally relied on the client to do checks prior to submitting a document, and server-side components enforced the integrity of the data they consumed. In web applications, however, we cannot count on the client because we don't always control the development of that code. Application components are under our control and do an excellent job, but their checks come late in the process, after the server has devoted resources to the incoming request. They rely, moreover, on rules embedded in their source code. That information is not easily circulated to client programming teams, and of course relies on custom implementation.

With strictly-written schemas, MSXML will provide a quick check of the incoming data without writing any new code. If a constraint is violated, you can reject the request before devoting too much time or too many resources to it. Better still, you can circulate the schema to your e-commerce partners without compromising your source code. Because you are providing text-based schema files (whether XDR or XSD format) and not source code, you can describe the permissible data structures without saying a word about the code that processes them. This enables your partners to write better code while your intellectual property remains protected.

In the following illustration, three concurrent clients are submitting requests in the form of XML documents written according to schemas A, B, or C. One, submitting a document from vocabulary B, is invalid due to a bad input that the client did not catch. The server application intercepts incoming requests and immediately validates them. To do this, it must have access to the three schemas. Since there are many requests arriving all the time, it is imperative that validation be efficient. To accomplish this, the application preloaded the schemas into a cache at startup. The invalid document is trapped and a brief error result returned to the submitting client. The valid documents, however, are passed on to the main body of the application, which might include other COM+ components and database access.

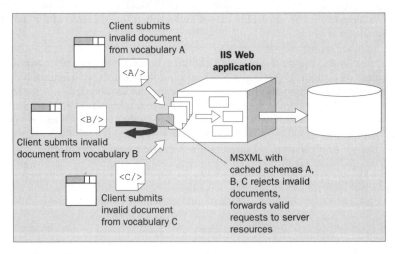

MSXML, then, has acted as a logical firewall, safeguarding server resources at minimal cost.

Threading Models

When you instantiate MSXML with the ProgID `Msxml2.XMLDOMDocument.4.0`, you get what COM+ programmers term a **rental-threaded** component. There are some subtle nuances to this threading model, but all you need to know about it is that it is only valid for use on the thread that creates it. Since it will only be used on one thread, the code can be lean, avoiding thread-safe code. It is faster and ties up fewer system resources. You use it in situations when you typically have a single user or application interested in the document.

This isn't an issue for client programming, and may not be an issue for server-side XML processing. If, however, you have globally useful documents, you need to be able to share them through the ASP `Application` and `Session` objects. IIS is, of course, a multi-threaded server, so COM+ components that are shared in application or session scope must be thread-safe (in other words, must be valid for use by any thread regardless of which thread created the component). Happily, MSXML offers a **thread-safe** version of the `DOMDocument` object. Such a component, once created, may be cached for global use without concern for whether the component is actually going to work when it is invoked on another thread. The JavaScript code to create such an object is:

```
var doc = new ActiveXObject("Msxml2.FreeThreadedDOMDocument.4.0");
```

This does not mean that you will automatically use the `Msxml2.FreeThreadedDOMDocument.4.0` ProgID for all server-side development. As you probably guessed, there are tradeoffs to consider. Thread safety comes at a price in COM+. Data passing between threads must be marshaled – or copied – from one thread to another. The COM+ runtime takes care of the details, but performance is adversely affected. Worse, of course, is data integrity. Store an XML document in global scope and we will almost certainly have multiple requests operating on it concurrently. If write access is desired, we must take steps to ensure document integrity is preserved. Locking and unlocking an ASP application, for example, takes additional time and may become a bottleneck.

What, then, is a good choice for free threading? Any read-only XML document, such as a frequently used XSLT stylesheet, is an excellent choice. Another use would be a large document that models some large system – perhaps the configuration of a manufacturing process – which must be shared by many processes. While many share the document, each application will only modify the portion of the document representing itd own data. By using a single free-threaded document instance, we avoid the issue of maintaining consistency between multiple small copies of the data, yet each process can update the document concurrently. A single-threaded instance would impose a grave penalty: each process would have to wait its turn, as the document would be tied to a specific thread.

We might also use small documents to provide read-only information to control the flow of execution in an application. An example would be a document describing the current contents of a site, or the location of available server resources. Usually though, there are native alternatives to XML documents (ActiveDirectory or SQL Server, for example) that will have better performance than an XML document. XML's virtue is its open and portable nature, not compactness and efficiency of representation. We'll take a practical trip through this decision-making process when we implement our sample application later in the chapter.

Schema Dialects Supported

The schema caching interfaces we are about to consider are so named because they work with XML schema documents, not DTDs. Schemas are themselves XML documents, whereas DTDs use an entirely different syntax. The need for an XML Schema language that takes data types and namespaces into account and uses XML syntax was recognized years ago. Unfortunately, forging consensus and pushing such a language through the W3C standardization process took rather longer than anyone in the XML community would like to recall. Many parties, Microsoft among them, were not shy in proposing their own schema languages. MSXML first provided full support for a schema language in version 2.6. This was Microsoft's own XML-Data Reduced (XDR), a simplified version of a language Microsoft had submitted to the W3C. This language saw wide use both in the community and in other Microsoft products such as SQL Server, Active Data Objects, and BizTalk Server. Support for XDR schemas continues in MSXML 4.0.

> *Chapter 3 covers the background to XDR and XSD support in greater detail. XDR schemas are described on the Microsoft Developer Network, starting with an introduction at http://msdn.microsoft.com/library/en-us/xmlsdk30/htm/xmconintroductiontoschemas.asp.*

The W3C finally reached the point of publishing its own schema language Recommendation on 2 May 2001. Microsoft followed through on its long-standing promise to adopt the W3C standard by including a substantial implementation of W3C XML Schema support in MSXML 4.0. This schema dialect is not only the de facto standard for XML schemas, but is considerably more robust than XDR. It provides for type extension and constraints, and even uses a regular expression syntax to constrain the form of string types. Validation rules for applications that could not be captured in DTD or XDR syntax can be written into W3C-style XML Schemas. We will use this schema language exclusively in this chapter, but it is worth remembering that MSXML 4.0 can cache schemas written in either language.

> *As discussed in Chapter 3, the W3C XML Schema Recommendation is published in three parts: an introduction and primer at http://www.w3.org/TR/xmlschema-0/, details of structure specification at http://www.w3.org/TR/xmlschema-1/, and a data types reference (explaining data type extension as well) at http://www.w3.org/TR/xmlschema-2/. The primer is the most useful section since it is a fast overview of the most useful parts, while the other two parts constitute the complete, definitive exposition of schemas. The latter two parts are more for users delving deep into XML Schemas or writing schema validating parsers. You can also find out more from "Professional XML Schemas" (Wrox Press, 1-861005-47-4).*

Schema Cache Interface

The two interfaces supported by MSXML 4.0 are IXMLDOMSchemaCollection and IXMLDOMSchemaCollection2. Despite the similarity in names, the two interfaces serve different purposes. The former is the one you will use to pre-load and cache schemas in order to improve performance, while the second provides an API, based on the terminology in the W3C XML Schemas Recommendation, to the schema documents contained in the former collection. It is the former interface we will discuss and demonstrate at some length in this chapter. It allows programmers to load schema files into a collection on demand. Schemas in this collection are available for document validation and may also be addressed by namespace URI. The latter interface has fewer uses on the server and is more directly applicable to schema investigation.

IXMLDOMSchemaCollection/XMLSchemaCache

MSXML version 2.6 introduced Microsoft's initial take on a schema caching interface, `IXMLDOMSchemaCollection`. This interface, with the ProgID `Msxml2.XMLSchemaCache`, offers a basic collection class for loaded and parsed schema files. The whole idea behind this interface is to give MSXML users the ability to load and unload schema files independently of any instance document and maintain them in their in-memory, parsed form for reference, as needed for validating DOM documents at run time. This interface offers the following properties and methods:

Properties

Property	Description
length	Number of schemas in the collection. Read-only.
namespaceURI	Takes a long integer index and returns the namespace URI found in the collection at that index. Read-only.
	Index: zero-based index into the collection.

Schemas are identified in both instance documents and the schema cache by their associated namespace URI. The ordinal position of the schema in the cache is not important. What you must focus on is the URI. The URI you provide as an index into the collection must match the namespace URI in the schema and is not, therefore, an arbitrary tag.

Methods

Method	Description
add()	Adds a schema to the collection and associates it with the provided namespace URI.
	URI: string containing the namespace URI to associate with the schema.
	Schema: variant representing the schema. This may take several forms. If the parameter is null, any schema associated with URI in the collection is removed. The effect is equivalent to calling remove(). If it is a string, the parameter is presumed to be a URL locating a schema. The schema will be loaded synchronously and, if no errors occur, will be added to the collection. If the parameters contain a reference to an IXMLDOMNode interface, the entire document to which the node belongs will be presumed to be a schema and will be added to the collection.
addCollection()	Adds the contents of the given schema collection (coll) to the current collection. If any URIs in the new collection collide with existing schemas, the old schemas are replaced with the new schemas.
	coll: the IXMLDOMSchemaCollection to add.

Table continued on following page

Method	Description
get()	Returns a schema associated with a given URI. The schema is returned as a DOM document element (IXMLDOMNode). URI: string containing the namespace URI associated with the desired schema.
remove()	Removes the schema associated with the URI from the collection. URI: string containing the namespace URI.

These comprise a fairly typical approach to a collection class. Note, however, there are three ways to go about building a schema collection. We will look at each in turn.

Using the add(), get(), and remove() Methods

First, the add(), get(), and remove() methods work with a single URI-schema file pair at a time. That is, each associates a schema file with the target namespace declared in it. These methods take a URI and perform the desired action on the schema associated with them. The add() method takes the pair and updates the collection.

You will need to be able to use these methods no matter what you do with this interface. Consider the following lines of code (found in basic_cache.asp in the chapter code download):

```
<%@ Language="JavaScript" %>
<%
   Response.ContentType = "text/xml";

   var cache = new ActiveXObject("Msxml2.XMLSchemaCache.4.0");

   // retrieve request parameters and load the schema
   var schemaName = Request.Item("schema");
   var schemaURI = Request.Item("uri");
   cache.add(schemaURI, Server.MapPath(schemaName));

   // retrieve the schema and return it
   var schemaRoot = cache.get(schemaURI);
   Response.Write(schemaRoot.xml);

   // clean up
   cache.remove(schemaURI);
   cache = null;
%>
```

This code takes an HTTP GET request containing the filename and target namespace URI of an XML schema, loads it into a schema collection, then returns the text of the schema to the requesting client. For example, you may view the text of the schema PO.xsd (in the chapter code download) with a request of the form:

```
http://hostname/virtual_dir/basic_cache.asp?schema=PO.xsd&uri=urn:xmlabs-com-po
```

Remember, of course, to substitute the appropriate machine name and IIS virtual folder for `hostname` and `virtual_dir`.

After creating an instance of the schema collection object, the code retrieves the `schema` filename and URI parameters from the HTTP request using the ASP `Request` object. These parameters are passed to `add()`. If the schema is found in the same directory as `basic_cache.asp` and the URI passed matches the value of the schema's `targetNamespace` attribute on the `schema` element, the call to `add()` succeeds and the schema resides in the cache. The subsequent call to `get()` retrieves the document element node of the schema. The `xml` property of that node is written back to the client using the ASP `Response` object's `Write()` method. Since the MIME type of the response document was set to `text/xml` in the first line of code, IE will display this document as a formatted tree. Finally, we call `remove()` to empty the cache, then set `cache` to `null` to allow ASP to free the COM+ object.

If you are using a browser other than Internet Explorer, it may be necessary to view the source of the page to see the full text of the schema document.

Using the DOMDocument Object's schemas Property

The next way to load a schema collection is to let MSXML do the work for you. If you load an XML instance document that references one or more schema files, the `schemas` property of the document interface will contain a schema collection. You can use this to initialize another instance of MSXML – say, for a pool of server-side XML processors – as follows (code available in `schemaValidate_basic.asp`):

```
var doc = new ActiveXObject("Msxml2.DOMDocument.4.0");
doc.async = false;
doc.load(Server.MapPath("sample_event.xml"));
if (doc.parseError.errorCode != 0)
   Response.Write(doc.parseError.reason);
else
{
   var cache = new ActiveXObject("Msxml2.XMLSchemaCache");
   cache = doc.schemas;
```

At this point we've initialized `doc` with an instance of the parser and set `async` to `false` so that our example can continue inline rather than moving off to an event handler. We call `load()` to pull in the file `sample_event.xml`. In the course of parsing that document, MSXML detects a schema file reference to `SocialFunctions.xsd` (through the `schemaLocation` attribute of the document element). This causes the component to load and parse that schema file. In the course of doing this, the parsed schema is automatically added to the schema cache maintained in the `schemas` property of `doc`. If the sample document was successfully loaded – as indicated by an `errorCode` value of zero – we create a new schema cache object (in the variable `cache`) and copy the schema cache held by `doc` into it.

Now let's see how this can help us in loading additional documents:

```
var newdoc = new ActiveXObject("Msxml2.DOMDocument.4.0");
newdoc.async = false;
newdoc.schemas = cache;
newdoc.load(Server.MapPath("sample_event.xml"));
}
```

Here we've created a new instance of MSXML and again set `async` to `false`. This time, rather than let MSXML set up its own schema cache in the course of loading documents, we pre-load it by copying the collection held in `cache` into the new document's `schemas` property. Next we try once again to load `sample_event.xml`. This time, upon encountering the reference to the schema file, MSXML will detect that a schema with the appropriate target namespace is already resident in the schema cache. If you were to profile this code, you'd find that the call to `load()` executes somewhat faster than the previous one. By pre-loading the schema, we bypass another disk access, file load, and parse of the schema file.

The code above (`schemaValidate_basic.asp`), uses one instance of MSXML to load the sample file `sample_event.xml`. We said that the `schemaLocation` attribute of the document element worked to associate a schema file with the instance document. This is part of the W3C XML Schemas Recommendation; here is what that reference looks like:

```
<Event xmlns="urn:xmlabs-com-functions" xmlns:evt="urn:xmlabs-com-functions"
       xmlns:xsi="http://www.w3.org/2001/XMLSchema-instance"
       xsi:schemaLocation="urn:xmlabs-com-functions SocialFunctions.xsd">
```

The last attribute, `xsi:schemaLocation`, does the trick. It associates the URI `urn:xmlabs-com-functions` with the schema file `SocialFunctions.xsd`. Note the whitespace in the attribute value separating the URI (`urn:xmlabs-com-functions`) from the schema filename (`SocialFunctions.xsd`). If the document required multiple schemas, we would add them as whitespace-delimited URI-filename pairs in the attribute value.

That schema, in turn, is built from two other namespaces described by schema files. We check the parse error object's error code to ensure nothing was amiss with either the instance document or the schema files, then create a schema cache object. At this point, `cache` references an empty schema collection. We initialize it with the contents of the first parser's `schemas` property, then use `cache` to set the value of the `schemas` property in a new instance of MSXML.

If you run `schemaValidate_basic.asp` (there are no HTTP parameters), you receive a count of the schemas found – four, one for the schemas' namespace and three for the schemas we provide – followed by a list of the schema URIs found. The namespace enumeration is accomplished by a function called `PunchNamespaces()`, which takes an instance of `IXMLDOMDocument` and outputs the schema cache's namespaces as an HTML table:

```
function PunchNamespaces(doc)
{
    Response.Write("<TABLE>");
    for (var i = 0; i < doc.namespaces.length; i++)
    {
        Response.Write("<TR><TD>");
        Response.Write(doc.namespaces.namespaceURI(i));
        Response.Write("</TD></TR>");
    }
    Response.Write("</TABLE>");
}
```

Although this function takes a DOM document instance, the `namespaces` property is the key to getting the namespaces. That property contains a reference to an `IXMLDOMSchemaCollection` object. The `namespaceURI` property is a collection of the namespace URIs found in the schemas associated with the document. We iterate through the collection until the upper bound (`length -1`) is reached, retrieving each URI and placing it in a cell of the HTML table.

This is repeated in the main body of the page for the new parser instance, showing that we short-circuited the schema load by preloading the parser with the schema collection. If you profile the ASP page, you will find that the second document loads faster because that instance of the parser does not have to go to disk, load the schema files, and parse them before it can perform validation.

Using the addCollection() Method

The final way to load a schema collection is through the addCollection() method. As with the previous example, we will be moving a complete collection object, but in this case we are adding a collection to another collection object. The code (found in addCollection.asp) looks like this:

```
var doc = new ActiveXObject("Msxml2.DOMDocument.4.0");
doc.async = false;

var schemaCol1 = new ActiveXObject("Msxml2.XMLSchemaCache.4.0");
schemaCol1.add("urn:xmlabs-com-functions",
              Server.MapPath("SocialFunctions.xsd"));

var schemaCol2 = new ActiveXObject("Msxml2.XMLSchemaCache.4.0");
schemaCol2.addCollection(schemaCol1);
doc.schemas = schemaCol2;
doc.load(Server.MapPath("sample_event.xml"));
```

So, when would we use the addCollection() method to load schemas into a cache? On a production server handling e-commerce, you are likely to have a number of schemas you would like to preload. Some will be core schemas that see frequent use, while others will be used only occasionally. You could load the core schemas into a globally scoped object (application or session scope in ASP), and preload the other schemas only when the web application heads down certain paths. In such cases, you could use addCollection() to place the core schemas into a new cache object, then use add() to load the remaining schemas. The resulting cache object would be used to handle specialized requests, while the original object remained dedicated to more common requests. The addCollection() method is just a shortcut to move commonly used schemas in a single method call.

IXMLDOMSchemaCollection2

MSXML 4.0 introduced IXMLDOMSchemaCollection2, which inherits from IXMLDOMSchemaCollection and adds a property and some methods. This interface is returned by default when you create or retrieve a schema collection using MSXML 4.0. The ProgID for this interface is XMLDOMSchemaCollection, bringing the ProgID into line with the interface name in contrast to the naming convention for the original interface.

You must use the proper ClassID in a Win32 CoCreateInstance call, or type an object as XMLSchemaCache in Visual Basic, if you wish to use only the IXMLDOMSchemaCollection interface.

IXMLDOMSchemaCollection2 has just one property, validateOnLoad. This read/write property controls whether documents are validated by MSXML using this collection when a document instance is loaded.

This property is not included in the written documentation for MSXML 4.0 and can only be found in the type library for the component.

The purpose of this new interface is to allow developers to gain access to the **Schema Object Model** (**SOM**) for the schema file. As discussed in Chapter 3, SOM is a Microsoft creation, largely influenced by the hierarchy appearing in the W3C Recommendation XML Schema Part 0: Primer (http://www.w3.org/TR/xmlschema-0/), an introduction to the two documents comprising the W3C XML Schemas Recommendation.

Since XML Schemas are themselves XML vocabularies, you can parse and traverse a schema using the DOM or SAX. SOM, though, embeds some knowledge of the XML Schema Recommendation, offering properties and methods specific to schemas. The methods for `IXMLDOMSchemaCollection2` are:

Method	Description
validate()	Forces immediate validation of any instance document to which this collection is attached using the schema collection.
getSchema()	Returns the schema associated with the given URI as an `ISchema` instance.
	URI: string containing the URI associated with the desired schema.
getDeclaration()	Returns the declaration in the schema that defines the given node in the instance document. The node representing the declaration is returned as an `ISchemaItem`.
	Node: the `IXMLDOMNode` for which the declaration is sought.

It is somewhat confusing, in our opinion, to name this interface after the original and suggest some continuity. While the `validateOnLoad` property and the `validate()` method may be used to fine-tune performance on the server, the ability to access the SOM is in no way related to caching. While there are occasions where it is useful to do meta data discovery at run time – such as when constraints frequently change or a schema is still evolving – you will be dealing with well known schemas on the server. The nature of the vocabularies that describe your application is well known, and any meta data you need to access is more usefully stored in a database for effective retrieval. The SOM is much more useful on the client in cases in which you may be dealing with unknown vocabularies. In such cases, you might traverse the unknown schema using the SOM to determine allowable structures.

> *An early example of such traversal using XDR-syntax schemas and the DOM is found in Chapter 5 of "Designing Distributed Applications" (Wrox Press, ISBN 1-861002-27-0), where it is used to create a default user interface for a class of XML documents.*

Working with Schemas on the Server

Let's return to the schematic with which we opened this chapter and develop a simple application that implements something like that semantic firewall, using `IXMLDOMSchemaCollection`. The points that are essential to this scheme are:

- ❑ Multiple XML vocabularies described by schemas.

- ❑ Server-side validation of client-originated documents via HTTP.

- ❑ Preloading and caching of schema files.

Rather than develop multiple clients, we will develop a lightweight client that allows us to simulate the creation of different XML documents. On the server we are only interested in the semantic firewall, so instead of developing some backend components and processing, the server will always return the results of validation to the client.

A real client would offer a friendly and effective user interface that mirrors how users interact with the data or task at hand, concealing all the gory details of XML. Since we are keenly interested in XML, and since we need an easy way to generate invalid XML with which to test our validation, it is far easier to design a client that displays an XML document in one edit field, while displaying the results of validation in another. Here is a screenshot of our stub client application, developed in Visual Basic:

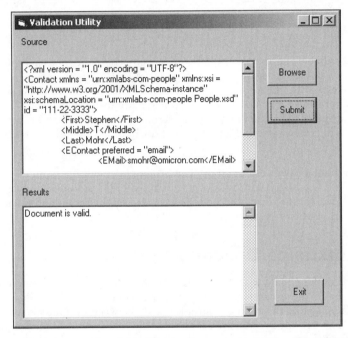

The edit field labeled Source is a multi-line edit box with a vertical scroll bar. While you are free to enter XML markup entirely by hand, it is useful to have a template. To this end, the Browse button invokes a common file dialog box, permitting the user to browse for an instance document on disk. The code download for this chapter provides samples for each of the included schemas. Each of the samples is valid according to its schema. To test validation, you may manually edit the text prior to submission.

When the Submit button is clicked, the text found in the Source box is submitted via HTTP to an ASP page that performs validation using a schema collection. The request is synchronous. The results returned by the ASP page are text messages intended for human consumption. If an error occurs during validation, the reason and file location is sent back. Otherwise, the success message depicted above appears.

The Visual Basic project has the following references:

❑   MSXML 4 (for HTTP support).

❑   Microsoft Scripting Runtime (for text file support).

Additionally, the common file dialog is implemented using the common dialog control, which appears in the Components dialog as Microsoft Common Dialog Control 6.0 (SP3).

Configuring the Sample

If you want to experiment with the sample first, you will find all the relevant files in the code download available from the Wrox web site. In particular, you are looking for:

- ❑ Validator.exe (built from the files Validator.vbp and Validator.frm) – client executable.

- ❑ Validator.asp – server-side validation script.

- ❑ sample_person.xml, sample_location.xml, sample_po.xml – sample instance documents.

- ❑ people.xsd, location.xsd, po.xsd – schemas defining the instance documents.

Place the client executable and the instance documents anywhere on your client machine. We're going to make use of one of MSXML's utility interfaces to make an HTTP request, so you will need to have MSXML 4.0 installed on the client machine if it is not the same computer as the server. On the server, create a virtual folder named schemaValidate in IIS. Place the ASP page and the schemas in that folder. The client assumes the virtual folder is hosted on the same machine as the client. If this is not the case, or you have a different virtual folder, alter the host URL found in the Submit_click subroutine in Validator.frm.

When you run the sample (Validator.exe), you browse to one of the sample instance documents and load it into the client. On submission, Validator.asp will load the submitted document into MSXML and attempt to validate it using copies of the schema found on the server and referenced by the instance document in the schemaLocation attribute.

Opening an Instance Document

This task really has nothing to do with XML and everything to do with the common dialog control and the scripting runtime FileSystemObject interface. The common dialog control presents no visible interface. On our application's form, the control is placed between the Submit and Exit buttons and is named FileDlg. The FileSystemObject offers a useful set of methods for accessing a disk file and reading its contents. We need to invoke the common dialog, obtain a fully qualified filename, then pass that name to a FileSystemObject instance. Using the methods of that object, we will open the file, read the contents into memory, then push the text into the Source edit box, named Src. The button handler for the Browse button starts like this:

```
Private Sub Browse_Click()
    Dim objFileSys As New FileSystemObject
    Dim objTextStream As TextStream

    FileDlg.FileName = ""
    FileDlg.ShowOpen
```

ShowOpen invokes the dialog box. If the user selects a file, the fully qualified pathname will be found in the FileName property. If the user cancels out of the dialog box without making a selection, no change will be made to the property's value. Hence, we inspect the property to see if we need to open the file:

```
            If FileDlg.FileName <> "" Then
                Set objTextStream = objFileSys.OpenTextFile(FileDlg.FileName,
                    ForReading)
                Src.Text = objTextStream.ReadAll
            End If
        End Sub
```

If we need to open the file, we use the `OpenTextFile()` method of the `FileSystemObject`, passing it the filename and an enumerated value telling it to open the file in read-only mode. Note that `objTextStream` is empty until we call `OpenTextFile()`. We had to explicitly create a `FileSystemObject` instance (with new in the `Dim` statement), but the return of the `OpenTextFile` method is a `TextStream` instance. That object's `ReadAll` method not only reads the file into the object, but also returns a string containing the full text of the file read. We assign this value to `Src.Text` and we are done.

Receiving the Document

To get the document to the server for validation, we need to grab the contents of the Source box (if any) and perform an HTTP POST of the document to the server page. The easiest way to do this is to make use of MSXML's client-side HTTP utility interface, `IXMLHTTPRequest`. Under the general declarations for the form (`Validator.frm`), in global scope, we have the following line:

```
Dim poster As New XMLHTTP40
```

This declares and instantiates an instance of the `IXMLHTTPRequest` interface when the application starts. The click handler for the Submit button starts like this, checking for the presence of some content:

```
If Src.Text = "" Then
    MsgBox "Must open a document first"
Else
```

If we have some text, we assume it is something we would like to submit to the server. If we were really conservative, we might load it into a DOM document with validation turned off to ensure well-formedness, but that is purely overhead for demonstration purposes.

In a production environment with a real client application, you would want to do field-level validation as information is entered. This is particularly true if the XML to be generated from user input is lengthy and the expected HTTP response time is significant (as when going across the public Internet rather than hitting the local host). Users will become frustrated if a lengthy input session is met with an error. Schema validation on the server is mostly to protect the server software and should not be expected to wholly replace client-side data checking.

Submitting a document using `IXMLHTTPRequest` involves two calls: one to initialize the connection parameters, and one to actually make the HTTP request:

```
Else
    Call poster.open("POST", _
        "http://localhost/schemaValidate/Validator.asp", False)
    poster.send (Src.Text)
    Results.Text = poster.responseText
End If
```

The open() call establishes the HTTP operation desired – POST – as well as the URL to send the document to. Be sure to modify this line to reflect the virtual directory in which you placed Validator.asp. The final parameter of our method call is the Boolean False, which tells poster to make a synchronous request. This simplifies our code as we don't have to do any event handling. Since this client is not intended for performance profiling, raw throughput is not a concern. If we had set the value to True, the client would be free to do other tasks while waiting for the reply, but this demonstration client has nothing else to do. Note that no socket connection is made when open() is called. That occurs in the following line, with send. This call takes the contents of the Source edit box and POSTs them to the server. When the results return, they will be found in the responseText property of IXMLHTTPRequest, from which property we can assign them to the Text property of the Results edit box (labeled Results in the user interface).

Now the flow of execution shifts to the server-side code, found in Validator.asp. We create an instance of a DOM document and synchronously load it with the contents sent to the page by the POST:

```
var indoc = new ActiveXObject("Msxml2.DOMDocument.4.0");
indoc.schemas = schemas;
indoc.async = false;
indoc.load(Request);
```

There's a lot to consider in these four little lines. First, we talked about free-threaded documents earlier in this chapter, yet we are using the old, reliable rental-threaded interface. Do we care so little about performance? This is one of those design-time tradeoffs you must make. In our application, the globally used objects will be the schemas. They are read-only and are needed for every request. The incoming messages, however, will result in some immediate processing of interest only to the current request. In a production system we would hand the message off to some component or function and process it at once. Here, we inspect the results of loading and parsing and return a verdict immediately. If we were passing the document off to a component for processing, we might use a free-threaded document so that the consumer could get a peek at the document as it is being parsed and validated, but that is not the case here, so the overhead of a free-threaded component is unwarranted.

Another concern is the effort to instantiate an instance of MSXML. We can't have two concurrent requests trying to use the same parser to load two different documents, so caching a single instance of MSXML in application scope is out of the question. Performance concerns aren't important for a sample application such as this, but they will be for most production applications. For those applications, you might consider maintaining a pool of parser instances, instantiated at application startup and protected by some sort of semaphore scheme to avoid collisions. Free-threading won't help you here as the issue is document integrity, not efficient use of system resources. We make do with instantiating a new instance with every request, freeing it when we are finished processing the XML document.

The next line prepares the document for validation by setting the schemas property to a schema collection. The initialization of that collection is the topic of the next section. For now, we merely note that we are short-circuiting MSXML's normal validation process (involving disk access) by providing access to a prepared schema collection residing in memory.

We know from Chapter 2 that script code can handle asynchronous document loading, and that is generally to be preferred to synchronous loads as it improves system responsiveness. In this case, though, there is little to be done until the document is loaded, so we set `async` to `false` to force MSXML to block until it completes the loading of the incoming document. This diminishes overall performance slightly, so in a production version you would want to go back and invest in the effort to make the load asynchronous. The processing code would be moved into an event handler for the `onreadystatechange` event (see Chapter 2 for a discussion and sample of such an event handler). If you have an asynchronous load, you can respond to a partially loaded document and begin working with the document while the rest of it loads, overlapping CPU-intensive processing with I/O-intensive file loading.

Finally, the call to `load()` takes advantage of the ASP `Request` object's support for stream interfaces to load the incoming document in one line of code. `Request` represents the contents of the HTTP submission.

Preparing the Cache

Now we reach the heart of the matter. This chapter is about schema collections, and we are about to set one up. Before we do, let's think about how we will scope the collection. The collection should be loaded as soon as possible, on start-up or on the first request. We will be loading a fixed set of schemas:

- ❑   `People.xsd` – a simplified vocabulary for describing people and contact information.

- ❑   `Location.xsd` – a simplified vocabulary for describing corporate locations.

- ❑   `PO.xsd` – a highly simplified vocabulary describing purchase orders.

The PO vocabulary, in particular, grossly oversimplifies purchase orders. There is nothing about billing or shipping, for example. The intent of these schemas is to provide enough markup to make validation interesting, but not so much as to make it burdensome to edit the instance documents.

These schemas apply in some sense to every application. Any request involves just a single schema, but the entire application deals with only these three schemas. The application will read the schemas but never modify them. There is no session-specific information. In fact, each request is a session in itself, carrying no state information forward. The ASP `Application` object is the right place to store the schema collection. The very first action to take in `Validator.asp`, then, is to check the application object for the presence of a schema collection variable:

```
var schemas = Application("schemas");
```

For every request except the first, schemas will be found in the `Application` object and the code may proceed to prepare for validation as described in the previous section. On the first request, though, nothing will be found and we will need to prepare the schema collection. This preparation is the same regardless of the threading model used:

```
if (schemas == null)
{
    schemas = new ActiveXObject("Msxml2.XMLSchemaCache.4.0");
    schemas.add("urn:xmlabs-com-people", Server.MapPath("People.xsd"));
    schemas.add("urn:xmlabs-com-loc", Server.MapPath("Location.xsd"));
    schemas.add("urn:xmlabs-com-po", Server.MapPath("PO.xsd"));
    Application("schemas") = schemas;
}
```

This should be familiar to you from our discussion of the IXMLDOMSchemaCollection interface. We instantiate a new component using the version-specific ProgID. Then we make three calls to load the known schema files and their target namespace URIs. Note that the schema files must be located in the same folder as the ASP. Finally, with our collection prepared, we add it to Application. Regardless of which path we take through the code, schemas will have an initialized schema collection when it reaches the code that follows the if statement. It is there that the code preparing the DOM document is found. This is the code that was described at the end of the last section:

```
if (schemas == null)
{
    // omitted for brevity
}

var indoc = new ActiveXObject("Msxml2.DOMDocument.4.0");
indoc.schemas = schemas;
indoc.async = false;
indoc.load(Request);
```

Notice that we have loaded all three schemas used in the application into a cache, which was assigned to a DOM document instance. When the document loads one of the sample documents, it will only need one of the three schemas, as each is based on a single schema. That reference in the document instance – the schemaLocation attribute – is key to MSXML's use of the schema cache. As it has a cache loaded, it is able to check the URI provided in the instance document against the namespace URIs in the cache. If it finds a match, it is able to retrieve the document from the cache rather than loading a new one from the source. If it does not find one but has a usable URL from the document instance, it will load the schema and add it to its cache. That is how the second method we discussed under the IXMLDOMSchemaCollection interface worked – letting MSXML do the loading for us.

Validation

For all our talk of validation, we do nothing to trigger it. We always want to validate the document when it is loaded, so we take advantage of the DOM document object's default setting of automatically performing validation. Since the schemas property of that interface is initialized, MSXML will not load the schemas from disk.

We've prepared a schema collection, prepared a DOM document for validation, loaded the incoming document, and performed validation. All that is left is to convey the results of validation back to the client. This is standard DOM programming:

```
if (indoc.parseError.errorCode != 0)
{
    Response.Write("Error: " + indoc.parseError.reason + "\r\n");
    Response.Write("Located in line " + indoc.parseError.line + ",
                    position " + indoc.parseError.linepos);
}
else
    Response.Write("Document is valid.");
```

The `parseError` property contains an object that encapsulates the results of document validation. If the `errorCode` property of that object is not zero, an error has occurred. The `errorCode` property is spectacularly unhelpful, so we rely instead on the human-readable string found in `reason`. This property is better than `errorCode`, but hardly infallible. To nudge the user in the right direction, we get the line number and position within the line where the error was detected from the `line` and `linepos` properties, respectively. The `\r\n` strings are JavaScript's way of indicating a newline character under Windows.

We have jumped around a bit to focus on various tasks performed on the server. Here is the full source code for `Validator.asp` so that you can see the tasks in their proper context:

```
<%@ Language="JavaScript" %>
<%
   var schemas = Application("schemas");
   if (schemas == null)
   {
      schemas = new ActiveXObject("Msxml2.XMLSchemaCache.4.0");
      schemas.add("urn:xmlabs-com-people", Server.MapPath("People.xsd"));
      schemas.add("urn:xmlabs-com-loc", Server.MapPath("Location.xsd"));
      schemas.add("urn:xmlabs-com-po", Server.MapPath("PO.xsd"));
      Application("schemas") = schemas;
   }

   var indoc = new ActiveXObject("Msxml2.DOMDocument.4.0");
   indoc.schemas = schemas;
   indoc.async = false;
   indoc.load(Request);
   if (indoc.parseError.errorCode != 0)
   {
      Response.Write("Error: " + indoc.parseError.reason + "\r\n");
      Response.Write("Located in line " + indoc.parseError.line +
         ", position " + indoc.parseError.linepos);
   }
   else
      Response.Write("Document is valid.");

   indoc = null;
%>
```

Summary

MSXML's schema caching capabilities are a basic but important feature of the component. Neither interface is a W3C standard, and schema caching has little utility on the client. On the server, however, the ability to cache schemas and control when they are loaded is an essential technique for scaling server-side XML applications. Early web applications that used XML tended to focus on the server to bypass differing levels of support for XML in browser-based clients, while the trend in XML development is toward sharing XML between the client and the server – indeed, using XML as the means of communication. This is seen in SOAP-based web services as well as in XML-based business-to-business e-commerce servers like Microsoft BizTalk or WebMethods. Just as the XSLT caching interfaces described in Chapter 13, "*Performance, Scalability, and Security*" allow XSLT applications to scale on the server, the interfaces discussed in this chapter allow us to scale applications that require server-side validation.

We introduced the idea of a semantic firewall (sometimes termed an XML firewall) as a way of protecting the server side of the application from bad or misdirected data. An incoming XML document may represent the results of an extended series of interactions between the user and the client application, or perhaps the results of a good deal of client-side processing. A browser-based client might require a user to fill out a lengthy HTML form to obtain the data for an XML request document. A SOAP client could conceivably be a desktop application that elicits the same information over the course of several dialogs or property pages. A user will not be happy if a single, simple error is not detected until the end of the interaction when the XML document is composed and sent to the server. Even so, while we hope that the client has performed adequate data integrity checks and is passing along clean data, we must protect the server from invalid inputs. Performing the appropriate integrity checks on the server may result in the consumption of significant resources if the integrity checks are distributed among the components and code that process the data on the server. This is typically the case. Instead, by enforcing adherence to a well-known schema, we can use XML validation as a fast way to screen for errors. This will become increasingly important as XML schemas become widespread through their advanced features for specifying data constraints. Turning on validation at the server imposes a performance penalty, though, so any measure that improves efficiency is welcome.

In this chapter we presented the following points:

- Servers face challenges unknown to clients when processing XML documents.

- XML validation as a semantic firewall is an important and increasingly common architectural practice.

- MSXML offers two threading models, and choosing between them is a serious design issue.

- MSXML's IXMLDOMSchemaCollection and, to a lesser extent, IXMLDOMSchemaCollection2 interfaces are a useful but proprietary way to improve validation performance on the server.

After discussing the various ways to load schemas and use the schema cache, we tied the interface discussion together with the architectural issues presented early in the chapter by looking at an example demonstrating the semantic firewall concept. The utility presented allows you to modify documents loaded from disk, submit them via HTTP for validation on the server, and receive the results of validation. Schema caches, though not needed to make the firewall concept work in theory, are in fact essential to making it work in practice on production servers due to scalability concerns.

Having spent a couple of chapters looking at working with XML on the server, and gaining an appreciation for what can be done server-side, we will now devote some time to working with data on the client, the subject of the next chapter.

XML Application Development with MSXML 4.0
SOAP SOAP SOAP SOAP SOAP SOAP
XHTML XHTML XHTML
XML Schemas DTDs XPath CSS
XML Namespaces XML Namespaces
XML 1.0 XML 1.0 XML 1.0
MSXML MSXML
MSXML

12

Working with Data on the Client

The previous three chapters focused on using MSXML to work with XML data on the server. In this chapter we'll change the spin and talk about various methods of handling XML data on the client. We'll start with a brief overview of XML encoding issues with MSXML, and some simple examples of processing and transforming XML documents client-side, and then we'll move on to look at dealing with MSXML version incompatibility issues. Next, we'll study XMLHTTP – a very useful class for sending HTTP requests and receiving the response. We'll then look at the data binding functionality of Internet Explorer and write a few snippets of code using XML Data Islands.

> *Note that we'll keep our focus on MSXML version 2.5+, and write examples for IE 5.0+. Most of the examples are written using either MSXML 3.0 or 4.0. The data island examples will work with IE 5.0+.*

Let's get started and first look at working with XML in IE with MSXML, starting with some encoding issues.

XML Encoding Issues with MSXML

According to the XML Recommendation, all XML parsers are required to support UTF-8 and UTF-16 encoding. MSXML supports these two and many other character encoding formats. However, there are still situations where we might run into problems with character encoding when working with MSXML. This section addresses such situations, but let's first briefly review how character encoding works.

Character Encoding Basics

For computer processing, the text characters are represented as numbers. The character encoding provides the mapping between the characters and the associated number. For instance, the letter "A" is represented as decimal 65 (hex 41) in character encoding schemes such as ASCII, Windows-1252, etc. The Universal Multiple-Octet Coded Character Set (UCS) defines a consistent way of representing text characters, including international characters and mathematical symbols. UCS-2 uses 2 octets (2 bytes), while UCS-4 uses 4 octets to represent a character. This scheme is specified by ISO/IEC 10646.

Unicode is another popular character encoding scheme, defined by the Unicode Consortium (http://www.unicode.org). The encoding scheme UTF-8 (UCS Transformation Format, 8-bit) is an alternative coded representation form for all of the characters of ISO/IEC 10646. UTF-8 encodes UCS-2 or UCS-4 characters as a varying number (1 to 6) of octets (bytes), where the number of octets, and the value of each, depends on the integer value assigned to the character in ISO/IEC 10646. The encoding scheme UTF-16 uses a fixed number of 2 bytes to represent any character. The two bytes are presented in either big-endian or little-endian, depending on the platform.

When an XML parser loads the XML document file, it looks for Byte-Order Mark (BOM) at the beginning of the file. If present, it can very easily decide if the file contains UTF-8 or UTF-16 data. If the file starts with 0xFF 0xFE or 0xFE 0xFF, it is assumed to be a UTF-16 document, while a UTF-8 document starts with a BOM of 0xEF 0xBB 0xBF.

> *Create any text document in Notepad and while saving it either select Unicode or UTF-8 from the Encoding combo box. Now when you try to open this file on a non-Unicode-aware program such as Edit on the DOS command prompt, you will see the BOM characters at the beginning of the file. The Unicode-aware tools know about the BOM and they hide it.*

If the XML parser does not find the Unicode BOM at the beginning of the file, it tries to find the `encoding` attribute in the XML declaration (`<?xml ...?>`). If this is not found, it can assume the UTF-8 encoding.

Let's say an XML file does not contain a BOM, does not specify the `encoding` attribute, but contains special characters (let's say from UTF-16 or ISO-8859-1 encoding). If we try to parse such an XML document, the MSXML parser returns the following error message:

An invalid character was found in text content.

The easiest solution to this problem is to specify the `encoding` attribute. Generally, it is good practice to specify the `encoding` attribute when creating the XML documents. Another common encoding error message returned by MSXML is:

Switch from current encoding to specified encoding not supported.

This means the XML file is saved using one encoding, while the `encoding` attribute in the `<?xml ...?>` declaration refers to a different encoding. For instance, if we save the file in Unicode UTF-16 format, but specify UTF-8 as the `encoding` attribute value in the XML declaration line, we will see the above error message while loading the XML document.

With this introduction, let's now look at encoding issues while working with MSXML.

The xml Property

MSXML DOM contains a property named xml that can be used to get the currently loaded XML document as a string. The xml property is of type BSTR and always returns the XML document in UTF-16 format without the BOM. It also removes the encoding attribute from the XML declaration (<?xml ...?>), if present. This can lead to problems in some situations. Consider the following ASP example in which we are loading an XML document from a disk file and sending it to the client:

Let's say the following XML file is available on the web server as Cust.xml:

```
<?xml version="1.0" encoding="ISO-8859-1"?>
<Customers>
    <Name>Comércio Mineiro</Name>
    <Name>Berglunds snabbköp</Name>
    <Name>Folk och fä HB</Name>
</Customers>
```

> *Note that the value of the encoding attribute is case-insensitive. Hence, ISO-8859-1 and ISO-8859-1 refer to the same thing.*

The above file contains some Latin 1 characters and hence specifies ISO-8859-1 as the encoding attribute value. If you directly browse to this file in IE, you will see it correctly. Next, let's say we wanted to use MSXML DOM to process this document before sending it to the client.

Let's now look at the ASP code that uses MSXML DOM to send this file to the client. For simplicity, we'll not do any processing here, but just send the XML to the client:

```
<%@ Language="VBScript" %>
<%
    Option Explicit
    Dim objXMLDOM

    Response.ContentType = "text/xml"

    Set objXMLDOM = Server.CreateObject("Msxml2.DOMDocument.4.0")

    objXMLDOM.load Server.MapPath("Cust.xml")

    Response.Write objXMLDOM.xml

    Set objXMLDOM = Nothing
%>
```

The above ASP code (GetCustomers.asp) simply loads the Cust.xml file using MSXML DOMDocument and sends the XML content to the client using Response.Write and the xml property. If we now try to access this ASP page, we'll see the following error message:

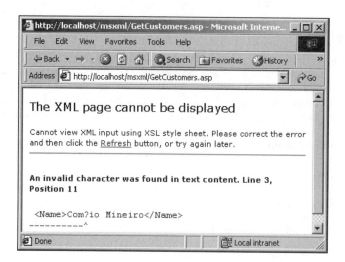

The source XML file properly contains the encoding attribute, so why do we get this error message? This is because the xml property removes the encoding attribute and sends the XML data string as UTF-16 Unicode format without the BOM. When IE (using MSXML) tries to load this XML text, since it does not find the BOM and the encoding attribute, it assumes the document to be UTF-8 encoded. As soon as it finds the special Latin characters, it stops parsing and issues the above error message.

The quick solution to this problem is to use the DOMDocument save method instead of the xml property. The DOMDocument save method preserves the encoding details.

In the above ASP page, change the Response.Write to the following line:

```
objXMLDOM.save Response
```

After this change, we see that the encoding attribute is preserved and IE (hence, MSXML) is able to load the XML document correctly:

Note that with MSXML version 2.5, 2.5 SP1, and 2.6, the DOMDocument loadXML *method can only load UTF-16 or UCS-2 encoded XML data. If we try to load XML data that is encoded with another encoding format (contains an encoding attribute with a value other than UTF-16), this results in a "Switch from current encoding to specified encoding not supported" error. This problem is fixed in MSXML version 3.0.*

Encoding and XSLT

MSXML DOM contains a method, transformNode(), that may be used to apply XSL stylesheets on the loaded XML document. This method, like the xml property, returns the results in a UTF-16 encoded BSTR value. Once again, this can lead to problems when we are using encoding other than UTF-16. Let's look at an example of this:

Here is our source XML document file (Cust2.xml):

```
<?xml version="1.0" encoding="ISO-8859-1"?>
<Customers>
    <Customer Name="Comércio Mineiro" />
    <Customer Name="Berglunds snabbköp" />
    <Customer Name="Folk och fä HB" />
</Customers>
```

Here is the XSL file (Cust2.xsl) to convert the attributes to elements:

```
<xsl:stylesheet
    xmlns:xsl="http://www.w3.org/1999/XSL/Transform"
    version="1.0">

    <xsl:output method="xml" encoding="ISO-8859-1"/>

    <xsl:template match="/">
        <Customers>
            <xsl:for-each select="/Customers/Customer">
                <xsl:element name="{name()}">
                    <xsl:for-each select="@*">
                        <xsl:element name="{name()}">
                            <xsl:value-of select="."/>
                        </xsl:element>
                    </xsl:for-each>
                </xsl:element>
            </xsl:for-each>
        </Customers>
    </xsl:template>
</xsl:stylesheet>
```

Finally, here is the ASP code (XSLCustomers.asp) that uses above XML and XSL files to do the transformation:

```
<%@ Language="VBScript" %>
<%
   Option Explicit
   Dim objXMLDOM
   Dim objXSLDOM

   Response.ContentType = "text/xml"

   Set objXMLDOM = Server.CreateObject("Msxml2.DOMDocument.4.0")
   Set objXSLDOM = Server.CreateObject("Msxml2.DOMDocument.4.0")

   objXMLDOM.load Server.MapPath("Cust2.xml")
   objXSLDOM.load Server.MapPath("Cust2.xsl")

   Response.Write objXMLDOM.transformNode(objXSLDOM)

   Set objXMLDOM = Nothing
   Set objXSLDOM = Nothing
%>
```

The above code simply loads the XML and XSL documents, uses the `transformNode()` method to apply the stylesheet and sends the results to the client using `Response.Write`. If we now browse to the above ASP page, we'll see the same "An invalid character was found in text content." error message. This is because the `transformNode()` method always returns the UTF-16 encoded BSTR string without the BOM, even though the XSL file contains the `<xsl:output>` tag with the correct encoding attribute value. Consequently, we run into the same problem we encountered earlier.

To fix this problem, use the `transformNodeToObject()` method, which preserves the encoding. Replace the `transformNode()` line above with:

```
objXMLDOM.transformNodeToObject objXSLDOM, Response
```

This now produces the following output:

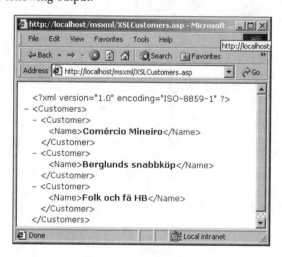

Note that the `encoding` attribute is preserved when we use the `transformNodeToObject()` method.

XML and Internet Explorer

IE 4.0 shipped with the first version of MSXML. MSXML 1.0 was a very basic, DOM-based, non-validating XML parser. MSXML has since undergone many changes to support the fast-changing XML standards. As we've seen so far, MSXML 4.0 is nowadays much more than a DOM XML parser. It offers improved performance as well as standards conformance with SAX 2.0, XPath, XSLT, and XSD Schemas. With this in mind, Microsoft has decided to rename MSXML and call it Microsoft XML Core Services.

Internet Explorer MSXML Versions

The following table lists the versions of MSXML that were shipped with various versions of IE:

Internet Explorer Version	MSXML Version	MSXML File Name (and Version)
IE 4.0	1.0	Msxml.dll (4.71.1712.5)
IE 4.0a	1.0a	Msxml.dll (4.72.2106.4)
IE 4.01 (SP1)	2.0a	Msxml.dll (5.0.2014.0206)
IE 5.0a	2.0a	Msxml.dll (5.0.2314.1000)
IE 5.0b (Windows 98 SE)	2.0b	Msxml.dll (5.0.2614.3500)
IE 5.01 (Windows 9x)	2.5a	Msxml.dll (5.0.2919.6303)
IE 5.01 (Windows NT 4.0)	2.5a	Msxml.dll (5.0.2919.6303)
IE 5.01 (Windows 2000)	2.5	Msxml.dll (5.0.2920.0)
5.01 SP1 (Windows 2000)	2.5 SP1	Msxml.dll (8.0.5226)
IE 5.5 (Windows 9x)	2.5 SP1	Msxml.dll (8.0.5226)
IE 5.5 (Windows NT 4.0)	2.5 SP1	Msxml.dll (8.0.5226)
IE 5.5 (Windows 2000)	2.5	Msxml.dll (5.0.2920.0)
IE 5.5 (Windows 2000 SP1)	2.5	Msxml.dll (8.0.5226)
IE 6.0	3.0 SP2	Msxml3.dll (8.20.8730.1)

In addition to IE, various other Microsoft products included versions of MSXML. For instance, MSXML 2.6 was bundled with SQL Server 2000 and BizTalk Server. Additionally, MSXML follows the web release model – in other words, various versions of MSXML were made available on the MSDN site as web releases, including the current MSXML 4.0.

> *Due to the rapidly evolving technologies around XML, Microsoft decided to make frequent releases of XML-related tools on its web site, in addition to bundling these tools with various products. This model is known as the Web Release model. Aside from MSXML, SQL Server2000 for XML (SQLXML) also follows this model.*

Let's now see what happens when we open XML files in IE.

Default Stylesheet

When an XML document is opened in IE, if the XML document does not specify any stylesheet, the browser uses a default stylesheet to "pretty print" the XML document as a hierarchical tree view. To view this stylesheet, type res://msxml.dll/defaultss.xsl or res://msxml3.dll/defaultss.xsl in the address bar of the browser.

Let's say we have the following XML document file saved on the server as music.xml:

```
<?xml version="1.0" encoding="utf-8"?>
<MusicTeachers>
   <Details>
      <Name>Daniela Mineva</Name>
      <Address>Denton , TX 76201</Address>
      <Phone>940.387.6967</Phone>
      <Email>danielamineva@hotmail.com</Email>
      <Type>Private Teacher</Type>
      <Teaches> Piano, Double Bass, Keyboard, Conducting</Teaches>
      <Style>Classical</Style>
      <Rates>$25 per Hour;</Rates>
   </Details>

   <Details>
      <Name>Sarah Engledow </Name>
      <Address>3400 Joyce Ln    Denton , TX 76207</Address>
      <Phone>940.323.1729</Phone>
      <Email>Slaalaa227@aol.com</Email>
      <Type>Private Teacher</Type>
      <Teaches>Piano, Theory, Ear Training</Teaches>
      <Style>Classical</Style>
      <Rates>$15 per 1/2 Hour;</Rates>
   </Details>
</MusicTeachers>
```

When this XML file is directly accessed from the browser, IE uses the defaultss.xsl stylesheet and displays it as shown:

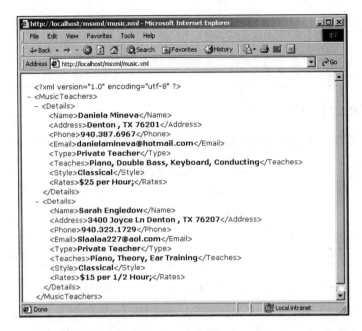

Note that the default stylesheet used by IE (`res://msxml3.dll/defaultss.xsl`) is written according to the XSL Working Draft. There is an updated version of this stylesheet available at http://www.dpawson.co.uk/xsl/sect2/microsoft.html#d156e206, which is written using the official XSLT Recommendation and also contains comments useful to understand the stylesheet. The updated stylesheet is also included in the code download for this chapter, saved as `defaultss_xslt.xsl`.

Custom Transformations

However, it is possible to specify either a CSS or XSL stylesheet along with the XML document, so that the browser will use that stylesheet file instead of the default:

```
<?xml version="1.0" encoding="utf-8"?>
<?xml-stylesheet href="music.xsl" type="text/xsl" ?>
<MusicTeachers>
    .....
```

We just added one line to the original `music.xml` file; this line refers to the `music.xsl` stylesheet, present in the same directory. Now when we browse the same XML file in IE, we see the following view:

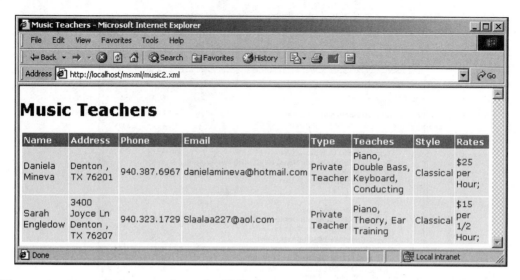

The `music.xsl` stylesheet transforms the XML document into HTML output.

When IE opens any XML file, if the XML document refers to a stylesheet, it automatically downloads the referred XSL file, applies the stylesheet on the XML document and shows the output, provided that the stylesheet is compatible with the version of MSXML used by IE.

The XSL implementation in MSXML (version 2.x) that shipped with IE 5.0 and 5.5 is based on the XSL Working Draft from December 1998 (IIRC). This uses http://www.w3.org/TR/WD-xsl as the namespace. Apart from many other changes, the final XSLT Recommendation uses http://www.w3.org/1999/XSL/Transform as the XSLT namespace. MSXML 3.0 was the first version of MSXML to fully support the final XSLT Recommendation, while providing backward compatibility for the Working Draft. However, MSXML 4.0 dropped support for the old Working Draft and now only supports the Recommendation version.

So, if we use the http://www.w3.org/1999/XSL/Transform namespace in our XSL and if the browser is not configured to use MSXML 3.0, our transformations might fail. The stylesheet used above (`music.xsl`) uses the http://www.w3.org/1999/XSL/Transform namespace, and still the browser transforms the XML document without any problems; this is because if you have MSXML 3.0 installed in replace mode on your machine, IE uses MSXML 3.0 to do the transformation.

So, how do we detect the version of MSXML used by the browser and how do we inform the browser to use a specific version of MSXML? Let's first talk about MSXML side-by-side and replace modes and then we'll see three ways to detect the MSXML version used by IE. We can have multiple installations of MSXML on one machine (side-by-side mode). Side-by-side mode is the only available mode in MSXML 4.0 and onwards.

Side-by-Side Versus Replace Mode

When two different versions of the same component are installed in **side-by-side mode**, it provides flexibility to switch back and forth between different versions of the component, by using the version-specific GUIDs/ProgIDs. For instance, if on a particular machine, we have both MSXML 3.0 and 4.0 installed, we may use the version-dependent ProgID `Msxml2.DOMDocument.3.0` to instantiate an MSXML 3.0 `DOMDocument`, and use `Msxml2.DOMDocument.4.0` to create an MSXML 4.0 `DOMDocument` object. With side-by-side mode, multiple registry entries are maintained for the component versions. MSXML 2.5 (or 2.5 SP1), 2.6, 3.0, and 4.0 can be run in side-by-side mode.

With MSXML 3.0, Microsoft also provided a tool, `xmlinst.exe`, to run MSXML 3.0 in **replace mode**. This tool updates the registry entries for previous versions of MSXML to map to MSXML 3.0, and hence applications using previous versions of XML parsers will start using MSXML 3.0. This tool helps to make sure that applications will readily use the latest parser, without the need to recompile the application. Also, as `xmlinst.exe` can help replace MSXML 2.0 and MSXML 2.5 objects with MSXML 3.0 objects, it ensures that IE (5.0 or above) supports XSLT and provides backward compatibility to XSL.

> *The `xmlinst.exe` replace mode tool can be downloaded from the MSDN web site at http://msdn.microsoft.com/downloads/default.asp?url=/downloads/sample.asp?url=/MSDN-FILES/027/001/469/msdncompositedoc.xml.*

Running `xmlinst.exe` can lead to various other problems When `xmlinst.exe` is used to run MSXML 3.0 in replace mode, it updates the registry (ProgID values) to make sure that all the references to any version of the MSXML parser point to MSXML 3.0. This might cause problems with applications that rely on previous version ProgIDs, such as SQL Server 2000 and Exchange Server 2000. Generally this problem can be fixed by running xmlinst.exe -u to remove the existing registry entries before installing the correct version of MSXML. More information about this can be found in the Microsoft Knowledge Base at http://support.microsoft.com/default.aspx?scid=kb;EN-US;q278636.

To install MSXML 3.0 in replace mode:

❑ Run `xmlinst.exe` with the -u option to uninstall all registry entries for MSXML.

❑ Next, register `msxml3.dll` by typing regsvr32 msxml3.dll at the DOS command prompt from the directory where the DLL is located.

❑ Finally, run `xmlinst.exe` without any parameters. This will update the registry to install MSXML 3.0 in replace mode.

To return to earlier versions of MSXML (and hence cancel the replace mode), simply run `xmlinst.exe` with the -u parameter, followed by regsvr32 on each MSXML DLL in order:

```
xmlinst -u
regsvr32 msxml.dll
regsvr32 msxml2.dll
regsvr32 msxml3.dll
```

Remember that MSXML 3.0 SP2 can only be installed in replace mode, and MSXML 4.0 can only be installed in side-by-side mode. MSXML 3.0 SP2 can be downloaded from http://msdn.microsoft.com/downloads/default.asp?URL=/code/sample.asp?url=/MSDN-FILES/027/001/772/msdncompositedoc.xml and MSXML 4.0 can be downloaded from http://msdn.microsoft.com/library/default.asp?url=/library/en-us/dnmsxml/html/whatsnew40rtm.asp.

As MSXML 4.0 is installed in side-by-side mode, the only disadvantage is that, until an Internet Explorer ships that makes use of MSXML 4.0, it cannot be made to use MSXML 4.0 for data island or native XSLT transformation functionality. However, we can still write client-side script and use MSXML 4.0-specific ProgIDs to process and transform XML documents, provided MSXML 4.0 is installed on the client.

Detecting MSXML Version

In this section we'll look at various ways to determine the MSXML version information.

XMLVersion ActiveX Control

Microsoft provides an ActiveX control, **XMLVersion**, which can be used to determine the MSXML parser versions installed on your computer. The ActiveX control may be downloaded from http://support.microsoft.com/default.aspx?scid=kb;EN-US;q278674. This link provides two versions of the same ActiveX control – one with a built-in user interface, and another without the user interface.

To use the XMLVersion ActiveX control, download the control from the above URL and extract it to a folder. To register the OCX control using `regsvr32.exe`, click Start and Run, then type **regsvr32 <pathofocx>\XMLVersions.ocx**.

To use the ActiveX control, type the following text into an HTML file:

```
<Object id=XMLVersion classid=clsid:A2ED8221-537B-4CE2-9D16-1977AD4921D1>
</Object>
```

Alternatively, open `xmlversion.html` in the code download and you will see output similar to the following:

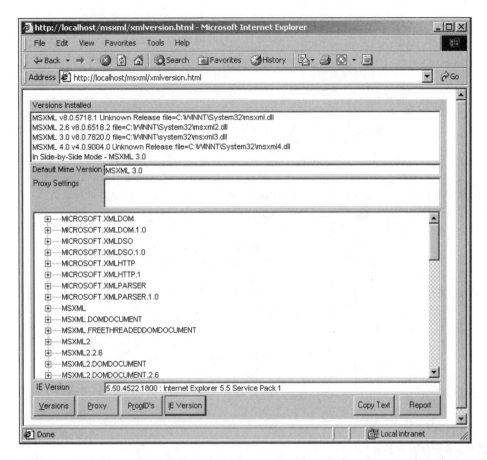

This ActiveX control has a built-in user interface; you may also try the other, text-based version of the ActiveX control. The minimum requirement to use the ActiveX control is the Visual Basic Runtime, IE 4.01 or higher, Microsoft Script Runtime (`scrrun.dll`), and MS Common Controls 1 and 2.

MSXML Version Used by Internet Explorer

The above ActiveX control simply lists all the MSXML versions installed on the machine, along with ProgIDs available. However, we are still not sure which version of MSXML (more specifically, which MSXML DLL file) is being used by IE.

One way to find out the version of MSXML used by IE is to monitor the DLL file loaded by the browser when we open an XML file. To do this we can use a utility such as **FileMon**, available from http://sysinternals.com/ntw2k/source/filemon.shtml. Filemon is a utility to monitor the file system activity on a system in real time. Download the FileMon utility, extract and run it, then set the filter by clicking on Edit | Filter/Highlight... so that it only shows file activity for any file named MSXML:

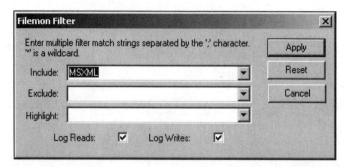

Next, open any XML file in IE and monitor the activity in FileMon. It will tell you the path and name of the MSXML DLL being used by the browser, and you will see output similar to this:

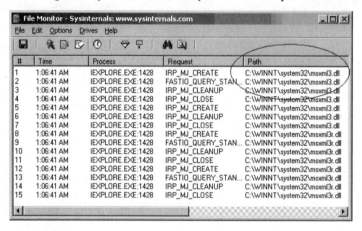

Using a JScript try...catch Block

The above two methods involve little human intervention and are suitable if we are debugging an application and want to get the MSXML version information. However, if we are writing a web page that uses MSXML and want to detect the MSXML version on the fly, we may use the following JScript `try...catch` trick.

Basically, we try to instantiate the MSXML DOMDocument object using the version-dependent ProgID, and try to load an XML document; if it succeeds then that parser version is available, but if it fails and raises an exception, we catch that and take the necessary action.

Let's say we are writing a web page that needs MSXML 3.0 to be installed on the client in order to work properly. We can use the following JScript code contained in `JScriptXMLVer1.html` to detect if MSXML 3.0 is installed:

```html
<html>
<head>
<title>MSXML Parser Version Test</title>
</head>
<body>
<script language="JScript">
try
{
```

```
    var strXML = "<?xml version='1.0'?><root>Test</root>";
    var objXMLDOM = new ActiveXObject("Msxml2.DOMDocument.3.0");
    objXMLDOM.loadXML(strXML);

    document.write("<font color=green>MSXML3 is Installed</font>");
}
catch(e)
{
    document.write("<font color=red>MSXML3 is NOT Installed</font>");
}
</script>
</body>
</html>
```

The above HTML page illustrates the use of JScript try...catch functionality to detect the MSXML version. We try to instantiate the MSXML 3.0 DOMDocument object, and then load the XML string into it. If the machine does not have MSXML 3.0 installed, the new ActiveXObject call will fail, raising an exception. Here we simply print the message that the parser is not installed. Alternatively, we could redirect to another page, or we could install the required version using the CAB file, which is discussed in the following section.

Deploying MSXML Solutions

It is strongly recommended that MSXML application developers should use at least MSXML 3.0, because this release offers better performance, is the most W3C-compliant, and provides support for various standards (such as SAX 2.0).

❑   MSXML 2.5 ships only with Windows 2000, though MSXML 2.5 SP1 is available to download at http://msdn.microsoft.com/code/sample.asp?url=/msdn-files/027/001/439/msdncompositedoc.xml.

❑   MSXML 2.6 is only available with the Microsoft Data Access (MDAC) 2.6 RTM redistribution package, available at http://www.microsoft.com/data.

❑   MSXML 3.0 English version is available to download at http://msdn.microsoft.com/downloads/default.asp?URL=/downloads/sample.asp?url=/msdn-files/027/001/596/msdncompositedoc.xml.

❑   A localized version for MSXML 3.0 is available at http://msdn.microsoft.com/downloads/default.asp?url=/downloads/sample.asp?url=/msdn-files/027/001/573/msdncompositedoc.xml.

The MSDN web site also provides the **MergeModule Redistribution Package** and the CAB file for various versions of the MSXML parser.

Microsoft Windows Installer installation technology makes use of .msi files, which are the application installation package files that contain code, files, resources, registry entries, and setup logic required to install the application. Merge modules are essentially simplified .msi files. They generally have an .msm file extension and cannot be installed alone, but need to be merged into an installation package using a merge tool (such as Orca.exe, available with MSI SDK). The MSXML MergeModule Redistribution Package is available from http://msdn.microsoft.com/downloads/sample.asp?url=/MSDN-FILES/027/001/716/msdncompositedoc.xml.

We may use MergeModule to bundle it with Windows applications that use MSXML. However, for web-based applications, **CAB file** deployment is the best option. Following are the locations from where you can download MSXML 3.0, MSXML 3.0 SP1, and SP2 `.cab` file redistribution packages:

- ❑ http://msdn.microsoft.com/downloads/default.asp?url=/downloads/sample.asp?url=/msdn-files/027/001/548/msdncompositedoc.xml

- ❑ http://msdn.microsoft.com/downloads/default.asp?url=/downloads/sample.asp?url=/MSDN-FILES/027/001/650/msdncompositedoc.xml

- ❑ http://msdn.microsoft.com/downloads/default.asp?url=/code/sample.asp?url=/MSDN-FILES/027/001/772/msdncompositedoc.xml

MSXML CAB file deployment is pretty straightforward, and requires writing the `<object>` tag on the web page and placing the CAB file on the server. For instance, to deploy MSXML 3.0 SP2, we may write the following lines in any web page:

```
<html>
<head>
    <title>MSXML 3.0 SP 2 Download Sample</title>
</head>

<body>

<object
    id="MSXML3"
    classid="clsid:f5078f32-c551-11d3-89b9-0000f81fe221"
    codebase="msxml3.cab#version=8,20,8730,0"
    type="application/x-oleobject"
    STYLE="display: none"
>
</object>

</body>
</html>
```

Remember to place the CAB file on the server! Now, when the above page is accessed, if the client does not have MSXML 3.0 SP2, it will be downloaded and installed on the client's machine seamlessly, and we can start using it. Note that MSXML 3.0 SP2 gets installed in replace mode, so be cautious while using the above HTML page.

With the basics covered, let's now look at some examples of using MSXML on the client side.

Script-based XML Data Access

IE 5.0+ provides two main ways to process XML data on the client. The first way is to write JScript, instantiate an MSXML DOM object, load the document, and process it. With this method, it is recommended to use version-dependent ProgIDs. This ensures that even if multiple versions of MSXML are installed, the script code still functions properly and uses the correct version. Also with this method, if the client has the latest version of MSXML, then the script can instantiate the objects from that version and use them.

The following table lists the ProgIDs for various classes present in MSXML 3.0 and 4.0:

Class	MSXML 3.0	**MSXML 4.0**
DOMDocument	Msxml2.DOMDocument.3.0 (version dependent)	Msxml2.DOMDocument.4.0
	Msxml2.DOMDocument (version independent)	
FreeThreaded DOMDocument	Msxml2.FreeThreadedDOM Document.3.0	Msxml2.FreeThreadedDOM Document.4.0
	Msxml2.FreeThreadedDOM Document	
DSOControl	Msxml2.DSOControl.3.0	Msxml2.DSOControl.4.0
	Msxml2.DSOControl	
XMLHTTP	Msxml2.XMLHTTP.3.0	Msxml2.XMLHTTP.4.0
	Msxml2.XMLHTTP	
ServerXMLHTTP	Msxml2.ServerXMLHTTP.3.0	Msxml2.ServerXMLHTTP.4.0
	Msxml2.ServerXMLHTTP	
XMLWriter	Msxml2.MXXMLWriter.3.0	Msxml2.MXXMLWriter.4.0
	Msxml2.MXXMLWriter	
XSLTemplate	Msxml2.XSLTemplate.3.0	Msxml2.XSLTemplate.4.0
	Msxml2.XSLTemplate	
XMLSchemaCache	Msxml2.XMLSchemaCache.3.0	Msxml2.XMLSchemaCache.4.0
	Msxml2.XMLSchemaCache	
XHTMLWriter	N/A	Msxml2.MXHTMLWriter.4.0
SAXAttributes	Msxml2.SAXAttributes.3.0	Msxml2.SAXAttributes.4.0
	Msxml2.SAXAttributes	
SAXXMLReader	Msxml2.SAXXMLReader.3.0	Msxml2.SAXXMLReader.4.0
	Msxml2.SAXXMLReader	
Namespace Manager	N/A	Msxml2.MXNamespaceManager.4.0

The other approach is to include XML data within the HTML, between the `<xml>` and `</xml>` tags. The browser loads the data specified using the `<xml>` and `</xml>` tags and automatically creates an XML DOM object, which is script-accessible via the ID attribute of the `<xml>` tag. IE also allows us to bind this data to various HTML controls. This method, known as data islands, is discussed later in the chapter. Let's first look at the script-based XML access method.

Loading an XML Document

The following example (`loadxml.html`) shows how to load an XML document from client-side JScript code:

```
<html>
<head>
    <title>Loading XML Example</title>
</head>
<body onLoad="GetAccountDetails()">
<div id="ActDetails"></div><br><br>

<script language="JScript">
function GetAccountDetails()
{
    try
    {
        var objXMLDOM = new ActiveXObject("Msxml2.DOMDocument.3.0");
        objXMLDOM.async = false;
        objXMLDOM.load("acct.xml");

        var loadResult = objXMLDOM.parseError;

        if (loadResult.errorCode == 0)
        {
            bal = objXMLDOM.documentElement.nodeTypedValue;
            ActDetails.innerHTML = "The balance is: " + bal;
        }
        else
        {
            ActDetails.innerHTML = "<font color=red>Error: " +
                        loadResult.reason;
        }
    }
    catch(e)
    {
        ActDetails.innerHTML = "<font color=red>Error: " +
                        e.description;
    }
}
</script>

<input type="button" value="Refresh Details" onClick="GetAccountDetails()">
</body>
</html>
```

The above HTML page contains a client-side JScript function named `GetAccountDetails()` that is called when the page is fully loaded and also when the "Refresh Details" button is clicked. The HTML page also uses a `<div>` tag, which is used to display the results.

The `GetAccountDetails()` function starts by instantiating an MSXML DOM object using the MSXML 3.0-specific ProgID. It then loads the XML document file named `acct.xml`, which is present in the same directory as the page on the server. The `acct.xml` file contains just one line:

```
<Balance>$2,608.77</Balance>
```

Next, the JScript code accesses the root node in the XML document (`Balance`) and prints its value using the `<div>` tag. If you change the balance value in the XML file and click on the **Refresh Details** button, it simply calls the same JScript function again, which loads the XML file from the server and prints the updated value of the root node. Using this method we are able to refresh part of a page, without loading the entire page again in order to refresh the data content.

We use the `try...catch` block to make sure that we can create the MSXML `DOMDocument`. Once the object is created, we load the XML file and use the `parseError` property to see if there were any errors while parsing the source XML document.

The above HTML code loads a static XML file, but it would be nice to point it to an ASP page that dynamically generates XML based on the parameters passed. To do this we just need to change the `load()` call as follows:

```
objXMLDOM.load("GetBalance.asp");
```

The above line makes a call to `GetBalance.asp`, on the same server (and same virtual directory). This page can then connect to the database, generate XML and return that to the client. It's also possible to load a page on a different server. For example:

```
objXMLDOM.load("http://p.moreover.com/cgi-
    local/page?c=XML%20and%20metadata%20news&o=xml")
```

Instead of using the DOM methods to access the XML data (as in the example above), let's now use an XSL stylesheet to do the transformation on the client-side.

Transformation on the Client

In Chapter 10, *Transformations on the Server*, we discussed doing the XSL transformation on the server and how it helps us to build client-independent web applications. However, there are some advantages to doing the transformation on the client and it is very well suited for intranet applications, where we can control the version of MSXML being used on the client.

The main benefits of doing client-side transformation include:

❑ Improved server performance – moving the transformation logic from the server to the client reduces processing requirements.

❑ Caching of the XSL document – let's say we have multiple XML documents, but they all use the same XSL stylesheet file. When the transformation is done on the client, the stylesheet is downloaded just once and the rest of the transformations will use the same cached XSL documents.

❑ Different views of the same XML data – the client-side transformation facilitates displaying multiple views of the same XML data, without reloading the entire page.

The only limitation is that we'll have to deal with the browsers' MSXML version incompatibilities and make sure that all clients have the required version of MSXML installed. Therefore, this solution is best suited for intranet web sites or for applications where we can control the MSXML version.

Let's look at an example of this. In the following example we have an HTML page (clientTransform.html), an XSL file (Orders.xsl), and an ASP page (GetOrdersInfo.asp). The ASP page connects to the SQL Server 2000 (NorthWind sample database), generates the order information as XML based on the input customer ID, and then sends that to the client.

Here is how the HTML page code looks:

```
<html>
<head>
<title>Client-side Transformation Example</title>
</head>

<body>

<form name="frmOrderDetails">
   Enter the customer ID:
   <input name="CustID" type="text" size="5" maxlength="5">
   <input type="button" value="Get Order Details" onClick="GetOrders()">
</form>

<div id="OrderDetails"></div>

<script language="JScript">
function GetOrders()
{
   var objXMLDOM = new ActiveXObject("Msxml2.DOMDocument.3.0");
   objXMLDOM.async = false;

   var objXSL    = new ActiveXObject("Msxml2.DOMDocument.3.0");
   objXSL.async = false;

   var CustID    = document.frmOrderDetails.CustID.value;

   objXMLDOM.load("getordersinfo.asp?CustID=" + CustID);
   objXSL.load ("Orders.xsl");

   OrderDetails.innerHTML = objXMLDOM.transformNode(objXSL);
}
</script>

</body>
</html>
```

The above HTML page starts with a form, which has a textbox and a button. The OnClick event handler function creates two XML DOM document objects – one to load the XML (using the ASP page) and another to load the stylesheet XSL file. Next, it calls the transformNode() method to transform the XML into HTML and display that using the div tag. We'll not discuss the ASP page or XSL file here, but they are included in the code download for this chapter. Note that when the customer ID is entered and the button is clicked, the entire page is not loaded again. Instead, the above HTML just uses MSXML to get what it wants (orders XML information) and applies the stylesheet to it, without posting the form and loading the entire page again.

The output looks like this:

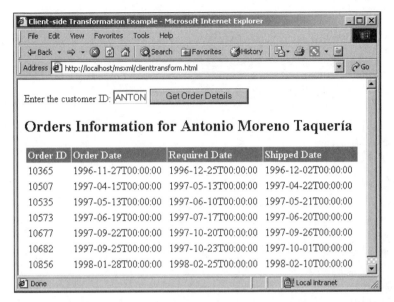

There is one more little glitch when using the client-side XSL transformation. If the transformed HTML needs to contain client-side script functions, those script blocks should have the `defer` attribute, and the script blocks should be written using the CDATA section enclosed inside the `<xsl:comment>` tag. Let's look at an example of this. Here is our source XML document (`favorites.xml`):

```
<?xml version="1.0" ?>
<Favorites>

    <WebLink>
        <Title>ASPToday</Title>
        <PageURL>http://www.asptoday.com</PageURL>
    </WebLink>

    <WebLink>
        <Title>C#Today</Title>
        <PageURL>http://www.csharptoday.com</PageURL>
    </WebLink>

</Favorites>
```

We need to transform the above XML to HTML that shows the list of favorite links from the above XML document. Clicking on a link will open up a new pop-up window (using the JavaScript `window.open()` method). Here is the XSL stylesheet (`favorites.xsl`) that we use to achieve this:

```
<xsl:stylesheet version="1.0"
    xmlns:xsl="http://www.w3.org/1999/XSL/Transform">
    <xsl:output method="html" />
    <xsl:template match="/">
        <html>
        <head>
```

```
        <title>My Favorites</title>
    </head>
    <body>
    My Favorites
    <ul>
    <xsl:for-each select="Favorites/WebLink">
        <li>
            <a href="javascript:openWin('{PageURL}')">
                <xsl:value-of select="Title" />
            </a>
        </li>
    </xsl:for-each>
    </ul>

    <script language="JScript" defer="true">
    <xsl:comment>
    <![CDATA[
        function openWin(strURL)
        {
            window.open(strURL, 'Favorite', 'top=0,left=0');
        }
    ]]>
    </xsl:comment>
    </script>

    </body>
    </html>
    </xsl:template>
</xsl:stylesheet>
```

As the client-side script may contain special characters (such as <, &, etc.) it needs to be enclosed inside a CDATA section in an XSL document. Also, the script code needs to be placed inside an <xsl:comment> tag, which translates to <!--...-->, in order to prevent the down-level browsers from displaying the script code.

When the transformation is applied on the client side using the script, and if the stylesheet file contains some script code, it is required to write the defer attribute, otherwise we'll get an "Object Expected" script error message when the script method present in the XSL file is called. If the defer attribute is not specified, the browser will try to find the function in the HTML file, while actually the function resides in the transformed document. The defer attribute is not required when applying the transformation on the server or if the stylesheet contains script code.

The following HTML page (favorites.html) uses the above XML and XSL files to perform client-side transformation:

```
<html>
<head>
    <title>Client-side Transformation Example #2</title>
</head>
<body>

<input type="button" onClick="DoTransform()" value="Transform">
```

```
<script language="JScript">
<!--
function DoTransform()
{
    var objXMLDOM = new ActiveXObject("Msxml2.DOMDocument.3.0");
    objXMLDOM.async = false;

    var objXSL    = new ActiveXObject("Msxml2.DOMDocument.3.0");
    objXSL.async = false;

    objXMLDOM.load("favorites.xml");
    objXSL.load ("favorites.xsl");

    document.body.innerHTML  = objXMLDOM.transformNode(objXSL);
}
//-->
</script>

</body>
</html>
```

The page is very similar to the previous example on client-side XSL transformation. Again, we simply load the XML and XSL document and call the transformNode() DOM method to actually perform the transformation.

When the HTML page is first called, you will see a page containing a button labeled "Transform". Clicking on the Transform button calls the JScript method, which performs the XSL transformation and updates the document body content with the transformed HTML. Below is the output you will see:

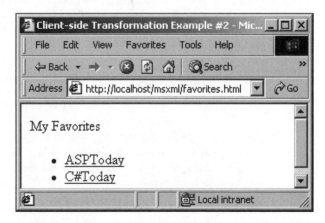

Clicking on the link opens up a JavaScript pop-up window, loading the homepage from either http://www.asptoday.com or http://www.csharptoday.com.

So far we have seen examples to read data from the server and use it on the client side, but what if we were to post the data to the server in XML format? MSXML provides a little class named XMLHTTP that can be used to do HTTP access from the client. Let's now look at some examples of using XMLHTTP from the client.

HTTP Access from the Client Using XMLHTTP

The XMLHTTP class provided with MSXML is a wrapper around the WinInet Internet API and can be used to do HTTP access from the client. It can be used to send an HTTP request to any web page and get the response. It can also be used to post the data over HTTP. It is designed for use with XML data, though it is not restricted to XML. It can be used to send, request, and receive any kind of data.

> *Note that XMLHTTP is designed (and is well-suited) for client-side HTTP access. It should be used from the client-side to make HTTP requests and get/send data. To perform server-side HTTP access, MSXML provides another class named ServerXMLHTTP, which is thread-safe and server-safe. While XMLHTTP is based on WinInet, ServerXMLHTTP is developed using a totally new HTTP protocol stack named WinHTTP. As XMLHTTP is based on WinInet, it has the limitations of WinInet (not thread-safe, restriction on number of connections, etc.). ServerXMLHTTP is discussed in detail in Chapters 9, 10, and 11.*

XMLHTTP Reference

The XMLHTTP co-class implements the IXMLHTTPRequest interface, which has the following methods in the order you're likely to use them:

Method/Property	Description
open()	This is the first method that is called on an XMLHTTP instance, and initializes the HTTP request by specifying the request type (GET, PUT, POST, PROPFIND, etc.) and the URL. The URL parameter may be either an absolute or a relative URL. The third parameter is a Boolean value that indicates if the call is asynchronous, and its default value is false. The final two parameters may be used to pass the user credentials for sites that require authentication.
	If the authentication information is not passed, and the site being accessed requires authentication, a logon screen is displayed.
setRequestHeader()	This method can be used to set the HTTP request headers.
send()	Actually establishes the HTTP connection, sends the request, and receives the response. Depending on the async parameter passed to the open() method call, this method functions either synchronously or asynchronously.
abort()	Cancels the current asynchronous HTTP request.
status	This read-only long integer property can be accessed after the call to the send() method to check the HTTP status code returned by the request.
statusText	This property is generally used in conjunction with status, to get the textual status.

Method/Property	Description
onReadyState Change	This Scripting clients use this property to specify invocation of an event handler when the readyState property changes.
readyState	A four-byte integer property indicating the state of an asynchronous request. The readyState value can be Loading (1), Loaded (2), Interactive (3), or Completed (4).
getResponse Header()	This method can be used to retrieve a particular HTTP response header.
getAllResponse Headers()	Retrieves all response headers as carriage return-line feed character separated name-value pairs.
responseText	After the send() method, this property contains the response body as a string.
responseXML	If you know that the response is going to be XML, use this property to get DOM access to the HTTP response XML.
responseStream	This property provides access to the HTTP response as an IStream.
responseBody	The response as an array of unsigned bytes. Useful for working with binary data.

The general sequence of using XMLHTTP is to first call its open() method, followed by optionally setting the request headers using the setRequestHeader() method call(s), and then calling the send() method to actually send the request.

If the request was sent as asynchronous (async parameter to open() method call was true), the send() method returns immediately and we may use the readyState property and onReadyStateChange event handler to wait until the document is loaded. However, if the request was sent synchronously (third parameter to open() method call was false), the send() method does not return until the HTTP request is complete.

Let's look at two simple examples using XMLHTTP, first to do an HTTP GET and then to send a POST request.

Retrieving Data

The following example (xmlhttp1.html) loads an XML document using XMLHTTP and sends a GET request for an XML document on some remote server:

```
<html>
<head>
<title>XMLHTTP Example 1</title>
</head>
<body>

<input value="Do GET" type="button" onClick="GetXML()" >
```

```
<script language="JScript">
function GetXML()
{
   var objXMLHTTP = new ActiveXObject("Msxml2.XMLHTTP.3.0");
   objXMLHTTP.open("GET", "http://www.PerfectXML.com/samples/product.xml",
                   false);
   objXMLHTTP.send();

   if (objXMLHTTP.status == 200)
   {
      alert(objXMLHTTP.responseXML.xml);
   }
   else
   {
      alert("Error: " + objXMLHTTP.status + ": " + objXMLHTTP.statusText);
   }
}
</script>

</body>
</html>
```

We use the MSXML 3.0-specific ProgID in the above HTML page to instantiate an XMLHTTP object. Next, we call the open() method with a GET request type and synchronous HTTP mode by passing false as the value for the third (async) parameter. The send() method then actually sends the HTTP request and finally, using the status property, we check if the HTTP access succeeded or not.

Remember that XMLHTTP is not just for XML data access; it can send an HTTP request for any kind of data and you can then play around with objects such as responseText, or responseBody to work with the returned results.

Posting the Data

The next example (xmlhttp2POST.html) illustrates using XMLHTTP to post data to a web page. The following code posts data to a publicly available web service to search for music teachers.

```
<html>
<head>
   <title>XMLHTTP Example 2</title>
</head>
<body>

<input value="Do POST" type="button" onClick="PostXML()" >

<script language="JScript">
<!--
function PostXML()
{
var objXMLHTTP = new ActiveXObject("Msxml2.XMLHTTP.3.0");

var PostData =
"ZipCode=60195&Instrument=Piano&SkillLevel=0&Style=0&Radius=0&RestrictResultsCount
=5";
```

```
objXMLHTTP.open
("POST",
"http://www.PerfectXML.net/WebServices/MusicTeachers/MusicTeachers.asmx/FindMusicT
eachers", false);

objXMLHTTP.setRequestHeader
("Content-Type", "application/x-www-form-urlencoded");

objXMLHTTP.setRequestHeader("Content-Length", PostData.length);

objXMLHTTP.send(PostData);
```

```
if (objXMLHTTP.status == 200)
{
    alert(objXMLHTTP.responseXML.xml);
}
else
{
    alert("Error: " + objXMLHTTP.status + ": " + objXMLHTTP.statusText);
}
}
//-->
</script>

</body>
</html>
```

Note that the open() method now has the first parameter as POST (instead of GET). In order to post a request (stimulate a form submission), it is required to send a header that indicates the proper content type. That proper content type is application/x-www-form-urlencoded. We do this by setting the Content-Type request header as application/x-www-form-urlencoded. Finally, we now pass a parameter to the send() method call (this parameter contains the data to be posted).

Asynchronous HTTP Access

Let's say we need to load a large amount of XML data on the client over HTTP and also update the UI as the data is being loaded. In that case, we cannot use the synchronous load like we have so far because with this approach, the send() method does not return until the entire data is received and we do not have any control until the send() method returns.

XMLHTTP can also be used to load the XML data asynchronously. We can then implement the onReadyStateChange event handler and keep checking the readyState property until it returns 4. We can then assume that the asynchronous request completed. The onReadyStateChange event handler is generally used with scripting clients and is not readily available with Microsoft Visual Basic or C++. However, we'll look at an example of how to implement it using Visual Basic. First, let's look at a simple web page (xmlhttp3Async.html) that sends an asynchronous HTTP request using XMLHTTP:

```
<html>
<head>
<title>XMLHTTP Example 3</title>
</head>
```

```
<body>

<input value="Do GET" type="button" onClick="GetLargeXML()">

<script language="JScript">
<!--
var objXMLHTTP = new ActiveXObject("Msxml2.XMLHTTP.3.0");
function GetLargeXML()
{
    objXMLHTTP.open("GET", "customers.xml", true);
    objXMLHTTP.onReadyStateChange= evtHandler;
    objXMLHTTP.send();
}

function evtHandler()
{
    if (objXMLHTTP.readyState == 4)
    {
        alert(objXMLHTTP.responseXML.xml);
    }
    else
    {
        alert(objXMLHTTP.readyState);
    }
}
//-->
</script>

</body>
</html>
```

Note that the third parameter to the open() method call is true, telling it to load the HTTP request asynchronously.

The onReadyStateChange property is designed mainly for use in scripting environments. We cannot directly use it in Visual Basic. The possible workarounds to this include using a timer control and polling the readyState until the entire response is received (readyState = 4).

The other workaround would be to create a class and add a single method that has the dispatch ID of 0 (default method). More specifically, to send an asynchronous XMLHTTP request from Visual Basic and handle the events involves the following steps:

❑ Add a wrapper class that implements the event handler method.

❑ Make the event handler method the default method of the class by assigning a dispatch ID of 0 to the method.

❑ Assign the instance of the above class to the onReadyStateChange property.

Start Visual Basic 6.0 and create a new standard EXE project. Add a reference to the MSXML 3.0 library. Add a class module and name it AsyncWrapper. Add a method in this class and name it evtHandler:

```
Public Sub evtHandler()
    If Form1.objXMLHTTP.readyState = 4 Then
```

```
        MsgBox Form1.objXMLHTTP.responseXML.xml
    Else
        MsgBox Form1.objXMLHTTP.readyState
    End If
End Sub
```

In the above method, we see if the document is fully loaded (readyState = 4). If so, we display the response XML text, whereas otherwise we just display the value of readyState. The possible values for readyState are:

❑ UNINITIALIZED (0): This means that the object has been created but has not been initialized by calling the open() method.

❑ LOADING (1): The send() method has not been called.

❑ LOADED (2): The send() method has been called, status and headers are available, but the actual response is still not available.

❑ INTERACTIVE (3): Partial data has been received. The responseBody and responseText can be used to get that partial response.

❑ COMPLETE (4): The complete response has been received and is available in responseBody, responseText, responseXML, and responseStream.

We now need to make this method the default method for the class by clicking on **Tools | Procedure Attributes**. Make sure that the evtHandler method is selected, click on the **Advanced** button, and select the **(Default)** entry from the **Procedure ID** combo box:

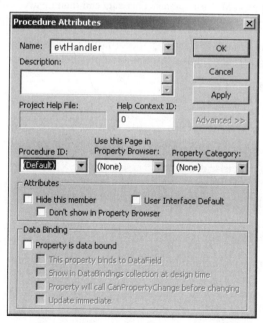

Now write the following code in the form file:

```
Public objXMLHTTP As New Msxml2.XMLHTTP30

Private Sub Form_Load()
   Dim WrapperObj As New AsyncWrapper

   objXMLHTTP.open "GET", "http://localhost/Demo/customers.xml", True
   objXMLHTTP.onReadyStateChange = WrapperObj
   objXMLHTTP.send
   Unload Me
End Sub
```

When we run the code, we'll see that the XMLHTTP event handling calls our evtHandler handler and the readyState property returns 1, 2, 3, and finally when the complete response is available, we display the received XML using the responseXML property.

So far, we have been manipulating XML data on the client through script, but we mentioned earlier that with IE 5.0+ there is a way to directly bind XML data to HTML controls. Let's now look at IE's data binding functionality.

XML Data Binding

HTML pages are mainly used as the presentation format. However, IE introduced a new concept of embedding XML data inside HTML documents. This data can then be accessed either from scripts or can be bound to HTML controls. This functionality is known as **data islands** and is supported by IE 5.0+.

We can use <XML></XML> syntax or <SCRIPT LANGUAGE="XML"></SCRIPT> syntax to hold chunks of XML data as part of HTML documents. All the examples below use the <XML></XML> syntax.

The basic syntax of a data island is:

```
<XML ID={SomeID} [SRC={URL}]>
[{XML data}]
</XML>
```

The XML data within the data island can be accessed as a MSXML DOMDocument from the client-side script. We'll see an example of this soon, but first let's learn how to display the data island data nicely using the data binding capabilities of IE, without writing a single line of script code.

Binding to a Table

Let's start with a very simple example of binding a data island with a table control. Below is the code for DataIsland1.html:

```
<html>
<head>
<title>Data Island Example 1</title>
</head>
<body>
```

```
<XML ID="Cal">
   <Calendar>
      <Event>
         <Day>Jan 1</Day>
         <Desc>New Year's Day</Desc>
      </Event>
      <Event>
         <Day>December 25</Day>
         <Desc>Christmas Day</Desc>
      </Event>
   </Calendar>
</XML>

<table DATASRC="#Cal" border="0" cellspacing="1" bgcolor="#FFFFFF">
   <thead>
      <th>Day</th>
      <th>Event</th>
   </thead>
   <tr>
      <td bgcolor="silver" width=200>
         <b><div DATAFLD="Day"></div></b>
      </td>
      <td bgcolor="silver" width=200>
         <div DATAFLD="Desc"></div>
      </td>
   </tr>
</table>
</body>
</html>
```

The file gives the following output:

The above HTML file contains calendar data as an XML data island and then DATASRC and DATAFLD attributes are used to bind this data with the HTML table. The <XML> tag has an ID attribute that is used as the value of the DATASRC attribute with the <table> element. This ID attribute can also be accessed from script as a DOM document object. Also, instead of the inline XML, we may use the SRC attribute with the data island and load the data from the URL. Let's look at an example (DataIsland2.html) that illustrates this:

```
<html>
<head>
   <title>Data Island Example 2</title>
</head>
<body>
<XML ID="Teachers" SRC="music.xml">
</XML>
```

```
<script language="JScript">
   iRecCnt = Teachers.documentElement.childNodes.length;
   document.write (iRecCnt + " records found!");
</script>
</body>

</html>
```

Make sure you have the `music.xml` file in the same folder. When you open the HTML file in IE you will see the output as "2 records found!"

In the above example we used a data island to refer to an external XML document using the `SRC` attribute, and used the data island as an XML DOM document object from the client JScript code.

While working with data islands, it is important to understand character encoding behavior when writing inline XML data as part of the HTML versus using the `SRC` attribute and referring to an external XML document. The inline XML uses the encoding of the surrounding HTML. Alternatively, if the `SRC` attribute is used, the referred XML file may contain the encoding declaration `<?xml version="1.0" encoding="..."?>` and so when we access that document from the script, MSXML will use the encoding specified in the external file.

Pagination

Another important use of data islands is to paginate the data on the client side. Let's look at an example of this (`DataIsland3.html`):

```
<html>
<head>
   <title>Data Island Example 3</title>
</head>
<body>
<XML ID="Books" SRC="books.xml">
</XML>
<table DATAPAGESIZE="1" border="0" cellspacing="1" bgcolor="#FFFFFF">
   <thead>
      <th>ISBN</th>
      <th>Title</th>
      <th>Price</th>
   </thead>
   <tr>
      <td width=200><b><div DATASRC="#Books"
               DATAFLD="ISBN"></div></b></td>
      <td width=200><div DATASRC="#Books" DATAFLD="TITLE"></div></td>
      <td width=200><div DATASRC="#Books" DATAFLD="PRICE"></div></td>
   </tr>
</table>

<button onClick="Books.recordset.moveFirst()"  >First Record</button>
<button onClick="movePrev();" >Previous Record</button>
<button onClick="moveNext();">Next Record</button>
<button onClick="Books.recordset.moveLast()"  >Last Record</button><br>
<script language="JScript">

   function movePrev()
```

```
    {
        if (Books.recordset.AbsolutePosition > 1)
            Books.recordset.movePrevious();
        else
            alert('No more records.')
    }

    function moveNext()
    {
        if (Books.recordset.AbsolutePosition <
            Books.recordset.RecordCount)
            Books.recordset.moveNext();
        else
            alert('No more records.');
    }
</script>
</body>
</html>
```

The file gives the following output:

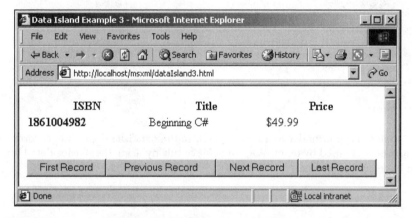

The XML data island in the above HTML file refers to an external XML document file named books.xml. We use the DATAPAGESIZE attribute with the <table> element to specify how many records we want to see at a time. Then, using the Next, Previous, Last, and First buttons we move between the records. We handle the button onClick events and use the data island recordset methods to move the current record position. In this example, we specify the DATAPAGESIZE as 1, so that one record will be shown at a time.

Master-Detail View

Consider the following XML file:

```
<?xml version="1.0" ?>
<Employees>
    <Team>
        <Title>eBusiness</Title>
        <Location>420</Location>
```

```
        <Members>
            <Employee>
                <Name>Kelly F</Name>
                <Role>Sr. Developer</Role>
            </Employee>

            <Employee>
                <Name>Jeff H</Name>
                <Role>Team Lead</Role>
            </Employee>
        </Members>
    </Team>

    <Team>
        <Title>Marketing</Title>
        <Location>205</Location>
        <Members>
            <Employee>
                <Name>Gerold F</Name>
                <Role>Manager</Role>
            </Employee>

            <Employee>
                <Name>Durriya S</Name>
                <Role>Copywriter</Role>
            </Employee>
        </Members>
    </Team>
</Employees>
```

Let's say we wish to keep a similar hierarchical view in the data island – in other words, we would like to see the members grouped by team. We can achieve this by using the master-detail functionality included in DataIsland4.html:

```
<html>
<head>
<title>Data Island Example 4</title>
</head>
<body>

<XML ID="Employees" SRC="emps.xml">
</XML>

<table DATASRC="#Employees" border="1" >
    <tr valign="top">
      <td><div DATAFLD="Title"></div></td>
      <td><div DATAFLD="Location"></div></td>
      <td>
        <table DATASRC="#Employees" DATAFLD="Members" border="1">
          <tr valign="top">
            <td>Team Members<br>
              <table DATASRC="#Employees" DATAFLD="Employee" border="1">
                <tr>
                  <td><div DATAFLD="Name"></div></td>
```

```
            <td><div DATAFLD="Role"></div></td>
          </tr>
        </table>
      </td>
    </tr>
  </table>
</td>
</tr>
</table>

</body>
</html>
```

The data island in the above HTML file once again refers to an external data file named emps.xml. The first table is assigned the DATASRC attribute as Employees, while the tables inside it have both DATASRC and DATAFLD attributes – this is the key to binding the lower level hierarchy. Basically, the key to master-detail view is to understand the structure of the data, create the tables accordingly, and assign the DATASRC and DATAFLD attribute values.

Title and Location are the unique nodes under the main Employees node. Hence, after setting the DATASRC as #Employees for the main table, we directly bind to these nodes using the DATAFLD attribute. Next, we want to work on the Members sub-tree and get the Name and Role for each employee. To do this, we create another table which now has DATASRC as #Employees (*creating the master link*) and DATAFLD as Employee (to allow binding to Employee sub-elements). Finally, we bind the Name and Role nodes using the DATAFLD attribute.

The above HTML file produces the following output:

XML data binding is well suited for simple XML structures, but as the XML becomes more complex, it is painfully hard to bind the data directly to HTML controls. However, we can still use XML data islands, and use the script approach to utilize the full DOM functionality. Since the first introduction of XML data islands in IE 5.0, little has changed and it is highly unlikely that other browser vendors will incorporate such functionality into their browsers.

If you are sure that you only need to support IE 5+ on the client-side, you may use data islands to dynamically generate the content on the client without making roundtrips to the server. If the XML structure is straightforward, you may directly bind the data to the HTML controls (such as a table) easily. However, if the XML structure is complex or you need to do some kind of processing on the document, you may access the data island from the script as an MSXML DOMDocument object.

Summary

The objective of this chapter was to study the various ways to work with XML on the client side. Today, IE is the only browser that has extensive support for working with XML on the client. IE 4.0 shipped with the first version of the MSXML 1.0 DOM-based parser, and today IE 6.0 bundles MSXML 3.0, which is much more than a parser. Different versions of IE and other products shipped different versions of MSXML. Hence, the biggest challenge while working with XML on the client-side is to make sure that the client has the correct version of the parser installed and that the correct version of the parser is being used.

This chapter started with a discussion of IE's native support for XML and how to detect which version of MSXML is being used. We then wrote a few sample web pages to process and transform XML on the client using MSXML. We also talked about options available to deploy MSXML applications.

We then learned about XMLHTTP – an interesting class provided by MSXML to do HTTP communication from the client. XMLHTTP can be used to retrieve data over HTTP or post data to a web page. We also talked about how to use XMLHTTP for asynchronous HTTP data access.

Finally, we looked at IE's data binding functionality and learned about various benefits of using Data Islands.

So far, we have learned the details of using MSXML on the server, and now in this chapter we learned about using MSXML on the client-side. Take a look back at Chapter 9, "*Sending and Retrieving XML*" *Data* for an example of working in a distributed environment. In the next chapter we'll move on to look at performance, scalability, and security issues when working with MSXML before moving on to some case studies.

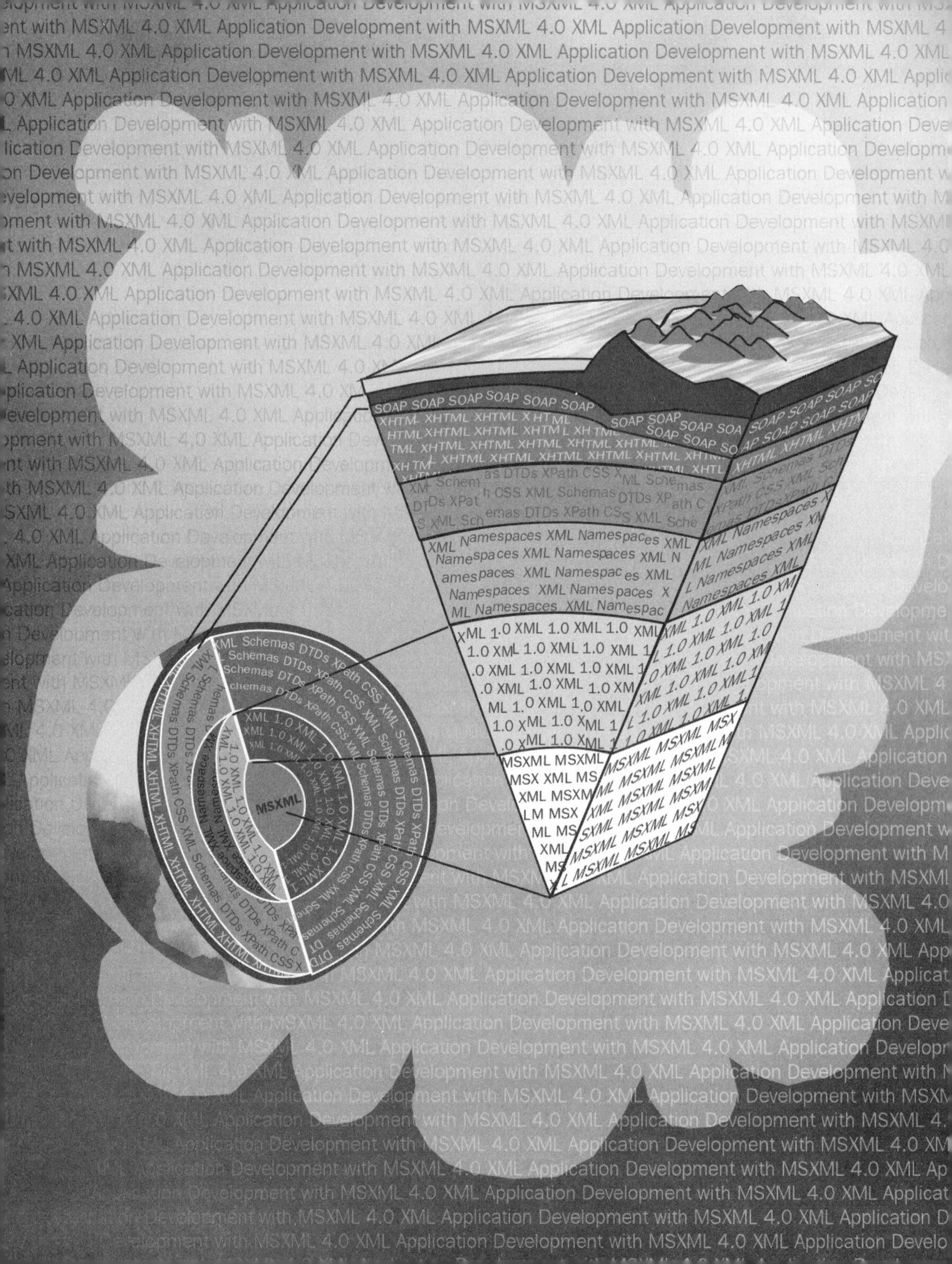
XML Application Development with MSXML 4.0
MSXML

13

Performance, Scalability, and Security

As monumental an achievement as it was, Newton's solution to the two-body problem in astronomy (understanding the gravitational interaction of two bodies such as Sun and Earth) pales against the challenge of the three-body problem (such as Sun, Earth, and Jupiter). Indeed, there is no general solution to the three-body problem (though there have been some surprises, such as a chaotic result from a known set of initial conditions). Needless to say, the complexity of the three-body problem is not linear. Programmers face their own two and three-body problems, though ours are far more tractable.

From physics to programming – the two-body problem for programmers is finding the equivalent to a "center of mass" for systems that *perform* for one and *scale* to all users. The three-body problem in programming is solving the two-body problem and adding the interaction of such a system with the various *security* models (which only get more sophisticated every day) without compromising the solution to the two-body problem.

Another challenge for any discussion of secure applications that perform at all scales is that there is an almost infinite combination of variables that any two systems can use to reach the same goal. This makes performance and scalability tuning a necessarily heuristic exercise; learning through discoveries made during investigative experimentation, rather than adopting a rules-based approach. This chapter can make suggestions, provide guidelines, and lay out tradeoffs, but it's up to each system architect to arrange the pieces in configurations that work.

There are also factors beyond the architects' control. Scale is clearly dependent on demand, and there are demand discontinuities. When Newton worked out the two-body problem, at least his numbers were stable; he knew the apogee and perigee of the Earth's orbit around the Sun. Architects may not be able to predict who will come to their site, how many will come to their site, at what time, or what they ask for. In a sense, architects are trying to solve the n-body problem.

> *The discussion here is taken in the context of scripting, not low-level languages like C++. This makes the chapter easier to read, but leaves us at the mercy of the intrinsic performance and scalability limitations of script.*

Another unusual thing about this chapter is that usually in Wrox multi-authored books, the author remains anonymous. However, this chapter is so full of blue-collar stories of XML at work that the Editors have asked me to go public with my identity and employer. I'm Michael Corning and I have one of the best jobs in the computer business. I work at Microsoft in Redmond, Washington. I work on the Test Infrastructure team in the Server Manager Group. My job is to apply Microsoft technologies to the development of Microsoft technologies. For the past four years, that work has brought me into close contact with the XML team, especially the technical lead, Derek Denny-Brown; the XSLT Program Manager, Jonathan Marsh; and even the XSLT developer, Andrew Kimball. If any of those lads read this book, they'll see their influence clearly – perhaps sometimes a bit too clearly.

So, let's now get to work.

Secure Applications that Perform for One and Scale to All

There is only one rule that must be followed when creating server applications: perfection. For at least a few more years, CPU cycles and network bandwidth are still scarce. This is still the age of parsimonious (or frugal) programming. So, when you see me suggest techniques that look like I'm picking nits on the client, remember that on the server the yields are measurable.

Some Definitions

Let's get a few definitions straight here: generally, **performance** is a measure of single use, and **scalability** is the ability of a system to handle an increasing number of users while leaving their performance unchanged.

Indeed, it is convenient to partition performance discussions mainly to the client, and scalability discussions to the server. We will follow such an approach in this chapter (although we shall note that some techniques both increase performance on both the client and enhance scalability on the server).

There is one subtlety in this distinction that needs highlighting: scale need not always be a function of the number of users; it can be the size of data on the client, for example. In the section of this chapter entitled *Cache XML in ASP Application Scope*, I describe a situation I found at work where my client application was fast because I only asked it to process sub-trees from my XML repository. Everything worked well, until my user came across one of those sub-trees that was very large. This discontinuity in size affected the scalability of the client, so we added some more caching on the server (reducing its scalability) to get back performance on the client in the presence of large data. Do you see why I characterize this point as a subtlety? The key to avoiding this performance/scale trap is to not lock us into a view of design that only looks to the server for scalability. Perhaps another example (covered below) will help make this distinction. About a year ago I wrote what turned out to be a huge 400 line transform that worked very well in its prototype stage, but failed at a mere 300kb XML file size. It appeared to me then that *XSLT* didn't scale, but then my mentor showed me "Matryoshka" variables. The transform ended up handling multi-megabyte scales of data. We'll look at Matryoshka variables later in the chapter.

Other Factors

We've seen how the number of users and the size of data can affect scalability (and performance), but there are other factors worth noting in passing. Hardware power, multiple processors, and the number of computers at your disposal also have dramatic impact on how fast your distributed applications run. I mention them in passing here because these other factors have little or no effect on programming techniques, and programming is the theme of this book.

A strong predictor of scale is hardware. Processor speed and memory capacity affect both server-side and client-side scale. For the server, an increase in CPU processing cycles available should increase the scalability. Theoretically, multi-processor servers will scale better than single processors. Two factors mitigate this assumption. First, the software must be properly architected to run more efficiently on multi-processor boxes, and this isn't easy to do. For example, `msxml.dll` (the version before `msxml3.dll`) had negative scale on multi-processor machines. Much of the work done on MSXML 3 and MSXML 4 has been to fix this problem, and the results of that work are nothing short of startling. The other mitigating factor relates to hardware architecture and to the amount of cycles the machine spends switching between threads or marshaling data between processors.

Multi-threading can also improve performance and scalability, but multi-threading requires synchronization, and synchronization mechanisms have differing levels of efficiency. Kernel-mode mechanisms like mutexes and semaphores are very fast, while user-mode controls like critical sections are comparatively slower. Most architects working with MSXML won't make choices about synchronization mechanisms, but they will have to live with the choices made by lower-level programmers. For example, the `FreeThreadedDOMDocument` uses a locking mechanism that is relatively easy to implement in the XML parser, but comparatively inefficient when compared to concurrency control (synchronization) mechanisms in SQL Server. So, application performance and scalability is dependent on architectural choices such as when and how to use the `FreeThreadedDOMDocument`. You'll see guidelines on this and other issues in the sections below.

World-class scalability (the ability to scale to global audiences) is impossible on a single computer, regardless of the manufacturer or the number of CPUs in the machine. For this level of scalability you must "scale out" using clusters of commodity servers. Microsoft's offering in this critical role is **Application Center 2000**. This chapter will discuss Application Center as it relates to applications that use `msxml4.dll`, and there's even a story from the Application Center Test Development team about how they replaced MSDE with `msxml3.dll` – to get *better* performance! For more details about scaling out web sites, see "*Professional Application Center 2000*' (ISBN 1-861004-47-8, Wrox Press).

So, now that we've covered the global issues and set a consistent definition of terms, it's now time to look more deeply into our three-body problem. The first body is performance. Following that, we'll see how to program with scale in mind and we'll complete this chapter by showing how to add security to XML applications without losing any ground gained in performance and scalability.

Performance

Appearance is fifty per cent of reality. It's also fifty per cent of performance. In other words, make your applications look fast first, and then work on the hard part – the real performance bottlenecks. On the client, the first way to make sluggish applications look fast was to spin off background tasks to separate threads. Multi-threading on the server is much tougher duty. Since we won't be working at a low-level of programming, we won't have to worry about using threads to improve perceived performance (though we do mention threads when we discuss SAX below). We will, however, see how to improve client-side perceived performance by working the user interface. This chapter contains several suggestions for doing this high-performance user interface work.

Real client-side performance can be enhanced by caching XML data on the server, such as if you are using ASP in Application Scope, for example. However, this comes at the price of reduced scalability. This XML data can be run-time data, schema data, or even the XML data that makes up XSLT transforms. It's situations like this that motivated the Microsoft XML team to add innovations like the `SchemaCache` and `XSLTemplate` classes to the XML parser. This chapter will show these real performance/scale enhancers in action.

So, get ready. In this chapter we'll also see how to improve perceived and real performance of XML-based applications. Specifically, we'll see how to:

❑ Use the Model-View-Controller design framework to make user interfaces sparkle.

❑ Use the fastest techniques for creating and loading XML DOMDocuments.

❑ Make XSLT transforms work as fast as possible.

❑ Get big returns from little changes, such as wisely choosing tag and attribute names, using delimited strings in node values, and taking maximum advantage of the operating system and your XML applications' host program.

❑ Exploit streams, a streaming API, and threads.

❑ Exploit upgrades from MSXML 3 to MSXML 4, and take advantage of managed XML (the `System.Xml` classes in the .NET frameworks).

❑ Make applications appear faster by using a very granular design framework.

When we're done with this section we'll see how paying close attention to the client actually improves server-side performance (the server saves the cycles from repeated parsing and compiling of XML data), and enables both better server-side scaling *and* better client-side performance. If only the rest of the programmer's three-body problems were so easy to solve!

Before delving into the technical details, I need to advocate a little architect's aid I've found very helpful: the "performance budget." In the next section I'll tell you why I think this budget is important, and in the "*Test, Test, Test*" section you'll see what counters I use to create the budget, the arithmetic I use to measure performance, and the application I run to gather performance data.

A Performance Budget

As we'll see throughout this chapter, there are many places where we can gain and also lose performance. One way to ensure optimal performance is to approach your design the way you approach your paycheck or your portfolio. If you create a budget that's flexible, you always know where the money is going each month – and where it's not. This way, when you have an unexpected need in one category you can take the money from a category with a positive variance; on balance, you stay even.

If you analyze and test your application carefully and you prepare a performance budget based on the results, you should have a good idea of how many users your application will support. For example, if you use a web stress tool (such as Application Center Test, as I elaborate below) you can increase the number of "users" programmatically until the time to first byte and time to last byte exceed some threshold; such as, fifteen seconds. In other words, you keep increasing the number in the connections property of your ACT test (in the property sheet at the lower right corner of the figure below) until the "Avg Time to Last Byte" measurement (see the test results window in the figure below) gets to 15,000. At this point your application is taking a whole fifteen seconds to respond to users, and we all know that fifteen seconds is now the limit of human patience.

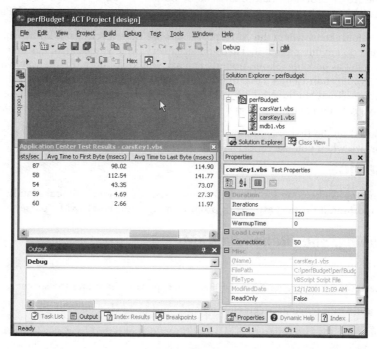

After deployment and after you review your web logs you can compare the actual number of users and you should (hopefully) see excess capacity (if not, see the *Scale Up/Scale Out/Scale Down* section below). This excess is your "performance savings account". That is, you can save the capacity so it's available later when your site becomes even more popular. Alternatively, you can use the capacity and spend the excess performance on more features or different architectures that are easier to implement, but less efficient. So take the time to assess how much power is latent in your design, and spend it, when you must, wisely.

Depending on the kinds of applications you're writing you will have some performance rigidities. For example, if you're writing document-centric XML applications such as a news service that handles news stories in some XML schema, you may have large instance XML files with node names infrequently used. This is one of the characteristics of document data (sometimes called semi-structured data). It's like the weather in the sense that you can anticipate it, but you can't control it. Given the way MSXML atomizes names (a feature that is explicit in managed XML when you use "Name Tables" in the System.Xml .NET classes), every instance of the same tag refers to a single object in memory; so a large file on the hard drive may be much smaller in memory. Data-centric files such as those generated by ADO enjoy this efficiency because elements like <row> are repeated frequently. Document-centric files like those news stories, on the other hand, may have lots of names used once or twice. With those news story files you lose this naming efficiency and your working set becomes larger than it would be with structured data.

Another consideration appears outside the context of performance rigidities. For example, besides having to deal with performance rigidities like infrequently used names, sometimes an innovation comes along that, by itself, might impose a performance hit, but in the context of a performance budget where we can "buy" cycles by being extra careful, the advantages of the innovation become a net increase in application effectiveness.

So, to keep your budget in balance, you go looking for other areas that can "pay" for this rigidity. You start, of course, with smaller tag names; if you're relying heavily on XSLT, you may switch from attribute normal form (such as default ADO) to element normal form (because all attributes are collected by the XSLT processor before any can be output). Even if you don't rely on XSLT, element normal form can be up to ten times faster than attribute normal form when using XPath.

The point is two-fold: know where the XML processors use more cycles, and know where your applications can't do anything about it. Then squeeze every cycle you can from as many places in your performance budget as possible. Shoot, nobody can ask you to do more. By the way, your "performance spreadsheet" is Application Center Test. In the *Test, Test, Test* section below, where I discuss this important tool (now a part of Visual Studio .NET), I will show you a performance metric that tells you just how many CPU cycles any given design costs you, and how many cycles you can save by changing little things.

So, let's get started on the first assignment in creating your performance budget. Let's see where you can save a cycle or two when you use `msxml4.dll`.

Back to Basics

Good programming is like good football and economics. It's based on fundamentals. This section reviews the important, if prosaic, aspects of programming with the MSXML parser.

Creating, Cloning, and (Re)loading XML

This section will show you:

- ❑ The fastest ways to create XML DOM objects on the client and the server
- ❑ The subtle difference between cloning and reusing XML data
- ❑ When to use the two different XML load functions exposed by `msxml4.dll`

Many applications that use XML start by instantiating an XML DOM and loading the DOM with data. Most programmers create XML DOMs using the standard COM-based methods: new `ActiveXObject()` in JScript and `CreateObject()` in VBScript. What's overlooked is that since the `msxml2.domdocument` is a COM component, developers can save cycles by minimizing COM overhead. These saved cycles add performance on the client and scale on the server. The trick is to create the first `domdocument` then call the `cloneNode()` method on that `domdocument` to create any other. Further details follow later in this section.

Incidentally, most ASP programmers create `domdocument` objects with the ASP function, `Server.CreateObject()`. This ASP function is not the `CreateObject()` method of VBScript and is different, of course, from the new `ActiveXObject()` of JScript. Unless the created object will be used with MTS and needs access to ASP intrinsics, using the `Server` object's `CreateObject()` method adds overhead to the object creation and maintenance. ASP programmers should generally use the simpler VBScript method, `CreateObject()`. Actually, ASP programmers should declare server-side objects using the `<OBJECT>` tag (instead of any of the script-based invocations) and should select the correct threading model and scope. Though we'll return to this again in the *Scalability* section, here's an example of using the `<OBJECT>` tag in `global.asa`:

```
<OBJECT
    ID="xmlRepository"
    SCOPE="APPLICATION"
    PROGID="MSXML2.FreeThreadedDOMDocument.4.0"
    RUNAT="SERVER" >
</OBJECT>
```

The reason we're using `<OBJECT>` tags like the one above is that the object becomes part of the `StaticObjects` collection, and the object doesn't get created until it's first used. Also, the only way to create an object for Application scope is the `<OBJECT>` tag. Objects created with `Server.CreateObject()` will raise an error if you try to give them Application scope, and as we'll see, if we can't get an object to Application scope, both performance and scalability on the server suffer.

At any rate, the only XML DOM that should be created with COM is the first one. All the rest should be clones of this seminal DOM. Here's an example that's explained in detail in just a moment:

```
var xml = new ActiveXObject("msxml2.domdocument.4.0");
xml.setProperty("SelectionLanguage","XPath");
xml.async=false;
xml.validateOnParse=false;
xml.load("testCases.xml");
var xmlClone=xml.cloneNode(true);
```

Using this `cloneNode()` trick also ensures that you never mix versions of MSXML. If you do forget to clone everything, and if you have an XML DOM based on both versions 3 and 4 of MSXML, you'll raise an error that doesn't point to the ultimate source of the problem, such as "The parameter is incorrect". When used with some related techniques, which we'll come onto later, this `cloneNode()` technique also makes upgrading your applications easier and safer.

A final point about cloning is that it saves typing (and parsing by the parser). That is, you really need at least four lines of code to instantiate an XML DOM in MSXML 3 and five lines with MSXML 4. So why keep typing these four or five lines each time you need a DOM? Each cloned DOM inherits all the properties of the seminal DOM. We'll cover these four or five lines of code in the *MSXML 4 Versus MSXML 3* section below.

Before getting into the code, there are two more fine points to consider in creating and using XML objects in code.

A Poor Man's SOAP

Besides the XML DOM, the second most popular objects are the `XMLHTTP` and the `ServerXMLHTTP` classes. I refer to these objects as a "poor man's SOAP". These objects permit XML messages to move from the client to the server and back again, or between two servers. When you use these two objects you tend to use them all through your application. So, instead of creating lots of page-level `XMLHTTP` objects, create them globally, and create a global XML DOM to use as the message payload. On the server, create the Application-scoped objects in `global.asa` with the `<OBJECT>` tag, like this:

```
<OBJECT
    ID="xmlHTTP"
    SCOPE="APPLICATION"
    PROGID="MSXML2.XMLHTTP.4.0"
    RUNAT="SERVER" >
</OBJECT>
```

```
<OBJECT
   ID="xmlPayload"
   SCOPE="APPLICATION"
   PROGID="MSXML2.DOMDocument.4.0"
   RUNAT="SERVER" >
</OBJECT>
<SCRIPT LANGUAGE=VBScript RUNAT=Server>
Sub Application_OnStart
   'set the properties of the payload used by xmlHTTP
   xmlPayload.setProperty("SelectionLanguage","XPath");
   xmlPayload.async=false;
   xmlPayload.validateOnParse=false;
End Sub
</SCRIPT>
```

Class-based XML

My second suggestion is to create script classes based on XML DOM objects. Simply expose your XML to functions in your applications through a class-based mechanism. This way you can do all your `selectSingleNode()` and `selectNodes()` functions in one place and handle any unexpected problems before dependent functions attempt to get their hands on the data.

Since, like C#, everything's an object in JScript, I tend to use JScript for object-oriented scripting. I'll explain each function from an example program that encapsulates an XML file into a class with specific properties exposing the underlying XML data.

This example (`classBasedXML.htm`) loads an XML document (`testCases.xml`) and gathers information from it using `selectNode()` and `selectSingleNode()`, which are given in this class that we are about to look at. The beginning of the program is self-evident:

```
<!DOCTYPE HTML PUBLIC "-//W3C//DTD HTML 4.0 Transitional//EN">
<html>
   <head>
   <title>Class-based XML Data Access</title>
   <script language="javascript">
   <!--
      window.onload=init;
```

The `init()` function creates an instance of the CXML class, then displays the properties of the XML-based object. Note that the token-oriented properties are taken at face value (we'll return to these two properties next). The `hlpn.xml` and `hlpn.holdingPlaces` references, on the other hand, are XML DOMDocument properties passed on through the class. Note that you're responsible for properly using the nodelist reference, a duty assumed by the class, as we'll examine next.

```
      function init()
      {
         var hlpn                    = new CXML();
         divXml.innerText            = hlpn.xml;
         divPlaces.innerText         = hlpn.places.length;
         divExtMailToken.innerText   = hlpn.extMailToken;
         divIntMailToken.innerText   = hlpn.intMailToken;
         var nod                     = hlpn.holdingPlaces[0];
         divHoldingPlaces.innerText  = nod?nod.text:"no holding place";
      }
```

The CXML() class function is the single place the testCases.xml file would be loaded in an application such as the current sample. This simple sample only references this data once, but industrial grade applications can make references to sub-trees many times in several different places. Many programmers repeat selectSingleNode() calls in those different places, and depending on the size of the XML, they're wasting a good many CPU cycles. In addition, if the XML file's schema should change, you have to search your entire application for any place where the data signature of a node selection call might need editing. When everything is in one class, maintainability and efficiency are as high as they can be.

The first part of this class uses the best practices regarding creation of an XML DOMDocument. Firstly, we ensure that it is created using the version-specific ProgIDs (MSXML2.DOMDocument.4.0). Then we set the correct SelectionLanguage property as being XPath. This allows the class to be upgraded from version 3 to version 4 without problems, though we could have encountered a problem because rather than XPath, version 3 used the old XSL Pattern language, which is deprecated in version 4.

```
function CXML()
{
    var xmlDOM   = new ActiveXObject("MSXML2.DOMDocument.4.0");
    xmlDOM.async = false;
    xmlDOM.setProperty("SelectionLanguage","XPath");
    xmlDOM.load("testCases.xml");
```

The next part of this function exposes nodelists and single nodes as public properties. Here's where the class ensures that the token-oriented properties always have some kind of text. These properties expose the xml property of the selected node. No other property exposed by the underlying XML is available to the class's client.

```
    this.xml           = xmlDOM.xml
    this.places        = xmlDOM.selectNodes("pnml/net/place");
    this.holdingPlaces = xmlDOM.selectNodes("pnml/net/place[token]");
    var nod            = xmlDOM.selectSingleNode("pnml/
                         net/place/token[n='externalMail']")
    this.extMailToken  = nod?nod.xml:"no external mail token";
    var nod            = xmlDOM.selectSingleNode("pnml/
                         net/place/token[n='internalMail']")
    this.intMailToken  = nod?nod.xml:"no internal mail token";
}
```

Again, the remainder of this program is self-explanatory.

```
        //-->
        </script>
        </head>
        <body>
            <p>
                <b>Number of places:</b>
                <div id="divPlaces"></div>
            </p>
            <p>
                <b>Text of first holding place:</b>
                <div id="divHoldingPlaces"></div>
            </p>
            <p>
```

```
            <b>External Mail Token:</b>
            <div id="divExtMailToken"></div>
        </p>
        <p>
            <b>Internal Mail Token:</b>
            <div id="divIntMailToken"></div>
        </p>
        <p>
            <b>XML of object:</b>
            <div id="divXml"></div>
        </p>
    </body>
</html>
```

Here's what that program produces:

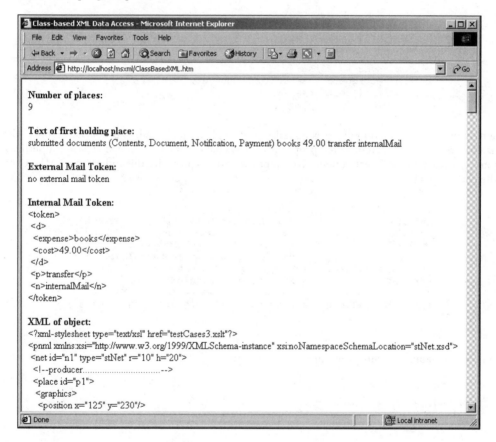

Here is the complete content of `ClassBasedXML.htm`:

```
<!DOCTYPE HTML PUBLIC "-//W3C//DTD HTML 4.0 Transitional//EN">
<html>
    <head>
    <title>Class-based XML Data Access</title>
    <script language="javascript">
```

```
<!--
    window.onload=init;

    function init()
    {
        var hlpn                    = new CXML();
        divXml.innerText            = hlpn.xml;
        divPlaces.innerText         = hlpn.places.length;
        divExtMailToken.innerText   = hlpn.extMailToken;
        divIntMailToken.innerText   = hlpn.intMailToken;
        var nod                     = hlpn.holdingPlaces[0];
        divHoldingPlaces.innerText  = nod?nod.text:"no holding place";
    }

    function CXML()
    {
        var xmlDOM    = new ActiveXObject("MSXML2.DOMDocument.4.0");
        xmlDOM.async  = false;
        xmlDOM.setProperty("SelectionLanguage","XPath");
        xmlDOM.load("testCases.xml");

        this.xml            = xmlDOM.xml
        this.places         = xmlDOM.selectNodes("pnml/net/place");
        this.holdingPlaces  = xmlDOM.selectNodes("pnml/net/place[token]");
        var nod             = xmlDOM.selectSingleNode("pnml/
                                net/place/token[n='externalMail']")
        this.extMailToken   = nod?nod.xml:"no external mail token";
        var nod             = xmlDOM.selectSingleNode("pnml/
                                net/place/token[n='internalMail']")
        this.intMailToken   = nod?nod.xml:"no internal mail token";
    }

//-->
</script>
</head>
<body MS_POSITIONING="GridLayout">
    <p>
        <b>Number of places:</b>
        <div id="divPlaces"></div>
    </p>
    <p>
        <b>Text of first holding place:</b>
        <div id="divHoldingPlaces"></div>
    </p>
    <p>
        <b>External Mail Token:</b>
        <div id="divExtMailToken"></div>
    </p>
    <p>
        <b>Internal Mail Token:</b>
        <div id="divIntMailToken"></div>
    </p>
    <p>
        <b>XML of object:</b>
        <div id="divXml"></div>
    </p>
</body>
</html>
```

Cloning versus Reusing XML

Again, let's begin with a few definitions. In this chapter, **cloned XML** is different from **reused XML** in one of two ways.

❑ An XML DOM can be cloned without data, whereas by definition, reused XML includes data.

❑ Cloned XML is precisely the same as the original XML; reused XML can be the same content, but can be validated against a different schema, potentially returning a validation error.

Cloned data can also come in two varieties.

❑ A cache of XML that is independent of the original, and an exact copy.

❑ A less common type of clone is one where the same XML DOM is accessed by different memory variables. Technically, this isn't a clone (it's an alias), but it's close enough to a clone that we'll continue to refer to it as such.

How to Clone or Reload XML

There are three ways to clone. The first two use the XML DOM's `cloneNode()` method. You clone only the DOM (without any data) using a call to `xmldom.cloneNode(false)`; and you create a fully populated clone with `xmldom.cloneNode(true)`.

To create the second type of clone, simply assign an XML DOM variable reference to a second, and different variable. If you change any node of the original, the corresponding nodes of the other XML DOM will change in the same way. For cloned copies of XML, the two values of the same node are independent. Let's look at the code in its constituent parts – the full code sample is displayed in a moment.

```
// create the first xml dom using COM
var xml = new ActiveXObject("msxml2.domdocument.4.0");
xml.setProperty("SelectionLanguage","XPath");
xml.async=false;
xml.validateOnParse=false;
xml.load("testCases.xml");

// create a complete copy of the xml - but skip COM
var xmlClone=xml.cloneNode(true);

// create a second reference to the original xml
var xml2=xml;

// create a third xml dom skipping COM and the data
var xmlReused=xml.cloneNode(false);

// this time, validate the same xml file during load
xmlReused.validateOnParse=true;
xmlReused.load(xml);
```

Reloading XML also has two XML DOM methods – `xmldom.load()` and `xmldom.loadXML()`. The `load()` method is much more efficient than `loadXML()` because `load()` does not require the entire XML representation to be in memory before parsing can even be started. With `load()`, parsing and writing out the XML happens in one function call. In addition, `loadXML()` has to manage the XML property of the host XML DOM, and that property uses the `BSTR` data type, (a data type that is especially CPU intensive).

```
// again, clone an empty xml dom
var xmlMsg= xml.cloneNode(false);

// but this time load the dom with a string of xml instead of a file
xmlMsg.loadXML("<msg/>");
var xmlMsg2= xml.cloneNode(false);
xmlMsg2.loadXML("<msg " + "date='" +new Date()+ "'/>");
```

When to loadXML() and When to load() XML

There are times when you need loadXML(), but those times usually don't exact a performance hit. I use loadXML() when I need to create an XML DOM with minimal data. Most frequently, this is when I need to create an XML DOM for a call to xmlhttp. The sample code above shows a typical example of this use. It also shows how simply enabling validation can change the outcome of loading the same XML data. A more common scenario is loading XML with different schemas, as we'll see later in the *Schema-based Security: XML Firewalls* section when we'll look at how to use the schemaCache object to effect some level of data security.

Examples of Cloning and Reusing XML

To put this all in perspective, here's the complete sample source code. Notice that by changing the value of the second XML DOM reference, the xml2 variable, we change the original XML DOM. This is because both variables point to the same address in memory.

The following source code is in the ClonedAndReusedXML.htm file:

```
<html>
<head>
<title></title>
<script language=javascript>
    var xml = new ActiveXObject("msxml2.domdocument.4.0");
    xml.setProperty("SelectionLanguage","XPath");
    xml.async=false;
    xml.validateOnParse=false;
    xml.load("testCases.xml");

    var xmlClone=xml.cloneNode(true);

    var xml2=xml;

    var xmlReused=xml.cloneNode(false);
    xmlReused.validateOnParse=true;
    xmlReused.load(xml);

    var xmlMsg= xml.cloneNode(false);
    xmlMsg.loadXML("<msg/>");
    var xmlMsg2= xml.cloneNode(false);
    xmlMsg2.loadXML("<msg " + "date='" +new Date()+ "'/>");

    window.onload=init;

    function init()
{
    var nod=xml.selectSingleNode("pnml/net/place[1]/name");
    var nod2=xml2.selectSingleNode("pnml/net/place[1]/name");

    var nodClone=xmlClone.selectSingleNode("pnml/net/place[1]/name");
    nodClone.text="checked documents"
    cloneTest.innerHTML="Clone's value: <b>"+nodClone.text.fontcolor("red")+
"</b><br/>Original value: <b>"+nod.text+
```

```
"</b><br/>Reference value: <b>"+nod2.text+"</b>";

    nod2.text="discarded documents"
    refTest.innerHTML="Referenced value: <b>"+nod2.text.fontcolor("red")+
"</b><br/>Original value: <b>"+nod.text.fontcolor("red")+
"</b><br/>Cloned value: <b>"+nodClone.text+"</b>";

    reuseTest.innerHTML="<b>xmlReused failed to load.</b><br/>".fontcolor("red")+
xmlReused.parseError.reason

    xmlMsgTest.innerText=xmlMsg.xml+"\nor\n\n"+xmlMsg2.xml
}
</script>

</head>

<body style="font-family:verdana">

<h3>Changing value of clone does not affect original or reference xml doms:</h3>
<div id="cloneTest"></div>
<p> </p>
<h3>But changing the reference node's value does change the original:</h3>
<div id="refTest"></div>
<p> </p>
<h3>Reloading permits you to validate previously unvalidated xml data:</h3>
<div id="reuseTest"></div>

<p> </p>
<h3>Here's some xml data that's created at runtime:</h3>
<div id="xmlMsgTest"></div>

</body>
</html>
```

Here's the output that the file produces:

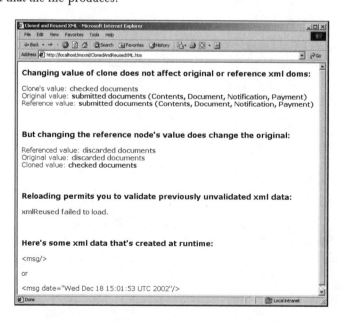

Fast XSLT

Microsoft changed the full name of `msxml4.dll` from the "Microsoft XML Parser" to "Microsoft XML Core Services" because `msxml4.dll` was the first product to ship W3C-compliant XML services far beyond mere parsing. Even though `msxml3.dll` shipped with a W3C-compliant XSLT processor, it still contained vestiges of a by-gone era of technology previews. With that in mind, I include XSLT tips and tricks in this performance chapter. Specifically, this XSLT section covers:

❑ The reason XSLT keys may be faster than XPath alone.

❑ How script eats up performance and how to avoid or minimize the impact.

❑ An easy-to-use operator you should almost never use (and what to use instead).

❑ Matryoshka variables (pronounced ma-trosh-ka).

❑ Just-In-Time Data and variables that have the single greatest impact on perceived performance for applications that render XML through XSLT.

The Key to Performance

There are three ways to get your hands on XML data while processing it in an XSLT transform:

❑ The most common is to simply evaluate an XPath expression.

❑ The second most common way is by assigning an XPath expression result to a variable and referencing that variable (instead of re-evaluating the XPath expression) in other parts of the transform.

❑ The least known/used way to use data is with the `key` element and `key()` function.

From time to time in this chapter, I mention a big 400-line transform I use at work. I'll talk about one way of implementing the grouping mechanism in the transform using Matryoshka variables in a moment. But first, here's how I can use keys to group the data in the transform. The following transform's forty lines of code replace almost 120 lines of code in the original transform.

Cutting the number of lines of code by two-thirds should have a measurable impact on performance, and early tests suggest the keyed approach listed below is 300% faster than the original version using Matryoshka variables. The first screenshot shows the test results of the variable-based design: a mere 0.2 Requests per Second. The second screenshot shows the key-based design comes in at 0.8 Requests per Second. Keep in mind that these two XSLT transforms are utility programs that don't interact with users, so nominal speed is not the issue: comparative speed is, and from the evidence in the application at hand, keys wins hands down.

Application Center Test Results – testKeyWithVar.vbs

Total Run Time	Total Iterations	Total Requests	Connections	Avg Requests/sec	Avg Time to First Byte (msecs)	Avg Time to Last Byte (msecs)
00:00:05:00	40	70	10	0.2	32,497.27	32,497.70

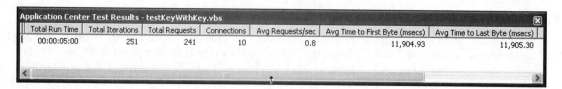

Total Run Time	Total Iterations	Total Requests	Connections	Avg Requests/sec	Avg Time to First Byte (msecs)	Avg Time to Last Byte (msecs)
00:00:05:00	251	241	10	0.8	11,904.93	11,905.30

These results are still provisional because the two versions don't yet produce absolutely the same output, but the outputs are darn close, and I don't expect a material change in the results of the `"testKeyWithKey"` test. Due to space limitations, we won't cover the code in the key-based transform below.

```xml
<xsl:stylesheet xmlns:xsl="http://www.w3.org/1999/XSL/Transform"
    version="1.0">
<xsl:output method="xml" indent="yes"/>

<xsl:key name="paths" match="problem" use="path"/>
<xsl:key name="pathFiles" match="problem" use="concat(path,file)"/>
<xsl:key name="pathFileProbids" match="problem"
      use="concat(path,file,probId)"/>
<xsl:key name="pathFileProbdescs" match="problem"
      use="concat(path,file,probDesc)"/>
<xsl:key name="pathFileContexts" match="problem"
      use="concat(path,file,context)"/>

<xsl:template match="/root" >
    <xmp>
    <product>
    <xsl:for-each select="problem[count(.| key('paths', path)[1])=1]">
       <folder>
       <name><xsl:value-of select="path" /></name>
       <xsl:for-each select="key('paths', path)[count(.| key('pathFiles',
           concat(path,file))[1])=1]">
       <file>
          <name><xsl:value-of select="file" /></name>
          <xsl:for-each select="key('pathFiles', concat(path,file))[count(.|
             key('pathFileProbids', concat(path,file,probId))[1])=1]">
          <problem>
             <id><xsl:value-of select="probId" /></id>
             <xsl:for-each select="key('pathFileProbids',
               concat(path,file,probId))[count(.| key('pathFileProbdescs',
               concat(path,file,probDesc))[1])=1]">
             <descrip><xsl:value-of select="probDesc" /></descrip>
             <context>
                <xsl:for-each select="key('pathFileProbdescs',
                     concat(path,file,probDesc))">
                <code><xsl:value-of select="context"/></code>
                </xsl:for-each>
             </context>
             </xsl:for-each>
          </problem>
          </xsl:for-each>
       </file>
       </xsl:for-each>
    </folder>
    </xsl:for-each>
    </product>
    </xmp>
</xsl:template>
</xsl:stylesheet>
```

Andrew Kimball, the Microsoft Developer who wrote the XSLT processor, has the following advice for when to use keys.

Using XPath expressions means that results of the query have to be recomputed each time. If the expression is evaluated only once, then using an XPath expression will always be faster than caching the result using variables or building an index using keys. If the same expression may be evaluated multiple times, then it's usually better to cache the result in a variable (global or local). However, if the expression is simple enough, the overhead of caching results might outweigh simply recomputing the result each time. If similar (but not exactly the same) expressions appear multiple times in the stylesheet, then using keys will usually be faster. Let's consider the example below:

```
//foo/bar[@id = 'val']
```

If this expression will only be evaluated once, just inline it in the stylesheet. If it appears multiple times, or appears within a loop (an explicit for-each loop or an implicit loop, such as an XPath predicate), then cache the result using a variable. If several variations of the expression exist, as in the code snippet below, then keys are probably best:

```
//foo/bar[@id = 'val2']
//foo/bar[@id = 'val3']
```

Keys are associated with input documents, not the stylesheet document. Therefore, caching the stylesheet doesn't affect the operation of keys. Remember that these are rules of thumb. No simple rule can replace specific scenario performance measurements.

No Scripts

Perhaps the biggest black hole of performance in XSLT is resorting to script. In the native world of MSXML, interpreted scripting engines still require too many CPU cycles to be used imprudently.

Considering the design constraints of the XSLT language and the increasingly broad range of applications that can exploit XSLT, it is inevitable that at some point you'll have to resort to script. When you do, ensure (if possible) that you assign the results of script to an XSL variable, and then use the variable's value (as an alternative to calling the script more than once). You only take the performance hit for script one time using this technique. Once the scripted fetch of data gets into an XSLT variable, the rest of the transform can use the data without any further calls to the scripting engine.

If you take the "limitations" of XSLT at face value you can often shortchange your transform. For instance, it is widely known that if you sum a nodelist that contains null values or values that cannot be coerced into numbers, the XPath sum() function returns a useless "NaN" result. This happened to me a year or two ago when I was building a version of my so-called "polymorphic XML spreadsheet" for the 1999 Wrox Web Developers Conference.

> *This is documented extensively in the "Performance" chapter of "Professional XSL" (ISBN 1-861003-57-9, Wrox Press) and you can also find out more at* http://www.topxml.com/conference/wrox/1999_dc/text/mikexml1.asp.

During a code review I learned that by filtering out those errant values, sum() would indeed return the correct result and I could finally jettison the last remaining script from my transform. So, use a [string(number(.))!="NaN"] predicate when using sum().

Here's an example of the technique:

```
<xsl:call-template name="displayValue">
    <xsl:with-param
        name="val"
        select=
            "sum($rows/@*[name()=current()/@name]
            [string(number(.))!='NaN'])"
    />
    <xsl:with-param name="dt" select="s:datatype/@dt:type"/>
</xsl:call-template>
```

Be Explicit

Another very common trap that saps a transform's power is the "recursive descent from root" operator (in XPath this is written as //). The recursive descent operator is necessary in semi-structured data when you cannot know at design time what a given node's ancestors will be. In structured data, // is rarely required at all, unless you're lazy and want to delegate the typing of a long data signature to the XSLT processor. So, to avoid this pitfall, express yourself fully by describing the complete path down to the node you want.

There are two related tricks if you do lots of work deep down in the tree. The first is the more powerful cousin of //, and that's the "recursive descent from here" operator. The // operator starts from the top of the XML tree and iterates the entire tree looking for all the nodes you want, even if you know there is only one. Alternatively, .// (notice the period before the // operator) will only start from the current context, but it will still search for all instances of the node you're looking for. Next, let's take a look at the second trick, Matryoshka variables.

Use Matryoshka Variables

If you have complex trees, and especially if your XSLT is highly abstract, you can get incredible performance improvements by using what I call **Matryoshka variables**. Matryoshka is the Russian word for "little mother", referring to those nesting dolls that start with Mom and go all the way down to baby sister. Anyway, in XSLT you can nest variables, creating new sub-trees from the root of previous sub-trees.

Matryoshka variables improve parsing efficiency because the amount of data the processor must traverse is constrained. Matryoshka variables improve programming efficiency because you can group your data into logically related islands, then combine these islands into archipelagoes of programs. A good example of the parsing efficiency comes from my direct personal experience. By using them, my transform went from burning up megabytes of virtual memory without completing its task to transforming multi-megabyte XML data in a matter of minutes.

First, let's look at how not to use variables (so that we can revisit the problem and take advantage of Matryoshka variables) – this is the way I used them myself, when my transform burned cycles like it was flushing a toilet. Each of these variables is defined as if they were independent of each other, even though they're not. Each variable is correct, but the process to define them is hideously inefficient, (especially on large node-sets) because **each** variable definition causes the XSLT parser to re-evaluate the **entire** tree.

```
<xsl:variable
    name="fileGroup"
    select="msxsl:node-set($root)/root/problem[path=$pathName]/file"
/>

<xsl:variable
```

```
     name="problemGroup"
     select="msxsl:node-set($root)/root/problem[path=$pathName]
             [file=$fileName]/probId"
  />

  <xsl:variable
     name="lineGroup"
     select="msxsl:node-set($root)/root/problem[path=$pathName]
             [file=$fileName][probId=$probId]
             [context=$contextName]/line"
  />
```

Now let's see a better way of using variables. Matryoshka variables enabled the transform to process all 5,000 nodes in about 15 seconds with no virtual memory used (instead of crashing in six minutes and consuming over 4Mb of VM).

The first transform is similar to the one above, but the `fileGroup` and `fileProblems` variables are derived separately below:

```
<xsl:variable
   name="problems"
   select="msxsl:node-set($root)/root/problem[path=$pathName]"
/>
<xsl:variable
   name="fileGroup"
 select="$problems/file"
/>
<xsl:variable
   name="fileProblems"
   select="$problems[file=$fileName]"
/>
```

So, the `fileProblems` variable is the base variable for the `problemIDs` variable...

```
<xsl:variable
   name="problemIDs"
   select="$fileProblems[probId=$probId]"
/>
```

...and the `problemIDs` variable is the base variable for the `thisContext` variable:

```
<xsl:variable
   name="thisContext"
   select="$problemIDs[context=$contextName]"
/>
```

Another good example of programming efficiency is my "High-Level Petri Net simulator", introduced in "Professional XSL" and thoroughly documented in my "Confessions of an XSLT Bigot" column in the "XML Developer" newsletter from Pinnacle Publishing and also available from http://www.xmldevelopernewsletter.com.

Exploit Just-In-Time Data

There are two ways to exploit JIT data. One is to get XML data into XSL variables in just the right amount at just the right time (meaning a screen full just before the user needs to see the page). The second way is to filter the screen-full of data, not the entire data set. In the first variable below, the `filteredRows` is used to create a distinct list of nodes. This list, the `distinctTree` variable, is then used in the second variable, `pk`. The third variable, `rowRange`, also uses the same just-in-time data that filled `filteredRows` with nodes. When these variables operate on very large XML files, only a subset of that data is actually processed. The first subset is a screen-full of data; namely, rows whose position is within an upper and lower bound, usually ten to twenty (out of thousands) rows. The second set of JIT data is based on this first – instead of making a distinct node-list from tens of thousands of nodes, the list is derived from ten to twenty.

So, the point of just-in-time data is to treat only the minimal amount of data at any one time; this way your application behaves as if it were small, even though it's huge. Generally, the user gets to tell the application what minimal is, and generally, that's specified by the number of records to display. Some readers prefer to scroll up and down using the elevator. I, personally, prefer to see all my data in one screen then use VCR buttons to move forward or back one screen full of data (or go to the beginning or end of the data).

```
<xsl:variable name="filteredRows" select="$rows[position() >= $lowerBound
    and position() < $upperBound]" />

<xsl:variable name="pk" select="msxsl:node-set($distinctTree)/distinct/*" />
<xsl:variable name="rowRange" select="$rows[position() >= $lowerBound and
    position() < $upperBound]" />
```

Optimize Tags:Text Ratio

The MSXML components have always been more sensitive to the number nodes than to the size of the data. This isn't surprising since each node is a comparatively complex object. However, there are other, even subtler issues to consider. Two of the most interesting are the frequency of tags with the same name and the ratio of tags to text. When MSXML parses an XML file it uses a single reference in memory for every element or attribute with the same name. This helps performance and minimizes the working set, unless you have a document with lots of unique tag names.

For XSLT, there's another interesting variable – the number of attributes. According to the XSLT Recommendation, all attributes must be loaded into memory before processing can begin on any of them. So, files with lots of long-named attributes are going to be a little harder for the parser to digest. In other words, the fewer attributes in the file, the faster the parser can start using them.

Backing Off

Sometimes a very simple and very significant performance improvement comes from going backwards. To illustrate what this means, consider the following three techniques:

❑ Present scalars as strings. For example, to reduce the number of tags and not lose any data, use a single node with delimited text, and then let the script engine's split() method separate the text in the node into an array. So, for example, instead of creating separate elements with simple scalar values (such as integers), just store all the integers in a space-delimited string value for a single node. Then, when your script or program uses the XML file, you can use the split() method to expand the string into separate elements of an array for further processing. Note that you should not (and should not have to) use script in an XSLT file. This trick is only intended for use in the XML file's host application.

Here's a good example of the trick in action: Years ago I upgraded and extended some old GWBasic programs Edgar Peters wrote for his book, *Chaos and Order in the Capital Markets*, John Wiley & Sons, 1991. These (now) VB 5 programs need another overhaul to VB .Net. The managed code versions of these programs will be web services, so users will send data up to the server using SOAP (originally the data files were simple text). Instead of having an XML element for each data element (and for Rescaled Range analysis you need tens of thousands of data points to get reliable results), the data stream will arrive in the SOAP message as a single node of comma-delimited text. Once inside the web service, this node will become an array with a single line of code (where DataPoints is the text value of the node in the SOAP payload that contains the comma-delimited string of values):

```
DataPointArray = DataPoints.Split(",");
```

The Lord willing, by the time you read this you should be able to see this code in action from the web service at http://aspalliance.com/mcorning/fma/.

Some developers may cringe at the thought of subverting XML like this, but it's really not subversion at all. It's a good example of creative use of text values normally stored in nodes. This approach has a measurable and positive affect on performance.

❑ Be a good host. I learned an important lesson last year – at work I do most of my XML programming with Word as my host. Some of my documents have tables that get populated at load time. My original design used the Word API to manipulate Word's table object. I didn't like the fact that manipulating a Word table's rows and columns directly was so slow that you could actually watch the table being built as the document loaded; it made the application literally look slow. Then I realized that I could use XSLT to convert the XML data (which I was using to plop into individual cells in the emerging Word table) into a comma-delimited text stream and pass that text to Word's table creation function. Word can create a table from text with blazing speed, and I never saw a table created (slowly) again; they just appeared in the document like Aphrodite rising from the sea fully formed!

❑ Use **XCopy** instead of HTTP. If your application works with multi-megabyte XML files from a remote share (as one of mine does at work), you can optimize file loads by using the operating system to copy the document to the machine where you host your application. The marginal gain here is that you save the overhead of streaming data across the wire in packets. Instead, you get the file across the wire in the fastest way possible. Keep in mind that I am not advocating this technique for applications whose users are outside the firewall; this is an intranet/distributed application scenario I have in mind here. My application at work, for example, grabs a multi-megabyte XML file from a colleague's application, and creates and then transforms its schema while merging its contents with the gigantic XML repository my application maintains. Since my colleague and I trust each other and we work for the same boss, we don't have any security issues to worry about. Besides, it was my boss who suggested I use XCopy instead of HTTP.

589

Test, Test, Test

Microsoft Application Center Test (ACT) is an indispensable tool (a developer version is available as part of Visual Studio .NET, and a more powerful version of ACT will ship with the Enterprise version of Application Center 2000) for the performance-obsessed architect. Indeed, the whole tool has been designed to enable developers to test their code *before* the code goes into production.

The key to using this tool with MSXML is to host your applications in ASP, even if they will ultimately be run from the client. In other words, while you're building your performance budget you will use ASP exclusively. You're not really building your system at this stage, you're assessing your various design options and looking to conserve every cycle you can.

When you use a performance budget to formulate design strategies, don't just compare one technique to another. Start by testing a single technique for scalability. In other words, for your first design, test it with one, ten, and one hundred users. Then repeat the process with your other design options. You may find some surprises when you compare two techniques at different levels of stress. Also, if you follow the best practice of using version-specific ProgIDs to create your MSXML objects you can add a dimension to your research by repeating the process using different versions of MSXML.

You may find that this extra dimension has value only the first time it's used – `msxml4.dll` is probably measurably faster than `msxml3.dll` in all applications. If your tests show this, then you can just standardize on MSXML 4 (or later). Regardless, setting up your laboratory to quickly and safely upgrade your XML Core Services will ensure that as the XML team continues to outdo itself, you will not only have the empirical evidence to justify the migration, but you'll also have a measure of the extra cycles that the latest version of MSXML saves your particular applications.

Once you know which techniques to use, you can return to your application development confident that you've done your homework and that few humans on Earth could write a similar application that performs faster than yours.

Incidentally, as you'll see later in this chapter, you gain scalability by pushing as much processing to the client as possible (for there's no better way to protect the performance of "the one" than by isolating "the one" from "the many"). So you'll return to ACT, using the same strategy you used while compiling your performance budget, in order to fine-tune the balance between client and server.

Use the following formula to quantify the performance of design strategy by measuring the number of processor cycles needed for each request. The formula divides the number of cycles spent on the task by the number of requests that were handled:

$$\frac{(\text{sum of processor speed} \times \text{processor use})}{\text{number of requests per second}} = \text{cost cycles/request (or Hz/rps)}$$

When you're evaluating various server-side strategies, you may be able to exploit multiprocessor machines. For example, stress tests on an ASP page might reach a maximum capacity at 800 requests per second, with 85 per cent processor use on the web server. If the web server has four 700 MHz (700,000,000 cycles per second) processors, we can calculate the strategy's cost as:

$$\frac{((4 \times 700,000,000 \text{ cycles/sec}) \times 0.85)}{800 \text{ requests/s}} = 2,975,000 \text{ cycles/request}$$

By the way, that 85 per cent factor above is somewhat arbitrary. The general rule is to keep your server utilization rate less than 100 per cent so you always have capacity for unusual peaks of demand. The key point in this discussion is to pick a number then stick with it for all your tests. In a sense, it doesn't matter much what factor you use because in preparing a performance budget you are interested in comparative numbers. Additionally, when you're using ASP to host test components that will run on the client, be sure to use a single processor machine, unless your clients have the luxury of using such heavy iron for desktop computers.

Streams, Streaming, and Threads

Streams are areas of buffered memory where applications can go for data. There is no need to convert this memory into concrete things like strings or BSTRs to get it to work in applications that know how to read streams directly. The main topics of this section are:

❑   ASP 3.0's Response and Request objects and their support of the IStream interface

❑   MSXML's support of the SAX API for streaming XML

This section also talks a little about threads, including another story told to me by the Technical Lead on the Microsoft XML team.

IStream Support in DOMDocument and IIS5+

The DOMDocument's load() method can take as its argument any object that supports the IStream COM interface. Since the DOMDocument itself supports IStream, you can use a memory variable that points to a DOMDocument as the source of the new XML. We saw that in action previously in the *How to Clone or Reload XML* section.

Beginning with IIS 5.0, you can also create a DOMDocument by loading the ASP Request object (before IIS 5.0 the Request object did not support the IStream interface). By the same token, you can save a DOMDocument via the IStream interface by passing the Response object to the DOMDocument's save() method. The code in the *ServerXMLHTTP* section below uses this strategy.

SAX and Threads

The Simple API for XML also uses streams, but these streams go in only one direction (some objects that support IStream can seek or otherwise behave in a manner less constrained than the streams used by SAX). The streams in SAX are similar to the streams in ADO created by read-only/forward-only cursors – so-called "firehose" cursors. So, SAX streams are the complement of the cache of data exposed by the DOMDocument. If you only need to stream through an XML file and you don't need to know anything about a node's ancestors, then the SAX stream may be just the ticket to significant performance gains.

There are, however, some costs to pay for this performance. If you're only interested in one node near the bottom of your file, you still need to process the entire file. In a sense, SAX pushes its data at you. In the world of native XML, the world of MSXML, this push model is the only alternative to a cache. Managed code in .NET's System.Xml classes, on the other hand, has a "pull" model where you process only those nodes of interest. Anyway, as this is a book about MSXML, I promise not to mention managed XML again.

In MSXML 4, the SAXXMLReader and MXXMLWriter (both SAX classes) are marked "Both" in the Registry. However, do not use them on the multiple threads simultaneously if you're sharing any data in the SAXXMLReader. Since AddRef/Release are not multithread-safe and there is no locking on any of the API entry points, the SAXXMLReader can't handle asynchronous processing. As a result, neither of these should be used in ASP Application scope. You can get some extra speed if you start up a SAXXMLReader on two threads in parallel – just release the object on each thread as soon as the thread no longer needs it. If you must share the SAXXMLReader on two threads, you're in charge of concurrency control.

An interesting side note on performance comes from the XML team. The only thing the lead developer on that team dislikes more than ActiveX security is OLE concurrency control. If you have ever written in a low-level language like C or C++ you know two things: Firstly, you'll probably mark all your threads multi-threaded, and secondly, multi-threaded programs are hard to write well. If you add to this the fact that your application must frequently deal with single-threaded apartment modeled applications, you have to deal with a double whammy.

The problem is that cross-thread marshaling exacts hideous sums of CPU cycles. One way to deal with this conundrum is to get resourceful in the way you mark your objects in the Windows registry. The "Neutral" threading model is the most efficient, but it's only available on Windows 2000 and later. The "Both" threading model is the next best bet, but this threading model is designed for thread-safe objects. For MSXML, this minimized the performance hit imposed by OLE, but since only the FreeThreadedDOMDocument is thread-safe (and it's locking mechanism can lock horns with OLE's thread-safety rules), this left concurrency control to the user of MSXML.

The moral of the story is that even the team that gave you MSXML has to deal with the same headaches that you – the user of MSXML – to deal with. The XML team opted for the best performance they could get with a strong dose of faith that those developers who need to worry about threads were competent to build sufficient controls on top of the platform MSXML provides.

Come to think of it, I shouldn't even be talking about this. This mess is exactly why this chapter was written under the policy of staying up at the scripting level (where you can't get into multi-threading trouble).

Regardless of my reservations about opening this can of threading worms, I do need to warn you about something (even scripters need to know). Don't use the SAXReader or the MXXMLWriter in Application scope in ASP. The reason is that though the component's threading model is marked "Both" in the registry, and even though you can use the SAXReader or the MXXMLWriter in a multi-threaded apartment, you cannot use them on more than one thread at once, and this is exactly what ASP would do if either component were in Application scope.

Finally, see http://support.microsoft.com/support/kb/articles/Q291/8/44.ASP to ensure you're not running into the double memory buffering problem that can be caused by using the SAXXMLReader to parse large XML files over HTTP (using the parseURL() method). This potential problem does not apply to using the file system as the source of the XML file.

Technology

When all else fails, upgrade. With MSXML, the upgrade strategy can be a very cost-effective way to get measurable improvements in your code. Or at least, it can be if you've taken some precautions when you created your XML DOMs. I've alluded to these precautions above and we'll discuss them in detail below.

MSXML 4 Versus MSXML 3

Microsoft customers get an added bonus when investing in Microsoft XML technology. The XSLT processor in MSXML 3 was as much as 300 per cent faster than earlier MSXML parsers and competitive XSLT processors on the market. There's a saying at Microsoft, "Our worst competitor is ourselves." By this, Microsoft acknowledges that if it produces a high quality product, to get customers to upgrade requires the upgrade to be significantly better. There is no better example of how this dynamic accrues to the benefit of the customer than with MSXML. Even as MSXML 3 was getting kudos for speed, the XML team was creating MSXML 4, and its XSLT processor is even faster. In fact, MSXML 4's XSLT processor is even faster than `System.Xml.Xsl` (I know, I promised). Not to be outdone by the native developers, the managed XML developers re-architected the managed XML classes to produce an optimized XPath cache so that managed transforms were even faster. Additionally, since managed XSL hasn't even shipped yet, there are more improvements in the works in the short term. Of course, this hasn't escaped the attention of the native guys, and they're already working on the even faster XSLT processor in MSXML 5.

So, with MSXML 4 you get:

❑ Faster XSLT. If MSXML 3's XSLT processor was three times faster than the competition, and if the Microsoft XML team's claim of four times faster XSLT processing over MSXML 3 is true, then in two engineering versions, customers have experienced more than an order of magnitude improvement in XSLT processing. You get this by changing one number in a single line of source code, as we'll see in a moment.

❑ Faster parser. Remember what I said about the managed XML team creating a separate `DOMDocument` optimized for XPath? Well, some of that spilled over into the MSXML 4 development effort, and this is one reason why MSXML 4's XSLT processing is so much faster. It's awfully nice, isn't it, when your code jumps up in performance because somebody else improved their product.

As with everything else in this chapter, there is a small admission charge to get your old applications into this world of supercharged XML processing. The smallest charge is one character on one line of code, like this:

```
// the original
var xml = new ActiveXObject("MSXML2.DOMDocument.3.0");
// the change
var xml = new ActiveXObject("MSXML2.DOMDocument.4.0");
```

You get away with this low cost of admission only if you've paid a slightly higher price in the past. If you haven't, you have a much steeper price to pay to retrofit all your old code to conform to the following best practice. Always create your first `DOMDocument` like this:

```
var xml = new ActiveXObject("MSXML2.DOMDocument.4.0");

// msxml3.dll defaulted to the old XSL Patterns language
// which msxml4 no longer supports.
xml.setProperty("SelectionLanguage", "XPath");

// the next line is required to take advantage of the new processor
// unless you need async loading, then you'll have to set this false.
xml.setProperty("NewParser", True);
```

```
// the next line has always been optional, but usually used.
xml.async=false

// note: currently, msxml4 does not support async loads and
// does not support DTD validation; both limitations will be lifted soon.
```

Here's how you'll pay if you don't create DOMDocuments this way. The old XSL Pattern language returned zero-based nodelists in selectNodes() and selectSingleNode() method calls. If you didn't override the default when you built your applications using msxml3.dll, those applications will break the first time you try to access the first node in a nodelist; XPath is one-based and so fails with an out-of-bounds error.

XSLT Versus DOM Versus .NET

I am a card-carrying XSLT bigot. To me everything is a transform. Sometimes, not surprisingly, I take my commitment too far. For example, my most ambitious transform so far can merge two ten-megabyte XML files, each with tens of thousands of nodes. The processing is so subtle that if I go away from the code for a few weeks, I'm lost when I try to explain exactly how it works. Though the transform runs to completion, it takes several hours. A colleague at work is intrigued with the idea of creating the same functionality in C++ or C# using the DOM instead of XSLT. It's too bad he barely has enough time to go sailing with me, let alone meet the challenge of writing the code. So I cannot, in this edition of the book, offer a definitive exemplar of the ultimate in high performance.

It doesn't take a Masters Degree in Computer Science to know that if you have to choose between script-based DOM navigation and XSLT, XSLT wins hands down. Additionally, in principle, since XSLT is a cache-based technology (meaning all the XML data is stored in memory in an XML DOM), it will usually not perform as well as a technology that does not consume memory and CPU cycles creating and maintaining a high overhead structure such as the XML DOM. Using a streaming API like SAX 2 (discussed previously) isn't designed for data transformation, but using System.Xml classes can easily support a streaming-like API that can transform data.

The point I'm trying to make here is simple: at this time of writing, System.Xml is not readily available on the client. Users can easily upgrade to msxml4.dll on the client, so for some time into the future you will need to develop XML-based applications for the client using native code running under msxml4.dll and later versions By the way, migrating from msxml4.dll to msxml5.dll should not be as problematic as is the migration from msxml3.dll to msxml4.dll. The difference is that msxml4.dll, as I've already noted, is the first version that completely eschews any "technology preview" bits like XSL Patterns and XDR. So use the server to exploit the power of managed XML by migrating as much processing as you can to ASP.NET.

Scalability

Scalability serves the many and leaves the performance of all unchanged. This is a delicate balance in general, but in the context of applications that are built on XML on the server and the client, the balance is easier to strike. This is because XML on the client works just as well as on the server, leaving the server able to handle more clients.

This section deals primarily with **caches**. You'll see ways to use caches of XML data, XSL data, and XML Schema data. Additional applications of the schemaCache object await you in the *Security* section where I'll show you how to use them to block access to data from those whose input you want (or need) to ignore.

This section concludes with a discussion of other server-side technologies besides ASP that can help make your applications serve more clients. In the process, I have a story to tell about my colleagues on the Application Center Test team. That story is the "Scale Down" part of the *Scale Up/Scale Out/Scale Down* section.

Caches

Caches are temporary storage areas of data. The life of these caches is generally controlled by time or by sensing changes to underlying long-term data stores. Caching mechanisms in an MSXML world are rather limited, but when you can move to ASP.NET you'll see an array of radically more effective caching mechanisms at your disposal. So, consider this section a warm up for when you move up to managed code.

Cache XML in ASP Application Scope

While building the user interface for my application that merges two multi-megabyte XML files using XSLT, I took some of my own advice: I only pared off from that big repository a sub-tree of data related to the selection made by the user. With or without a sub-tree, that parcel of data was sometimes very large – a fact that didn't become apparent until I saw how sluggish a simple edit was. It turns out the problem was that each edit was saved in the repository on the server and the data was reloaded from disk to ensure the user could see the latest version of the data, possibly edited by other users.

My solution was to cache the sub-tree in Application scope. More than that, I created a secondary XML DOM in Application scope and appended my sub-trees to that cache. This way, if the user navigated to a different sub-tree and then back to one they'd seen before, I didn't have to take the file input/output (I/O) hit and DOM load hit; I simply queried the cache with the node value I needed and transformed that node into HTML for the client. It's a simple approach, but effective nonetheless.

The essence of this approach is that the code tries to match an incoming string (identifying the repository of interest to the user) to the identity of the `xmlRepository` in memory. My application supports all combinations of several static code analysis tools and several Microsoft products (such as Application Center 2000 and Application Center Test). Therefore, I can have many different large XML repositories available to the user. So, once they choose one of these repositories to work in, ASP caches the contents of sub-trees of that repository.

If the user remains in the context of a single tool/product repository, then the second thing the `try` block does is search for the sub-tree the user is currently interested in.

```
try
{
    // xmlRepository is an App scope, FreeThreadedDOMDocument
    //    initialized with an <OBJECT> tag in global.asa
    if(strPathName.toLowerCase()==
        xmlRepository.documentElement.getAttribute("id").toLowerCase())
    {
        nodFolder = xmlRepository.selectSingleNode(strFolderPath);
    }
}
```

If the attempt to fetch a sub-tree fails, ASP loads the entire repository of interest and selects the sub-tree. The cached repository gets recreated by loading a new document element, `<xml>`, setting this new element's `id` property to the current tool/product repository, and adds the selected sub-tree to the cache.

```
    catch(e)
    {
        xmlFolder.load(strPathName);
        nodFolder= xmlFolder.selectSingleNode(strFolderPath);

        xmlRepository.loadXML("<xml/>");
        xmlRepository.documentElement.setAttribute("id",strPathName);
        xmlRepository.documentElement.appendChild(xmlFolder.documentElement);
    }
```

The final step (re)uses the `xmlFolder` node; again, by creating a new XML DOM instance and appending the `nodFolder` element created in either the `try` or `catch` block.

```
    // reuse xmlFolder
    xmlFolder.loadXML("<xml/>");
    xmlFolder.documentElement.appendChild(nodFolder.cloneNode(true));
    xmlFolder.save(Response);
```

Incidentally, that `cloneNode(true)` call was not used for speed. This is an example of the second most commonly used scenario: the `appendChild()` method actually removes the node from its source – in my case, that would usually be the Application-scope repository. To avoid this, I create a clone of the node from the repository, leaving the repository unharmed.

Cache XSLT Transformations in XSLTemplate Objects

The next two caches I'll describe were innovations inspired by the drive to make MSXML 3 significantly faster than previous versions. They were both created with the server in mind, though they can both be used on the client if necessary.

The `XSLTemplate` object is especially interesting. It is a free-threaded object that can manage (within available memory) a virtually unlimited number of different stylesheets for different clients. The key aspect of the `XSLTemplate` object is that its `stylesheet` property is an address of an address to a stylesheet. This extra indirection makes it possible for two different clients to access the same template and get different stylesheets.

The performance and scalability enhancements accrue because the stylesheet is loaded and compiled only once, regardless of the number of times it's accessed. For large stylesheets (and the one of mine that I've been mentioning in this chapter that is almost 400 lines long), this can be a huge saving.

As we'll see a little later, you should not use I/O-intensive XSLT operations such as `<xsl:include>` or `<xsl.import>` tags. If you must use these mechanisms, then by all means use the `XSLTemplate` objects so you load, parse, and compile the transform only once. If you have to use the XSLT `document()` method, try whenever it's possible, to use an ASP file as the source of the data, and see that the ASP file is using an Application-scope cache of data. (IIS will buffer data to some extent, but you can't control that and you don't know when it won't happen, so cache data yourself.)

Cache XML Schema in SchemaCache Objects

In a way, **schemas** are a lot like XSLT transforms. They're both (usually) static XML data, and when they're used, they're used the same way over and over again. This makes them perfect candidates for caching, and that's just what the Microsoft XML team did. The `SchemaCache` object saves applications that need to validate data from repeatedly loading and parsing schema files. This is especially important on the server because file I/O is a huge performance pit, into which much time and many cycles will fall. In other words, a general rule for server-side XML processing is to minimize the times you have to go to the file system. The `SchemaCache` and `XSLTemplate` objects are two extremely effective ways to obey this rule.

When to Cache and When to Stream

The obvious downside to caches is that they can consume considerable memory. Further, if the data is dynamic (such as a cache of XML data), then you also have to consider synchronization overhead; that is, you'll need to use the `FreeThreadedDOMDocument` and its locking mechanism. As I noted above, exploit the hierarchical nature of XML and cache only those sub-trees you last used. If you're using XSLT, you have to cache, otherwise you can use SAX on the server and switch to a streaming strategy.

If you're really paranoid, you could allocate a `FreeThreadedDOMDocument` for XML data of some optimal size (depending on your situation). Then, use an associative array to hold the XML DOMs, each identified with a name. If a request for data comes in that's not cached in one of the DOMs, spin up another one (using `cloneNode(false)`, of course) and add it to the cache. You can timestamp each element in the array and flush it after a specified interval of idleness. Alternatively, you can pick the DOM with the largest relative size (measured in the length of its `xml` property). The key is that you lock only that data in the sub-tree, not the whole tree. The locking mechanism used in the `FreeThreadedDOMDocument` doesn't implement the most sophisticated strategy, so you can offset this by limiting the data that it can lock.

Scale Up/Scale Out/Scale Down

This section takes a look at scalability from yet another vantage. Here I'll survey the other Microsoft technologies that can come to the aid of developers using MSXML in their applications. Besides being important assets separately, there is an initiative inside Microsoft called "better together" that is working toward making all the .NET servers and web data technologies work as a seamless, well-oiled machine (how's that for mixing metaphors?).

SQL Server 2000

SQL Server 2000 is the obvious choice when it comes to scaling up your XML-based systems when either the filesystem or a flatfile database like Microsoft Access 2002 fail to support your users. The key feature of SQL Server 2000, at least as far as this book is concerned, is its strong support for XML. Indeed, future versions of SQL Server promise to be far more XML-centric than it is today. By using XML templates, you may not have to change your applications. As long as your application loads an XML file, it can load a template (which is nothing more than a `.xml` file, itself).

For example, I'm beginning to stretch the limits of prudence as I insist on using my big industrial scale XML files from the filesystem alone. Very soon, especially if my XML files grow much bigger than the current twenty megabytes some of them get to, I'll be forced to switch to storing and retrieving my XML data in SQL Server 2000. When I do scale up to SQL, I'll wrap my SQL statements in XML and I won't have to change a line of code in my application. In other words, calling `xmlRepository.load("repository.xml")` still works because I've replaced my old huge repository XML file with a tiny template by the same name; and now the `load()` method is invoking the SQLXML ISAPI instead of going to the file system. The result is still 20 megabytes of (the same) XML data.

Application Center 2000

A second option for improving the scalability of your web applications is to increase the number of web servers; this is the "scale out" option. The trick is to avoid the hassles and risks of managing several servers separately. Application Center 2000 is a magician that permits you to deploy applications on clusters of commodity hardware as if there was only one machine. This helps to form part of the "better together" initiative I just alluded to, and both SQL Server 2000 and Application Center 2000 are charter members of the all-new Microsoft .NET Servers. The .NET Servers represent a full-court press by Microsoft to ship products that are actually easier to use in groups than they are separately.

Years ago I remember reading from a PC columnist that if you want a multi-processor computer, buy two machines. Well, that option is now feasible.

XML versus MSDE

My friends on the Application Center Test team told me a fascinating story. If you've read this chapter from the beginning, you'll know ACT is the tool that helps you test your applications by running them under test scenarios that match (and in some cases actually duplicate) actual user scenarios. For developers using ACT, the "client" is simply a machine that's calling on the tested application. The client is not an actual user, and the client machines tend to be slimmed down so they can put all their resources into participating in a stress test. For this reason, working set size is important.

The problem my ACT colleagues faced was that early versions of ACT used MSDE – a scaled down SQL Server 2000. MSDE is designed to configure itself to optimize all available memory, so its footprint not only tends to be large, but as large as it can be! Additionally, knowledge of SQL was required in order to use the MSDE features of ACT – an assumption you cannot safely make for all web developers. Finally, the set up time for ACT using MSDE took 60 megabytes and ten to fifteen minutes. All of these factors got the ACT team to reconsider MSDE. Did they really need that entire horsepower, and was the horsepower worth the cost?

The ACT team decided to scale down. In the end, they had developed their own memory management algorithm that streamed in data from the tests run (this is what MSDE was doing in the earlier versions of ACT). This data in memory was serialized to the file system as XML using SAX. The advantages were substantial. First, they ended up with persisted data that was simply text and could easily be moved around via e-mail, transformed with XSLT into any report needed, and even loaded into SQL Server 2000, if necessary. By focusing on their specific data needs (and not on how that data fit the SQL model), the ACT developers could optimize the data management of ACT and improve ACT's run-time performance. Finally, the set up footprint went down to less than six megabytes and about three minutes to install.

This story has a lot to tell us about our assumptions. Clients can be different things, and the differences can make a difference to designs. Power is relative, and is part of the performance budget, sometimes in a surprising way. As Richard Buckminster Fuller once noted, "sometimes less is more".

Security

This final section has some caveats. Strictly speaking, the security features of MSXML are practically non-existent. The main goal of the MSXML team was to avoid introducing any security holes through the XML mechanism. Second, to quote the lead developer on the XML team, "*...the ActiveX security architecture is a mess, not well thought out, not well documented, and a royal pain ... to implement.*" Considering the bounds of this chapter, that we will not be discussing low-level programming interfaces, the ActiveX security we *will* discuss does not include things like IObjectWithSite, IInternetSecurityManager, and IInternetHostSecurityManager. That said, there's still plenty to talk about in this section, and there are a few interesting script-related security facts that you should be aware of.

The focus of our attention in this section is:

❑ The ServerXMLHTTP component and how it interacts with IIS and NT security

❑ Security issues related to script (including script used by XSLT)

❑   How IE helps keeps things secure

❑   How ASP adds some extra security features to your applications

This general dearth of MSXML-specific security material also motivates the writing of the section's final demonstration: something called "**XML firewalls**". XML firewalls basically bind XML Schemas to XML instance documents at run time to validate incoming data. This technique is most often used for so-called "**updategrams**" because XML Schemas make it easy to match user identities to various maintenance capabilities. By the same token, if your applications want to expose only certain data to certain people, storing the rest of the data in a FreeThreadedDOMDocument in the middle tier, then XML firewalls give you a convenient way to expose only permissible views of that data.

ServerXMLHTTP

A big problem with MSXML 3 happened when using XMLHTTP between servers. If you could get it to work at all (and I never could), you were on borrowed time. The issue arose from the fact that XMLHTTP is based on URLMon and WinInet – two client-side technologies. URLMon didn't work at all on the server, and that's why you can't load an XML file from a URL when the load is called from inside an ASP file. WinInet was not thread-safe, so eventually you'd get into trouble, and since threading issues are one of the hardest to troubleshoot, getting to the root cause of your failure would probably be difficult and time-consuming.

Microsoft addressed this by developing the ServerXMLHTTP component. ServerXMLHTTP uses Microsoft Windows HTTP Services (WinHTTP) 5.0 as an alternative to the older WinInet stack (that's still used on the client).

Since XMLHTTP is based on URLMon that is based on WinInet, XMLHTTP can rely on the URLMon and WinInet stacks to interact with the ActiveX security infrastructure. The configurable part of this security infrastructure comes from the **security zones** of IE, which we'll discuss shortly.

ServerXMLHTTP was not designed to run on the client. It has been optimized for thread-safe server-side processing and does not implement all the necessary security checks typically done on the client. For example, in the tests below, data is captured across domains – something not (usually) permitted in the client world. However, ServerXMLHTTP is capable of using client certificates controlling this interaction through the ServerXMLHTTP getOption() and setOption() methods.

ServerXMLHTTP Running Under Proxy Server

WinHTTP can work with proxy servers when the ServerXMLHTTP component is on an intranet that uses a proxy server to safely connect with ASP servers (or any other XML-aware servers) on the Internet. To work, the Registry must be set up to support proxy settings. To do this, run the proxycfg.exe utility – usually in the System32 folder of the folder in the WINDIR environment variable. In my case, the pathname is C:\WINNT\system32\proxycfg.exe). Give the utility the name of the proxy server and any addresses with which you want to bypass the proxy.

As you'll see a little later, you will probably need to run the proxycfg.exe, even when you're developing from a laptop. So, the general rule is always run the proxycfg.exe utility on any machine that will use ServerXMLHTTP. It can't hurt, and it will be one less thing to worry about later.

Refer back to Chapter 9, "Sending and Retrieving XML Data" for further information on proxycfg.exe.

ServerXMLHTTP and Basic Authentication

Basic authentication is the type you use if someone is coming to your server who is either not in your domain, or using some non-Windows platform. The user ID and password are passed in the clear, encoded with base64 encoding. So, to call a site secure that is based on basic authentication is being generous. If you've never used basic authentication before, and now find that you need to, then follow these steps to get the basics. By the way, if you don't already have a shortcut on your desktop to Inetmgr.exe, right-click your desktop, select "New Shortcut" and enter the following string for the location: C:\WINNT\system32\inetsrv\inetmgr.exe (you may have to change the string to match your computer's configuration).

1. Right-click the "My Computer" icon on your desktop, then select "Manage" to open the Microsoft Management Console. Go to the Local Users and Groups node and right-click the Users node to add a new NT user account. Create a new user entry for user "wrox" and use "msxml4..7" as the password.

2. Create a virtual directory in IIS named "remoteServer". Disable its anonymous and NT authentication and enable basic authentication by unchecking and checking the appropriate boxes in the Directory Security dialog of the Properties dialog for the remoteServer virtual root. You get to the virtual root's Properties with the Inetmgr.exe application.

3. In the remoteServer virtual root's physical folder, add a file called remoteServer.asp and enter this script:

```
<%@ Language=JScript %>
<%
Response.ContentType="text/xml";
var xml = new ActiveXObject("msxml2.domdocument.4.0");
xml.async=false;
xml.loadXML("<msg URL='"+
Request.ServerVariables("SERVER_NAME")+Request.ServerVariables("URL")+"'
type='"+Request.ServerVariables("AUTH_TYPE")+"'
uid='"+Request.ServerVariables("AUTH_USER")+"'
pwd='"+Request.ServerVariables("AUTH_PASSWORD")+"'/>");
xml.save(Response);
%>
```

4. In some other virtual directory (if you don't have any on your machine, use the inetpub\wwwroot folder), put a file named serverDirect.asp that has this code:

```
<%@ Language=JScript %>
<%
var objSrvHTTP;
objSrvHTTP = new ActiveXObject("MSXML2.ServerXMLHTTP.4.0");
objSrvHTTP.open ("GET","http://localhost/remoteServer/remoteServer.asp", false,
"wrox", "msxml4..7");
objSrvHTTP.send ();
Response.ContentType = "text/xml";
Response.Write("<msg><status>" +objSrvHTTP.status+"</status>");
objSrvHTTP.responseXML.save(Response);
Response.Write("</msg>")
%>
```

5. After you run `serverDirect.asp` you will see this is the output:

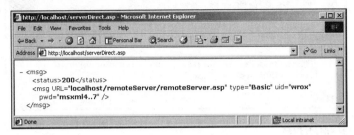

ServerXMLHTTP Gumption Traps

Dealing with system security can be a taxing if not downright vexing experience. This tribulation subsides with experience, but the process of gaining that experience is fraught with gumption traps. If you fall into those traps often enough, you are tempted to just forget about implementing security, and all you can do then is hope for the best.

In this section I'll share some of the traps I've fallen into. Perhaps in reading these stories you can avoid losing any precious gumption of your own. You'll need it.

Credentials and the Indirect Method

If you don't pass a userID and password you won't get any return value (other than "401" as the status property of the `ServerXMLHTTP` object) because ASP can't prompt you for credentials in the middle of processing a page.

There is an indirect method of using `ServerXMLHTTP` (see the bold line of code below):

```
<%@ Language=JScript %>
<%
var xml = new ActiveXObject("msxml2.domdocument.4.0");
xml.async=false;
xml.setProperty("ServerHTTPRequest", true);
if (xml.load("http://localhost/remoteServer/remoteServer.asp"))
{
    Response.ContentType="text/xml";
    xml.save(Response);
}
else
    Response.Write(xml.parseError.reason)
%>
```

If you use this approach you will raise this error: "System error: -2146697208". The indirect method only works when you use anonymous authentication (since no credentials are passed by the `ServerHTTPRequest` object). If you add NT authentication to the remoteServer virtual directory, then this code will return data, though not exactly the same data as basic authentication returns (since NT authentication is processing the NT security token, not the data passed in via the ASP `Request` object).

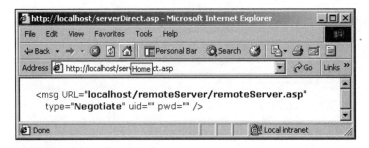

Asynchronous ServerXMLHTTP

You can't use an asynchronous load of the XML DOM when it's using a background `ServerXMLHTTP` object. You can, however, do asynchronous direct access using an explicit `ServerXMLHTTP`, as I show here in `asynchrousDirect.asp`:

```
<%@ Language=JScript %>
<%
var objSrvHTTP= new ActiveXObject("MSXML2.ServerXMLHTTP.4.0");
objSrvHTTP.open ("GET","http://localhost/remoteServer/remoteServer.asp", true,
"wrox", "msxml4..7");
objSrvHTTP.send ();
while (objSrvHTTP.readyState != 4)
{
    objSrvHTTP.waitForResponse(1000);
}
render();

function render()
{
    Response.ContentType = "text/xml";
    Response.Write("" +objSrvHTTP.status+"");
    objSrvHTTP.responseXML.save(Response);
    Response.Write("")
}
%>
```

The asynchronous code above only works when NT authentication is disabled, and it displays user data only when anonymous authentication is disabled, as well. Here's what the code does: the second argument to the `ServerXMLHTTP` `open()` method informs the component to use asynchronous processing. This means the program calling the `ServerXMLHTTP` component continues processing while the `ServerXMLHTTP` component does its work. When the remote server completes its work it calls back to the `objSrvHTTP` object and changes the `readyState` property to the value of 4. The code above actually makes the `async` call into a synchronous one by using the `waitForResponse()` method. After some number of seconds, the program calls the `render()` function to display the results of processing on the remote server.

Also note that if you're using MSXML 3, you may have trouble with improper security contexts between two users. For details, see: http://support.microsoft.com/support/kb/articles/Q292/5/21.ASP

NT Authentication and Proxy Servers

Take a close look at the IE screenshots above – they both use the localhost machine name. I developed these samples on my laptop at home. Unless I'm logged onto the Microsoft corporate network, I don't have a proxy server to contend with. When I tried to use my machine name in the URLs above, I kept getting 401 – Access Denied errors. Then I remembered a Knowledge Base article that I'd read. At the end of http://support.microsoft.com/support/kb/articles/Q291/0/08.ASP are instructions for guys like me. To make a long KB article short, as soon as I executed the following command the results were as shown:

```
Command Prompt                                                    _ □ X

C:\Documents and Settings>proxycfg -d -p "<local>" "<c1714119-a>"
Updating proxy settings

Current WinHTTP proxy settings under

  HKEY_LOCAL_MACHINE\
    SOFTWARE\Microsoft\Windows\CurrentVersion\Internet Settings\Connections\
      WinHttpSettings :

    Flags       = PROXY_TYPE_DIRECT | PROXY_TYPE_PROXY
    Proxy Server = <local>
    Bypass List = <c1714119-a>


C:\Documents and Settings>_
```

When we run the proxy configuration tool from the command line, the second parameter (after local) is the list of machines you want the proxy to bypass, separated by a semi-colon. Even if your machine is not using a proxy server, you might need to run proxycfg.exe, and then restart your IIS Admin Service and the W3C Service for the proxy configuration settings to take effect.

I was able to use machine names in my samples when I switched the samples' virtual roots to NT authentication only. The only thing you'll change in the command is the name of your machine in the by-pass list, instead of "c1714119-a" which is my laptop's name.

Cached Credentials

As you're experimenting with these security features, be sure you close IE before trying your next experiment. IE often caches credentials, so the best way to ensure you're testing what you think you're testing is to have ASP create a new client each time.

Relative URLs

If you're using ServerXMLHTTP to bind ASP files (that are all on the same server) together like objects (the same way you can treat an ASP file like an object using XMLHTTP from the client), don't try to save typing by using relative references. For example, if you had the calling ASP page and the called ASP page on the same virtual root, you'll see the results below if you try this call:

```
objSrvHTTP.open ("GET","remoteServer.asp", true, "wrox", "msxml4..7");
```

Debugging and Domains

Two more little things that will drive you stark raving mad if you forget are, firstly, if your user ID includes a domain and your script is written in JScript, be sure you escape the "\" character, otherwise your domain name merges with your user name and authentication fails. The second caveat is don't enable ASP Debugging (enabled from the Debugging tab on the Application Configuration dialog of the virtual root in the IIS MMC) and use the VisualInterDev Debugger if you're using `ServerXMLHTTP` to call an ASP *in the same virtual root* that is being debugged. You'll deadlock both the first and second server requests because the debugger serializes all requests to the server. The first request has the ASP processor and calls the second one, but the second can't return its value because the first request holds the thread. Classic deadlock.

XSLT Security Through Scripting Engines

For those times when you simply must resort to script in your XSLT transforms, be advised that the scripting engine, not the XSLT processor, is responsible for maintaining security.

Client-side Security Through Internet Explorer Security Zones

You can't use MSXML all by itself; MSXML relies on two host environments in which to execute and to provide virtually all of its security. On the client tier, this host is usually Internet Explorer. Internet Explorer 5.0+ provides security through its so-called "security zones". ASP, on the other hand, provides most of the security when it hosts MSXML on the server.

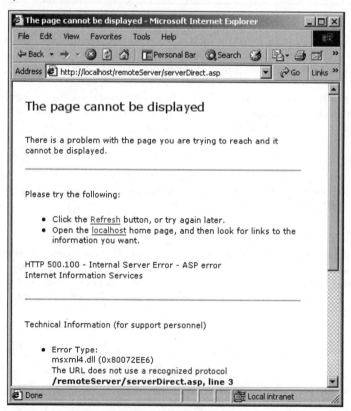

Local File System Access

IE plays in a sandbox. The most common mistake made is when you try to open an XML file from the client's file system. Try running this code from `clientDestinedToFail`.htm:

```
<HTML>
<HEAD>
<META NAME="GENERATOR" Content="Microsoft Visual Studio 6.0">
<TITLE>Thou Shalt Not Play Outside the Sandbox</TITLE>
<SCRIPT LANGUAGE=javascript>
<!--
window.onload=init;
function init()
{
    var xml = new ActiveXObject ("MSXML2.DOMDocument.4.0");
    xml.async=false;
    try
    {
        xml.load("c:\\inetpub\\wwwroot\\msxml4\\root.xml");
        alert(xml.xml);
    }
    catch(e)
    {
        alert("Error loading xml ("+xml.parseError.url+") from file
            system:\n"+xml.parseError.reason);
    }
}
//-->
</SCRIPT>

</HEAD>
<BODY>
</BODY>
</HTML>
```

Here's a real puzzler when you first see it – if you give an XML instance document a local file pathname for the value of its document element's noNamespaceSchemaLocation attribute, you'll get an **Access denied** error when you try to load the XML file in IE. If you change the attribute to use a fully qualified URL or a relative URL (or simply refer to the schema file by name alone), IE will load the schema and be able to validate your instance document. So this won't work in IE:

```
<catalog xmlns:xsi="http://www.w3.org/2001/XMLSchema-instance"
    xsi:noNamespaceSchemaLocation="C:\Inetpub\wwwroot\msxml4\booksMPC.xsd">
```

But this will:

```
<catalog xmlns:xsi="http://www.w3.org/2001/XMLSchema-instance"
    xsi:noNamespaceSchemaLocation="booksMPC.xsd">
```

So if you're not alert, sometimes a general error like **Access denied** can leave you (as it did me) scratching your head.

Remote Server File Access

The most common need of IE is to access XML from a source other than the server that rendered the HTML page. Using the two virtual roots from the previous `ServerXMLHTTP` section, place `clientMayFail.htm` in the virtual root from which you called the remoteServer virtual root. Create a `root.xml` file on the remoteServer share, and set the "Local Intranet" security zone to the "High" setting, or set the cross-domain security setting manually, as in the screenshot below:

When you try to access the remote XML, IE will deny you access if cross-domain access is disabled.

```
<HTML>
<HEAD>
<TITLE>Thou Shalt Not Play With What is Not Yours</TITLE>
<SCRIPT LANGUAGE=javascript>
<!--
window.onload=init;
function init()
{
    var xml = new ActiveXObject ("MSXML2.DOMDocument.4.0");
    xml.async=false;
    try
    {
        xml.load("http://c1714119-a/remoteServer/root.xml");
        alert(xml.xml);
    }
    catch(e)
    {
        alert("Error loading xml from file system:\n"+xml.parseError.reason);
    }
}
//-->
</SCRIPT>

</HEAD>
<BODY>
</BODY>
</HTML>
```

Note the use of the machine name in the script above (and in the error dialog below), along with "localhost" in the URL of the screenshot, below. You can force a cross across domains by using these two different identities for the host. If you use localhost in the script above (or use the machine name in the URL), you'll be granted access and will see the XML. So, if you have localhost for both, it requests data from the same resource, whereas giving the machine name in the script will allow a similar operation to a cross-domain call. This is because IE treats local files as being in their own security zone.

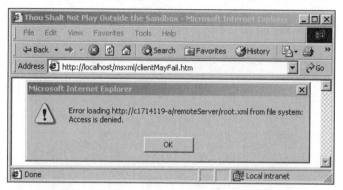

Server-side Security

I'll now move outside the domain of MSXML, per se, and into the middle tier where you often find that, once again, you need to come to terms with the Security Cop that lives inside every computer. In the following discussion I'll show you two ways that solve the perennial remote file access problem:

❑ Remote file access

❑ UNC-based Virtual Roots

For one of my applications at work I chose remote file access. That application needs to convert source code into well-formed HTML. That particular application accesses the source code for Application Center 2000, renders that source code as well-formed HTML, and returns it to the client via XMLHTTP so I can display the source code in the browser. I use this technique when I can't control the machine where my files come from. When I am in control of the infrastructure, I vastly prefer the second method: creating a virtual root that uses a Universal Naming Convention (UNC) share for its directory.

Remote File Access

Sometimes security is a pain in the area just above the hamstrings. Remote file access is a fairly common requirement, and in ASP applications that can take some work or some creativity. For instance, in the application I mentioned above, to access source code from a server that was not a web server I used the **Windows Script Host** (**WSH**) filesystem object to create a null file share – a file share that is not mapped to a folder. My script then sends the network an authenticated user and password, and my application is granted access to the files. To protect passwords a little bit we use a component that keeps passwords in a database and all our applications request a specified user's password from the component, passing the results to the WSH network command. This component is all the more handy because we change passwords at regular intervals, and this way we don't have to go to every program that uses credentials to edit the password after we change it.

Remote Virtual Directories

If you can control the server where your remote XML files will come from, then use IIS's ability to accept content from a UNC file share. This technique lets the operating system handle the security issues for you, making the web site appear as if it were locally hosted. By pressing the "Connect As..." button shown in the following screen shot, you can fill in the server and share names, and you can assign an authenticated user's credentials to the file access.

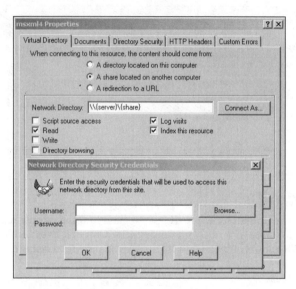

One problem with this approach is that if your network administrators are doing their jobs well, you will have to change your password periodically. If you forget to go to this, of course, file access through the web server will fail, and the IIS MMC will show you a little stop sign, as you can see here:

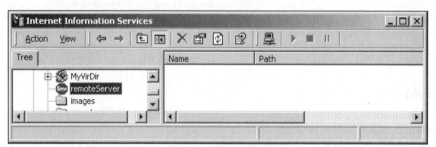

Schema-based Security: XML Firewalls

The most common use of XML firewalls is to limit updates to XML repositories. The key to this feature is that the limitations can be very well defined. That is, through a schema you can tell the system exactly what individual users can change. The simplest way to demonstrate this strategy is to simply have schemas for three kinds of global updates. The first schema permits only inserting data. The second schema permits the user to change data, and the third enables a user to delete data. Using XML firewalls to read only certain data is left to the enterprising reader.

Furthermore, an XML firewall handles this schema binding at run time; the firewall does not use schema references in the incoming XML data. So, the firewall needs some way to know who's asking to update the data. For the following demonstration, the user ID is passed through an HTTP header; in the real world the most reliable source of user ID will be the logged on user.

The firewall resides inside an ASP page. The `xmlFirewall.asp` page (below) has two roles. First, it caches an `XMLSchemaCache` object in Application scope. Again, in the real world, this cache should be created in `global.asa`. The second role of `xmlFirewall.asp` has two parts: it adds (or replaces) one or more XSD files to one or more namespaces, and secondly, it binds the `SchemaCache` object to the `schemas` property of the incoming updategram. If the updategram actually loads into an XML DOM, then the firewall has permitted the user to conduct their business; otherwise, `xmlFirewall.asp` tells the user why they were stopped and which actions they are permitted to take. So, let's look at some code.

The `xmlFirewall.asp` accepts an incoming stream of XML from the client. The `xmlFirewall.htm` file uses the XMLHTTP component to do this. Here's the relevant code from `xmlFirewall.htm`:

```
// change the url to reflect the vroot on your machine
xmlHttp.Open ("POST", "http://localhost/msxml4/xmlFirewall.asp",
    false);
xmlHttp.setRequestHeader ("Content-type", "application/xml");
xmlHttp.setRequestHeader ("User-ID", selUser.value);
xmlHttp.send (xmlDoc);

result.innerHTML  = xmlHttp.responseText;
```

The `xmlDoc` was loaded either from an XML file or from XML generated within the `.htm` file. The client application allows you to select one of two users and one of four actions. From those choices in the UI, data is fed to `xmlFirewall.asp`. Note the use of the `xmlHttp.setRequestHeader()` method to send the value of the user's ID to `xmlFirewall.asp`.

It seems a shame to have a perfectly good, free-threaded component, and not use it in Application scope. So, if you adopt XML firewalls, note the opening comment below.

```
<%@ language="jscript"%>
<%

/*
    this caching really should be done in the global.asa using

    <object id="schemaCache" progid="MSXML2.XMLSchemaCache.4.0"
    scope="Application" runat="server"></object>

    and if you use global.asa, remove the next if block.
*/
if(Application("SchemaCache"))
{
    var schemaCache = Application("SchemaCache");
}
else
{
    var schemaCache = new ActiveXObject("MSXML2.XMLSchemaCache.4.0");
    Application("SchemaCache") = schemaCache;
}
```

Next, we create the XML DOM (remember to set the `async` property, and don't worry about setting the `SelectionLanguage` property on the DOM – `msxml4.dll` only uses XPath). Then we fetch the HTTP header used to send the identity of the user to `xmlFirewall.asp`.

```
var xmlUpdateGram = new ActiveXObject("msxml2.domdocument.4.0");
xmlUpdateGram.async=false;

var userID=Request.ServerVariables("HTTP_User_ID").item;
```

Now `xmlFirewall.asp` is ready to start binding XSD files to namespaces. There are three namespaces – update, delete, and insert. These namespaces are like the key rack we might find in the entry area of someone's home. When I come home, I hook my car keys on the far left hook of the rack, while my wife hooks hers on the next one over. When I leave in the morning, I grab the keys on the far left hook (and hopefully I've grabbed the correct keys, otherwise my poor wife won't make it in to her office that morning). The three namespaces used by the `schemaCache` object serve the same purpose. Upon each namespace hangs a schema. Later, when `xmlFirewall.asp` processes the incoming XML data, it will look to the namespace in the XML and then go to the correct "hook" for the XML Schema. If there is no schema on that hook, nothing happens and the XML opens without being validated.

> *I wasted more than an hour while writing this section because I forgot to keep track of my namespaces. Be sure any incoming XML has a namespace from the list you use to add a schema to the* schemaCache.

```
switch(userID)
{
    case "mcorning":
        schemaCache.add("update", Server.MapPath("updateGram.xsd"));
        schemaCache.add("delete", Server.MapPath("deleteGram.xsd"));
        schemaCache.add("insert", Server.MapPath("insertGram.xsd"));
        break
    case "kcorning":
        schemaCache.add("delete", Server.MapPath("noCanDoGram.xsd"));
        schemaCache.add("update", Server.MapPath("updateGram.xsd"));
        schemaCache.add("insert", Server.MapPath("insertGram.xsd"));
        break
}
```

Note the bold XSD file. This schema contains only one thing: an empty tag. Here's the `noCanDoGram.xsd` file.

```
<?xml version="1.0" encoding="UTF-8" ?>
<xs:schema xmlns:xs="http://www.w3.org/2001/XMLSchema"
        elementFormDefault="qualified">
    <xs:element name="ROOT">
        <xs:complexType />
    </xs:element>
</xs:schema>
```

No editing is possible if an instance XML document gets the `noCanDoGram.xsd` file bound to it. Since my wife, Katy (referred to in the code as `kcorning`) does not have permission to delete files, the `noCanDoGram.xsd` is the schema that `xmlFirehose.asp` will bind to any updategram from my wife that tries to delete data from the repository.

So, assuming `xmlFirewall.asp` binds some other XSD file to the incoming updategram, the following `load()` method will succeed. If the load fails, the `xmlFirewall.asp` will run the first clause in the following `if` block. If the load succeeds, you enter your actual updating code to the beginning of the `else` clause of the following `if` block.

```
// bind schema to xmlUpdateGram XMLDOM
xmlUpdateGram.schemas = schemaCache;
// attempt to load
xmlUpdateGram.load(Request);

/*
    if the user identity didn't permit a schema to be bound that matched
    the updategram coming in, then return the relevant info to the user
*/
if(xmlUpdateGram.parseError.reason)
{
    // display the reason the parse fialed
    Response.Write("<h3>Status</h3><div style='color:red; font-weight:
        bolder'>Parse Error: " + xmlUpdateGram.parseError.reason+"</div>")
    Response.Write("<h3>Available Schema</h3>")
    Response.ContentType="text/xml";
    Response.Write("<xmp>");

    // list out the schema for all namespaces available to the user
    for (var i=0; i<schemaCache.length; i++)
    Response.Write("<"+schemaCache.namespaceURI(i)+">\n"+schemaCache.get
        (schemaCache.namespaceURI(i)).xml+"\n
        </"+schemaCache.namespaceURI(i)+">\n");
    Response.Write("</xmp>");
}
else
{
    // this is where you'd put your xml update routines

    // return information to user
    Response.Write("<h3>Status</h3>No Parse Error<h3>Data and Schema</h3>")
    Response.ContentType="text/xml";

    // xmp tag enables the returning xml to be rendered in IE
    Response.Write("<xmp>");

    //return the updategram
    xmlUpdateGram.save(Response);

    // get the namespaceURI of the updategram (indicating the action
        requested)

    var ns = xmlUpdateGram.documentElement.namespaceURI;
    if (schemaCache.get(ns))

        // return the xml of the schema bound to the incoming updategram
      Response.Write("\n<"+ns+">\n"+schemaCache.get(schemaCache.namespaceURI(i))
        .xml+"\n</"+ns+">\n");
    else
        Response.Write("<error>there is no known schema for "+ns+"
            operation</error>");
    Response.Write("</xmp>");
}

%>
```

Here's an example screenshot of a successful update:

Here's what happens when a user oversteps their bounds:

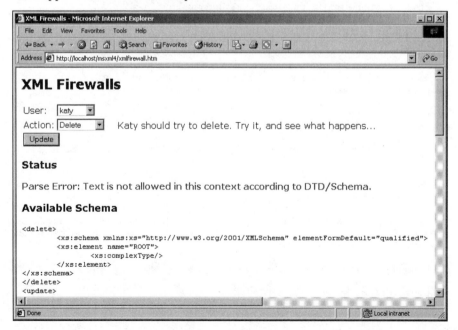

As you can see, XML Firewalls are a fairly straightforward security measure that, like everything else in schema-based programming, uses only XML to enforce data integrity. There are only a couple of gotchas to worry about:

❑ Ensure your incoming data uses one of the SchemaCache namespaces; otherwise, no validation will occur.

❑ Ensure all users have a schema bound to all namespaces, and if there is a proscribed action for a user, bind the noCanDoGram.xsd file to that action.

Remember that I just said that no validation occurs if an unknown namespace gets into the xmlFirewall.asp? Well, the firewall traps that condition near the end of the file, but an exercise you can carry out is to figure out how to change the firewall so no loading ever happens when a rogue namespace is sent by the user.

Security Futures

Though usually not life-threatening, software security is still a serious issue. About the only good thing that comes from hackers is better software (hopefully, that's the main reason most hackers ply their trade), and better software comes from an evolving security infrastructure. This final section looks into what's coming in the short and long term.

Common Language Runtime

By the time you read this book, Microsoft will have shipped what is arguably the most important innovation in the company's history – the .NET Framework and the **Common Language Runtime** (**CLR**). The security features of this runtime are notable. In many ways Microsoft has pulled off a major coup: many security techniques in the CLR are both more effective and easier to implement than security in, say, ActiveX. For example, remote file access for an ASP.NET application is far simpler and more direct than the hack I mentioned above. It requires a few settings in the web.config file and the machine name being added as a user on the remote machine. In addition, security becomes part of the declaration of assemblies, so it becomes easier to configure and more granular. This will make CLR-based clients more adaptable and flexible than those depending on the relatively higher level of security zones in IE. CLR security is based on applications, not on environments.

Binary XML

The W3C and its affiliates are hard at work making XML work harder at making hackers work harder at breaking into your intellectual property. Take a look at the XML security page at http://www.nue.et-inf.uni-siegen.de/~geuer-pollmann/xml_security.html and you will see just how broad and deep work is to make XML far more secure than the naive text files of today.

W3C XML security initiatives follow the same basic lines as any other security-oriented work. The **XML Encryption** work is focused on data and its integrity, and the **XML Signature** work is focused on the authenticity of the source of the data, mainly in terms of authentication of either the message or the signer.

Until this work gets out of the Requirements and Working Draft stages, we'll have to keep using things like XML firewalls and system-level security to ensure the data we share is shared only with those with a need to know, and that the data is changed only by those we know and to the extent we trust them.

Summary

This chapter studied the "three-body problem" in programming that uses MSXML. Performance, scalability, and security were our three problems. Like our brethren in astrophysics, understanding how all three interact with each other takes persistence and perspicacity. This chapter generally partitioned performance issues to the client and scalability issues to the server. Security covers both tiers, and in a multi-tier environment the user context is different depending on the tier. Anonymous and authenticated users, and other applications/systems must all interoperate smoothly, because it might not just be a person on the end giving a password; it may be another folder on the same machine, or even a different machine in a server-to-server scenario.

The other point made in this chapter is that performance, scalability, and security can no longer be afterthoughts; they have to be first-class issues in the design and implementation of web-based applications.

A powerful tool to aid good design is the performance budget. Based on best practices on the client and server, the performance budget strives to provide reliable and accurate measurements of the number of cycles different design strategies exact from the system. Combined with traffic data, the performance budget enables architects and developers to trade off cycles for other real goods, such as usability in user interfaces.

Writing this chapter and applying its recommendations is challenging, primarily because there is no clear-cut correct answer to the question of how performance, scale, and security interact. Each of our applications is a little star system of its own, with each having its own "center of mass". Yet, like recent evidence that even galaxies have a thread-like structure; our "independent" star systems are really part of a larger constellation. As such, they all interact with each other. Well-designed systems tend to take traffic away from poor performers. The underlying goal of this chapter has been to give you the tools you need to be a super star. May the force be with you.

> *You can gain further support for the concepts and techniques illustrated in this chapter from the support page at my site, http://www.aspalliance.com/mcorning/books/msxml4.*

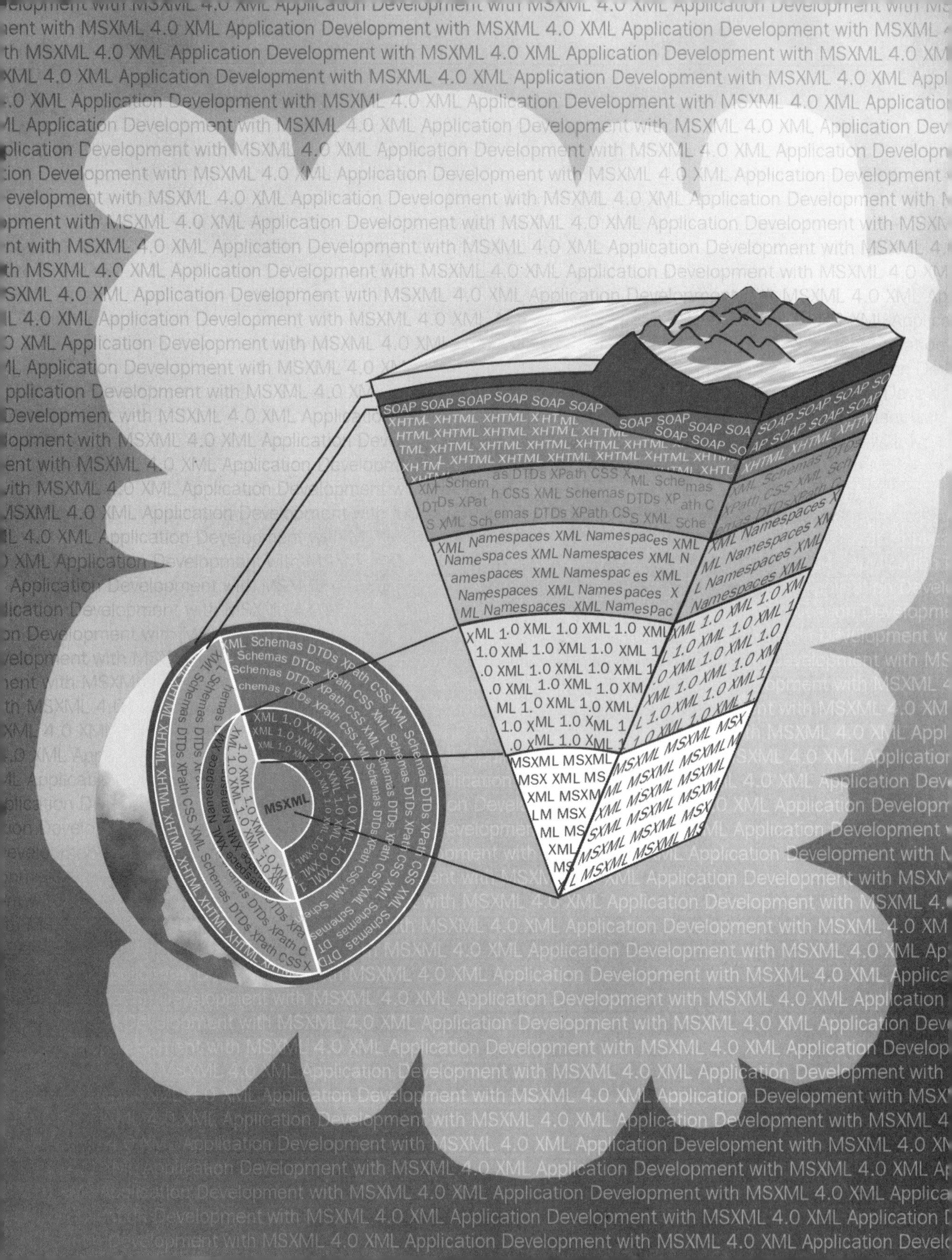

XML Application Development with MSXML 4.0
SOAP
XHTML
XML Schemas DTDs XPath CSS
XML Namespaces
XML 1.0
MSXML

14

Case Study: An Information Portal

This case study will look at an information portal system that registers, indexes, and generates content for multiple browsers. We will look at how content syndication and batch retrieval can be used to retrieve HTML or XML content from a remote site and (for XML), validate it against our local XSD Schema definition. Valid content is converted to our local standard XML format and an index of available documents is created. Furthermore, device-specific XSLT stylesheets are used to create pre-generated HTML versions of the content and when users hit the portal, some device detection will be used to retrieve the appropriate XML and XSLT to create the front page that links to these pre-generated HTML pages. It uses most of the concepts discussed in this book to varying levels, and shows how they are all needed to produce a successful real-world application.

We will look at how to integrate a portal with content from remote web sites using MSXML's XMLHTTP and ServerXMLHTTP objects. We will consider how to improve the performance and flexibility of the site by doing most of the work offline and creating pre-generated pages for various browsers using XSLT transforms. We will show how to dramatically improve performance by using the MSXML IXSLTemplate and IXSLProcessor objects and application-level caching, as well as how to determine browser types and map these directly to XSLT stylesheets. Finally, the application will demonstrate how to link in other utility processes, such as a term finder/thesaurus, to improve the content richness.

Let's get started by setting up the portal!

Setting up "ProPortal"

There are a number of pre-requisites for running this sample application:

❑   (Compulsory) MSXML 4.0 installed on the server (this is fine even if the "client" and "server" are running on the same PC).

❑   (Compulsory) IE 5+ and/or Navigator 6.0 installed. IE 6.0 is recommended, along with Navigator 6.0 on the client.

❑   (Compulsory) The latest version of the Windows Script Components is required on the server (not required if IE 6.0 is installed on the server). You can download this from http://msdn.microsft.com and search for "Windows Script Components".

❑   (Optional) Any MSXML version on the client (for IE only).

❑   (Optional) Scheduling software installed – such as the Scheduler built into Windows 2000.

❑   (Optional) Microsoft Word installed.

❑   (Compulsory) Have read the chapters in this book!

Portal Configuration

This section is provided only to get you up and running with the portal – you may have questions on some of the things done here, but these will be fully explained and demonstrated later in the chapter!

Also, the way we will work in this chapter is to demonstrate how a section of the portal is used and how it looks prior to investigating the code that produces it – this is mainly to allow you to visualize the results, as pure code can sometimes be confusing.

First, unzip the code download for this chapter. When you do this, a folder called ProPortal will be created, containing all of the files required. You should put this folder, with all of its contents, in a suitable place as we are now going to map to it a virtual directory on your web server.

Web Server Setup

The first thing to do is to create a virtual directory called ProPortal in Internet Information Server (or other preferred web server, as long as it supports ASP). In Internet Information Server you can do this by launching the Internet Services Manager from Start | Settings | Control Panel | Administrative Tools and expanding the computer name that the web site you are using is on. Next, right-click on the icon displaying the web site name ("Default Web Site", for example) and choose New | Virtual Directory from the context menu. The wizard will take you through the rest of the process. Ensure that you point this virtual directory to the physical location of the ProPortal directory that was created when you unzipped the code download.

This would be enough in most cases, but we want to add some access restrictions to the remote3 folder, specifically to the file mondonews.xml. In a real-world case, this would be like some syndicate content provider putting restrictions on access to a file on their web server – not your web server.

To do this, launch Internet Information Services from Start | Settings | Control Panel | Administrative Tools and click on the virtual directory called ProPortal. Next, click on the folder remote3, right-click on the file mondonews.xml, and click the Properties item. When the Properties window launches, click the File Security tab to obtain a screen like the one shown here:

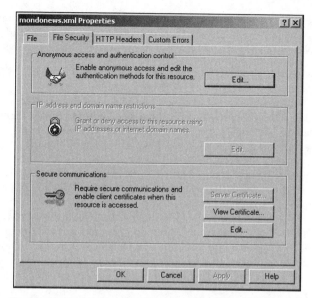

Next, click the Edit... button in the Anonymous access and authentication control section to launch the Authentication Methods window. Uncheck the Anonymous access and Integrated Windows authentication checkboxes and click the Basic Authentication box – say yes to the dialog box that appears when you check Basic authentication (below).

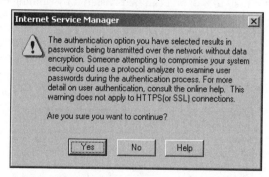

Basic authentication actually transmits in clear text but it is the simplest method to illustrate authentication on our site – MSXML 4.0 also supports anonymous certificate authentication. Finally, click OK on the window and, when it closes, click OK on the second window to return to the Internet Information Services explorer window.

This may be all you have to do if you intend to use the administrator username and password to authenticate when you want to access this file. If you don't, you should ensure that the username and password combination required to access this file exists and has log on locally privileges – most likely a member of the Guest group or some custom group. You can equally well use the administrator account of the machine (or some other account with appropriate privileges) – of course, on a live site you would not use the administrator account, but it is likely that for now you are running this portal on a single machine and this is the main assumption when working through the case study (but doesn't limit you from extending to multiple servers if desired). In our case, an account called wroxuser with password wroxuser was created and will be used in the application.

Finally, if your user is not a member of the Administrators or Guests groups, then you will have to use Windows Explorer to navigate to the physical location of mondonews.xml and set the access privileges on this file. Consult Windows Help if you have questions on setting access privileges.

Write Permissions

One other thing that must be done that will affect the running of the site is to set appropriate write permissions on the XML files. There are two files that are written to in this application. The first, index.xml, is populated by the batch script CreateIndex.vbs and generally doesn't require any modification if the user who runs the script has write permissions to this file.

The other file *does* require a change in permissions – this is the config.xml file used in the registration process. At the moment, the simplest way to achieve this is to navigate to the physical location of this file (it sits in the root of the ProPortal folder) using Windows Explorer. Right-click on the file and select **Properties**. Click the **Security** tab, click on the **Internet Guest Account** (usually **IUSER_COMPUTERNAME**) in the **Name** section, and give this user write permissions to the file by clicking the **Allow** checkbox in the **Write** option. Click **OK** to confirm this. In an actual application it is more likely that the user would have a username and password mapped to this file with appropriate permissions set on it and would *not* be using the Internet Guest account.

File Registration

The final thing you have to do is register a DLL that will be used to discover synonyms for given words on your web page from Microsoft Word (if you have it installed). This is called Livingstone.dll (so my imagination isn't what it used to be!) and can be registered by running the RegSvr32 utility at the command line. Simply open the **Command Prompt**, change to the directory containing the DLL (unzipped from the download into the **ProPortal** folder), and type:

```
>RegSvr32 Livingstone.dll
```

You will then get a message indicating success, as below:

Now we are set! The application has been configured, so let's go on and look at the operation of the site.

Working with ProPortal

You can run the site now by navigating to http://*localhost*/ProPortal/default.asp. Substitute "*localhost*" with the relevant web server name – it will be assumed for the remainder of the chapter that you have entered the appropriate server name.

The following pages are displayed when viewed with IE 5+ and Navigator 6.0:

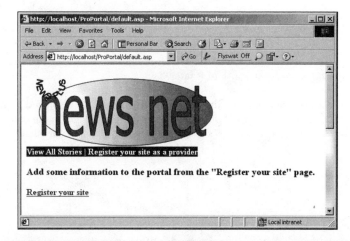

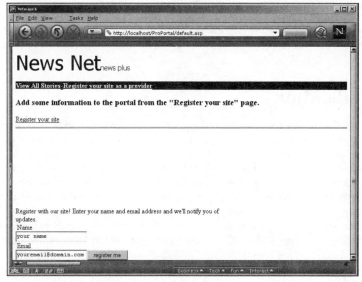

We are not going to look at how this screen is output just yet – that involves a complex series of events that we will investigate in detail later on. However, it is useful to understand the basic building blocks of the portal so we can see why no output is yet available.

The entire site revolves around the XML file called `config.xml`, which contains an index of all of the remote web sites and web pages that are to be stored in the information portal, and this indexing is used later by a batch process to get content from each of the pages specified within this index. Hence, it acts as the definition of the syndicate sites from which information should be gathered. However, because we haven't actually registered any sites or files yet, it follows that we have no information – we have an empty portal. The code listing overleaf shows the `config.xml` file at the start – effectively an empty template (this is also stored in `configStart.xml`, which doesn't actually get used by the portal, but allows you to copy its contents and overwrite the contents of `config.xml` to start the portal from scratch):

```
<?xml version="1.0" encoding="utf-8" ?>
<siteconfig>
   <indexsites />
</siteconfig>
```

The root element is `<siteconfig>` and at the start it contains a single `<indexsites>` child element – this is a placeholder and we will see more of it later.

The actual generation of the index of pages that determines what is to be displayed in the portal is stored in a file called `index.xml`. There are no pages yet indexed, so the index page (in the code download at `ProPortal\index\indexStart.xml`) is shown below, and is a holder for what we will look at later on:

```
<?xml version="1.0" encoding="utf-8" ?>
<?xml-stylesheet type="text/css" href="/ProPortal/index/index.css" ?>
<Index>
   <entry />
</Index>
```

The significance of the `xml-stylesheet` processing instruction is discussed near the end of the chapter. It follows that if there are no portal files yet indexed, there is nothing to display in the portal – that is why it is empty just now. To register a site we can click the **Register your site** link – but we don't know anything about the entire registration process yet, so let's look at the next section – content syndication.

Content Syndication

There are three sites that we are going to be working with in this example to provide content for the information portal, although the design of the portal means that we can have as many providers as we wish. Furthermore, because it is unlikely that you have three spare web servers on a network that can be used for testing, the sample also works on one single server. Let it be clear though – this portal can be distributed over three (or more) servers anywhere across the world and, except for a slight performance hit, you will not notice any difference. In this case, the servers will be represented as three different folders on the same web server. Alternatively, you could create multiple web sites on your local Internet Information web server and modify the URLs as appropriate in the application. As will be seen, this is only necessary for the sample files, as you actually register the location of the files so they can reside at any (accessible) location in the world.

The folders `remote1`, `remote2`, and `remote3` represent the three remote servers and the sample files listed below were put in these folders – note that these locations can equally be http://www.remoteaddress1.com, http://www.remoteaddress2.com, and http://www.remoteaddress3.com as long as the sample files can be located in the given site. The contents of each "remote" location are shown below:

remote1

- ❏ `businessheadlines.htm` – business news page
- ❏ `sportheadlines.htm` – sports news page
- ❏ `financeheadlines.htm` – finance news page
- ❏ `register.asp` – register user with site page
- ❏ `registerXML.asp` – register user with site XML interface

remote2

- ❏ euronews.htm – European business news page
- ❏ eurosport.htm – European sports news page
- ❏ eurofinance.htm – European financial news page
- ❏ euroglobal.htm – European global news page
- ❏ register.asp – register user with site page
- ❏ registerXML.asp – register user with site XML interface

remote3

- ❏ mondonews.xml – World news page
- ❏ mondotech.xml – World technology news page
- ❏ mondoTV.xml – World TV news page
- ❏ register.asp – register user with site page
- ❏ registerXML.asp – register user with site XML interface

Rather than looking at all of the sample files, let's consider two representative files – an HTML example and an XML example. The register.asp and registerXML.asp pages are discussed later in the chapter.

The first file we'll look at here is called businessheadlines.htm and is available in the remote1 folder. Users of the portal don't directly access this remote page, but the portal itself uses it to build its content. The HTML of this page is shown below:

```
<!DOCTYPE HTML PUBLIC "-//W3C//DTD HTML 4.0 Transitional//EN" >
<html>
    <head>
        <title>Glasgow hosts XML Convention</title>
        <meta NAME="NewsItem" Content="business">
        <meta NAME="Keywords" Content="Glasgow,XML,agent">
        <meta NAME="registerURL" Content="register.asp">
        <meta NAME="EntryTime" Content="12:23:00">
        <meta NAME="LastUpdateTime" Content="23:23:00">
    </head>
    <body>
        <h1>
            Glasgow hosts XML Exhibition
        </h1>
        <p>
            Glasgow is to host the world renowned XML Expert Convention
            in March at the Exhibition Center - an XML first for the
            city. Mayor of the town Graham Livingpebble said that it
            was "a step forward for the large technical community of
            Glasgow ".
            <br/>
            Dr. Xavier Michel Lineas of Strathclyde University who has
            invested heavily with XML in his Agent technologies will
            provide the keynote which is expected to focus on his
            XML-based Agent technology, which can inform you just
            before your toast burns.
            <br/>
```

```
             For more information, visit the web site at
             http:www.xmlinglasgow.gla
         </p>
      </body>
   </html>
```

There is nothing greatly exciting about this page – in fact, it can be any HTML page as long as the TITLE and META information is entered. The content of the TITLE element is used to represent the story within the portal – the META tags are defined as follows:

`<meta>` Tag	Valid Values	Description
NewsItem	global finance sport business technology	Identifies the type of content that is being provided.
Keywords	Text strings	Contains keywords within the content.
registerURL	URL	The URL where users can submit their username and e-mail address for site updates.
EntryTime	HH:MM:SS	Time when content was first entered. HH hours, MM minutes, SS seconds.
LastUpdateTime	HH:MM:SS	Last time the content was updated. HH hours, MM minutes, SS seconds.

The following figure shows how this page looks when viewed at
`http://localhost/ProPortal/remote1/businessheadlines.htm`:

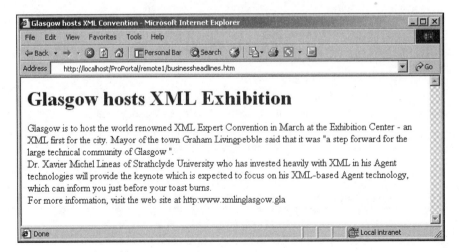

The other HTML pages are not much different from this one – they may be worth a read though to familiarize yourself with the content (and my creative writing abilities). We assume that they follow the format defined by our site. In a real-world example you may publish a template so that web page creators follow the correct format; or you may simply publish the guidelines.

The third server, remote3, is where things are a little different from the other two. The first thing is that the first two servers (remote1 and remote2) contain HTML files, and the third server (remote3), contains XML files. Another difference is that some access to files on the third server will actually require validation – you should remember this from the configuration phase where we set basic authentication on the mondonews.xml file that sits in the folder remote3.

The third site, remote3, stores information in XML format and one of the files mondotech.xml is shown below:

```xml
<?xml version="1.0" encoding="utf-8" ?>
<story NewsItem="technology" registerURL="register.asp" entryTime="08:21:00"
       LastUpdateTime="10:25:00"
       xmlns="http://sightkeys.com/schema/newsnet.xsd">
   <keywords>
      <keyword>deltabis</keyword>
      <keyword>WishAFish</keyword>
      <keyword>portal</keyword>
      <keyword>exchange</keyword>
   </keywords>
   <name>Deltabis Technology Extension</name>
   <text><![CDATA[
      <h1>Deltabis Technology Extension</h1>
      Deltabis, the Internet's number one exchange portal for Southern
      American fish has announced a range of new breakthrough services
      targetting whales.
      <br />
      Called "A Whale of a time", the company will offer a trip to see
      whales off the coast of Chile for the CEO of any company
      purchasing over $10,000 US using its business exchange technology.
      <br />
      Partners WishAFish Technologies plan to provide over 1000
      visits in the first year and plan to put the money towards
      their goal of producing "Bad Dream Bay", a film that combines
      the stories of Free Willy and Nightmare on Elm Street.
   ]]></text>
</story>
```

All stories must have a root <story> element with some attributes – you will notice that the names of these attributes and the child <keywords> elements correspond with the <meta> tags discussed above. Notice that the default namespace in the file is set as xmlns="http://sightkeys.com/schema/newsnet.xsd" – we will later see why this is used. Also, the <name> element corresponds to the <title> HTML tag and the <text> element contains the same information as the <body> HTML tag. However, because this is an XML document and HTML 4.0 is not always well-formed XML, the entire content of the <text> element is wrapped in a CDATA section.

Up to this point we have looked at how the site looks prior to any content registration, and have seen how the information providers are structured. It's about time the portal was populated with some information. After all, an information portal is not half as exciting when there is no information.

Registering a Remote Site

In order for content to be present within the information portal, the owners of the pages on remote sites must register them using the portal registration page. Also, the owner of the portal will want to ensure that valid and appropriate content is in their portal and so control where the information comes from. The last time we checked the portal entry page, it told us that no pages had yet been registered and that we should click the Register your site link to populate the site content. Let's now look at doing this, by navigating to http://*localhost*/ProPortal/default.asp using IE or Netscape and clicking on the Register your site link. This will take you to the page http://*localhost*/ProPortal/RegRemote/register.asp, which allows a user to register any accessible web site in HTML or XML format. It works on a two-phased approach.

- ❑ Phase 1 allows the submitted pages to be validated (everything from checking their actual existence to their syntax).

- ❑ Phase 2 displays the results and allows confirmation of the pages that are being submitted.

We are now going to demonstrate page registration for the web pages at the location remote1 – the process for remote2 is the same and you'll be given details below. The process for registering the files in remote1 is quite simple. First, here are the details:

Name:
NewsLine InfoServe

Base URL:
http://localhost/ProPortal/remote1/

Pages to Register:
businessheadlines.htm
sportheadlines.htm
financeheadlines.htm
radioHeadlines.htm

Enter these details into the registration page, and then click the Check Compliancy button. The result should be as shown in the following figure:

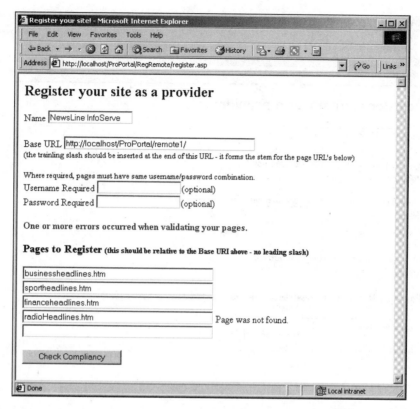

So we got an error here – why? Well, a message is shown next to the URL that caused the problem – in this case we can see it was in fact the fourth URL. The reason is relatively straightforward (although the registration supports more advanced problems with registration such as the indication that there has been a server error). The page does not exist because the sample only has the first three files entered at the URL location given. Now, delete the entry for this fourth URL and click the Check Compliancy button again. This time you should get the same screen, but instead of the error message, you will get another message indicating that the pages were successfully validated, and the Check Compliancy button will change to a Submit button. Click the Submit button and you will receive a message to confirm that all pages were successfully submitted, as overleaf:

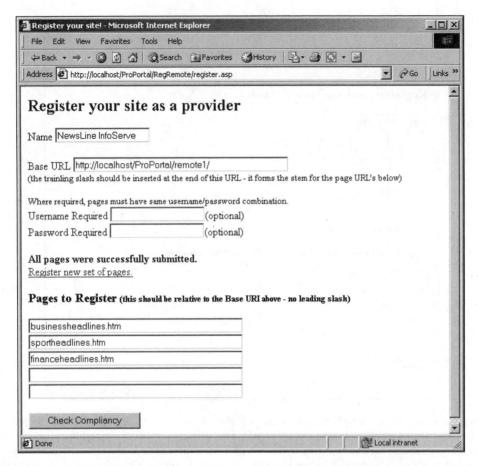

Our first set of pages has now been registered and we will see what happens next later on. Let's first register the pages at site 2 – those in the `remote2` folder. The details are listed below, so click the **Register new set of pages** link, go ahead and enter and submit these details, and then we can move on to submission of the XML pages. The details for `remote2` are as follows (you may have to alter the server name or more if you have altered the set up):

Name:
Euro InfoNet

Base URL:
http://localhost/ProPortal/remote2/

Pages to Register:
euronews.htm
eurosport.htm
eurofinance.htm
euroglobal.htm

There is no validation of the .htm files; only a check is done to ensure they exist and then information is effectively "screen scraped" from them. The registration of XML files is similar from a user perspective, but the possibility of error messages is much greater because (as mentioned earlier), schema validation is carried out – we'll look at this soon. Additionally, in our case, the registration for files in remote3 requires username and password authentication, as we discussed earlier. Go ahead and enter the following details to register the following XML pages from the site:

Name:
Mondo Syndication

Base URL:
http://localhost/ProPortal/remote3/

Username:
wroxuser (or your admin/custom account)

Password:
wroxuser (or your admin/custom account)

Pages to Register:
mondonews.xml
mondotech.xml
mondoTV.xml

When you click the Check Compliancy button you will get the following screen:

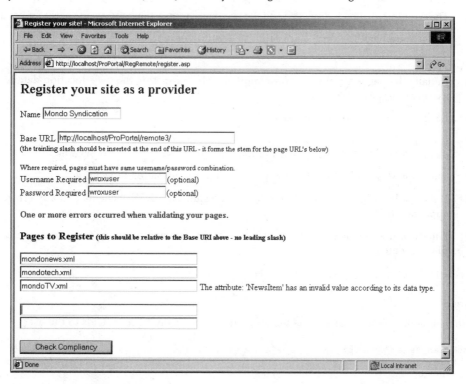

So once again you have been given some bogus registration information – we learn the most from our mistakes! The first two files were great, but the last file (mondoTV.xml) caused us problems. It exists, but it defines its NewsItem attribute type (an identifier for the type of news this is) as "tv", and this is not registered as an acceptable type of information for the portal (as we will see when we discuss the XSD Schema below); so it fails. If we try to register a page that does not exist, we would simply return an "Object Not Found" error. Incidentally, entering a username and password that is not allowed to access the page will result in an Access Denied error for those pages that actually require authentication.

Remove the last entry and click the Check Compliancy button. This will validate and you can then click the Submit button to have the site and pages registered.

The user interaction with the web site is now complete for setup, but a lot actually happened while we were registering the pages. Let's look under the cover and see what we did.

Registering a Remote Site – the Building Blocks

As we saw above, the registration of a remote site and page(s) starts with the ASP file register.asp (in the ProPortal\RegRemote directory). Let's look at the HTML portion of this file first.

An Overview

The following steps are performed in the site registration section:

On the Client

❑   User uses HTML output from register.asp to input the site data (including username/password information) and checks for compliancy.

❑   The error information is displayed and the user makes corrections and again checks for compliancy.

❑   When compliant, the details are submitted to the server.

On the Server

❑   Initially the pages are checked for compliancy by extracting the page location details and any username or password.

❑   Each page is iterated through as a collection.

❑   If the file is an XML file, an MSXML 4.0 DOMDocument instance with ServerXMLHTTPRequest is used to load the NewsNet.xsd XML Schema file.

❑   The request is made – passing the authentication information as required.

❑   If the file is an XML file, the file is validated against the XML Schema and any errors are appended to the ParseError array.

❑   Finally, if the page is submitted and has no validation errors, the config.xml configuration file is updated.

Let's now look at register.asp in more detail.

register.asp

First there is some HTML that accepts the input and displays the various fields to the user:

```
<%@ Language="JScript"%>
<html>
    <head>
```

```
        <title>Register your site!</title>
    </head>
    <body>
        <h2>
            Register your site as a provider
        </h2>
        <form action="register.asp" method="post">
            <p>
                Name
                <input type="text" name="name"
                    value="<%=Request.Form("name")%>">
            </P>
```

Next, some messages are displayed to the user, depending on the current posting position (checking compliancy or submitting):

```
            <%if (Request.Form.Count>0)
                if (ParseErr.length>0)
                    Response.Write("<b style='color:red'>One or
                        more errors occurred when validating your
                        pages.</b><br/>")
                else if (Request.Form("Submit")=="Submit")
                    Response.Write("<b style='color:darkblue'>
                    All pages were successfully
                        submitted.</b><br/><a href='register.asp'>
                        Register new set of pages.</a>")
                else
                    Response.Write("<b style='color:darkblue'>
                        All pages were successfully validated.
                        </b><br/>")
            %>
            <h3>
                Pages to Register <font size="-1">(this should
                    be relative to the Base URI above - no leading
                    slash)</font>
            </h3>
```

Each input field for the pages is then displayed – the `disabled` "attribute" prevents the user from changing the values once they have been validated, as well as outputting any error messages that are present in the `ParseErr` object – this will contain information on page availability and XML Schema validation:

```
            <input <%=disabled%> type="text" name="page"
            value="<%if (Request.Form.Count>0)
            Response.Write(Request.Form("page")(1))%>"
            size="50"> <%=ParseErr[0]%>
        ...
            </p>
```

Finally, the appropriate button (Check Compliancy) is displayed if the pages have not yet been checked, and Submit if they have been successfully validated:

```
    <p>
            <%if (bolCheckCompliancy == true)
                Response.Write("<input type=\"submit\"
                                    value=\"Submit\" name=\"submit\">")
            else
```

```
                    Response.Write("<input type=\"submit\"
                                    value=\"Check Compliancy\"
                                    name=\"CheckCompliancy\">")
            %>
          </p>
        </form>
      </body>
    </html>
```

Let's now look at the server code that processes the submissions. `ParseErr` is an array object containing all errors that occur during checking. So, when a user actually posts some values, the ASP checks to see whether they are in "check compliancy" mode or "submit" mode:

```
<%
    var ParseErr = new Array();
    var disabled = "";

    if (Request.Form.Count>0)
    {
```

In "check compliancy" mode any username and password is extracted from the form (used in getting authorization for protected web resources) as well as the base URI that was posted:

```
    if (Request.Form("CheckCompliancy") == "Check Compliancy")
    {
        //for each go through each page element and use
        //ServerXMLHTTP to validate
        //against some schema and "correct" each one.

        var strUsername = "";
        var strPassword = "";
        strUsername = Request.Form("username").Item;
        strPassword = Request.Form("password").Item;
        strURI = Request.Form("uri").Item;
```

We then iterate through each page (they were all given the name "page" in the HTML form, so they will arrive as a collection of values). The first thing that is done is a check to see what kind of page we are working with, and we first assume that if it does not have an extension of `.htm` then it is an XML file – fairly basic, but useful for the sample. In the real word you would have to support ASP pages and JSP pages as well as others. However, as the output is HTML or XML, the methods shouldn't differ too much.

```
    var colPages = Request.Form("page")

    for (var intPages=1;intPages<colPages.Count+1;intPages++)
    {
      if (colPages(intPages)!="" &&
        (colPages(intPages).indexOf(".htm")==-1))
        {
```

Next, an MSXML 4.0 `DOMDocument` instance is instantiated and its `serverHTTPRequest` property is set to make any HTTP requests server-safe. In this case, this is not strictly necessary as we are getting a local file, but just to be safe for the future (when the file loaded may be remote), we will stick with this. The actual file that is loaded is an XSD file called `NewsNet.xsd` (available in the `ProPortal\schema` folder). Following this, an `XMLSchemaCache` object is created and the XSD Schema we just loaded is added to the cache collection and associated with the namespace `http://sightkeys.com/schema/newsnet.xsd`. This is needed to match the `targetNamespace` attribute of the XSD Schema that we will look at a little later. Note that it would be useful to cache the `XMLSchemaCache` object using the techniques discussed in Chapter 11, "*Schemas on the Server*".

```
var xmlXSD = Server.CreateObject("Msxml2.DOMDocument.4.0");
xmlXSD.async = false;
xmlXSD.setProperty("ServerHTTPRequest", true);
bol = xmlXSD.load(Server.MapPath
  ("/ProPortal/schema/NewsNet.xsd"));

var cache = Server.CreateObject("MSXML2.XMLSchemaCache.4.0");
cache.add("http://sightkeys.com/schema/newsnet.xsd", xmlXSD)
```

Next, we have to get the actual XML file we wish to validate. This is a remote file (at locations `remote1`, `remote2`, and `remote3`) so an instance of `ServerXMLHTTP` is created. There are now two situations – either a username/password combination has been sent to provide authentication, or not. In the latter case, the `open()` method of this object is used with `GET` and the full URL (`BaseURL` page name in `colPages` collection). In the first case, the same call is used, but the username and password variables are also passed. Following this, the `send()` method invokes the call to the remote page. If the response is not an HTML "OK" code (HTML status 200), then the appropriate error is added to the `ParseErr` collection using the `statusText` property and the `continue` keyword is used to jump to the next page:

```
//Assume is an XML page and info can be got directly

    var objXMLHTTPSrv = Server.CreateObject
        ("MSXML2.ServerXMLHTTP.4.0")
if (strUsername == "")
 objXMLHTTPSrv.open("GET", strURI+colPages(intPages), false);
else
   objXMLHTTPSrv.open("GET", strURI + colPages(intPages),
    false, strUsername, strPassword);

    objXMLHTTPSrv.send();

    if (objXMLHTTPSrv.status != 200)
    {
            ParseErr[intPages-1] = objXMLHTTPSrv.statusText;
            continue;
    }
```

By this point we know we have retrieved a page, so we want to get the result into a format that will allow us to validate it against our schema! Again, a `DOMDocument` instance is created with the `validateOnParse` property set to `true` (and this is the default). The `schemas` property is set to the `XMLSchemaCache` object we created earlier. This means that when the `load()` method is called, with the `responseXML` property returning the XML of the page, this XML will be validated against the XSD(s) in the `XMLSchemaCache` object. Any error that occurs is inserted into the `ParseErr` object. This is the array we created above and each index corresponds to an HTML `input` element that was submitted. Hence, we can associate a given error with the element that was posted by simply assigning the error value to the index. We see the result of this output later on.

```
            var xmlPageDoc = Server.CreateObject ("Msxml2.DOMDocument.4.0");
                xmlPageDoc.async = false;
                xmlPageDoc.setProperty("ServerHTTPRequest", true);
                xmlPageDoc.validateOnParse = true;
                xmlPageDoc.schemas = cache;
            var bol = xmlPageDoc.load(objXMLHTTPSrv.responseXML);

                if (xmlPageDoc.parseError.reason != "")
                    ParseErr[intPages-1] = xmlPageDoc.parseError.reason;

                var xmlPageDoc = null;
            }
```

Alternatively, if the page *is* an HTML page, then a similar call is done – you should look at the source to see this, as it is similar to the above, without the validation. Next, the variable `bolCheckCompliancy` is initialized to `true`, meaning that the pages are initially regarded as being successful. However, if the `ParseErr` object has members then something has failed and so this variable is changed to `false`:

```
            else if (colPages(intPages).indexOf(".htm") != -1)
            {
                ...
            }

            var bolCheckCompliancy = true;

            if (ParseErr.length > 0)
                bolCheckCompliancy = false;
        }
    }
    else
    {
```

If the user did not click the **Check Compliancy** button and instead is now at the submission part, then a method called `BuildRegistration()` builds an XML string from the posted form – this method is in the `postHTML.asp` include file. This include file is also available in the source code for Chapter 10, but we don't look at it here – have a look at it and compare it with the similar code in Chapter 10, "*Transformations on the Server*". Once this XML string has been created it is loaded into a `DOMDocument` using the `loadXML()` method:

```
        var str = BuildRegistration(Request.Form)

        var xmlDoc = Server.CreateObject("Msxml2.DOMDocument.4.0");
        xmlDoc.async = false;
        xmlDoc.loadXML(str);
```

As the user is registering a page, the details must be entered in the `config.xml` file, as this contains a listing of all the registered pages for the portal indexer. So, this file is loaded next and then the `appendChild()` method is used to insert the `<site>` element node and its children as a child of the `<indexsites>` element in `config.xml`. Finally, `config.xml` is saved with the new information:

```
            var xmlConfigDoc =Server.CreateObject
                ("Msxml2.DOMDocument.4.0");
        xmlConfigDoc.async = false;
        xmlConfigDoc.load(Server.MapPath("/ProPortal/config.xml"));
```

```
        var o = xmlConfigDoc.documentElement.childNodes[0].
           appendChild(xmlDoc.documentElement.childNodes[0].
           childNodes[0]);

        //Make sure you have set access rights to WRITE for
        //Internet Guest Account

        xmlConfigDoc.save(Server.MapPath("/ProPortal/config.xml"));
     }
   }
%>
<!--#include file="postHTML.asp"-->
```

This is an administration section and for this reason, and to make the sample simpler, we don't deal with concurrency issues, such as two administrators updating at the same time. However, in full production this would likely be necessary (unless you are the only administrator).

A fragment of config.xml is shown below:

```
<?xml version="1.0" encoding="utf-8" ?>
<siteconfig>
   <indexsites>
      <site name="NewsLine InfoServe"
         uri="http://localhost/ProPortal/remote1/">
         <page name="businessheadlines.htm" />
         <page name="sportheadlines.htm" />
      </site>
   ...
   </indexsites>
</siteconfig>
```

We mentioned that the XML pages are validated against some XML Schema – this is called NewsNet.xsd and we look at this next.

NewsNet.xsd

NewsNetTypes.xsd is a schema that contains basic types used in NetNews.xsd, and is a library that could be used in several schemas for NewsNet, not just NewsNet.xsd. The namespace and targetNamespace attributes are set to http://sightkeys.com/schema/newsnet.xsd, which you should remember is the namespace used when we added the schema to the XMLSchemaCache object earlier in register.asp. A namespace for xmlns:newsnettypes is also defined to allow us to qualify types used in the imported NewsNetTypes.xsd file. In fact, the xsd:import element imports this schema and associates it with this namespace, so we need to qualify it in the root. Here we used the prefix newsnettypes. The namespace on the imported element must also match the targetNamespace of the imported XSD.

```
<?xml version="1.0" encoding="utf-8" ?>
<xsd:schema id="newsnet" targetNamespace="http://sightkeys.com/schema/newsnet.xsd"
elementFormDefault="qualified" xmlns="http://sightkeys.com/schema/newsnet.xsd"
xmlns:xsd="http://www.w3.org/2001/XMLSchema"
xmlns:newsnettypes="http://sightkeys.com/schema/NewsNetTypes.xsd">

   <xsd:import namespace="http://sightkeys.com/schema/NewsNetTypes.xsd"
      schemaLocation="newsnetTypes.xsd" />
```

```
<xsd:annotation>
    <xsd:documentation>News Net Syndicate Schema</xsd:documentation>
</xsd:annotation>
```

We then conveniently group the `NewsItem`, `registerURL`, `entryTime`, and `LastUpdateTime` attribute definitions as an `attributeGroup` called `g_storyInfo`. Notice that the first of these attributes, `NewsItem`, actually uses a qualified custom type from the imported Schema:

```
<xsd:attributeGroup name="g_storyInfo">
    <xsd:attribute name="NewsItem" type="newsnettypes:NewsItems" />
    <xsd:attribute name="registerURL" type="xsd:anyURI" />
    <xsd:attribute name="entryTime" type="xsd:anyURI" />
    <xsd:attribute name="LastUpdateTime" type="xsd:anyURI" />
</xsd:attributeGroup>
```

Next, the `<story>` element, which is the root element, is defined to contain the elements in the `keywords` definition, followed by a name element and the text of the story. Finally, the `attributeGroup` we just defined is attached to this element:

```
<xsd:element name="story">
    <xsd:complexType>
        <xsd:sequence>
            <xsd:element ref="keywords" minOccurs="1" maxOccurs="1" />
            <xsd:element name="name" type="xsd:string" />
            <xsd:element name="text" type="xsd:string" />
        </xsd:sequence>
        <xsd:attributeGroup ref="g_storyInfo" />
    </xsd:complexType>
</xsd:element>
```

The `keywords` element definition consists of a `complexType` sequence of keywords:

```
<xsd:element name="keywords">
    <xsd:complexType>
        <xsd:sequence minOccurs="1" maxOccurs="unbounded">
            <xsd:element name="keyword" type="xsd:string" />
        </xsd:sequence>
    </xsd:complexType>
</xsd:element>
</xsd:schema>
```

NewsNetTypes.xsd

The `NewsNetTypes.xsd` Schema that was imported into the above Schema is fairly simple, but very important in the running of the site, as it defines the story types available in the portal. It does this by defining a `simpleType` called `NewsItems`, which is restricted to a string enumeration of a set of values. If the portal is to be extended to support other types, then this enumeration must be updated. Notice that its `targetNamespace` is the same as the `namespace` attribute on the `xsd:import` element above:

```
<?xml version="1.0" encoding="utf-8" ?>
<xsd:schema id="NewsNetTypes"
            targetNamespace="http://sightkeys.com/schema/NewsNetTypes.xsd"
            elementFormDefault="qualified"
```

```
              xmlns="http://sightkeys.com/schema/NewsNetTypes.xsd"
              xmlns:xsd="http://www.w3.org/2001/XMLSchema">
   <xsd:annotation>
      <xsd:documentation>
         News Net Syndicate Schema Types Supplement
      </xsd:documentation>
   </xsd:annotation>
   <xsd:simpleType name="NewsItems">
      <xsd:restriction base="xsd:string">
         <xsd:enumeration value="global" />
         <xsd:enumeration value="finance" />
         <xsd:enumeration value="sport" />
         <xsd:enumeration value="business" />
         <xsd:enumeration value="technology" />
      </xsd:restriction>
   </xsd:simpleType>
</xsd:schema>
```

Have a look at the `MondoTech.xml` file above (in the registering section) or any of the XML files to see examples of files that successfully validate against this schema. In fact, you also saw an example of an XML file that does *not* validate against this schema – you should now understand why this happened.

We have now seen how registration is accomplished, and we have a list of sites that are to be our content syndicate sites in `config.xml`. The next stage in the process is actually getting this content and indexing it.

Information Population

For the ProPortal system to display any information, an index must be created because, as we saw earlier, the `index.xml` file is currently empty. We have successfully registered sites and pages to be used, as we saw above in `config.xml`, but a further stage is required to create the index itself.

Creating an Index

The script is actually a Windows Scripting Host (WSH) file called `CreateIndex.vbs` – it was created as such because the index creation is *not* something you want to do when a user hits the site – it should produce pre-generated information to minimize the impact on performance. There are two ways you can use this file – in this sample we will simply navigate to it and click on it to invoke the indexing process. In a real-world situation, you would most likely use the Windows 2000 Scheduler in the control panel (or the "AT" command at the command line) to make it run once every morning, or twice a day, or whatever parameters are appropriate for your situation. With NT4, this is installed with IE 5 and can be found in My Computer.

Open up Windows Explorer, navigate to the `\ProPortal\Index` directory, and double-click on the `CreateIndex.vbs` WSH file. This invokes a series of silent processes to create the index and when it is completed a message box will appear indicating that the indexing was successfully done. If any problems occur you will be shown an error message and processing will be terminated.

When you have done this, you can now browse to the front page of the portal at http://*localhost*/ProPortal/default.asp and you should see something like the following figure:

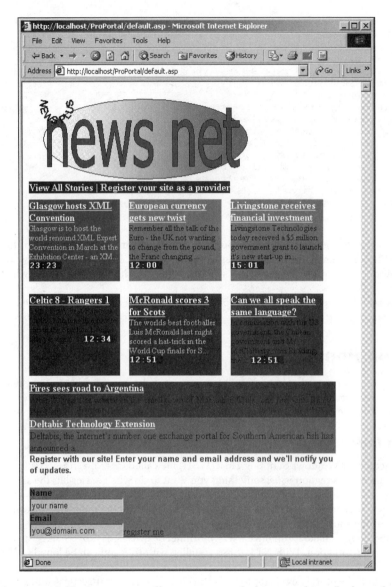

If you view the site with Navigator you will get pretty much the same thing. Let's see how all this is created. There is more to this than just the front page, but let's look at the site bit by bit, as it will be a lot easier to understand what is going on.

Populating the portal is actually a two-part process – the first is an offline process and the second is a dynamic process when the user views the site. We are first going to look at the offline process – this offline process creates the information basis for the portal and hence has many constituent parts. We are going to consider an overview of these parts as we work through the indexing process to show you how they are created. After this, we can then look in turn at each process and then how it works for the user.

Creating a Site Index – Under the Hood

This is the offline part of the portal creation process mentioned earlier, and creates a summary index of the content of the sites that were visited by the application. We should first warn you that this is a fairly hefty piece of code, but it makes extensive use of MSXML 4.0 and other objects to create a real-world application, so understanding it will be of great benefit to you in developing your own applications.

We won't cover the entire script as there is quite a bit to it – we will look at the major parts and you can have a look at the source to understand more. Where you see an ellipsis (. . .) some less important code (to our discussion at least, for example, error testing) has been omitted from what is in the source.

An Overview

The following steps are performed in the indexing process:

- ❑ The `config.xml` configuration file is loaded as a DOM Document and the sites that have to be indexed are selected from it.

- ❑ The `Livingstone.dll` COM DLL that integrates with Microsoft Word is created.

- ❑ We iterate through each site node returned from the first step above and get username/password information, and invoke a remote request for the page using the `GetRemotePage()` method.

- ❑ The `GetRemotePage()` method determines whether it is an HTML page or XML page and if the file is a HTML file, then it is retrieved using the IE `WebBrowser` object. Any errors in its retrieval are put in the `ParseError` array. Any XML file is retrieved using the `IXMLServerXMLHTTP` object.

- ❑ If the file is an HTML file, the `GetHTMLMetaInformation()` method gets META information from the HTML page. If it's an XML file, the `GetXMLMetaInformation()` method gets the META information.

- ❑ The `StoreMetaInIndex()` takes either the HTML or XML version and creates a standard XML fragment, which is inserted into the `index.xml` file. In addition, the actual content of these files is persisted in a unique file in XML format.

- ❑ Following this, the `CreateBrowsableDocuments()` method is used to create HTML versions of the files – this uses the locally stored XML version of the story and browser-specific stylesheets to generate the output. During this process, the `InsertThesaurusTerms()` method inserts equivalent terms into the HTML documents. These can be seen using DHTML.

Let's look at the process in detail.

CreateIndex.vbs

The entire process is kicked off by a call to the main function at the start of the script, so let's take a more detailed look at it. The basis of the indexing process is the registered sites defined in `config.xml`, so this file is first loaded, and an XPath query is used in the `selectNodes()` method to get back all of the site nodes that contain the registration details:

```
main
...
function main()
Set objXML = WScript.CreateObject ("MSXML2.DomDocument.4.0")
objXML.async=false
```

639

```
objXML.load("../config.xml")

Set objSiteNodes = objXML.selectNodes("siteconfig/indexsites/site")
...
```

Following this, the thesaurus object is created – we discuss this in more detail later, but this allows you to use Microsoft Office capabilities to improve the semantic value (or meaning) of the data in your web page. The variable intMaxWords contains an integer variable determining the number of words that should have associated words checked for – don't go too crazy with this as it can have a serious effect on processing time.

```
'Open data checker and set global
Set obj = CreateObject("Livingstone.Data")
bolOK = obj.InitializeComponent()
...
intMaxWords=25
```

Following this, each <site> element is iterated through, and the URI, username, and password for the site are obtained:

```
For i=0 To objSiteNodes.length-1
    Set objNode = objSiteNodes(i)

    strSiteURL = objNode.getAttribute("uri")

    strUserName=""
    strPassword=""
    If objNode.getAttribute("username") <> "" Then
        strUserName=objNode.getAttribute("username")
        strPassword=objNode.getAttribute("password")
    End If
```

With these details, each <page> child element of the <site> element is iterated through to get the page name. With this name, as well as the URI and username/password details, a call to the method GetRemotePage() is made (discussed below) and this gets the page concerned and invokes the indexing process. Once all remote pages have been indexed, the SaveIndexPage() method very simply persists the XML file. The thesaurus component is ended and a success message box is shown:

```
    For j=0 To objNode.childNodes.length-1
        Set objSiteNode = objNode.childNodes(j)
        strPageName=objSiteNode.getAttribute("name")
        GetRemotePage strSiteURL,strPageName,strUserName,strPassword
    Next
Next

SaveIndexPage

'Close data checker
If bolOK Then
    obj.KillComponent
End If

Msgbox "Procesing Completed!"
end function
```

The `GetRemotePage()` method we mentioned determines the page type (`htm` or `xml`), gets the data from that remote page, and calls the appropriate method to handle the data returned. The first test is for `.htm` pages – when this is the case, an instance of the `InternetExplorer.Application` object is created and the `Navigate()` method is used, with the URL, to get the remote HTML web page. You may ask why we used this for HTML pages rather than just using `ServerXMLHTTP` and getting the `responseText`. This is because HTML is often not valid XML, so `responseXML` could fail. The `InternetExplorer.Application` object allows us to access the web page programmatically as a web document and so DHTML can be used – this is illustrated later on. We used the `Busy` property and `sleep` method to wait for the page to be fully downloaded before continuing. When the page is complete, the `GetHTMLMetaInformation()` method is called – notice that the final parameter is the `Document` property of the object, which is the same as the DHTML document object.

```
Dim objIE
Dim keep_going
function GetRemotePage(strSiteURL,strPageURL,strUsername,strPassword)
    keep_going=true
    Dim strServerPath

    strServerPath = strSiteURL & strPageURL

    'If HTML doc then use web browser to get META info
    If instr(1,strPageURL,".htm") Then
        Set objIE = WScript.CreateObject("InternetExplorer.Application")
        objIE.Navigate strServerPath

        While objIE.Busy
            WScript.Sleep 100
        Wend

        GetHTMLMetaInformation strSiteURL,strPageURL,objIE.Document
    Else
```

A similar process to that above is used for XML documents, but the `ServerXMLHTTP` approach is used instead. We won't go into this because we used the same process in the registration stage, but when the remote XML page has been downloaded, it is passed into the `GetXMLMetaInformation()` method. One thing worth noting is that the `SelectionNamespaces` property has been set to `xmlns:nw="http://sightkeys.com/schema/newsnet.xsd"`, which is required because this is the default namespace of the XML documents that are created – future XPath queries on this document will use this.

```
        ... 'get Remote page using serverXMLHTTP
        Set objMetaXML = WScript.CreateObject ("MSXML2.DomDocument.4.0")
        objMetaXML.async=false
        objMetaXML.setProperty "SelectionNamespaces",
                        "xmlns:nw='http://sightkeys.com/schema/newsnet.xsd'"
        objMetaXML.load(objXMLHTTPSrv.responseXML)

        GetXMLMetaInformation objMetaXML,strSiteURL,strPageURL
    End If
end function
```

In the previous method, the handler for HTML documents is called `GetHTMLMetaInformation()`, which performs the task of extracting meta data from the web document. Firstly, it gets all the `<meta>` element tags and iterates through each element, setting appropriate variables based on the `Name` (for example, `"NewsItem"`) and `Content` (for example, `"global"`) of the `<meta>` tag. Similarly, the `<title>` and `<body>` of the document are stored in the variables `strTitle` and `strBody` respectively. Also, a shortened version of the `<body>` text is stored in the `strPreview` variable – this is the summary text you see on the front page of the portal.

```
function GetHTMLMetaInformation(strSiteURI,strFilePath,objDocument)
    Set objMeta = objDocument.getElementsByTagName("meta")

    For intMetaLen=0 To objMeta.length-1
        strName =  objMeta(intMetaLen).getAttribute("Name")
        strContent =  objMeta(intMetaLen).getAttribute("Content")
        ...
    Next

    strTitle = objDocument.getElementsByTagName("title")(0).innerHTML
    strBody = objDocument.getElementsByTagName("body")(0).innerHTML
    strPreview = Left(objDocument.getElementsByTagName("body")(0)_
                    .innerText,100) & "..."
```

Following this, three methods are called that are at the core of the portal. `StoreMetaInIndex()` populates the site index XML file with summary details of the pages, returns a site-unique local URL to the entry, and stores it in `strUniqueURL`. The index page is what is used to create the front page of the site. `SaveXMLDocument()` stores the information retrieved from the HTML source in a site-wide common XML structure using the unique URL in `strUniqueURL`. Finally, the `CreateBrowsableDocuments()` method uses the `strUniqueURL` to locate the common XML document format of the story to create a series of documents that users can browse. We'll look at these shortly.

```
    strUniqueURL = StoreMetaInIndex(strTitle,strPreview, strSiteURI, _
            strFilePath,strItem,strRegisterURL,strEntryTime, _
            strLastUpdateTime,arrKeywords)

    SaveXMLDocument strUniqueURL,strTitle,strBody,strRegisterURL, _
        strEntryTime,strLastUpdateTime

    'Create HTML, Netscape & WAP
    CreateBrowsableDocuments(strUniqueURL)
end function
```

The `GetXMLMetaInformation()` method does a very similar thing to the HTML-based method above. It first gets the values of the appropriate attributes and then creates an array of the keywords in the XML document. It gets the title and body content from the file, but must use a qualified namespace to do this. We defined the `SelectionNamespaces` property in the `GetRemotePage()` method above and this is where it is used. (Remember, this is because the story has a default namespace and we cannot use default empty namespaces in this way in XPath. We must assign it some prefix, although this prefix doesn't need to be the same as the prefix in the document, because it is the expanded namespaces that are compared and *not* the name of the prefix). When this is done, the three methods called at the end of `GetHTMLMetaInformation()` are also called. At this point, there is no difference in the type of source document as all documents are now in a single XML format.

```
function GetXMLMetaInformation(objXML,strSiteURI,strFilePath)
   Dim arrKeywords()

   strItem = objXML.documentElement.selectSingleNode("@NewsItem").text
   ... 'Other attributes

   Set objKeywordNode = objXML.documentElement.childNodes(0)
   For intKeywords=0 To objKeywordNode.childNodes.length-1
      ReDim Preserve arrKeywords(intKeywords+1)
      arrKeywords(intKeywords) = objKeywordNode.childNodes(intKeywords).text
   Next

   strTitle = objXML.documentElement.selectSingleNode("//nw:name").text
   strBody = objXML.documentElement.selectSingleNode("//nw:text") _
      .childNodes(0).text
   strPreview = Left(strBody,100) & "..."

   ...
end function
```

The `StoreMetaInIndex()` method loads the `index.xml` portal repository document. A new `<entry>` element is created and a portal-unique string is created that will be the physical location of the XML file – it is based on date and file information to ensure uniqueness (though daily iterative uniqueness has not yet been dealt with). Next, attributes are assigned to the new `<entry>` element, and the `title`, `body`, and `keyword` values are also appended as child element nodes to this `<entry>` element. Finally, the populated `<entry>` element is appended to the `index.xml` document and the unique URL to the XML document is returned:

```
Dim objIndexXML
function StoreMetaInIndex(strTitle,strPreview,strSiteURI,strFilePath,strItem,
   strRegisterURL,strEntryTime,strLastUpdate,arrKeywords)

   If NOT IsObject(objIndexXML) Then
      Set objIndexXML = WScript.CreateObject ("MSXML2.DomDocument.4.0")
      objIndexXML.async=false
      objIndexXML.load("index.xml")
      ... 'remove previous entries
   End If

   Set objNewNode = objIndexXML.createElement("entry")
   strUnique = Day(Date) & "_" & MonthName(Month(Date)) & "_" & Year(Date) &
      "_" & replace(mid(strSiteURI,8) & left(strFilePath,Len(strFilePath)-4)
      ,"/","_") & ".xml"

   objNewNode.setAttribute "LocalURL",strUnique
   ... 'other attribute values entered

   objNewNode.text=strPreview

   Set objTitleNode = objIndexXML.createElement("title")
   objTitleNode.text=strTitle
   Set objNewKWNode = objNewNode.appendChild(objTitleNode)

   Dim intCountarrKeywords
   intCountarrKeywords = UBOUND(arrKeywords)
   For intKeys=0 To intCountarrKeywords-1
      Set objKWNode = objIndexXML.createElement("keyword")
      objKWNode.text=arrKeywords(intKeys)
```

```
        Set objNewKWNode = objNewNode.appendChild(objKWNode)
        Set objResNode = objNewNode.appendChild(objNewKWNode)
    Next

    objIndexXML.documentElement.appendChild(objNewNode)

    StoreMetaInIndex = strUnique
end function
```

The `SaveXMLDocument()` builds a string to represent the story, loads this as a `DOMDocument` instance, and saves this as an XML document at the location defined by the `strLocation` argument (the unique URL). Notice that a method called `InsertThesaurusTerms()` is called, which we'll briefly discuss next.

```
function SaveXMLDocument(strLocation,strTitle,strBody,strRegisterURL,
strEntryTime,
    strLastUpdateTime)
    ...
    strNewXML = "<?xml-stylesheet type='text/xsl' href='IE60.xsl' ?>"
    ...
    strNewXML = strNewXML & "<body><![CDATA[" &
    InsertThesaurusTerms(strBody) &
    "]]></body>"
    ...

    objNewXML.Save(strLocation)
end function
```

We won't be going into the `InsertThesaurusTerms()` method much – the section entitled "*Dynamic Thesaurus*" below discusses how it is used. Basically, it iterates through each word in the body of text that is passed to it and does two things. Firstly, it uses the `terms.xml` document to find custom definitions of words, and outputs these custom definitions using JavaScript. It also uses the `Livingstone.dll` we registered earlier (stored in the `obj` global variable) to check for associated word definitions using Microsoft Office Thesaurus (if it is installed).

```
function InsertThesaurusTerms(strText)
    ...
    Set objThesaurusXML = Wscript.CreateObject
("MSXML2.FreeThreadedDomDocument.4.0")
    objThesaurusXML.async=false
    objThesaurusXML.load("../Thesaurus/terms.xml")
    ...
    InsertThesaurusTerms = strText
end function
```

Finally, the `CreateBrowsableDocuments()` method is where the documents that most users will see are actually created! The unique URL to the local XML document is passed as an argument. First, an array is created that has a comma-separated list of the browser types that are to have an HTML document created for them by the stylesheet named after the pipe symbol. There are other ways of doing this and perhaps an improvement on this would be similar to the `devices.xml` file that is discussed in Chapter 10, "*Transformations on the Server*" and briefly below. However, in this case, the stylesheet is determined and `IE50` and `IE60` are actually used to make the result of the transforms unique for each browser, so you can make use of any advanced techniques available in IE 6 and not IE 5 (such as element behaviors).

```
function CreateBrowsableDocuments(strUniqueURL)
    Dim BrowsArray(2)
    BrowsArray(0) = "IE50,IE60|IE60.xsl"
    BrowsArray(1) = "Netscape60|Netscape60.xsl"
```

Next, the XML document instance (determined by the unique URL we talked about earlier) is loaded. The `BrowsArray` array is then iterated through and the XSL associated with each index is loaded. A `FileSystemObject` instance is then created (assuming the account that is running has the privileges to create an instance of this) for each browser type using the unique XML name as a basis for the new file name, but `.htm` files are created instead for each browser. The `Write` method of the `TextStream` object takes the actual transform result as its argument – resulting in the creation of an HTML version. Finally, the `TextStream` is closed and the offline process is completed.

```
    Set objBrowserXML = CreateObject("MSXML2.DomDocument.4.0")
    objBrowserXML.async=false
    objBrowserXML.load(strUniqueURL)

    Dim intCountBrowsArray
    intCountBrowsArray = UBOUND(BrowsArray)
    For intBrowsers=0 To intCountBrowsArray-1
        strCurrentFile=Split(BrowsArray(intBrowsers),"|")(1)
        strTargetArray=Split(Split(BrowsArray(intBrowsers),"|")(0),",")

        Set objBrowserXSL = WScript.CreateObject ("MSXML2.DomDocument.4.0")
        objBrowserXSL.async=false
        objBrowserXSL.load(strCurrentFile)

        set fso = WScript.CreateObject ("Scripting.FileSystemObject")

        Dim intCountstrTargetArray
        intCountstrTargetArray = UBOUND(strTargetArray)
        For intNumFiles=0 To intCountstrTargetArray
          Set TextStream = FSO.CreateTextFile(Replace(strUniqueURL,".xml","_" &
            Left(strTargetArray(intNumFiles),Len(strTargetArray(intNumFiles)))
              & ".htm"))

          TextStream.Write objBrowserXML.transformNode(objBrowserXSL)
          TextStream.Close
        Next
    Next
end function
```

`CreateIndex.vbs` script has used many resources and produced quite a lot of output, so where do we start to analyze these? Let's first look at the updates to `index.xml` – remember that this file contains all the files that were in `config.xml` and were successfully indexed.

The new `index.xml` is shown below, though not all of the entry elements are shown here, to save space. They are really all the same as the one below with slightly different data. Notice the `LocalURL` attribute, which contains the unique URL to the XML instance we have been talking about.

index.xml

```
<?xml version="1.0" encoding="utf-8" ?>
<?xml-stylesheet type="text/css" href="/ProPortal/index/index.css" ?>
<Index>
    <entry>
```

```
        LocalURL="7_November_2001_localhost_ProPortal_remote1_businessheadlines.xml"
    source="http://localhost/ProPortal/remote1/businessheadlines.htm"
    type="business"
    registerURL="http://localhost/ProPortal/remote1/register.asp"
    EntryTime="12:23:00" LastUpdate="23:23:00">
    Glasgow hosts XML Exhibition
Glasgow is to host the world renound XML Expert Convention in March
a...<title>Glasgow hosts XML
Convention</title><keyword>Glasgow</keyword><keyword>XML</keyword></entry>
...
</Index>
```

As was mentioned earlier, an XML document for every story is also persisted in the index section in order to provide an independent store of the story – this also happens for XML sources that have been indexed. Effectively the pages are cached. The template XML document for a story instance is shown below:

```
<?xml-stylesheet type='text/xsl' href='IE60.xsl' ?>
<story registerURL="" EntryTime="" LastUpdateTime="">
   <title></title>
   <body>
      <![CDATA[ ... ]]>
   </body>
</story>
```

The portal primarily targets IE 6.0 users, and so there is a default stylesheet processing instruction pointing to IE60.xsl (discussed later) – this is overridden for any other type of browser. A root <story> element has three attributes – the registerURL, the EntryTime, and the LastUpdateTime. Finally, any story should consist of a <title> and <body>, the latter containing a CDATA section to escape special characters as this will be an HTML section.

This result (just a fragment as the output is quite large) is shown below for our sample story businessHeadlines.htm in the remote1 location, which has been stored in the index as 7_November_2001_localhost_ProPortal_remote1_businessheadlines.xml (this will be slightly different depending on when you run it).

```
<?xml-stylesheet type='text/xsl' href='IE60.xsl' ?>
<story registerURL="http://localhost/ProPortal/remote1/register.asp"
   EntryTime="12:23:00" LastUpdateTime="23:23:00"><title>Glasgow hosts XML
   Convention</title><body>

<![CDATA[<H1><span class='glossary'
   onmouseover="ShowGlossary(this,unescape
   ('European%20country%20with%20population%20of%20approx.
   %2016%20million.%20Native%20Spanish%20language.'));">Glasgow</span> hosts
   <span class='glossary' onmouseover="ShowGlossary(this,unescape
   ('Extensible%20Markup%20Language.'));">XML</span> <span
class='glossaryT' onmouseover="ShowGlossary(this,unescape('%3Cwords%20type
count%3D%221%22%3E%3Ctype%20num%3D%221%22%3E%3Cword%20index%3D%221%22%3
Edisplay%3C/word%3E%3Cword%20index%3D%222%22%3Eshow%3C/word%3E%3Cword%20
index%3D%223%22%3Eshowing%3C/word%3E%3Cword%20index%3D%224%22%3
Edemonstration%3C/word%3E%3Cword%20index%3D%225%22%3Eexposition%3C/word
%3E%3Cword%20index%3D%226%22%3Etrade%20fair%3C/word%3E%3Cword%20index%3D%
227%22%3Epresentation%3C/word%3E%3Cword%20index%3D%228%22%3Efair%3C/word%
3E%3Cword%20index%3D%229%22%3Eretrospective%3C/word%3E%3Cword%20index%3D%
2210%22%3Eshowcase%3C/word%3E%3C/type%3E%3C/words%3E'))">Exhibition</span> </H1>
.
]]></body></story>
```

First thing – don't worry about the %XX characters all over the place – it has worked correctly and these characters simply escape the characters within the JScript code (such as quotes)! This is to prevent various types of character clashes I was getting when mixing scripting with my XML output – the most notable being various quote characters. Also, you will notice a lot of ShowGlossary() JavaScript code fragments – this is related to the thesaurus we talked about earlier and which we will detail later on.

You will see many files in the /ProPortal/index/ directory, not only like the XML file discussed above, but with _IE50.htm, _IE60.htm, and _Netscape60.htm endings also. What has happened? Well, the portal is multi-browser (and easily multi-device) and the XML file discussed above has been the basis for XSLT transformations into the various browser formats. In fact, there is an XML, IE 5, IE 6 and Netscape file created for every page that was indexed.

There is an XSLT stylesheet in the /ProPortal/index directory for IE 6 (including 5.0/5.5) and Netscape 6.0, although it is very easy to add more – all of these stylesheets produce almost exactly the same results, although the methods used to do this vary based on browser functionality. In fact, it is recommended that specific stylesheets be created for IE 5, so you can take advantage of client-side XML capabilities. However, due to time constraints (and the fact this is a chapter and not the entire MSDN Library), this was not done. You *can* see a very detailed example of this for the creation of the front page discussed further below, which does use specific stylesheets and client-side XML capabilities.

> One point that needs making is the remarkable cross-functionality available between the latest versions of IE and Netscape. In fact, much of the styling and DHTML worked immediately, although some very basic modifications were sometimes required. However, with the experiences of prior version incompatibility, the later version saved a lot of time, effort, patience, and hair.

The IE 6 stylesheet is the most powerful and uses an array of XML-based technologies used in this book, including the Vector Markup Language, element behaviors, the XML DOM, as well as DHTML and various other techniques. The Netscape stylesheet is a toned-down version of the IE 6 stylesheet, inserting the actual HTML rather than using element behaviors, for example. However, don't let this put you off the power of using element behaviors, because it was not any more difficult than copying the code from the element behavior and removing a few pieces of text! Have a look at the Netscape stylesheet to compare the code.

Rather than look at them all, let's consider the most powerful and exciting – the IE 6 stylesheet. Remember that this stylesheet is never actually used when a user comes to the site – it is part of the offline process. This is called IE60.xsl in the /ProPortal/index directory. The output is set to HTML 4.0 and an xsl:apply-templates starts processing from the document root. The first template match finds <story> elements, which start by defining a child HTML element with two namespace definitions. The first is for our own custom element behaviors and is defined as xmlns:ProPortal, and the second references the VML namespace:

```
<?xml version="1.0" ?>
<xsl:stylesheet version="1.0"
    xmlns:xsl="http://www.w3.org/1999/XSL/Transform">
    <xsl:output method="html" version="4.0" />
    <xsl:template match="/">
        <xsl:apply-templates />
    </xsl:template>
    <xsl:template match="story">
        <html xmlns:ProPortal="uri:ProPortal"
            xmlns:vml="urn:schemas-microsoft-com:vml">
            <head>
```

As you read in Chapter 7, *Styling XML Content*, you have to import the namespace definitions for any element behaviors you are going to use. These are of the format:

```
<?IMPORT namespace="name" implementation="location">
```

There are two ways to do this – the first is to use the xsl:processing-instruction element to create a PI, as was done in the IE50.xsl file. As you can see, there is no question mark at the end of the behavior import (as defined by Microsoft in MSDN) the xsl:text element with output escaping disabled, allows both register.htc and navbar.htc to be imported. A stylesheet, IEStyle.css, is also referenced and this contains some basic DHTML behaviors. There is also a block of JavaScript code that is output to the HTML client – this works with the thesaurus definitions covered below, so we won't touch on it here. Additionally, there is some VML that is used to display a logo for the page in the same manner as was discussed in Chapter 7.

```
            <xsl:text disable-output-escaping="yes">
              <![CDATA[<?IMPORT namespace="ProPortal"
                  implementation="../behav/register.htc">
              <?IMPORT namespace="ProPortal"
                  implementation="/ProPortal/behav/navbar.htc">]]>
            </xsl:text>
          <link rel="stylesheet" type="text/css" href="IEStyle.css" />

<script language="JavaScript">
   <xsl:comment><![CDATA[
      ...//JavaScript code
   ]]>//</xsl:comment>
</script>
            <title>
               <xsl:value-of select="title" />
            </title>
          </head>
          ... <!-- VML LOGO -->
            </p>
            <hr />
```

So, immediately after the logo the navigation bar is displayed, using the navbar behavior we imported above, with the appropriate attributes – we'll look at this shortly. The entry and update times are inserted, as is the body (or content) of the document, with output escaping disabled so the markup is persisted:

```
            <div>
               <ProPortal:navbar
                    nav1="Front Page|/ProPortal/default.asp|false"/>
            </div>
            <i>Entered At : <xsl:value-of select="@EntryTime" /> -
               <b>Last Updated At
               <xsl:value-of select="@LastUpdateTime" />
               </b>
            </i>
            <br />
            <xsl:value-of select="body"
                    disable-output-escaping="yes" />
            <hr />
```

Finally, the `register` element behavior is inserted, which allows the user to enter their name and e-mail address, and have it sent to the provider of the content they are reading. The `postTo` attribute determines the URL the content will be sent to – the XPath `substring-before()` function allows us to extract the stem from the `registerURL` attribute and add the `XML.asp` to this stem. This says that we want to use the XML interface of the content provider's site rather than the default `POST` interface (as is used in Netscape). This displays the individual story pages we can see in the portal.

```
                <ProPortal:register
                    postTo="{substring-before(@registerURL,'.asp')}XML.asp"
                    stylefile="/ProPortal/behav/RegisterNameEmail.css">
                    <span class="message">Liked this story?
                        Enter your name and email address and we'll
                        notify you of updates.
                    </span>
                </ProPortal:register>
            </body>
        </html>
    </xsl:template>
    <xsl:template match="text()" />
</xsl:stylesheet>
```

There were some interesting components that made up this XSLT file. The CSS file `IEStyle.css` contains some style and DHTML behavior detail and you should look at this source on your own – there is nothing complicated about it. The two element behaviors are interesting, though – first look at `navbar.htc` (in `\ProPortal\behav`), which was used in the XSLT document as follows:

```
<ProPortal:navbar nav1="Front Page|/ProPortal/default.asp|false"/>
```

We want to prevent the navigation bar from being part of the hosting document, mainly because it is a separate component, and so encapsulating it and preventing outside forces from modifying it is better design; so the `viewLinkContent` is set to `true`. The `DoInit()` method is attached to the `ondocumentready` event of the hosting document. Also, six properties are created – this means that we can have six items in the navigation menu and they must be named `na1`, `nav2`, through to `nav6`.

```
<PUBLIC:COMPONENT tagName="navbar">
    <PUBLIC:DEFAULTS viewLinkContent="True" />
    <PUBLIC:ATTACH EVENT="ondocumentready" ONEVENT="DoInit()" />
    <PUBLIC:PROPERTY NAME="nav1" />
    <PUBLIC:PROPERTY NAME="nav2" />
    <PUBLIC:PROPERTY NAME="nav3" />
    <PUBLIC:PROPERTY NAME="nav4" />
    <PUBLIC:PROPERTY NAME="nav5" />
    <PUBLIC:PROPERTY NAME="nav6" />
    <SCRIPT LANGUAGE="jscript">

function DoInit() {
    NavBarDefaults();
    CreateNavBar();
}
```

The `NavBarDefaults()` method puts each valid `navX` property into a `NavItems` array – because often, less than six items will be used, and we will only want to process a couple.

```
var NavItems = new Array();
function NavBarDefaults() {
   var i=0;

   if (nav1!=null)
      NavItems[i++]=nav1;
   if (nav2!=null)
      NavItems[i++]=nav2;
   if (nav3!=null)
      NavItems[i++]=nav3;
   if (nav4!=null)
      NavItems[i++]=nav4;
   if (nav5!=null)
      NavItems[i++]=nav5;
   if (nav6!=null)
      NavItems[i++]=nav6;
}
```

Finally, the navigation menu can actually be created using the `CreateNavBar()` method. The `htmTxt` variable is gradually built up as iterations through each of the items in the `NavItems` array are made:

```
function CreateNavBar() {

   var htmTxt="";
   htmTxt += "<div style='background-color:darkblue;'>"
   for (var i=0;i<NavItems.length;i++)
   {
```

Each array item (and hence nav item) actually takes a pre-defined format of `"Display Name|Link URL|NewWindow"`; the `NewWindow` is a Boolean indicating whether the link should open in a new window. So, with each value extracted from the array item, the link item is created, separated by a `"|"` character.

```
      var strText = NavItems[i].split("|")[0];
      var strLink = NavItems[i].split("|")[1];
      var strNewWin = NavItems[i].split("|")[2];

      htmTxt += "<a style='color:White;text-decoration:none;
         font-weight:bold;behavior:url(/ProPortal/behav/hiLite.htc)'
          class='navItem'"
      if (strNewWin=="true")
         htmTxt += " onclick=\"window.open('" + strLink
            + "');return(false);\">" + strText
      else
         htmTxt += " href='" + strLink + "'>" + strText

         if (i+1<NavItems.length)
            htmTxt += "<b> | </b>"

         htmTxt +="</a>"
   }
   htmTxt += "</div>"
```

Finally, the resulting `DIV` navigation bar is displayed to the user within the element behavior tag, by setting the `innerHTML` property of the `body` element to the value of the string `htmTxt`:

```
      document.body.innerHTML = htmTxt;
   }

   </SCRIPT>
   </PUBLIC:COMPONENT>
```

The other behavior, `register.htc`, is used in the source document as follows:

```
<ProPortal:register postTo="{substring-before(@registerURL,'.asp')}XML.asp"
    stylefile="/ProPortal/behav/RegisterNameEmail.css">
    <span class="message">Liked this story?
       Enter your name and e-mail address and we'll notify you of updates.
    </span>
</ProPortal:register>
```

The component is defined as shown below with a `tagName` value of `register`. It also has `viewLinkContent` as `true` and uses the `DoInit()` method, with some attributes attached to the document, all of which are self-explanatory. The `LogonDefaults()` function sets some initial values for the fields if nothing is passed when it is instanced, and the `CreateLogon()` form works in a similar way to the `navbar` behavior, showing the form fields for the user to enter their values into.

```
<PUBLIC:COMPONENT tagName="register">
    <PUBLIC:DEFAULTS viewLinkContent="True" />
    <PUBLIC:ATTACH EVENT="ondocumentready" ONEVENT="DoInit()" />
    <PUBLIC:PROPERTY NAME="name" />
    <PUBLIC:PROPERTY NAME="email" />
    <PUBLIC:PROPERTY NAME="postTo" />
    <PUBLIC:PROPERTY NAME="stylefile" />
    <SCRIPT LANGUAGE="jscript">

function DoInit()
{
   LoginDefaults();
   CreateLogin();
}

function LoginDefaults()
{
...
}

function CreateLogin()
{
   var htmTxt="";
   htmTxt += "<link rel='stylesheet' type='text/css' href='" + stylefile +
      "' />"
   htmTxt += "<div id='message'></div>"
   htmTxt += "<form id='form' name='' method='post' action='" + postTo +
      "'>"
   htmTxt += "<label id='' for=''>Name</label><br />"
   htmTxt += "<input type='text' id='name' name='name' value='" + name +
      "'></input>"
   htmTxt += "<br />"
   htmTxt += "<label id='' for=''>Email</label><br />"
   htmTxt += "<input type='text' id='email' name='email' value='" + email +
      "'></input>"
```

The submission, however, is done by clicking on the **register me** link, which calls the `PostInfo()` method:

```
    htmTxt += "<a href='' onclick='PostInfo();return(false);'>register
        me</a>"
    htmTxt += "</form>"

    document.body.innerHTML = element.innerHTML + htmTxt;
}
```

The `PostInfo()` method takes the newly entered user's name and e-mail address and builds a short XML string wrapping these values. It is this string that is then loaded as a full XML `DOMDocument` into the `xmlDoc` variable. An `XMLHTTP` instance is then created (remember this will be executed on the client, not server) and the `xmlDoc` document is `POST`ed to the address given in the `postTo` attribute. Finally, the `responseText` from the `XMLHTTP` instance is replaced as the element display – currently this shows a simple message, but the display message can be changed on the server anyway.

```
function PostInfo()
{
    strName=document.all("name").value;
    strEmail=document.all("email").value;

    var strXMLUser = "<UserInfo><name>"+strName
    strXMLUser+="</name><email>"+strEmail+"</email></UserInfo>"

    var xmlDoc = new ActiveXObject("Msxml2.DOMDocument.4.0");
    xmlDoc.async = false;
    xmlDoc.loadXML(strXMLUser);

        var xmlhttp = new ActiveXObject("Msxml2.XMLHTTP.4.0");
    xmlhttp.Open("POST", postTo, false);
        xmlhttp.Send(xmlDoc);

    document.all("form").style.display="none";
    document.all("message").innerHTML=xmlhttp.responseText;
}

</SCRIPT>
</PUBLIC:COMPONENT>
```

Before continuing with more code, let's check the portal to see how it looks at this point – once again we are going to concentrate on IE – the Netscape version is similar. Navigate to the ProPortal front page and click on the **Glasgow hosts XML Convention** link to take you to the output generated from the `businessHeadlines.htm` page found at `remote1`. You will see a screen like this – the notes in boxes indicate some XML technologies that are used in the page:

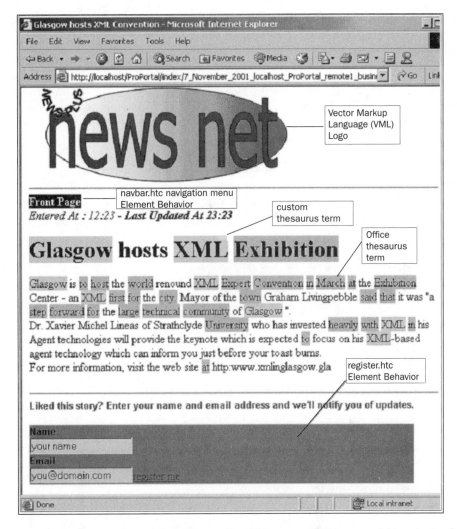

For the moment don't question why there is shading (there is actually gray and blue shading) over the words in the document – that will be explained in the dynamic thesaurus section next.

Dynamic Thesaurus

There is something we never touched much on when working with the indexing process above, although it does work within the offline process, and that is the portal's thesaurus. As part of every page that is indexed in the portal, an additional feature is the "term finder". The intention of this is to insert some semantic information on top of the content provided to the site. Currently this comes in two forms – the first is based on the thesaurus provided with Microsoft Word and the latter is your own custom thesaurus.

For example, a document may contain the word "delineate", but a reader may not know what this means, or it may be a different vocabulary from what they're used to – a good example being the various technical words used in many documents we read! What the term finder does (during the offline process we discussed earlier) is to look up words that are similar to this and present them within the document, so that the user can move the mouse over a given word with terms associated with it (hence the shading) and DHTML is used to show the user the word. In the case of the Office-based utility, the Microsoft Word thesaurus is used to get associated words – remember that you can define your own custom dictionaries in MS Word, so this utility can be very powerful. An example is shown in the figure below for the word "technical" – the mouse was moved over this word:

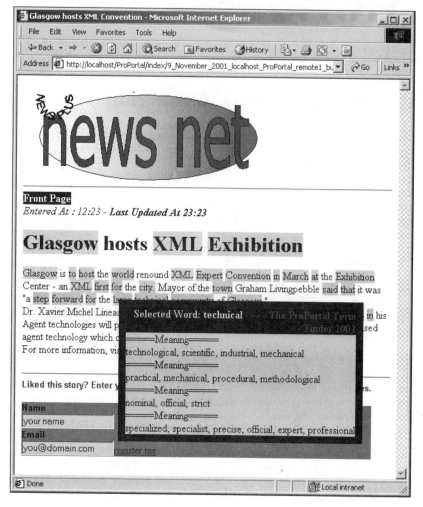

Furthermore, the portal allows you to define your own words in a thesaurus XML file we will look at shortly – the sample opposite is how the custom definition of XML may appear in Netscape – of course you would probably add more to this definition.

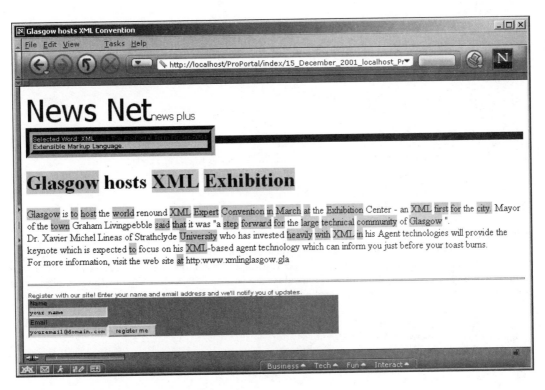

How the Dynamic Thesaurus Works

There are two methods to determine which words are to be highlighted when working with the thesaurus. The first is out of your command and basically works through the words in the text of the document and checks if there is some equivalent word(s) in the Microsoft Word thesaurus. The second is by explicit definition in the `terms.xml` file – this is discussed below.

Earlier, when looking at the `IE60.xsl` document, we delayed looking at how the thesaurus script worked. In fact, in the output any words that have been matched are shaded in gray and blue, and moving your mouse over these produces a visible `DIV` tag with the terms that are associated with this word – we saw this above. It has been commented that a round trip may be better rather than having all the words initially – it really depends on the user's knowledge of the subject base – I sure would want a lot for an essay on "Cooking Japanese-Style" (and my family equally for "Symptoms of food poisoning")! The terms are within some JavaScript placed in a `<SPAN>` element round each word that has associated terms – viewing the source of the HTML document will show you this – an example for the `XML` term is shown below:

```
<span class='glossary'
      onmouseover="ShowGlossary
                   (this,unescape('Extensible%20Markup%20Language.'));">
    XML
</span>
```

The code that actually displays this information is the JavaScript below. The `ShowGlossary()` method starts by getting the text of the element that caused the event using the `innerHTML` property, and also gets a reference to the (initially hidden) `DIV` tag that will pop up to display the information to the user. Some header information is then built up that you can see at the top of this `DIV` tag:

```
<SCRIPT LANGUAGE="JavaScript">
<!--
   var objLast="";
   var word="";
   function ShowGlossary(obj,strTerm)
      {
         strWord = obj.innerHTML;
         word = document.getElementById("worddef");
         word.style.display="block";

         strHeader+="<div align='right' "
         strHeader+="style='background-color:black;color:red;"
         strHeader+="font-weight:bold;'>"
         strHeader+="<span style='color:lightblue'>Selected Word:"
         strHeader+="<span style='color:yellow'>"+ strWord + "</span>"
         strHeader+="</span> ---- The ProPortal Term Finder 2001</div>"
```

Following this, the `charAt()` method determines if the term string that was passed starts with a "<" character. This is because the custom elements return a simple string (we will this see below) and the Office-based word checks return an XML string. The XML string is passed into the `XMLToText()` method and the result is written to the output; the simple string values are written out directly. Finally, the `DIV` element is correctly positioned and the window is scrolled (useful when the `DIV` moved out of the screen).

```
         if (strTerm.charAt(0)=="<")
            word.innerHTML=strHeader + XMLToText(strTerm);
         else
            word.innerHTML=strHeader + strTerm;

         word.style.left=event.x-50;
         word.style.top=event.y-10;
         objLast=event.srcElement;

         window.scrollTo(600, window.top)
      }
```

The `XMLToText()` method accepts the XML term string and loads it as a document. It then simply iterates through each node and writes it to the output:

```
   function XMLToText(strTerm)
   {
         var strHTML="";

         var obj = new ActiveXObject("Microsoft.XMLDOM");
         obj.async=false;
         bol = obj.loadXML(strTerm);

         ...

      return strHTML;
   }
//--></SCRIPT>
```

Defining custom words is quite simple and you need know nothing about the programming interface. This is done in the `terms.xml` file and a fragment of the one given with the sample is shown:

```
<?xml version="1.0" encoding="utf-8" ?>
<Thesaurus>
    <PreferredTerm>
        <text>Chile</text>
        <gloss>South American country with population of approx. 16 million.
            Native Spanish language.
        </gloss>
    </PreferredTerm>
    <PreferredTerm>
        <text>glasgow</text>
        <gloss>European city in Scotland with population of approx. 1 million.
            Native English language.
        </gloss>
    </PreferredTerm>
    <PreferredTerm>
        <text>XML</text>
        <gloss>Extensible Markup Language.</gloss>
    </PreferredTerm>
    .
</Thesaurus>
```

To have some custom term added to this document, simply create a new `<PreferredTerm>` element and enter the string of the text value to match in the `<text>` element, along with its definition in the `<gloss>` element. The next time the offline process is run, your new definitions will be added to the output documents where appropriate. We discussed the process briefly above in the `InsertThesaurusTerms()` method.

The Front Page

Finally we get back to the front page, `default.asp`, which we saw in an earlier figure. This brings the portal together and is the first page users hit when they visit the site.

default.asp

The variable `intNumDisplayItems` is quite important. On the front page you will see colored blocks of news slots. The maximum number of these blocks is defined by this variable and when this value is reached, the remaining headlines are places as text lines below these blocks. This is also the default value in the stylesheets if this value is not set. As we keep saying, the `index.xml` is what the site revolves around and so this is loaded – it is loaded each time, but as this data rarely changes (relatively speaking) there is no good reason not to cache this as some application-wide object!

```
<%@ Language="JScript"%>
<%
var intNumDisplayItems=6;

var xmlDoc = Server.CreateObject("Msxml2.DOMDocument.4.0");
xmlDoc.async = false;
bol = xmlDoc.load(Server.MapPath("/ProPortal/index/index.xml"));
```

So, once this is done, a method called `GetDeviceInfo()` returns the browser name and version (see below), which is stored in variables. Next, it gets a bit more exciting – there are three possible things that happen now. If the number of items to display is 6 (the default in the XSLT document) and the browser is IE 6.0, then a processing instruction is created to associate the `index_IE60.xsl` stylesheet with the XML index document, and the XML document is written directly to the XML-enabled browser. This is the best performance option as almost no server work is required.

```
var objDictDevice = GetDeviceInfo()
var strB = objDictDevice("browser")
var strV = objDictDevice("version")

if (intNumDisplayItems==6 && strB=="IE" && parseInt(strV)==parseInt("6.0"))
{
   Response.ContentType="text/xml";

   var pi = xmlDoc.createProcessingInstruction("xml-
      stylesheet","type=\"text/xsl\" href=\"/ProPortal/Index_IE60.xsl\"")
   var oNew = xmlDoc.insertBefore(pi, xmlDoc.childNodes.item(1));

   Response.Write(xmlDoc.xml)
}
```

Another alternative is that the client is IE 5.0 or 5.5 and therefore supports the earlier version of XSL. We have to do a little more in this case – we can't load it on the server using MSXML 4.0 because it doesn't support the old XSL language. In addition, the old language doesn't support passing parameters (which the IE 6 XSL version did!). So, to simulate this and allow display of the variable that specifies the number of item blocks, the XML DOM is used to get the first child node of the stylesheet element, which is in fact a JavaScript block. The text inside this is set to "var i=X", where X is the number of items to display and so i is now a global variable that can be (and is) accessed in the XSL scripting. This update is saved to disk to update the stylesheet (as it is unlikely to happen very often) and finally, as in the IE 6.0 method above, a processing instruction is appended and the XML written directly to the client.

```
else if (intNumDisplayItems==6 && strB=="IE" && ((parseInt(strV)==parseInt("5.0"))
|| parseInt(strV)==parseInt("5.5")))
{
   Response.ContentType="text/xml";

   if (intNumDisplayItems!=Application("IE50NumItems"))
   {
      var xslDoc = Server.CreateObject ("Msxml2.FreeThreadedDOMDocument.4.0")
      xslDoc.async = false
      xslDoc.resolveExternals=false
      xslDoc.validateOnParse=false;
      bol = xslDoc.load(server.MapPath("/ProPortal/Index_IE50.xsl"))
      xslDoc.childNodes(1).childNodes(0).text="var i=" + intNumDisplayItems
         + ";";
      xslDoc.save(server.MapPath("/ProPortal/Index_IE50.xsl"))   //must
         have "write" rights to this file

      Application.Lock
      Application("IE50NumItems")=intNumDisplayItems;
      Application.UnLock
   }

   var pi = xmlDoc.createProcessingInstruction("xml-
      stylesheet","type=\"text/xsl\" href=\"/ProPortal/Index_IE50.xsl\"")
   var oNew = xmlDoc.insertBefore(pi, xmlDoc.childNodes.item(1));

   Response.Write(xmlDoc.xml);
}
```

Finally, the other option catches all other considerations and is probably the most common method used. It does not involve any XML on the client and instead uses HTML or whatever language is supported to display the page. The GetTemplate() method (defined in the getxsl.asp file) actually returns an instance of a relevant cached stylesheet (a similar technique was discussed in detail in Chapter 10, "*Transformations on the Server*"). The ShowResult() method creates a processor object and defines the xmlDoc object as the input XML document. The number of items to display is added as a parameter called maxViews, the transformation is initiated, and the result written to the output:

```
else
{
    var xslTemplate = GetTemplate();

    ShowResult(xmlDoc,xslTemplate);
}

function ShowResult(objXML,objTemplate)
{
    var xslProc = objTemplate.createProcessor();
    xslProc.input=objXML;
    xslProc.output=Response;

    xslProc.addParameter("maxViews",intNumDisplayItems);
    xslProc.transform();
}
%>
<!--#include file="getxsl.asp"-->
```

At the end of this file the getxsl.asp file is included and although this is similar to the getxsl.asp file we looked at earlier in Chapter 10, there are some differences. However, the GetDeviceInfo() and GetStyleSheet() methods are the same, so we won't repeat them here – look back at the earlier chapter for detailed information on these.

```
<script language="vbscript" runat="server">
Dim objInfo
Set objInfo = Server.CreateObject("Scripting.Dictionary")

Function GetDeviceInfo()
...
End Function

Function GetStyleSheet(g_strBrowser,g_strVersion)
...
End Function
```

The GetTemplate() method is not significantly different, but rather than storing the template object for each stylesheet in the user's session, they are stored at application level, hence improving performance and not using all of the computer's memory! Each application object for each stylesheet is identified by its browser and version names, and if some application object or a given browser version does not exist, then the XSLTemplate object is created and stored in a relevant application object for access next time.

```
Function GetTemplate()
    Set objDictDevice = GetDeviceInfo()

    g_strBrowser=objDictDevice("browser")
    g_strVersion=objDictDevice("version")
```

```
      'Cache Stylesheet in Application
      strIdentifier = "StyleSheet" & "_" & g_strBrowser & "_" & g_strVersion

   If (IsNull(Application(strIdentifier)) OR
       IsEmpty(Application(strIdentifier))) Then
       Set objXSL_L = GetStyleSheet(g_strBrowser,g_strVersion)

       Set objTemplate = CreateObject("Msxml2.XSLTemplate.4.0")
       objTemplate.stylesheet = objXSL_L

       Application.Lock
       Set Application(strIdentifier) = objTemplate
       Application.UnLock
   Else
       Set objTemplate = Application(strIdentifier)
   End If

   Set GetTemplate = objTemplate
End Function

</script>
```

The `GetDeviceInfo()` method we mentioned uses the file `devices.xml`, which is shown below for the ProPortal example. Although it is similar to that in Chapter 10, it's modified for this application:

```xml
<?xml version="1.0" ?>
<DisplayDevices>
   <device browser="Netscape" version="6" Name="Netscape 6.00">
      <page url="default.asp" href="index_Netscape6.xsl" />
      <page url="multi.asp" href="index/index_Netscape6.xsl" />
   </device>
   <device browser="IE" version="6.0" Name="Internet Explorer 6.0">
      <page url="default.asp" href="index_IE60.xsl" />
      <page url="multi.asp" href="index/index_IE60.xsl" />
   </device>
   <device browser="IE" version="5.0" Name="Internet Explorer 5.0">
      <page url="default.asp" href="index_IE50.xsl" />
      <page url="multi.asp" href="index/index_IE50.xsl" />
   </device>
   ...
</DisplayDevices>
```

The `Index_IE50.xsl` file is very much similar in functionality to the `index_IE60.xsl` file we are going to look at. However, the `index_IE50.xsl` file uses the older XSL implementation (unlike the IE 6.0 stylesheet which uses the W3C Recommendation) and is designed to work client-side, and not server-side on IE 5.0 or 5.5. In fact, if you try to load it server-side with MSXML 4.0 it will fail, as MSXML 4.0 does not support the older XSL language. The `Index_Netscape.xsl` file is also similar in functionality, but targets the less XML-aware Netscape browsers. Let's look at `index_IE60.xsl` – the heart of the front page, and arguably the most important component for user interaction.

The root `xsl:stylesheet` element contains the `xsl` namespace, the `msxsl` namespace required when using scripting, and my own user-defined namespace to define my script sections with the prefix `style`:

```
<?xml version="1.0" ?>
<xsl:stylesheet version="1.0"
                xmlns:xsl="http://www.w3.org/1999/XSL/Transform"
                xmlns:msxsl="urn:schemas-microsoft-com:xslt"
                xmlns:style="http://sightkeys.com/styles">
```

The `maxViews` parameter is defaulted to 6, but it is possible that this can be overridden by the `addParameter()` method in the `default.asp` page. This is controlled by the variable at the top of the `default.asp` file:

```
var intNumDisplayItems=6;
```

This means that there will be six blocks of news items and the rest will go in the "Other News" at the bottom.

Back to the XSLT we are working with. The first template matches the root `index` element and the HTML document is defined below this. The namespace definitions on this refer to our customer element behavior namespace and the VML namespace; we won't say more about this because it was discussed in the section on `IE60.xsl` and nothing is different. The majority of the HTML that is output is very similar to that in `IE60.xsl` discussed above, so let's look instead at what's different.

```
<xsl:param name="maxViews" select="6" />
<xsl:output method="html" version="4.0" />
<xsl:template match="Index">
    <HTML xmlns:ProPortal="urn:ProPortal"
        xmlns:vml="urn:schemas-microsoft-com:vml">
    ...
    </HTML>
</xsl:template>
```

The `<entry>` element is matched and immediately an `<xsl:choose>` element is used to determine whether the content position of the entry element within the node-list of entry nodes is less than or equal to the `maxViews` parameter, which determines the number of colored block news slots to be displayed on the page. When this is true, a `DIV` class is created with the class name set to the concatenation of the string `NewsItem` with the integer value of the context position. This is done to uniquely identify each `DIV` element, and the CSS associated with this stylesheet actually defines styles for six `DIV` elements to determine their placement on the page. (This is currently a maximum of six blocks. Beyond this, a simple line headline and description format is used to save having to scroll down when there are many headlines.)

```
<xsl:template match="entry">
    <xsl:choose>
        <xsl:when test="position()&lt;=$maxViews">
            <div class="NewsItem{position()}">
```

The background color of the `DIV` element is dynamic, based on the news item type, and the custom script method `GetColor()` is used here. This method is shown a little later on, but you must pass the context node as well as qualifying the call with the custom style namespace:

```
<xsl:attribute name="style">
    background-color:
    <xsl:value-of select="style:GetColor(.)" />
</xsl:attribute>
```

The link to each news story is the original unique URL to the XML document with the `.xml` replaced with the `_IE60.htm` string. This is achieved using the XPath `substring-before()` method to get the stem before the `.xml` and add this to the `_IE60.htm` string instead:

```
<a href="/ProPortal/index/
    {substring-before(@LocalURL,'.xml')}_IE60.htm">
    <xsl:value-of select="./title" />
</a>
<br />
```

The child `text()` node is then output and this is in fact the story summary we created during the offline process. Finally, if an update time has been specified, then this is added to the output. Otherwise, we assume the document has not been updated yet and so we display the time it was entered:

```
<font size="2">
    <xsl:value-of select="./text()" />
</font>
<b style="background-color:darkblue;
    color:white;font-family:courier;font-size:8px;">
    <xsl:choose>
        <xsl:when test="@LastUpdate!=''">
            <xsl:value-of select="@LastUpdate" />
        </xsl:when>
        <xsl:otherwise>
            <xsl:value-of select="@EntryTime" />
        </xsl:otherwise>
    </xsl:choose>
</b>
</div>
</xsl:when>
```

If the content position of the current `<entry>` element is beyond the `maxViews` parameter, then we fall into the `xsl:otherwise` element, which simply displays the story link as a row of links and text:

```
<xsl:otherwise>
    <div class="OtherNews">
        <xsl:attribute name="style">
            color:<xsl:value-of select="style:GetColor(.)" />
        </xsl:attribute>
        <a href="/ProPortal/index/
            {substring-before(@LocalURL,'.xml')}_IE60.htm">
            <xsl:attribute name="style">
            color:
            <xsl:value-of select="style:GetColor(.)" />
            </xsl:attribute>
            <xsl:value-of select="./title" />
        </a>
        <br />
        <xsl:value-of select="./text()" />
    </div>
</xsl:otherwise>
</xsl:choose>
</xsl:template>
<xsl:template match="text()" />
```

The script that gets the appropriate background color based on the type of NewsItem is shown below. Note that the implements-prefix attribute must be set to style to associate it with our custom namespace definition. The name of the type attribute is obtained from the context node and then a switch statement is executed that checks the type against some predefined values and returns an appropriate color.

```
<msxsl:script language="JScript" implements-prefix="style">
    function GetColor(nodelist)
    {
        var color =
            nodelist.item(0).attributes.getNamedItem("type").value;

        switch (color)
        {
            case "sport":
                strColor="Maroon";
                break;
            case "business":
                strColor="Red";
                break;
            case "finance":
                strColor="Gray";
                break;
            case "global":
                strColor="Purple";
                break;
            case "technology":
                strColor="Olive";
                break;
            default:
                strColor="green";
        }

        return strColor;
    }
</msxsl:script>
</xsl:stylesheet>
```

One final useful link is the View all stories link. This is a direct link to an XML page, which is a CSS-styled list of the stories that have been indexed; most useful for administrators, syndicates, or users looking for a quick overview of what's on the site.

The coolest thing is that exactly the same XML file and CSS work almost the same on IE 6 and Netscape 6, as shown overleaf:

663

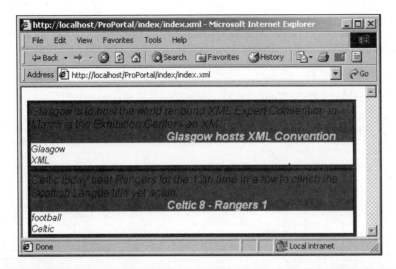

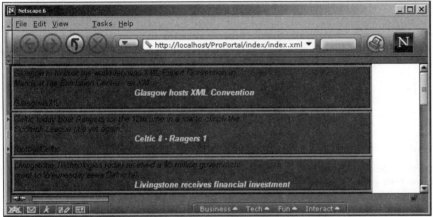

The fact that both Netscape and IE can view our XML files directly using CSS should allow us to produce some pretty useful cross-browser XML applications with no re-writing. Chapter 7, "*Styling XML Content*", shows how to create CSS and XML output.

The index.xml file has a CSS processing instruction at the top of the file:

```
<?xml version="1.0" encoding="utf-8"?>
<?xml-stylesheet type="text/css" href="/ProPortal/index/index.css" ?>
<Index>
.
</Index>
```

The CSS (index.css) displays the page to the user where the CSS-defined items match element names within the XML index.xml document, and applies some appropriate style. Looking at the title style element, we can see that we can even apply behaviors, so this could be quite powerful.

```
Index
{
   display: block;
   color: black;
   font-family: Arial;
   font-style: italic;
   text-align: left;
   font-size:medium;}

entry
   {
      background-color: green;
         display: block;
         font-family: Arial, Helvetica, sans-serif;
         font-size: small;
         width: 30em;
         border: groove 5px darkgreen;
         position:relative;
   }

title
{
   display: block;
   position:relative;
   top:0px;
   left:200px;
   font-style: italic;
   font-weight:bold;
   color:yellow;
   behavior:url(../behav/alink.htc)};
}

keyword
{
   display: block;
   background-color: white;
   font-size:smaller;
}
```

This takes us to the end of our look at the ProPortal Information Portal System. It is a fairly complex and realistic use of MSXML and related technologies, and can be extended in many ways. The next section provides information on how you can find out more about extending what is already available to you.

Further Details

The ProPortal Information Portal is a freely available, open source system available and downloadable at http://www.deltabis.com/. You can get help and advice, contribute opinions and/or code to its development, and download the latest version from there. The version used in this chapter is available in the book's code download. More details can be found in the file VersionInformation.txt at the root of the ProPortal virtual directory.

Summary

This chapter looked at a real-world information portal and the various technologies required when creating a live application.

We looked at how to integrate a portal with content from remote web sites using MSXML's XMLHTTP and ServerXMLHTTP objects, as well as improving the performance and flexibility of the site by doing most of the work offline and creating pre-generated pages for various browsers using XSLT transforms.

We also saw how to dramatically improve performance by using the template and processor object and Application-level caching (more information is available on this in Chapter 10, "*Transformations on the Server*"), as well as how to determine browser types and map these directly to XSLT stylesheets.

Finally, the application demonstrated how to link in other utility processes, such as the term finder, to improve the content richness. There is much more potential in this application and many of the principles can be applied to any XML application with MSXML 4.0 as its basis.

XML Application Development with MSXML 4.0
SOAP
XHTML
XML Schemas DTDs XPath CSS
XML Namespaces
XML 1.0
MSXML

Case Study: Attendance Tracking System

The goal of this case study is to demonstrate the use of MSXML in a 3-tier web application. We'll build a web-based system to track employee absences and leave accruals – an integral part of Human Resources (HR) and Payroll in any organization. This system will allow employees to log in and see the number of days off they are allowed to take, review their past vacation details, and also submit new time-off requests. The time-off requests can then be approved or rejected by the respective manager, and HR can generate reports and use them for payroll purposes.

In this case study we'll see XML used as a data transfer mechanism, and also how separating content from presentation leads to effective application design. We'll be using MSXML only on the server-side and on the middle tier. In other words, we will not be relying on any client-side manipulation of XML.

In this classic three-tier web application, we'll start by gathering the application requirements, and move on to look at the database and application flow design. We'll then begin implementation by creating a Visual Basic COM object, which will provide the data access services and implement business logic. This COM object will then be used from ASP pages.

All the "get" methods in the COM object return the data as an XML string, and the "add/update" methods take XML-formatted data strings as their input. The ASP code calls the COM object methods, receives XML, applies stylesheets on it, and sends HTML to the client. On the other hand, when the web form is posted, the ASP code builds XML strings from the form fields and passes that XML text to the "add/update" methods in the COM object. The benefits of sending and accepting XML are multifold. For example, it enables data access from any platform, in any language. For instance, we can use the WSDL Generator utility (that comes with the Microsoft SOAP Toolkit) to create a WSDL (Web Service Description Language) file and supporting code to instantly turn our Visual Basic COM object into a web service. Then this web service can be accessed from any platform, any language, by using SOAP messaging.

> *To learn more about SOAP and web services refer to "Professional XML Web Services" published by Wrox Press (ISBN 1-861005-09-1).*

Let's now first review the system requirements for this case study before taking a more detailed look at the application itself and its implementation.

Requirements

To build and test this case study we will need the following:

- ❑ Microsoft Windows (NT/2000/XP).
- ❑ Internet Information Server (IIS) 4.0 or higher.
- ❑ Microsoft XML Core Services (MSXML) 4.0.
- ❑ A database. We have used Microsoft Access 2000, but an alternative such as SQL Server, Access 97, or some other database system can be used with minor modifications to the connection string in the configuration XML file (discussed later).
- ❑ Visual Basic 6.0.
- ❑ Microsoft Data Access Components (MDAC 2.6) or higher.
- ❑ Internet Explorer 5 or higher.

> *Although IIS 4.0 is mentioned above, the case study will also work with Personal Web Server (PWS) on a Win 98 platform.*

When a new absence request is submitted, the application uses e-mail to send notification to the appropriate manager. Also, when a request is updated (approved/rejected) by a manager, an e-mail is sent to the employee who submitted the request. The case study uses the free **AspEmail 4.5 component** from Persits Software, Inc. (http://www.persits.com). You will need to download and install it if you want to see the full application in operation. However, the code can easily be modified to use the Microsoft-provided Collaboration Data Objects (CDO) or any other third-party e-mailing component, such as AspMail by ServerObjects Inc. (http://www.serverobjects.com/).

The case study assumes some familiarity with creating COM components in Visual Basic and data access using ADO.

> We will not include a complete listing of all of the code in the final working program. The
> Visual Basic COM object (middle-tier) code, ASP pages, a Microsoft Access database file,
> and XSL stylesheet files are all available in the code download for this chapter.

Application Specification

The Human Resources department at ABC Software Corp. (a fictitious company) has used a paper-based
absence tracking system for quite some time now. With this approach, whenever an employee needs to
request a term of absence, they print a particular Word document and fill it with time-off dates and type of
absence information before getting it signed by the manager and submitting it to the HR department.

Within this process, the employee often forgets to pass the document to HR after getting it signed by
their manager (you know how developers get busy when they return to their desks!). The HR group also
tried asking managers to collect the signed requests and submit them to HR later on, but that did not
work either. On top of this, employees and HR have always struggled to instantly calculate the
information about leave available and time-off taken. Finally, using this time-off information during
Payroll was a tedious task and involved a lot of manual work.

The HR group has now decided to create a small intranet web site to track employees' time-off details.
This allows employees to view their absence details and submit new requests. The system will later be
integrated with Payroll.

Employee Benefits

The date of joining is a very important factor for calculating the number of days paid vacation that an
employee at ABC Software Corp. can enjoy. Employees begin to accrue vacation time on the first day
of the month following the date of hire. For the first twelve months, employees are offered 0.83 days per
month (equivalent to a total of ten days for the first year). Each year, on the anniversary of an
employee's date of hire, the employee receives an additional two days of vacation.

The following table lists the exact schedule offered for paid vacation:

Months of Service	Days per Month (Annualized Earnings)
1-12	0.83 (10)
13-23	1.00 (12)
24-35	1.17 (14)
36-47	1.33 (16)
48-71	Fixed number of 16 per annum
71-107	Fixed number of 18 per annum
108 and above	Fixed number of 20 per annum

Each employee is also entitled to take two floating holidays, apart from the standard holidays observed
during the year. However, if an employee starts on or after July 1, only one floating holiday is granted.

Apart from floating holidays and paid vacation, employees are eligible to take a half day per month sick leave, up to a maximum of six days, a maximum of three days bereavement leave, and two days of wedding holiday. The wedding holiday is only offered if the employee has finished six months of service.

For this case study we'll assume that ABC Software Corp. has just five employees, displayed in the following organization chart:

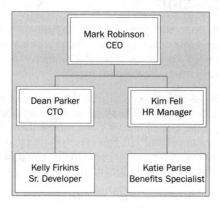

Database Schema

We have a very simple database schema for this case study, with just five tables, as shown in the following database schema diagram:

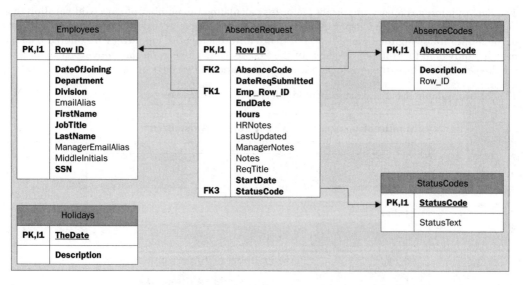

The two most important fields in the Employees table are DateOfJoining and SSN (Social Security Number). The DateOfJoining field is used to calculate the number of days off allowed for a particular employee. And the last four digits of the SSN are used as the employee's password for this system. Other fields include EmailAlias (employee's e-mail alias), and ManagerEmailAlias (employee's manager's e-mail alias). The following table details some of the columns in the Employees table:

Row_ID	LastName	FirstName	SSN	Email Alias	Manager EmailAlias
1	Firkins	Kelly	111-11-1111	kelly	dean
2	Parker	Dean	222-22-2222	dean	mark
3	Fell	Kim	333-33-3333	kim	mark
4	Parise	Katie	444-44-4444	katie	kim
5	Robinson	Mark	555-55-5555	mark	

Note that the ManagerEmailAlias *for Mark Robinson has been intentionally left blank. As CEO, Mark has no manager to report to.*

The AbsenceRequest table holds the employees' time-off details and new requests. The standard holidays observed are stored in the Holidays table. Finally, the AbsenceCodes and StatusCodes tables have the following contents:

AbsenceCode	Description
B	Bereavement
COMP	Compensatory Time
FH	Floating Holiday
O	Other
S	Sick/Illness
V	Vacation
WED	Wedding

StatusCode	StatusText
0	New
1	Approved
2	Rejected

Application Flow

The application flows as described:

- ❏ An employee registers with the system by typing their e-mail alias. The system generates an e-mail that contains the employee's login information, where the login ID is the same as the e-mail alias and the password is the last four digits of the employee's social security number (SSN). This e-mail is then sent to the employee.

- ❏ The employee logs onto the system using the information provided in the e-mail. The system business logic calculates the days off taken and leave available by looking at the `AbsenceRequest` table. We then display these details along with a link to add a new absence request.

- ❏ Let's say an employee submits a new absence request. The details are saved in the `AbsenceRequest` table and an e-mail is sent to the employee's manager (by using the `ManagerEmailAlias` field).

- ❏ When a manager logs onto the system they can view their employees' absence details and new requests. The manager either approves or rejects the request by updating the request. The details in the `AbsenceRequest` table record are updated and an e-mail is generated and sent to the employee.

- ❏ The designated HR members can view any employee's absence records and can generate reports.

- ❏ Employees are not allowed to update the request once it is approved or rejected. The HR team is not allowed to change the request status because only the appropriate manager is permitted to approve/reject requests. Special fields are provided to allow employees, managers, and the HR team to write notes with each request.

Getting Ready

The case study code and sample database file are included in the code download available from the Wrox Press web site. When you unzip the download file, within the `chapter15` folder you will find a `CaseStudy` folder, with the directory structure shown:

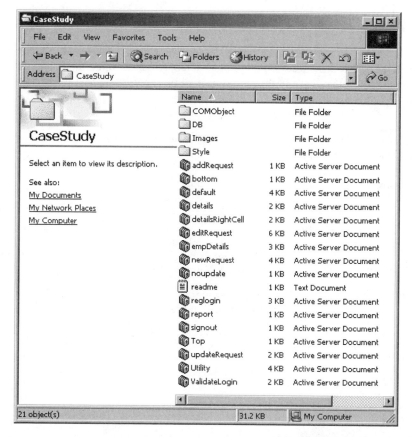

- Create a new virtual directory in IIS and point it to the directory where you unzipped the files. (If necessary, refer back to Chapter 14 for details of how to do this.)

- Make sure you have MSXML 4.0 and ADO 2.6 or higher installed.

- The COMObject folder has the middle-tier COM component, Vacation.dll. Register the DLL using the RegSvr32.exe tool.

- If you placed the files in a folder other than C:\CaseStudy, make sure to update the connection string in the XML configuration file (CaseStudy.config file under the COMObject folder).

- Make sure that the IIS user for this virtual directory has read/write permissions on the DB folder, because we'll be running INSERT and UPDATE statements on the Access database saved in the DB folder.

- Finally, remember to update the e-mail server information in the XML configuration file. This is an optional step – if you don't want e-mails to be sent, the rest of the application can still be run without doing so.

With this understanding of the application and database structure, let's now get our hands dirty with some code and see how MSXML is used in this application.

Middle-Tier COM Component

As mentioned earlier, we will write a COM object in Visual Basic 6.0 that will then be called from ASP pages. This COM object provides services such as database access and e-mail, and also has business logic implementation. In addition to this, it has a small but interesting class to get and set values from a configuration XML file.

For this case study we'll not be using Component Services (MTS/COM+), but if you want to you can put the COM component inside MTS to use the scalability and security features offered by MTS/COM+.

The COM component has the following five class modules:

Class Module Name	Description
BusinessLogic.cls	Provides methods to get time-off details, implements business logic to calculate time-off days allowed and days off taken.
ConfigSettings.cls	Provides methods to read or update XML configuration file.
DBAccess.cls	Database access methods.
RegisterOrLogin.cls	This class has just two methods, Register() and Login().
Utility.cls	Some utility functions, such as sending e-mails.

Configuration XML File

If you have looked at Microsoft's .NET initiative, you might have noticed that it makes extensive use of XML in various places. One such interesting application of XML in .NET is in **configuration files**. The application configuration details are stored in a text file written using XML syntax.

As this is a plain text file, it can be easily read and edited in any text editor (compare this with the Registry, which requires special tools to view or edit its contents). There are many other benefits of using XML configuration files, including easy deployment and configuration replication. In addition, any XML parser (like MSXML) can be easily used to parse and read the information from the XML configuration file.

To learn more about XML configuration files in .NET, refer to "Professional XML for .NET Developers" by Wrox Press (ISBN 1861005-31-8). That book is dedicated to covering XML features in .NET and also talks about how .NET itself makes use of XML.

This case study makes use of a similar XML configuration file; it is named `CaseStudy.config` and looks like this:

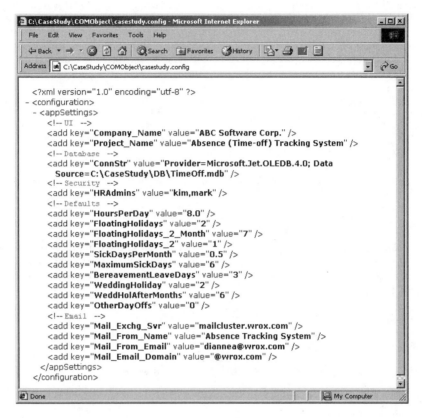

We use the XML configuration file to hold the database connection string, some user interface (UI) details, default values used for the business logic, e-mail server information, and the list of HR administrators.

> *For simplicity, we have written the information as plain text, but if security is a major concern, you should encrypt the information in the XML configuration file and decrypt it in the COM object after reading it using MSXML.*

Begin by creating a new ActiveX DLL project in Visual Basic 6.0, add a reference (Project | References) to MSXML 4.0, Microsoft ActiveX Data Objects (ADO) 2.6 (or higher), and if you would like to use the mailing functionality, add the reference to the respective COM component (for example Persits Software AspEmail 4.5).

Let's start with a class module that provides functionality to read and update the above configuration file. When we create the ActiveX DLL project, it creates a class named `Class1`; simply rename that class to `ConfigSettings` and save the project as `Vacation`.

ConfigSettings.cls

This class is used to read and update configuration values stored in an XML-formatted configuration file. It has just two methods: GetValue() and SetValue().

In the class initialization we create the MSXML DOMDocument object and load the configuration XML file. The application assumes that the CaseStudy.config file is in the same directory as the COM DLL file.

```
Option Explicit
Dim objXMLDoc As MSXML2.DOMDocument40
Dim objRootElem As MSXML2.IXMLDOMElement

Private Sub Class_Initialize()
    Set objXMLDoc = New MSXML2.DOMDocument40
    objXMLDoc.async = False
    objXMLDoc.Load App.Path & "\casestudy.config"

    Set objRootElem = objXMLDoc.documentElement
End Sub
```

Each <add> element under /configuration/appSettings in the configuration file has two attributes: key and value. The GetValue() method uses an XPath expression and the selectSingleNode() method to get the element based on the key attribute and then, using the Attributes collection, we get the content of the value attribute:

```
Public Function GetValue(ByVal KeyName As String)
    Dim objNode As MSXML2.IXMLDOMNode

    Set objNode = objRootElem.selectSingleNode _
    ("/configuration/appSettings/add[@key='" & KeyName & "']")

    If objNode Is Nothing Then
        GetValue = "-"
    Else
        GetValue = objNode.Attributes(1).nodeTypedValue
    End If

End Function
```

Similarly, the SetValue() function uses an XPath expression to locate the element. If found, we update the node value and save the XML file back to disk:

```
Public Sub SetValue(ByVal KeyName As String, ByVal NewValue As String)
    Dim objNode As MSXML2.IXMLDOMNode

    Set objNode = objRootElem.selectSingleNode _
        ("/configuration/appSettings/add[@key='" & KeyName & "']")

    If Not objNode Is Nothing Then
        objNode.Attributes(1).nodeTypedValue = NewValue

        objXMLDoc.save App.Path & "\casestudy.config"
    End If
```

```
   End Sub

   Private Sub Class_Terminate()
      Set objXMLDoc = Nothing
   End Sub
```

The `GetValue()` and `SetValue()` methods provide the basic functionality of reading and updating the XML configuration file. In our application we'll not be using `SetValue()`, only `GetValue()`. But the goal here was to illustrate how easy it is to write a few lines of code and build a flexible application configuration mechanism.

Database Access

Let's now look at `DBAccess.cls` – another very important class module inside the middle-tier COM component.

DBAccess.cls

The `DBAccess` class mainly provides the database access services, and at the heart of this class is the method `RSToXML()`.

First, in the component initialization we connect to the database:

```
Option Explicit
Dim objADOConn As ADODB.Connection

Private Sub Class_Initialize()
   Dim ConnStr As String
   Dim objConfig As New ConfigSettings

   Set objADOConn = New ADODB.Connection

   ConnStr = objConfig.GetValue("ConnStr")

   'Connect to the database
   objADOConn.Open ConnStr

   Set objConfig = Nothing

End Sub
```

We simply get the database connection string from the XML configuration file and then call the `open()` method on the `ADODB.Connection` object.

Let's now look at the `RSToXML()` method, which is used throughout the `DBAccess` class to convert the ADO recordset into an XML string:

```
Public Function RSToXML(ByVal SQLStmt As String, _
                        ByVal RootNodeName As String)
   Dim objADORS As New ADODB.Recordset
   Dim objFields As ADODB.Fields
   Dim objField As ADODB.Field
```

```
Dim objTempDOM As New MSXML2.DOMDocument40
Dim objXMLDecl As MSXML2.IXMLDOMProcessingInstruction
Dim RootElement As MSXML2.IXMLDOMElement
Dim RecElement As MSXML2.IXMLDOMElement
Dim FieldElement As MSXML2.IXMLDOMElement
Dim TextCDATASec As MSXML2.IXMLDOMCDATASection

Dim FieldVal As String
Dim FldType As Integer
```

The function accepts two parameters: a SQL statement that is used to generate the recordset, and the name of the top document element in the resultant XML document. The function starts with a sequence of variable declaration statements. Next, we create the root node:

```
Set RootElement = objTempDOM.createElement(RootNodeName)
Set objTempDOM.documentElement = RootElement
```

Now, we execute the SQL statement to generate the ADO recordset:

```
Set objADORS.ActiveConnection = objADOConn
objADORS.Open SQLStmt
```

Finally, we iterate over each record in the recordset and build the XML document:

```
'For each record
While Not objADORS.EOF

    'Create the "Record" sub-element
    Set RecElement = objTempDOM.createElement("Record")

    Set objFields = objADORS.fields

    'For each field
    For Each objField In objFields

        'Create an element with same name is that of field
        Set FieldElement = objTempDOM.createElement(objField.Name)

        FldType = objField.Type

        If Not (IsNull(objField.Value)) Then
            FieldVal = objField.Value

            'Binary data gets Base64 encoded
            'Large textual data is sent as CDATA section
            'All other field values are simply node values

            If FldType = adBinary Or FldType = adLongVarBinary Then
                FieldElement.dataType = "bin.base64"
                FieldElement.nodeTypedValue = FieldVal
```

```
        Else

            If FldType = adLongVarChar Or FldType = adLongVarWChar Then
                Set TextCDATASec = _
                objTempDOM.createCDATASection(FieldVal)
                FieldElement.appendChild TextCDATASec

            Else
                FieldVal = Trim(CStr(FieldVal))
                FieldElement.nodeTypedValue = FieldVal
            End If
        End If
    End If

    'Append the field sub-element
    RecElement.appendChild FieldElement
  Next

  objADORS.MoveNext

  'Append the record sub-element
  RootElement.appendChild RecElement
Wend
```

For each record in the recordset, we first create an element named <Record>, then we get the `Fields`
collection for the current record and iterate over each field, adding the sub-element with the name
matching the field name.

> *Note that if you are using SQL Server 2000, you may use the* FOR XML *clause with a* SELECT
> *SQL statement and directly get the data in XML format. The above method for converting a
> recordset to XML is useful if you are programming against a database system that does not natively
> support XML (like SQL Server 7 or Microsoft Access) or when you want better control over the
> generated XML structure and its content.*

Remember that XML documents are text documents. What if one of the database fields contains binary
data and we want that to be part of the generated XML document? In order to include binary data as
part of an XML document, it needs to be text-encoded. A well-known scheme for this is base64
encoding. Base64 encoding maps binary bits into one of 64 characters (A-Z, a-z, 0-9, and +/).

The good news is that we don't have to write the encoding code. MSXML supports converting binary
data to base64 and back again. In the above code, we check if the field type is binary, then we simply
set the element's `dataType` to `bin.base64` – the rest is taken care of by MSXML.

Another point to note in the above code is that, if the field type is `Memo` (long varchar or Unicode long
varchar) we create a CDATA section for that field's value, simply to avoid taking care of characters that
are special to XML. In a CDATA section we can have characters such as <, >, &, etc. and we don't have
to worry about escaping them, since the parser simply doesn't parse that content.

For all other field types we directly use the field values.

Finally, we close the recordset and return the generated XML by assigning the value of DOMDocument's
xml property to the function name:

```
      objADORS.Close

   RSToXML = objTempDOM.xml

   Set objTempDOM = Nothing
   Set objADORS = Nothing
   Set objFields = Nothing
   Set objField = Nothing
End Function
```

The `xml` property of the `DOMDocument` object returns the generated XML as a string.

> *Note that, starting with version 2.1, ADO also provides a mechanism to persist a recordset as XML. We are not using that built-in functionality here, simply to avoid the schema overhead, and to control the final structure of the resultant XML document.*

With this useful function now available, the rest of the data-access `"get"` methods simply make a call to the `RSToXML()` function:

```
Public Function GetHolidays(ByVal ForYear As Integer)
   Dim SQLStmt As String

   SQLStmt = "SELECT * FROM Holidays WHERE Year(TheDate)=" & ForYear & _
               " ORDER BY TheDate"

   GetHolidays = RSToXML(SQLStmt, "Holidays")

End Function

Public Function GetAbsenceCodes()
   Dim SQLStmt As String

   SQLStmt = "SELECT * FROM AbsenceCodes ORDER BY AbsenceCode"
   GetAbsenceCodes = RSToXML(SQLStmt, "AbsenceCodes")
End Function

Public Function GetStatusCodes()
   Dim SQLStmt As String

   SQLStmt = "SELECT * FROM StatusCodes ORDER BY StatusCode"
   GetStatusCodes = RSToXML(SQLStmt, "StatusCodes")
End Function

Public Function GetAllEmpDetails()
   Dim SQLStmt As String

   SQLStmt = "SELECT * FROM Employees ORDER BY FirstName "
   GetAllEmpDetails = RSToXML(SQLStmt, "EmpDetails")
End Function

Public Function GetEmpDetailsByID(ByVal EmpID As String)
   Dim SQLStmt As String
   SQLStmt = "SELECT * FROM Employees WHERE Row_ID = " & EmpID
   GetEmpDetailsByID = RSToXML(SQLStmt, "EmpDetails")
```

```
End Function

Public Function GetEmpDetailsByEmail(ByVal EmailAlias As String)
   Dim SQLStmt As String

   SQLStmt = "SELECT * FROM Employees WHERE EmailAlias='" & _
             EmailAlias & "'"
   GetEmpDetailsByEmail = RSToXML(SQLStmt, "EmpDetails")
End Function

'And so on ...
'Refer to DBAccess.cls file for implementation of other Get methods.
```

For instance, if the DBAccess GetHolidays(2002) method is called, the resultant XML string will look like this:

```
<?xml version="1.0"?>
<Holidays>
   <Record>
      <TheDate>1/1/2002</TheDate>
      <Description>New Years Day</Description>
   </Record>
   <Record>
      <TheDate>5/27/2002</TheDate>
      <Description>Memorial Day</Description>
   </Record>


</Holidays>
```

In addition to the "get" functions, the DBAccess class has two other important methods: AddAbsenceRequest() and UpdateAbsenceRequest(). These methods are called from the ASP pages in response to the form posts to add or update an absence request. Both these methods take just one parameter – RequestData, which is an XML string containing form data.

```
Public Function AddAbsenceRequest(ByVal RequestData As String)

   Dim objUtility As New Utility
   Dim objAbsReqXMLDom As New MSXML2.DOMDocument40

   Dim EmpID As String
   Dim AbsCode As String
   Dim StDate As String
   Dim EnDate As String
   Dim Hours As String
   Dim Notes As String


   Dim InsertSQLStmt As String
   Dim ReqTitle As String
```

The function starts with the variable declarations. Next, we load the input XML string into a DOM document and then get the form field values, and generate and execute the INSERT SQL statement:

```
        objAbsReqXMLDom.async = False
        objAbsReqXMLDom.loadXML RequestData

        EmpID = objAbsReqXMLDom.selectSingleNode _
                    ("/AbsenceRequest/Emp_Row_ID").nodeTypedValue
        ReqTitle = objAbsReqXMLDom.selectSingleNode _
                    ("/AbsenceRequest/ReqTitle").nodeTypedValue
        AbsCode = objAbsReqXMLDom.selectSingleNode _
                    ("/AbsenceRequest/AbsenceCode").nodeTypedValue
        StDate = objAbsReqXMLDom.selectSingleNode _
                    ("/AbsenceRequest/StartDate").nodeTypedValue
        EnDate = objAbsReqXMLDom.selectSingleNode _
                    ("/AbsenceRequest/EndDate").nodeTypedValue
        Hours = objAbsReqXMLDom.selectSingleNode _
                    ("/AbsenceRequest/Hours").nodeTypedValue
        Notes = objAbsReqXMLDom.selectSingleNode _
                    ("/AbsenceRequest/Notes").nodeTypedValue

        ReqTitle = Replace(ReqTitle, "'", "''")
        Notes = Replace(Notes, "'", "''")

        InsertSQLStmt = "INSERT INTO AbsenceRequest " & _
                    "(Emp_Row_ID, ReqTitle, AbsenceCode, StartDate" & _
                    ", EndDate, Hours, Notes) VALUES (" & EmpID & _
                    ", '" & ReqTitle & "', '" & AbsCode & "', '" & _
                    StDate & "', '" & EnDate & "', " & Hours & ", '" & _
                    Notes & "') "

    objADOConn.Execute InsertSQLStmt
```

We synchronously load the XML document and then, using the `selectSingleNode()` method and `nodeTypedValue` property, we retrieve the form field values and use them with the INSERT statement.

Finally, we need to send an e-mail to the respective manager. We use the utility class method `SendEmailToManager()` to do this:

```
        objUtility.SendEmailToManager EmpID

        If Err = 0 Then
            AddAbsenceRequest = "OK"
        Else
            AddAbsenceRequest = "Error : (" & Err.Number & ") " & _
                    Err.Description
        End If

        Set objAbsReqXMLDom = Nothing
    End Function
```

The `UpdateAbsenceRequest()` function implementation is similar to the above method. In that method we again load the input XML string into a `DOMDocument`, use `selectSingleNode()` and `nodeTypedValue` to get the form values, and finally execute the SQL statement, in this case UPDATE. Refer to the section describing the `DBAccess.cls` file for more implementation details.

Other Supporting Classes

The other three classes (`Utility.cls`, `BusinessLogic.cls`, and `RegisterOrLogin.cls`) contain the methods to send e-mails, calculate days off available, and vacation taken, etc.

We'll discuss these classes very briefly here, because they make very minimal or no use of MSXML, but simply implement the business logic or supporting functionality. Let's start with the utility class (`Utility.cls`) that is mainly used to send e-mails.

Utility.cls

In the `Class_Initialize` method, we initialize the mailer component by getting the e-mail settings from the XML configuration file (using the XML configuration helper class):

```
Option Explicit
Dim objMailer As Object

Private Sub Class_Initialize()
    Dim objConfig As New ConfigSettings

    On Error Resume Next
    Set objMailer = CreateObject("Persits.MailSender.4")
    objMailer.IsHTML = True

    objMailer.Host = objConfig.GetValue("Mail_Exchg_Svr")
    objMailer.From = objConfig.GetValue("Mail_From_Email")
    objMailer.FromName = objConfig.GetValue("Mail_From_Name")

    Set objConfig = Nothing
End Sub
```

When the new absence request is submitted, an e-mail is sent to that particular employee's manager. The following function in the `Utility.cls` is used to achieve this:

```
Public Function SendEmailToManager(ByVal EmpID As Integer)
    Dim MgrEmail As String
    Dim EmpName As String
    Dim MailDomain As String
    Dim SubjectLine As String
    Dim BodyText As String

    Dim objConfig As New ConfigSettings
    Dim objDBAccess As New DBAccess
    Dim objXMLDOM As New MSXML2.DOMDocument40

    On Error Resume Next

    objXMLDOM.async = False
    objXMLDOM.loadXML objDBAccess.GetEmpDetailsByID(EmpID)

    MgrEmail = objXMLDOM.selectSingleNode _
        ("/EmpDetails/Record/ManagerEmailAlias").nodeTypedValue
```

```
        EmpName = objXMLDOM.selectSingleNode _
            ("/EmpDetails/Record/FirstName").nodeTypedValue

        SubjectLine = EmpName & " just submitted a vacation request!"

        BodyText = "<font face=verdana size=2><b>Greetings!</b><br>" & _
                   "<blockquote>" & SubjectLine & "</b></font>" & _
                   "</blockquote><hr>"

        MailDomain = objConfig.GetValue("Mail_Email_Domain")

        SendEmailToManager = SendMail(MgrEmail & MailDomain, _
                                      SubjectLine, BodyText)

        Set objConfig = Nothing
        Set objDBAccess = Nothing
        Set objXMLDOM = Nothing

    End Function
```

The above function receives an employee ID as the input parameter, which is then used to get the employee details by calling the GetEmpDetailsByID() method of the DBAccess class. Remember that GetEmpDetailsByID() returns employee details in XML format, as a string. We then load that XML string into a DOMDocument and, using an XPath expression and the selectSingleNode method, we extract the values for the employee's first name and their manager's e-mail alias. Finally, we get the mail domain name from the configuration file, build the e-mail subject line and body text, and then actually send an e-mail.

The Utility.cls file contains one more function, SendEmailToEmployee(), which is very similar to the above method and is used to send an e-mail to an employee when their vacation request is updated. And finally, in the Class_Terminate() method we release the mailer object:

```
    Private Sub Class_Terminate()
        On Error Resume Next
        Set objMailer = Nothing
    End Sub
```

RegisterOrLogin.cls

This file contains just two methods: Register() and Login(). The Register() method is used when the employee signs up by typing their e-mail address. It takes the e-mail alias as input, gets the employee details from the database using the GetEmpDetailsByEmail() method in DBAccess, and sends an e-mail containing the login information (e-mail alias as login ID and last four digits of SSN as the password) to the employee. The Register() method implementation is similar to the Login() method so we won't look at them both in detail.

The Login Method

The Login() method takes the e-mail alias (which is the login ID) and password strings as input parameters. The employee details will be returned if the login succeeds, else an error will be returned (in XML format) if the login failed:

```
Public Function Login(ByVal EmailAlias As String, ByVal PWD As String)
    Dim objEmpXMLDom As New MSXML2.DOMDocument40
    Dim SSN, DBEmailAlias As String
    Dim EmpDetails As String

    Dim objDBAcc As New DBAccess

    On Error Resume Next
```

The above lines of code create a new DOMDocument object and a DBAccess object. Next, we call the GetEmpDetailsByEmail() function from the DBAccess class and load the returned XML string into the DOMDocument:

```
EmpDetails = objDBAcc.GetEmpDetailsByEmail(EmailAlias)

objEmpXMLDom.async = False
objEmpXMLDom.loadXML EmpDetails
```

If the GetEmpDetailsByEmail() method succeeds, we should get back an XML string similar to this:

```
<?xml version="1.0"?>
<EmpDetails>
    <Record>
        <Row_ID>1</Row_ID>
        <LastName>Firkins</LastName>
        <FirstName>Kelly</FirstName>
        <MiddleInitials/>
        <SSN>111-11-1111</SSN>
        <EmailAlias>kelly</EmailAlias>
        <DateOfJoining>2/12/1998</DateOfJoining>
        ...
    </Record>
</EmpDetails>
```

If the method fails to locate the employee record based on the e-mail alias, we simply get:

```
<?xml version="1.0"?>
<EmpDetails/>
```

The Login() method, after loading the XML string returned by the GetEmpDetailsByEmail() function, tries to match the e-mail alias and password (last four digits of employee's SSN):

```
SSN = objEmpXMLDom.selectSingleNode _
    ("/EmpDetails/Record/SSN").nodeTypedValue

SSN = Right(SSN, 4)

DBEmailAlias = objEmpXMLDom.selectSingleNode _
    ("/EmpDetails/Record/EmailAlias").nodeTypedValue

DBEmailAlias = UCase(DBEmailAlias)
```

```
        If UCase(EmailAlias) = DBEmailAlias And SSN = PWD Then
            Login = EmpDetails
        Else
            Login = "<Error>Login failed!</Error>"
        End If
End Function
```

If the login details match, the above function returns the employee details as an XML string, else it returns the <Error>Login failed!</Error> string.

The ASP Code

It's now time to look at the ASP pages that make use of the above COM component. Here also, we'll only discuss the code where we use MSXML, and we'll skip the user-interface-specific code. You can look at the individual ASP files for further details.

Let's first look at Utility.asp, which contains some VBScript utility functions.

Helper Functions

There are about a dozen functions in Utility.asp, of which the following two are functions that help the other ten:

```
<%
Function ApplyXSL(XMLText, XSLFile)
    Dim objXMLDOM
    Dim objXSLDOM

    Set objXMLDOM = Server.CreateObject("Msxml2.DOMDocument.4.0")
    Set objXSLDOM = Server.CreateObject("Msxml2.DOMDocument.4.0")

    objXMLDOM.async = False
    objXMLDOM.loadXML XMLText

    objXSLDOM.async = False
    objXSLDOM.Load XSLFile

    ApplyXSL = objXMLDOM.transformNode(objXSLDOM)

End Function

Function ApplyXSLWithParam(XMLText, XSLFile, paramName, paramValue)
    Dim objXMLDOM
    Dim objXSLDOM
    Dim objXSLTemplate
    Dim objXSLProcessor

    Set objXMLDOM = Server.CreateObject("Msxml2.DOMDocument.4.0")
    Set objXSLDOM = _
        Server.CreateObject("Msxml2.FreeThreadedDOMDocument.4.0")
```

```
    Set objXSLTemplate = _
        Server.CreateObject("Msxml2.XSLTemplate.4.0")

    objXMLDOM.async = False
    objXMLDOM.loadXML XMLText

    objXSLDOM.async = False
    objXSLDOM.Load XSLFile

    Set objXSLTemplate.stylesheet = objXSLDOM
    Set objXSLProcessor = objXSLTemplate.createProcessor()

    objXSLProcessor.input = objXMLDOM
    objXSLProcessor.addParameter paramName, paramValue
    objXSLProcessor.Transform

    ApplyXSLWithParam = objXSLProcessor.output
End Function
```

As you might remember, most of the "get" methods in the COM component return an XML string. After we receive the XML we want to apply a stylesheet on that XML string and send the transformed HTML to the client. The above two methods are used for this purpose.

The ApplyXSL() method takes the XML string as the first parameter and the XSL file name (full path as obtained by Server.MapPath in the calling ASP code) as the second parameter. It then loads the XML string and XSL file, applies the transformation, and sends the transformed text back to the caller as the result.

The ApplyXSLWithParam() method is similar in functionality to the first one, except it allows a single parameter to be passed to the XSL file. This method can be easily modified to accept multiple parameters and values. We use this method when building HTML combo boxes (such as a combo box for absence codes or status codes) and to select a particular item in it. The item to be selected is passed as the parameter to the stylesheet. The XSL transformation features with MSXML 4.0 are described in greater detail in Chapter 5, "*XSLT in MSXML*".

> *Note that we use the version-dependent ProgIDs throughout this application, which saves us from encountering lots of problems that the version-independent ProgIDs can create. The other important reason is that MSXML 4.0 completely removes support for version-independent ProgIDs and GUIDs. It is installed in side-by-side mode, allowing the applications to choose the version of MSXML to use by specifying the version-dependent ProgIDs/GUIDs. This is a cleaner, more dependable and manageable approach.*

One example of where the ApplyXSL() method is used is yet another supporting function (in Utility.asp), named PrintHolidays():

```
Sub PrintHolidays(ForYear)
    Dim objDBAcc
    Set objDBAcc = Server.CreateObject("Vacation.DBAccess")

    Response.Write ApplyXSL _
        (objDBAcc.GetHolidays(ForYear), _
        Server.MapPath("./Style/holidays.xsl"))
```

```
      Set objDBAcc = Nothing
   End Sub
```

The above method uses the `DBAccess` class from the COM component and calls the `GetHolidays()` method, which returns the holiday details as an XML string. Next, it calls the `ApplyXSL()` method with the holidays XML string and the `holidays.xsl` file (located in the `Style` sub-directory). The `ApplyXSL()` method returns HTML, which is then sent to the client using the `Response.Write()` method.

The `PrintHolidays()` utility function is called from `default.asp`, the very first page that a user would see:

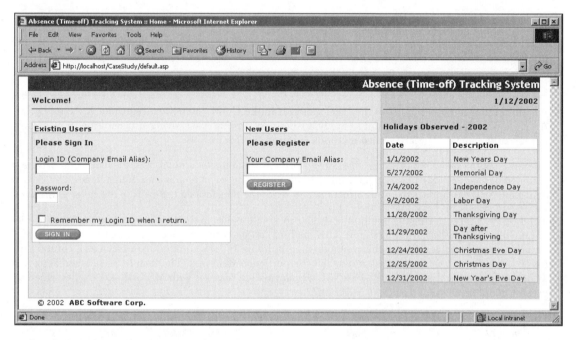

Similarly, other utility functions also make use of the `ApplyXSL()` function:

```
Sub PrintPendingReqs(EmpID, ForYear)
   Dim objDBAcc
   Set objDBAcc = Server.CreateObject("Vacation.DBAccess")

   Response.Write ApplyXSL _
      (objDBAcc.GetEmpPendingReqs(EmpID, ForYear), _
      Server.MapPath("./Style/TimeOffDetails.xsl"))

   Set objDBAcc = Nothing
End Sub


Sub PrintRejectedReqs(EmpID, ForYear)
   Dim objDBAcc
   Set objDBAcc = Server.CreateObject("Vacation.DBAccess")
```

```
      Response.Write ApplyXSL _
         (objDBAcc.GetEmpRejectedReqs(EmpID, ForYear), _
          Server.MapPath("./Style/TimeOffDetails.xsl"))

      Set objDBAcc = Nothing
   End Sub


   Sub PrintTimeOffDetails(EmpID, ForYear)
      Dim objDBAcc
      Set objDBAcc = Server.CreateObject("Vacation.DBAccess")

      Response.Write ApplyXSL _
         (objDBAcc.GetEmpAbsenceReqs(EmpID, ForYear), _
          Server.MapPath("./Style/TimeOffDetails.xsl"))

      Set objDBAcc = Nothing
   End Sub


   Sub PrintTimeOffSummary(EmpID, ForYear)
      Dim objBusLogic
      Set objBusLogic = Server.CreateObject("Vacation.BusinessLogic")

      Response.Write ApplyXSL _
         (objBusLogic.GetDaysOffFullDetails(EmpID, ForYear), _
          Server.MapPath("./Style/TimeOffSummary.xsl"))

      Set objBusLogic = Nothing
   End Sub
```

Signing In

The login form is posted to `reglogin.asp`, which includes the following lines of code that use the `RegisterOrLogin` component class:

```
Set objRegLogin = Server.CreateObject("Vacation.RegisterOrLogin")

Set LoginResultXMLDOM = Server.CreateObject("Msxml2.DOMDocument.4.0")

LoginResultXMLDOM.async = False
LoginResultXMLDOM.loadXML objRegLogin.Login(EmailAlias, PWD)

On Error Resume Next
EmpID = LoginResultXMLDOM.selectSingleNode _
      ("/EmpDetails/Record/Row_ID").nodeTypedValue

If (Not Err.Number = 0) Then
   'Display error message
Else
   Session("EMPID") = EmpID
   Response.Redirect ("details.asp")
End If
```

The e-mail alias and password are sent as input parameters to the Login() method, which as we know, if it succeeds, will return the employee details as an XML string. We load that XML string into a DOMDocument object and then try to retrieve the employee ID (Row_ID field) value. If we find it, we save that value into a Session variable and transfer control to details.asp; otherwise we simply show an error message.

> *The download zip file for this case study contains the Microsoft Access database used here. You may look in the* employee *table for the login ID (e-mail alias) and password (last four digits of SSN) information.*

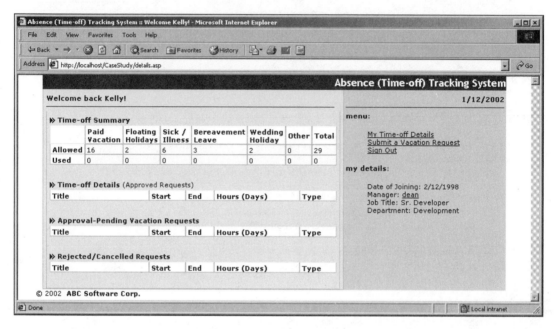

The details.asp page simply makes utility function calls such as PrintTimeOffSummary(), PrintTimeOffDetails(), PrintPendingReqs(), PrintRejectedReqs(), etc., which all use the COM component to get data as an XML string and then call the ApplyXSL() utility function to transform the XML string into HTML text.

Submitting a New Request

After logging-in, employees can then submit new vacation requests:

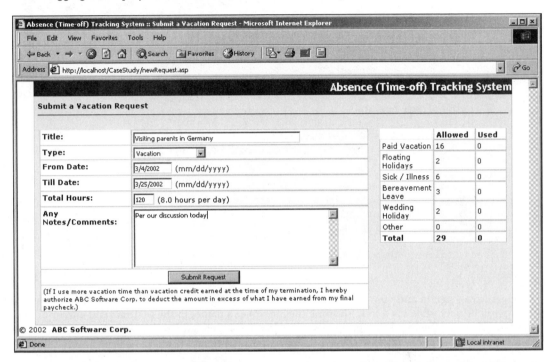

The above page illustrates how the separation of content from presentation can help to show different views of the same data. The time-off summary table on the right-hand side calls the same BusinessLogic method (GetDaysOffFullDetails()) as in the details.asp page above, but applies a different stylesheet to show a vertical view instead of a horizontal view of the time-off summary.

The vacation type combo box is generated using the following utility function from Utility.asp:

```
Sub BuildAbsenceCodeComboBox(selAbsenceCode)
   Dim objDBAcc
   Set objDBAcc = Server.CreateObject("Vacation.DBAccess")

   Response.Write _
      ApplyXSLWithParam(objDBAcc.GetAbsenceCodes, _
      Server.MapPath("./Style/ACCombo.xsl"), _
      "selIndex", selAbsenceCode)
End Sub
```

The above method uses the GetAbsenceCodes() method from the DBAccess class and passes the returned XML string to the ApplyXSLWithParam() utility function. The same function is used to show the absence codes combo box and select a particular item (based on the parameter passed).

When the above form is submitted it is posted to addRequest.asp, which builds the XML string from the form data and sends that XML string to the AddAbsenceRequest() method in the DBAccess class.

```
<%@ Language=VBScript %>
<%
Option Explicit

Dim PostXMLStr
Dim objDBAcc
Set objDBAcc = Server.CreateObject("Vacation.DBAccess")

PostXMLStr = "<AbsenceRequest>"

PostXMLStr = PostXMLStr & "<Emp_Row_ID>" & Request("Emp_Row_ID") & _
             "</Emp_Row_ID>"

PostXMLStr = PostXMLStr & "<ReqTitle>" & _
         Server.HTMLEncode(Request("ReqTitle")) & "</ReqTitle>"

...

PostXMLStr = PostXMLStr & "</AbsenceRequest>"

objDBAcc.AddAbsenceRequest PostXMLStr

Response.Redirect "details.asp"
%>
```

A manager can sign-in and view the vacation requests for all their employees – all their team members' details will be accessible via a link (showing the employee's name) in the bottom right corner of the window. They can then update (approve/reject/add notes to, etc.) the requests. In the following screen, Dean (Kelly's manager) signs in and views Kelly's vacation requests:

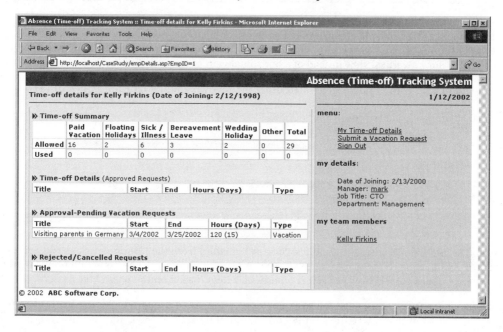

A manager can then update the request:

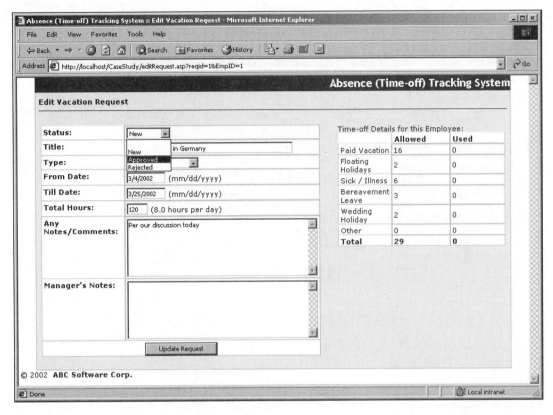

The above form is submitted to `updateRequest.asp`, which, like `addRequest.asp`, builds the XML string from the posted data and sends it to the `UpdateAbsenceRequest()` method in the `DBAccess` class.

When a member of the HR Administrators group signs in, they can view the absence details for any employee and generate reports. In the following screen, Kim (one of the HR Administrators) signs in and views the vacation details for Dean (another employee):

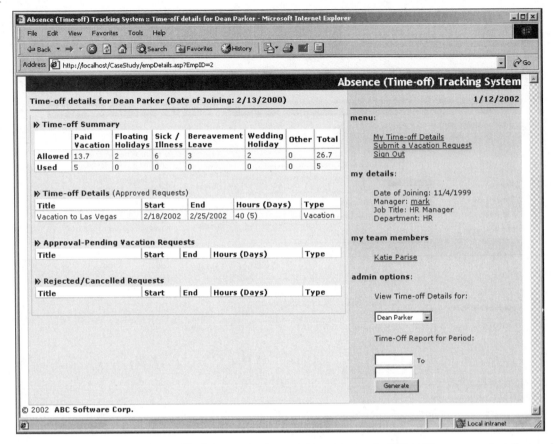

The empDetails.asp page calls the GetEmpDetailsByID() method from the DBAccess class and loads the resultant employee details into the DOMDocument. Then, using the selectSingleNode() method and nodeTypedValue property, we get the employee's first name, last name, and date of joining, etc.

Like in details.asp, in empDetails.asp we also use the utility functions, such as PrintTimeOffSummary() to output the time-off details.

Generating Reports

Members of the HR Administrators group can generate a report to view all the approved vacation requests for a particular date period and then they can use that information during the payroll. If we wish, we can easily integrate this information with the Payroll system, since the COM object returns the information in XML format and we can use it in whatever way we prefer, from any platform or language.

The report.asp page code simply calls the GetAbsenceReqsBetween() method from the DBAccess class and applies a particular stylesheet to show the details nicely in the browser:

```
<!--#include file="top.asp"-->
<!--#include file="utility.asp"-->
<!--#include file="ValidateLogin.asp"-->


<%
   If IsHRAdmin Then
   Else
      Response.Redirect "details.asp"
   End If

   Dim FromDate, ToDate, objXMLDOMAbsReq
   FromDate = Request("FromDate")
   ToDate = Request("ToDate")
%>
<center><h3>Report for Period: <%=FromDate%> To  <%=ToDate%></h3></center>
<%
   Response.Write ApplyXSL _
      (objDBAcc.GetAbsenceReqsBetween(FromDate, ToDate), _
      Server.MapPath("./Style/report.xsl"))
%>
<!--#include file="bottom.asp"-->
```

Once again, we use the `ApplyXSL()` function from `Utility.asp` to transform the XML into HTML.

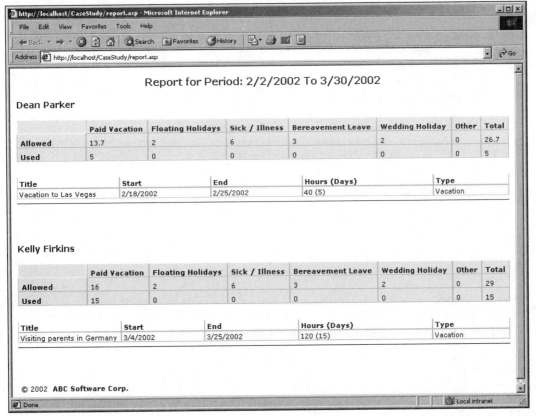

XSLT Stylesheets

The stylesheet file (`report.xsl`) used for the report above, and all other XSL files, are available under the `Style` directory. Let's look at a couple of stylesheet files, and then you may spend some time reviewing the others. They illustrate some interesting concepts, such as using stylesheet parameters and including client-side JavaScript as part of an XSL stylesheet.

MyTeam.xsl

When a manager logs in, we show a list of their immediate subordinates. They can then click on individual team members and view or update their vacation details. The DBAccess class has a member method, `GetMyTeamMembers()`, which is first used to get the details of subordinates in XML format and then the following stylesheet is applied to generate the HTML.

```xml
<?xml version="1.0"?>

<xsl:stylesheet xmlns:xsl="http://www.w3.org/1999/XSL/Transform"
     version="1.0">
<xsl:output method="html"/>

<xsl:template match="/">
     <xsl:apply-templates />
</xsl:template>

<xsl:template match="/MyTeam">
     <b>my team members</b>

     <blockquote>

     <xsl:for-each select="Record">
          <a href="empDetails.asp?EmpID={Row_ID}" class="stdlink">
               <xsl:value-of select="FirstName" />
                    <xsl:text> </xsl:text>
               <xsl:value-of select="LastName" />
          </a>
          <br />
     </xsl:for-each>

     </blockquote>

</xsl:template>

</xsl:stylesheet>
```

For each <Record> element, we generate an anchor link (<a> tag) referencing empDetails.asp with the value of Row_ID passed as a parameter to the ASP page. Note the usage of an attribute value template to get the value of ROW_ID while building the anchor link.

ACCombo.xsl

While entering a new vacation (time-off) request or updating an existing entry, we want to show the list of absence codes in a combo box. If you recall, the absence codes are available in the database in the AbsenceCodes table. We first use the GetAbsenceCodes() function from the DBAccess COM class, which returns absence code details as XML, and we then apply the following stylesheet to build an HTML combo box:

```xsl
<xsl:stylesheet
    xmlns:xsl="http://www.w3.org/1999/XSL/Transform"
    version="1.0" >

    <xsl:output method="html"/>

    <xsl:param name="selIndex"/>

    <xsl:template match="/">

        <select id="AbsenceCode" name="AbsenceCode">
            <option value="" ></option>

            <xsl:for-each select="AbsenceCodes/Record">

                <xsl:element name="option">

                    <xsl:attribute name="value">
                        <xsl:value-of select="AbsenceCode"/>
                    </xsl:attribute>

                    <xsl:if test="AbsenceCode = $selIndex">
                        <xsl:attribute name="selected"/>
                    </xsl:if>

                    <xsl:value-of select="Description"/>

                </xsl:element>

            </xsl:for-each>

        </select>

    </xsl:template>
</xsl:stylesheet>
```

The above stylesheet accepts a parameter (selIndex) that is used to select the item in the combo box. We use the <xsl:if> syntax to match the input parameter while creating the combo box, and add the selected attribute if the condition matches.

Summary

In this case study we saw how MSXML can be used to facilitate XML data transfer, and to build components that can be used for today's applications yet still be ready for future application integration. We created a simple intranet web application to track employee absence details.

The Visual Basic COM component that we wrote used XML for almost all class methods. The "get" methods returned data as an XML string and the "add/update" methods accepted XML formatted data as input parameters. This COM component was frequently used in this application (from ASP pages). At the same time it can be very easily used from other applications, including over the Internet (for instance using SOAP).

We used MSXML to build XML documents, to separate the content from the presentation, and to parse and retrieve data from XML documents. We also learned about saving application settings into an XML configuration file and how we can very easily access that information using MSXML.

XML offers interesting benefits when it comes to data transfer and application integration, separating data from presentation, and building simple but flexible applications. MSXML helps us actually use those benefits easily and efficiently. From its beginnings as a very basic DOM-based XML parser, today MSXML has become an essential component for any kind of XML application development on a Windows platform.

XML Application Development with MSXML 4.0
SOAP
XHTML
XML Schemas DTDs XPath CSS
XML Namespaces
XML 1.0
MSXML

16

Case Study: XML Messaging System (Helpdesk)

It is easy to get the impression that to use XML it is necessary to modify infrastructure at an enterprise level and plug into larger-scale standards, such as ebXML.

Nothing could be farther from the truth. With tools like MSXML, it is possible to take advantage of XML for applications with any kind of scope, and even use the same kind of models used in large systems but on a smaller scale. With the effort it would have taken a few years ago to create a simple desktop application, we can now produce scalable and interoperable distributed systems with the aid of XML APIs and Internet protocols. In the hope of supporting this claim, this case study provides an application that is simple in purpose and implementation (as it stands it is very much a conceptual application) but approached in such a way that while designing for the present, future doors are left wide open.

This case study will look at a simple **web-based helpdesk application**. The end result will be functional, but not suitable for deployment without considerable additional work, in particular on error handling and the user interface. To keep things simple, the server file system is used for data persistence – for scalability and reliability a database (RDBMS or native XML) would be much more appropriate. We are assuming that the target audience is a smallish business, where in-house programmers are available for further development and maintenance of the code. In spite of these omissions, it will demonstrate some useful functionality that can be achieved with MSXML. It will use MSXML and ASP 3.0 on Windows 2000 technologies and take a message-based, modular approach. We will look at:

- ❑ The requirements of a simple helpdesk application, described through use cases.
- ❑ Generation of XML text from a light client, without using MSXML.

❏ Using JScript and XSLT in a complementary fashion to build, interpret, and transform XML messages.

❏ The use of a broker to coordinate message routing and transformation.

❏ Chaining ASP pages for synchronous communications.

❏ Unchained ASP pages for messaging.

❏ How to communicate with remote, non-MS systems.

Requirements

Before we get started looking at the implementation of this case study, let's consider the requirements – firstly what you need to run the code for yourself, and then the general requirements of a message-based helpdesk system.

Development Environment

The code in this chapter comprises JScript and XSLT scripts. The JScript was developed using the **Coda** tool from Xoology at http://www.xoology.com, a free version of which is available for download. Visual InterDev or any decent text editor could easily have been used instead. It is possible to develop XSL scripts using a text editor, perhaps with a command-line tool to test the transforms, but it is unlikely that any MS-platform developer would dream of going back to the basic kit once they have used **XML Cooktop**, available from http://www.xmleverywhere.com. XML Cooktop is a Windows application (95/98/98SE/ME/NT4/2000) for writing and testing XSLT stylesheets, XML documents, DTDs, and XPaths.

Developing on a local IIS web server avoids upsetting system administrators. The application in this case study sends e-mail programmatically – we used the IIS Default SMTP server and an existing mail server, but a local (SMTP/POP3) mail server could be used instead. For example, you can download a freeware version of a suitable product from **ArGoSoft** (http://www.argosoft.com). The web server used was Internet Information Services (IIS) 5.0, with ASP as supplied. MSXML SDK 4.0 and Microsoft Windows HTTP Services SDK 5 were installed (both from http://msdn.microsoft.com/downloads).

The code described is this case study is available in the code download for this book, from http://www.wrox.com/.

The Helpdesk

Despite having washing machines with alleged intelligence and semantics being added to the Web, if any machine breaks down, we're likely to need the assistance of a human expert. One way of providing this assistance is through a helpdesk, where it is possible for a small number of experts to help a large number of clients. The traditional mode of communication with a helpdesk is via a telephone, where the expert on the end of the line is able to give immediate assistance. For various reasons this can be an inefficient use of resources, and in many situations it can be the case that the expert cannot produce the answer straight away. Such a situation is crying out for a software solution, and of course helpdesk-support packages are available, though as requirements are likely to vary and the task isn't particularly complex, this makes a good candidate for in-house development. The application described in this case study is designed to provide a simple web interface for a helpdesk, where a client can report a problem and the recipient can provide the solution online.

Messaging Systems

The helpdesk can be seen as an archetypal messaging system, where a **message** is sent to report a problem and a message is returned with the solution to the problem: in other words, a kind of workflow system. Different views of the data will be required (so that helpdesk personnel can check on open jobs, for example), but software for such a system will be more about *routing* than *processing* data. Data, as it becomes available, will be delivered from one point to another with little or no modification. In other words we are looking at software that will usually be idle, until events drive some kind of action. Other characteristics that are common with most messaging systems are that they use a peer-to-peer model rather than client-server, and communication between the peers is asynchronous. In human terms, e-mail shares a lot of these characteristics – e-mail is normally peer-to-peer (person to person) and asynchronous, that is, the recipient of the e-mail isn't obliged to acknowledge receipt. Under normal circumstances the recipient of an e-mail doesn't care which machine or machines actually deliver it the information contained within the e-mail itself is what is important. Similarly, in messaging-based applications, the recipient of a message doesn't really care about where it originated, only the content, so little coupling between peers is needed. A significant benefit of this is that messaging-based applications lend themselves to modularization and to being distributed, with different operations taking place on different, loosely coupled peers in the network. In other words, such systems are inherently extensible (a functional unit can be added without affecting other parts of the application) and scalable (if a particular unit is overworked, then another unit that carries out the same operation can be added and the workload shared). In this case study we will refer to the discrete functional units as 'modules'.

A key part of a messaging system is the routing of messages, and there is a tried and tested pattern for the part(s) of a system that deal with this: the **broker**. Essentially the broker will receive all messages, examine relevant parts of the content, and, based on a set of predetermined rules, forward the message to the proper location. It is convenient to include within the broker other functionality, such as validation of the messages and manipulation of those messages into a form that will be understood by the ultimate recipient. In this case study we won't be looking at message validation or any other kinds of error checking, but there will be plenty of message manipulation.

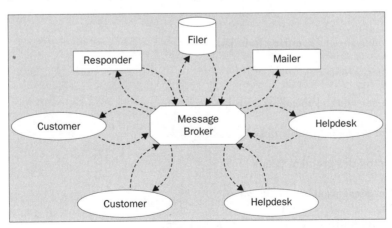

This diagram shows the key modules in the system, together with two customers and two members of the helpdesk staff. Customers will report problems and helpdesk personnel will supply solutions from browsers. Modules on the server will respond to browser submissions, look after storage of reported problems, and provide e-mail notifications as appropriate. Essentially, as far as the broker is concerned, all these entities are given equal status as peers in the system. Compromises are made in the implementation described here, but in principle the physical location of the broker, modules (on one or more servers), and clients is irrelevant; all the broker cares about is the messages it receives and the rules it has been given for manipulating and routing these. We will be looking at how this set-up was arrived at next, and then the actual implementation details.

Requirements Specification

Where a system involves a fair amount of human interaction, the 'use case' based approach to requirements specification has proved its worth many times. Described by the pioneer Ivar Jacobson as "*a behaviorally related sequence of transactions in a dialogue with the system*", the use case is basically an easy way of tying down what it is you want a system to do. Use cases play a key role in many of the leading software development methodologies, and have their own diagram format within the UML family, but for our purposes we only really need their basic form – a list of interactions between the user and the system.

Use Cases

Five basic cases (and two alternatives) were determined, and here each is presented broken down into numbered steps. As we are only dealing with a prototype system here, we are only attempting to describe the normal flow of operations, and no effort is made to cover errors or *abuse* cases. Before it is possible to realistically take this system much further it's necessary to identify the causes of exceptions, the sequence of events following these, and the end results.

Use Case Name: Report a Problem

Participating Actors: Customer, System
Entry Conditions: Use case is initiated when customer wishes to report a problem.
Flow of Events:

1. Customer goes to company help page.

2. System presents help options.

3. Customer chooses to report a problem after finding no diagnosis with the online FAQ.

4. System presents 'trouble ticket' form.

5. User provides problem details.

6. System presents acknowledgement.

7. System initializes job history for this problem.

Postconditions: Problem recorded in system.

Alternative: Report a critical problem. As above up to step 5, when the user has selected 'Urgent' for priority on the 'trouble ticket' form, then:

6. System e-mails appropriate helpdesk personnel.

Postconditions: Problem recorded in system, helpdesk notified.

Use Case Name: Check Status of Job

Participating Actors: Customer, System
Entry Conditions: Use case is initiated when customer wishes to check status of previously submitted problem.
Flow of Events:

1. Customer goes to company help page.

2. System presents help options.

3. Customer chooses to check status.

4. System requests user and/or 'trouble ticket' identification.

5. User enters personal or ticket identification.

6. System presents requested status details (job history).

Postconditions: No change.

Alternative: Close job. As above, then:

7. User closes job.

8. System records status.

Postconditions: Job recorded as closed.

The following use cases are interactions between helpdesk personnel and the application.

Use Case Name: Problem Update

Participating Actors: Helpdesk, System
Entry Conditions: Helpdesk personnel available.
Flow of Events:

1. Helpdesk goes to login page.

2. Helpdesk enters authorization information.

3. System displays list of open jobs for helpdesk's department.

Postconditions: Job history updated, customer notified.

Use Case Name: View Job

Participating Actors: Helpdesk, System
Entry Conditions: Helpdesk logged in.
Flow of Events:

1. Helpdesk clicks on required job.

2. System returns job history.

Postconditions: None.

Use Case Name: Add Proposed Solution

Participating Actors: Helpdesk, System
Entry Conditions: Helpdesk logged in.
Flow of Events:

1. Helpdesk views job.

2. Helpdesk enters solution to problem.

3. System updates job history.

4. System sends e-mail to customer.

Postconditions: Job history updated, customer notified.

Alternative: Close job. As above, but:

5. Helpdesk specifies job is closed.

Postconditions: Job status updated.

Other Requirements

Other requirements that govern our system include response times and logging, which we'll consider next.

Response Time

As mentioned earlier, a helpdesk system falls very much into that class of applications where most of the system's time will be spent doing nothing, waiting for user input. The real processing in a helpdesk system is actually carried out by the helpdesk personnel – human rather than electronic agents. For these reasons the requirements are quite slack here, but like all applications it will be desirable for the user (customer or helpdesk) to receive some feedback from their actions as soon as expected. For web applications this means providing a page in response to a form submission within a few seconds.

Ticket Logging

For most systems it is desirable to include infrastructure that is not needed for normal operation, but which will allow recovery or repair when something goes wrong. One such facility is a logging mechanism. As programmers we are familiar with fairly low-level logging, for instance that provided with a web server. If system actions are logged, then it allows problems to be traced back to their cause. As it happens, such a mechanism at a higher level within a system can sometimes offer a significant value-add. For instance, in a helpdesk system, it might be the case that a customer's problem has apparently been resolved satisfactorily, but then the problem reappears in the same or a slightly different form a few months later. For our system, we will simply log all new problem reports ('trouble tickets').

A Simple Messaging Framework

We will now look at the implementation of the helpdesk system. Firstly we have two important considerations:

❏ To use procedural or declarative programming? As you will by now be aware, MSXML is seriously versatile. At its heart we have tools for manipulating XML either using procedural programming on DOM objects or declarative programming using XSLT. There are disadvantages to each technique – making changes to a document procedurally by addressing and manipulating nodes can soon become messy, and stylesheets are pretty limited when it comes to dealing with things like the file system. However, we can take the best of both worlds, and use XSLT for document transforms. We can use procedural code to interface with the world outside of stylesheets and to act as glue to tie everything together. In the helpdesk application there are operations carried out by procedural script that could fairly easily have been done by XSLT and vice versa.

❏ Persistence – how to retaining data between interactions? Typically the first choice in a server-side system would be a relational database, with efficiency, security, and transactional isolation available. The present version of the requirements does not consider these factors an issue (it is likely a later version would), so following the 'keep it simple' rule for this application we will just use the file system to store our data as XML text files.

Modules

Looking through the requirements it is relatively easy to identify discrete functional units that will be needed in the system. As mentioned earlier, we'll call these "modules". At the heart there will be our broker. As we're using the file system for persistence we'll write a module called "**filer**". We also need to somehow build up job histories, that is, the original trouble ticket plus any advice the helpdesk has added. The facility to send e-mails will be handled by another module we'll call "**mailer**". We also need a way of providing the user with some kind of feedback, and for this we have the "**responder**" module. To summarize:

❏ broker – handles message routing, in other words invocation of other modules and transforms.

❏ responder – passes back a message to a client browser.

❏ filer – saves a message to disk.

❏ mailer – sends an e-mail.

The key part of this application is the broker module. Its usual behavior is to receive a message, do things to it, and pass it elsewhere. Different messaging systems choose to handle messages differently. It may be that the source of the message has relevance, or some other factor such as the time of day, but in the abstract, the actions taken will be a combination of the contents of the message and some predetermined rules. When we talk of doing things to a message and sending it elsewhere, we are talking about transformation and routing.

Views

Again, looking through the requirements we can identify various views that have to be presented to the user, whether they are a customer or a member of the helpdesk personnel. These views may be static HTML pages or dynamically generated through ASP. Either way, they will present information to the user and have a facility for the user to respond. Where the same basic data may be presented to either the customer or a helpdesk person, the fact that we can dynamically generate the pages means that it will be relatively straightforward to reuse the same underlying page, just modifying the presentation as appropriate. This is the case for "joblist" and "jobview" below. The pages are as follows:

❑ **welcome** – starting page for customers.

❑ **ticket** – form for the customer to report a problem.

❑ **acknowledge** – acknowledgement of problem reported.

❑ **helpdesk login** – helpdesk personnel login.

❑ **joblist** – list of individual job histories.

❑ **jobview** – individual job history.

XML from the Client

For a customer to report a problem, we need a way of allowing them to type in the details and then pump these into the system. Our helpdesk system will be based around passing XML trees between various subsystems, and as we are using MSXML and JScript anyway, there is a great temptation to build a DOM object at the client side using these technologies and to pass this to the server. Unfortunately this approach is likely to fall at the first hurdle; to use MSXML on the client demands that these libraries be installed on the client – in many circumstances it might be reasonable to insist on this type of set up in a controlled (or controllable) environment, but in others (for example, where clients use a Mozilla browser on Linux) it may be an impossibility. Fortunately, XML is a text-based format, and it is inconceivable that a client won't be able to handle text. Something else that is reasonable to assume today is that the browser the clients are using will support JavaScript.

The usual way of passing data between a client browser and a web server is by means of the HTTP GET and POST methods of a form. The W3C guidelines suggest that GET is reserved for situations where a transaction doesn't have side effects, such as updating a database. By reporting a problem we do want to make some changes on the server side, so this suggests we should use the POST method. Therefore, what we are looking at is a way of the customer typing their problem into a standard HTML form, and this data being somehow converted into XML with JavaScript and sent via the POST method to the server. The use of POST rather than GET is also a pragmatic choice – HTTP server and user agent vendors limit the number of characters that can passed using a GET method.

The problem reporting or 'trouble ticket' form for our helpdesk (`ticket.htm`) looks like this:

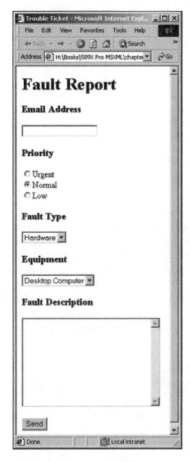

The body code is straightforward and is displayed below:

```
<body>
<h1>Fault Report</h1>
<form name="userForm">
    <h3>Email Address</h3>
    <input type="text" name="sender">

    <h3>Priority</h3>
    <input type="radio" name="priority" value="urgent">Urgent<br />
    <input type="radio" name="priority" value="normal" checked>Normal<br />
    <input type="radio" name="priority" value="low">Low<br />

    <h3>Fault Type</h3>
    <select name="system">
        <option>Hardware</option>
        <option>Software</option>
    </select>
```

```
    <h3>Equipment</h3>
    <select name="component">
        <option>Desktop Computer</option>
        <option>Notepad</option>
        <option>PDA</option>
    </select>

    <h3>Fault Description</h3>
    <textarea name="description" cols="30" rows="10"></textarea>
</form>
<br /><br />
<form name="submitForm" method="post" action="broker.asp"
        onsubmit="return send()">
    <input type="submit" value="Send">
    <input type="hidden" name="message">
</form>
</body>
```

There are a couple of minor deviations from the minimal HTML form. We have two forms here; the first displays the visual controls, and the second looks after the button-clicking action. This second form includes a call to a JavaScript method, send(). In this case study we're not going to bother about data validation, but for future reference, the value returned within the onsubmit, if equivalent to false, will abort the POST submission operation. Another thing to note about the HTML above is that on the surface we appear to be forgetting about all the form data, and instead are including in the data POSTed a hidden element called message, that doesn't even have a value. Whatever this value is, clicking on the button will POST it to the URL specified in the action attribute. If we now look at the script contained in the head of this HTML document, things might start to make sense.

```
<html>
<head>
<title>Trouble Ticket</title>
<script language="JavaScript">

var root = "message";

function Message(){
    var rnd = Math.random();
    this.id = (new String(rnd)).slice(3,9);
    this.sender = userForm.sender.value;

    this.priority = getRadioValue(userForm.priority);
    this.date = numericDate();

    var selector = userForm.system;
    this.system = selector.options[selector.selectedIndex].text;

    selector = userForm.component;
    this.component = selector.options[selector.selectedIndex].text;

    this.description = userForm.description.value;
}

Message.prototype.type = "ticket";
Message.prototype.status = "new";
Message.prototype.responded = "false";
```

```
function getValueSet(){
   var message = new Message();
   return message;
}

</script>
<script language="JavaScript" src="xmlWrapper.js"></script>

</head>
```

The `root` value will later become the root element of the XML we construct. The `getValueSet()` method creates a new `Message` object which will contain the data. Some values, which may be thought of as constants, are put in place as prototypes, others are assembled in the `Message` constructor block. The `id` value is just a six-digit random number represented as a string. The `sender` value is taken from the form controls in the listing above (an e-mail address); `type` and `status` are given hard-coded values. The `priority` value is taken from the corresponding radio button controls. This uses a utility function (in the external script) to obtain the name of the radio button selected. The `date` value is generated by another utility function, which returns the current date in a `yyyy-mm-dd` format. The `system`, `component`, and `description` values are taken from the form above. The `responded` property will be used later when we need to check if a user request has been acknowledged by the system.

The included script (`xmlWrapper.js`), as well as containing the utility functions used above, also does the XML formatting. The reason for including this as a separate file, rather than within the HTML page, is that it will make the reuse of the code easier – the properties of an object are set in the HTML, the script converts this into an XML string.

Generally speaking it isn't good practice to create XML using text that 'just happens to be XML', but here we are operating on the assumption that the client hasn't got MSXML, and the only real alternative would be to build an object that emulated the DOM model to generate XML. This approach would have advantages in terms of maintenance and reuse, but hasn't been attempted here in the interests of keeping the code simple in this version.

It begins by setting a pair of strings that will define the "outside" of the XML document:

```
// xmlWrapper.js
var head = "<?xml version=\"1.0\" encoding=\"iso-8859-1\"?>\n<"+root+">\n";
var tail = "</"+root+">";
```

The JavaScript object might not be to the taste of OO purists, but it can make some tasks very easy to code. After initializing the string which will contain the XML with the header value, the `toXml()` method takes an object and then steps through its properties, calling the `wrapTags()` method (below) on each property name and value, so for instance the `message.type` property set in the HTML above will in effect be used like so: `wrapTags("type", "ticket")`.

```
function toXml(object)
{
   var xml = head;
   for (prop in object)
   {
       xml += wrapTags(prop, object[prop]);
   }
   return xml+tail;
}
```

The `wrapTags()` method does a simple bit of formatting, so if called with `wrapTags("type", "ticket")`, it will return the string `"<type>ticket</type>"`.

```
function wrapTags(name, value)
{
    return  "\t<" + name + ">" + value + "</" + name + ">\n";
}
```

Basically the `toXml()` method above calls `wrapTags` for each property in the object, accumulating a series of XML elements between preset head and tail strings.

The `send()` method calls `getValueSet()`, which is listed within the HTML document; as we have seen this loads the `message` object with properties. This object is converted to an XML string by `toXml()`, and this string is placed in the (hidden) form field message, which is what gets POSTed by the form.

```
function send()
{
var valueSet = getValueSet();
    submitForm.message.value = toXml(valueSet);
    // alert(toXml(valueSet));
    return true;
}
```

Note the commented `alert()` call above; if we uncomment this open `ticket.htm` in IE, and fill in the form with the details of a possible problem, clicking on the **Send** button will produce a pop-up like this:

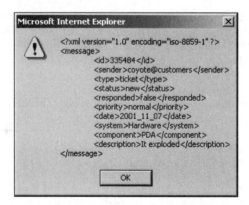

The remainder of the script contains two utility functions, `getRadioValue()` which will return the value of whichever of a group of radio buttons is checked, and `numericDate()` which creates a new `Date` object (which will contain today's date) and uses it to build an ISO 8601 formatted string, such as `"2002-01-14"`.

```
// utility functions

function getRadioValue(radioGroup){
    var value = null;
        if(radioGroup.length) {
            // is false if radioGroup not an array
            for (var index = 0; index < radioGroup.length; index++) {
                if (radioGroup[index].checked) value = radioGroup[index].value;
```

```
            }
        }
        else {
            value = radioGroup.value;
        }
    return value;
}

function numericDate(){
    var date = new Date();
    var day = new String(date.getDate());
    day = day.length > 1 ? day : "0"+day;
    var month = new String(date.getMonth()+1);
    month = month.length > 1 ? month : "0" + month;
    var year = date.getYear();
    if (year < 1000) year += 1900; // y2k safety
    return year + "-" + month + "-" + day;
}
```

So to summarize, the `ticket.htm` page and the included `xmlWrapper.js` script allows the customer to enter the details of their problem, which when they click on 'Send' will be formatted as a string containing XML which will be POSTed to a server.

Receiving the POST

So what happens to the POSTed data when it gets to the server? The "modules" of the system will be passing around DOM objects, so we have a piece of script to convert the POSTed string data into such an object. To keep this side of the system open, we will include a script in each module that will check whether or not data POSTed is a string, in which case a DOM object will be created. The server will get its data through an HTTP Request, and in the code we can access the data through the Request object. This will be passed to the methods below. We need to check on the type of data POSTed, which will be in the HTTP as the value of HTTP_CONTENT_TYPE, and this we extract in a little initialization function. If this variable has the value "application/x-www-form-urlencoded" we know the data is coming from a form, otherwise we will assume that the data is a DOM object. We are going to be passing back a DOM object either way, so we also create one of these here:

```
<!-- converter.asp -->
<%
var type;
var doc;

function init(req){
    type = req.ServerVariables("HTTP_CONTENT_TYPE");
    doc = Server.CreateObject("Msxml2.DOMDocument.4.0");
    doc.async = false;
}
```

To get a DOM object, our module pages will be making a call like this, which will pass a reference to the Request object into the `init(req)` function:

```
var messageDoc = getDoc(Request);
```

The variables above are initialized, and Request is checked to see if it contains text sent from a form. If this is the case then the text itself will be obtained by name. The client-side code above included a form object called message, and this is the name used to get hold of the data, which all being well will be a string containing XML. The DOM document object will then be loaded with this data. We are only allowing for two possibilities within the application – that the data POSTed is text from a form or it is a DOM object. The DOM object is then loaded from the Request.

```
function getDoc(req){
    init(req);
    if(type == "application/x-www-form-urlencoded")
    {
    // text sent
    var text = req.Form("message");
    doc.loadXML(text);
}
else{
    // object sent
        doc.load(req);
    }
    return doc;
} %>
```

Return to Sender

To use a messaging approach throughout requires that modules have the ability to POST a message back to the broker once the module has done its work. There is another architectural issue here, relating to ASP in general. Once the client has POSTed a message from their browser, we have to present them with something. It would be possible to link in a static page, but we can make the system a little more versatile by giving the broker another responsibility, that of returning the required page to the browser once a message has been sent. This, and the message posting facility, will be handled in another little script, which will be included in the modules:

```
<% // post.asp
function post(document, target){
    var postObject = Server.CreateObject("MSXML2.ServerXMLHTTP.4.0");
    postObject.open("POST", target, false);
    postObject.send(document);
    return postObject.responseText;
}

function postback(document, target, resp){
    var respText = post(document, target);
    resp.Write(respText);
    resp.End();
}
%>
```

The post() function takes two parameters, a DOM document object and the target URL (which in this application will always be the broker). An instance of ServerXMLHTTP is created, its open method prepares the request, and its send method POSTs the document. After the request has been carried out, the ServerXMLHTTP object will contain the response of the target URL. The postback() function takes the same document and target values as post, and a third value will be the Response object from a calling page. The post method is called to pass on the message, and then the response from whichever page the message went to is written back to the Response of the page that called this function.

The postback() method is thus intimately connected (through the Response object) to whatever page called it. On the other hand, some of the modules will call post() directly and not make use of the returned value. This is a kind of quasi-asynchronous call – though in reality the program flow will wait for a response from the called server, it is treated as if a message has been sent and forgotten about. A true asynchronous call would be preferable here, in other words postObject.open("POST", target, true), completely decoupling the post from the local program flow, but the problem with that in this context is that the script will have completed and the postObject will be destroyed before the posting operation has completed. The approach taken here is something of a workaround – if a system like this were to be implemented across several servers then this would need reviewing.

Broker

The function of the broker is to receive, transform, and dispatch messages to the required target. We will now have a look at the design of the broker in this application, beginning with the way its routing and transformation rules are specified. This will be followed by the broker's source code, and a look at how it handles a message. We will then move on to code and operation of the modules with which the broker will be interacting.

Rules

In the helpdesk application we use an XML file rules.xml to specify these rules. The following snippet contains a single rule, which is comprised of one or more pattern-matching blocks, followed by an action that is to be carried out all if the matching conditions are satisfied:

```
<rules>

    <!-- respond to new ticket -->
    <rule>
        <match>
            <path>message/status</path>
            <value>new</value>
        </match>
        <match>
            <path>message/type</path>
            <value>ticket</value>
        </match>
        <match>
            <path>message/responded</path>
            <value>false</value>
        </match>

    <target>http://localhost/tickets/control/responder.asp</target>
        <transform>../xsl/ticketresponse.xsl</transform>
    </rule>
...
</rules>
```

The <match> subsection contains a <path> element and a <value> element used to test the incoming message. Each rule can contain an arbitrary number of <match> subsections. The path is an XPath statement, which the broker will apply to an incoming message. If the value returned by this is equal to the value specified in the <value> element, then the incoming message will have passed that test, and the next <match> subsection will be tried. If all the <match> subsections are successful, then the rule is triggered – the stylesheet specified in the <transform> element is applied to the message and the result is posted on to the URL specified in <target>. The path and value test could perhaps be reduced down to a single test line, something like //path/[text()='value'], though in this version of the application at least it was decided to opt for human-readability.

As mentioned earlier, the MSXML programmer often has the luxury of choice between using procedural operations on DOM objects or declarative operations through XSLT. The way rules are defined and used is a case in point. The broker here will test the <match> parts of rules using script on DOM objects.

An alternative would have been to specify an XSL transform here, apply it to the message, and, based on the result, decide subsequent transforms and routing. For the helpdesk application it was decided that the tests required only needed to be quite simple, and there was significant benefit from being able to specify them all in one place, in a format that was easy to read.

The source code for the broker itself begins by getting the message that has been posted as a DOM object, using the getDoc() method in converter.asp:

```
<%@ LANGUAGE=JScript %>
<!-- broker.asp -->
<!-- #INCLUDE FILE="converter.asp" -->
<!-- #INCLUDE FILE="post.asp" -->
<%
   var messageDoc = getDoc(Request);
```

Next the message will be checked against the rules. The rules data will not change after the application has been deployed, so to avoid having to reload this every time the broker is called the data is stored as a DOM object in an Application variable, effectively caching it. The getRules() method takes care of this caching. At development time we may wish to modify the rules as we go along, so we can disable the caching by initially setting the variable to null, forcing a reload.

The rules themselves are pulled out into a node list, which is stepped through, each rule being tested in turn using the testRule() method, which we will see in a moment. If a match is successful then the invoke() method is called to carry out the operations (transform and target) given in the rule.

```
   Application("rules") = null; // remove after deployment

   var rules = getRules();
   var ruleList = rules.documentElement.selectNodes("rule");

   for (var i=0; i<ruleList.length; i++)
{
   if (testRule(messageDoc, ruleList.item(i)))
   {
      invoke(messageDoc, ruleList.item(i));
   }
}

function getRules(){
   if(!Application("rules"))
   {
      var rulesDoc =
         Server.CreateObject("Msxml2.FreeThreadedDOMDocument.4.0");
      rulesDoc.async = false;
      rulesDoc.load(Server.MapPath("rules.xml"));
      Application("rules") = rulesDoc;
   }
   return Application("rules");
}
```

There can be any number of `<match>` subsections for a given rule. So, we test each of these in turn, pulling out the values from the rule data and comparing them with the values retrieved from the message with the XPath criteria contained in the `<path>` element, so from the rule example above, this test:

```
<match>
    <path>message/status</path>
    <value>new</value>
</match>
```

would be satisfied by a document with root `<message>` containing the element `<status>new</status>`.

The test picks up the path and value from the rules document using XPath expressions, using the value obtained for `path` as an XPath expression itself, and applying it to the document under test. A simple string comparison is then made between the value contained in the rule and the value retrieved from the document under test:

```
function testRule(messageDoc, rule){
    var tests = rule.selectNodes("match");
    var path;
    var value;
    var test;

    for(var i=0;i<tests.length;i++){
        path = tests.item(i).selectSingleNode("path").text;
        value = tests.item(i).selectSingleNode("value").text;
        if((value.length == 0) && (path.length == 0)) return true;
        test = messageDoc.selectSingleNode(path);
        if(test == null) return false;
        if(test.text != value) return false;
    }
    return true;
}
```

The `invoke()` method begins by getting the strings containing the name of the XSLT transform and the target URL. If a transform has been specified (that is, the `<transform>` element isn't empty) then one `DOMDocument` object is created to hold the transform and another for the result of applying the transform to the message. The transform is applied using the `transformNodeToObject()` method.

```
function invoke(messageDoc, rule){
    var target = rule.selectSingleNode("target").text;
    var transform = rule.selectSingleNode("transform").text;

    if(transform != ""){
    var result = Server.CreateObject("MSXML2.DOMDocument.4.0");
    var styleFile = Server.MapPath(transform);
    var style = Server.CreateObject("MSXML2.DOMDocument.4.0");
    style.async = false;
    style.load(styleFile);
    messageDoc.transformNodeToObject(style, result);
    messageDoc = result;
}
```

Finally the result of the transformation (or the original message, if no transform was specified) is POSTed on to the target URL specified in the `<target>` element in the rule using the `postback()` function (included from `post.asp`). This page's Response object is also passed; we will see later what happens to this.

```
        postback(messageDoc, target, Response);
    }
%>
```

The Broker in Action

We will now look at how the broker handles a message, in this case:

```
<?xml version="1.0" encoding="ISO-8859-1"?>
<message>
   <id>710727</id>
   <sender>roadrunner@customers</sender>
   <type>ticketresponse</type>
   <status>new</status>
   <responded>true</responded>
   <priority>low</priority>
   <date>2001-10-18</date>
   <system>Software</system>
   <component>Notepad</component>
   <description>Too slow.</description>
</message>
```

The `<responded>` value of `true` here signifies that a client submission has been acknowledged – we will see how a message of this form might occur shortly.

Running through the rule list, let's say the broker encounters the following:

```
    <!-- Log new tickets-->
    <rule>
       <match>
          <path>message/type</path>
          <value>ticketresponse</value>
       </match>
       <match>
          <path>message/status</path>
          <value>new</value>
       </match>
       <match>
          <path>message/responded</path>
          <value>true</value>
       </match>
       <target>http://localhost/tickets/control/filer.asp</target>
       <transform>../xsl/logger.xsl</transform>
    </rule>
```

The content of the `<type>` element in the message is obtained with the `message/type` path, and has the value "`ticketresponse`". This does match the contents of the `<value>` tag in the rule, and the other two tests are also successful, so the transform (`logger.xsl`) is applied and the result is passed on to the target URL.

The `filer.asp` module will take care of saving the message to disk, and this module will need to know where to save the data. The module will simply use the filename provided in the message it receives, which will be in the form of an element, for example:

```
<filename>path/filename.xml</filename>
```

This element will be generated and added to the message before it is sent to the filer module using a stylesheet `logger.xsl`. The filer will pass back a message to the broker, and to let it be known that the message has been logged, the stylesheet transform will also change the content of the `<status>` element from `new` into `logged`.

The stylesheet begins with the `<xsl:stylesheet>` element, with a namespace declaration to identify the document as a stylesheet. The `<xsl:output>` element controls the format of the stylesheet output: this has attributes to give us the output as XML, and indenting is switched on (which makes the output much easier to read – not necessary, but handy while developing). The `encoding` is forced to ISO-8859-1 (Latin 1 character set) which helps overcome minor inconsistencies in Microsoft's XML support (see http://support.microsoft.com/support/kb/articles/Q275/8/83.asp for more information).

```
<?xml version="1.0"?>
<!-- logger.xsl -->
<xsl:stylesheet version="1.0"
                xmlns:xsl="http://www.w3.org/1999/XSL/Transform">
<xsl:output method="xml" indent="yes" encoding="ISO-8859-1"/>
```

The first template will match the `<message>` element at the root of the message, and uses the `<xsl:copy>` instruction to make copy of this element (without its children). The `<xsl:apply-templates>` then runs the contents of the XML through the other templates, looking for matches in the XPath expressions. The matching template with highest precedence (the most specific in this case) is given by the path `message/status`. The contents of this template are used to modify the `<status>` element (use of `<xsl:element>` or simply providing the element literally, for example, `<status>logged</status>`, is largely a matter of personal preference in this case). The next template to match has the XPath expression `"*"`, which will pick up all the elements and, using the `<xsl:copy-of>` instruction, copy these unchanged through for the output. The `"."` here signifies the current context. Now the other templates have been applied, the first template continues its instructions and inserts a `<filename>` element derived from various parts of the source document.

```
<xsl:template match="message">
<xsl:copy>
   <xsl:apply-templates/>
   <xsl:element name="filename">../log/<xsl:value-of
          select="date"/>_<xsl:value-of select="type"/>_<xsl:value-of
          select="id"/>.xml</xsl:element>
</xsl:copy>
</xsl:template>

<xsl:template match="message/status">
   <xsl:element name="status">logged</xsl:element>
</xsl:template>

<xsl:template match="*">
   <xsl:copy-of select="."/>
</xsl:template>

</xsl:stylesheet>
```

If we apply this transform to the message listed at the start of this section, we get the modified result:

```xml
<?xml version="1.0" encoding="ISO-8859-1"?>
<message>
<id>710727</id>
<sender>roadrunner@customers</sender>
<type>ticketresponse</type>
<status>logged</status>
<responded>true</responded>
<priority>low</priority>
<date>2001-10-18</date>
<system>Software</system>
<component>Notepad</component>
<description>Too slow.</description>
<filename>../log/2001-10-18_ticketresponse_710727.xml</filename>
</message>
```

Filer Module

The filer module is pretty trivial – it receives a message as a DOM object, pulls out the value of the `<filename>` element, and, using `DOMDocument`'s convenient `save()` method, writes the data to disk (note you will have to set write permissions on the target folder for this to work). Finally it `POST`s the message back to the broker:

```asp
<%@ LANGUAGE=JScript %>
<!-- filer.asp -->
<!-- #INCLUDE FILE="converter.asp" -->
<!-- #INCLUDE FILE="post.asp" -->
<%
    var target = "http://localhost/tickets/control/broker.asp";
    var messageDoc = getDoc(Request);

    var filename = messageDoc.selectSingleNode("//filename").text;
    messageDoc.save(Server.MapPath(filename));
    post(messageDoc, target);
%>
```

The code above covers our requirement that new problem reports should be logged.

Responder Module

With problem reports that are posted by a customer, the system has to return an acknowledgement back to the customer. This is a synchronous operation, but we want the message to be passed on for other processing, such as the logging we have just looked at, which is intended to operate asynchronously. The answer to this dichotomy lies in the responder module. Let's first see how a message will find its way to the responder.

The first rule of the helpdesk system will apply to the messages sent when a new problem is reported. Checking whether their `<status>` element contains the value "new" identifies these messages. The broker will transform these messages using the `ticketresponse.xsl` stylesheet, and the result will be passed to `responder.asp`.

```xml
<!-- respond to new ticket -->
<rule>
    <match>
        <path>message/status</path>
```

```
         <value>new</value>
    </match>
    <match>
       <path>message/type</path>
       <value>ticket</value>
    </match>
    <match>
       <path>message/responded</path>
       <value>false</value>
    </match>
    <target>http://localhost/tickets/control/responder.asp</target>
    <transform>../xsl/ticketresponse.xsl</transform>
</rule>
```

The stylesheet is as follows:

```
<?xml version="1.0"?>
<!-- ticketresponse.xsl -->
<xsl:stylesheet version="1.0"
                xmlns:xsl="http://www.w3.org/1999/XSL/Transform">
<xsl:output method="xml" indent="yes" encoding="ISO-8859-1"/>

<xsl:template match="message">
<xsl:copy>
   <xsl:apply-templates/>
</xsl:copy>
</xsl:template>

<xsl:template match="message/*">
   <xsl:copy-of select="."/>
</xsl:template>

<xsl:template match="message/status">
   <xsl:element name="status">ticketresponse</xsl:element>
</xsl:template>

</xsl:stylesheet>
```

All this transform does is change the value of the <status> element to ticketresponse, copying everything else unchanged. Such an operation formed part of logger.xsl, but it is worth repeating in its purer form, as one of the operations carried out procedurally by the responder is virtually identical. Here is the responder code:

```
<%@ LANGUAGE=JScript %>
<!-- responder.asp -->
<!-- #INCLUDE FILE="converter.asp" -->
<!-- #INCLUDE FILE="post.asp" -->
<%
   var target = "http://localhost/tickets/control/broker.asp";

   var messageDoc = getDoc(Request);

   var responseDoc = messageDoc.cloneNode(true);

   var statusNode = messageDoc.selectSingleNode("message/status");
   statusNode.text = "responded";
```

```
      post(messageDoc, target);
      postback(responseDoc, target, Response);
%>
```

The script obtains the message as a DOM object, `messageDoc`. This it duplicates into `responseDoc` using the `cloneNode()` method. Remember that `responseDoc = messageDoc` would have merely copied the reference to the object, not the object itself. The parameter taken by `cloneNode()` specifies whether to recursively copy all the descendents of this node (`true`), or just the node itself (`false`). Now we have two messages. We obtain the `<status>` element from `messageDoc`, and as we know that this node is an element that contains a child text node (the content) we can change its content directly by addressing the `text` property of the parent. These two lines essentially carry out the same operation as the stylesheet above, though of course we have already created a document object and loaded in the data.

The modified document (containing `<status>responded</status>`) is posted back to the broker (and forgotten about) and the unmodified copy (containing `<status>ticketresponse</status>`) is posted back to the broker, along with the `Response` object of this page.

What the responder is in effect creating is a fork in the execution path – the message passed to the broker using the `post()` function will be handled independently as a fresh incoming message, whereas the message sent using the `postback()` function is effectively tied to the current page, with its `Response` object as an argument to the `postback` call.

In the helpdesk system, a message with a `<status>` value of `ticketresponse` and `<responded>` value of `false` will be picked up by the second rule:

```
<!-- acknowledge ticket -->
<rule>
   <match>
      <path>message/type</path>
      <value>ticketresponse</value>
   </match>
   <match>
      <path>message/responded</path>
      <value>false</value>
   </match>
   <target>http://localhost/tickets/control/acknowledge.asp</target>
   <transform>../xsl/acknowledge.xsl</transform>
</rule>
```

This rule applies the following stylesheet, which will prepare an acknowledgement for the customer:

```
<xsl:stylesheet version="1.0"
                xmlns:xsl="http://www.w3.org/1999/XSL/Transform">
<!-- acknowledge.xsl -->
<xsl:output method="xml" encoding="ISO-8859-1"/>

<xsl:template match="/">

   <html>
   <head><title>Acknowledgement</title></head>
   <body>
   <h3>Thank you!</h3>
   <b>Your report has been passed to the appropriate department.</b>
      <p>
```

```
        Reference : <xsl:value-of select="message/id"/>
     </p><p>
        User: <xsl:value-of select=" message/sender"/>
     </p><p>
        Priority : <xsl:value-of select=" message/priority"/>
     </p><p>
        Date : <xsl:value-of select="message/date"/>
     </p>
   </body>
   </html>
</xsl:template>
</xsl:stylesheet>
```

Note that although HTML tags are used, they are all paired so that the result of this stylesheet will be valid XML (the `xsl:output` method attribute reflects this), which is essential to allow the data to be returned through the modules using `ServerXMLHTTP.send(document)` in the `postback()` method.

The acknowledgement page looks like this:

```
<%@ LANGUAGE=JScript %>
<!-- acknowledge.asp -->
<!-- #INCLUDE FILE="converter.asp" -->
<%
   var messageDoc = getDoc(Request);
   Response.Write(messageDoc.xml);
   Response.End();
%>
```

All this does is write the message it has received to its response object. However, this page hasn't been called by the usual kind of route – its response is passed back through the series of `postback()` methods to the first broker, which was looking after the original POST. From the browser's point of view, all that has happened is that the first broker has been called and the response from that page is the content of the message that ended up at `acknowledge.asp`. In other words, what we are looking at here is **ASP page chaining**.

The result of applying this stylesheet to the message and passing it to `acknowledge.asp` looks like this in the browser:

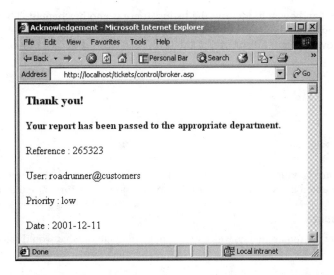

The message flow can be seen in the following diagram. The ticket message is POSTed to the broker, which calls the responder module. All the while the browser from which the ticket was sent is awaiting a response. Following the right fork in the diagram, the responder in turn calls another instance of the broker, which arrives at the acknowledge.asp page above. The data written by this page is passed back down the chain to supply the response that appears in the customer's browser. However, along the way, another POST of the message has been made by the responder module, which goes to a broker instance for subsequent handling. The dotted line on the diagram shows how the response created by the acknowledgement code gets passed back to the broker page. Operation through the left-hand fork will continue largely independently.

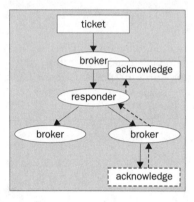

The customer starts at a static HTML page, ticket.htm. They will fill out the form and click the 'Send' button. The message will be posted to the broker, and following its rules it will call the responder. The responder in turn will call another instance of the broker, which following its rules this time will call the acknowledgement page.

You may have noticed in the code of the modules that the name of the module appeared as an XML comment, for example:

```
<!-- broker.asp -->
```

Apart from being a handy way to identify the listing, there is another benefit. These comments get transparently passed along the chain, accumulating in what becomes the final response. Viewing the source of the acknowledgement displayed in the browser reveals that the code proper is preceded by:

```
<!-- broker.asp -->

<!-- responder.asp -->

<!-- broker.asp -->

<!-- acknowledge.asp -->
```

Thus the modules are leaving a trail, which is useful while building a chained set of broker rules, but it is hoped the commented lines in the modules would be removed before a system like this went live.

Choosing a Department

Looking way back at the requirements, we can work out a diagram of what would satisfy the first use case:

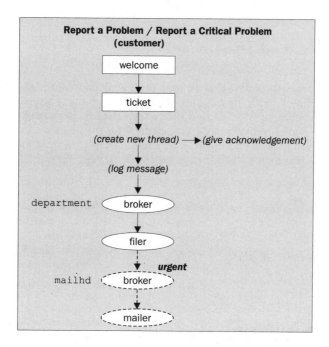

The customer will be presented with a welcome page, from where they can choose whether to check the status of the job or, in this use case, submit a new problem using the trouble ticket form. The responder module will then be called into play, and the ASP chain used to give the customer an acknowledgement. The message is being logged using the filer, which posts the message back to the broker. At this point the message will look something like this:

```xml
<?xml version="1.0" encoding="ISO-8859-1"?>
<message>
    <id>710727</id>
    <sender>roadrunner@customers</sender>
    <type>ticketresponse</type>
    <status>ticketresponse</status>
    <responded>true</responded>
    <priority>low</priority>
    <date>2001-10-18</date>
    <system>Software</system>
    <component>Notepad</component>
    <description>Too slow.</description>
    <filename>../log/2001-10-18_ticketresponse_710727.xml</filename>
</message>
```

The next requirement is for this message to be passed to the appropriate department. Here this will mean writing the message to disk again, this time in a location particular to the department. The rule that will recognize a message at this point once more only needs to check the `<status>` element:

```xml
<!-- Save for particular dept -->
<rule>
    <match>
        <path>message/status</path>
        <value>logged</value>
```

```
      </match>
      <target>http://localhost/tickets/control/filer.asp</target>
      <transform>../xsl/department.xsl</transform>
   </rule>
```

To keep things simple, we will assume that we have just two departments, "Hardware" and "Software", and these correspond directly with the contents of the `<system>` tag. The stylesheet to prepare the message for the filer is quite similar to those we have seen already, beginning with the code to copy the message. This time we don't need to create a new element for the filename, we can modify the element that `logger.xsl` created earlier. The `<system>` element is replaced by a `<department>` element with the same content. This time we will change the status to 'reported'.

```
<?xml version="1.0"?>
<!-- department.xsl -->
<xsl:stylesheet version="1.0"
                xmlns:xsl="http://www.w3.org/1999/XSL/Transform">
<xsl:output method="xml" indent="yes" encoding="ISO-8859-1"/>

<xsl:template match="message">
   <xsl:copy>
      <xsl:apply-templates/>
   </xsl:copy>
</xsl:template>

<xsl:template match="message/*">
   <xsl:copy-of select="."/>
</xsl:template>

<xsl:template match="message/filename">
   <xsl:element name="filename">../jobs/<xsl:value-of
      select="//system"/>/<xsl:value-of select="//id"/>.xml</xsl:element>
</xsl:template>

<xsl:template match="message/system">
   <xsl:element name="department"><xsl:value-of select="."/></xsl:element>
</xsl:template>

<xsl:template match="message/status">
   <xsl:element name="status">reported</xsl:element>
</xsl:template>

</xsl:stylesheet>
```

So now the message looks like this:

```
<?xml version="1.0" encoding="ISO-8859-1"?>
<message>
<id>710727</id>
<sender>roadrunner@customers</sender>
<type>ticketresponse</type>
<status>reported</status>
<responded>true</responded>
<priority>low</priority>
<date>2001-10-18</date>
<department>Software</department>
<component>Notepad</component>
<description>Too slow.</description>
<filename>../jobs/Software/710727.xml</filename>
</message>
```

In the diagram above, the lower steps describe what we want to happen to the message after it has been reported if its `<priority>` element has the value `urgent`. If this isn't the case, then the broker will ignore the message. Here is the rule:

```
<!-- notify hd of urgent jobs -->
   <rule>
      <match>
         <path>message/status</path>
         <value>reported</value>
      </match>
      <match>
         <path>message/priority</path>
         <value>urgent</value>
      </match>
      <target>http://localhost/tickets/control/mailer.asp</target>
      <transform>../xsl/mailhd.xsl</transform>
   </rule>
```

The target of the rule, that is, the module that will handle the messages that trigger this rule, is another ASP page, `mailer.asp`. The message will be pre-processed with the transform contained in `mailhd.xsl`.

Mailer Module

Two of the use cases require that the system sends an e-mail: when a user reports an urgent job, helpdesk personnel should be notified by this means, and when a job has been updated by the helpdesk personnel, the customer should be notified. If either of these situations arise (as specified in the rule list), then the broker will send an appropriate message to the mailer module, which will dispatch an e-mail according to the contents of the message.

The mailer module is fairly straightforward, largely thanks to existing Win32 components. With a default install of IIS it is possible to use the **CDONTS** (**Collaboration Data Objects NT Server**) component to send SMTP mail, though this won't work from behind proxies or firewalls. With Windows 2000 the **CDO** component is a more versatile alternative. In this we used the popular **JMail** component from Dimac (http://tech.dimac.net). For a basic e-mail we need a value for the To, From, Subject, and Body fields. To keep the mailer simple, we will just let it work on four XML elements corresponding to each of these fields, in other words `<to>`, `<from>`, `<subject>`, and `<body>`.

The stylesheet looks like this (note that you will need to change the domain name to suit your mail server setup, in our case we used @helpdesk):

```
<?xml version="1.0"?>
<!-- mailhd.xsl -->
<xsl:stylesheet version="1.0"
                xmlns:xsl="http://www.w3.org/1999/XSL/Transform">
<xsl:output method="xml" indent="yes" encoding="ISO-8859-1"/>

<xsl:template match="message">
<xsl:copy>
   <xsl:apply-templates/>
   <xsl:element name="to">
      <xsl:value-of select="//department"/>@helpdesk</xsl:element>
   <xsl:element name="from"><xsl:value-of select="//sender"/></xsl:element>
   <xsl:element name="subject">Urgent Problem</xsl:element>
   <xsl:element name="body">Job <xsl:value-of select="//id"/> is
   URGENT</xsl:element>
```

```
    </xsl:copy>
  </xsl:template>

  <xsl:template match="message/*">
    <xsl:copy-of select="."/>
  </xsl:template>

  <xsl:template match="message/status">
    <xsl:element name="status">hdmailed</xsl:element>
  </xsl:template>

</xsl:stylesheet>
```

A straight copy is made of the source XML, and a series of tags for the attention of the mailer are
added, some derived from the source document and some hard-coded. The `<status>` element is again
updated to reflect the new status. The result of this transformation on a typical message (the example we
used before, except with the priority changed to `urgent`) looks like this:

```
<?xml version="1.0" encoding="ISO-8859-1"?>
<message>
<id>710727</id>
<sender>roadrunner@customers</sender>
<type>ticketresponse</type>
<status>hdmailed</status>
<responded>true</responded>
<priority>low</priority>
<date>2001-10-18</date>
<department>Software</department>
<component>Notepad</component>
<description>Too slow.</description>
<filename>../jobs/Software/710727.xml</filename>
<to>Software@helpdesk</to>
<from>roadrunner@customers</from>
<subject>Urgent Problem</subject>
<body>Job 710727 is URGENT</body>
</message>
```

The mailer module code begins like this (note it does need to be customized for your own setup – more
on this in a while):

```
<%@ LANGUAGE=JScript %>
<!-- mailer.asp -->
<!-- #INCLUDE FILE="converter.asp" -->
<!-- #INCLUDE FILE="post.asp" -->
<%
    var mailServer = "mail.myServer.com"; // only used by Jmail

    var target = "http://localhost/tickets/control/broker.asp";
    var messageDoc = getDoc(Request);

    var from = messageDoc.selectSingleNode("//from").text;
    var to = messageDoc.selectSingleNode("//to").text;
    var subject = messageDoc.selectSingleNode("//subject").text;
    var body = messageDoc.selectSingleNode("//body").text;
```

Here we have got hold of the DOM document object from the HTTP request, and we extract the contents of the individual elements.

There are differences in the use of the different e-mail components, but whichever is chosen, the code we need to build and send an e-mail is straightforward. We begin by creating the `mail` object, then set its properties, and finally call the appropriate method to send the mail. You should comment/uncomment the appropriate section for your particular setup.

Here is the JMail version:

```
// JMail version
   var mail =  Server.CreateObject("JMail.Message");

   mail.AddRecipient(to);
   mail.from = from;
   mail.subject = subject;
   mail.body = body;
   mail.Send(mailServer);
```

The CDO/Win2K version is very similar, with only a few changes:

```
/* CDO Win2k version
   var mail = Server.CreateObject("CDO.Message")

   mail.to = to;
   mail.from = from;
   mail.subject = subject;
   mail.textBody = body;
   mail.send();
*/
```

The CDONTS version is along the same lines:

```
/*
   var mail = Server.CreateObject("CDONTS.NewMail");

   mail.to = to;
   mail.from = from;
   mail.subject = subject;
   mail.body = body;
   mail.send();
*/
```

The only significant difference is that for JMail the domain name or IP address of the e-mail server must be provided. At present its value is declared in this ASP file, though (if JMail is used) this should be moved to the `Global.asa` file before deployment.

Once the message has been sent, we can POST back to the broker the DOM document, to deal with as it pleases – in this use case it will be ignored.

```
   post(messageDoc, target, Response);
%>
```

If someone in the software department now cares to check their e-mail, they will see they have a message:

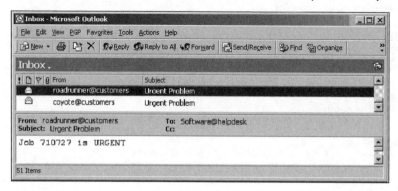

Helpdesk Login

The next thing liable to happen to the system is that someone at the helpdesk wants to see if they have any jobs to do. Here is the use case again:

Login

1. Helpdesk goes to login page.

2. Helpdesk enters their login name, password, and department.

3. System displays list of open jobs for helpdesk's department.

The login page will be a static HTML page, containing script that will generate XML appropriate to the operation. Like the trouble ticket form, we will build the message as an object, then use functions in xmlWrapper.js to express this in XML. This file is helpdesk.htm:

```
<html>
<head>
    <title>Helpdesk</title>

<script language="JavaScript">

var root = "message";

function Message(){
    this.sender = userForm.sender.value;
    this.password = userForm.password.value;
    var selector = userForm.department;
    this.department = selector.options[selector.selectedIndex].text;
}

Message.prototype.type= "joblistreq";
Message.prototype.category = "helpdesk";

function getValueSet(){
    var message = new Message();
    return message;
}
```

```
    </script>
    <script language="JavaScript"  src="xmlWrapper.js"></script>
    </head>
    <body>

    <form name="userForm">
        <table>
            <tr>
                <td>
                    Name :
                </td><td>
                    <input type="text" name="sender">
                </td>
            </tr><tr>
                <td>
                    Password :
                </td><td>
                    <input type="password" name="password">
                </td>
            </tr><tr>
                <td>
                    Department :
                </td><td>
                    <select name="department">
                        <option>Hardware</option>
                        <option>Software</option>
                    </select>
                </td>
            </tr>
        </table>
    </form>

    <form method="post" action="broker.asp" name="submitForm"
        onsubmit="return send();">
        <input type="submit" value="Login">
        <input type="hidden" name="message">
    </form>
    </body>
    </html>
```

The person on the helpdesk will be presented with the following:

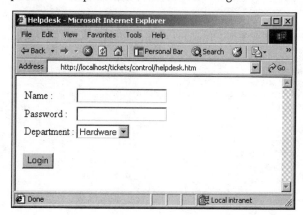

When they enter their details, the script will generate XML, which we can display in an alert box (triggered by the send() function):

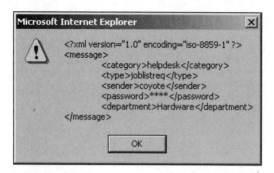

The XML message is POSTed to the broker, and in the broker's rule list (rules.xml) are the following:

```
<!-- show helpdesk list of jobs -->
<rule>
   <match>
      <path>message/type</path>
      <value>joblistreq</value>
   </match>
   <match>
      <path>message/category</path>
      <value>helpdesk</value>
   </match>
   <target>http://localhost/tickets/control/joblist.asp</target>
   <transform>../xsl/joblisthd.xsl</transform>
</rule>
```

After comparing the match sections with the contents of the DOM tree in the message, the broker will apply the transform joblisthd.xsl:

```
<?xml version="1.0"?>
<!-- joblisthd.xsl -->
<xsl:stylesheet version="1.0"
                xmlns:xsl="http://www.w3.org/1999/XSL/Transform">
<xsl:output method="xml" indent="yes" encoding="ISO-8859-1"/>

<xsl:template match="message">
   <xsl:copy>
      <xsl:apply-templates/>
      <xsl:element name="testpath">//department</xsl:element>
      <xsl:element name="testvalue">
         <xsl:value-of select="//department"/>
      </xsl:element>
   </xsl:copy>
</xsl:template>

<xsl:template match="message/*">
   <xsl:copy-of select="."/>
</xsl:template>

</xsl:stylesheet>
```

This stylesheet copies the message as received, adding a `<testpath>` and a `<testvalue>` element. These elements will contain the criteria on which we select the jobs to view. The elements that would be generated from the XML shown in the alert box above would be:

```
<testpath>//department</testpath>
<testvalue>Hardware</testvalue>
```

This might look familiar – we are going to use the same kind of testing to recognize jobs to list as the broker uses to decide which rules to apply. To keep things simple here, we've got a search criteria that would match any messages that are being handled by the particular department, in this case any document containing the following element:

```
<department>Hardware</department>
```

This is passed to an ASP page, `joblist.asp`, that will load all the XML files in a specified directory into a DOM document, test each to see if the above criteria ap plies, and if so show the filenames in a list, alongside radio buttons, like so:

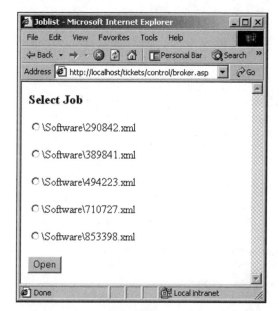

We want the user's selection to generate a message, so here we have a page very similar to those of `ticket.htm` and `helpdesk.htm`, only this time it will be generated dynamically. The first section initializes a handful of variables, including some which have values extracted from the DOM object this page has received as a message:

```
<%@ LANGUAGE=JScript %>
<!-- joblist.asp -->
<!-- #INCLUDE FILE="converter.asp" -->
<%
    var target = "http://localhost/tickets/control/broker.asp";
    var messageDoc = getDoc(Request);
    var testpath = messageDoc.documentElement.
                   selectSingleNode("//testpath").text;
```

```
        var testvalue = messageDoc.documentElement.
                    selectSingleNode("//testvalue").text;
        var category = messageDoc.documentElement.
                    selectSingleNode("//category").text;

        var base = "http://localhost/tickets/jobs";
```

We're going to be looking at the server's file system, for which we use a `FileSystemObject`. The base of the directory tree we will examine, relative to this ASP page, is `'../jobs/'`. The `getContainedFiles` function (listed below) will place into the `jobs` array references to all the files contained in this directory and all its subdirectories that meet the `testpath/testvalue` criterion.

```
        var fsObject = Server.CreateObject("Scripting.FileSystemObject");

        var folderName = Server.MapPath("../jobs/");
        var baseLength = folderName.length;
        var topFolder = fsObject.getFolder(folderName);

        var jobs = new Array();
        getContainedFiles(topFolder, jobs);

        var radio;
        var job;
    %>
```

The head section of the HTML sent to the browser is essentially the same as that of the pages we saw earlier. The properties of a message object are built up in exactly the same way, and what the browser gets will contain something like this:

```
message.type = "jobloadreq";
message.status = "new";
message.category = "helpdesk";
message.testpath = "//department";
message.testvalue = "Hardware";
message.filename = getRadioValue(userForm.jobselect);
```

which will be the result of the `Response.Write` lines here:

```
<html><head><title>Joblist</title>
<script language="JavaScript">

var root = "message";
var message = new Message();
function Message(){};

function getValueSet()
{

<%
    Response.Write("message.type = \"jobloadreq\";");
    Response.Write("message.status = \"new\";");
    Response.Write("message.category = \""+category+"\";");
    Response.Write("message.testpath = \""+testpath+"\";");
    Response.Write("message.testvalue = \""+testvalue+"\";");
%>
```

```
    message.filename = getRadioValue(userForm.jobselect);

    return message;
}
</script>
<script language="JavaScript" src="xmlWrapper.js"></script>
</head>
<body>
```

A form is put together using values taken from the array of file references. The references will contain the full path of the files, so the common base path is sliced off before writing the line to the browser:

```
<form name="userForm">
    <h3>Select Job</h3>
<%
// draw radio buttons
    for (var i = 0; i < jobs.length; i++)
{
    job = (new String(jobs[i])).slice(baseLength);
    radio = "<input type=\"radio\" value=\""+job+"\" name=\"jobselect\">";
    Response.Write("<p>"+radio+job);
}
Response.Write("<input type=\"hidden\" name=\"message\">");
%>
    </form>
```

The second form is virtually identical to those we used already:

```
<form name="submitForm" method="post" action="broker.asp"
        onsubmit="return send()">
    <input type="submit" value="Open">
    <input type="hidden" name="message">
</form>
</body></html>
```

We now have the function that will collect references to files contained in a specified folder. The function steps through the files and folders in the current directory, and if the result of the test() method on a particular file is true, the file reference will be pushed into an array. The function is recursive – any folders within the current folder will also be used as parameters for further calls to the function. Note that the array variable has been declared outside of the function, effectively global to this page, so it can collect the file references from whatever depth of recursion the function gets into.

```
<%
function getContainedFiles(folder, array){
    var innerFile;
    var innerFolder;
    var innerFiles;
    var subFolders = new Enumerator(folder.SubFolders);

    for (;!subFolders.atEnd(); subFolders.moveNext())
    {
        innerFolder = subFolders.item();
        innerFiles = new Enumerator(innerFolder.files);
        for (;!innerFiles.atEnd(); innerFiles.moveNext())
        {
```

```
            innerFile = innerFiles.item();
            if(test(innerFile)) array.push(innerFile);
        }
        getContainedFiles(innerFolder, array);
    }
}
```

The test carried out on each file reference starts by loading the file into a DOM object. An XPath operator in `testpath` gets hold of the part of the document in question and compares it to the required content in `value`. If there is a match, the function will check whether the content of the `<status>` element in the object tested has the value `"closed"` (we will see later that this signifies a closed job). If the content passes the test and the job hasn't been closed then the function will return `true`.

```
function test(file){
    var url = "file:///"+file;
    var doc = Server.CreateObject("Msxml2.DOMDocument.4.0");
    doc.async = false;
    doc.load(url);
    var value = doc.selectSingleNode(testpath).text;
    var status = doc.selectSingleNode("//status").text;
    if((value == testvalue) && (status != "closed")) return true;
}
%>
```

The XML that will be passed to the broker by the preceding code will look something like this:

The broker knows a rule about this kind of message:

```
<!-- load individual job -->
<rule>
    <match>
        <path>message/type</path>
        <value>jobloadreq</value>
    </match>
    <match>
        <path>message/status</path>
        <value>new</value>
    </match>
    <target>http://localhost/tickets/control/jobload.asp</target>
    <transform>../xsl/jobload.xsl</transform>
</rule>
```

The transform here simply changes the text of the `<type>` element from "jobloadreq" to "jobviewreq". This isn't very awe-inspiring, but if the value wasn't changed in this kind of circumstance then we could see the same message sent from the broker back to the broker in a loop – likely results would be a rapid slowdown and failure of the server's operation, and/or the maximum number of users permitted on the server would be reached, the message rejected, and the loop broken.

```
<?xml version="1.0"?>
<!-- jobload.xsl -->
<xsl:stylesheet version="1.0"
                xmlns:xsl="http://www.w3.org/1999/XSL/Transform">
<xsl:output method="xml" indent="yes" encoding="ISO-8859-1"/>

<xsl:template match="message">
<xsl:copy>
   <xsl:apply-templates/>
</xsl:copy>
</xsl:template>

<xsl:template match="message/*">
   <xsl:copy-of select="."/>
</xsl:template>

<xsl:template match="message/type">
   <xsl:element name="type">jobviewreq</xsl:element>
</xsl:template>

</xsl:stylesheet>
```

We are in a short chain of ASP pages here, and the `jobload.asp` file doesn't itself present the browser anything to look at directly (apart from a comment line). The message is loaded as an object once again, and the value of its `<status>` element changed. The name of the file containing the job we are interested in is reconstituted from a relative path reference (`../jobs`) and the contents of the `<filename>` element in the message. The file this refers to is then loaded into another DOM object, `doc`. A new element node `<job>` is created in the document containing the message (`messageDoc`). All the child nodes of the document loaded from file are selected using the `'*'` XPath wildcard, and then each of these is appended to the newly created `job` node. This node is finally added to the message document, which is posted back to the broker.

```
<%@ LANGUAGE=JScript %>
<!-- #INCLUDE FILE="converter.asp" -->
<!-- #INCLUDE FILE="post.asp" -->
<%
   var target = "http://localhost/tickets/control/broker.asp";
   var messageDoc = getDoc(Request);

   var statusNode = messageDoc.selectSingleNode("message/status");
   statusNode.text = "loaded";

   var filename = "../jobs" + messageDoc.documentElement.
                  selectSingleNode("//filename").text;
   var doc = Server.CreateObject("Msxml2.DOMDocument.4.0");
   doc.async = false;
   doc.load(Server.MapPath(filename));

   var jobNode = messageDoc.createNode(1, "job", "");
```

```
    var childNodes = doc.documentElement.selectNodes("*");
    for(var i=0;i<childNodes.length;i++){
        jobNode.appendChild(childNodes.item(i));
    }
    messageDoc.documentElement.appendChild(jobNode);
    postback(messageDoc, target, Response);
%>
```

The result of these operations can be seen here:

```
<!-- broker.asp  -->
<?xml version="1.0" ?>
<message>
    <type>jobviewreq</type>
    <status>loaded</status>
    <category>helpdesk</category>
    <testpath>//department</testpath>
    <testvalue>Hardware</testvalue>
    <filename>\Hardware\026124.xml</filename>
    <job>
    <id>026124</id>
    <sender>roadrunner@customers</sender>
    <type>ticket</type>
    <status>reported</status>
    <priority>urgent</priority>
    <date>2001-10-22</date>
    <department>Hardware</department>
    <component>Desktop Computer</component>
    <description>Too slow.</description>
    <filename>../jobs/Hardware/026124.xml</filename>
    </job>
</message>
```

Elements of the message loaded from file have been placed in a branch of the current message. The message will trigger the following rule:

```
<!-- show individual job -->
<rule>
    <match>
        <path>message/type</path>
        <value>jobviewreq</value>
    </match>
    <match>
        <path>message/status</path>
        <value>loaded</value>
    </match>
    <target>http://localhost/tickets/control/jobview.asp</target>
    <transform></transform>
</rule>
```

This rule doesn't name a transform, so the received message is passed directly on to `jobview.asp`. Before seeing the code for this page, we'll just backtrack a little to the use cases.

It isn't hard to see considerable overlap in what we want the system to do when the helpdesk wants to look at a job and when the customer wants to look at a job. Similarly, the customer closing a job is essentially the same operation as the helpdesk closing a job, and the end result of either of these can be affected by giving the job a status of 'closed'. We can put all this functionality together in one page, with minor adjustments made depending on whether the user is a customer or helpdesk person. Going a small step further, when the helpdesk adds a solution to a problem, this can be seen as essentially the same operation as closing a job – we simply need to append some more data to the job record. We will wrap up the user interface side of all these points in the jobview.asp page. We want to be able to discriminate between helpdesk and user, so once we've loaded the document we will make a Boolean we can test by using an XPath operation to find out from the message document whether or not the client is a customer:

```
<%@ LANGUAGE=JScript %>
<!-- jobview.asp -->
<!-- #INCLUDE FILE="converter.asp" -->
<%
    var target = "http://localhost/tickets/control/broker.asp";
    var messageDoc = getDoc(Request);
    var isCustomer =
        (messageDoc.selectSingleNode("message/category").text = = "customer");
    var solution;
%>
```

The page is again a largely dynamically generated relative of the ticket.htm form. In this case, we are going to pass all the details of the job in question back to the server. This can be achieved quite neatly by getting the nodes into a list, and then making a series of variable assignments using the name and value of each property in turn. So the JavaScript in the HTML head begins literally:

```
<html><head><title>Jobview</title>
<script language="JavaScript">

var root = "message";
var message = new Message();

function Message(){};

function getValueSet(){
```

Now we have the impressive bit, with JavaScript *source* generated dynamically:

```
<%
var jobNodes = messageDoc.selectNodes("message/job/*");
var name;
var value;
for(var i=0;i<jobNodes.length;i++){
    name = jobNodes.item(i).nodeName;
    value = jobNodes.item(i).text;
    if((name != "type") && (name != "status") )   {
        Response.Write( "\n\tmessage." + name + " = \"" + value + "\";"  );
    }
}
%>
```

Each name in the list will be pre-pended with "message." so we end up with script of this form:

```
message.id = "026124";
message.sender = "roadrunner@customers";
message.priority = "urgent";
message.date = "2001-10-22";
message.department = "Hardware";
message.component = "Desktop Computer";
message.description = "Leg fell off.";
message.filename = "../jobs/Hardware/026124.xml";
```

The rest of the `message` object properties are added more conventionally, some in hard-wired JavaScript while others will gain their values later through calls to the `updateJob()` and `closeJob()` functions:

```
message.type = "updatereq";
message.responded = "false";
    return message;
}

function updateJob(){
    message.solution = userForm.solution.value;
    message.status = "updated";
}

function closeJob(){
    message.status = "closed";
}
</script>
<script language="JavaScript"  src="xmlWrapper.js"></script>
</head>
```

The first part of the body of this page will present the details of the job in question, using the same kind of `for` loop as above. Here we want to treat some of the properties in slightly different ways – the `<id>` is used as part of a heading, the contents of the `<filename>` and `<status>` elements are ignored, but the default is to write the property names and values on screen:

```
<body>
<%
var jobNodes = messageDoc.selectNodes("message/job/*");
var name;
var value;
for(var i=0;i<jobNodes.length;i++){
    name = jobNodes.item(i).nodeName;
    value = jobNodes.item(i).text;

    switch(name){
      case "id":
      Response.Write("<h3>Job No. "+value+"</h3>");
      break;

      case "filename":
      break;

      case "status":
      break;

      case "solution":
      solution = value;
      break;
```

```
        default :
        Response.Write("<p><b>"+name+"</b> : "+value);
        break;
    }
}
%>
```

The first form on this page is a slightly modified version of what has come before. We have a button labeled 'Close', and upon clicking this button the closeJob() function above will be called (setting the status to 'closed'), followed by send() (preparing the XML), and finally the submit() function of this form, which will post the message to the broker. The reason for using this approach is that we can call the submit() function from elsewhere, and we don't always want the closeJob() method to be called.

```
<form name="submitForm" method="post" action="broker.asp">
<input type="button" value="Close Job" onclick="closeJob();
        send(); submit();">
<input type="hidden" name="message">
</form>
```

Next comes a little trick – if the viewer of this page is a customer (as stated in the message received) then the closing HTML tag will be sent back to the browser, followed by notification of the end of the response. Thus for a customer, the page stops here.

```
<%
if(isCustomer)
{
    Response.Write("</html>");
    Response.End();
}
%>
```

For the helpdesk, on the other hand, we have an extra form, into which they can give the solution to the problem displayed above. Again we have a button, which this time will first call the updateJob() function above (which will add a solution property/element to the outgoing message, and set the status to "updated"). The send() function is then called, followed by a call to the submit() function of the form above.

```
<h4>Enter Proposed Solution</h4>
<form name="userForm">
    <textarea name="solution" cols="30" rows="10"></textarea>
    <input type="button" value="Update" onclick="updateJob();
        send(); submitForm.submit();">
</form>
</body></html>
```

If the client is from the helpdesk, then they will have this browser view:

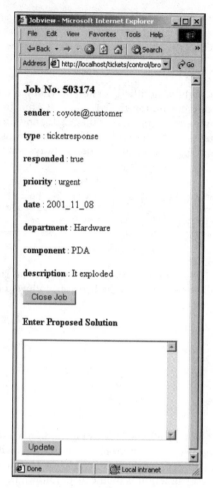

If the client is a customer, they will not see the text-entry box and 'Update' button.

If text is entered into the box and 'Update' clicked, then the text is placed in a new field in an XML message which is passed back to the broker, which in turn calls `filer.asp` to update the file on disk and `mailer.asp` to send a mail to the customer advising them of this update. The processing is carried in essentially the same manner as we have seen so far, the only difference being in the content of the message.

If the **Close Job** button is clicked, we have the following XML:

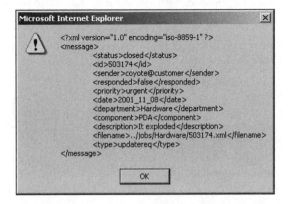

Closure of the job calls for three actions by the system – acknowledge the operation, update the job record, and send e-mail notification to the customer who submitted the problem in the first place. This scenario is similar to that when a trouble ticket is sent to the system, and this is reflected in the corresponding rules:

```
<!-- respond to update request -->
<rule>
    <match>
        <path>message/type</path>
        <value>updatereq</value>
    </match>
    <match>
        <path>message/responded</path>
        <value>false</value>
    </match>
    <target>http://localhost/tickets/control/responder.asp</target>
    <transform>../xsl/updateresponse.xsl</transform>
</rule>
```

The stylesheet here merely copies the source document, apart from changing the content of the `<type>` element to "updateresponse" following the same pattern as `jobload.xsl`. The responder is called, which will fork the message into two operational threads, one of which will send an acknowledgement back to the user through the chain of ASP pages:

```
<!-- acknowledge update -->
<rule>
    <match>
        <path>message/type</path>
        <value>updateresponse</value>
    </match>
    <match>
        <path>message/responded</path>
        <value>false</value>
    </match>

<target>http://localhost/tickets/control/acknowledge.asp</target>
    <transform>../xsl/update_ackn.xsl</transform>
</rule>
```

The `update_ackn.xsl` stylesheet is virtually identical to `acknowledge.xsl` that we saw earlier, except that rather than presenting the user with "Your report has been passed to the appropriate department." the user will see a message stating "The job has been updated."

The untethered message will go on to trigger the following rule, which will cause the filer module to overwrite the job record with the new message:

```
<!-- update job -->
<rule>
   <match>
      <path>message/type</path>
      <value>updateresponse</value>
   </match>
   <match>
      <path>message/responded</path>
      <value>true</value>
   </match>

   <target>http://localhost/tickets/control/filer.asp</target>
   <transform>../xsl/updated.xsl</transform>
</rule>
```

When the filer has carried out its operations, it will send a message back to the broker. The message will have previously been filtered by the `updated.xsl` stylesheet, which again simply modifies the content of a single element, in this case making the `<type>` element `mailreq`.

Finally we have a call to the mailer message, giving the user the details of the changes made to their job:

```
<!-- mail user -->
<rule>
   <match>
      <path>message/type</path>
      <value>mailreq</value>
   </match>

   <target>http://localhost/tickets/control/mailer.asp</target>
   <transform>../xsl/mailcust.xsl</transform>
</rule>

</rules>
```

The stylesheet here is largely a copy of `mailhd.xsl`, except that the e-mail fields are taken from different parts of the message:

```
<?xml version="1.0"?>
<!-- mailcust.xsl -->
<xsl:stylesheet version="1.0"
                xmlns:xsl="http://www.w3.org/1999/XSL/Transform">
<xsl:output method="xml" indent="yes" encoding="ISO-8859-1"/>

<xsl:template match="message">
<xsl:copy>
   <xsl:apply-templates/>
   <xsl:element name="to"><xsl:value-of select="//sender"/></xsl:element>
   <xsl:element name="from">Helpdesk</xsl:element>
   <xsl:element name="subject">Job <xsl:value-of select="//id"/>
```

```
      </xsl:element>
      <xsl:element name="body">
         <xsl:value-of select="//solution"/>
      </xsl:element>
   </xsl:copy>
</xsl:template>

<xsl:template match="message/*">
   <xsl:copy-of select="."/>

</xsl:template>

<xsl:template match="message/type">
   <xsl:element name="status">done</xsl:element>
</xsl:template>

</xsl:stylesheet>
```

We have already seen the target ASP pages called by each of these rules, and the first three stylesheets do no more than change the content of a single element. The fourth is a rearrangement of a stylesheet we have already seen. With a very small amount of new code we have fulfilled quite a significant chunk of the requirements. There's more to come.

Customer Welcome

Our use cases talk of the customer going to a company help page. OK, so this company won't win any prizes for style or accessibility:

The 'click here' link takes the customer to the `ticket.htm` page we saw earlier. The Submit Query button causes an XML message to be sent to the broker. The code, like `ticket.htm`, is based around a static form:

```
<html>
<head>
   <title>Helpdesk</title>

<script language="JavaScript">
```

```
var root = "message";
var message = new Message();
function Message(){};

function getValueSet(){
   message.type = "joblistreq";
   message.category = "customer";
   message.responded = "false";
   message.sender = userForm.sender.value;
   return message;
}
</script>
<script language="JavaScript"  src="xmlWrapper.js"></script>
</head>

<body>
<h2>Welcome to the Helpdesk</h2>
To report a new problem, please <a href="ticket.htm">click here</a>
<p>
To view the status of an existing problem, please enter your email address and
click the button below.

<form name="userForm">

Email address :
<input type=text name="sender">
</form>

<form method="post" action="../control/broker.asp" name="submitForm"
      onsubmit="return send()">
<input type="submit">
<input type="hidden" name="message">
</form>
</body>
</html>
```

Here we have an example of the XML generated:

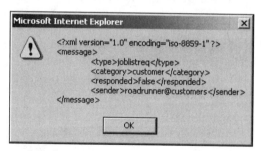

You will probably not be surprised to find we have a rule that matches this:

```
<!-- show customer list of jobs -->
<rule>
   <match>
      <path>message/type</path>
      <value>joblistreq</value>
   </match>
   <match>
```

```
            <path>message/category</path>
            <value>customer</value>
        </match>
        <target>http://localhost/tickets/control/joblist.asp</target>
        <transform>../xsl/joblistcust.xsl</transform>
    </rule>
```

We are again calling the `joblistreq.asp` page, only this time a customer is doing the calling so the stylesheet is slightly different to `joblisthd.xsl`:

```
<?xml version="1.0"?>
<!-- joblistcust.xsl -->
<xsl:stylesheet version="1.0"
                xmlns:xsl="http://www.w3.org/1999/XSL/Transform">
<xsl:output method="xml" indent="yes" encoding="ISO-8859-1"/>

<xsl:template match="message">
<xsl:copy>
   <xsl:apply-templates/>
   <xsl:element name="testpath">//sender</xsl:element>
   <xsl:element name="testvalue">
      <xsl:value-of select="//sender"/>
   </xsl:element>
</xsl:copy>
</xsl:template>

<xsl:template match="message/*">
   <xsl:copy-of select="."/>
</xsl:template>
</xsl:stylesheet>
```

Here the jobs selected from the file system will be checked to see if the name of the sender of the original job matches the e-mail address of the person that is now requesting the view.

We already have the code that shows the list of jobs and an individual job view, so we've just added another sizable portion of the use case requirements by reusing the same basic pages with a little customization. In the system, we are reusing the core modules (broker, filer, mailer) and much of the other code is more or less repeated. Generally speaking, having copies of large chunks of code with the same functionality is not a good idea (and isn't really reuse), but what we are looking at here are separate pages that may be modified, for instance to make the UI a little nicer, or even may be called upon to perform a very different function at a later date. The modular and loosely coupled nature of the approach we take here means that such changes are possible with minimum side effects on other parts of the system.

Running the Application

This application in its current form is very much experimental, and quite a lot of work would be required to develop it for live use. It is therefore strongly recommended that the application is run in a 'sandbox' environment, where other systems are not likely to be affected – either on an IIS server set aside for development purposes or on a local desktop host.

749

Mail Server

The application will send out e-mail (using CDONTS, CDO, or JMail) to notify the helpdesk of urgent jobs or customers of updates, and for it to receive accounts corresponding to the helpdesk and customers it will need to exist on a mail server. If a standard SMTP/POP server is already available then this may be used, but following the sandbox principle it is better to set up a local server, away from existing systems. A free product that is suitable is available from http://www.argosoft.com. This will provide the SMTP/POP service required and is very straightforward to set up. Once installed and run, it can be configured by double-clicking its icon in the Windows system tray. Whatever mail server you use, the examples in this text use two local domains, 'helpdesk' and 'customers', and four users, coyote, roadrunner, hardware, and software.

If you are using a local server such as ArgoSoft Mail Server, to be able to receive the mails sent through this server, it will be necessary to add accounts to an e-mail client, such as Microsoft Outlook. You will need to add the address (for example, roadrunner@customers) and the server domain name or IP address of the machine on which the e-mail server is being run (on a local machine this will probably be '127.0.0.1'). The e-mail server can be tested by simply sending an e-mail between the users that have been set up (also see the "*Troubleshooting*" section later in the chapter).

File Locations

The whole application should be contained in a virtual directory called `tickets`. There should be the following subdirectories:

❑   `tickets\control` – the application's `.asp` and `.htm` pages.

❑   `tickets\xsl` – stylesheets used in the application.

❑   `tickets\log` – files generated from incoming problem reports.

❑   `tickets\jobs\Hardware` – job files generated for this department.

❑   `tickets\jobs\Software` – job files generated for this department.

Assuming that IIS is running on the local host, and MSXML and whichever e-mail delivery component chosen are installed, the system should now run by pointing a browser at either http://localhost/tickets/control/welcome.htm (customer view) or http://localhost/tickets/control/helpdesk.htm (helpdesk view) and entering the appropriate details.

Troubleshooting

If problems are encountered with this system, it is straightforward to narrow down the location of the problem. First of all the various system components used should be checked. That IIS is working correctly can be confirmed by simply pointing a browser at the host's address (http://localhost). The basic functionality of the COM components required can be checked using simple scripts run on IIS.

MSXML

That MSXML is installed and basically working can be confirmed by running a simple ASP script on IIS:

```
<%@ LANGUAGE=JScript %>
<%
    var xmlDoc = Server.CreateObject("Msxml2.DOMDocument.4.0");
```

```
    xmlDoc.async = false;
    xmlDoc.loadXML("<h1>MSXML Works</h1>");
    Response.Write(xmlDoc.xml);
    Response.End();
%>
```

A piece of XML is loaded into a DOM object, and then serialized back out to the calling browser. Pointing a browser at the page should show the message 'MSXML Works'.

WinHTTP

In the final section of this chapter below we will be using the WinHTTP component, and to keep the troubleshooting information together we have a test script here. If this component is installed, then pointing a browser at the following should show the page given as target. Of course if the target is on the Internet, as here, then the host being tested must have a connection to the Internet (for example, the local host machine will need to be online).

```
<%@ LANGUAGE=JScript %>
<%
    var target = "http://www.wrox.com";
    var postObject = Server.CreateObject("MSXML2.ServerXMLHTTP.4.0");
    postObject.open("GET", target, false);
    postObject.send();
    Response.Write(postObject.responseText);
    Response.End();
%>
```

Mail System

The e-mail server can be tested by sending and receiving e-mail through it using a standard e-mail client as described above. The e-mail component used in mailer.asp can be testing by writing a simple script to send a message with the contents hard-coded. This will be a little different depending on which e-mail component has been chosen, but for JMail it would look something like this:

```
<%@ LANGUAGE=JScript %>
<%

    var mailServer = "mailserveraddress"; // address of mail server
    var mail =  Server.CreateObject("JMail.Message");

    mail.AddRecipient("coyote@customers");
    mail.from = "Test Script";
    mail.subject = "Test Message";
    mail.body = "This is a test message";
    var result = mail.Send(mailServer);
    Response.Write("Result = "+result);
    Response.End();
%>
```

Here the recipient given is one on the local e-mail server, but a 'real' e-mail address could be used instead, as long as the e-mail server address is known. If the e-mail component and server are functioning correctly, then pointing a browser at the above script will show 'Result = true'. Checking the e-mail for the address given should show a new message has been delivered (this may take a few minutes, depending on the e-mail server).

ASP Script Problems

The scripts as supplied should work as described, but if problems are encountered when modifying the system then the simplest way of checking that things are happening as they should is by passing variables to the Response object, that is, inserting Response.Write(*variable*) statements into the code. If a particular page won't display at all, then statements like this can be followed with Response.End(), which will ensure that at least the calling browser receives a complete HTTP message. An alternative is to write these variables to the web server's log with Response.AppendToLog(*variable*).

In general, script problems are often caused by JScript's interpretation differing from what was actually intended. For instance, say the following appeared in a script:

```
if(x = 10) {
    // do something
}
```

JScript will (correctly) see x = 10 as an assignment rather than a comparison (x == 10), and the contents of the if block will always be run. A slightly more sophisticated version of variable checking in a script is to include assertions, where the contents variable is tested against the value it is meant to have, for example, Response.Write(x == 10). If a false value is displayed, then something is amiss, though of course after development these lines will have to be deleted or commented out. Better still, it is possible to declare a flag at the start of the script or at the start of an application in an application or session variable that will be set during development, and write the assert messages to the server log, for example:

```
var logging = true;

    if(logging) Response.AppendToLog(x == 10);.
```

XSLT Problems

It can be very difficult to spot errors in stylesheets, and one approach to troubleshooting here is to create some sample data and run this through the transform using a tool such as Cooktop (http://www.xmleverywhere.com). Once the transformation has been isolated from its application, it is much quicker to modify and test it. Often it helps to have a look at the contents of a particular context within a template, for example:

```
<xsl:template match="/blah">
   <xsl:copy-of select="."/>
   <!-- rest of template operations -->
</xsl:template>
```

As with troubleshooting in general, a methodical breaking down and isolation of faulty components is usually the best way forward.

All being well the system is now working correctly, so we can start to consider how it may be extended.

Communicating with Non-Microsoft Servers

The server-to-server code we have seen so far all makes use of MSXML, specifically `ServerXMLHTTP`, to pass DOM documents as complete objects. For our helpdesk system this was all that was required, but if we want true system interoperability we need a little more. For the sake of completeness, that's what we'll look at now.

The DOM objects we've been using are artifacts of the Microsoft MSXML API, and as such it is rather unlikely that a non-Microsoft system will be able to understand them. It is also worth remembering that even if the external server is an IIS installation, it could quite easily be the case that the programmers of the server don't wish to use MSXML, or the administrators don't want to install it. What we need to communicate with other systems is a way of converting these objects to and from standard HTTP messages. As it happens, we have already covered the *from* part of this to handle HTTP POST messages from client forms (in `converter.asp`). The system modules as they stand will be able to make sense of incoming messages from other servers, as long as the HTTP type is `"application/x-www-form-urlencoded"` and the data has been posted as a form element called `"message"` (and of course the XML sent actually means something to the system). To post out data in this same standard HTTP format we can use another Microsoft COM component, `WinHTTP`, which offers facilities very similar to those of `XMLHTTP` but without the XML wrapping. This is to be found in the Windows HTTP SDK, which provides a high-level interface to this protocol. Rather than including the conversion in all modules (which would require extra switching logic to decide whether the data was sent as an MSXML DOM object or as text in a POST message) we will have a small utility script that will receive a DOM object and forward the decoded XML to a specified target.

The following code requires Microsoft Windows HTTP Services SDK 5.0. The executable package available from http://msdn.microsoft.com/downloads/ will install and register all the required libraries.

```
<%
<%
// sendext.asp

function sendExt(data, target){

   var messageText;
   if (typeof(data) == "string"){
      messageText = data;
   } else {
      messageText = data.xml;
   }
   var winHttpReq = Server.CreateObject("WinHttp.WinHttpRequest.5");
   winHttpReq.Open("POST", target, false);
   winHttpReq.SetRequestHeader("Content-Type",
                               "application/x-www-form-urlencoded");
   winHttpReq.Send("message="+messageText);
   return winHttpReq.responseText;
}
%>
```

This function takes two parameters – the data we wish to transmit and the target URL. If the data sent is already in text format (that is, a string) then this will be the text we send. The other alternative is that the data is a DOM object, in which case the message text is obtained using the DOMDocument.xml() property. We then create an instance of WinHttpRequest, which is a plain cousin of the ServerXMLHTTP we saw earlier. We then open it for POSTing, specifying the target URL and that the async option is false. The next line makes the request object look more like a message POSTed from a form by setting the HTTP content header to the appropriate value. To thoroughly mimic a form POST, we prefix the message with a string that will allow the recipient to retrieve the message by name, in this case "message". Finally the function returns whatever the receiving server has passed back as a response.

The helpdesk application as it stands does communicate with any non-Microsoft servers, but we can easily demonstrate how the above script would be used. Below we have a simple script to create a DOM document and load it from a little hard-coded XML. It will pass this document to the sendExt() function, along with the address on a non-Microsoft server.

```
<!-- sendexttest.asp -->
<%@ LANGUAGE=JScript %>
<!-- #INCLUDE FILE="sendext.asp" -->

<%
var text = "<test><p>Hello non-MS World!</p></test>";
var target = "http://localhost:8080/iis/test.php";

var doc = Server.CreateObject("Msxml2.DOMDocument.4.0");
doc.async = false;
doc.loadXML(text);

var responseText = sendExt(doc, target);
Response.Write(responseText);
Response.End();
%>
```

The target URL for this demonstration happens to be looked after by a local installation (on port 8080) of the Apache web server, and the page test.php contains the following PHP script:

```
<html><head><title>test.php</title></head>
    <body>
        <? echo $message; ?>
    </body>
</html>
```

This isn't a book about PHP, so suffice to say that the script above will display the contents of a POSTed variable named "message" in the browser window. If we point a browser at sendexttest.asp, in its window we see:

Hello non-MS World!

If we view the source we have:

```
<!-- sendexttest.asp -->
<html><head><title>test.php</title></head>
    <body>
        <test>Hello non-MS World!</test>
    </body>
</html>
```

This clearly shows that the XML message has got through. The `sendExt()` function above will thus allow us to convert an MSXML DOM object into a message that any standard HTTP server can understand. From the receiver's point of view, the message we sent above could just as easily have come from the following HTML:

```
<form name="submitForm" method="post"
      action="http://localhost:8080/iis/test.php">
<input type="submit" value="Send">
<input type="hidden" name="message"
       value="<test>Hello non-MS World!</test>">
</form>
```

Summary

We have seen various ways in which MSXML can be used in a messaging system – allowing the DOM object to act as a message container, and the use of an XML file to contain rules on how the parts of the system should be joined together. We created modules to carry out a single function as prescribed by the use cases, operating directly in a procedural manner on the message. These modules can be easily reused through applying stylesheet transforms to change the data they receive, and thus the operation carried out. From a higher viewpoint, we have seen that the versatility of MSXML allows us to concentrate on the system requirements – we know the implementation of any XML-based system is likely to be comparatively straightforward using MSXML.

XML Application Development with MSXML 4.0
SOAP
XHTML
XML Schemas DTDs XPath CSS
XML Namespaces
XML 1.0
MSXML

Index

Z

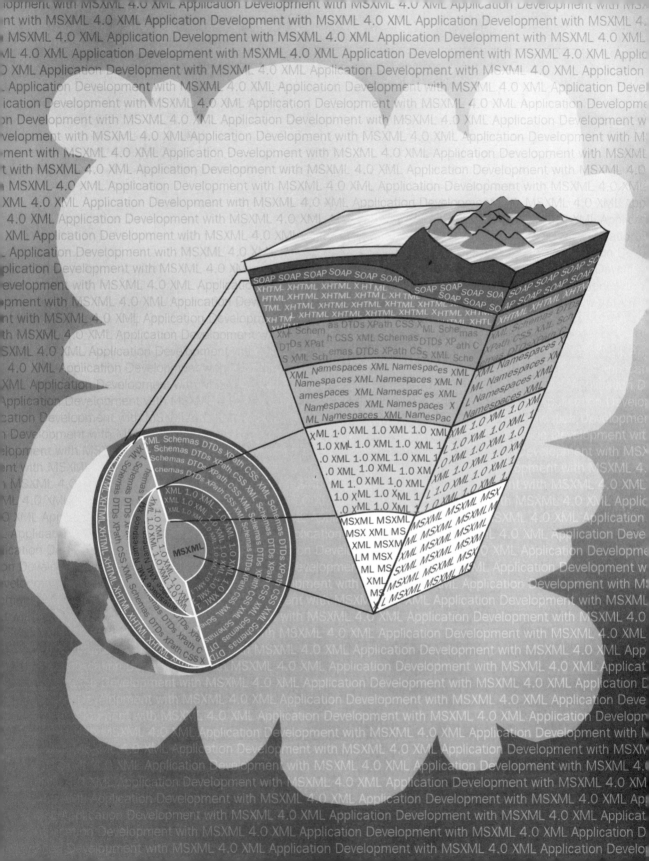

p2p.wrox.com
The programmer's resource centre

A unique free service from Wrox Press
With the aim of helping programmers to help each other

Wrox Press aims to provide timely and practical information to today's programmer. P2P is a list server offering a host of targeted mailing lists where you can share knowledge with four fellow programmers and find solutions to your problems. Whatever the level of your programming knowledge, and whatever technology you use P2P can provide you with the information you need.

ASP Support for beginners and professionals, including a resource page with hundreds of links, and a popular ASP.NET mailing list.

DATABASES For database programmers, offering support on SQL Server, mySQL, and Oracle.

MOBILE Software development for the mobile market is growing rapidly. We provide lists for the several current standards, including WAP, Windows CE, and Symbian.

JAVA A complete set of Java lists, covering beginners, professionals, and server-side programmers (including JSP, servlets and EJBs)

.NET Microsoft's new OS platform, covering topics such as ASP.NET, C#, and general .NET discussion.

VISUAL BASIC Covers all aspects of VB programming, from programming Office macros to creating components for the .NET platform.

WEB DESIGN As web page requirements become more complex, programmer's are taking a more important role in creating web sites. For these programmers, we offer lists covering technologies such as Flash, Coldfusion, and JavaScript.

XML Covering all aspects of XML, including XSLT and schemas.

OPEN SOURCE Many Open Source topics covered including PHP, Apache, Perl, Linux, Python and more.

FOREIGN LANGUAGE Several lists dedicated to Spanish and German speaking programmers, categories include. NET, Java, XML, PHP and XML

How to subscribe
Simply visit the P2P site, at http://p2p.wrox.com/

wrox

Programmer to Programmer™

Wrox writes books for you. Any suggestions, or ideas about how you want information given in your ideal book will be studied by our team. Your comments are always valued at Wrox.

Free phone in USA 800-USE-WROX
Fax (312) 893 8001

UK Tel.: (0121) 687 4100   Fax: (0121) 687 4101

XML Application Development with MSXML 4.0 – Registration Card

Name _____

Address _____

_____

_____

City _____ State/Region _____

Country _____ Postcode/Zip _____

E-Mail _____

Occupation _____

How did you hear about this book?

☐ Book review (name) _____

☐ Advertisement (name) _____

☐ Recommendation _____

☐ Catalog _____

☐ Other _____

Where did you buy this book?

☐ Bookstore (name) _____ City _____

☐ Computer store (name) _____

☐ Mail order _____

☐ Other _____

What influenced you in the purchase of this book?

☐ Cover Design ☐ Contents ☐ Other (please specify):

_____

How did you rate the overall content of this book?

☐ Excellent ☐ Good ☐ Average ☐ Poor

What did you find most useful about this book? _____

_____

What did you find least useful about this book? _____

_____

Please add any additional comments. _____

_____

What other subjects will you buy a computer book on soon?

_____

What is the best computer book you have used this year?

_____

Note: This information will only be used to keep you updated about new Wrox Press titles and will not be used for any other purpose or passed to any other third party.

589X   Check here if you DO NOT want to receive support for this book ■   **589X**

wrox

Programmer to Programmer™

Note: If you post the bounce back card below in the UK, please send it to:

Wrox Press Limited, Arden House, 1102 Warwick Road,
Acocks Green, Birmingham B27 6HB. UK.

Computer Book Publishers